Original Enlightenment and the
Transformation of Medieval Japanese Buddhism

Kuroda Institute
Studies in East Asian Buddhism

STUDIES IN EAST ASIAN BUDDHISM 12

Original Enlightenment and the Transformation of Medieval Japanese Buddhism

Jacqueline I. Stone

A KURODA INSTITUTE BOOK
University of Hawai'i Press
Honolulu

Publication of this book has been
assisted by a grant from the
Suntory Foundation.

04 03 02 01 00 99   5 4 3 2 1

Library of Congress Cataloging-in-Publication Data

Stone, Jacqueline Ilyse.
Original enlightenment and the transformation of medieval Japanese
Buddhism / Jacqueline I. Stone.
p.   cm.—(Studies in East Asian Buddhism ; 12)
"A Kuroda Institute book."
Includes bibliographical references and index.
ISBN 0–8248–2026–6 (cloth : alk. paper)
1. Tendai (Sect)—Doctrines—History. 2. Buddhahood—History.
3. Buddhism—Japan—History—1185–1600. 4. Tendai (Sect)—
Relations—History. I. Title. II. Series: Studies in East Asian
Buddhism ; no. 12.
BQ9118.6.S76   1999   98–54333
294.3'92—dc21   CIP

The Kuroda Institute for the Study of Buddhism and Human Values is a non-
profit, educational corporation founded in 1976. One of its primary objectives
is to promote scholarship on the historical, philosophical, and cultural
ramifications of Buddhism. In association with the University of Hawai'i Press,
the Institute also publishes Classics in East Asian Buddhism, a series devoted to
the translation of significant texts in the East Asian Buddhist tradition.

Designed by Kenneth Miyamoto

Printed by The Maple-Vail Book Manufacturing Group

For my father, Morris J. Ehrlich,
and my stepmother, Jane H. Ehrlich

In memoriam

Contents

Contents

Charts and Illustrations

Preface

ANYONE WHO HAS read even a little about medieval Japanese religion has no doubt encountered at least one reference to the immensely influential Tendai Buddhist discourse of "original enlightenment" *(hongaku)*, the assertion that all beings are Buddhas inherently. And anyone who has studied a bit further may well have been struck by the profound ambivalence surrounding "original enlightenment thought" *(hongaku shisō)* as discussed in modern scholarship. On one hand, it has been touted as the pinnacle of Buddhist philosophical achievement, the quintessential expression of Japanese spirituality, and the basis of medieval aesthetics. On the other, it has been condemned as a pernicious influence that corrupted orthodox Buddhist scholarship, undermined morality, and even legitimized political oppression. Nowhere has this ambivalence appeared more strikingly than in discussions of the relationship between Tendai *hongaku* thought and the Pure Land, Zen, and Nichiren Buddhist movements that emerged during the Kamakura period (1185–1333). Original enlightenment thought, one reads, was the intellectual matrix from which these new movements emerged, but they found their true identity in rejecting it.

This book represents an attempt to make sense of the original enlightenment discourse, its place in medieval Japanese religion, and the issues involved in its study. I have found it necessary to consider this subject in two broad contexts: that of the medieval Buddhist world, in which ideas of original enlightenment emerged and flourished, and that of twentieth-century scholarship, whose methods and assumptions have shaped the way medieval Japanese Buddhism has been understood. In both contexts, the subject of original enlightenment thought intersects another issue that has generated much scholarly interest of late: that of rethinking the nature of the Buddhist developments of the Kamakura period, long considered the formative moment in Japanese Buddhist history. The present study is thus as much about Kamakura Buddhism as it is about original enlightenment thought. It does not offer a grand unified theory of Kamakura Buddhism; probably no single theory could do justice to a subject of such richness and complexity. It does, however, call into question several entrenched assumptions that have informed our study of this period and suggests new perspectives.

This volume is divided into three parts. Part 1, "Perspectives and Problems," outlines the background of medieval Tendai original enlightenment discourse and the major trends in scholarship on this subject. Chapter 1 traces the genealogy of Tendai *hongaku* thought and the extent of its influence on medieval Japanese culture, as well as the problems—textual, definitional, and methodological—that confront the researcher in this area. Chapter 2 outlines the issues involved in scholarship on the relationship of Tendai original enlightenment thought to the new Kamakura Buddhism. Despite its influence as the most powerful religious institution of its day and the immense impact of its teachings on medieval art and culture, Tendai Buddhism has for a long time garnered interest chiefly as the "womb" of the new movements and the "mother" of their five great founders—Eisai, Dōgen, Hōnen, Shinran, and Nichiren—who all began their religious career as Tendai monks. Ever since Tendai original enlightenment discourse first began to attract scholarly attention early in this century, some connection between *hongaku* ideas and the doctrines of the new Kamakura Buddhism has been assumed. However, the nature of that connection has been much disputed. This chapter introduces the competing scholarly theories on this subject and points out their underlying assumptions, especially the tendency to frame the issue in ways that privilege the new schools as somehow more authentically "religious" than the parent, Tendai tradition.

Part 2, "The World of Medieval Tendai," contextualizes ideas of original enlightenment by locating them within the historical, institutional, and intellectual framework of medieval Tendai Buddhism. Chapter 3 explores the "culture of secret transmission," the tradition of master-disciple lineages in which such ideas were developed and disseminated, centering on the great Tendai center at Mt. Hiei northeast of the imperial capital. It examines the origins of this culture in the formation of lineages of esoteric ritual, in the monopolizing by aristocrats of the highest clerical ranks, and in the Tendai tradition of religious debate. It also considers the politics of succession in monastic lineages and the rise of competing Tendai institutions in eastern Japan. The medieval period has often been considered a time of Tendai scholarly decline, but in fact, evidence points to considerable intellectual activity. Chapter 4 addresses the hermeneutical techniques employed in medieval Tendai oral transmission *(kuden)* texts and specific doctrinal formulations in which notions of original enlightenment were expressed. My concerns in these two chapters are to redress a tendency to treat the *hongaku* literature as an abstract body of philosophy or "thought" by clarifying its specific contexts, and to show that medieval Tendai, long condemned in modern scholarship as elitist and decadent, was actually a vital and innovative religious tradition.

Whatever their differences, most theories to date about the relationship of Tendai original enlightenment ideas to doctrines of the new Kamakura Buddhism have found in the former a tendency toward "uncritical world affirmation," which, in declaring all beings to be innately enlightened just as they are, in effect denied the necessity of Buddhist practice and legitimated evil conduct. In contrast, the founders of the new Buddhist movements are characterized as having restored the primacy of practice and ethical considerations. Chapter 5 calls this characterization into question through an examination of specific texts. It also suggests a new perspective for understanding the relation of original enlightenment thought to the new Kamakura Buddhism, in which both *hongaku* ideas and the teachings of the new movements are seen as part of a larger, particularly medieval concern with reimagining liberation in a "nonlinear" fashion, that is, as directly accessible in the present moment and not dependent on moral cultivation or the long-term accumulation of merit.

Part 3, "Nichiren and His Successors," shifts focus from medieval Tendai to one of the new Kamakura founders, Nichiren (1222–1282), and the tradition that emerged from his early following. Much of the debate over the relationship between the new Kamakura Buddhism and Tendai *hongaku* thought has taken place in the context of the scholarly study of Nichiren, who has been alternatively characterized as upholding, rejecting, or reforming Tendai original enlightenment doctrine. This chapter refocuses this discussion by presenting Nichiren's thought as expressive of the same sort of Kamakura-period reimagining of enlightenment found in *hongaku* thought but transformed by assimilation to a very different social context and set of ideological concerns.

Original enlightenment thought, in a broad sense, was not exclusive to Tendai Buddhism, nor is the question of its relationship to the new Kamakura Buddhism limited to the Kamakura period. Chapter 7 moves beyond the thirteenth century to examine how, in the process of institutionalization, scholar-monks in the various lineages of Nichiren's new Buddhism, the Hokkeshū, appropriated the interpretive techniques and doctrinal formulations of Tendai *hongaku* thought, thoroughly assimilating them to Nichiren's teaching of exclusive faith in the *Lotus Sūtra* and the practice of chanting its title or *daimoku*. In so doing, they developed a distinctively Nichiren Buddhist mode of original enlightenment discourse.

I have delimited this study by focusing on ideas of original enlightenment solely within the context of Tendai and one of the new movements that emerged from it. Needless to say, there is far more to the original enlightenment discourse, and to Kamakura Buddhism, than this. This volume should be taken as a preliminary, rather than a definitive, study; if it prompts further inquiry in any of the areas it touches upon, I will be very happy.

Acknowledgments

THIS STUDY would not have been undertaken, let alone completed, without the interest and support of many people. William LaFleur first alerted me, when I was still a graduate student, to the importance of original enlightenment thought in the medieval Japanese Buddhist tradition and introduced me to the work of Tamura Yoshirō. Professor Tamura himself took time to meet and talk with me about his research not long before his last illness. The late Shioiri Ryōdō, then head of the Sōgō Bukkyō Kenkyūjo (Institute for Comprehensive Studies of Buddhism) at Taishō University, took me in as a visiting research fellow from 1988 to 1990. Though I was not yet seriously investigating the subject of original enlightenment thought, Professor Shioiri's insistence that the study of Buddhism should be *sōgōteki*—integrative and not bound by sectarian considerations—made a deep impact on me and influenced the eventual direction of this study. He also enabled me to join the Tendai Kuden Hōmon Kenkyūkai, a study group engaged in reading medieval Tendai Buddhist texts in the *kuden hōmon* (orally transmitted doctrines) genre, which sparked my interest in the subject. Tonegawa Kōgyō went out of his way to introduce me to Ōkubo Ryōjun, a leading senior scholar of medieval Japanese Tendai. Though already retired, Professor Ōkubo kindly met with me, recommended readings, and advised me about issues involved in the study of *kuden hōmon*. Others I met at Taishō University at that time who have continued to encourage my studies in this area include Ichishima Masao, Saitō Enshin, and Hirokawa Gyōbin.

The actual research and writing of this study, which began a few years later, also owes much to others' knowledge and assistance. Peter Gregory, executive director of the Kuroda Institute for the Study of Buddhism and Human Values, was wonderfully helpful and encouraging throughout. A timely conversation with Robert Buswell inspired me to proceed with this new project. I am especially indebted to the three read-

ers who reviewed the manuscript for the Kuroda Institute—Carl Bielefeldt, William Bodiford, and Paul Groner—for their insightful responses.
Will Bodiford in particular offered many detailed and cogent suggestions; to the extent that I have been able to implement them, the book
has been much improved. Others who read all or part of the manuscript
at various stages and offered helpful suggestions include the late Philip
B. Yampolsky, Masatoshi Nagatomi, Helen Hardacre, Stephen ("Buzzy")
F. Teiser, and Susan Mattis. I also benefited from the knowledge of colleagues in Japan, especially Sueki Fumihiko and Imai Masaharu. This
study has been refined and strengthened by the excellent advice and
criticism I have received. For its errors and shortcomings, I alone am
responsible.

I would also like to express my gratitude to those Japanese scholars,
both living and deceased, whose work I have drawn on in preparing this
study, such as Shimaji Daitō, Hazama Jikō, Asai Yōrin, Shigyō Kaishū,
Ogami Kanchū, and many others. My own study of the medieval Tendai
and Nichiren traditions would be sadly limited without the benefit of
Japanese secondary scholarship.

This project has also received material assistance in various forms. The
D. T. Suzuki Preceptorship in Buddhist Studies, granted to me by Princeton University from 1992 to 1995, provided extra leave time for the re-
searching and writing of this project and helped to cover expenses. Additional support was provided by the Princeton University Committee
on Research in the Humanities and Social Sciences. For their help in locating sources, I would like to thank the library staff at Taishō and Risshō universities, as well as Soowon Kim, then the Japanese and Korean
bibliographer at Princeton's Gest Library. Fumiko Nazikian and Reiko
Sono corrected my Japanese for the many letters I wrote in the course
of completing this study. Jay Ford initiated me into the use of Twinbridge
for Windows 95. Anita O'Brien's patient copy-editing has improved the
clarity of the manuscript. I would particularly like to thank Patricia
Crosby, executive editor at University of Hawai'i Press, for all that she
has done to make publication of the book possible. Thanks are due also
to Masako Ikeda, managing editor, for her help and patience, and to
Mary Mortensen for preparing the index. I am also grateful to the editors of *Journal of Asian Culture* and *Epoché* for permission to include in
this volume material drawn from my early articles, "Mystical Interpretations of the *Lotus Sūtra* in the Thought of Nichiren" and "An Introduction to the Poetry of Jien," published in the 1984 and 1986 issues of these
journals, respectively.

The photographs in this volume were added at the suggestion of my
readers. My thanks to Professor Nakao Takashi of the History Department of Risshō University for his advice on which of Nichiren's holo-

graphic mandalas to include. The *rinmetsu doji honzon,* whose photograph appears in this book, was reproduced from the frontispiece of *Uchi no otera wa Nichirenshū* (Our family temple belongs to the Nichiren sect) in the series *Waga ie no shūkyō o shiru* (Know your family religion), published in 1997 by Futabasha. My thanks to the mandala's owner, Myōhonji in Kamakura, and to Futabasha, for granting permission to reproduce it. Other temples and shrines who graciously gave permission to include photographs of icons in their possession are Ryūhonji (Kyoto), Senshūji (Mie), Kōsanji (Kyoto), Taisanji (Hyōgo), Hasadera (Nara), Yokokuraji (Gifu), and Togakushi Jinja (Nagano). For providing the photographs, I would like to thank Hōzōkan Publishers, Kyoto National Museum, Nara National Museum, and George Tanabe. I am indebted to Yoshida Koichirō and Okazaki Kazuyo of Kōsei Shuppan for their kind help in mediating communications among me, Nara National Museum, and the owners of those icons whose photographs also appear in Tamura Yoshirō and Kurata Bunsaku's *Hokekyō no bijutsu* (The art of the *Lotus Sūtra,* Kōsei Shuppan, 1981). My thanks, too, to Yoshiaki Shimizu, Karen Brock, and George Tanabe for specific advice on obtaining photographs and permissions.

I am also grateful to several of my colleagues at Princeton in the departments of Religion and East Asian Studies for their encouragement during the writing of the manuscript. Those not yet mentioned include Jeffrey Stout, Victor Preller, Martin Collcutt, Shaun Marmon, and Mark Larrimore. Shaun Marmon's friendship in particular provided intellectual stimulation and much appreciated emotional support. Finally, I wish to thank my husband, Kelley L. Ross of the Philosophy Department of Los Angeles Valley College, whose companionship and unflagging enthusiasm have sustained me throughout this project. His thoughtful responses often helped me to clarify my thinking. He proofread two versions of the entire manuscript and also did the lineage charts.

Abbreviations and Conventions

BD	*Bukkyō daijiten*
BKD	*Busshō kaisetsu daijiten*
Chi	*Fa-hua wen-chü chi*
Chih-kuan	*Mo-ho chih-kuan*
DDZ	*Dengyō Daishi zenshū*
DZZ	*Dōgen Zenshi zenshū*
DNBZ	*Dai Nihon Bukkyō zensho*
ESZ	*Eshin Sōzu zenshū*
FSY	*Fuji shūgaku yōshū*
GR	*Gunsho ruijū*
Hsüan-i	*Miao-fa lien-hua ching hsüan-i*
HTC	*Hsü tsang ching*
Hung-chüeh	*Chih-kuan fu-hsing ch'uan-hung chüeh*
Hurvitz	Leon Hurvitz, *Scripture of the Lotus Blossom of the Fine Dharma (The Lotus Sūtra), Translated from the Chinese of Kumārajīva*
IBK	*Indogaku Bukkyōgaku kenkyū*
KDZ	*Kōbō Daishi zenshū*
Major Writings	*The Major Writings of Nichiren Daishonin*
MFLHC	*Miao-fa lien-hua ching*
NJ	*Nichirenshū jiten*
NSIJ	*Nichiren Shōnin ibun jiten*
NSZ	*Nichirenshū shūgaku zensho*
SCZ	*Shinran chosaku zenshū*
Shih-ch'ien	*Fa-hua hsüan-i shih-ch'ien*
SSH	*Shōwa shinshū Hōnen Shōnin zenshū*
STN	*Shōwa teihon Nichiren Shōnin ibun*
SZ	*Sōtōshū zensho*
T	*Taishō shinshū daizōkyō*

Tendai zasu ki	*Kōtei zōho Tendai zasu ki*
THR	*Tendai hongaku ron*
TZ	*Tendaishū zensho*
Watson and Yampolsky	Burton Watson and others, trans., and Philip B. Yampolsky, ed., *Selected Writings of Nichiren*
Wen-chü	*Miao-fa lien-hua ching wen-chü*
Zenshi	*Nichiren kyōdan zenshi*, vol. 1, ed. Risshō Daigaku Nichiren Kyōgaku Kenkyūjo
ZG	*Zoku gunsho ruijū*
ZTZ	*Zoku Tendaishū zensho*

Specific passages from the *Taishō* canon are cited by title, *Taishō* volume number, page number, column (a, b, or c), and, where appropriate, line numbers. *Taishō* serial numbers are given in the bibliography. Titles of canonical works compiled or translated in China or Korea are cited in Chinese; Sanskrit or Korean titles have been given in parentheses in the bibliography. Where relevant, fascicle *(chüan)* numbers are given in citations; in the case of citations from the *Lotus Sūtra* alone, chapter *(p'in)* numbers are given instead, as the identification of individual chapters is often important to the discussion. Unless otherwise indicated, all references to the *Lotus Sūtra* refer to Kumārajīva's translation, *Miao-fa lien-hua ching* (*T* no. 262).

Works by or attributed to Nichiren have been cited from the four-volume, 1988 revised version of *Shōwa teihon Nichiren shōnin ibun,* giving volume and page numbers. Serial numbers of individual works in this collection are provided in the bibliography. *Selected Writings of Nichiren,* translated by Burton Watson and edited by Philip B. Yampolsky, is based on the earlier *Major Writings of Nichiren Daishonin;* where a particular writing has been translated in both collections, it is cited only from the Watson and Yampolsky version.

Chinese names and terms have been romanized according to the Wade-Giles system; a modified Hepburn has been used for Japanese. In general, technical terms used in reference to a Chinese context are given in Chinese, while Japanese pronunciations have been used in reference to Japan. Pronunciation of Japanese names and terms are given according to the following reference works: Nakamura Hajime, ed., *Bukkyōgo daijiten;* Mochizuki Shinkō, *Bukkyō daijiten;* Ono Genmyō, ed., *Bussho kaisetsu daijiten;* Shibuya Ryōtei, ed., *Shōwa genson Tendai shoseki sōgō mokuroku;* and *Nichirenshū jiten.* Alternative pronunciations appear in parentheses.

In giving dates, years have generally been converted to the Western Gregorian calendar, while months and days are given according to the Japanese lunar calendar. For example, 4/28/1253 would refer to the twenty-eighth day of the fourth lunar month in the year corresponding to 1253 (Kenchō 5). Converted to the day and month of the Gregorian calendar, this would correspond to May 26; however, such conversions have not been given. The ages of individuals are given so as to accord with traditional biographies.

Part One

Perspectives and Problems

Chapter One

What Is "Original Enlightenment Thought"?

IN THE EARLY DECADES of the twentieth century, Buddhologist Shimaji Daitō (1875–1927) introduced to the Japanese academic world a new interpretive category, which he called "original enlightenment thought" (Jpn. *hongaku shisō*).[1] By this term he meant, in general, those strands of Buddhist thought, most prominent in East Asia and especially in Japan, that regard enlightenment or the ideal state as inherent from the outset and as accessible in the present, rather than as the fruit of a long process of cultivation. More specifically, Shimaji used "original enlightenment thought" to designate the intellectual mainstream of medieval Japanese Tendai Buddhism.[2] In this medieval Tendai context, "original enlightenment thought" denotes an array of doctrines and concepts associated with the proposition that all beings are enlightened inherently. Not only human beings, but ants and crickets, mountains and rivers, grasses and trees are all innately Buddhas. The Buddhas who appear in sūtras, radiating light and endowed with excellent marks, are merely provisional signs. The "real" Buddha is the ordinary worldling. Indeed, the whole phenomenal world is the primordially enlightened Tathâgata. Seen in their true light, all forms of daily conduct, even one's delusive thoughts, are, without transformation, the expressions of original enlightenment. Liberation is reimagined, not as the eradication of mental defilements or as achieving birth in a pure land after death, but as the insight, or even the faith, that one has been enlightened from the very beginning. Shimaji saw original enlightenment thought as representing the "climax" of Buddhist philosophy and argued that research in this area would shed light, not only on the development of Japanese Buddhism, but on medieval Japanese culture itself, including Buddhist-Shintō interactions, ethics and morality, literature, and the arts.[3]

Subsequent studies have confirmed Shimaji's assertions about the profound influence of original enlightenment thought, or "*hongaku* thought," to use the shorter expression.[4] But there has been little consensus as to how that importance should be understood and evaluated. Periodically, debates over this subject have burst the confines of Tendai studies to enliven the usually staid world of academic Buddhism in Japan with heated controversy. At issue is how the original enlightenment discourse was related to broader trends in Japanese religion and culture. One school of thought has found in notions of original enlightenment an expression, couched in Buddhistic terms, of a pre-Buddhist, archaic Japanese mentality or psychological orientation characterized by the affirmation of nature and accommodation to phenomenal realities. This tendency to harmonize with outer reality is sometimes said to have originated in primitive responses to Japan's scenic beauty and mild climate, with its orderly progression of the seasons, and even to hold the key to healing the rift between humans and the natural world said to have precipitated the ecological problems of the West.[5] More recently, another group of scholars has made original enlightenment thought the target of a scathing critique. These are the exponents of the intellectual movement known as "critical Buddhism" *(hihan Bukkyō),* of which more will be said in the next chapter. Critical Buddhism charges that notions of original enlightenment introduce into Buddhism the non-Buddhist concept of an *ātman* or metaphysical substrate, subverting the normative Buddhist teaching that all things are empty of independent self-essence. Moreover, despite its superficial semblance of egalitarianism, the claim that all phenomena are enlightened inherently serves to sacralize the given order and thus legitimates social inequities. Notions of original enlightenment, say the critical Buddhists, have served to bolster the emperor system, wartime imperial aggression, and uncritical, self-glorifying Japanism.[6]

These rival polemics have overlapped and interacted with an older controversy about original enlightenment thought, one that concerns its relationship to the new Pure Land, Zen, and Nichiren Buddhist movements of the Kamakura period (1185–1333). These new movements emerged at a time when original enlightenment thought was flourishing, and the writings of their founders contain some points of similarity with medieval Tendai *hongaku* doctrine. What exactly was the relationship between the two? This essay represents an attempt to understand the Tendai original enlightenment discourse, to locate it in its medieval context, and to reconceive the problem of its relation to the new Kamakura Buddhism. First, however, it will be necessary to provide a fairly detailed background. Where did medieval Tendai original enlightenment thought come from? And what are the particular problems—textual and methodological—that confront the researcher in this area? These are the issues addressed in this opening chapter.

A Genealogy of Original Enlightenment Thought

The original enlightenment thought that characterized medieval Japanese Tendai Buddhism emerged in the latter part of the Heian period (794–1185). It had antecedents in the Buddhist traditions of the Asian continent and in those—particularly Tendai and Shingon—of early Heian Japan. Here, only the intellectual influences contributing to the emergence of medieval Tendai *hongaku* thought will be outlined; its institutional and social contexts will be addressed later.[7]

Continental Antecedents: The Awakening of Faith, *Hua-yen and T'ien-t'ai*

Early references to "original enlightenment" (Ch. *pen-chüeh*, Kor. *pon'gak*) occur in the sinitic apocryphal sūtras *Chin-kang san-mei ching* (Sūtra of adamantine absorption) and that version of the *Jen-wang ching* (Sūtra of the benevolent kings) said to have been translated by Amoghavajra (705–774); however, the most influential early source for the term "original enlightenment" is the treatise *Ta-sheng ch'i-hsin lun* or *Awakening of Faith in the Mahāyāna.*[8] Traditionally attributed to the Indian master Aśvaghoṣa, the *Awakening of Faith* is now generally thought to be a sixth-century Chinese apocryphon[9] and represents part of a larger attempt on the part of Chinese Buddhists to clarify the relation between the mind, understood as originally pure, and ignorance.[10] It synthesizes two influential streams of Mahāyāna thought, one concerning the intrinsic nature of enlightenment, and the other, the source of delusion and suffering. The first was expressed as the doctrine of the *tathâgata-garbha,* the originally pure, enlightened mind intrinsic to all sentient beings, conceptualized as the "womb" or "embryo" of Buddhahood. In ordinary worldlings, it is the potential for enlightenment; in Buddhas, the fully realized truth or *dharma-kāya.* In China, *tathâgata-garbha* thought would develop into a major Mahāyāna tradition, ranking beside those of Madhyamaka and Yogācāra. It reflects an attempt to clarify the ontological basis upon which ordinary worldlings can realize Buddhahood.

However, emphasis on an innate basis for enlightenment gave rise to the question of how ignorance arises in the first place. Within the Indian Mahāyāna, this question had been addressed most explicitly by the Yogācāra doctrine of the *ālaya-vijñāna* or "store consciousness." This level of mind is imagined as the repository in which all past experiences, wholesome and unwholesome, pure and defiled, are deposited as "seeds" *(bīja)* that shape future deeds. Ignorance has its source in the defiled seeds that have accumulated in the store consciousness since the inconceivably distant past. Only their thorough extirpation can transform and purify consciousness, a process thought to require many successive lifetimes—three incalculable aeons *(asaṃkhyeya-kalpas)* being a common estimate. Many Chinese Buddhists of the Sui (581–617) and T'ang (618–907) dynasties were dismayed by so remote a vision of liberation and sought to reimagine it in more accessible ways.[11] In approaching this problem, the *Awakening of Faith* subsumes the *ālaya-vijñāna* concept within that of the *tathāgata-garbha* by redefining the former as the none other than the one pure mind as perceived through unenlightened consciousness. The treatise begins by positing two inseparable aspects of the one mind: the mind as suchness or the mind in terms of the absolute, and the mind as arising and perishing (that is, the *ālaya-vijñāna*). These two aspects correspond respectively to the ultimate truth *(paramārtha-satya)* and conventional truth *(saṃvṛti-satya)* in Madhyamaka thought. Because the mind as arising and perishing is grounded in the mind as suchness or the *dharma-kāya,* it is said to possess the aspect of "original enlightenment," the "essence of the mind free from [deluded] thoughts."[12] However, because of not realizing this identity with suchness, deluded thoughts emerge; this state is called nonenlightenment *(pu-chüeh)*. Through contemplative practice, one is able to realize that deluded thoughts have no real status; they are in essence none other than the mind as suchness, which is innately pure. The process of cultivation by which one arrives at such insight is termed "acquired" or "actualized" enlightenment *(shih-chüeh)*. As the text says, "Grounded on the original enlightenment is nonenlightenment. And because of nonenlightenment, the process of actualization of enlightenment can be spoken of."[13] When enlightenment is actualized, one realizes that it is identical to "original enlightenment," the mind of suchness that one has possessed all along. Thus, in the *Awakening of Faith,* "original enlightenment" is posited in distinction to "actualized enlightenment"; it represents the inherence of suchness in the deluded mind and thus the ever-present possibility of transforming that mind into the mind of awakening.

Via the *Awakening of Faith,* the notion of original enlightenment exerted a formative influence on the development of Chinese and Korean Buddhist thought. It became especially important in the Hua-yen school, which—in addition to its central scripture, the *Hua-yen ching (Avataṃ-saka-sūtra,* Flower Ornament Sūtra)—takes the *Awakening of Faith* as a basic text. The concept undergoes development in the thought of Chih-yen (602–668) and Fa-tsang (643–712), counted as the second and third Hua-yen patriarchs, and of later Hua-yen masters such as Ch'eng-kuan (738–839) and Tsung-mi (780–841), both of whom brought Ch'an elements to bear in their interpretations.[14]

Japanese *hongaku* thought would be indebted not only to the specific category of "original enlightenment" set forth in the *Awakening of Faith* and developed in its commentaries, but more broadly to the great totalistic systems of Chinese Buddhist thought, especially those of Hua-yen and T'ien-t'ai, which envision the world as a cosmos in which all things, being empty of independent existence, interpenetrate and encompass one another. These systems are both ontological, in explaining all concrete phenomena *(shih)* as nondual with truth or principle *(li)*, and soteriological, in showing liberation to consist of insight into this unity.

Hua-yen thought sees all phenomena as expressions of an originally pure and undifferentiated one mind. As Robert Gimello has expressed it: "[T]he full diversity of sentient experience and the experienced world—the subjective and the objective, the true and the false, the pure and the defiled, the latent and the manifest—is seen to rest upon or to grow from a common noetic source."[15] Hua-yen thinkers developed new theories of dependent origination *(pratītya-samutpāda, yüan-ch'i)*, such as "dharma realm origination" *(fa-chieh yüan-ch'i)*, "tathâgata-garbha origination" *(ju-lai-tsang yüan-ch'i)*, or "nature origination" *(hsing-ch'i)*, to clarify how the one mind manifests itself as the phenomenal world.[16] Often cited in Japanese *hongaku*-related literature is Fa-tsang's formulation of the two aspects of suchness. In his commentary on the *Awakening of Faith* and elsewhere, Fa-tsang interpreted the two aspects of the one mind as suchness that is absolute or unchanging *(pu-pien)* and suchness that accords with conditions *(sui-yüan)*, equating them with principle *(li)* and phenomena *(shih)*, respectively.[17] Suchness in its unchanging, quiescent mode is the one pure mind; in its dynamic mode, responding to the ignorance that is the condition of sentient beings, it manifests the phenomenal world. Notions of origination from the mind or suchness are often illustrated with the metaphor of water and waves that occurs in the *Awakening of Faith:* when the water of true suchness or principle *(li)* is stirred by the winds of ignorance, the waves of differentiated phenomena *(shih)* arise, but the waves are no different in substance from the water.[18] Origination from suchness stands in contrast to both the classic "twelve-linked" model of dependent origination as the arising of birth, old age, sickness, and death in dependence upon ignorance, craving, and so forth, and the Yogācāra model in which differentiated phenomena arise from seeds stored within the *ālaya-vijñāna* and are independent of suchness. Both these understandings see the empirical world as inherently delusory, something that must be literally undone if liberation is to be achieved. The teaching of origination from suchness in effect grounds the arising of phenomena in the one pure mind and thus obliterates any ontological distinction between them. It is only because of adventitious nonenlightenment that deluded thoughts appear, producing the distinction of subject and object and thus leading to the notion of self and other as real entities, and to craving, attachment, and enmeshment in samsaric misery. Liberation lies in discerning that the differentiated phenomena of the samsaric world are, in their essence, no different from the one mind and thus originally pure.

The nonduality of principle *(li)* and phenomena *(shih)* as set forth in much of Hua-yen thought is heavily weighted toward the former. The mind is original, pure, and true, while phenomena are in contrast unreal, arising only as the one mind is perceived through human ignorance. A different sort of totalistic vision occurs in the T'ien-t'ai school, whose central scripture is the *Lotus Sūtra,* and which is deeply rooted in Madhyamaka thinking concerning the nonduality of absolute and conventional truth. "Original enlightenment" does not appear as a category in early Chinese T'ien-t'ai, nor was the *Awakening of Faith* an important inspiration for early T'ien-t'ai thinkers. Nonetheless, the T'ien-t'ai tradition represents a crucial antecedent to the development of Japanese *hongaku* thought. In contrast to Hua-yen emphasis on all things arising from the mind, early T'ien-t'ai—as well as the later T'ien-t'ai thought of Ssu-ming Chih-li (960–1028), who attempted to counter Hua-yen influences—denies that the mind is a pure, undifferentiated cosmic principle from which all things arise. In the words of Chih-i (538–597), regarded as the founder of the T'ien-t'ai school: "One may say neither that the one mind is prior and all dharmas posterior nor that all dharmas are prior and the mind posterior. . . . All one can say is that the mind is all dharmas and all dharmas are the mind. Therefore the relationship is neither vertical nor horizontal, neither the same nor different."[19]

For Chih-i, phenomena do not "arise" from principle. Principle is that form and mind are always nondual and mutually inclusive *(hu-chü);* the mutual encompassing of good and evil, delusion and enlightenment, is the "true aspect" *(shih-hsiang)* of all things. This emphasis on the mutually inclusive nature of dharmas and the mind can be seen in the structure of the threefold truth or threefold contemplation that lies at the heart of Chih-i's interpretation of the *Lotus Sūtra* and the Indian Madhyamaka tradition.[20] It will be discussed in more detail in chapters 3 and 4. In Chih-i's system of meditation, one contemplates all phenomena from the three perspectives of emptiness *(k'ung),* conventional existence *(chia),* and the middle *(chung).* By contemplating the phenomena of conventional existence as arising through dependent origination, one discerns that they are empty of self-nature; this move, termed "entering emptiness from conventional existence," frees one from attachment to samsaric existence. By a reverse discernment, "[re]entering conventional existence from emptiness," one is freed from attachment to reified notions of emptiness and is able to reengage the myriad phenomena of the world in a soteriologically effective way. And by contemplation of the middle, one gains both discernments simultaneously, the perspectives of "emptiness" and "conventional existence" being mutually illuminated but also negated as one-sided extremes. The status of "conventional existence" as the point from which one begins contemplation, and to which one "returns" for bodhisattva practice, reflects T'ien-t'ai emphasis on concrete particulars as instantiating ultimate truth: "Of every form and fragrance, there is none that is not the Middle Way."[21]

T'ien-t'ai emphasis on the mutual inclusiveness of mind and all dharmas obviously ruled out Hua-yen-style notions of a primal purity. "Mind" as the object of contemplation was for Chih-i the deluded thought-moment of ordinary worldlings, which he saw as naturally endowed *(hsing-chü)* with the ten dharma realms from hell to Buddhahood. In T'ien-t'ai thought, even the single thought-moment of the Buddha is endowed with these ten realms and thus continues to possess evil as an innate, though nonmanifested, potential *(hsing-o, shōaku)*.[22] Thus purity and impurity are always mutually encompassing. Where Hua-yen develops a discourse of origination from the one pure mind *(yüan-ch'i lun, engi ron)*, T'ien-t'ai maintains that all dharmas manifest the true aspect of reality *(shih-hsiang lun, jissō ron)*, or that the mind by nature is endowed with all dharmas *(hsing-chü-shuo, shōgu setsu)*.

Hua-yen Buddhism had not yet taken shape as an independent tradition in Chih-i's time; his critique of the position that held the mind to be prior to the dharmas was aimed rather at the mind-only doctrines of the Ti-lun and She-lun schools, which exerted a formative influence on Hua-yen.[23] However, when Hua-yen began to emerge as a rival tradition and sectarian consciousness gained strength, Chih-i's rejection of an originally pure mind prior to the arising of the dharmas became an axis along which his later followers would define T'ien-t'ai orthodoxy, especially over and against Hua-yen. The sixth T'ien-t'ai patriarch Chan-jan (711–782) drew on the *Awakening of Faith* and also borrowed key Hua-yen terms such as "mind only" and "nature origination"—but he appropriated them, vis-à-vis a largely Hua-yen audience, in the service of a T'ien-t'ai position that "take(s) issue with a one-sided [notion] of a clean and pure suchness."[24] For example, in his treatise *Chin-kang pei* (The diamond scalpel), Chan-jan used Fa-tsang's concept of "suchness according with conditions" to assert his famous doctrine that insentient beings have the Buddha nature. If all phenomena are none other than suchness, he argued, then it becomes meaningless to say that sentient beings have the Buddha nature but insentient beings do not.[25] With this doctrine, Chan-jan asserted the superior inclusivity of T'ien-t'ai Buddhism. In its distinctively Japanese incarnation as "the realization of Buddhahood by grasses and trees" *(sōmoku jōbutsu)*, the doctrine of the Buddha nature of insentient beings would exert a profound influence on both Tendai thought and Japanese Buddhism generally. After Chan-jan's time, his use of Hua-yen terminology and concepts tended increasingly to be interpreted by some among his followers in light of *tathâgata-garbha* notions of an originally pure mind. This led, during the Sung dynasty, to doctrinal conflict between the so-called mountain-school *(shan-chia)* and off-mountain *(shan-wai)* factions within T'ien-tai Buddhism. The mountain school, led by Chih-li (960–1028), identified themselves as the champi-ons of an orthodox T'ien-t'ai definition of "mind" as the mind of the or-dinary worldling, over and against the off-mountain side who advocated a more "Hua-yen"-style interpretation in light of notions of an originally pure *tathâgata-garbha*.[26]

In his study of the antecedents of Japanese original enlightenment thought, Tamura Yoshirō has characterized the Hua-yen totalistic vision as "dynamic," in that it explains how the one mind, by encountering conditions, manifests the myriad phenomena. T'ien-t'ai, on the other hand, he characterizes as "concrete," in that form and mind are mutu-ally identified in every phenomenal particular. Hua-yen, Tamura says, moves from *li* to *shih*, emphasizing the exfoliation of particulars from the one mind, while T'ien-t'ai moves from *shih* to *li*, stressing that each particular as it stands encompasses the true aspect of reality.[27] Though their approaches differ, the two traditions addressed similar issues, and the similarity increased with mutual exchanges and borrowings from the latter T'ang period into the Sung. Both T'ien-t'ai and Hua-yen can be seen as attempts to reconceive Indian Mahāyāna insights about the empty and dependent nature of the dharmas and express them in terms of Chi-nese intellectual categories such as principle *(li)* and phenomena *(shih)*, essence *(t'i)* and function *(yung)*, or nature *(hsing)* and outward form *(hsiang)*.[28] This involved a significant shift away from the apophatic lan-guage of Indian Madhyamaka—which maintains, in its extreme wariness about the limitations of language, that truth can be verbally illuminated only by stating what it is not—to more kataphatic modes of expression. These new modes attempt neither to reimport into Buddhism notions of metaphysical essence nor to claim that there can be adequate verbal descriptions for truth, but to employ positive language in soteriologically effective ways. Moreover, since principle and phenomena are seen as non-dual, and this nonduality is expressed in every particular form, the Hua-yen and T'ien-t'ai totalistic visions also entailed a reconception of the empirical world. No longer was it the product of delusion or a place of suffering to be escaped, but the very realm where truth is to be realized and liberation achieved. This reconception was critical to the sinification of Buddhism and exerted an immense impact on the subsequent de-velopment of Buddhism in East Asia.[29]

Japanese Beginnings: Saichō and Kūkai

Original enlightenment thought in Japan may be said properly to have begun in the time of Saichō (767–822) and Kūkai (774–835). These two men are revered as the founders, respectively, of the Japa-nese Tendai and Shingon schools, which rose to prominence during the Heian period.[30] The "six schools" of Buddhism in the preceding Nara period (710–794) were largely under state control, and their temples were located in the capital at Nara. In contrast, the monastic centers established by Kūkai on Mt. Kōya and by Saichō on Mt. Hiei stood at some remove from the new capital of Heian-kyō and enjoyed greater independence from the government. Both Tendai and Shingon introduced remarkable innovations in doctrine and practice. Over and against the gradualist models of liberation upheld by the Nara schools, they regarded enlightenment as accessible in the near future, perhaps even in this lifetime.

Kūkai must be acknowledged as the first Japanese Buddhist to engage seriously the concept of original enlightenment. Heir to a continental tradition of Hua-yen and Chen-yen (Jpn. Shingon) interactions, Kūkai ranked Hua-yen (Jpn. Kegon) just below the esoteric teachings in his doctrinal classification of the "ten stages of mind" and drew heavily on Hua-yen thought in his systematization of the esoteric teachings.[31] In particular, he drew extensively on the *Shih Mo-ho-yen lun* (Treatise interpreting the Mahāyāna), said to be Nāgārjuna's commentary on the *Awakening of Faith* as translated by Vṛddhimata (dates unknown), but probably an eighth-century Korean apocryphon.[32] This treatise relativizes the distinction drawn in the *Awakening of Faith* between the "mind as suchness" and the "mind as arising and perishing" by postulating a third term, the "nondual Mahāyāna" *(pu-erh mo-ho-yen, funi makaen)* in which both are subsumed; Kūkai identified this "nondual Mahāyāna" with the esoteric teachings. The *Shih Mo-ho-yen lun* also elaborates in great detail on "original enlightenment," for example, by dividing it into a number of subcategories.[33] Basic to these is a distinction between "original enlightenment as [both] tainted and pure," and "original enlightenment as clean and pure." The former is very close to the meaning of "original enlightenment" as it appears in the *Awakening of Faith:* the potential for enlightenment inherent in the deluded mind. In the latter sense, however, it is given a more absolute reading, much closer to suchness itself, or to the ontological basis of the nonduality of beings and the Buddha: "The Buddha nature that is original enlightenment encompasses countless merits and neither increases nor decreases. . . . Since the beginningless past, original enlightenment that is clean and pure has not depended on practice, nor is it obtained by the power of another."[34] Kūkai drew especially on this latter usage of "original enlightenment" from the *Shih Mo-ho-yen-lun* and read it in an esoteric light, for example, as the Dharma body of the Tathâgata Vairocana which is one's own nature.[35] Where continental thought concerning "original enlightenment," especially that of Hua-yen tradition, had interpreted this concept in light of the "one mind," in Kūkai's thought, it is linked to the esoteric doctrines of identity with the cosmic Buddha and of realizing Buddhahood with this very body *(sokushin jōbutsu).*[36] Kūkai's understanding of "original enlightenment" and his use of the *Shih Mo-ho-yen lun* would eventually influence thinkers within the Japanese Tendai tradition, such as Annen (841–?).

Saichō, the founder of Japanese Tendai, did not develop *hongaku* as a doctrinal category; the term as such occurs only once in his authenticated writings, and there, in a quotation from another source.[37] Nevertheless, he is important to the development of medieval Tendai original enlightenment thought. Though he journeyed to China to further his study of T'ien-t'ai teachings and presented himself as a transmitter of T'ien-t'ai Buddhism to Japan, Saichō was responsible for a number of innovations in thought and practice that, over time, would deeply differentiate Japanese Tendai from its continental predecessor. Without these innovations, Japanese Tendai original enlightenment thought would not have emerged. Medieval Tendai *hongaku* thought thus has two major Japanese Buddhist sources: Kūkai's appropriation of continental original enlightenment thought as expressed in the *Shih Mo-ho-yen lun,* and Saichō's innovations in Tendai Buddhism. Among the latter, the most significant are Saichō's understanding of the one vehicle, his advocacy of bodhisattva precept ordinations, and his insistence on the unity of esoteric and exoteric teachings.

Saichō and the One Vehicle

The *Lotus Sūtra* is central to the T'ien-t'ai/Tendai tradition, which regards it as the culmination of the Buddha's teachings, preached during the last eight years of his life. Some Mahāyāna sūtras deny the validity of the two "lesser vehicles" (Hīnayāna)—the vehicle of the *śrāvaka* or voice-hearer, culminating in the state of the *arhat* and, at life's end, in final nirvāṇa, and the vehicle of the *pratyeka-buddha* or independently enlightened "private Buddha," also culminating at death in final nirvāṇa—and supplant both with the bodhisattva vehicle, which leads to supreme Buddhahood. The *Lotus,* however, while maintaining the superiority of the bodhisattva vehicle, subsumes all three within the "one Buddha vehicle." "Within the Buddha lands of the ten directions," it says, "there is the Dharma of only One Vehicle. There are not two, nor are there yet three."[38] The sūtra acknowledges that the Buddha did indeed teach three paths or vehicles, yet this threefold division of the Dharma was apparent, not real; it represents the Buddha's skillful means (*upāya, hōben*) set forth in response to the varying capacities of his followers. His true intention was to lead all beings to the supreme enlightenment represented by the one Buddha vehicle.[39]

Saichō understood the one vehicle in terms of the universal potential for Buddhahood. This was by no means a new idea; virtually all Chinese Mahāyāna traditions upheld that Buddhahood is ultimately attainable by all. The sole exception was the Fa-hsiang (Jpn. Hossō) school, the branch of Yogācāra that had been established by Hsüan-tsang (602–664) and his disciple K'uei-chi (632–682). In Japan, Hossō had become the most influential of the Nara Buddhist schools, and Saichō developed unique arguments for the universality of Buddhahood in written debate with a Hossō scholar named Tokuitsu. Their debate spanned only four years, from 817 through 821, but Saichō produced the vast majority of his doctrinal writings in this context.[40]

As a Hossō scholar, Tokuitsu distinguished two kinds of Buddha nature: Buddha nature as suchness or principle *(ri-busshō),* which is universal, and active Buddha nature *(gyō-busshō),* which is not. *Ri-busshō* is quiescent and does not manifest itself in the phenomenal world; thus the universality of the Buddha nature in this sense does not mean that all people can become Buddhas. Realizing Buddhahood depends on *gyō-busshō,* which consists of "untainted seeds" present in the *ālaya* consciousness since the beginningless past. Those who possess such seeds can become Buddhas; those who lack them can never attain Buddhahood, no matter how hard they may strive. Hossō thought additionally postulates two other kinds of untainted seeds that a person might possess: seeds enabling one to become a *śrāvaka* or a *pratyeka-buddha.* Some individuals are presumed to have two or three of these different kinds of untainted seeds. Such persons are said to be of undetermined nature *(fujōshō),* in that which of the three kinds of seeds will develop in them— that is, whether they will become śrāvakas or pratyeka-buddhas, who can achieve arhatship, or bodhisattvas, who can achieve Buddhahood—is uncertain. There are also persons lacking untainted seeds altogether, who can never attain liberation of any kind. They can, however, achieve improved rebirths in the human and heavenly realms through religious efforts.

From the perspective of this Hossō doctrine, called "the distinction of five natures" *(goshō kakubetsu),* Tokuitsu argued that the division of the Dharma into three vehicles represented the Buddha's true intent: some people really were destined to become arhats, pratyeka-buddhas, or bodhisattvas. On the other hand, the *Lotus Sūtra*'s teaching of the one vehicle was a provisional expedient set forth to encourage those of the undetermined group, some of whom might be capable of practicing the bodhisattva path and becoming Buddhas. For Saichō, however, it was just as the *Lotus* declared: the three vehicles were provisional and the one vehicle, true; Buddhahood was the final destiny of all. In support of his position, Saichō drew on a variety of sources. One was Fa-tsang's commentary on the *Awakening of Faith,* specifically, its distinction between suchness that is unchanging *(fuhen shinnyo)* and suchness that accords with conditions *(zuien shinnyo).* Like Fa-tsang, Saichō argued that suchness has a dynamic as well as a quiescent aspect. In its dynamic aspect, it expresses itself as all phenomena and also has the nature of realizing and knowing *(kakuchi shō).*[41] Thus there is no need to postulate seeds in the *ālaya* consciousness as the source of the phenomenal world or as the cause, in some individuals, for achieving Buddhahood. Saichō equated suchness in its dynamic aspect with *gyō-busshō;* since suchness is universal, he argued, everyone has the potential to realize Buddhahood.

Saichō's appropriation of the two aspects of suchness was reminiscent of the move made by Chan-jan, who had also drawn on this aspect of Fa-tsang's thought to argue the Buddha nature of insentient beings. Saichō had been ordained under the Kegon (Ch. Hua-yen) master Gyōhyō and had studied texts of the Kegon/Hua-yen tradition—including the *Awakening of Faith* and Fa-tsang's commentary—before being drawn to T'ien-t'ai thought. He also studied in China with two of Chan-jan's disciples, Tao-sui and Hsing-man, who belonged to a generation when Hua-yen terminology and concepts were being incorporated into T'ien-t'ai Buddhism. Thus it is hardly surprising that Saichō's Tendai doctrine reflects some Kegon/Hua-yen ideas.[42] Along with the classic T'ien-t'ai emphasis on the nonduality of pure and impure, delusion and enlightenment, inherent in every concrete phenomenon, Japanese Tendai writings from Saichō on would include elements of a more "Kegon" style, such as notions of an originally pure mind. In this case, however, Saichō's understanding of "suchness according with conditions" had a unique twist not found either in Chan-jan's *Chin-kang pei* or in Hua-yen teachings. Saichō referred to the unchanging, quiescent view of suchness as a "one-sided truth" *(hen shinri)* pertaining to the three vehicles, and to the dynamic view of suchness as "truth according with the middle" *(chū shinri)* and the teaching of the one vehicle.[43] This reading not only acknowledges two aspects of suchness but establishes a hierarchy between the two in identifying the dynamic aspect of suchness—its expression as the phenomenal world—with the T'ien-t'ai category of the "middle" and with the one vehicle of the *Lotus.* This represents a crucial step toward the profound valorization of empirical reality found in medieval Tendai original enlightenment thought.[44]

Exclusive and Inclusive Readings

Saichō's interpretation of the one vehicle is also reflected in his contributions to doctrinal classification. The project of doctrinal classification (Ch. *p'an-chiao* or *chiao-p'an;* Jpn. *kyōhan*) developed in China through the efforts of Chinese Buddhists to organize into coherent systems the mass of Buddhist texts introduced from India and Central Asia.[45] Peter N. Gregory has pointed out that these doctrinal classifications served three kinds of purposes: hermeneutical, sectarian, and soteriological. Hermeneutically, they attempt to uncover a unified framework underlying the diversity of Buddhist teachings and within which those teachings can be systematized. Typically, the framework takes the form of a hierarchy or graded sequence of teachings; thus schemes of doctrinal classification also work to legitimize the claims of particular sectarian traditions to be the most authoritative. And soteriologically, they function as models of the path, in which successive levels of teachings correspond to stages of attainment traversed by the practitioner.[46] Doctrinal classifications range from simple binary schemes (e.g., "sudden" and "gradual") to highly elaborate systems, such as the "five periods and eight teachings" *(wu-shih pa-chiao, goji hakkyō)* of the T'ien-t'ai tradition.[47]

Within the T'ien-t'ai/Tendai tradition, doctrinal classifications have drawn on the claim that all teachings are "opened and integrated in the one vehicle" *(ichijō kaie)* of the *Lotus Sūtra*. Historically, interpretations of this "opening and integration" have developed in two general directions. From an absolute standpoint *(zettai kaie)*, because the one vehicle is all-encompassing, nothing exists outside it to which it might be contrasted. Once grounded in the one vehicle, the distinction between "true" and "provisional" is dissolved; understood in this light, all teachings become expressions of the one vehicle. This is an inclusive reading, in which all teachings in effect become "true." But from a relative standpoint *(sōtai kaie)*, the distinction is preserved between the provisional teachings, which are opened and integrated, and the true teaching, which opens and integrates them. This is an exclusive reading, one that emphasizes the superiority of the *Lotus Sūtra* over all other teachings.[48] Both kinds of interpretations recur throughout the T'ien-t'ai/Tendai tradition, though one mode may predominate depending on the individual work or thinker as well as on historical circumstances. Unsurprisingly, exclusive readings come to the fore in sectarian polemics, where T'ien-t'ai or Tendai positions are being argued against those of other traditions. However, both inclusive and exclusive readings exhibit all three aspects of doctrinal classification schemes—hermeneutical, sectarian, and soteriological—that Gregory has noted.

In his schemes of doctrinal classification, Saichō developed both exclusive and inclusive readings of the one vehicle that would be important to the development of medieval Tendai thought and practice. In his written debates with Tokuitsu, Saichō argued the superiority of the *Lotus* over all other teachings from a number of angles. For example, he asserted that the *Lotus* alone represents the standpoint of "effect," or the Buddha's enlightenment *(kabun);* other sūtras, such as the *Avataṃsaka*, reflect the standpoint of "cause," or of those still in the stages of cultivation *(inbun).*[49] He also distinguished the *Lotus* as the "direct path" *(jikidō)* or "great direct path" *(daijikidō)* to enlightenment, in contrast to both the "roundabout path" of the Hīnayāna and the "path requiring kalpas" followed by bodhisattvas of provisional Mahāyāna.[50] In Saichō's view, a practitioner of the *Lotus* endowed with unusually keen faculties might even be able to realize Buddhahood with this very body *(sokushin jōbutsu),* though he confined this possibility to persons who had already achieved the first abode, or the fifth of the six stages of identity, which, according to T'ien-t'ai doctrine, comprise the Buddhist path.[51] Practitioners of lesser faculties would be able to realize Buddhahood in the next lifetime, or in the lifetime after that.[52] As discussed below, the doctrine of realizing Buddhahood with this very body, as interpreted by Saichō's disciples, was crucial to the development of medieval Tendai original enlightenment thought. Saichō also interpreted the *Lotus Sūtra* as particularly suited to the time and to the capacities of the Japanese people, claims that would be further developed in the thought of Nichiren (1222–1282).[53]

However, based on the idea of its superiority to all other teachings, Saichō also developed inclusive readings of the *Lotus Sūtra.* One sees this, for example, in his concept of the "three kinds of *Lotus Sūtra*" *(sanshu Hokke),* by which he interpreted the sūtra passage: "The Buddhas, by their power of skillful means, with respect to the one Buddha vehicle make distinctions and preach it as three. . . . There is only the one Buddha vehicle."[54] Saichō wrote: "'With respect to the one Buddha vehicle' indicates the fundamental *Lotus (konpon Hokke);* 'make distinctions and preach it as three,' the hidden and secret *Lotus (onmitsu Hokke);* and 'there is only the one Buddha vehicle,' the *Lotus* that was explicitly preached *(kensetsu Hokke).* Apart from the [*Sūtra of the Lotus*] *Blossom of the Wonderful Dharma,* there exists not [even] a single phrase of another sūtra."[55] From this inclusive standpoint, *"Lotus Sūtra"* means not only the actual text of that name (i.e., "the *Lotus* that was explicitly preached"), but the consistent intent underlying the Buddha's lifetime teachings ("the fundamental *Lotus*"), as well as all sūtras other than the *Lotus,* in which, due to the immaturity of his hearers' capacity, that intention is not fully revealed ("the hidden and secret *Lotus*"). This reading would inform doctrinal classifications that developed in the context of medieval Tendai original enlightenment thought.

Most important to the later Tendai tradition, Saichō's attempts to integrate all teachings within the one vehicle of the *Lotus Sūtra* were not merely conceptual but also extended to practice. While in China, he received instruction or ordination in four traditions: T'ien-t'ai doctrine proper; esoteric teachings; Ch'an, of the Ox-head and Northern schools; and the bodhisattva precepts.[56] To some extent, these multiple transmissions reflect the tendency of Chinese T'ien-t'ai monks of the time to adopt elements from other traditions.[57] But they also suggest Saichō's conviction that all teachings could be unified within the one vehicle. It is not altogether clear how Saichō himself envisioned the integration of these four. Based on the *Naishō Buppō kechimyaku fu,* Saichō's record of the lineages of the transmissions he had received, Paul Groner has suggested that Saichō may have intended to unify them by tracing all four back to a single Buddha—Śākyamuni, identified with Vairocana (Ru-shana or Birushana in Japanese), who is the Buddha asssociated with both the *Fan-wang ching* and the esoteric teachings.[58] The task of systemati-cally unifying these four traditions would fall to Saichō's disciples and led to distinctive developments within Japanese Tendai that sharply dif-ferentiate it from the continental T'ien-t'ai tradition.

The Bodhisattva Precepts

In Saichō's day, Buddhist ordinations in East Asia were usually per-formed by conferring the precepts of the *Ssu fen lü* (Vinaya in four parts), the *vinaya* or monastic code of the Dharmagupta school, comprising 250 rules for monks and 348 for nuns. Many monastics subsequently received an additional set of "bodhisattva precepts"—guidelines for conduct found in a number of Mahāyāna sūtras—to confirm their commitment to the Mahāyāna. These same bodhisattva precepts were also conferred on lay people to enable them to form a closer connection with Buddhism. The most widely used set of bodhisattva precepts occurs in the fifth-century apocryphal *Fan-wang ching* (Brahmā-Net Sūtra), which includes a list of ten major and forty-eight minor precepts.[59] The Chinese *vinaya* master Chien-chen (Jpn. Ganjin, 688–763), invited by the Japanese court to help regularize monastic ordinations in Japan, is thought to have con-ferred the *Fan-wang* precepts on Emperor Kōken and more than four hundred others, as well as on Japanese monks whom he had previously ordained with the precepts of the *Ssu-fen lü*.[60] While the *Ssu-fen lü* pre-cepts technically represented the *vinaya* of a "Hīnayāna" school, they were seldom regarded as Hinayanist—a pejorative term—but were in-terpreted in a Mahāyāna light.[61]

Saichō, as is well known, deprecated the *Ssu-fen lü* as "Hīnayāna pre-cepts" and argued that Tendai novices should be ordained as "bodhi-sattva monks" with the precepts of the *Fan-wang ching*. With this radical move, Saichō challenged the authority of the Nara schools, who con-trolled the three state-sponsored ordination platforms, and freed his dis-ciples from the need to interrupt their training on Mt. Hiei to journey to Nara for ordination. He also sought to remove his newly inaugurated Tendai school and its program of education from the jurisdiction of the government Office of Monastic Affairs (Sōgō), which was dominated by prominent monks of the Nara schools, especially of the rival Hossō school.

However, Saichō also had doctrinal grounds for his advocacy of the bodhisattva precepts. He called them the "perfect precepts" *(enkai)*, meaning that he assimilated them to the *Lotus Sūtra* and the T'ien-t'ai/Tendai teaching of universal Buddha nature.[62] Of the three kinds of learning *(sangaku)* that comprise the Buddha Way, Saichō held that per-fect meditation and perfect wisdom (i.e., doctrinal teachings) had al-

ready emerged within T'ien-t'ai Buddhism; the perfect precepts, however, had yet to be established.[63]

In this connection, Shirato Waka has suggested a possible link between
Saichō's understanding of the *Fan-wang* precepts and the later emergence of Tendai original enlightenment thought.[64] The *Fan-wang ching*
describes its bodhisattva precepts as "the fundamental source of all Buddhas, the fundamental source of all bodhisattvas, the seeds of the Buddha nature. All sentient beings have the Buddha nature. All things with
consciousness, form and mental activity, all sentient [beings] with mental activity, are all included within [the purview of] these Buddha-nature
precepts. . . . The fundamental source of precepts for all sentient beings
is pure in itself."[65] Here the bodhisattva precepts are said to be grounded
in the Buddha nature. Since all beings have the Buddha nature, they in-
cline naturally toward these precepts. Saichō further developed this argument: "These are the precepts which are [based on] the constantly
abiding Buddha nature, the original source of all living beings, pure in
its self-nature and unmoving like empty space. Therefore, by means of
these precepts, one manifests and attains the original, inherent, constantly abiding Dharma body endowed with the thirty-two marks."[66] In
this reading, the precepts are no longer an externally imposed set of regulations or moral guidelines, but an expression of innate Buddhahood
and also the direct cause for its realization. Because the Buddha nature
is innate, all people, clerics and laity alike, can readily practice the bodhisattva precepts, and by practicing these precepts, innate Buddhahood
is naturally manifested. This theme is related to Saichō's idea of the *Lotus*
as opening the "direct path" (*jikidō*) to the speedy realization of Buddhahood.[67] This view of practice (in this case, of the precepts) as simultaneously both the effect and the cause of Buddhahood would be developed in later Tendai *hongaku* thought.

Saichō's reception of the bodhisattva precepts appears to have influenced later original enlightenment discourse in another way as well.
The *Fan-wang ching* precepts stress attitude and intention; they do not
include instructions in protocol for monastic assemblies and were not
designed to serve as the sole guideline for regulating a renunciate community. In adopting them for purposes of initiating "bodhisattva monks,"
Saichō himself clearly never intended that high standards of monastic
discipline be compromised. He not only mandated twelve years' uninterrupted study on Mt. Hiei but left final instructions for his disciples
exhorting them to extreme frugality in matters of food, clothing, bed-
ding, and the like.[68] He also instructed that, after twelve years of training on Mt. Hiei, when they would no longer be in danger of "backsliding,"
monks should provisionally receive the "Hīnayāna" *Ssu-fen lü* ordination.[69] However, Saichō died before he could fully elaborate his interpretation of the precepts in terms of either doctrine or practical appli-

cation, and understandings differed considerably even among his immediate disciples.[70] Before many decades had passed, under the influence of esoteric interpretations of the precepts and the need to accommodate the lifestyles of growing numbers of aristocrats seeking
careers as Tendai monks, lenient readings would prevail. Especially
influential in this regard was the *Futsū jubosatsukai kōshaku* (Extensive explanation of the bodhisattva precept ordination) of the ninth-century
Tendai monk Annen, systematizer of Tendai esoteric thought, which interprets the bodhisattva precepts as instilling a Mahāyāna attitude, rather
than mandating particular forms of conduct.[71] Annen, for example, held
that all precepts are inherent in the precept-essence *(kaitai);* by receiving the precept-essence, one realizes Buddhahood in this very body.
Through such interpretations, emphasis shifted from observance of the
precepts as moral guidelines or institutional regulations to the ceremony
of ordination itself, understood increasingly as esoteric initiation and a
guarantee of realizing Buddhahood. By the medieval period, notions of
formless, originally inherent "perfect and sudden precepts" *(endonkai),*
"*Lotus* one-vehicle precepts" *(Hokke ichijōkai),* or "unproduced diamond
precepts" *(musa kongō hōkai)* came to supersede literal adherence to the
specifics of the *Fan-wang ching* precepts.[72] These "formless readings" of
the precepts put forth within the influential T'ien-t'ai school influenced
other Buddhist traditions as well and have been seen by many scholars
as contributing to a decline in monastic discipline in the latter Heian
period.[73] "Formless" understandings of the precepts, rooted remotely in
Saichō's advocacy of bodhisattva precept ordinations, were also linked
to an important strand of early medieval Buddhist discourse, found in
both Tendai and some of the new Kamakura Buddhist movements, which
denies the validity of precepts in the Final Dharma age *(mappō mukai)*
and makes liberation dependent on faith or insight, rather than on the
cultivation of morality or the accumulation of merit through good
deeds.[74]

Saichō and the Esoteric Teachings

The esoteric teachings *(mikkyō)* are also known as the Vajrayāna (Diamond Vehicle), Mantrayāna (Mantra Vehicle), Tantric Buddhism, or,
in Japan, *shingon.*[75] The major forms of Mikkyō to be established in
Japan—the great esoteric systems of Shingon and Tendai—center on
Dainichi Nyorai (Skt. Vairocana or Mahāvairocana Tathâgata), who is neither a historical figure nor a supramundane being but the Buddha as
Dharma body, that is, the truth without beginning or end that is inherent in all things. All other Buddhas are seen as manifestations of this cosmic Buddha; so indeed is the universe itself. All visible forms are the Buddha's body, all sounds are the Buddha's voice, and all thoughts are the
Buddha's mind, though the unenlightened do not discern this. How-

ever, through the practice of the three mysteries *(sanmitsu)*—mūdras, or ritual hand gestures; mantras, sacred syllables or phrases; and meditations on specific objects of worship *(honzon)*—the initiate is able to realize his identity with the cosmic Buddha.[76] Esoteric ritual was also highly valued for its magical achievement of worldly ends, such as good harvests, healing, timely rainful, the prevention of disaster, prosperity, subjugation of enemies, placation of vengeful spirits, and sexual fulfillment. The perceived power of esoteric rites to effect these and other concrete ends led to widespread patronage of Mikkyō ritualists by the court and by powerful aristocrats. Modern scholars have tended to dismiss esoteric rituals conducted for apotropaic or other wish-fulfilling purposes as inferior to, or even a corruption of, the high soteriologial aspects of the Mikkyō tradition; however, there is little indication that esoteric adepts of the premodern period shared this view. To the contrary, the performance of esoteric rites for both spiritual liberation and practical, worldly ends reflected Mikkyō emphasis on the nonduality of saṃsāra and nirvāṇa, and of ultimate and mundane truth.[77]

While various strands of esoteric Buddhism had existed in Japan since the Nara period, Saichō and Kūkai are generally credited with its formal introduction and establishment. In China, Kūkai was initiated into a recently developed *ryōbu* (two-part) esoteric system that united the lineages of the Diamond Realm (Skt. Vajradhātu, Jpn. Kongōkai) and Matrix Realm (Garbhadhātu, Taizōkai) mandalas, which are based respectively on the esoteric scriptures *Chin-kang-ting ching* (Skt. *Vajraśekhara-sūtra;* Jpn. *Kongōchō-kyō*) and *Ta-p'i-lu-che-na ching* or simply *Ta-jih ching (Mahāvairocana-sūtra, Dainichi-kyō).*[78] The *ryōbu* tradition was handed down within Kūkai's Shingon school, while the Tendai school was to adopt a three-part system that joined to the lineages of the Diamond and Matrix Realms a third esoteric tradition based on the *Su-hsi-ti ching (Soshitsuji-kyō),* a scripture related to the *Ta-jih-ching.* Saichō's own initiation in China into the esoteric teachings had not been as detailed as Kūkai's.[79] Thus for seven years, from 809 through 816, he made a point of borrowing and copying esoteric texts from Kūkai and even received an *abhiṣekha* or esoteric initiation from him, as did several of his leading disciples. However, the initially cordial relations between the two men eventually broke down as a result of their divergent understandings of Mikkyō.[80] Where Kūkai saw the esoteric teachings as fundamentally distinct from and superior to the exoteric teachings *(kengyō),* Saichō maintained the unity of the two and sought to integrate Mikkyō within the framework of the *Lotus*-based teachings of the Tendai school.[81] During Saichō's lifetime, monastic training on Mt. Hiei was divided into two areas of specialization, whereby monks followed either the "meditation course" *(shikangō),* based on Chih-i's great treatise on meditation, the *Mo-ho chih-kuan* (Jpn. *Maka shikan,* Great Calming and Contemplation) or the "esoteric course" *(shanagō)*, focusing on the *Ta-p'i-lu-che-na ching* (Jpn. *Daibirushana-kyō*), on which the Matrix Realm mandala is based.[82] Saichō did not live long enough to work out a thorough synthesis of esoteric Buddhism and the one-vehicle teaching of the *Lotus Sūtra*, and the task would be carried on by his disciples. The integration of Tendai/*Lotus* doctrine and the esoteric teachings *(enmitsu itchi)* would become a major feature distinguishing Taimitsu—the Mikkyō that developed within Tendai—from that of Tōmitsu, the Mikkyō of Kūkai's Shingon tradition, and was essential to the development of medieval Tendai *hongaku* thought.[83]

Roots in Early Japanese Tendai

The major figures in the development of Taimitsu thought were Ennin (794–864), Enchin (814–891), and Annen (841–?). Like Saichō, Ennin and Enchin employed the term "original enlightenment" only rarely; even in the works of Annen, where it appears more frequently, most ocurrences are in quotations from other writings, and the term is used not in a distinctive sense, but in a manner synonymous with other terms for inherent liberative potential, such as "suchness" or "Buddha nature."[84] Nevertheless, the work of these men, especially Annen, laid the necessary intellectual foundation for the emergence of a distinct "Tendai original enlightenment thought" in the medieval period. Taimitsu thought is too complex to discuss in detail here, nor is it feasible to explore the ideas of these three systematizers one by one. However, it will be useful to outline those general developments within Taimitsu thought that were to prove most significant in shaping the medieval *hongaku* discourse.

Estericizing the *Lotus Sūtra*

In his *Jūjūshin ron* (Treatise on the ten stages of mind), Kūkai established ten stages of religious development, corresponding to ten levels of teaching, among which he ranked Mikkyō the highest.[85] He relegated the Tendai-*Lotus* teachings to stage eight. In contrast, the Taimitsu thinkers, following Saichō, were concerned to establish that the *Lotus Sūtra* and Mikkyō formed a unity. Traditional T'ien-t'ai schemes of doctrinal classification had been developed before the introduction of the esoteric teachings to China and so did not take account of them. Thus, establishing the relationship of the *Lotus* to the esoteric teachings demanded of the Taimitsu scholars a creative rethinking of existing doctrinal classifications and the postulating of new ones. While their arguments varied, all in effect sought to redefine the *Lotus* as an esoteric scripture.

The first to attempt this systematically was Saichō's disciple Ennin. Ennin put forth the notion of the "one great perfect teaching" *(ichidai en-*

gyō), in which the whole of Buddhism was encompassed.[86] Based on this
underlying unity, however, a distinction was to be drawn between esoteric
and exoteric teachings. Ennin drew this distinction in various ways: for
example, he wrote, the exoteric teachings were expounded in accord with
their auditors' capacity *(zuitai),* while the esoteric teachings were expounded from the Buddha's own enlightenment *(zuijii);* exoteric teachings require many kalpas of practice to attain Buddhahood, while in the
esoteric teachings, Buddhahood can be realized immediately; exoteric
teachings elucidate suchness only in its quiescent aspect *(shinnyo fuhen)*
and thus separate the true nature of things from their outward appearance, while the esoteric teachings reveal that suchness manifests the phenomenal world in accordance with conditions *(shinnyo zuien),* thus teaching the nonduality of nature and appearance, and so forth.[87] Within the
category of "esoteric teachings," Ennin included such Mahāyāna sūtras
as the *Avataṃsaka,* the *Vimalakīrti,* the *prajñā-pāramitā* sūtras, and of course
the *Lotus,* along with the *Ta-jih ching* and the *Chin-kang-ting ching.* However, the *Lotus* in fact says nothing about esoteric ritual performance. Having defined it as an esoteric scripture, Ennin found another distinction
to be necessary. All esoteric scriptures were equal in principle, he said,
in that they taught the nonduality of worldly and ultimate truth, but they
differed in their treatment of specific practices. That is, the *Lotus* was esoteric in principle alone *(rimitsu),* while the *Ta-jih ching* and other sūtras
that set forth the specifics of mūdras, mantras, and mandalas to be used
in esoteric performance were esoteric in both principle and actual
specifics *(jiri gumitsu).*[88] In short, Ennin borrowed Saichō's argument that
the three vehicles are provisional and the one vehicle is true, and recast
it to assert that the three vehicles are exoteric, and the one vehicle, esoteric. However, where Saichō had relegated Mahāyāna sūtras other than
the *Lotus* (such as the *Avataṃsaka*) to the status of provisional teachings,
Ennin included them in the one, esoteric vehicle; but where Saichō had
seen the *Lotus* and the esoteric teachings as equally representing the category of "true teaching," Ennin's distinction between sūtras that are esoteric in principle *(rimitsu)* and sūtras that are esoteric in both principle
and practice *(jiri gumitsu)* made it possible to regard the *Ta-jih ching* and
Chin-kang-ting ching as superior to the *Lotus* in clarifying matters of esoteric performance. This distinction was further developed in the writings
of Enchin.[89] Enchin also addressed the issue of where the *Ta-jih ching* was
to be placed in the traditional T'ien-t'ai classification of the "five periods" *(goji)* and concluded that it belonged in the fifth and highest period, along with the *Lotus* and *Nivāṇa* sūtras. In so doing, he sought to
rebut the arguments of Chinese T'ien-t'ai masters Kuang-hsiu (770–844?)
and his disciple Wei-chūan (d.u.), who had relegated it to the third, *vaipulya* period, which in Enchin's view did not give sufficient weight to the
esoteric teachings. But he sought also to counter the claims of Kūkai, who

had ranked the Tendai/*Lotus* teachings in eighth place, two steps below the esoteric teachings, in his ten stages of mind.[90]

A further development in the notion of the "one great perfect teaching" occurs in Annen's *Shingonshū kyōji gi* (The meaning of teaching and time in the *shingon* school), with his concept of the "four ones"—one Buddha, one time, one place, and one teaching:

> All Buddhas are called the one Buddha; all times are called the one time; all places are called the one place; all teachings are called the one teaching. . . . The originally inherent, constantly abiding Buddha who is without beginning or end is called all Buddhas; the [always] equal time that is without beginning or end is referred to as all times; the palace of the dharma realm that is without center or periphery is called all places; and the teaching that pervades all vehicles and makes one's mind realize Buddhahood is called all teachings.[91]

Annen's subsuming of all teachings in the one great perfect teaching goes beyond the earlier interpretations of the one vehicle put forth by Saichō and Ennin, in that it includes not only the teachings attributed to the historical Buddha Śākyamuni but those of "all Buddhas throughout the three time periods [past, present and future] and the ten directions [the eight points of the compass, up and down]." Nor is it about the unity of the teaching alone, but of the whole of time and space, which is affirmed as the realm where the originally inherent Buddha constantly and universally preaches to living beings. Annen's "four ones" were clearly influenced by esoteric concepts of the Dharma-body Buddha whose body and mind are identified with the entire phenomenal world.

Annen's affirmation of all teachings as the one teaching is made from the standpoint of what he understood to be the Buddha's own intent. From the standpoint of the Buddha's preaching according to his listeners' capacity, however, distinctions were to be drawn.[92] On this basis, Annen established a hierarchical scheme of five doctrinal categories: Tripiṭaka, shared, specific, perfect, and esoteric. These represent the four categories of teaching in the classic T'ien-t'ai *p'an-chiao* scheme, with Mikkyō superimposed as the highest category. Unlike Enchin, who had included Mikkyō and the *Lotus* in the same category, Annen used the distinction between "Mikkyō in principle alone" and "Mikkyō in both principle and actuality" to rank the latter in highest place.[93] Since Mikkyō represented the "one great perfect teaching" of all Buddhas, transcending both time and space, it could not, in his estimation, properly be fitted into a categorization of the teachings of the historical Buddha but must be placed above them. So thoroughly esotericized did Tendai doctrine become in Annen's thought that he habitually designated his school not as Tendai/*Lotus,* but as *shingon (shingonshū).*

In this way, among Saichō's later followers, the traditional T'ien-t'ai "perfect teaching" *(engyō)* based on the *Lotus Sūtra* was fused with Mikkyō in the "one great perfect teaching." Their writings recapitulate Saichō's move to incorporate all teachings within the *Lotus,* but in esoteric terms. That is, rather than encompassing Mikkyō within the framework of the one vehicle of the *Lotus* as Saichō had intended, Taimitsu developed an esoteric reading of the one vehicle that tended to subsume the *Lotus* within Mikkyō, a tendency especially evident in Annen's writings. In any event, the two traditions became inseparably intertwined and came to share a common vocabulary. Medieval Tendai *hongaku* thought would emerge in large part as an attempt to reinterpret traditional T'ien-t'ai/Tendai doctrines through the lense of an esotericized sensibility.

Redefining the Buddha

As the *Lotus* came to be understood within Taimitsu as an esoteric scripture, a corollary need was perceived to identify its Buddha with the Buddha of the esoteric teachings. Kūkai had argued, as part of his claim for the superiority of the esoteric teachings, that exoteric sūtras (which for Kūkai included the *Lotus)* had been preached by Śākyamuni as the "manifested body" *(nirmāṇa-kāya),* the human Buddha who appears in this world, while the esoteric teachings were preached by Dainichi as the "Dharma body," that is, universal and timeless truth conceived of as the Buddha's "body." If the *Lotus Sūtra* were to be claimed as an esoteric sūtra, it was necessary for the Taimitsu thinkers to overcome this distinction. This they did by finding ways to identify the two Buddhas.

The Buddha of the *Lotus Sūtra* appears in that text in two forms. First he is presented simply as the historical Buddha, Śākyamuni, who attained enlightenment at the age of thirty under the Bodhi tree. But the eleventh chapter suggests that he is more than this: all Buddhas in the worlds of the ten directions are shown to be his emanations.[94] This foreshadows the dramatic revelation of the sixteenth chapter, called "Fathoming the Lifespan of the Tathâgata" *(Nyorai juryō-hon),* in which Śākyamuni declares that countless myriads of kalpas have passed since he attained Buddhahood, and that ever since then, he has been constantly in this world, preaching the Dharma in various guises and by various skillful means. Chih-i had divided the sūtra into two parts of fourteen chapters each, according to these two presentations of the Buddha.[95] The first fourteen chapters, called the "trace teaching" *(shakumon),* present the Buddha as a "manifest trace" *(suijaku)* or historical appearance, while the latter fourteen chapters, called the "origin teaching" *(honmon),* present him in his original ground *(honji)* as the Buddha who first attained enlightenment in the inconceivably remote past. The relevant passage of the "Fathoming the Lifespan" chapter reads:

> In all the worlds, gods, men, and asuras all say that the present Śākya-munibuddha left the palace of the Śākya clan and at a place not far removed from the city of Gayā, seated on the Platform of the Path, attained anuttarasanmyakusaṃbodhi. And yet, O good men, since I in fact achieved Buddhahood it has been incalculable, limitless hundreds of thousands of myriads of millions of nayutas of kalpas. For example, one might imagine that in the five hundred thousand myriads of millions of nayutas of asaṃkheyas of thousand-millionfold worlds there is a man who pounds them all to atoms, and then, only after passing eastward over five hundred thousand myriads of millions of nayutas of asaṃkheyas of realms, deposits one atom, in this way in his eastward movement exhausting all these atoms. . . . If these world-spheres [that the man has passed], whether an atom was deposited in them or not, were all reduced to atoms, and if each atom were a kalpa, the time since my achievement of Buddhahood would exceed even this. . . . My life-span is incalculable asaṃkhyeyakalpas, ever enduring, never perishing. O good men! The life-span I achieved in my former treading of the bodhisattva path even now is not exhausted, for it is twice the above number.[96]

A literal reading of this passage suggests that this original realization, however inconceivably long ago, did indeed take place at a specific point in time and thus must be said to have a beginning. Nonetheless, this "original Buddha" *(honbutsu)* of the "Fathoming the Lifespan" chapter lent himself more readily than did the historical Śākyamuni to identification with the beginningless Dharma body of Dainichi or Mahāvairocana. Thus one finds, in Taimitsu writings, the development of a distinct *"honmon* thought" centering on the latter fourteen chapters of the sūtra and its original Buddha.[97] In time, the Buddha of the "Fathoming of the Lifespan" chapter came to be understood, like the cosmic Buddha Dainichi, as timeless, having neither beginning nor end.

Long before the emergence of Japanese Taimitsu, or even of esoteric Buddhism in East Asia, attempts had been made to identify Śākyamuni with the Buddha Vairocana, whose name is transliterated in Chinese versions of the sūtra as either Lu-che-na (Jpn. Rushana) or P'i-lu-che-na (Birushana). Such identifications begin in the sūtra literature. The sixty-fascicle *Hua-yen ching* says that the names "Śākyamuni" and "Vairocana" refer to the same Buddha.[98] The *Fo-shuo kuan P'u-hsien P'u-sa hsing-fa ching* (Sūtra of the Buddha's preaching on the method of contemplating Bodhisattva Samantabhadra), the capping sūtra to the *Lotus,* reads, "At that time the voice in space will speak these words [to the meditator]: 'Śākyamuni is called Vairocana Pervading All Places, and that Buddha's dwelling place is called Ever-Tranquil Light.'"[99] The *Fan-wang ching* presents Vairocana as manifesting individual Śākyamuni Buddhas as his ema-

nations in billions of worlds. Because he is said to have attained these
powers as the reward of long efforts in cultivation, Vairocana in this
depiction may properly be regarded as a recompense body (saṃbhoga-
kāya, hōjin)—the wisdom and supernatural attainments of a Buddha
achieved through practice, imagined as a subtle body.[100]

Chinese commentators advanced various theories about the relationship of these Buddhas, often in connection with discussions about
the various kinds of "bodies" that Buddhas were said to possess.[101]
Chih-i, for example, citing various sources, identified P'i-lu-che-na as the
Dharma body, Lu-che-na as the recompense body, and Śākyamuni as the
manifested body—noting, however, that the three bodies were inseparable.[102] Elsewhere, in a dynamic synthesis, he interpreted Śākyamuni
Buddha of the "Fathoming the Lifespan" chapter as embodying all three
bodies in one. When the Buddha's wisdom grasps the ultimate reality,
that which is realized is the Dharma body; and the wisdom that realizes
it is the recompense body. For the sake of living beings, this wisdom manifests itself in physical form as human Buddha who teaches in the world;
this is the manifested body. Since the recompense body both realizes the
truth that is the Dharma body and responds to aspirations of the beings
in the form of the manifested body, Chih-i regarded it as central. However, he also rejected any notion of hierarchy among the three bodies,
denying that one can be seen as prior to the others.[103] Chih-i's theories
no doubt contributed to Taimitsu developments on three grounds: in
strengthening the identification of Śākyamuni with Vairocana; in identifying Śākyamuni with the Dharma body as well as with the manifested
and recompense bodies; and in denying that the Dharma body can be
seen as prior to the other two. The identification of Śākyamuni with Vairocana was also made by Chinese monks specializing in the esoteric teachings, such as I-hsing (683–727) and possibly Yüan-cheng (d.u.), under
whom Ennin studied.[104]

In Japan, this identification is also found in Saichō's writing.[105] As
noted earlier, he may even have seen it as a way to unify the various transmissions and initiations he had received in China by tracing them to a
single source.[106] After Saichō's death, his successors continued to elaborate in esoteric terms the unity of the two Buddhas. While their diverse
arguments are too complex to discuss at length, in essence, they redefined Śākyamuni of the Lotus Sūtra, not as an individual person who
had once cultivated bodhisattva practice and achieved Buddhahood, but
as an originally inherent Buddha, without beginning or end.[107] He is, in
Annen's words, the one Buddha who is all Buddhas, who preaches continuously throughout all space and time. And, since the Dharma body
is originally inherent in all phenomena, ordinary worldlings are in
essence Buddhas, too; between the enlightened and the unenlightened,
no ontological distinction whatever can be made. Redefinition of the

Buddha of the "Fathoming the Lifespan" chapter as an originally inherent Buddha would help give rise to medieval understandings of the *Lotus Sūtra* as a teaching of original enlightenment.

In passing, we may note an early and influential Tendai text that reflects both the esotericizing of the *Lotus* and the redefining of its Buddha. This is the esoteric scripture *Myōhō-renge sanmai himitsu sanmaya kyō* (Sūtra of the secret *samaya* [symbols] of the samādhi of the lotus blossom of the Wonderful Dharma), or simply *Renge sanmai-kyō*. Though traditionally said to have been translated by the esoteric master Amoghavajra (Ch. Pu-k'ung, 705–774) and brought to Japan by either Kūkai or Enchin, it is almost certainly a Japanese apocryphon. Only its opening verse, known today as the *Hongaku san* ([Hymn] in praise of original enlightenment), is cited in Heian- and Kamakura-period texts and is thought to have been composed around Annen's time, perhaps even by Annen himself.[108] The verse is as follows:

kimyō hongaku shin hosshin	I take refuge in the Dharma-body [Buddha], the mind of original enlightenment,
jōjū myōhō shin rendai	who ever resides on the lotus pedestal of the mind, which is the Wonderful Dharma.
honrai gusoku sanjin toku	Innately adorned with the virtues of the triple [Tathâgata] body,
sanjū shichison jū shinjō	The thirty-seven honored ones[109] dwell in the palace of the mind.
fumon jinju shozanmai onri inga hōnengu	The countless universal samādhis are naturally inherent, independent of cause and effect.
muhen tokkai hon enman	The boundless sea of virtues is originally perfect and full
gen ga chōrai shin shobutsu	Reverently I salute the Buddhas of the mind.

The idea that the various samādhis or contemplations are all "naturally inherent" and "independent of cause and effect" would be further developed within medieval Tendai original enlightenment thought. The *Renge sanmai* verse is widely cited in Tendai *hongaku*-related literature, and commentaries on it were retrospectively attributed to major Tendai figures.[110]

Valorizing the Phenomenal World

As discussed above, the T'ien-t'ai philosophical tradition approached the universality of truth from the standpoint of phenomena *(shih, ji)*, in that each concrete phenomenon is held to embody in itself the three-fold truth of emptiness, conventional existence, and the middle. This emphasis on the phenomenal was underscored in Saichō's appropriation of the doctrine of "suchness according with conditions" in a way that gave priority to the dynamic aspect of suchness, that is, its expression as the phenomenal world.

With the development of Taimitsu, the concrete world of visible phenomena was accorded still greater importance. This move had a major source in esoteric understandings of the sensory world. Kūkai had taught the esoteric doctrine of the six great elements—earth, water, fire, wind, space, and consciousness—which comprise all things in the cosmos and are the body and mind of Dainichi Nyorai. To see colors, shapes, thoughts, and so forth as body of the originally inherent Buddha is to endow them with heightened sacrality; Kūkai took this one step further to argue that all phenomena were in fact the "preaching" of the Dharma body (hosshin seppō), by which Dainichi is revealed. Such ideas were also eventually incorporated into Taimitsu.

The valorization of the phenomenal world in Mikkyō thought was grounded in the bivalent meaning of the "three mysteries." On the one hand, the three mysteries are all forms, sounds, and thoughts, that is, the entire phenomenal world, equated with the body, speech, and mind of the cosmic Buddha Dainichi. On the other hand, the three mysteries are the concrete forms of esoteric practice by which identity with Dainichi is realized: the intricate mūdras formed with the hands and body; the vocally recited mantras and dharanis; and the mental contemplations of the holy figures represented on the mandalas. In this connection, the categories of ri and ji, in addition to their earlier meanings of "principle" and "phenomena," assumed new connotations in the realm of esoteric practice, ri being the timeless paradigm to be contemplated inwardly, and ji, its physical and temporal imitation or expression in actual practice. For example, ri is the mental visualization of the Buddha, while ji is the Buddha image standing on the altar.[111] Hence the Taimitsu distinction between the Lotus, which is "esoteric in principle" (rimitsu), and the Ta-jih ching, which, including as it does descriptions of mūdras and mantras, is "esoteric in concrete form" (jimitsu). Esoteric practice, with its ritual gestures, chanting of sacred formulas, and elaborate mandalas, was valorized as the secret language and gestures of the Buddha. Its strong sensory and aesthetic appeal, as well as its presumed efficacy in both soteriological and worldly matters, contributed greatly to its spread and patronage. Under its influence, one sees in the latter Heian period a general shift across Buddhist traditions away from silent, introspective contemplation toward practices having concrete form. This is evident, for example, in the way that the T'ien-t'ai contemplative methods introduced by Saichō were gradually supplemented and then surpassed in popularity by such tangible acts as reading, reciting, and copying the *Lotus Sūtra,* and in the way that the chanting of the *nenbutsu,* the name of the Buddha Amida, emerged alongside, and eventually superseded, the silent contemplation or visualization of the Buddha.[112]

This emphasis, rooted in Mikkyō, on *ji* as the concrete forms of practice by which enlightenment is said to be realized experientially also enhanced the value accorded to *ji* in the broader sense as the actualities of the phenomenal world. The phenomenal world as the locus of truth was expressed in the Tendai tradition by such terms as "the real is identical with phenomena" *(sokuji nishin)* or—an expression especially popular in the medieval period—the "constant abiding of the worldly truth" *(zokutai jōjū).*[113] These doctrines were explicitly associated with the origin teaching *(honmon),* or latter fourteen chapters of the *Lotus Sūtra,*[114] and were often supported with a passage from the sūtra that reads: "The dharmas dwell in a Dharma-position, / and the worldly aspect constantly abides" *(ze hō jū hōi / seken sō jōjū).*[115] Along with the verse from the *Renge sanmai-kyō,* this is one of the textual passages most frequently quoted in medieval Tendai *hongaku* literature.

A particular example of the valorizing of the phenomenal world that occurred in early and medieval Japanese Tendai thought may be found in doctrinal discussion of the realization of Buddhahood by grasses and trees *(sōmoku jōbutsu).*[116] This doctrine had its origins in the attempts of Chinese Buddhist exegetes to extend the potential for Buddhahood universally. Tao-sheng (d. 434), disciple of the great translator Kumārajīva, argued that Buddha-nature is inherent even in the *icchantika,* people of incorrigible disbelief who lack the aspiration for enlightenment; Chitsang (549–623) of the San-lun school argued that insentient beings have the Buddha nature as well.[117] However, the Chinese thinker most closely connected with the idea that insentient beings have the Buddha nature is Chan-jan, whose discussion of this doctrine in his *Chin-kang pei* has been noted above. Chan-jan also develops the idea in his commentary on Chih-i's *Mo-ho chih-kuan,* in discussing the passage, "Of every form and fragrance, there is none that is not the Middle Way."[118] However, even among those Chinese Buddhists who upheld the possibility of the realization of Buddhahood by insentient beings, this was thought to depend on the realization of Buddhahood by sentient beings: because self and the outer world are nondual, when the practitioner manifests Buddhahood, so will that person's environment.

In Japan, the problem of the Buddhahood of insentient beings— refocused as the Buddhahood of grasses and trees—garnered greater interest and moved in a different direction. Kūkai saw plants and trees as participating ontologically in the five great elements that compose the Dharma body and that "therefore, without change in their essence, they may without objection be referred to as 'Buddha.'"[119] On the Tendai side, beginning with Saichō, the discussion evolved in more complex fashion. Saichō had been pressed to address the issue in his debates with Hossō scholars. His opponents demanded: If, as Saichō maintained, universal suchness has the nature of awakening and knowing, was he then claiming that even insentient beings such as grasses and trees should be able, of themselves, to realize Buddhahood?[120] From Saichō's time on, Tendai scholars would argue the position that grasses and trees can indeed, of themselves, arouse the aspiration for enlightenment (bodhicitta, bodai-shin), cultivate practice, and achieve enlightenment. Annen in particular devoted great attention to this issue.[121] The doctrine of the Buddhahood of grasses and trees would eventually spread beyond monastic circles and influence first medieval poetry and later the Nō drama.[122]

Ideas about the enlightenment of plants are taken up in the later, medieval Tendai original enlightenment discourse, and it is there that one first finds concrete explanation of what exactly the enlightenment of plants might mean. In response to the question of how plants arouse the bodhicitta, cultivate practice, and realize enlightenment, one text responds: "Grasses and trees already have the four aspects of emergence, abiding, change, and extinction. These are [respectively] the awakening of aspiration, the cultivation of practice, the [realization of] enlightened wisdom (bodai), and the nirvāṇa of grasses and trees. How could they not belong to the category of sentient beings?"[123]

Here the doctrine of the Buddhahood of trees and grasses has been assimilated to hongaku discourse, in which, to the enlightened eye, the moment-to-moment arising and perishing of the phenomenal world is none other than the true aspect of original enlightenment.

In contrast to Chinese discussions of the Buddha nature of insentient beings, which aimed at asserting the universality of the Buddha nature, Japanese debates focused primarily on "grasses and trees." This focus, it has been suggested, may have reflected ancient, pre-Buddhist Japanese experience of the numinous presence of the deities or kami in nature and was reinforced in early medieval times by an increasing valorization of the natural world as a place of reclusion and enhanced soteriological meaning, in contrast to the turmoil and political scheming that marked the imperial capital of Heian-kyō in the eleventh and twelfth centuries.[124] This suggestion may have some validity, especially in later appropriations of the sōmoku jōbutsu discourse outside the realm of monastic scholarship. However, it should be borne in mind that notions of the "Buddhahood of grasses and trees" originated not as responses to "nature," but in doctrinal debate over the implications of claims for universal Buddhahood, and developed as a specific example of a larger tendency, emerging within Taimitsu and esoteric Buddhist thought more generally, to see the ordinary phenomena of the world as the locus of ultimate truth.

As discussed earlier, both Chinese T'ien-t'ai and Hua-yen intellectual traditions saw concrete particulars *(shih)* and universal principle *(li)* as nondual, though they approached this nonduality from different standpoints. By asserting this nonduality, they were able to "reclaim" the phenomenal world, not as a realm of suffering to be escaped, but as the locus of Buddhist practice and realization. Nonetheless, in the polarity of *li* and *shih,* concrete phenomena were still acknowledged as insubstantial, fleeting, and in that sense inferior or subordinate to "mind" or "true aspect." With the development of Japanese Mikkyō, however, this polarity began to shift, with increasing emphasis being placed upon the realm of the sensory and the phenomenal. In the Tendai tradition, this shift in emphasis would culminate in the medieval discourse of original enlightenment.[125]

"Shortening the Path"

A fourth critical development in early Tendai thought was a progressive reduction, in doctrinal interpretation, of the length of time and level of achievement deemed necessary to realize enlightenment. Paul Groner has aptly termed this move "shortening the path" in an article of the same name. Discussion of this issue focused on the concept of "realizing Buddhahood with this very body" *(sokushin jōbutsu).* This concept had been introduced to Japan by both Kūkai and Saichō and contrasted sharply with the views of the Nara schools, which emphasized gradualist models of the Buddhist path.

It is extremely difficult to determine which of the two men, Saichō or Kūkai, first advocated the concept.[126] However, their sources clearly differed. Kūkai based himself on the *P'u-t'i-hsin lun* (Treatise on the aspiration for enlightenment), an apocryphal treatise attributed to Nāgārjuna, which contains the term.[127] Kūkai's own treatise on the subject, *Sokushin jōbutsu gi* (The meaning of realizing Buddhahood with this very body), argues the direct realization of Buddhahood on the basis of the universality of the six great elements that compose the body and mind of both Dainichi and the practitioner; in the performance of the three mysteries, the identity of the body, speech, and mind of the esoteric adept with those of Dainichi Nyorai is realized.[128] Saichō, however, drew on the episode in the *Lotus Sūtra* of the eight-year-old Nāga princess, who in the space of a moment changes into a male, completes the eight phases of a Buddha's life, and manifests perfect enlightenment.[129] In his writings, the realization of Buddhahood with this very body is linked not to esoteric practices, but to the power of the *Lotus Sūtra.* The Nāga girl, Saichō points out, had a threefold hindrance: she was born into the animal realm as a *nāga* (a serpent or dragon), clearly the result of unfavorable karma; she was female and of poor faculties; and she was young and therefore had not been able to devote many years to religious practice. Nevertheless, through the wondrous power of the *Lotus,* she was able to attain Buddhahood.[130]

We have already seen that Saichō saw the *Lotus Sūtra* as the "direct path" or "great direct path," over and against the Hossō view of enlightenment as requiring three incalculable aeons to achieve. He was not optimistic about most people actually realizing Buddhahood with this very body, a possibility he saw as open only to those who had reached the stage of partial realization, the fifth of the six stages of identity, which corresponds to the first abode or *bhūmi* in the fifty-seven stages of bodhisattva practice of the perfect teaching.[131] The fifth stage of identity and the first abode both denote the point of transition from the level of an ordinary worldling *(pṛthag-jana, bonbu)* bound by defilements to that of the sage *(ārya-sattva, shō),* who has eliminated all defilements except ignorance *(mumyō-waku)* and begun to experience true insight. Where the birth and death of the ordinary worldling is determined by karma *(bundan shōji),* that of the sage is chosen in accordance with his aspiration for enlightenment and intent to benefit others *(hennyaku shōji).* "Realizing Buddhahood with this very body" for Saichō thus referred to the partial enlightenment of those who had already made the transition from ordinary worldling to sage. However, he also maintained that, even in the case of deluded worldlings, through the power of the *Lotus Sūtra* the process of enlightenment could be vastly accelerated, being fulfilled in the next lifetime or at latest the lifetime after that. This concern, even on a theoretical level, with the possibility of Buddhahood for ordinary worldlings would eventually emerge as a major characteristic of Japanese Buddhism as a whole.[132]

After Saichō's death, his followers enthusiastically discussed and elaborated the concept of realizing Buddhahood with this very body. Among the issues of debate was whether *sokushin jōbutsu* should be understood as full or partial realization; whether it referred to enlightenment in this lifetime or in a subsequent lifetime; whether or not it was accompanied by a Buddha's distinguishing physical marks; whether or not stages of the path might be skipped by advanced practitioners; whether emphasis should be placed on eradicating defilements or on manifesting innate Buddha nature; and what sort of practices would actually enable the realization of Buddhahood in this body.[133] While opinions varied, a general tendency emerged to define *sokushin jōbutsu* as occurring in this single lifetime *(isshō jōbutsu)* and as accessible at increasingly lower stages of the path. Thus it came to be understood as a possibility for ordinary worldlings as well as sages. Especially from the time of Annen, Tendai discussions of *sokushin jōbutsu,* though still grounded textually in the *Lotus Sūtra*'s story of the Nāga girl, came increasingly to be associated with esoteric practices.

This stress on the possibility of realizing Buddhahood with this very body greatly influenced the development of medieval Tendai thought. In *hongaku* discourse, all beings are considered to be enlightened from the outset; what counts, then, is the moment when, whether hearing this doctrine from a teacher or reading it in texts, one realizes (or takes faith in) one's originally enlightened nature. Thus medieval Tendai texts would speak of "realizing Buddhahood in a single moment" *(ichinen jōbutsu).*

Of the four characteristics of early Tendai thought outlined above, the esotericizing of the *Lotus Sūtra* and the identification of its Buddha with the Dharma body of Dainichi are specifically characteristic of Tai-mitsu, though they also illustrate the incorporation of esoteric elements that occurred more broadly in all "exoteric" schools. The other two characteristics—emphasis on phenomenal world as the locus of truth and the possibility of realizing enlightenment quickly—transcended Tendai doctrine and emerged as prominent themes in Japanese Buddhism more generally. Also broadly influential was the culture of secret transmission that surrounded Tendai esoteric practice, of which more will be said in chapter 3. Esoteric teachings and ritual, being esoteric, were not published universally but were passed on secretly from master to disciple. In the medieval period, this mode of transmitting knowledge would become normative not only for religion but in the arts, crafts, and other branches of knowledge as well.

Tendai Pure Land Thought

One more element should be mentioned that helped lay the ground for the emergence of medieval Tendai *hongaku* thought. This was the Pure Land Buddhism, focused on the Buddha Amida (Skt. Amitābha), that developed within the Tendai tradition.[134] Pure Land practices had existed in Japan in some form almost from the time of Buddhism's introduction. Within the Tendai school, Saichō himself may be said to have introduced such practices in the context of the "four kinds of samādhi," the meditation system established by Chih-i.[135] Of these four kinds of meditation, the "constantly walking samādhi" is performed while circumambulating an image of Amida Buddha. It entails visualization of Amida's thirty-two major and eighty minor excellent marks and leads to insight into the nonduality of the visualized Buddha and the visualizing subject. Later, Saichō's disciple Ennin introduced to Japan the *nenbutsu* practice of Mt. Wu-t'ai, which involved group recitation of the *A-mi-t'o ching* (*Amida-kyō*, Sūtra of Amitābha) for a fixed number of days and was practiced while contemplating Amida Buddha. This was called the "uninterrupted nenbutsu" *(fudan nenbutsu)* and was instituted on Mt. Hiei as a form of the constantly walking samādhi.[136] Tendai Pure Land thought was greatly stimulated by the famous treatise of Genshin (942–1017), *Ōjō yōshū* (Essentials of birth in the Pure Land), which emphasized aspiring to birth in Amida's Pure Land after death by relying on contemplative *nenbutsu* practice or, for those less capable, the repeated recitation of Amida's name.[137] Tendai Pure Land thought was further influenced by popular practices that employed the chanted *nenbutsu* as an offering for the salvation of the dead and the pacification of vengeful ghosts.[138] Also associated with Tendai were a number of famous itinerant *nenbutsu hijiri* or holy men such as Kōya (or Kūya, 903–972) and Ryōnin (1072–1132), who traveled widely in Japan and spread the chanted *nenbutsu* among the populace.

Medieval Pure Land thought, especially that of Hōnen (1133–1212) and Shinran (1173–1262), has often been seen as a response to the Final Dharma age *(mappō)*, thought to have begun in 1052 and to mark the beginning of the third and last stage in a three-stage process of Buddhism's decline.[139] It is often associated with belief in human limitations, in the depravity of the times, in salvation after death, and in the need to rely on the power of the Buddha. It would seem, at first glance, to be the very opposite of *hongaku* doctrine. However, as seen in the "constantly walking samādhi," there had also existed within Tendai Buddhism almost from the outset another, older strand of Pure Land thought emphasizing the nonduality of Amida and the practitioner, which would later be assimilated to and developed within Mikkyō thought. Original enlightenment discourse drew on this tradition and was also influenced by later popular Pure Land concerns about the salvation of ordinary worldlings. Several important *hongaku* texts are cast in an Amidist mode. These texts interpret the present world as the Pure Land, and Amida as the Buddha originally inherent in all phenomena, for example, by equating the three characters of the name *A-mi-da* with the three truths of emptiness, conventional existence, and the middle.[140] They may in fact represent some of the earliest Tendai *hongaku* literature.

The Emergence of Medieval Tendai
Original Enlightenment Thought

A distinct tradition within Japanese Tendai that centered on the idea of original enlightenment emerged in the latter Heian period. Although heavily influenced by earlier Mikkyō developments, notions of original enlightenment were developed under the rubric of Tendai/*Lotus* studies and were presented as the *Lotus Sūtra*'s ultimate intent. This tradition evolved its own rituals and doctrines and produced its own texts. Since it forms the chief subject of this study, it will not be discussed in detail in this introductory genealogy. However, three of its salient characteristics should be noted here at the outset.

First, original enlightenment thought is distinctive of that period in Tendai history known as "medieval Tendai" *(chūko Tendai)*. What constitutes Japan's "medieval period" *(chūsei)* has been the subject of some controversy, and definitions have varied among disciplines.[141] At one time said to have begun with the establishment of the Kamakura *bakufu* or samurai government in 1185, the "medieval period" has now been pushed back by some historians to the eleventh or even tenth century in connection with the breakdown of the Ritsuryō system of imperial control of public lands and the beginnings of the private estates *(shōen)* system. "Medieval Tendai," while intimately related to changes in the larger society, has its own parameters. The term was first proposed by Shimaji Daitō, who argued the need for periodicization in the study of Japanese Tendai intellectual history. *Chūko* or "medieval" in his view represented the period from Saichō up until the adoption during the mid-Edo period of the Sung T'ien-t'ai thought of Ssu-ming Chih-li and was characterized by the fusion of esoteric and exoteric Buddhism, emphasis on the origin teaching of the *Lotus Sūtra,* and the doctrine of original enlightenment.[142] The category was further refined by Shimaji's student and scholar of Tendai Buddhism, Hazama Jikō (1895–1946), who defined "medieval Tendai" as extending roughly from the period of Insei or rule by retired emperors (1086–1185) up until about the Genroku through Kyōhō eras (1688–1735) of the Edo period, a usage that has now become widely accepted.[143] In Hazama's view, three characteristics distinguished Tendai thought during this period: the development of "original enlightenment thought" *(hongaku shisō);* a particular interpretive style based on personal insight rather than fidelity to texts *(kanjin-shugi);* and an emphasis on the authority of oral transmissions *(kuden).*[144] Hazama further divided this *hongaku*-dominated "medieval Tendai" into three stages: (1) The period of emergence and establishment, extending from the mid-Insei through the late Kamakura period. During this stage, oral transmissions of the teachings of medieval Tendai thinkers began to be written down and collected. Two main lineages, the Eshin and the Danna, appeared and divided into several subbranches. Within these lineages, specific doctrines were formulated and systematized, and distinctive transmission rituals took shape. (2) The period of development and decline. In this period, lasting from roughly the Nanbokuchō (1336–1392) through the Muromachi (1333–1568) period, doctrines underwent further elaboration, extensive collections of, and commentaries on, oral transmission literature were produced, and rituals of transmission became increasingly formalized. Medieval Tendai *hongaku* thought developed in conjunction with distinctive practices of Mt. Hiei, including the cult of Sannō Shintō, the *kaihōgyō* walking meditation, and mountain asceticism. According to Hazama, in this period, especially in the later Muromachi, abuses were becoming evident, including increasingly arbitrary interpretations, the forging and selling of transmissions, and the general ossification of formal aspects of the tradition. (3) The period of transmission and maintenance, lasting from the early to the mid-Edo period. During this time, despite occasional new developments, emphasis was on maintaining the tradition. In the Genroku (1685–1703) and Kyōhō (1716–35) periods, the priest Myōryū (1637–1690) and his disciple Reikū (1652–1739), leader of a faction on Mt. Hiei called the Anraku school, advocated the *Ssu-fen lü* precepts in addition to the bodhisattva precepts and championed the Sung T'ien-t'ai doctrine of Chih-li as a new orthodoxy superseding that of the medieval *kuden*.[145] These events marked a shift away from the characteristically medieval modes of Tendai thought and practice and ushered in the "modern period" of Japanese Tendai history.

A second point to be noted is that the literature of this *hongaku*-based medieval Tendai tradition, especially in its earlier stages, is largely a literature of apocryphal texts. Specific teachings of this tradition were at first passed down from master to disciple in the form of oral transmissions *(kuden)*, perhaps beginning around the middle of the eleventh century. (The chronology given here was proposed by Tamura Yoshirō and will be discussed below.[146]) Eventually *kuden* were written down in a few sentences on single sheets of paper, called *kirikami* (or *kirigami*), which the master would then give to his disciple. *Kirikami* were inscribed on a single sheet and wrapped in a separate piece of paper, on which would be written an outer title *(gedai)*, or the original sheet would simply be folded and the outer title inscribed on the outside. In some *kirikami* collections, such as the *Sanjū shika no kotogaki* (Notes on thirty-four articles), the outer titles of some of the original *kirikami* are preserved. Beginning probably around the mid-twelfth century, numbers of *kirikami* were collected together to form larger texts, assigned a collective title, and attributed retrospectively to a great Tendai master of the past, such as Saichō, Ennin, or Genshin. Some compilations made during the mid- to late-Kamakura period were similarly attributed to later Tendai figures, such as Chūjin (1065–1138), the forty-sixth *zasu* or chief abbot of Mt. Hiei, or his disciple Kōkaku. Once set down in writing, they of course became textual records, rather than oral transmissions, but they continued to be called *kuden*, probably in testament to the authority surrounding one-to-one master-disciple transmission. Works dealing with original enlightenment thought other than *kuden* collections were also produced; these include a number of essays interpreting Pure Land thought from an original enlightenment perspective, several of which were retrospectively attributed to Genshin, the great Tendai Pure Land figure of the mid-Heian period. By the mid-Kamakura period, systematizations of doctrine were beginning to take shape. These are the so-called *kuden hōmon*, or orally transmitted doctrines. Best known among these are the comparative classification of the "fourfold rise and fall" *(shijū kōhai)* and the system of the "threefold seven great matters" *(sanjū shichika no daiji),* both of which developed within the Eshin school.[147] In the fourteenth and fifteenth centuries—that is, from the end of the Kamakura through the Nanbokuchō and Muromachi periods—a variety of extensive commentaries informed by *hongaku* ideas was produced on classical T'ien-t'ai works, on the *Lotus Sūtra,* and on earlier *kuden hōmon.* Some of these later works were signed by their actual authors or compilers, though works whose attribution appears dubious still continued to appear.[148] Thus for medieval Tendai Buddhism, apocryphal texts were the norm rather than the exception, a fact that has had significant consequences for the study of this literature.

Third, it must be mentioned that, in medieval Tendai thought, the category *"hongaku"* assumes a distinctive meaning different from its usage in earlier contexts. First to note this was Shimaji Daitō, who distinguished between "original enlightenment" as used in medieval Tendai texts and in the *Awakening of Faith.*[149] In the *Awakening of Faith,* he pointed out, "original enlightenment" refers to the one mind considered from the perspective of conventional consciousness, or the "mind as arising and perishing," and not from the absolute perspective of the mind as suchness. "Original enlightenment" is paired with "nonenlightenment" as one of two inseparable aspects of the *ālaya-vijñāna* or store consciousness, in which innate purity and delusion are conjoined; moreover, "original enlightenment" must be realized through the knowledge cultivated by practice in the process called "acquired enlightenment." Thus in the *Awakening of Faith,* "original enlightenment" remains merely the potential for enlightenment in deluded beings. In the medieval Tendai *kuden* literature, however, Shimaji found that *hongaku* is equated with suchness itself and assigned an absolute meaning; it is no longer merely an abstract principle but the actual, true aspect of all things *(ji jissō)*—a development he attributed, via Kūkai's appropriations, to the *Shih Mo-ho-yen lun.* He also noted that the terms "original enlightenment" and "acquired enlightenment" had been assimilated in medieval Tendai to the project of doctrinal classification: "original enlightenment" was defined as the profound insight of the origin teaching of the *Lotus Sūtra,* and "acquired enlightenment," as representing an inferior level of teaching.

Shimaji's observations were further elaborated by Tamura Yoshirō, who saw a clear line dividing medieval Tendai original enlightenment thought and its antecedents both on the continent and in Japanese Tendai up through Annen.[150] In his view, medieval Tendai *hongaku* thought represented the thorough conflation of two streams of thought: the notion of mind or suchness as an absolute principle *(ri)* that had developed within Hua-yen Buddhism, and the emphasis on the world of concrete phenomena *(ji)* found in T'ien-t'ai and associated since Chan-jan's time with the origin teaching of the *Lotus Sūtra* and the Buddha's revelation of his original enlightenment in the remote past. First, said Tamura, the idea of original enlightenment was identified as an absolute principle *(ri);* then the monism of this absolute principle was applied directly to concrete actualities *(ji),* so that the arising and perishing of phenomena, just as they are, were valorized absolutely as the expressions of original enlightenment. Tamura found this "absolute monism" or "absolute affirmation" of the phenomenal world to be exemplified by passages such as this one, from the *kuden* collection *Sanjū shika no kotogaki:*

> The revelation of [the Buddha's original enlightenment as] principle *(ri kenpon)* means that hell dwellers are [none other than] hell dwellers, hungry ghosts are none other than hungry ghosts, and so on, on up to Buddhas and bodhisattvas being [none other than] Buddhas and bodhisattvas. Because the ten realms [of living beings] from the outset constantly abide, the ten realms, without transformation, represent the original essence *(hontai).*[151]

Hell dwellers, hungry ghosts, and other deluded beings do not change and become Buddhas; all beings just as they are manifest the true aspect, which is original enlightenment. This entails the "absolute affirmation of reality" and the "affirmation of the deluded ordinary worldling" that Tamura sees as central to original enlightenment thought.

Whether or not it is accurate to characterize original enlightenment as a doctrine of "absolute affirmation" will be among the questions raised by this study. Here we may simply note that the shift in the meaning of "original enlightenment" found in medieval Tendai thought may also be described from a different perspective. Once the Buddha nature has been defined as innate in all beings, the question arises as to whether awakening depends on removing the attachments and false views that obstruct one from discerning the Buddha nature, or on a direct realization of the Buddha nature, as whose consequence the mental defilements will naturally be dispelled or transformed. The *Awakening of Faith* clearly takes the former position, as, to a lesser extent, does early Tendai thought. By the medieval period of Tendai history, however, largely under Mikkyō influence, emphasis had shifted heavily in the other direction. All one must do is discern, or even simply have faith in, original enlightenment; then the defilements and hindrances appear in their true light as its nondual manifestations.

While the perspective of original enlightenment dominated the medieval Tendai tradition, it was not universally accepted. An important critic was Hōchi-bō Shōshin (fl. 12th cent.), a scrupulous exegete who was the author of voluminous commentaries on the major works of Chih-i.[152] Shōshin framed his criticism in response to "many among those who study *shingon*," hinting at the esoteric roots of Tendai original enlightenment thought. Original enlightenment, he said, was to be understood in terms of the *Awakening of Faith,* as a potential within deluded worldlings to be realized by the practice of acquired enlightenment. In particular, Shōshin criticized the claim that the ordinary worldling is "originally the Buddha of self-awakening" *(honrai jikaku-butsu),* a position he denounced as a denial of the causality of practice and attainment and "the same as heterodox teachings" *(gedō-setsu).* Shōshin also opposed definitions of Śākyamuni of the "Fathoming the Lifespan" chapter of the *Lotus Sūtra* as an originally inherent Buddha, which, he said, clearly went against the sūtra's statement that Śākyamuni had practiced the bodhisattva way and attained Buddhahood in the remote past. Shōshin's criticisms form an important external reference point for gauging how far original enlightenment thought had developed by the late Heian period. For convenience' sake, this book will use the term "medieval Tendai thought" to refer to the tradition's *hongaku*-dominated mainstream, but with the understanding that not all medieval Tendai thinkers accepted contemporary notions of original enlightenment.

Original Enlightenment Thought and Broader Intellectual Currents

Thus far, this genealogy has traced in vertical, diachronic fashion the origins and development of ideas important to the emergence of medieval Tendai original thought. Here, it is appropriate to note some of its horizontal branches, that is, the synchronous influence of *hongaku* thought on the broader intellectual life of medieval Japan. This discourse did not remain confined to Buddhist scholastic circles but was quickly assimilated to other vocabularies and found other modes of expression. It can be found, for example, in didactic tales and poetry of the medieval period. *Shasekishū* (Sand and pebbles), a collection of *setsuwa* (tales) by Mujū Ichien (a.k.a. Dōgyō, 1226–1312), relates the following:

> The *Shou-leng-yen ching* tells the story of Yajñadattā, who looked in a mirror one morning and could not see her face because of the way she was holding the mirror. Believing that her head had been taken by a demon, she ran about distractedly until someone showed her how to hold the mirror correctly. Then she thought that her head had been restored. Both her wretchedness and her delight were without foundation. The unenlightened man is like one who looks for his lost head. The mind of original enlightenment *(hongaku)* is not lost; the loss comes only from thinking that this is so. Thinking that we have discovered and attained something for the first time is what we feel when we experience enlightenment for the first time *(shikaku).* But how can

we attain it for the very first time [when it has been there since the beginning]?[153]

Ideas of original enlightenment are also found occasionally in verse, such as these poems of Shōtetsu (1381–1459), where the Sinitic Buddhist terms *hongaku* and *honbutsu* are transformed into their Japanese equivalents, *moto no satori* and *moto no hotoke:*

> *Hotoke to mo*   He who knows nothing
> *nori to mo shiranu*   of "Buddha" or "Dharma"—
> *hito ni koso*   he is the one in whom
> *moto no satori wa*   original enlightenment
> *fukaku miekere*   appears profoundly.

> *Yama mo mina*   Mountains and tiny river shells
> *moto no hotoke no*   are all the forms
> *sugata ni te*   of the original Buddha,
> *taezu minori o*   and the storm ceaselessly
> *toku arashi kana* [154]   preaches the Dharma.

A detailed discussion of the impact of original enlightenment thought on the broader intellectual culture of medieval Japan would exceed the scope of this study. Here it will suffice to touch briefly on two important areas of influence: Shintō theory and poetics.

Hongaku Thought and Shintō Theory

In the late Kamakura and Muromachi periods, a body of literature began to take shape detailing various secret transmissions and theories concerning the nature of *kami* or local deities. The threat of Mongol attack in the late thirteenth century may well have stimulated a heightened interest in the *kami* as sources of numinous power to be invoked for nation protection, and who—after typhoons thwarted two invasion attempts in 1274 and 1281—were seen as having indeed repelled Japan's enemies. This new literature was chiefly a development within Buddhism. Buddhist monks were among the few educated people who could both travel widely and communicate with people of different social classes. Thus they helped initiate the practice of making pilgrimages to major shrines such as Ise and Kumano, played a key role in the dissemination of stories about the miraculous powers of the *gongen* or local manifestations of the deities, and did much to popularize the worship of shrines beyond those of the family or village.[155] They were also the major producers of the new transmission literature concerning the shrines and their deities. Its two main streams are those of Sannō Shintō, which concerns the *kami* of the Hie shrine complex worshipped on Mt. Hiei, and Ryōbu Shintō, which originated within the Shingon school as an attempt to assert the identity of the inner and outer shrines of Ise with the Diamond- and Matrix-Realm mandalas. Similar literature was also compiled within the families of hereditary shrine priests, though their ideas too were strongly influenced by Buddhism.[156] Central to these Shintō theories and transmissions is the doctrine of original enlightenment.[157] While this remains a vast and largely unexplored area within the field of medieval Japanese religion, a few examples can be given here.

First, notions of original enlightenment were invoked in attempts to establish the preeminence of the Ise shrine. For example, a Ryōbu Shintō transmission text retrospectively attributed to Kūkai outlines three categories of *kami*. The first category is the *kami* of original enlightenment *(hongaku)*. This refers to the deity of the great shrine of Ise, the "constantly abiding and unchanging subtle essence of the principle or nature that is originally pure." Second are the *kami* of nonenlightenment *(fukaku)*, ignorant, boisterous, and deluded demons who "never emerge from the four evil [realms]" and "lose their minds on hearing the pure voice of the Buddhas' [preaching]." Third are the *kami* of acquired enlightenment *(shikaku)*, the deities of the various other shrines, who, after undergoing transmigration, by means of the Buddhist teachings "awake from the sleep of ignorance and return to the principle of original enlightenment."[158] The categories of original enlightenment, nonenlightenment, and acquired enlightenment of course come from the *Awakening of Faith*. This threefold categorization of *kami (sanjin-setsu)* appears in other transmission texts of the late Kamakura period and influenced the development of Ise Shintō doctrine.[159]

Second, original enlightenment thought influenced a shift in how the unity of *kami* and Buddhas was understood. During the Nara and Heian periods, the Buddhas and bodhisattvas, who transcend time and space, had increasingly come to be identified with specific local deities and thus grounded, as it were, in the temporal and geographical realities of Japan. The logic of these identifications was eventually expressed in terms of *honji-suijaku*, language borrowed from T'ien-t'ai/Tendai *Lotus Sūtra* exegesis. The Buddha of the latter fourteen chapters of the sūtra, or "origin teaching" *(honmon)*, who attained enlightenment countless kalpas ago, is the Buddha in his original ground *(honji)*, while the Buddha of the first fourteen chapters, or "trace teaching" *(shakumon)*, is the "manifest trace" *(suijaku)* who appeared in this world as the historical Buddha. Chih-i had likened the relation of the two to that of the moon in the sky and its reflection on a pond.[160] When this relation was applied to that of Buddhas and *kami*, it became possible to conceive of the deities, not merely as protectors of Buddhism or as suffering beings in need of Buddhist salvation, but as local manifestations of the transcendent Buddhas and bodhisattvas, compassionately projected as a "skillful means" to lead the people of Japan to enlightenment. Correspondences between specific Buddhas or bodhisattvas and *kami* were elaborated on geographic, political, and economic grounds, as well as those of linguistic association.[161]

In the polarity of *honji-suijaku* thought, Buddhas and bodhisattvas are clearly valorized over *kami*. The transcendent Buddhas are regarded as the origin, and the local *kami* as their manifested traces *(buppon shinjaku)*. With the emergence of theories and transmissions about the *kami* in the late Kamakura period, however, the polarity of this relationship began to shift in favor of the *kami* who compassionately "dim their light and mingle with the dust of the world" *(wakō dōjin)*. Interpretations of the identity of Buddhas and *kami* paralleled those of the nonduality of abstract principle *(ri)* and concrete phenomena *(ji)* in medieval Tendai thought; as concrete phenomena came to be stressed over their invisible ground, so did *kami* over Buddhas. Eventually, in the Muromachi period, there emerged what modern scholars have called "reverse" or *han honji-suijaku* theory. Here the original relationship is inverted: the local *kami* are seen as the original ground, and the transcendent Buddhas, as their manifestations *(shinpon busshaku)*. The role of *hongaku* thought in arguing this reversal is well expressed in the following passage from Sonshun (1451–1514):

> Buddhas achieve the way by acquired enlightenment; thus they are regarded as traces *(suijaku)*. *Kami* convert and teach by virtue of original enlightenment; thus they are called "original ground" *(honji)*. . . . *Kami* have worldly forms, and Buddhas, the forms of renunciates *(shukke)*. "Renunciation" means that one corrects one's worldly form; it takes the shape of a shaven head and [black]-dyed robes, of discarding evil and upholding good. This is the practice of acquired enlightenment. But the lay state *(zaike)* entails behavior stemming from the virtue of one's innate nature and demonstrates the practice of one's present status being precisely the [stage of] wondrous enlightenment *(tōtai soku myōkaku)*. . . . Tenshō Daijin [Amaterasu Ōmikami] is the honest and upright, originally inherent deity; therefore [this *kami*] rejects the twisted mind of acquired enlightenment and takes the straight way of original enlightenment as fundamental.[162]

It should be noted that Sonshun was a Tendai monk, and that this passage occurs in a commentary on the *Lotus Sūtra,* a Buddhist text. Reverse *honji-suijaku* thought did not originate in an independent Shintō world defining itself over and against Buddhism, though such claims have long been made. It emerged within the Buddhist realm, as Shimaji Daitō asserted nearly a century ago.[163] It also occurs in the school of Yuiitsu Shintō established by Yoshida Kanetomo (1435–1511) of the sacerdotal lineage of the Yoshida Shrine; however, Yuiitsu Shintō theories were also clearly shaped by medieval Tendai original enlightenment thought.[164]

Third, one finds myths and legends of the *kami* reinterpreted in light of *hongaku* doctrine. For example, the Tendai monk Ryōhen wrote in 1424: "All sentient beings are also known as the eight million *kami*. Opening one's mouth [to assert] that the momentary deluded thoughts of all living beings are unmoving original enlightenment is what is meant by the opening of the rock cave."[165] In the myths related in the eighth-century imperially commissioned chronicles *Kojiki* (Record of ancient matters) and *Nihon shoki* (Chronicles of Japan), when the Sun Goddess hid herself in the rock cave, all was in darkness. The opening of the rock cave, which restored light to the world, is here likened to the revelation of original enlightenment.

Hongaku Thought and Medieval Poetics

The doctrine of original enlightenment not only appeared as a theme in individual poems, as noted above, but also informed medieval poetic theory.[166] Some monastics regarded the composing of poetry, or "floating phrases and fictive utterances" *(kyōgen kigo),* as an obstacle to Buddhist practice. Devotion to poetry inevitably involved one in "sins of the mouth"—false or exaggerated expressions—and in the realm of the senses, as well as in such worldly pursuits as poetry competitions. It also consumed time that could perhaps be more profitably spent in contemplative practices.[167] Original enlightenment thought and its attendant valorization of concrete phenomena provided one rationale by which some poets were able to reclaim the composition of verse, not only as an activity valid for Buddhists, but as a form of Buddhist practice in its own right.

A suggestive work in this regard is the *Korai fūtei shō* (Poetic styles past and present, 1197) by the poet Fujiwara no Shunzei (1114–1204). Shunzei is credited with having introduced into Japanese verse the elusive aesthetic quality of *yūgen,* connoting mystery and depth. The relevant section of his treatise begins by likening the composition of poetry to "calming and contemplation" *(shikan)* as set forth in Chih-i's *Mo-ho chih-kuan* (Great calming and contemplation). Chih-i's work begins with a recitation of the Dharma lineage transmitted from Śākyamuni Buddha down to the present; in like manner, Shunzei declares, the Japanese *uta* or verse has been handed down since antiquity:

[Some might say] that the one [i.e., the *Mo-ho chih-kuan*] addresses the profound truth transmitted by writings on the Dharma and by the [Buddha's own] golden mouth, while the other [that is, the tradition of poetry] resembles the game of "floating phrases and fictive utterances." But it is here that the deep meaning of things becomes apparent, for poetry as a connection *(en)* can bring one even to the Buddha Way. Hence the teaching that "the worldly passions are precisely enlightenment" *(bonnō soku bodai).* Thus the *Lotus Sūtra* states, "If he [the practitioner of the sūtra] preaches secular classics, pronounce-ments on the governance of the world, occupations that sustain life and things of that sort, he shall in every case accord with the True Dharma."[168] And the *Contemplation of Samantabhadra* says, "What is sin? And what is good fortune? The mind itself being empty, sins and for-tune are without substance."[169] For these reasons, I can now definitively state that the profound way of poetry resembles the three truths of emptiness, conventional existence, and the middle.[170]

The connection between Shunzei's poetics of *yūgen* and T'ien-t'ai/Tendai concepts of nonduality has long been noted. The threefold truth, as mentioned above, denies both the real existence of phenomena and one-sided attachment to emptiness, affirming all things as simultaneously empty of substance but also existing provisionally as elements of con-ventional reality. Scholars have noted a number of structural similarities between this concept and Shunzei's verse, which are also reflected in the work of other medieval poets. One such similarity is a collapse of the dis-tinction between observer and observed to reveal the "mind" in which both subject and object are encompassed. Konishi Jin'ichi has pointed to this development in Shunzei as representing a new direction in me-dieval poetry.[171] William LaFleur has additionally noted a denial of hi-erarchy between signifier and signified, or between poetic imagery and what it alludes to, that characterizes medieval poetry in the *yūgen* mode. Such verse, like the threefold truth itself, "aims at a kind of ontological egalitarianism" in which "the abstract is no more and no less real than the concrete" and "surfaces are never merely superficial."[172] A symbol, while being a symbol, simultaneously embodies the reality it represents. To apply LaFleur's mode of analysis to a single poem, one might con-sider this verse by the Tendai prelate Jien (1155–1225) on the brevity of summer nights:

Musubu te ni	In my cupped hands,
kage midare yuku	the moon's reflections scatters
yama no i no	in this mountain well:
akademo tsuki no	While I am still unsatisfied,
katabuki ni keru[173]	the moon sinks from view.

To anyone familiar with T'ien-t'ai/Tendai doctrine, the poem imme-diately suggests the analogy of the moon and its reflection that Chih-i employed in his exegesis of the *Lotus Sūtra* to explain the relation be-tween the original Buddha and his historical manifestation in this world. However, one point of that analogy is that historical manifestation and origin are neither separate nor hierarchical. A similar "nondual" struc-ture informs the poem; thus it does not merely allude to the analogy of the unity of origin and manifestation as expressed in Chih-i's commentary but is also about the moon on a summer night and its reflection in a mountain well. In a manner similar to the trajectory of the threefold contemplation, which proceeds from conventional existence to emptiness and then reverses, returning to conventional existence, so the poem points to the classic allusion beyond itself only to turn and redirect the attention back to its immediate imagery. This rejection of hierarchy between image and the truth to which it alludes mirrors, as LaFleur has noted, the Tendai idea that "phenomena are none other than the true aspect" *(genshō soku jissō).*[174] This verse of Jien's also illustrates the denial of observer/observed duality noted by Konishi. As the reflected moon breaks apart in the poet's hands, the "real" moon vanishes from sight, simultaneously cutting off perceiver and perceived, object and reflection.

Yet another, deeper structural similarity is to be found between medieval Tendai thought and medieval poetics. This is the claim that poetry, even art itself, is not a second-level representation of a higher, "religious" truth but, when approached with the proper attitude, is equivalent to Buddhist practice and is the expression of enlightenment. Shunzei's suggestion that "the profound way of poetry" resembles the threefold truth soon found expression in the phrase "the way of poetry is itself the Buddha Way" *(kadō soku butsudō).* In other words, the same sort of nondual relationship thought to obtain between *ji* and *ri,* or between *kami* and Buddhas, was applied to the relationship of artistic expression and Buddhist truth.[175]

Shunzei's reference to the threefold truth has usually been interpreted in terms of the methods of contemplation set forth in Chih-i's *Mo-ho chih-kuan.* However, by Shunzei's time, "calming and contemplation" and the "threefold truth" had emerged as central themes in the medieval Tendai *kuden* literature, where they were often interpreted from a *hongaku* perspective, not as actual forms of contemplative discipline, but as innate from the outset: for the person who has realized original enlightenment, all ordinary activities are "calming and contemplation." It seems possible, even likely, that Shunzei understood the contemplation of poetry in this sense.

The influence on poetics of Tendai thought generally and original enlightenment thought in particular is also evident in the writings of other leading medieval poets concerning their art. Jien asserted that the principle of the nonduality of ultimate and worldly truths was expressed in the composition of *uta.*[176] Jakuzen (fl. 12th cent.) wrote, "'Of every form and fragrance, there is none that is not the Middle Way.' [To compose poetry on] on green leaves or scarlet blossoms is an instance of this principle."[177] *Nomori no kagami,* a thirteenth-century treatise on poetics, suggests that sincerity of expression in composing verse is equivalent to the threefold truth of emptiness, conventional existence, and the mid-

dle, and to the heart of esoteric Buddhist practice. "To endow with mind
that which is without mind, to give voice to things that cannot speak, is
the realization of Buddhahood in this very body by both sentient and
insentient beings." Composing a thirty-one-syllable *waka* is equivalent to
reciting an esoteric mantra.[178] A somewhat later poet, Shūgi (1421-1502),
wrote in his treatise on linked verse *(renga):*

> As for the way of poetry, by simply fixing compassion in one's mind
> and contemplating the principle of birth and death, even when watch-
> ing the scattering blossoms and falling leaves, the demons in one's
> mind will be calmed and will return to the principle of suchness which
> is original enlightenment. Because "in every case there will be no con-
> tradiction to the true aspect," whatever the path to which he is devoted,
> one should not deviate from this mind.[179]

The relationship between original enlightenment thought and the
broader cultural milieu has yet to be fully explored. However, even a brief
examination brings to light striking similarities between the collapsing
of the distinction between ultimate reality and concrete phenomena seen
in medieval Tendai *hongaku* thought; the identification of Buddhas with
kami; and the equation of the Buddha Way with poetry. All three discourses participate in a shared "nondual" matrix in which immediate
particulars are valorized as instantiating the whole of enlightened reality. This way of thinking appears to have characterized much of medieval
intellectual activity.

Problems in the Study of Tendai Hongaku Thought

Thus far, the term Tendai "original enlightenment thought" has been
used as though it were unproblematic, but what it represents is far more
complex and less unified than this single rubric would suggest. At this
point, it will be well to give some idea of the sources involved in the study
of this subject and the problems they present, as well as the difficulties
entailed by the use of "original enlightenment thought" as a scholarly
category. An awareness of such problems is essential, because they affect
how the subject of "original enlightenment thought" has been constructed in modern scholarship.

Problems with the Texts

Medieval Tendai *hongaku* thought is developed primarily in a diverse
body of texts known as orally transmitted doctrines *(kuden hōmon)*. Some
of these texts deal explicitly with the concept of original enlightenment,
while in others this idea is present only as a tacit premise informing a
discussion of other subjects, such as the Sannō cult, the chanting of
hymns *(shōmyō),* precept initiation, or topics of doctrinal debate. There

are also works dealing with original enlightenment notions that do not take the form of oral transmissions. Much of the *hongaku*-related Pure Land material attributed to Genshin falls into this category.

Modern academic study of the Tendai *kuden hōmon* began around the same time that the topic of "original enlightenment thought" began to draw scholarly attention.[180] Scholarly research thus far, however, has illuminated merely the proverbial tip of the iceberg. Oral transmission texts account for an estimated 20 percent of the Tendai sect's Eizan Library holdings, and this is only one of several archives in Japan housing such documents.[181] Only a small percentage of these texts has been made available in printed editions.[182] The sole annotated volume of such literature, *Tendai hongaku ron* (Tendai original enlightenment discourse), was published in 1973; it has since come to be regarded in the nature of a canon and has done much to stimulate interest in original enlightenment thought.[183] However, it contains only seven complete texts and two substantial portions of larger texts—a fraction of the extant *hongaku*-related literature. It is well to bear in mind that our understanding of "original enlightenment thought," and of medieval Tendai more broadly, is still based on a limited sampling of data. As more manuscripts are edited and published, a more detailed picture should emerge.

Another, formidable difficulty with the Tendai oral transmission literature concerns the dating and attribution of individual texts. As outlined above, *kuden* were first relayed orally from master to disciple, then written down as *kirikami,* and finally assembled into collections that were retrospectively attributed to Saichō, Enchin, Kōkaku, or other prominent Tendai figures. During this period of compilation, oral transmission and the production of new *kirikami* were still continuing, and these transmissions would in turn be incorporated into compiled texts. Thus not all *kirikami* included in a particular collection necessarily date from the same period.[184] Later works systematizing and commenting on *hongaku*-related doctrines sometimes carry reliable attribution; these begin to appear from around the fourteenth century. Before that, however, lie two hundred years or more of texts whose exact chronology and authorship, in most cases, are simply not known. Internal clues will occasionally establish an upper or lower limit for the date of a text's compilation or the sequence of two or more texts. In a few cases there are external references. For example, in his commentary on Chih-i's *Fa-hua wen-chü* (Words and phrases of the *Lotus Sūtra*), written between 1165 and 1207, Hōchi-bō Shōshin questions the authenticity of a collection of *kuden* attributed to Ennin called *Juketsu entaragishū tōketsu;*[185] thus some version of the *Entaragishū* must have been written before that time. For the most part, however, dating is a matter of elaborate guesswork as to the sequence of texts based on what appear to be earlier or later stages in the development of the doctrines and arguments they contain. Connections

among texts are often so complex that tentatively dating one can affect
the placement of several others.

Drawing upon the work of earlier scholars and on his own comparison of texts, the late Tamura Yoshirō (1921–1989) established a tentative chronology of some of the major texts considered representative of
medieval Japanese original enlightenment thought, dividing the production of this literature into six fifty-year periods from 1100 to 1400.[186]
Tamura notes that his dating is tentative and his list of texts far from exhaustive. His dating of certain individual writings has been debated.
Nonetheless, his represents the most detailed chronology to date and is
heuristically useful as a framework for discussing the development of
Tendai *hongaku* thought. It has been cited so widely that it is worth examining some of the evidence on which it is based and the major uncertainties involved.

Dating of some texts from Tamura's fifth and sixth periods—from
1300 to 1400—can be established with relative certainty, as by this late
stage, some works were signed by their actual compilers. Fixing the upper limits of the tradition is much more difficult. Tamura's choice of
"1100" as a starting point for the process of textual compilation derives
from his analysis of the *kuden* collection *Honri taikōshū* (Collection in outline of the original principle). As a collection of *kirikami* transmissions
said to have been received by Saichō in China, it clearly belongs to the
medieval Tendai *kuden* tradition. However, because it does not yet exhibit the characteristic vocabulary of *hongaku* thought, it is obviously a
very early example of the genre. Tamura finds great similarity between
the *Taikōshū* and the ideas of Annen, who died in the late ninth century.
However, the *Taikōshū* says that it represents "the doctrinal interpretations of Eshin's followers," a reference to Eshin Sōzu or Genshin, who
died in 1017. Considering that it must then have been compiled by Genshin's followers after his death, Tamura places the *Taikōshū* "around
1100" and begins his dating of the *kuden* literature from that point.[187]

If the compiling of oral transmissions and *kirikami* into larger texts began "around 1100," then when did Tendai oral transmission itself begin?
Perhaps, Tamura suggests, from about the mid-eleventh century, that is,
from the time of the Tendai monk Kōkei or Kōgyō (977–1049) and his
disciple Shōhan (996–1077). Kōkei, known as a systematizer of Taimitsu
ritual, is said to have transmitted his teachings on esoteric rites verbally
to his disciples. This convention of oral transmission may then have been
applied to Tendai doctrinal interpretations as well. Shōhan, under the
name of his lodging temple, the Renjitsu-bō, is mentioned frequently in
medieval Tendai *kuden* texts as the source of various oral transmissions.[188]

Central to Tamura's scheme is his proposed dating of the *kuden* collection *Sanjū shika no kotogaki* (Notes on thirty-four articles), attributed
to Kōkaku (fl. 1150). Tamura considered the *Kotogaki* to be a watershed

work. In his view, all the essentials of *hongaku* thought are fully present in this work: later texts may be seen as developing not new ideas, but systematizations and commentaries on doctrinal positions already present in the *Kotogaki*. In this text, says Tamura, the monism of *hongaku* as principle *(ri)* is applied directly to the world of changing phenomena *(ji)*, which are then absolutized as the expressions of original enlightenment. However, he notes, this absolutizing of concrete phenomena is not among those aspects of *hongaku* doctrine criticized by Shōshin in his commentary on Chih-i's *Hsüan-i,* completed in 1207. Thus, Tamura concludes, this idea had probably not emerged by Shōshin's time. He accordingly dates the *Kotogaki* between 1200 and 1250, probably closer to 1250.[189]

However, Tamura's dating of the *Kotogaki* is by no means universally accepted, and other scholars push it back to the late Heian period.[190] At stake is the issue of when Tendai *hongaku* thought reached its full point of development. Over and against earlier scholars such as Hazama Jikō, who had placed this flourishing in the late Heian or early Kamakura period, Tamura, by his relatively late dating of the *Kotogaki* and other significant texts, pushed it forward to the mid-Kamakura period.[191] This in turn may hold implications for the relationship of original enlightenment thought to that of the new Kamakura-period Buddhist movements, whose founders—apart from Nichiren and Ippen (if one includes him)—were active well before 1250.

Most disagreements with Tamura's proposed chronological sequence have taken the form of disputes over the dating of individual texts.[192] One scholar, however—Hanano Michiaki—has challenged the entire scheme. Hanano, like Hazama before him, sees *hongaku* thought as coming into flower during the late Heian or Insei period. Hanano has developed his own six-stage chronology in the compilation of medieval Tendai texts. It is similar to Tamura's except that the dates of a number of significant works are pushed back between fifty and a hundred years.[193] One of the more intriguing aspects of Hanano's argument concerns the body of Amidist *hongaku* literature, which is chiefly attributed to Genshin.[194] Pointing out that this literature differs stylistically from the Tendai *kuden hōmon* and does not take the form of collected oral transmissions, Hanano maintains that it should be regarded as forming an independent and earlier lineage of Tendai *hongaku* literature, dating from very shortly after Genshin's time. This possibility is supported by the datings tentatively proposed by other scholars of specific texts in the Tendai *hongaku*–Pure Land genre, though again, there is little firm agreement.[195]

Further study and comparison of texts, it is hoped, may shed some additional light on the chronology of stages in the development of *hongaku* thought and the compilation of related literature. At present, however, it is virtually impossible to say with exactitude who compiled a particular text or when. As a result of such uncertainties, the Tendai *hongaku*-related literature in its formative stages comes to us in a state of dislocation, removed from its original contexts. Problems of dating and attribution compound the difficulty of knowing why particular texts were written or under what circumstances, who read them, what their ritual or institutional contexts may have been, or what part they may have played in the careers of those who transmitted them. These are limitations that must be borne in mind in thinking about notions of original enlightenment.

Problems with the Category

The *kuden hōmon* literature and other medieval Tendai texts often use the term "original enlightenment" and, occasionally, "original enlightenment teaching" *(hongakumon)* or "original enlightenment doctrine" *(hongaku hōmon)*. "Original enlightenment *thought*," however, is a modern category, first popularized by Shimaji Daitō's studies. Introducing an expression that would be echoed by decades of later scholarship, Shimaji characterized original enlightenment thought as "absolute affirmation" of the phenomenal world. Tamura Yoshirō, as already noted, saw this "absolute affirmation" as a thorough-going monism in which the realm of principle *(ri)* and the realm of phenomena *(ji)* were utterly conflated. He also expanded upon this characterization in an attempt to define "original enlightenment thought" more precisely. It consists, says Tamura, in two philosophical moves.[196] First, the Mahāyāna idea of nonduality is pushed to its ultimate conclusion. All existents, being empty of independent self-nature, are seen as interpenetrating and mutually identified. This move negates any ontological difference whatsoever between the ordinary person and the Buddha, the mundane world and the pure land, self and other, and so on. All conventional distinctions of the phenomenal world are thus collapsed in a breakthrough into an undifferentiated, nondual realm. Second, based on this insight into absolute nonduality, one "returns," as it were, to the phenomenal world, affirming its relative distinctions, just as they are, as expressions of ultimate nondual reality or original enlightenment. In other words, one negates two levels of distinctions to reveal two levels of nonduality: (1) the distinctions among phenomena (e.g., between body and mind, or between self and objective world) are negated to reveal their absolute nonduality; and (2) the distinction between this absolute nondual realm and the empirical world of differentiated phenomena (e.g., body/mind, subject/object, birth/death) is also negated, revealing the nonduality of phenomena and the ultimate truth. Thus far, this might seem indistinguishable from earlier Mahāyāna formulations of nonduality, especially the T'ien-t'ai threefold truth. The difference for Tamura lies in the extent to which the second move is carried in medieval Tendai thought. The "return" to the phenomenal world affirms as the expressions of original enlightenment not only the "existential" aspects of that world, such as "birth" and "death," or "self" and "other," but also its delusive aspects, such as ignorance and the mental defilements. Thus the deluded ordinary worldling *qua* ordinary worldling and the Buddha *qua* Buddha are both affirmed as manifestations of nondual original enlightenment. In fact, as Tamura points out, it is the ordinary worldling living in the actual world who is identified as the "true Buddha," while the transcendent Buddha of the sūtras is reduced to the status of a provisional Buddha. This affirmation of ordinary worldlings, in Tamura's view, establishes all activities of daily life as the Buddha's conduct and in effect denies the need for any specific religious practice. He concludes that, while the first of these two philosophical moves is "grounded in traditional Buddhist thought," the second, in affirming deluded worldlings, "oversteps the boundary of Buddhist thinking patterns and is due more to the influence of Japanese thinking patterns."[197] This definition has come to enjoy considerable currency. For example, it appears under the entry *"hongaku shisō"* in the recently published Iwanami Buddhist dictionary, reputed to be the most outstanding Buddhist dictionary in Japan directed toward the nonspecialist.[198]

Tamura's definition is helpful in illuminating common conceptual structures underlying a mass of diverse materials. Nonetheless, certain reservations are in order and will be discussed in the course of this study. Here, it is appropriate to note the problems entailed in the attempt to establish a singular or unified definition of "original enlightenment thought."

First is the danger of excessive reification. The term "original enlightenment thought," especially when supported by a very systematized definition such as Tamura's, may tend to suggest a greater degree of unity in the source materials than they actually possess.[199] For example, the above-mentioned Iwanami *Tendai hongaku ron* contains nine texts that all participate, as the title indicates, in something called "Tendai original enlightenment discourse." Close examination, however, reveals important differences in approach. Among the selections, the *Tendai Hokkeshū gozu hōmon yōsan* (Essentials of the Oxhead doctrine of the Tendai-*Lotus* school) and the *Sanju shika no kotogaki* are clearly collections of oral transmissions or *kirikami*. However, the *Shinnyo kan* (The contemplation of suchness) takes an essay form, rather than that of a *kuden* collection. It is also written in the mixed Japanese style *(kana majiri bun),* rather than the literary Chinese employed in most medieval Tendai doctrinal writings, and it may have been written for an educated lay reader. Among those selections that are classifiable as *kuden hōmon,* the *Shuzenji-ketsu* (Decisions of Hsiu-ch'an-ssu) contains instructions for a range of meditative practices, while the *Kankō ruijū* (Digest of the Light of Han) appears to be closely related to the Tendai tradition of doctrinal examination and debate.[200] The *Honri taikōshū, Shuzenji-ketsu, Kankō ruijū,* and others focus on interpretation of traditional Tendai/*Lotus* doctrine, while the *Shinnyo kan* incorporates Pure Land elements. Such diversity increases when a wider range of texts is considered. The use of the single rubric "original enlightenment thought" can easily obscure the plurality of approaches, genres, and subject matter of the writings informed by a *hongaku* perspective.[201]

A second problem lies in the notion of "original enlightenment *thought*," which gives the impression of a primarily or even purely philosophical enterprise, independent of practice, ritual, or institution. Until quite recently, the discipline of Buddhist studies in both Japan and the West tended to stress doctrine to the exclusion of other concerns. In the case of medieval Tendai, this tendency has been exacerbated by the scarcity of information surrounding the production of texts, which makes their ideas particularly difficult to contextualize. There may also be historical reasons why *hongaku* thought has so often been presented in a chiefly philosophical light. Shimaji, who characterized it as the "climax" of Buddhist philosophy in Japan, saw it as the perfect counter to a criticism, evidently current in his day, that "Japan has religion but no philosophy."[202] The category of "*hongaku* thought" thus easily becomes a double abstraction: due to problems of dating and attribution, many of the relevant texts have in effect been abstracted from their original contexts; then, the idea of a unified "original enlightenment thought" is abstracted from the texts.

"*Hongaku* thought" is best understood not as a monolithic philosophy, but as a multivalent discourse, albeit one that included among its many forms some highly developed doctrinal formulations. It was, moreover, a discourse embodied in specific practices, lineages, and concerns about authority and legitimacy. "Original enlightenment thought" is a convenient designation for the great range of concepts, perspectives, arguments, and doctrinal formulations informed by ideas of original enlightenment, but it was by no means either unified or an exclusively philosophical enterprise. The term will be used in this study based on this understanding.

Is Original Enlightenment Thought "Japanese"?

Tamura Yoshirō, as seen above, maintained that the affirmation of deluded worldlings as equal to the Buddha "oversteps the boundary of Buddhist thinking patterns and is due more to the influence of Japanese thinking patterns." This affirmation, he suggests, is rooted in "the Japanese ability to accommodate themselves to nature," a characteristic that, when applied to the actual world, "becomes one of accommodation to the actual world, and even an affirmation of the actual world."[203] Nor is Tamura the only scholar to make such assertions.[204] Others, while not claiming that *hongaku* thought departs from Buddhism, still see it as representative of a quintessential Japanese spirit.[205] Of all attempts to shed light on the discourse of original enlightenment, those linking it to a reified Japanese mentality are probably the least useful, and it is appropriate to note here some of the difficulties that such efforts present.

First is the problem of cultural essentialism. To inflate to the status of "Japanese thinking patterns" the ideas of certain influential producers of discourse is to run the risk of obscuring less powerful, and thus less vocal, social groups who may not have shared those ideas. In discussing medieval Tendai *hongaku* thought, we are talking primarily about the ideas of a privileged group within medieval society: almost exclusively male, predominantly clerical, and in many cases of noble birth. Not all involved were aristocrats, to be sure, but they were nonetheless well educated and in that sense represented a cultural elite. How far other medieval Japanese may have shared in their views is a question very difficult to answer.

Philosophically speaking, doctrinal positions affirming the phenomenal world as the locus of truth did indeed come to predominate in Japanese religious thought. However, this should not blind us to significant exceptions, nor to the very common disjunctures between doctrinal argument and "on-the-ground" religious activity. Medieval Tendai original enlightenment thought coexisted, especially in the late Heian period, with the radically different discourse of "shunning this defiled world and aspiring to the Pure Land" *(enri edo gongu jōdo),* celebrated in the collections of "tales of those who achieved birth in the Pure Land" *(ōjōden).* It also flourished in a society where reclusion was a respected course of action. Nor was this coexistence always a simple divide between those holding immanentalist views and an opposing camp seeking salvation beyond this world. The same individual might hold one view or the other according to context, for example, by displaying increasing concern with birth in Amida's Western Pure Land as he or she approached death.

Lastly one must ask: Is *hongaku* thought of the sort found in medieval Tendai something unique to Japan? May there not have been parallel developments in other countries? While such comparative issues go beyond the scope of this study, it may be noted in passing that some very similar ideas can be found in the work of some Chinese Buddhist thinkers. Tsung-mi, for example, in his criticism of the Hung-chou lineage of Ch'an originating with Ma-tsu Tao-i (709–788), represented its position as follows:

> The arising of mental activity, the movement of thought, snapping the fingers, or moving the eyes, all actions and activities are the function-

ing of the entire essence of the Buddha nature. Since there is no other
kind of functioning, greed, anger, and folly, the performance of good
and bad actions and the experiencing of their pleasurable and painful
consequences are all, in their entirety, Buddha nature.[206]

This statement closely resembles a number of passages in medieval
Tendai texts. Tendai *hongaku* thought, as Tamura himself has amply
demonstrated, emerged out of a long tradition of interpretation of the
Mahāyāna teaching of nonduality; one does not need to invoke "Japanese thought patterns" to account for it. Nonetheless, like any Buddhist
tradition, medieval Tendai was grounded in the specifics of a particular
culture and a particular historical moment, apart from which it cannot
be fully understood. Tendai *hongaku* thought is indeed "Japanese," not
in embodying some putatively timeless and essentialized Japanese mentality, but in terms of the medieval Japanese historical, social, and institutional context in which it developed. Locating original enlightenment
thought within that context is a major aim of this study.

Chapter Two

Tendai Hongaku Thought and the New Kamakura Buddhism: Rival Theories

DESPITE DIFFERENCES of opinion on the chronology of individual texts, it appears that medieval Tendai *hongaku* thought underwent its most creative phase from roughly the late eleventh or twelfth centuries through the early fourteenth—the period in the history of medieval Tendai thought that Hazama terms "emergence and development." This period begins somewhat before and then coincides with "Kamakura Buddhism," a term often taken as encompassing, not only the Buddhist forms that emerged during the Kamakura period (1185 to 1333) *per se,* but their precursors of the late Heian period as well. No moment in the history of Japanese Buddhism has attracted more scholarly attention. Understanding original enlightenment thought thus demands that one locate it, not only within its medieval Tendai Buddhist context, but also within the context of modern scholarship about Kamakura Buddhism.

The Kamakura period has often been depicted as a particularly dramatic moment in Japanese history, a time of social and political upheaval. It was marked, first of all, by the rise to power of the *bushi,* a class of military professionals who had steadily been gaining influence in the provinces as local peacekeepers and administrators. The Kamakura period is dated from 1185, when the warrior Minamoto clan defeated their rivals, the Taira, who had gained unprecedented influence by winning imperial appointments to provincial governorships and other offices and through marriage politics at court. Long depicted as a struggle between two leading warrior houses, the Genpei War (1180–1185) is now better understood as a challenge on the part of provincial warriors to the Kyoto-centered and courtier-administered system of land tenure.[1] The Minamoto leader, Minamoto no Yoritomo, established his *bakufu* or "tent govenment" at the town of Kamakura in eastern Japan and in 1192 was granted the title Seii Taishōgun (barbarian-subduing great general) by the imperial court. After his death, power in Kamakura came to rest with

55

the Hōjō clan, who monopolized the office of regent *(shikken)* to successive shoguns. Throughout the thirteenth century, Kamakura would function as a second locus of political authority, intertwined with that of the court in Kyoto. A major landmark in the solidification of Kamakura power was the "Jōkyū Disturbance" *(Jōkyū no ran)* of 1221, when the retired emperor Gotoba sought to challenge growing *bushi* authority. His forces were routed by the Hōjō, and Gotoba himself was exiled to the island of Oki in the Japan Sea. While aristocratic and imperial rule was not eclipsed by *bushi* power until the succeeding Muromachi period (1333–1568), the establishment of the Kamakura *bakufu* opened the way for warrior ascendancy. In addition to constituting a recently empowered social and political force, the *bushi* represented a new clientele eager and able to sponsor religious services, and their patronage had great influence on Buddhist developments of the day.

The Kamakura period has also been characterized, especially in studies of Buddhist history, as a period of cataclysms and disasters. These included not only the social change wrought by the rise of *bushi* power but a number of natural calamities recorded in mid-century sources such as the *Azuma kagami* (Mirror of the East), such as drought, famine, epidemics, and the great earthquake of Shōka 1 (1257), which leveled much of Kamakura. In addition, there were the Mongol invasion attempts of 1274 and another in 1281, Japan's most serious confrontation with an external threat in the premodern period. Whether the natural disasters of the Kamakura period were in fact worse than those of previous eras is open to question, but the social transformations accompanying the establishment of the *bakufu* and the need to defend against foreign invasion were new in Japanese experience. All such disruptions and uncertainties were assimilated to the polemics of competing agendas within the Buddhist world. In some quarters they were taken as evidence that the world had further entered a period of decline, and in others they were blamed directly on the spread of rival interpretations of the Buddha-Dharma.

Scholars of Buddhism in Japan and their Western counterparts have long been fascinated by the religious ferment that accompanied the political and social changes of this era and found expression in a burgeoning of new practices, doctrines, iconic forms, and types of religious organization. Much of the research to date has focused on the emergence, during this time, of a variety of new Buddhist movements. Some remained within existing Buddhist institutions, while others broke away to form independent organizations. Some did not survive the Kamakura period, while others, though small and relatively insignificant in the thirteenth century, gained institutional prominence in the Muromachi period and eventually numbered among the most powerful Buddhist denominations in Japan. Among those groups that achieved institutional independence are the Jōdoshū or Pure Land sect founded by Hōnen (1133–1212); the Jōdo Shinshū or True Pure Land sect, which takes as its founder Hōnen's disciple, Shinran (1173–1262); and the Nichiren-shū or Nichiren sect, named after the monk Nichiren (1222–1282), with whom it originated. These three groups in particular represent a radical move known as "exclusive choice" *(senchaku* or *senju),* the rejection of the plurality of available Buddhist practices in favor of a single form, which thereby acquires absolute status. For the Pure Land teachers Hōnen and Shinran, this meant exclusive devotion to the Buddha Amida and the sole practice of the vocal *nenbutsu* or recitation of Amida's name. For Nichiren, it was exclusive devotion to the *Lotus Sūtra* and the chanting of its title. Hōnen, Shinran, and Nichiren all invoked rhetoric about the difficulties of salvation in the age of the Final Dharma *(mappō)* and emphasized faith, rather than moral conduct and merit accumulation, as the basis of liberation. Another, less well known Pure Land movement of this time that would acquire independent sectarian status and survive up to the present was the Jishū founded by Ippen (1239–1289), who had originally studied with Shōtatsu, a disciple of Hōnen's follower Shōkū. While emphasizing the chanting of the *nenbutsu* as Hōnen and Shinran had done, Ippen actively incorporated into his Pure Land teaching practices associated with the *kami,* which Hōnen and Shinran had not.

In contrast to the "faith alone" orientation of the Pure Land and Nichiren movements, the same period also witnessed a number of efforts to revive the Buddhist precepts, both to restore the ideal of pure and orderly monastic life through observance of the *vinaya* and to enable numbers of lay people to form a karmic connection to Buddhism through precept ordination. Precept revival crossed Buddhist denominational lines and included the efforts of such figures as Eizon (or Eison, 1201–1290) of the Saidaiji, a reviver of the Risshū or "precepts school"; Eizon's disciple Ninshō (1217–1303), active in Kamakura, who enlisted the support of *bakufu* authorities for a range of charitable projects; Myōe (1173–1232), known as a "restorer" of the Kegon tradition; Jōkei (1155–1213), a scholar of Hossō doctrine also active in Pure Land practices, Maitreya worship, and devotion to the deity of the Kasuga Shrine; Shunjō (1166–1227), an advocate of the Risshū based in Kyoto; and the Tendai monks Eikū and Ejin (d. 1289?) of Mt. Hiei, who sought to restore strict observance of the bodhisattva precepts. Precept revival efforts did not in themselves develop into lasting independent religious movements; they did, however, play a role in the establishment of Zen. Zen Buddhism first acquired the beginnings of an independent institutional presence in the Kamakura period through the efforts of men like Eisai (or Yōsai, 1151–1215) and Dōgen (1200–1253), regarded as the founders, respectively, of the Rinzan and Sōtō sects of Japanese Zen. Both men emphasized strict observance of the monastic precepts; Eisai, however, promoted Zen in conjuction with *shingon* and Tendai practices, while Dōgen, who emphasized Zen exclusively, is sometimes grouped for this reason with Hōnen, Shinran, and Nichiren as a teacher of single practice. (Unlike these three, however, Dōgen gave but little attention to *mappō* discourse.) In contrast to both Eisai and Dōgen is Dainichi Nōnin (fl. late 12th cent.), founder of the short-lived and much maligned Darumashū or Bodhidharma school, an independent Zen movement but one that, in its denial of the necessity of keeping precepts and the antinomian character of its doctrine, exhibited some similarities to the Pure Land teachings of men like Shinran.

Whether or not Buddhist precepts were essential to practice and realization, whether liberation was deemed accessible through a variety of practices or depended on one practice alone, whether or not the discourse of *mappō* played a significant role in the formation of doctrine and the interpretation of events, whether or not faith in the *kami* was actively incorporated, whether a movement defined itself within existing Buddhist institutions or broke away to achieve independence, are some of the lenses through which Buddhist developments in this period have been analyzed. Because such concerns crossed institutional lines and were joined in different combinations, the Buddhist movements of the Kamakura period have proved hard to categorize. Viewed from one perspective, any one of them exhibits affinities with certain others, but when the perspective is shifted, it will be seen to differ from these and instead show affinities to others.

Trends in Interpreting Kamakura Buddhism

Since the postwar era, two major trends have emerged in the historiography of Kamakura Buddhism.[2] The first has focused on the careers and teachings of those men regarded as the founders of the new Buddhist sectarian movements of the Kamakura period that have survived to the present—Eisai, Hōnen, Shinran, Dōgen, and Nichiren—and characterized them as representative of medieval Japanese Buddhism. Several of these studies have highlighted Pure Land figures as paradigmatic for the new movements, an approach taken by such scholars as Ienaga Saburō and Inoue Mitsusada. Founder-centered studies of Kamakura Buddhism have done much to illuminate the life and thought of those individuals who initiated what would become, in time, some of the most influential Buddhist traditions in Japan. In general, this approach has regarded these new sectarian movements as a significant departure from the Buddhism of earlier times and therefore speaks of them collectively as the "new Buddhism" *(shin Bukkyō)*. This category has in turn demanded the construction of its opposite—"old Buddhism" *(kyū Bukkyō)*—a term that replaced the older and less wieldy though more neutral expression *nanto hokurei* (i.e., the Buddhism of the temples of Nara and Mt. Hiei). The way in which modern scholarly construction of "new Buddhism" called into being an opposing "old Buddhism" has aptly been likened to the way in which the formation of the Mahāyāna engendered the category of "Hīnayāna."[3] The opposition of *shin* and *kyū* in modern studies of Kamakura Buddhism has supported a number of academic stereotypes about a democratic, reformist "new Buddhism" arising in reaction to an elitist, degenerate, and outmoded "old Buddhism." These clichés have become enshrined in a number of basic reference sources, such as the *Encyclopedia of Religion,* which asserts that founders such as Hōnen and Shinran were moved to seek new directions in faith because they "had become disillusioned by the empty ceremonialism, scholasticism and moral corruption that characterized the monastic life of their times."[4]

Assumptions about the "corruption" of older Buddhist institutions have profoundly affected the study of medieval Japanese Buddhism. Prewar sources of these assumptions include the influence on the historiography of Japanese religions of the modern Buddhism sectarian scholarship *(shūgaku)* conducted within the "new" schools, which tends to regard the entire history of Buddhism as culminating in the teachings of a given tradition's founder, such as Shinran, Dōgen, or Nichiren. Another source is the lingering effect of notions about the new Kamakura Buddhism as a "reformation." The comparison of the rise of the new Kamakura Buddhism with the Protestant Reformation was first proposed by Hara Katsurō in 1911 and enjoyed considerable vogue among both Japanese and Western scholars.[5] While both parties have now largely abandoned comparisons with the European Protestant Reformation in favor of more historically contextualized approaches to Kamakura Buddhism, the image of the new Buddhist founders as "reformers" persists. Still another source may be the recurring tendency to see the new Kamakura Buddhism as inherently more "Japanese" than older forms, representing the moment when "Buddhism in Japan" became "Japanese Buddhism." This reading can probably be traced to Meiji-period refigurations of the new Kamakura founders as Japanese cultural heroes. It ignores both the extent to which Buddhism had already become assimilated and "indigenized" in the Heian period and even earlier, as well as the fact that some of the new Kamakura founders were inspired by Chinese models. More than two decades ago, James H. Foard quipped that this reading of the new Buddhism had "passed away in Japan only to find eternal life in the West" and urged that it "be laid to permanent rest."[6] However, it has shown a disturbing tendency to rise from the grave.[7] Sometimes it has been coupled with the equally persistent and similarly problematic claim that, where "old Buddhism" catered only to the aristocracy, the "new Buddhism" reached out to the common people. Alicia and Daigan Matsunaga, for example, write that in the Kamakura period "Buddhism in Japan assumed a truly Japanese character by embracing the majority of the populace."[8]

Postwar intellectual trends have also played a role in reinforcing images of the "old Buddhism" as decadent. Retrospective reflection on Buddhist institutional cooperation with militant imperialism during the prewar period and World War II encouraged a negative evaluation of premodern Buddhism's official role of thaumaturgical "nation protection" (chingo kokka). Older Buddhist institutions that had provided nation-protection rites, such as those of Tendai and Shingon, were compared unfavorably with the new movements, which had in several cases resisted established religious and political authority. In this connection, the "old Buddhism" has been treated primarily as an institution, while the "new Buddhism" has been characterized in terms of the great men who were its founders. This dichotomy of "institution" versus "founder" has fostered images of an "old Buddhism" engaged in chiefly "political" activity over and against a "new Buddhism" concerned with the genuinely "religious" issue of personal salvation.[9] One can also point to the influence of Marxist-inspired postwar historiography, which has tended to characterize "old Buddhism" as lending ritual and ideological support to ruling elites, and "new Buddhism," as representing the interests of the common people.

Notions of the older Buddhist institutions as "corrupt" are not altogether modern constructions. There is abundant contemporary evidence for widespread monastic laxity and misconduct, as well as a sense of crisis—at least in some circles—in human capacity to observe Buddhist precepts and ethical conduct, often associated with belief in the advent of the degenerate Final Dharma age (mappō). Criticism of religious institutions is also implicit in the conduct of some hijiri or "holy men," monks who left the monastic establishment to practice in reclusion. However, such evidence is not sufficient to warrant the assumptions of thorough-going decadence found in many "new Buddhism"-centered studies.

An approach to Kamakura Buddhism radically different from that of the founder-centered studies was developed by the late historian Kuroda Toshio (1926–1993) and those who have been influenced by his work.[10] Kuroda conclusively demonstrated that the representative forms of medieval Japanese Buddhism were not the new Kamakura movements, but what he termed the kenmitsu taisei, the "exoteric-esoteric" system that characterized the older Buddhist institutions—Tendai, Shingon, and the Nara schools. It consisted of a shared base in esoteric Buddhist teachings and practices, which all these schools had incorporated, joined to an emphasis by each school on its particular distinguishing exoteric doctrine. Fundamental to the kenmitsu system were the perceived magical powers of Mikkyō ritual to ward off danger and invite prosperity. This emphasis on Mikkyō apotropaic ritual enabled the incorporation into the *kenmitsu* system of local thaumaturgical rites, such as those for the pacification of vengeful spirits *(goryō);* yin-yang divination practices (Onmyōdō); and cults of the *kami,* subsuming them all within the universality of the Mahāyāna. *Kenmitsu* Buddhism, Kuroda has argued, not only was an all-encompassing religious system but had important political dimensions as well. The leading temple-shrine complexes *(jisha)* performed esoteric rituals for the benefit of their aristocratic patrons, thus providing thaumaturgical and ideological support for the ruling powers. In return they received grants of extensive private estates *(shōen),* enabling their emergence as significant political and economic forces in medieval society. In fact, Kuroda has shown that the major temple-shrine complexes, along with the court and the *bakufu,* formed part of the system of medieval ruling elites *(kenmon taisei). Kenmitsu* Buddhism thus represented the side of religious orthodoxy *(seitō-ha).* Within this system, the new Kamakura Buddhist movements began only as small, marginal heterodoxies *(itan-ha).*

Kuroda's work has served as a vital corrective, not only in demonstrating that the "old," rather than the "new," forms of Buddhism predominated in the Kamakura period, but also in calling attention to often neglected political, economic, and ideological aspects of medieval Japanese religion. Ironically, however, in focusing on the powerful political and economic role of the major temple-shrine complexes, *kenmitsu taisei* theory, despite its revisionary nature, has worked to reinforce older images that privilege the "new Buddhism" over the old as champions of the common people against the forces of authority.[11] As Sueki Fumihiko wryly observes, "It does not readily escape the formulation that the *itan-ha* (or new Buddhism) equals the good guys, and the *seitō-ha* (or old Buddhism), the bad guys."[12]

The labels "new Buddhism" and "old Buddhism" are, as Sueki notes, a convenience. They enable one to speak collectively of movements newly arisen in the Kamakura period as distinguished from those with a prior institutional presence. In this sense, the problem may lie not as much with the categories themselves as with the assumptions that inform them. However, in addition to perpetuating the stereotypes already discussed, there are several matters that the reification of Kamakura Buddhism into "old" and "new" obscures. First, it ignores new developments within the so-called old traditions. Where innovators within the established traditions (such as Myōe or Eizon) have been studied, they have all too often been cast in the role of "reformers"—a characterization that in effect both reinforces the notion of "old Buddhism" as decadent and assimilates these figures to the model of the new Buddhist founders as challengers of the status quo. Second, the division into "new Buddhism" and "old Buddhism" overlooks ground shared by the two. Such common ground includes not merely those elements that newer movements derived from older institutions, but also synchronous developments occurring across the "new"/"old" divide that were peculiarly characteristic of the medieval period. And third, the separation fails to note the extent to which "new" movements, having achieved institutional independence from the "old" traditions, proceeded to borrow from them in the process of becoming established.

For some years, scholars both in Japan and other countries have begun to redress these problems inherent in the "old" versus "new" model of Kamakura Buddhism. Such challenges have taken two major forms. One is serious study of the religious thought and practice of the "old Buddhism." The publication of the *Kamakura kyū Bukkyō* volume of *Nihon shisō taikei* in 1971 was a milestone in this endeavor and has been followed by studies of specific figures. Such studies began with major figures within the established Buddhist traditions, such as Myōe, but are now expanding to deal with broader aspects of the "old Buddhism."[13] A second approach attempts in various ways to problematize, redefine, or transcend the "new"/"old" distinction.[14] James Foard, for example, in a landmark essay critiquing the "Reformation" model of Kamakura Buddhism, drew attention to new developments common to both "new" and "old": simplified forms of practice, new forms of religious organization, and new proselytizing techniques.[15] More recently, Matsuo Kenji has suggested that the *vinaya* revival movement of such monks as Eizon and Ninshō, long considered a conservative movement within "old Buddhism," should in fact be considered part of "new Buddhism" because its advocates, like the adherents of the new sectarian movements, adopted new forms of ordination outside the official state-sponsored ordination system.[16] Sasaki Kaoru has drawn attention such figures as Saigyō, Chōgen, and Ippen as representative of a "trans-establishment Buddhism" *(chō-taisei Bukkyō),* a third element cutting across the opposition of the "establishment Buddhism" *(taisei Bukkyō)* of nobles and *bakufu* and the "anti-establishment Buddhism" *(han-taisei Bukkyō)* comprised by the single-practice movements.[17]

In addressing the subject of original enlightenment discourse, the present study combines both these recent approaches. On one hand, it investigates the contexts of this discourse in the medieval Tendai tradition, the most influential representative of the "old Buddhism." On the other, it attempts to undermine reification of the "new"/"old" distinction by considering original enlightenment as one example of innovative, shared ways of reconceiving enlightenment or salvation that were emerging concurrently in both "old" and "new" Buddhist institutions. First, however, it will be useful to outline the major trends in scholarship on this issue to date.

Tendai Hongaku Thought and the New Kamakura Buddhism

The men regarded as the founders of the new Kamakura Buddhist sects—Eisai, Hōnen, Shinran, Dōgen, and Nichiren—began their careers as Tendai monks and studied on Mt. Hiei, where *hongaku* thought was flourishing. Moreover, some of their ideas share points of similarity with certain medieval Tendai *hongaku* writings, including the primacy of faith, the direct accessibility of Buddhahood, the nonduality of practice and enlightenment, and optimism about the possibility of salvation for ignorant and evil persons. What, exactly, was the nature of the connection between the new Kamakura Buddhism and medieval Tendai *hongaku* thought? This question has now been debated for some decades. Rather than attempting to detail the views of every scholar who has taken part in this discussion or to present a precise chronology of their arguments, I will summarize the major theories on this issue. At the risk of some oversimplification, these may be regarded as falling into three basic positions, which for convenience' sake I have termed "Tendai as matrix," "the radical break," and "dialectical emergence." In reality, there is considerable shading and overlap, rather than absolute confrontation, among the three.

Theory One: Tendai as Matrix

This position sees the new Kamakura Buddhist movements as emerging out of a common intellectual basis in medieval Tendai original enlightenment thought. It was first advanced by Shimaji Daitō in a seminal essay published in 1926 called "Nihon ko Tendai kenkyū no hitsuyō o ronzu" (An argument for the need to study early Japanese Tendai). In this essay, Shimaji proposed that original enlightenment thought had been the "womb" or "matrix" of the new Kamakura Buddhism. Many scholars at the time assumed a close relationship between Nichiren's thought and medieval Tendai doctrine, but Kamakura Zen had been understood as a Chinese import, and the Pure Land movements, as having been inspired largely by the Pure Land thought of the Chinese master Shan-tao (613–681). Shimaji argued that both these traditions had deep connections with medieval Tendai *hongaku* thought, especially in the case of Dōgen's Zen and the Pure Land teachings of Hōnen's disciples Shōkō, Kōsai, and Shinran. Prior to Shimaji's research, antecedents of the new Kamakura schools had been sought in medieval responses to anxieties about the Final Dharma age *(mappō),* or in the activities of *hijiri* or holy men, whether wanderers or recluses, who lived apart from the official monastic establishment. Shimaji's claim that the new schools had a common intellectual foundation in Tendai *hongaku* thought made it possible to discuss them within a unified, transsectarian framework, and it quickly gained wide acceptance.

Along with the "womb" or "matrix" metaphor, other expressions Shimaji employed in this essay would become standard vocabulary in discussing original enlightenment thought. He was the first to characterize it as "absolute affirmation" and the "climax" of Buddhist philosophy. Several of the suggestions made in "Nihon ko Tendai kenkyū no hitsuyō o ronzu," such as the possibility of intellectual connections between *hongaku* thought and developments in Kamakura Zen and Pure Land teachings, have been explored productively in the work of later scholars, especially Tamura Yoshirō. The aspect of Shimaji's work on *hongaku* thought that has come under the greatest revision is his dating of texts. A pioneer in the field, Shimaji worked without printed editions, noting that his research was frequently obstructed by "the difficulty of obtaining sources, and, when by chance they are obtained, most are of doubtful authenticity."[18] Shimaji was among the first to recognize that many of the Tendai oral transmission texts attributed to Saichō and Genshin were apocryphal, but he nevertheless tended to regard as authentic those attributed to later Tendai masters such as Chūjin (1065–1138), an assumption that later researchers have questioned. Shimaji accordingly placed the developmental phase of Tendai original enlightenment thought in the period between the flourishing of the Tendai and Shingon schools in the early Heian period and the rise of the new Kamakura Buddhism.[19] This chronology supported his idea that the new Kamakura movements emerged from the matrix of mature *hongaku* thought. Later researchers in this area, beginning with Shimaji's student Hazama Jikō, would see Tendai *hongaku* thought as emerging later, in the latter part of the Heian, and then developing during the Kamakura period, coevally with the new movements.

Although Shimaji characterized original enlightenment thought as the "climax" of Buddhist philosophy in Japan and the "matrix" of the new Kamakura Buddhism, he perceived a moral danger in an idea that affirmed all activities of life as precisely the activities of the originally inherent Tathâgata. Tendai thought concerning an inherently enlightened Buddha, Shimaji said, had proceeded in two major directions: "One took form as the bright Kamakura Buddhism that purified original enlightenment thought, while the other sank to a naturalistic, corrupt thought and brought about the deterioration of the Buddhism of Mt. Hiei."[20] Elsewhere—using "original enlightenment thought" in a very broad sense to encompass all the immanentalist forms of Buddhism that had developed in East Asia—Shimaji suggested that the notion of all things as inherently enlightened had encouraged an incorporation of non-Buddhist elements that inevitably brought about the destruction of Buddhism.[21] In the case of Japan, he said, this process had fortunately been halted at the critical moment by the emergence of the new Kamakura movements, which "were able to remove the danger that inevitably accompanies original enlightenment thought, purify and actualize it, skillfully harmonizing it with the idea that enlightenment is acquired."[22] Scattered throughout Shimaji's writings are indications that, despite his conviction of their philosophical indebtedness to Tendai *hongaku* thought, he considered the Kamakura thinkers superior in the areas of practice and ethics. In the case of Nichiren, for example, while judging that "the content of his doctrine scarcely differs from medieval Tendai thought," Shimaji wrote that Nichiren had brought the vitality of faith to a medieval Tendai that had not transcended philosophical conceptualizing, and introduced national concerns to an original enlightenment doctrine that had hitherto been concerned purely with individual salvation.[23]

A variation on the "Tendai as matrix" theory was advanced by Tendai scholar Uesugi Bunshū (1867–1936), who worked extensively on medieval Tendai transmission texts of the Eshin and Danna schools. Like Shimaji before him, Uesugi saw the period dominated by original enlightenment thought and oral transmission literature as one of decline in traditional Tendai scholarship. The one-to-one master-disciple form of transmission, he suggested, had encouraged rote memorization rather than real learning. Uesugi also noted that many transmission texts employ the highly subjective *kanjin* style of interpretation, which will be discussed in greater detail in chapter 4. Rather than taking classic texts as the basis of interpretation, *kanjin*-style hermeneutics first establishes a normative principle (in this case, the premise of original enlightenment) and then seeks textual passages to support it, deriving these where necessary from the invention of proof texts, out-of-context quotation, or imaginative repunctuating of Chinese sources. While allowing scope for creativity to insightful teachers, in the hands of the less skillful, Uesugi said, this approach merely gave rise to bizarre statements, production of spurious writings, and a general decline of scholarship, marking the medieval period as "the dark ages" of Tendai doctrinal studies. This darkness had been illuminated, claimed Uesugi, by the founders of the new Kamakura Buddhist movements, as well as by scholars such as Hōchi-bō Shōshin, who had sought to revive traditional Tendai exegetical studies.[24] Uesugi saw the rise of the new Buddhism as "restoring the honor" of Tendai and returning to the original spirit of Saichō and the universality of the One Vehicle. Among the founders of the new movements, he said, "there was none who was not a scholar ensuring the eternal perpetuation of [the Buddhism of] Mt. Hiei."[25]

For Uesugi, the "Tendai matrix" from which the new thinkers sprang was not that of medieval *hongaku* thought, as Shimaji had suggested, but the original Japanese Tendai of Saichō. His suggestion represents a variation on the long-influential view of the new Kamakura Buddhism as a reform movement attempting to rectify abuses in the existing Buddhist establishment. It stands midway between Shimaji's "matrix" argument and the second theory outlined below.

Theory Two: The Radical Break

In criticism of Shimaji's "*hongaku* thought as matrix" idea, Buddhologist Nishi Giyū (b. 1897) wrote:

> The sectarian founders of the newly emergent Buddhism of the Kamakura period—Hōnen, Eisai, Shinran, Dōgen, and Nichiren—all originally studied on Mt. Hiei, so in some sense, the new Buddhism represents their expansion of the medieval Tendai that had developed on Mt. Hiei. From this perspective, to regard medieval Tendai as having functioned as the matrix of the new Buddhism is a common-sense idea, which anyone might readily conceive. However, in that these men all left the mountain and eventually started their own sects, they were people who rejected medieval Tendai. Thus, though there may in some sense have been influence [from medieval Tendai on the new Kamakura Buddhism], it is more appropriate to view that influence as [engendering] a reaction against medieval Tendai.[26]

This position may be called the "radical break" theory. It maintains that the emergence of the new Kamakura Buddhism is to be understood as a rejection of medieval Tendai thought, especially the doctrine of original enlightenment. While not confined to sectarian scholars, arguments for this position have been advanced most vigorously on two sectarian fronts, having been initiated within the academic wing of Nichirenshū and later taken up by several scholars of Sōtō Zen.[27] As mentioned above, Tendai Pure Land thought played an important role in some strands of original enlightenment discourse, and the question of *hongaku* influence on the teachings of Hōnen, Shinran, and their later disciples has been explored by scholars within both Jōdoshū and Jōdo Shinshū.[28] Thus far, however, their work on this issue has not generated major controversy or polemical heat comparable in any degree to that surrounding arguments about the relationship of Tendai *hongaku* thought to the teachings of Nichiren or Dōgen, as encountered in Nichirenshū and Sōtōshū scholarship. Because of the sectarian contexts of these arguments, it is appropriate here to touch briefly on the subject of sectarian scholarship (*shūgaku*) and its influence on modern studies of Japanese Buddhism.

Modern *shūgaku* has its roots in the Edo period (1600–1868), when Buddhist temples were organized along sectarian lines into the main-temple branch-temple system and brought under *bakufu* control. Forbidden from disrupting the public order by engaging in intersectarian debate, scholar-monks based at their respective sect's official seminaries (*danrin*) devoted themselves to systematizing the doctrines of their traditions. This period saw a massive effort in the collecting, editing, and publishing of each sect's important texts and the production of voluminous commentaries.

The methods and categories of this early modern *shūgaku* continue to influence the normative study of Buddhist doctrine today. Contemporary *shūgaku* is conducted chiefly at Buddhist universities, which originated as seminaries and—along with their more recently acquired role as liberal arts colleges—retain the function of educating future priests in the teachings of their own sect and of Buddhism generally. Among the more prominent are, in Tokyo, Risshō University, affiliated with Nichirenshū, and Komazawa University, with Sōtō Zen; and in Kyoto, Hanazono University, affiliated with Rinzai Zen; Bukkyō University, with Jōdoshū; Ōtani University, with the Ōtani branch of Jōdo Shinshū; and Ryūkoku University, with Jōdo Shinshū's Nishi Honganji branch. Taishō University in Tokyo is unique among such institutions in being administered by the cooperative efforts of four sects: Tendai, Jōdo, and the Chizan and Buzan branches of Shingon.

Contemporary *shūgaku* is like Western theology in that it assumes the truth claims of its tradition, but broader in that it encompasses not only textual and doctrinal studies but also Buddhist institutional history. Practitioners of *shūgaku* command a historical and textual expertise in their respective traditions seldom rivaled by Buddhist scholars of purely secular institutions, and their work provides a vital resource for anyone studying Japanese Buddhism. However, certain biases are built into the sectarian scholarly enterprise. These include a tendency to privilege the sect's founder as unique, along with a teleological approach to its own history that views prior developments as leading up to the founder's thought and measures subsequent ones against it, often overlooking similar phenomena occurring synchronously in other traditions. Such sectarian concerns are very much at work in "radical break" theories of the relationship between original enlightenment thought and the new Kamakura Buddhism.

ARGUMENTS FROM NICHIRENSHŪ Among the large corpus of writings traditionally attributed to Nichiren (1222–1282) are many that deal with original enlightenment thought. In 1926, when Shimaji published "Nihon ko Tendai kenkyū no hitsuyō o ronzu," it was generally accepted both inside and outside Nichirenshū that Nichiren had taught the doctrine of original enlightenment. Some difference of opinion existed as to whether he stood closer to the doctrinal position of the Eshin or the Danna school, but the influence of medieval Tendai on his thinking was virtually unquestioned.[29]

Nonetheless, within Nichirenshū, scholars had for some time been engaged in attempting to establish the existence of clear differences between medieval Tendai *hongaku* thought and the *hongaku* thought of Nichiren, making use of the distinction between *ri,* or "principle," and *ji,* meaning "phenomena" or "concrete actuality." Over and above their importance to East Asian Buddhism generally, these categories held a time-honored place in the Nichiren tradition, having been used by Nichiren himself to distinguish between the "contemplation of the mind" *(kanjin)* set forth by the Chinese T'ien-t'ai founder Chih-i (538–597) and his own form of practice. Where Chih-i's form of meditative discipline was that of "principle," or introspective contemplation to perceive the true aspect of reality in one's own mind, Nichiren's was that of "actuality," or the chanting of the *daimoku,* the title of the *Lotus Sūtra,* said to embody the reality of the Buddha's enlightenment and the seed of Buddhahood.[30] Nichiren's usage reflects the strong influence of esoteric Buddhism, in which *ri* refers to formless truth that is contemplated inwardly, and *ji,* to its expression in outwardly manifest practices involving concrete forms.[31] The categories of "principle" and "actuality" had also been used extensively by later Edo period Nichiren scholars such as Udana-in Nichiki (1800–1859), who sought to systematize Nichiren doctrine in a way that would emancipate it from the T'ien-t'ai/Tendai studies that had dominated Nichiren seminaries since the beginning of the early modern period.[32] Applied to the issue of distinguishing between medieval Tendai and Nichirenist versions of *hongaku* thought, however, the *ri/ji* distinction became not a contrasting of two modes of practice, as Nichiren had used the terms, but a distinction of theory and practice. An example concerned medieval Tendai versus Nichirenist readings of the "original Buddha" *(honbutsu)* of the sixteenth or "Fathoming the Lifespan of the Tathâgata" chapter of the *Lotus Sūtra,* enlightened since the unimaginably remote past. For medieval Tendai thinkers, this Buddha was the "Tathâgata of original enlightenment" who is equated with the cosmos or dharma realm itself; the sūtra's revelation of his "original attainment" of Buddhahood countless kalpas ago was no more than a revelation in principle *(ri kenpon),* a skillful means or metaphor to show that all beings are enlightened from the outset. Such an interpretation, the Nichiren scholars argued, reduced the eternal Buddha of the *Lotus Sūtra* to no more than an abstract Dharma body (Skt. *dharmakāya,* Jpn. *hosshin)* or truth as principle; in their reading, the "original attainment" was actual *(ji kenpon)* and emphasized the centrality, among the Buddha's three bodies, of the "reward body" *(saṃbhogakāya, hōjin),* the Buddha wisdom acquired through practice by which the Dharma is realized. Tendai original enlightenment thought was accordingly characterized as a mere theoretical, abstract statement that beings are inherently enlightened by nature *(jinen hongaku),* while Nichiren's teaching was presented as the actualization of inherent enlightenment through faith and practice *(shikaku soku hongaku).*[33]

In the eyes of scholars outside Nichirenshū, however, the clear presence of original enlightenment discourse in writings attributed to Nichiren tended to reduce him to an offshoot of medieval Tendai. Maeda Eun (1857–1930), for example, wrote that the doctrines of the Nichiren sect are "in fact based on original enlightenment thought" and "completely inherited from the original enlightenment doctrine of our teacher Saichō."[34]

Similarly, Shimaji Daitō, while acknowledging points unique to Nichiren in his approach to practice and application, nevertheless thought that "the content of his doctrine hardly differs from medieval Tendai thought,"[35] while Uesugi Bunshū saw Nichiren's doctrine as "a derivation of the oral transmission literature of Mt. Hiei."[36] This reduction of Nichiren's thought to an offshoot of medieval Tendai was galling to Nichirenshū scholars, especially when Maeda and Shimaji made remarks to this effect while speaking as guest lecturers at the Nichirenshū Academy (later Risshō University).[37] New efforts were made to clarify distinctions between medieval Tendai and Nichiren's *hongaku* thought, such as Shimizu Ryūzan's *Tendai Nichiren taishō ronjutsu Hokekyō yōgi* (Essentials of the *Lotus Sūtra*, outlining doctrinal differences between Tendai and Nichiren), written in hopes of persuading scholars outside the sect of the need to consider Nichiren on his own terms.[38] But the first effective ammunition for counterattack was to come from an entirely new scholarly methodology: critical studies of the Nichiren canon.

Such studies were pioneered by the Nichirenshū scholar Asai Yōrin (1883–1942), who aimed at recovering a "pure" Nichiren doctrine based on "scientific" investigation of the canon and the identification and elimination of apocryphal texts. Asai's findings, which he began to publish in the 1930s, were startling and revisionist. He pointed out that, of the works traditionally attributed to Nichiren that deal with original enlightenment thought, most do not exist in Nichiren's autograph or in transcriptions made by his immediate disciples, nor do they appear in the earliest indices of his writings. Moreover, they employ terminology and concepts that, while common to medieval Tendai oral transmission texts, appear only infrequently or not at all in those of Nichiren's writings whose authenticity can be verified. Maeda, Shimaji, and Uesugi were in error, Asai declared, because they had assumed that the essence of Nichiren's doctrine was expressed by writings in his corpus reflecting the influence of medieval Tendai *hongaku* thought. In fact, Asai argued, these writings were not Nichiren's work at all but the forgeries of later disciples who, influenced by their study on Mt. Hiei or at Tendai seminaries in eastern Japan, had incorporated *hongaku* thought into their understanding of Nichiren's teaching. Even if some of these texts should conceivably be Nichiren's writings, they did not represent his "primary thought," as expressed in his two major treatises, which Asai held should be normative:

the *Kaimoku shō* (Opening of the eyes) and the *Kanjin honzon shō* (The contemplation of the mind and the object of worship).[39] While presenting itself as objective and scientific, Asai's argument proved a timely and effective weapon in defending Nichiren against the charge of being derivative of medieval Tendai.

On the whole, the textual evidence marshaled by Asai does indeed suggest that many Nichiren-attributed writings showing the influence of medieval Tendai *hongaku* thought may be apocryphal. Asai, however, went to the extreme of arguing not only that the issue of original enlightenment thought was peripheral to Nichiren's concerns, but that he had actively rejected it. Original enlightenment thought, in Asai's estimation, was little more than esotericism decked out in new terminology. Nichiren, who had sharply criticized post-Saichō Japanese Tendai for its incorporation of Mikkyō, would never have made use of elements originating in a tradition he himself had rejected, Asai said; Nichiren's doctrinal studies were indebted to no one except the orthodox T'ien-t'ai/Tendai tradition represented by the Chih-i, Chan-jan, and Saichō. Hence Asai questioned the authenticity of any Nichiren-attributed text that contained terminology related to original enlightenment discourse.

For Asai, *hongaku* thought was a defilement that had to be removed if the original purity of Nichiren's doctrine were to be restored. He was vehement about its corruptive tendencies. The *kanjin* style of interpretation that it fostered had contributed not only to a decline in faithful scholarly exegesis, he said, but also to the degeneracy of monks who took advantage of the decline of imperial authority in the Insei period to flaunt their power.[40] "From the outset, the original enlightenment doctrine of medieval Tendai actually spurred on corruption." Asai saw its claim that "the worldly passions are enlightenment" as serving to rationalize widespread monastic license in the Muromachi period, such as descents from Mt. Hiei on nightly pleasure-seeking forays or homosexual relations with male novices *(chigo)*.[41] Nichiren, he argued, had stressed text-based exegesis, not subjective interpretation; the primordial Buddha of the *Lotus Sūtra* was for him a transcendent object of faith, not equated with the mind of deluded beings. In short, Nichiren's thought was not to be grasped within the same frame as medieval Tendai, which was permeated throughout by the very Mikkyō that Nichiren had so bitterly criticized.

Asai's project of recovering a "pure" and "normative" Nichiren doctrine has drawn criticism on both historical and hermeneutical grounds, and his criteria for judging textual authenticity were not always as clear or objective as he maintained.[42] But in bringing critical methods to bear on the study of his tradition's sacred canon, he transformed the scholarly study of Nichiren. While a detailed discussion of his work must wait for another occasion, he should be noted here as probably the first scholar to characterize the thought of one of the new Kamakura Buddhist founders in opposition to—rather than as emerging from—original enlightenment thought.

Asai Yōrin's locating of Nichiren in opposition to medieval Tendai was explicitly extended to the other Kamakura founders by one of his disciples, Shigyō Kaishū (1907–1968). In a brief essay published in 1954, Shigyō challenged the idea that original enlightenment thought could be regarded as the matrix or womb of the new Kamakura Buddhism.[43] Shigyō suggested later datings than had thus far been proposed for certain key medieval Tendai texts, such as the *Shuzenji-ketsu,* traditionally attributed to Saichō. Where Hazama Jikō had dated it from the late Heian period, Shigyō placed it in the mid- to late Kamakura period. The new Kamakura schools had not, Shigyō said, branched off from a mature tradition of medieval Tendai *hongaku* thought as Shimaji, Uesugi, and Hazama had suggested; rather, while the idea of original enlightenment had already been implicit in Tendai studies, its development and systematization were stimulated by the need to confront and resist the newly emerged schools of Kamakura Buddhism.[44] Shigyō offered little evidence in support of this highly speculative theory, nor has anyone seriously developed it since. There is altogether too much evidence that *hongaku* thought was being actively advanced by the late Heian period, as Hōchi-bō Shōshin's criticism indicates. Moreover, while there probably was some "reverse influence" from the new Kamakura Buddhist movements on medieval Tendai thought, recent scholarship, such as that of Kuroda Toshio, has dispelled the idea that the newly emergent Kamakura movements immediately became powerful enough seriously to threaten the religious establishment. Shigyō's contribution in this essay was to underscore the fact, already pointed out by Hazama, that Tendai *hongaku* thought had continued to develop during and after the emergence of the new Kamakura movements. His relatively late dating of certain key medieval Tendai texts such as the *Shuzenji-ketsu* has been upheld by Tamura Yoshirō. Shigyō also preceded Tamura in suggesting that Tendai *hongaku* thought had not reached its peak of development until well after the end of the Heian period. Shigyō saw original enlightenment thought as absolute affirmation of all phenomena, a doctrine that "cuts off discrimination between good and evil, right and wrong" and seeks to "reject all effort by human agency and dwell peacefully in the unconditioned, natural realm just as it is given, not acknowledging concepts of value distinction."[45] The *kanjin* style of interpretation for him had "no sort of logic" and "falls into a game of concepts."[46] The esoteric claim of original enlightenment thought that "this body is itself Buddha" had done nothing to alleviate the samsaric suffering of ordinary persons. In contrast, the new Kamakura schools "developed as a shift from theoretical Buddhism to practical Buddhism, looking squarely at reality and concentrating on the problem of how to change it." Hōnen's and Shinran's deep awareness of human sinfulness "must be seen as a reconsideration and reaction against original enlightenment thought" with its too-facile identification of the mind of living beings with the originally enlightened Buddha.[47] Where, according to Shigyō, medieval Tendai simply declared that the defilements are expressions of original enlightenment just as they are (*jinen hongaku*), in Dōgen's thought, original enlightenment is mediated by practice and self-awakening, and in Shinran's thought, by the relinquishing of egotistical reliance on one's own efforts (*jiriki*). In addition, where medieval Tendai thought had taught contemplation of the mind of ordinary persons, the new Kamakura schools stressed faith in the enlightenment of the Buddha.[48]

Similar statements have continued to emerge from the Nichirenshū academic circle based at Risshō University and appear to represent a certain orthodoxy. Asai Endō, for example, writing twenty years after Shigyō, claims that medieval Tendai stressed only the Buddhahood inherent in ordinary people and "disregarded even [the stage of] hearing the Dharma and embracing it with faith," which he terms "a confusion of theory and practice, a pernicious equality."[49] Its insistence on the identity of ordinary persons with an originally enlightened Buddha "became an empty theory divorced from the times," unable to bring about positive spiritual results in an age of turmoil accompanying the rise of the warrior class.[50] "The founders of the new Kamakura Buddhism left Mount Hiei, weary of this kind of Buddhist thought that gave priority to theory, being divorced from reality. Therefore, while Hōnen, Shinran, Dōgen, and Nichiren each have their own unique religious qualities, they are all alike in the point of having resolved to overthrow abstract theory."[51]

ARGUMENTS FROM SŌTŌ ZEN Similar arguments for a radical break between medieval Tendai original enlightenment thought and the new Kamakura Buddhism have been forthcoming from some scholars of Sōtō Zen who characterize their founder, Dōgen, as a critic of the *hongaku* doctrine. Often cited as a basis for this characterization is the "great doubt" that, according to traditional hagiography, led Dōgen as a young man to abandon his Tendai training on Mt. Hiei: "Both exoteric and esoteric teachings say that the original Dharma-nature is naturally innate within oneself. If this is the case, then why do the Buddhas of the three time periods arouse the aspiration for and seek enlightenment? At that time, he asked this of senior teachers, but there was none who could answer or explain it."[52] Dōgen's failure to obtain a satisfactory response is said to have prompted him to leave Mt. Hiei and go first to Kōin Sōjō (1145–1216), a Tendai prelate of the Onjōji, and then to the Zen teacher

Eisai. After Eisai's death, Dōgen studied under his disciple Myōzen and then finally went to China, where he met his true master, Ju-ching.

This story appears in a hagiographical account written after Dōgen's death and contains numerous problems. Dōgen himself does not cite this "great doubt" as the reason for his departure from Mt. Hiei. His own writings suggest that he was troubled by the contradiction between his ideal of an authentic teacher and the worldly aspirations of the monks around him.[53] Or, he may have left Mt. Hiei in connection with the fact that the teacher from whom he had recieved ordination—Kōen, the *zasu* or chief abbot of the Enryakuji—had been forced to resign toward the end of 1213.[54] It is also highly unlikely that no one on Mt. Hiei was capable of addressing the relationship of practice and original enlightenment, a topic explicitly addressed in a number of medieval Tendai texts. Whatever the case, it seems probable that the "great doubt" represents a hagiographical "reading back," into the beginnings of Dōgen's career, of his later concern with the relationship between practice and innate Buddha nature.[55] In the last few decades, however, it has become commonplace, among Sōtōshū scholars and others, to cite the "great doubt" as evidence for characterizing Dōgen from his earliest years as a critic of Tendai original enlightenment thought, which is in turn seen as compromising the need for practice.[56]

Like the anti-*hongaku* arguments of their Nichirenshū counterparts, this contemporary Sōtō position has remote roots in Edo period sectarian scholarship, particularly that of Menzan Zuihō (1683–1769), who sought to eliminate from his systematization of Sōtō doctrine all elements resonant of Tendai or other traditions and to establish a pure, Dōgen-centered orthodoxy. Menzan's edited version of the *Kenzei ki* (Kenzei's record), a traditional biography of Dōgen, appears deliberately to minimize the extent of Dōgen's exposure to medieval Tendai.[57] However, Menzan in no way characterized Dōgen as a critic of *hongaku* doctrine—a development that would have to await the twentieth century.

Sōtō arguments about Dōgen as a critic of original enlightenment thought have grown particularly heated in the postwar period. These postwar discussions appear to have been stimulated largely by the work of Tamura Yoshirō, who carried on Shimaji Daitō's project of using original enlightenment thought as a framework for understanding the doctrines of the new Kamakura Buddhism in an integrated fashion. (Tamura's own theory of the relationship between original enlightenment thought and the new Kamakura Buddhism, including Dōgen's thought, will be discussed in a later section of this chapter.) Tamura saw several points of resemblance between Dōgen's ideas and those found in Tendai *kuden* texts, including Dōgen's equation of the moment-to-moment rising and perishing of the phenomenal world with the Buddha nature;

his concept of the eternal present, or "Absolute now" *(nikon);* his emphasis on "dwelling in a Dharma-position" *(jūhōi);* and in particular his teaching of "original realization and wondrous practice" *(honshō myōshu),* or the unity of practice and realization *(shushō ittō).* Nonetheless, despite these similarities, Tamura took seriously as a critique of *hongaku* doctrine the story of Dōgen's "great doubt" that had supposedly precipitated his departure from Hiei. Tamura also found passages in Dōgen's essay collection *Shōbō genzō* (Eye and treasury of the true Dharma) critical of the position that beings are enlightened a priori, as well as a passage from the *Hōkyō ki,* Dōgen's record of his studies in China, which reports that his master Ju-ching dismissed such ideas as a naturalist heresy.[58] Tamura concluded,

> Dōgen's connection with Tendai original enlightenment thought lies in his criticism and rebuttal of original enlightenment thought. If one closely examines the points of similarity between the two, differences in emphasis become apparent. In contrast to the Tendai *hongaku* doctrine, which emphasized original enlightenment thought exclusively, ... Dōgen maintained this [original enlightenment thought] as his foundation, but reversed the direction [of its interpretation].[59]

In Tamura's view, medieval Tendai had argued the oneness of practice and enlightenment in a manner that negated the need for practice, while Dōgen held that because practice and enlightenment are inseparable, there can be no enlightenment apart from practice.

The responses of Sōtō sectarian scholars to Tamura's argument has been ambivalent. On the one hand, there has been some readiness to acknowledge his claim for a historical connection between Dōgen's thought and that of medieval Tendai. On the other hand—even though Tamura by no means saw Dōgen as uncritically accepting the original enlightenment position—it has also been argued that he unduly stressed the continuities and did not sufficiently elaborate the differences. An early response came from Kagamishima Genryū, who sought to illuminate what Tamura had termed the "reverse direction" in Dōgen's understanding of *hongaku.* Kagamishima argues that Dōgen found himself "stymied" by Japanese Tendai *hongaku* thought, which had "fallen into a naturalistic view of practice and enlightenment that held practice to be unnecessary," and turned instead to Chinese Ch'an. However, after the time of Bodhidharma and the sixth patriarch Hui-neng—both of whom Kagamishima understands as taking a position close to that of original enlightenment thought—Chinese Ch'an had developed an orientation of *shikaku,* that is, approaching enlightenment as a future goal to be realized. While Dōgen's emphasis on the importance of practice derived from Chinese Ch'an, his exposure to Japanese Tendai original enlightenment thought made it impossible for him to accept this *shi-*

kaku approach, maintaining instead that practice and enlightenment are one. In this sense, Kagamishima claims that Dōgen "transcended the view of practice and enlightenment of Ch'inese Ch'an, developing it in a Japanese way."[60]

Tamura's position has been addressed at greater length by Yamanouchi (or Yamauchi) Shun'yū (1920–), a Sōtō scholar specializing in Chinese T'ien-t'ai, in his voluminous *Dōgen Zen to Tendai hongaku hōmon* (Dōgen Zen and the Tendai original enlightenment doctrine).[61] While acknowledging the importance of original enlightenment thought as part of Dōgen's intellectual background, Yamanouchi questions the idea that Dōgen "maintained it in his foundation."[62] Yamanouchi acknowledges the story of Dōgen's "great doubt"—why the need for practice if one is enlightened inherently—to be the creation of later hagiographers; it is not adequate ground, he says, for assuming that Dōgen, before the age of twenty, had fully thought out and rejected Tendai original enlightenment thought.[63] Nonetheless, Yamanouchi holds that, despite some superficial similarities, an attitude critical to original enlightenment thought pervades Dōgen's writings, and it is here that Dōgen's uniqueness lies.

For Yamanouchi, the essence of Dōgen's teaching is the onenes of "original realization and wondrous practice."[64] Where Tamura saw this teaching as incorporating original enlightenment thought, Yamanouchi sees it as embodying a severe criticism of it. In discussing the *Kankō ruijū,* a Tendai text of Dōgen's time or perhaps a bit later, Yamanouchi writes that "by the sole emphasis on persons at the stage of identity in principle (*ri-soku,* i.e., prior to practice) being equal to the original Buddha, practice is completely nullified. . . . This was precisely the object of Dōgen Zenji's criticism and bears no structural similarity to his thought."[65] "Even if, from a hundred paces off, one were to acknowledge a certain resemblance to the pattern of original enlightenment thought, original enlightenment thought itself was for Dōgen Zenji an object of criticism and censure, something completely heterogenous."[66] In what is perhaps the most novel part of his argument, Yamanouchi suggests that Dōgen's teaching of original realization and wondrous practice should be understood as belonging to the same intellectual stream as Hōchi-bō Shōshin's critique of original enlightenment thought. Shōshin, in a manner consistent with the *Awakening of Faith,* saw *hongaku* as the Buddha-potential of sentient beings to be realized in practice, and not as actual Buddhahood itself. Both Shōshin and Dōgen's teacher Ju-ching, Yamanouchi points out, criticized the idea of original enlightenment as a "naturalist heresy."[67]

Dōgen's Zen, which teaches practice with body and mind and stresses the sole practice of sitting in meditation, had no room to incorporate

the *hongaku* mode of thought. If one seeks the source of "original realization and wondrous practice" in medieval Tendai, it is to be found
in the interpretation, based on traditional doctrinal studies, of Shōshin, who denied *hongaku* and stressed realization in actuality *(genjō),*
and rejected inherent enlightenment in favor of actual awakening
(genshō).[68]

However, drawing on earlier work by Kagamishima Genryū, Yamanouchi argues that Dōgen's original critical attitude toward original enlightenment thought was compromised in the first layers of *Shōbō genzō*
commentary, the *Shōbō genzō gokikigaki* by Dōgen's disciple Senne (n.d.)
and the *Shōbō genzō shō* by Senne's successor Kyōgō (n.d.)—often referred
to together as the *Gokikigakishō* or simply *Goshō.*[69] In contrast to Dōgen's
"doctrine of resistance," Yamanouchi sees the *Goshō* as contributing to
the formation of a "docile" Sōtō doctrine that accommodated itself to
the "old system."[70] Senne and Kyōgō are both thought to have received
extensive training in medieval Tendai and may well have been influenced
by its teachings in their reading of Dōgen. In interpreting such influence
as a compromise of Dōgen's original stance, Yamanouchi's argument parallels that of Nichirenshū scholars such as Asai Yōrin who held that
Nichiren's successors had imported into their reading of his thought the
very original enlightenment thought he had allegedly rejected.

Yamanouchi also extends Dōgen's presumed criticism of Tendai *hongaku* thought to the rest of the new Kamakura Buddhist thinkers:

> In order to remove themselves from a state of affairs intellectually sat-
> urated by original enlightenment doctrine, the founders of the new
> Kamakura schools put forth a rigorous emphasis on practice. In this
> sense, aiming toward the ideal with their feet planted in reality, they
> maintained throughout a vigorous emphasis on action. . . . In order
> to overcome original enlightenment, they believed dualism [of ordi-
> nary persons and the Buddha] to be permissible.[71]

This particular strand of Sōtō argumentation takes issue with Tamura
in maintaining that criticism of *hongaku* thought, rather than *hongaku*
thought itself, forms the basis of Dōgen's teaching. Like Tamura, it
identifies Dōgen's distinguishing characteristic as an emphasis on practice over and against an original enlightenment doctrine assumed to
deny the need for practice. The difference lies in the identification of
Dōgen's sources of inspiration. Where Tamura has seen Dōgen's thought
as Dōgen's individual response to a contemporary Japanese context, that
of medieval Tendai, Sōtō scholars have tended to regard it as Dōgen's
distinctively Japanese development of the heritage of Chinese Ch'an. A
related argument, one that we shall not explore here, maintains that Dōgen did indeed draw on Tendai sources—not the *hongaku*-centered me-

dieval Tendai of his own day, but the "orthodox" Chinese T'ien-t'ai of Chih-i and Chan-jan.[72]

Several structural similarities can be identified between the "radical break" arguments of both Nichirenshū and Sōtōshū scholars. In both cases, the founder—whether Nichiren or Dōgen—is seen as a critic of medieval Tendai *hongaku* thought. Specifically, he is seen as restoring a normative emphasis on practice that medieval Tendai is said to have lost sight of in a one-sided emphasis on original enlightenment. This move is then more broadly ascribed to all the founders of the new Kamakura Buddhist movements. The sources of the founder's inspiration are located not in the "corrupt" religious milieu of his own time and place, which he is said to have rejected, but in an "orthodox" tradition rooted in China, which he reformulates in a distinctive way. Lastly, his later medieval successors who bring *hongaku* discourse to bear on their interpretation of his work—and whose readings become normative for the premodern period and beyond—are seen not as developing possibilities latent in his thought, but as betraying his original critical stance. These parallels suggest that similar concerns have informed the scholarship on both sides.

Hongaku Thought as Substantialist Heresy

A different sort of argument serving to bolster the "radical break" position over and against the Tendai-as-matrix theory is one confined to the difference specifically between Dōgen and medieval Tendai thought. This is the claim that the idea of original enlightenment represents a substantialist heterodoxy—a claim for a permanent, underlying essence or *ātman*—over and against which Dōgen reasserted the normative Buddhist position of nonsubstantiality and impermanence. This argument had its beginning not in Sōtō Zen sectarian studies, but in a 1942 essay by the Tendai scholar Hazama Jikō.[73] Hazama called attention to the tenth in a series of questions raised and answered in Dōgen's early essay *Bendōwa* (A tale of the Way), which addresses the legitimacy of claims for the "constant abiding of the mind-nature" *(shinshō jōjū)*. The gist of this doctrine, says the questioner, is that the body perishes but the mind-nature is forever unchanging; one who realizes this will put an end to transmigration and, on the body's death, be released into the ocean of original nature. Dōgen condemns this view as equivalent to the "Śrenika heresy" *(senni gedō)*, which he describes as belief in a "spiritual intelligence" *(reichi)* abiding within the body, an "inner knower" that distinguishes pain and pleasure, hot and cold, and which, on the death of this body, is reborn in another. "The Buddha-Dharma from the outset expounds that body and mind are a single suchness, nature and form are nondual."[74] Passages of the *Shōbō genzō* also warn against the "Śrenika heresy."[75]

Śrenika is said to have been a heterodox teacher, contemporary with the Buddha, who taught the existence of an immortal soul that reincarnates in successive bodies.[76] But Dōgen must have been criticizing some person or persons among his contemporaries. Who, then, was his polemical target? Hazama suggests that Dōgen may have been making a veiled criticism of the idea of "original no birth-and-death" *(hon mu-shōji),* which appears in a number of Tendai *kirikami* collections and is thought to represent part of the early stratum of the medieval Tendai oral transmissions.[77] To quote a part of one such transmission cited by Hazama:

> Birth and death are the wondrous functions of the one mind. Being and nothingness are the real virtues of original enlightenment. "Mind" is the dharma without coming or going; "spirit" is the principle that pervades the dharma realm. Thus, at the time of birth, there is no coming, and at the time of death, there is no going. When this mind that is without coming or going displays the function of being, then "mind" is precisely the individual consisting of six sense faculties; this is called "birth." When "spirit" that pervades the dharma realm displays the function of emptiness, then spirit is precisely the destruction of the body composed of the five *skandhas;* this is spoken of as "death." This is the subtle coming that is without coming, the true birth that is without birth, the perfect going that is without going, the great death that is without dying. Birth and death are one, emptiness and being are nondual. To know and see thus, to contemplate and understand thus, is to realize the mind as Buddha and be free in the samsaric realm. . . .
>
> Originally inherent, unproduced *(musa)* birth and death is without beginning or end; it is the constantly abiding mind-essence of being and nothingness. It is neither annihilation nor permanence, without coming or going. . . . Do not desire to abide in birth and death, for the sufferings of transmigration are hard to endure. But do not desire to escape birth and death, for it is then difficult to avoid the error of the view of annihilationism. Therefore you should awaken to the essence of the one mind and quickly escape the errors of the two views [of annihilationism and eternalism].[78]

While acknowledging points difficult of interpretation in the passage, Hazama concludes that it is setting forth a dualistic view in which the body is born and perishes while the mind constantly abides. He suggests that substantialist ideas such as the "constant abiding mind-nature" were representative of original enlightenment thought and may have prompted the doubts that led Dōgen to abandon Mt. Hiei. Hazama's hypothesis has been well received by scholars within the Sōtō sect.[79]

A reading of the passage alternative to Hazama's—and one arguably more convincing in light of the passage as a whole—would be to take "mind" to indicate not "mind" as an underlying essence as opposed to "body," but "mind" as the nondual truth of reality. Even so, some of its language, such as the terminology of "essence and function" or "mind-essence," does contain substantialist overtones. Such language was adopted in Chinese formulations of the Mahāyāna partly to counteract what were seen as nihilistic understandings of the Madhyamaka and characterizes a very wide range of East Asian Buddhist philosophical writing. Whether the kataphatic or "positive" expressions for ultimate reality common in East Asian Buddhism carry substantialist implications is a large philosophical issue and well exceeds the scope of this study.

Was Dōgen's critique of the "Śrenika heresy" indeed directed at Tendai original enlightenment thought, or had he another target in mind? It is worth noting here that, in both *Bendōwa* and the "Sokushin ze butsu" ("This very mind is Buddha") fascicle of the *Shōbō genzō*, Dōgen closely modeled his denunciation of the "Śrenika heresy" on the recorded words of a Chinese predecessor, National Teacher Nan-yang Hui-chung (d. 775). Hui-chung attacked as "no different from that heretic Śrenika" those who maintain that the body perishes while the mind-nature *(hsin-hsing, shinshō)* continues, "just as a snake sheds its skin or a man leaves an old house." He also clearly identified the targets of his criticism—Ch'an teachers of the South who arbitrarily interpret the *Platform Sūtra* and teach that "this very mind is Buddha."[80] In Dōgen's time, "this very mind is Buddha" formed a central doctrine of the Darumashū founded in the twelfth century by Dainichi Nōnin, the first person to establish an independent Zen group in Japan. Nōnin is said to have achieved awakening through his own efforts but was criticized because he had not studied under a teacher. Therefore, in 1189 he sent two disciples to Sung China carrying a poem expressing his understanding, and they obtained a Dharma lineage for him from Fo-chao Te-kuang (1121–1203), a teacher of the Lin-chi (Rinzai) branch of Ch'an. This is a form of Dharma transmission known as "conferring from afar" *(yōfu)*. The Darumashū is said to have denied the necessity of monastic precepts, held Zen to represent a transmission independent of the scriptures, and asserted that ordinary worldlings are innately Buddhas. It achieved wide popularity and soon came under attack by monks of the established temples. After Nōnin's death his followers were dispersed, and a number of them joined Dōgen's community. The influx of these new disciples may well have affected Dōgen's teachings and prompted his growing criticism of the Rinzai tradition. It seems entirely possible that Dōgen's criticisms of the "Śrenika heresy" were aimed not primarily at medieval Tendai, but at the teachings of rival Zen lineages, especially the Darumashū.[81]

The claim that original enlightenment thought represents a substantialist heresy, and Dōgen's thought a return to normative Buddhist ideas of impermanence and contingency, has recently garnered wide attention through the intellectual movement known as "critical Buddhism" *(hihan Bukkyō),* spearheaded by Hakamaya Noriaki, formerly of Komazawa University, in close association with his colleague Matsumoto Shirō.[82] "Critical Buddhism" is not concerned with defining the relationship between medieval Tendai and the new Kamakura Buddhist movements; its issues are normatively philosophical and ethical, not historical. At the time of this writing, the brief tempest generated by "critical Buddhism" in academic Buddhist circles in the late 1980s and early 1990s seems to have abated somewhat, though it remains an issue within the Sōtō sect. Nevertheless, "original enlightenment" first came to the attention of many, especially Western, scholars through Hakamaya's writing, and his critique of *hongaku* thought has served in effect to bolster the "radical break" position, at least with regard to Dōgen. For these reasons, it is worth mentioning here.

The premise of the term "critical Buddhism" is that to be Buddhist (in a normative sense) means to be critical, that is, to make distinctions, to choose between what is right and what is wrong, what is liberative and what is not. The specific object of criticism here is anything corresponding to a "topos," that is, an unchanging or substantial locus or basis, or pretemporal condition, which all things are held to arise from and depend upon. Notions of "topos" are said to originate at a very early stage in the development of human consciousness and to be characteristic of "indigenous" or "native" thought.[83] Any philosophical or religious system based on the notion of a "topos" is termed a "topical philosophy." (Matsumoto has also introduced the neo-Sanskritism "dhātu-vāda," a teaching premised upon a locus or *dhātu.*) Examples include the concepts of *ātman* and *brahman* in Indian thought, the idea of "nature" in Lao-tzu or Chuang-tzu, and, of course, the doctrine of original enlightenment. "Original enlightenment thought," Hakamaya bluntly asserts, "is not Buddhism." Since he uses the term in an extremely broad, cross-cultural sense to mean any immanentalist form of Buddhist thought, including notions of Buddha-nature, *tathâgata-garbha,* one mind, and so forth, Hakamaya's critique encompasses virtually the entire Japanese Buddhist tradition and many of its continental antecedents. Hakamaya has outlined three major ways in which original enlightenment thought deviates from what he understands as normative Buddhism.[84]

First, in holding all things to be expressions of an unconditionally postulated primordial enlightenment, *hongaku* thought represents a "topos." As such, it contradicts the basic Buddhist teaching of causation, or dependent origination *(pratītya-samutpāda),* by which Hakamaya means not Hua-yen-style models of all phenomena simultaneously interpenetrating and giving rise to one another, but a temporal sequence of causally related events without underlying ground. In the course of Chinese assimilation of Buddhism, says Hakamaya, these definitive concepts of causality and dependent origination were obscured. "Original enlightenment thought" is no more than ancient Chinese "topical" ideas of "nature," resurfacing in a Buddhist context. *Hongaku* thought also undermines normative Buddhist teachings of impermanence by asserting that "birth" and "death" are the functions of inherent principle.[85]

Second, since "original enlightenment" represents a topos given unconditionally and without logical examination, it tends uncritically to affirm both oneself and the authority of one's tradition. Normative Buddhist ideas of nonself and dependent origination, which deny the existence of "topos," imply a moral imperative to be critical of self and of authoritarian claims, as well as to work for others' welfare. Such moral imperatives are undercut, says Hakamaya, by the self- and tradition-affirming tendencies of original enlightenment thought. To say that "rivers and mountains, grasses and trees, have all attained the Buddha Way" may sound egalitarian, but the claim that "all things, just as they are, are Buddha" sacralizes the given social order and thus works to legitimate discrimination and other injustices.[86] The moral critique of specific ways in which "topical philosophy" has been used in Japanese history to bolster the status quo seems to have been the most persuasive aspect of critical Buddhism to date.

Third, Hakamaya sees original enlightenment thought as an "experiential" philosophy stressing the ineffability of suchness. Thus in his view it makes light of faith, intellect, and the use of language, by which the truth of dependent origination is to be discerned and investigated. Hakamaya sees the critical use of intellect and language as inseparable from normative Buddhism: Śākyamuni's hesitation to preach was not because his realization was ineffable, but because of the difficulty of communicating a teaching that goes "against the current" of the reality-affirming ideas that most people hold, based on the notion of topos. Without words, error cannot be criticized nor truth demonstrated. Moreover, without language, we would not only be unable to recall and reflect critically upon the past but would lose all sense of time itself, becoming locked in a timeless, eternal present—a loss of the very faculty that distinguishes us as humans.[87]

Hakamaya uses the term "original enlightenment thought" in a sweeping, ahistorical sense; thus his criticisms cannot readily be evaluated with regard to specific cases such as medieval Tendai *hongaku* thought, which is by no means itself a unified discourse. What is important to the present discussion is that Hakamaya sees Dōgen as taking a stand against a hegemonic "original enlightenment thought" that has dominated the Japanese Buddhist tradition. "Original realization and wondrous practice," which Yamanouchi values as Dōgen's distinguishing characteristic, appears only in the *Bendōwa* essay, while criticism of *hongaku* thought—

Hakamaya argues—can be found throughout the entire *Shōbō genzō* collection and is the "definitive perspective for understanding Dōgen." Dōgen, in Hakamaya's view, opposed not only the original enlightenment thought of medieval Tendai, but also the sort of original enlightenment thought set forth in the *Awakening of Faith,* which Yamanouchi describes as "orthodox *hongaku* thought." Yamanouchi's attempt to trace the roots of "original realization and wondrous practice" to Shōshin's work merely obscures the extent to which Dōgen was critical of all immanentalist positions.[88] Dōgen, in Hakamaya's view, "passed his life seeking a simple and clear determination of truth and falsehood." "The enemy he staked his life on attempting to negate" was a "thoroughly compromising original enlightenment thought" that was "completely unconcerned with the determination of right and wrong" in a Buddhist sense. Dōgen was "unshakeable in his blunt criticism that this was not Buddhism."[89] Hakamaya says that this lifelong criticism, first articulated in *Bendōwa,* composed immediately after Dōgen's return from China, remains muted or is not explicitly developed in interim works but resurfaces and is most fully articulated in the twelve-fascicle *Shōbo genzō,* the work of Dōgen's final years.[90] For Hakamaya, that work shows a clear rejection of original enlightenment thought and represents "the authentic Buddhism of Dōgen."[91]

Given the multivocality of medieval Tendai texts, it may be difficult to make accurate generalizations about whether or not original enlightenment thought represents a substantialist position. Moreover, this question is embedded in the larger, normative issue of whether or not such doctrines as the one mind, Buddha nature, *tathâgatha-garbha,* and suchness represent substantialist positions. Others have argued, in response to Hakamaya and Matsumoto, that such language, while appearing to presuppose a substantial ground, was in fact premised upon an understanding of emptiness and thus does not violate the normative Buddhist position.[92] Such issues, while of great importance, cannot be explored here. It will suffice to note in passing the argument of one American scholar, Ruben Habito, who has recently challenged the view of Tendai *hongaku* thought as substantialist.[93] Drawing on the work of Frederic Streng, C. W. Huntington, Jr., and other scholars of the Madhyamaka who have emphasized the soteriological thrust of emptiness discourse as a skillful device *(upāya)* for engendering transformative understanding, Habito argues that certain medieval *hongaku* texts, when read with the assumption that they were produced in a context of "enlightenment practice," can be seen as undermining attachments and encouraging liberative nondual insight. It is of great interest that Habito, like Hazama, chooses for his primary illustration a passage from a transmission related to the notion of "original no birth-and-death" but uses it to make a virtually opposite argument:

All the awakened ones are not separate from the realm of birth-death, and at the same time are separated from birth-death; they do not cling to nirvāṇa, and thus attain nirvāṇa. Having abandoned the way and its practice, they are in Eternity, Bliss, Self, and Purity.

The living beings of the three worlds, due to their views of birth and death, are submerged in the six realms; wishing to cut themselves off from birth and death, they do not escape birth and death; wishing to hold on to nirvāṇa, they do not attain nirvāṇa.

The Effortless *(musa)* birth-death is from the outset *(moto)* beginningless and endless. In the Perfect Teaching [of our school] the phenomenal world and emptiness fall into neither the eternalistic nor the nihilistic view. Contemplate this, and do not fear birth and death. Birth-death is originary bliss *(shōji wa moto raku nari)*. Human beings are deluded and perceive this as suffering. Remove this erroneous view at once, and you will arrive at the Buddha-land.[94]

The logic of such passages, Habito argues, is threefold. First, dualistic views of "nirvāṇa" and "saṃsāra" are rejected as false and delusive. Second, the nonduality of the two is affirmed. While a surface reading of statements such as "eternity, bliss, self, purity"—the four predicates of nirvāṇa set forth in the *Mahāparinirvāṇa-sūtra*[95]—or "birth-death is originary bliss" may suggest a naive, substantialist affirmation, the possibility of such hypostasis is undercut by a "deconstructive disclaimer" embedded in the text: "The phenomenal world and emptiness fall into neither the eternalistic nor the nihilistic view." Such disclaimers represent what Habito sees as the third step in the logic of this and similar medieval Tendai texts, an "emptying of concepts" that obviates both the rejection of birth-and-death as antithetical to nirvāṇa (annihilationism) *and* its essentializing as "originary bliss" (eternalism), and thus becomes the occasion of transformative nondual insight. Habito therefore argues that original enlightenment thought need not be read as endorsing a substantialist position. He is also one of very few interpreters to suggest that these texts were read and studied in a context of meditative practice, and thus, by implication, that Tendai *hongaku* thought was far more consistent with traditional Mahāyāna than has often been acknowledged.

As the above discussion indicates, "radical break" arguments tend to serve sectarian interestedness by emphasizing the intellectual independence of the founder—Nichiren or Dōgen, as the case may be—from the parent Tendai tradition. Their contribution has been to call attention to the distinguishing characteristics of individual Kamakura-period Buddhist founders, countering the tendency to reduce them to simple emanations of original enlightenment thought as the "matrix" position

might suggest. Nonetheless, there are problems with the attempt to
define the new Kamakura Buddhism as a reaction against original enlightenment discourse. It is true that Dōgen's writings contain passages
critical of the claim that ordinary worldlings are Buddhas prior to practice, or that enlightenment represents a return to an "original source."
It is also true that some elements in teachings of new Buddhist founders
do not square readily with the *hongaku* position, Hōnen's emphasis on
the transcendent "Other-power" of Amida's Original Vow being an obvious instance. Yet nowhere in the writings of any of these men do we
find the sort of explicit condemnation of *hongaku* doctrine found, for
example, in the commentaries of Hōchi-bō Shōshin. Thus it remains
questionable just how far the new Buddhist movements can be seen as
a deliberate reaction against *hongaku* thought.

Before moving on to the third theory, we may note one further strand
of scholarly argument that, while neither sectarian nor theological, has
worked to reinforce the idea of the new Kamakura Buddhism as a reaction against original enlightenment thought. This is the scholarship
of historians of the *kenmitsu taisei,* the system of exoteric doctrine and
esoteric ritual that characterized the established schools of Buddhism
in the medieval period and served ideologically to support the ruling
parties. Kuroda Toshio, who originated this approach, wrote that "*kenmitsu* ideology in its most archetypal form is found in the Tendai doctrine known as *hongaku shisō.*"[96] Satō Hiroo has argued that nondual *hongaku* ideas equating this world with the pure land were employed to
legitimize established systems of rule.[97] Taira Masayuki sees *hongaku*
thought as contributing both to aristocratic monopolizing of high clerical offices and to a climate in which strict observance of monastic precepts was devalued:

> Novices who were scions of the nobility, having received the secret
> transmission of arcane rites, were easily able to lord it over the most
> senior monks accomplished in difficult and austere practices. This was
> because of original enlightenment thought. The discourse of absolute
> affirmation found in original enlightenment thought readily translated
> into an immediate affirmation of personal desires, becoming an excuse
> for precept-breaking and the excesses of aristocratic monks. It was fur-
> ther employed to rationalize the attack and razing of rival temple-
> shrine complexes and became the intellectual basis for the activities
> of warrior monks *(akusō).*[98]

Being concerned primarily with the institutional and ideological aspects of medieval religion, *kenmitsu taisei* historians have not focused on
the issue of what continuities and discontinuities obtain between Tendai
hongaku thought and the teachings of the new Kamakura Buddhist leaders. However, in that they have treated *hongaku* thought as an ideology

of the dominant *kenmitsu* Buddhism, and the *itan-ha* or marginal heterodoxies as resisting *kenmitsu* authority, their work has contributed to
the picture of the two as standing in opposition.[99]

Theory Three: Dialectical Emergence

We come now to the work of Tamura Yoshirō, who has already been
mentioned. A specialist in Buddhist studies and Japanese Budddhist
thought related to the *Lotus Sūtra* in particular, Tamura devoted a great
part of his scholarly career to exploring, testing, and developing the suggestions made earlier by Shimaji Daitō about the relationship of original enlightenment thought to the new schools of Kamakura Buddhism.
Tamura's work on original enlightenment thought may be divided into
three major areas of contribution. First, he helped clarify the geneaol-
ogy of *"hongaku"* by tracing its antecedents in East Asian Mahāyāna
thought.[100] Second, as noted above, he proposed the most detailed
chronology to date of key medieval Tendai texts. His third major contribution, and the one that concerns us here, is his theory about the relationship of the new Kamakura Buddhism, especially that of Shinran,
Dōgen, and Nichiren, to Tendai original enlightenment thought. By contrasting the teachings of these three men with the *hongaku* ideas assumed
to have constituted their common intellectual background, Tamura
sought to clarify the individuality and uniqueness of each. Tamura himself did not use the term "dialectic" to describe how he saw the teachings of Shinran, Dōgen and Nichiren emerging out of original enlightenment thought, but its appropriateness will soon become apparent.
Because Tamura's argument has been extremely influential, it is worth
presenting in some detail.[101]

Tamura, like Shimaji, characterizes Tendai original enlightenment
thought as "absolute affirmation of reality" and the "climax" of Buddhist
philosophy, a synthesis of Tendai, Kegon, esoteric, and Zen elements that
carried to the farthest possible point the denial of any separation between
ordinary worldlings and the Buddha's enlightened reality. Tamura himself terms original enlightenment thought a teaching of "absolute nonduality" *(zettai funi)* or "absolute monism" *(zettai ichigen ron)*, a term now
commonly used in Japanese scholarly writing in reference to Tendai *hongaku* thought. By "absolute monism," Tamura means not a single entity
or essence underlying all phenomena, but that the realm of the Buddha's enlightenment (i.e., the realm of principle, or *ri*) and the conventional realm of changing phenomena *(ji)* are thoroughly conflated.
This identification is on the one hand ontological, consistent with classic Madhyamaka teachings about the emptiness of the dharmas and the
nonduality of ultimate and conventional truth, as expressed in the
phrase "saṃsāra is nirvāṇa." But in Tendai *hongaku* thought, the identification holds on the existential level as well: the deluded thoughts of

ordinary beings *as such* are the Buddha's enlightenment. In Tamura's terms, both the "existential aspect" and "illusional aspect" of reality are "absolutely affirmed." Tamura writes:

> Tendai original enlightenment thought . . . sought to go to the utmost heights, and also to the foundation, in breaking through every sort of relativistic conception. In having reached the ultimate of nondual absolutism, it may be said to encompass the highest level of philosophical principle. However, for the same reason, it gave rise to problems in the realm of ethics and practice. As we have seen, from the late Kamakura into the Nanbokuchō and Muromachi periods, in response to the secularization of society in general, the absolute monism of original enlightenment thought became mere affirmation of reality. The secular realm and secular affairs, even the defilements, were regarded as true. . . .
>
> While showing respect for the intellectual heights of Tendai original enlightenment thought, in order to revive the dynamism of practice and salvation in the real world, it may be said that the founders of the new Kamakura Buddhism descended from the peak of nondual absolutism to reassert in some way a dualistic relativism.[102]

This "descent from nondual absolutism," according to Tamura, occurred in two stages. The first stage is represented by Hōnen (1133–1212), founder of the Jōdo or Pure Land sect. Acutely conscious of human limitations and depravity, and believing his time to be that of the degenerate Final Dharma age, Hōnen broke with the contemplative Pure Land traditions of Tendai and Shingon, which identify Amida Buddha with the practitioner's mind and the Pure Land with the present world, and taught men and women to seek salvation through a power that is "Other" *(tariki)*. Hōnen reasserted the realm of relative distinctions: between this defiled world, which is to be abhorred, and the Pure Land, which is to be desired; between sinful beings, incapable of achieving salvation through their own efforts, and the Buddha Amida, in whom all trust and reliance are to be placed. Tamura argues that, while Hōnen's message is liable to appear a crude dualism, he did not in fact abandon the traditional Mahāyāna nonduality taught in the Lotus, Kegon, Shingon, *prajñā pāramitā*, and Zen traditions; he merely held these teachings to be beyond the limited capacity of those born into the Final Dharma age. The essential thing was to attain birth after death in the Western Pure Land, where such teachings could then be practiced easily.[103] Thus, over and against the absolute nondualism of original enlightenment thought, Hōnen as a matter of perceived soteriological necessity asserted the relative dualism of his distinctive Pure Land teaching.

The second stage in the "descent from nondual absolutism" is represented by Shinran, Dōgen, and Nichiren. Unlike Hōnen, who lived during the troubled and uncertain times of the late Heian, these three teachers were active in a more "positive" age. Tamura sees the Jōkyū Disturbance of 1221 as a turning point; after this event, which firmly established the authority of the Kamakura *bakufu,* people realized that, for better or worse, a new order had come into being, and they sought new principles *(dōri)* appropriate to it. The "world-affirming" stance of Tendai *hongaku* thought, as well as its philosophical sophistication, exerted a renewed attraction. Shinran, Dōgen, and Nichiren, in Tamura's view, appreciated the high philosophical achievement of nondualistic Tendai original enlightenment thought but also saw the soteriological necessity for acknowledging human sinfulness and limitations as Hōnen's dualistic Pure Land thought had done; thus they strove to reconcile the two. The teachings of all three, Tamura says, can thus be seen as syntheses of the absolute nondualism of Tendai original enlightenment thought and the relative dualism seen in Hōnen. It is in the differences in their respective syntheses that the distinctive character of the thought of each of these three teachers becomes apparent.

SHINRAN Shinran (1173–1262) has often been characterized as someone who developed in full the implications of Hōnen's teaching of absolute reliance on the "Other Power" of Amida's vow. He rejected the monastic state as a vain, self-calculating attempt to further salvation through one's own efforts and denied the efficacy of the deathbed *nenbutsu,* holding that the Pure Land is attained in the moment faith first arises in one's heart. This awakening of faith Shinran saw not as due to the virtue of the believer, but as the gift of Amida. The *nenbutsu* itself he is said to have regarded as "neither a practice nor a good deed," for to understand the *nenbutsu* in this way would be to suggest that salvation does not come wholly from Amida but is in some way dependent upon the believer's own efforts.[104] Tamura, however, sees Shinran's uniqueness not as an absolute emphasis on Other Power, but as a return from Hōnen's dualism to the nondual structure of Tendai *hongaku* thought.[105] He points to passages in Shinran's writings that identify Amida with suchness or the Dharma nature, "pervading the ten directions," and that identify faith with this omnipresent Buddha body.[106] The "Other" on whom Shinran taught his followers to rely is not "Other" as opposed to "self" but an Other in which self/other distinctions are dissolved. At the moment of relinquishing utterly all self-calculation, one is seized by the compassionate working of Amida's vow, never to be let go; such a person has in that moment become one with Amida, "equal to Tathâgatas."[107] The starting point for this union, however, is the painful experience of separation or duality, that is, of the sinfulness of self and the impossibility of salvation apart from the Other Power of Amida's original vow. Thus

Tamura characterizes Shinran's teaching as "the absolute based upon the relative" or a move toward nonduality premised upon duality. Shinran's nonduality is not an "essentialistic monism"; he does not "brandish nondual absolutism in the abstract." Rather, Shinran grasped original enlightenment through the "existential depths" of his own painful experience of human evil and limitation; his is an "existential" rather than a theoretical grasp of nonduality.[108]

Tamura's argument about Shinran's relationship to Tendai *hongaku* thought has drawn criticism from Jōdo Shinshū scholar Nakanishi Chikai. Nakanishi accuses Tamura of failing adequately to grasp Shinran's existential standpoint, which is rooted in a profound sense of human sinfulness and karmic limitations.[109] According to Nakanishi, Shinran's teachings of being "equal to the Tathâgatas" and of achieving birth in the Pure Land in this present world derive not from a "return" to *hongaku* nonduality, but from his transformative religious experience of salvation through the absolute compassion of Amida's vow. Tamura's argument does occasionally convey the impression that Shinran, Dōgen, and Nichiren set out deliberately to resolve a perceived tension between *hongaku* nonduality and Hōnen's duality as a philosophical problem, which seems dubious and overly intellectualized. Nakanishi, speaking from within the Shin tradition, insists rather on Shinran's sense of his existential position as the source for his doctrine of absolute Other Power. However, in that Tamura saw Shinran as grasping nondual *hongaku* thought "existentially," and that Nakanishi does not deny *hongaku* thought as a part of Shinran's intellectual background, the disagreement appears to be not about Shinran's message per se, but about the chief source of its inspiration: Tamura arguing for the influence of Tendai *hongaku* thought, and Nakanishi, for that of Shinran's own religious awakening.

Where Shinran took the position of "the absolute based upon the relative" or "nonduality premised upon duality," Dōgen and Nichiren are characterized by Tamura as setting forth "the relative based upon the absolute" or "duality premised upon nonduality." That is, they maintained the absolute monism of Tendai *hongaku* thought, the ontological nonduality of the Buddha and the ordinary person, as the basis of their thought, but in the realm of practice they asserted a distinction between the two. Their fundamental positions are very similar; however, while Dōgen's focus was the individual's personal practice, Nichiren stressed the transformation of society into a "Buddha land."

DŌGEN We have already touched on Tamura's comparison of Dōgen's teaching and Tendai original enlightenment thought and his noting of similarities between them. First of these is the unity of practice and realization, as expressed in Dōgen's famous statement: "To think that practice and realization are not one is a heterodox view. In the Buddha-Dharma, practice and realization are identical."[110] This finds resonance in medieval Tendai *kuden* texts such as the *Makura sōshi*, attributed to Genshin, which asserts that "practice and realization are a single time."[111] Dōgen held saṃsāra and nirvāṇa to be nondual, writing, for example, that "When one realizes that birth and death are nirvāṇa, there is no birth and death to abhor, and no nirvāṇa to seek."[112] Similar ideas can be found throughout the Tendai *kuden* literature. For example, "There is no birth and death that is to be abandoned, and no nirvāṇa that is to be sought."[113] Another point of similarity with Tendai *hongaku* thought is the idea that all things "dwell in a Dharma-position," meaning that the particular spatiotemporal events constituting a given moment are seen as the total manifestation of nondual reality.[114] Dōgen writes, "When all dharmas are the Buddha-Dharma, there are delusion and awakening, cultivation and practice, birth and death, Buddhas and living beings."[115] Similarly, in the *kuden* literature: "The defilements and saṃsāra, bodhi and nirvāṇa, all [abide] in their inherent Dharma-position."[116] Tamura also finds parallels in the Tendai *hongaku* literature with Dōgen's denial of the linear flow of time and his concept of the "absolute now" *(nikon),* as well as his equation of "all living beings" with "the Buddha nature," listing numerous examples.[117]

Nonetheless, Tamura also identifies several passages from Dōgen's writings critical of an unconditional identification of Buddhas and ordinary beings. For example:

> The thoughts of ordinary worldlings and the thoughts of the Buddhas differ greatly. They are not to be compared. To calculate the original enlightenment of ordinary beings, and to realize the original enlightenment of the Buddhas, are as remote as heaven and earth.[118]

> Although people are abundantly endowed with this Dharma, if they do not practice, it will not be manifested, and if it is not realized, it will not be attained.[119]

> The Buddha nature is not possessed prior to realizing Buddhahood. After realizing Buddhahood, one is endowed with it. The Buddha nature and attaining Buddhahood always occur simultaneously.[120]

For Dōgen, the practice of ordinary beings and the Buddha's enlightened state are always identified, as stated in the famous passage from *Bendōwa:*

> In the Buddha-Dharma, practice and realization are identical. Because one's present practice is practice on the basis of realization, one's initial negotiation of the Way in itself is the whole of original realization. Thus, even while one is given instruction in practice, he is taught not

to anticipate realization apart from practice, because practice points directly to original realization. Because it is already the realization of practice, realization is endless; as it is the practice of realization, practice is beginningless.[121]

Tamura argues that, while Dōgen maintains the nondual ontological structure of original enlightenment thought, his teaching of the oneness of "original realization and wondrous practice" represents a "revival" of practice. He thus sees Dōgen as provisionally reasserting a relative duality. Moreover, where Tendai emphasizes the "concrete" (*ji*) in the sense of affirming all phenomena as expressions of original enlightenment, in Dōgen "concreteness" becomes an emphasis on the necessity of practice. Reactions to Tamura's theory on the part of Sōtō scholars have already been discussed.

NICHIREN In Tamura's view, Nichiren ultimately arrived at a position extremely similar to Dōgen's; however, Nichiren's relationship to original enlightenment thought must be understood as undergoing change and development over the course of his career.[122] Nichiren's early writings suggest that he was at first strongly drawn to *hongaku* ideas, especially the identification of the pure land with the present world. His earliest extant essay, written at age twenty, reads:

> When one attains the enlightenment of the *Lotus Sūtra,* then one realizes that one's body and mind that arise and perish are precisely unborn and undying. And the land is also thus. Its horses, cows and the others of the six kinds of domestic animals are all Buddhas, and the grasses and trees, the sun and moon, are all their holy retinue. The sūtra states, "The dharmas dwell in a Dharma position, and the worldly aspect constantly abides."[123]

Nichiren's early writings often employ this nondual standpoint to attack the exclusive *nenbutsu* doctrine of Hōnen, which he saw as antithetical to the traditional Tendai vision of a Buddhism united in the One Vehicle of the *Lotus Sūtra.* However, as Nichiren himself grew more exclusivistic in his claims for the sole validity of the *Lotus* and more critical of other teachings, he came into conflict with the authorities. Beginning around the time of his first exile (1261–1264), Tamura says, Nichiren became less concerned with monistic *hongaku* thought and increasingly attentive to problems in the realm of relative distinctions, such as time and human capacity. This can be seen in his growing concern with such issues as comparative classification of the Buddhist scriptures; the age of *mappō;* the capacity of beings living in that age; and the karma of the specific country of Japan. Nichiren's writings from this time also show an emerging sense of his own mission as the "votary of the *Lotus Sūtra*"

(Hokekyō no gyōja), who propagates its teachings even at the risk of his life. Especially from the time of his exile to Sado Island (1271–1274), he became critical of the nondual Taimitsu tradition that had formed the basis of his earlier thought.

As noted above in connection with the work of Asai Yōrin, the question of Nichiren's relation to the doctrine of original enlightenment is mediated by the complex problem of textual authenticity. Numerous writings attributed to the later period of his life uphold the *hongaku* doctrine. However, few survive in Nichiren's holograph or appear in early indices. Following Asai and Shigyō Kaishū, Tamura questions the authenticity of any work attributed to Nichiren, especially if dated in the latter period of his life, that contains concepts or expressions associated with *hongaku* thought. Could these writings be proved authentic, Tamura's thesis would have to be modified. However, based on a consideration only of verifiable documents, it would seem that original enlightenment thought became less central to Nichiren's thinking in his later years.

Tamura acknowledges the presence of certain passages strongly suggestive of *hongaku* thought even in unimpeachable documents from the latter part of Nichiren's career. Nichiren writes, for example, that "this world is the [Buddha's] original land; the pure lands of the ten directions are defiled worlds that are its traces,"[124] or, "Śākyamuni of wondrous awakening *(myōkaku)* is our blood and flesh. Are not the merits of his causes [practice] and effects [enlightenment] our bones and marrow?"[125] However, Tamura says, on close examination such writings, "while maintaining nondual original enlightenment as their basis, in fact emerge from it."[126] Nichiren's "Śākyamuni of wondrous awakening" is no mere abstract, all-pervasive Dharma-body but also encompasses the virtues of the reward-body Buddha who has traversed practice and attainment, as well as the concreteness of the manifested body, the historical Buddha who appeared in this world. Nor was Nichiren content merely to assert that this world is the Buddha's pure land; he attempted actually to realize the pure land in this present world through bodhisattva conduct, by spreading faith in the *Lotus Sūtra.* As in the case of Dōgen, Nichiren's emphasis on the concrete *(ji)* is not the affirmation of the phenomenal world seen in medieval Tendai *hongaku* thought but an emphasis on action that "restored the dynamic power of practice in the actual world."[127] Like Dōgen, Nichiren maintained the ontological nonduality of the Buddha and living beings as his basis, but "descended" to confront the relative distinctions of the world.

The major critic of Tamura's presentation of Nichiren is Hanano Michiaki, a scholar of both Nichiren and medieval Tendai. Hanano opposes the move of Asai, Shigyō, Tamura, and others to exclude from the consideration of Nichiren's thought those texts attributed to him that deal with *hongaku* ideas. In contrast to Tamura and the Nichirenshū scholars, Hanano positions Nichiren firmly within the intellectual tradition of Tendai original enlightenment thought.[128] Like them, however, Hanano sees Nichiren as emphasizing practice, in contrast to a purely theoretical and abstract Tendai *hongaku* doctrine, thus "elevating it [original enlightenment thought] to the realm of religion."[129]

It will now be clear why "dialectic" is an appropriate term to describe Tamura's theory. First Tendai original enlightenment thought establishes the "thesis" of absolute nonduality: ordinary worldlings, just as they are, are the originally enlightened Buddha. Then in a counterreaction, out of soteriological concern and as a sort of "skillful means," Hōnen asserts the "antithesis" of duality: the Buddha is "Other," and salvation is both temporally and spatially removed from the present world. Shinran, Dōgen, and Nichiren represent "synthesis." They are the ones shown as uniting the best in both "nondualistic" and "dualistic" systems, retaining the philosophical subtleties of Tendai *hongaku* thought while obviating its moral ambiguities and tendency uncritically to affirm the world by a renewed emphasis on practice and an acute existential awareness of human limitations. Tamura's theory unites elements of both the "matrix" and "radical break" positions, arguing that the thought of Shinran, Dōgen, and Nichiren was neither simply an extended development of original enlightenment thought nor merely a reaction aganst it, but contained elements of both. Using as its organizing principle the question of the relationship between the absolute and the relative, the nondual and the dual, and the Buddha and the ordinary worldling, Tamura's scheme provides a useful framework for considering both similarities and differences in the thought of these three figures and their common basis in Tendai *hongaku* doctrine. It represents the most comprehensive treatment thus far of the relationship of original enlightenment thought to the new Kamakura Buddhism, and subsequent studies, this one included, must inevitably be indebted to it. Nevertheless, as do earlier theories, it presents certain problems, to which we shall now turn.

Above we have outlined the major theories put forth to date concerning the relationship between medieval Japanese Tendai original enlightenment thought and the new Kamakura Buddhism. After Shimaji first suggested that *hongaku* thought represents the matrix of the new Kamakura Buddhism, all contributions to the discussion have been made in dialogue with one another, sometimes disagreeing with considerable heat. Nevertheless, it should by now be clear that these rival theories share several interrelated assumptions and have more in common than they may acknowledge. First and most obvious is the assumption that original enlightenment thought represents a denial of the need for Buddhist practice. Since *hongaku* doctrine asserts that deluded beings, without transformation, are Buddhas, it has been taken as a claim that no efforts in religious discipline are necessary. Over and against so clearly problematic a stance, the teachers of the new Kamakura Buddhism, especially Dōgen and Nichiren, are presented as reasserting the primacy of Buddhist practice. Second, whether it is exalted as the "climax" of Buddhist philosophy or condemned as a "game of concepts," we find a tendency to treat *hongaku* thought as an intellectual abstraction. In contrast, the founders of the new Kamakura Buddhism are seen as "breaking through" abstraction: mediated by their personal experience as seekers of religious truth, nondual metaphysics acquire an "existential depth," to borrow Tamura's term. There seems to be an implicit assumption here that, where medieval Tendai is mere philosophy, the new Kamakura Buddhism is true religion. Third, Tendai *hongaku* thought is seen as an absolute and uncritical "world affirmation," while the teachers of the new Kamakura schools are presented as actively grappling with the contradictions and sufferings of real existence. Either by their alleged "revival" of Buddhist practice or by their deep humility in the face of human shortcomings, they are assumed to have avoided the moral ambiguity of nondual *hongaku* thought. Lastly, related to all the above, is the pervasive assumption that *hongaku* thought was deeply implicated in monastic corruption, both as a major contributing cause and as its expression. Its emphasis on *kanjin*-style interpretation is seen as perverting orthodox exegetical scholarship, and its equation of the deluded behavior of unenlightened beings with the expression of inherent enlightenment is said to have legitimized, even encouraged, moral laxity. The influence of *hongaku* thought has been detected in virtually every medieval departure from the monastic ideal, from the sexual license of ranking clerics to the predations of warrior monks. How, one begins to wonder, did so decadent an intellectual tradition manage to survive and flourish for nearly six hundred years?

In fact, the characterization outlined above is a two-dimensional picture of the incredibly rich tradition of medieval Tendai, in effect reducing it to a cardboard backdrop against which to depict the more fully embodied personae of the new Buddhist founders. The doctrine of original enlightenment may indeed have served at times to rationalize misconduct, or have been used ideologically to support the authority of ruling elites. Charges that this discourse undermined traditional scholarship, denied the necessity of practice, and contributed to moral corruption are not altogether groundless. But they need to be reexamined and seriously qualified in the light of both primary documents and the historical context. This will be the task of subsequent chapters. Here, however, we will merely note how characterizing Tendai *hongaku* thought in this manner serves in the most dramatic fashion to privilege the new Buddhism. Beneath this characterization lies the unstated meta-assumption that the new schools of Kamakura Buddhism represent not merely the emergence of new forms, but a higher stage of religious development. Whether the new schools are seen as emerging from the "womb" of Tendai original enlightenment thought, or taking form as a reaction against it, or developing out of it by dialectical process, all these views reflect the influence of an evolutionary model of Buddhist history in which the new Kamakura Buddhism represents the apex. Occasionally there is even a hint of telos at work, as though the very raison d'être of Tendai original enlightenment thought was to give rise to the new Kamakura Buddhism. *Hongaku* thought thus becomes merely one more locus from which to reassert tired stereotypes of a vibrant, reformist "new Buddhism" reacting against a corrupt, elitist "old Buddhism."

To point out that existing models of the relationship between Tendai *hongaku* thought and the new Kamakura schools serve to privilege the latter is in no way to disparage the achievements of men like Shinran, Dōgen, and Nichiren. Nevertheless, such assumptions prejudice our understanding and need to be reexamined if a more balanced view is to be obtained. Let us turn, then, to the world of medieval Tendai, and a fuller understanding of the contexts—institutional, cultural, and doctrinal— in which original enlightenment discourse was conducted.

Part Two

The World of Medieval Tendai

Chapter Three

The Culture of Secret Transmission

STRADDLING THE BOUNDARY between Kyoto and Shiga Prefecture (formerly Ōmi Province) stands a group of peaks ranging north and south called "Mt. Hiei." Here is located the extensive temple complex Enryakuji, main headquarters of Tendai Buddhism. So closely has the Enryakuji been associated with Mt. Hiei that the two names are often used interchangeably. While the name Enryakuji (after the Enryaku era) was conferred by Emperor Saga in 823, the temple's founding dates from 788. In that year Saichō—who had gone to practice in retreat on Mt. Hiei following his ordination in 785 at the Tōdaiji in Nara—is said to have carved an image of the Buddha of Healing (Bhaiṣajyaguru, Yakushi Nyorai) and enshrined it in a small hall that he named the Hieizanji. When Emperor Kanmu moved the capital from Nara and reestablished it at Heian-kyō (modern Kyoto) in 794, the talented young monk came to his attention. Following his return from China, Saichō rose to prominence under Kanmu's patronage, and the newly established Tendai school was allotted yearly ordinands by the court. Mt. Hiei's location—roughly ten kilometers to the northeast of Heian-kyō—placed it so as to protect the capital from the malign influences that, according to contemporary geomantic thought, could enter from the northeast. The Enryakuji emerged as the leading center for the performance of nation-protecting rituals.[1]

During the Heian period, Mt. Hiei developed into a major institution of religion, learning, and culture. A schism in the late tenth century divided the Tendai school into two branches—the Sanmon (mountain branch) based at the Enryakuji, and the Jimon (temple branch), which established a rival center, the Onjōji or Miidera, located in the town of Ōtsu about six kilometers southeast of Hiei.[2] However, the split did not substantially undermine the growing influence and prosperity of Mt. Hiei. The eighteenth *zasu* or chief abbot Ryōgen (912–985) built new temple

structures, promoted doctrinal study, and furthered the monastery's relations with the nobility; in his time, the Enryakuji assumed the complex
organizational structure that would characterize it throughout the medieval period. Geographically and administratively it was divided into
three precincts or "pagodas."[3] The Eastern Pagoda (Tōtō) included the
ordination platform and the Enryakuji's main hall or Konpon Chūdō.
Not quite two kilometers away was the Western Pagoda (Saitō), while the
third precinct, Yokawa, lay at some distance from the other two. Following the topography of the mountain, each pagoda precinct encompassed
a number of valleys, five each in the Eastern and Western pagoda precincts and six in Yokawa. Each of the sixteen valleys had its own main temple (collectively called the *jūrokuin*), as well as other temple buildings
and monks' cloisters, and was organized around master-disciple lines,
developing distinctive rituals and doctrines. The "three pagodas and sixteen valleys" were central to the mountain's three-tiered organizational
structure. Presiding over Enryakuji was the *zasu* or chief abbot and his
head administrators, while a second tier consisted of representatives of
the sixteen valleys. The third, most fundamental level was the entire
monastic assembly. Since Heian times, Mt. Hiei was said to have boasted
"three thousand monks": an early twelfth-century source divides this into
1,813 monks at the Eastern Pagoda, 717 at the Western Pagoda, and 470
at Yokawa.[4] The assembly was broadly divided into the *gakuryō* (or
gakushō), an elite consisting of scholar-monks and ritual specialists, often
of noble birth, and the more numerous *dōshū*, lower-ranking clergy who
performed a variety of routine liturgical and other services. In addition
to the *gakuryō* and *dōshū* were others who might be loosely grouped into
a third category called *hijiri* or *shōnin*—"holy men."[5] While the term was
also used to indicate "unofficial" monks including a range of mendicants
and shamanic practitioners, in the context of temple-shrine communities, *hijiri* designated those monks who had withdrawn from the official
temple organization to practice in reclusion at *bessho*, literally "detached
places," affiliated with the main temple-shrine institution but removed
from it geographically and administratively. Mt. Hiei had several *bessho*,
located both on the mountain itself and in the capital.

Also significant were the *jinnin*, or service people attached to the mountain's shrines. Like virtually all major medieval Buddhist institutions, the
Enryakuji was in fact a temple-shrine complex *(jisha)*.[6] Central to these
shrines was the Hiesha or Hie Shrine—"Hie" being a more ancient form
of the sinicized "Hiei"—a group of 7 shrines that grew up at the foot of
the mountain's eastern slope. The presence of shrines on the mountain
had long preceded the founding of the Tendai school. The oldest of these
appear to have been dedicated to Ōyamagui-no-mikoto, or Yamasue-no-
ōnushi, a *kami* of agriculture, and Ōnamuchi-no-mikoto, a protector of
imperial residences. By the late tenth century, the 7 Hie shrines had been

merged institutionally with the Enryakuji, and the worship of their divinities was gradually integrated into Tendai doctrine and practice. During the medieval period, the Hie shrine system expanded into 21 shrines in three groups of 7 shrines each, then into 108 inner shrines and 108 outer shrines. The shrine system added immensely to Mt. Hiei's spiritual authority, and the sacred palanquins *(omikoshi)* of the *kami* of the original 7 shrines were often carried by Enryakuji monks down into the capital to lend numinous force to their appeals to the imperial court.[7]

Mt. Hiei was not only a major religious center but a powerful political and economic force. Originally supported by court patronage, with the privatization of land and political power that developed in the early medieval period, Mt. Hiei, like other temple-shrine complexes, was forced to rely increasingly on its own resources. In addition to its vast networks of branch and subsidiary temples and shrines throughout the country, the Enryakuji was a major proprietor of *shōen* or private estates. Due to a lack of surviving documentation, the full extent of its landholdings is not clear, but it is known to have controlled some 270 estates during the premodern period.[8] The Enryakuji was also linked economically to Sakamoto, the *monzen-machi* or "gate town" located at its eastern foot.[9] A thriving port on the southwest shore of Lake Biwa, Sakamoto linked the eastern and northern provinces to the area of the capital and served as a vital economic nexus for the Enryakuji, supplying the material needs of its large community and acting as the collection point for the land tax and other revenues sent in from its outlying estates. Mt. Hiei also regulated and taxed the inhabitants' commercial and manufacturing activities while providing them with judicial immunities and other protections.

Like other major landholders and ruling elites of the early medieval period, the Enryakuji had both the need and the ability to defend its interests by force of arms. The warrior monks of Mt. Hiei—known as *shuto* or *daishu,* both collective terms for a temple's monastic assembly, or peroratively as *akusō* ("evil monks")—were at first deployed chiefly against perceived external threats, for example, to settle disputes with rival institutions, such as the Onjōji, and later the great temples of Nara, or to guard against local intrusion onto Enryakuji *shōen* in the provinces. Later they took part increasingly in internecine disputes. From the Insei period on, fighting broke out sporadically between the monks of the Eastern and Western Pagoda precincts; between the factions represented by the major imperial residence temples *(monzeki jiin),* the Kajii and the Shōren-in, over their respective candidates for the position of *zasu;* and between the *gakuryō* and the *dōshū.*[10] These internal armed conflicts, while divisive, also contributed overall to the development of the Enryakuji's military power.[11]

For a long time modern scholars of Japanese Buddhism tended to

see the amassing of wealth and political involvements of major temple-
shrine complexes such as the Enryakuji, and particularly the activities
of their armed monks, as evidence of a growing trend toward corruption
and "secularization" within the so-called old Buddhism.[12] This approach has called attention to an acute anxiety that prevailed during
the late Heian and early Kamakura periods, at least in some monastic
and aristocractic circles, over a perceived decline in Buddhist observances and an accompanying sense of crisis with regard to the Final
Dharma age—although the ideological, as opposed to existential, aspects of *mappō* discourse have not always been recognized.[13] Claims
about monastic corruption are not altogether without validity, in that
contemporary records do bear witness to some glaring instances of clerical misbehavior.[14] However, as Neil McMullin has pointed out, arguments
about the decline and secularization of the older medieval Buddhist institutions rest on the very modern, and largely Western, academic construction of religion as a category divorced from the realm of politics
and economics:

> It is incorrect to assume that the acquisition of political, economic,
> and military power on the part of clerics and the monastery-shrine
> complexes is ipso facto a sign of corruption, degeneration and/or
> secularization, and equally incorrect to assume that there was once
> a time in Japan—or even, for that matter, in India—when religious
> communities were utterly devoid of "secular" power (assuming, for the
> sake of this point, that there was a notion of purely secular power in
> pre-modern Japan and India). . . . There has been a tendency in the
> field of Japanese Religious Studies to preserve religion from the muck
> and mire of politics and economics, as is evidenced by a preoccupa-
> tion on the part of some scholars with keeping religion—especially
> Buddhism . . . —"pure."[15]

In the context of the present study, it may be noted that the "rhetoric
of decadence," as Richard Payne aptly terms it, has often been used uncritically to support unwarranted assumptions about precipitous decline
on the part of the older Buddhist institutions during the Kamakura period.[16] It has also served as a convenient backdrop against which to high-
light the activities of those individuals defined as the religious heroes of
the age: the founders of the new Kamakura Buddhism, and, to a lesser
extent, "reformers" within the older schools, such as Myōei or Eizon.

A very different perspective, however, has been advanced by the late
historian Kuroda Toshio and others influenced by his work. Kuroda argued that the political entanglements of Mt. Hiei and other major temple-shrine complexes, their accumulation of private wealth, and their em-
ployment of warrior monks should be understood not as deviations from
normative Buddhist ideals, but in terms of the changing structures of

medieval Japanese society. With the rise of the *shōen* system of privately owned tax-exempt estates, temple-shrine complexes could no longer rely on the economic support of the court and instead acquired major land-holdings in their own right. In some provinces, more than 60 percent of the cultivated land was under the administration of temple-shrine complexes.[17] Like the *bushi* who protected the provincial estates held by aristocrats in the capital, armed monks protected the landholdings of temple-shrine complexes; both were born of the same political and economic circumstances of the latter Heian.[18] In this way, temple-shrine complexes emerged as powerful participants in the *kenmon taisei,* the order of "ruling elites" or "influential parties" system.[19] Kuroda cautions against a scholarly standpoint that "will not acknowledge as Buddhism that which deviates from Buddhism's ideal form." "We need," he writes, "to grasp the social and political influence of the temple-shrine complexes, not simply as a corrupt form, but as a basic and also quotidian form of medieval society."[20]

The work of Kuroda and other *kenmitsu* historians has served as a needed corrective in demonstrating that the temple-shrine complexes of the "old Buddhism"—the *kenmitsu taisei*—represented the dominant religious forms of the age, while the new Kamakura Buddhist movements remained fairly marginal heterodoxies until much later in the medieval period. This strand of scholarship has shed considerable light on the political, institutional, and ideological aspects of *kenmitsu* Buddhism, including Tendai and the Enryakuji. However, it has not yet generated a major investigation into the cultural and intellectual activities of these temple-shrine complexes. This section of the present study represents an effort in this direction. The present chapter examines the development within medieval Tendai of what might be termed a culture of secret transmission, organized around master-disciple lineages and the production of *kuden* or oral teachings. This culture grew from within the *kenmitsu* Buddhism of the latter Heian period and became the normative mode for transmitting knowledge in the medieval period. It dictated the forms within which rituals and doctrines shaped by notions of original enlightenment were communicated, and represents the historical context from which *hongaku* discourse emerged. This chapter will first outline the emergence, during the Kamakura period, of the Eshin and Danna schools, the major doctrinal lineages of medieval Tendai in which ideas of original enlightenment were elaborated and transmitted. It will consider their origins in earlier, Heian-period developments including the formation of rival schools of Taimitsu ritual, the aristocraticization of the clergy, and the debate traditions of Mt. Hiei, as well as their creative "reinvention" of Saichō's heritage as a basis for their transmissions. Further, it will introduce other, overlapping Tendai lineages involved in the production of *hongaku* discourse, including lineages of chroniclers, precept keepers, and chanters of *shōmyō,* or sacred hymns, and also the rituals of initiation by which medieval Tendai lineages sought to define and preserve their legitimacy. Lastly, it will examine the politics of secret transmission, how lineages were defined and perpetuated, and the challenges posed by the rise of the rival "provincial Tendai" of eastern Japan, which emerged with the establishment of the Kamakura *bakufu* as a new center of political power. In the interests of limiting this discussion to what is manageable, it will be confined chiefly to the Sanmon or "mountain branch," that is, the Tendai of Mt. Hiei, together with its offshoots in the Kantō, and will not extend to the Jimon or "temple branch" (*jimon*) based at the Onjōji.[21]

Eshin and Danna Schools:
Lineage Formation and Origin Myths

As the medieval Tendai *kuden* tradition developed, various schools and teaching lines emerged. First to take shape were the Eshin and the Danna schools, which remained the most important. When exactly they appeared is not easy to determine, and there is little scholarly consensus. The names "Eshin" and "Danna" are well attested by the latter part of the thirteenth century.[22] Hazama Jikō proposed that the two schools began to emerge around the middle of the Insei period.[23] However, Ōkubo Ryōjun has suggested that they did not take shape as clearly defined, rival entities until the very end of the Kamakura period.[24]

Both schools retrospectively produced mythic narratives of their origins to serve the purposes of legitimization. The first known internal narrative of Eshin/Danna origins occurs in the Eshin text *Kankō ruijū*, which probably dates from around the latter part of the thirteenth century.[25] As related in this text, the story has two parts. The first deals with the common origin of the two schools. This it locates in mythic time, when Śākyamuni Buddha sat beside the Tathâgata Many Jewels (Prabhūtaratna, Tahō Nyorai) in the jeweled stūpa that had emerged into open space from beneath the earth and preached the *Lotus Sūtra* to the assembly, who, by his supernatural powers, he had raised into the air above Sacred Eagle Peak.[26] Present in the assembly, it says, was Nan-yüeh Tashih Hui-ssu, who at that time directly received the transmission of the Buddha's enlightenment. Also present in the assembly was Chih-i. Later Hui-ssu and Chih-i were born in China as master and disciple, and the transmission in historical time passed from Hui-ssu to Chih-i to the successive T'ien-t'ai patriarchs, down to Chan-jan.[27] Mythic and historical time are thus conjoined in the person of Chih-i (538–597), founder of the T'ien-t'ai school.

This part of the story has antecedents in T'ien-t'ai/Tendai sources. The earliest is the biography of Chih-i by his disciple Kuan-ting (561–

632), according to which Hui-ssu (515–577) welcomed Chih-i as a disciple, saying, "In the past, we heard the *Lotus* together on Sacred [Eagle] Peak; impelled by this karmic connection, you have now come again!"[28] The tradition that Hui-ssu and Chih-i had together heard the Buddha's original preaching of the *Lotus Sūtra* was widespread in China, even outside the T'ien-t-'ai school, and appears to have represented their shared mastery of the "*Lotus* samādhi," the insight into the profound meaning of the *Lotus Sūtra* that Chih-i would later express as the threefold truth.[29] Prominent among Japanese antecedents for the incorporation of this account into the Eshin and Danna origin myth is the lineage that Saichō drew up for his newly established Tendai school, which identifies Hui-ssu and Chih-i in the line of transmission as "auditors on Sacred [Eagle] Peak in India."[30] Saichō traced the historical roots of his lineage to Hui-ssu and Chih-i; however, the Buddha with whom he began the lineage is not the historical Śākyamuni, but, in the words of the *Fo-shūo kuan P'u-hsien P'u-sa hsing-fa ching*, Śākyamuni who is "Vairocana Pervading All Places."[31] As noted in chapter 1, this early conflation of the historical Śākyamuni with the omnipresent cosmic Buddha would undergo major development in Tendai esoteric thought. Eventually it also gave rise to the tradition, recurring in medieval Tendai ritual and doctrinal transmission texts, that "the assembly on Sacred [Eagle] Peak is solemnly [present] and has not yet dispersed" (*ryōzen ichie gennen misan*).[32]

The *Tendai Hokkeshū denbō ge* (Verses of Dharma transmission of the Tendai-*Lotus* lineage), a latter Heian period work retrospectively attributed to Saichō, says that Chih-i, while practicing the *Lotus* samādhi under Hui-ssu's instruction on Mt. Ta-su, perceived himself, together with Hui-ssu, at the assembly on Eagle Peak, listening to the Buddha preach the *Lotus Sūtra*.[33] This work, along with the sources just mentioned, also seems to have strongly influenced the formation of medieval Tendai notions about a direct Dharma transmission from Śākyamuni Buddha to Hui-ssu and Chih-i. This direct transmission from Śākyamuni in the jeweled stūpa above Eagle Peak to the two T'ien-t'ai masters forms a standard feature of the origin myths, not only of the Eshin and Danna schools, but also of medieval Tendai precept lineages.[34] In grounding the origins of the lineage in mythic rather than historical time, it also parallels the Shingon origin myth of the bodhisattva Vajrasatta, who, having been directly initiated into the esoteric teachings by Mahāvairocana, hid himself in an iron stūpa in southern India; there Nāgārjuna eventually discovered him and received the transmission of the esoteric lineage.[35]

The second part of the origin story accounts for how there came to be two schools, the Eshin and the Danna. When Saichō journeyed to T'ang China, he studied under two T'ien-t'ai masters, Tao-sui and Hsing-man, both disciples of the ninth patriarch Chan-jan (711–782). According to the *Kankō ruijū*, he received from Hsing-man the transmission of the doctrinal teachings of the school *(shūkyō)*, and from Tao-sui, the transmission of the school's essential purport *(shūshi)*, or meditative insight. Both transmissions were then passed down in a direct line from Saichō to Ryōgen, eighteenth *zasu* of Mt. Hiei. Here a split is said to have occurred. Ryōgen had two chief disciples: Genshin (942–1017), called Eshin Sōzu after his temple, the Eshin-in at Yokawa; and Kakuun (953–1007), called Danna Sōzu or Danna Sōjō for his temple, the Danna-in of the Eastern Pagoda precinct (*sōjō* and *sōzu* were, respectively, the highest and second highest ranks in the Office of Monastic Affairs). To Genshin, Ryōgen transmitted the teachings on both meditation and on doctrine; this transmission was handed down by the Eshin school. But to Kakuun, Ryōgen transmitted only the teachings on doctrine; these were transmitted by the Danna school.[36] Later medieval Tendai texts elaborate on this distinction, saying, for example, that the Eshin school transmitted the doctrine of original enlightenment, and the Danna, that of acquired enlightenment; that the Eshin took as the basis of meditation the ninth consciousness, and the Danna, the sixth consciousness; that the Eshin valued oral transmissions and meditative insight, and the Danna doctrine and texts; that the Eshin privileged the "origin teaching" *(honmon)* or latter fourteen chapters of the *Lotus Sūtra* over the "trace teaching" *(shakumon)* or first fourteen chapters, while the Danna regarded both sections as equally important; and so forth.[37] Similar distinctions also appear in external sources, for example, in this passage from a letter attributed to Nichiren:

> The eighteenth *zasu* [of Mt. Hiei] was Jie Daishi [Ryōgen]. He had many disciples, of whom four—Danna, Eshin, Zōga and Zen'yū—were the most outstanding. [At that time, the Tendai] teachings were also divided into two. Danna Sōjō inherited the doctrinal teachings *(kyō);* Eshin Sōzu learned the meditative disciplines *(kan).* Now doctrinal teachings and meditative disciplines are like the sun and moon. Doctrine is shallow, while meditation is deep. Thus the Danna teaching is broad and shallow, while the Eshin teaching is narrow and deep.[38]

However, a number of these distinctions occur in Eshin texts and appear to represent attempts on the part of Eshin scholars to claim superiority for their tradition over the rival, Danna school. At least one Danna text reverses the comparison and asserts that the Danna school transmitted the origin teaching and the Eshin school, the trace teaching.[39] In fact, complete doctrinal unanimity did not exist in either school. Moreover, while the teachings of the Danna school in particular have yet to be more fully investigated, it is clear that both schools transmitted the doctrine of original enlightenment, valued meditative insight over strict textual exegesis, and based their authority on oral transmissions. Extensive borrowing between the two schools also militates against the likelihood that clear doctrinal distinctions existed between them.[40] Their chief differences appear to have been those of lineage and ritual forms, rather than of doctrinal content.

The *Kankō ruijū*'s account of the origin of the two schools seems to have been widely accepted throughout the medieval period.[41] However, modern scholarly investigation has failed to unearth factual support for the supposed double transmission to Saichō.[42] Saichō did study under both Tao-sui and Hsing-man, and what he learned from Tao-sui was connected at least in part with meditation, for he wrote that Tao-sui had taught him the "threefold contemplation in a single mind" *(isshin sangan)*.[43] Moreover, a comparison of the few surviving works of these two men suggests that while Hsing-man was a conservative and faithful transmitter of doctrines, Tao-sui was given to more personal interpretations.[44] Yet these fragmentary data are not sufficient to confirm the tradition that Saichō received two separate transmissions, from Tao-sui and Hsing-man, respectively. Rather, they seem to represent the elements out of which that tradition was constructed. Before the rise of the medieval *kuden* tradition, Hsing-man's role as one of Saichō's teachers had come to be virtually ignored. It seems possible that he was resurrected by E-shin scholars for polemical reasons, to serve as the source of the "inferior," rival Danna school.[45]

Similarly, there is no evidence that the Eshin and Danna schools originated with Genshin and Kakuun. The authenticated works of these two men show little evidence of anything resembling medieval Tendai *hongaku* thought and reveal no major points of doctrinal difference between them; both wrote on traditional Tendai studies—reflecting, in contrast to earlier esoteric Tendai, the renewed emphasis on the *Lotus Sūtra* brought about by Ryōgen's promotion of doctrinal study—and also on Pure Land practice as suitable to the approaching last age.[46]

Hazama Jikō has proposed that the names "Eshin" and "Danna" may reflect a nostalgia for the prosperity of Mt. Hiei and the flourishing of Tendai studies in Ryōgen's time, which, in his view, had subsequently declined together with the fortunes of the Fujiwara regental family, who were Hiei's leading patrons. Hazama also suggests that the names "E-shin" and "Danna" may derive not from Genshin and Kakuun, but from the cloisters Eshin-in and Danna-in, located, respectively, in the areas of Yokawa and the Eastern Pagoda precincts. The geographic location of these two temples, Hazama says, may point to a possible connection, respectively, between the Eshin and Danna schools and the Kawa and Tani schools, the two major lineages into which the various lines of Tai-mitsu ritual were divided. Genshin's disciple Kakuchō (953/960–1034) of Yokawa was regarded as the founder of the Kawa (river) school, and

Kakuun's disciple Kōkei (or Kōgyō) of the Minamidani (south valley) area of the Eastern Pagoda was the founder of the Tani (valley) school. Kakuchō, like Genshin, was based at Yokawa, and Kōkei, like his teacher Kakuun, at the Eastern Pagoda.[47] According to traditional Tendai accounts, the areas of Yokawa, the Western Pagoda, and the Mudōji valley of the Eastern Pagoda were dominated by the Eshin school, while the north, south, east, and west valleys of the Eastern Pagoda precinct belonged to the Danna school.[48]

Both schools divided into a number of sublineages. Tradition speaks of the "eight schools of Eshin and Danna" (see chart); in actuality, there were many more.[49] Like the emergence of the parent Eshin and Danna schools themselves, the chronology of these subsidiary lineages is difficult to establish. Contemporary sources testify to the existence of several of these subbranches by the latter part of the thirteenth century, and on this basis Hazama suggested that many such divisions must have been in place earlier, by the early Kamakura period.[50] However, as noted above, where Hazama believed that the Eshin and Danna schools had begun to emerge in the mid-Insei period, Ōkubo Ryōjun has suggested that they did not take firm shape as self-conscious traditions until late in the Kamakura period. If Ōkubo is correct, this would obviously affect the chronology of the sublineages as well. In fact, some of the earliest sources to mention the Eshin and Danna schools also mention the names of sublineages.[51] This raises the possibility that these subsidiary lineages were retrospectively constructed around the same time as those of the Eshin and Danna schools, beginning with existing teaching lines whose origins were then projected into the past. Sueki Fumihiko has pointed out that the putative founders of the "eight schools of Eshin and Danna" are people of either the Insei or the mid-Kamakura period, which correspond to two important junctures in the development of the medieval *kuden hōmon:* the writing down of oral transmissions in the Insei period, and the systematizing of doctrine in the mid-Kamakura period.[52] This finding strengthens the suggestion that, at least to some extent, retrospective lineage construction was taking place. A clear instance is the Hōchi-bō line, which appropriates, as the founder of a *kuden* lineage, Hōchi-bō Shōshin—a staunch critic of the very original enlightenment doctrine that the *kuden* tradition represented.[53]

In short, lineage formation in medieval Tendai was a complex process occurring simultaneously in two directions, forward and back, as a given teacher's disciples in the first, second, or subsequent generations of historical time retrospectively constructed a lineage for him, traced back through his own teacher to great masters of the earlier eras. One also finds an interplay between expansion and divergence, on the one hand, as teachers chose disciples and conferred transmissions, succession disputes broke out, and rival lineages took shape; and unification through

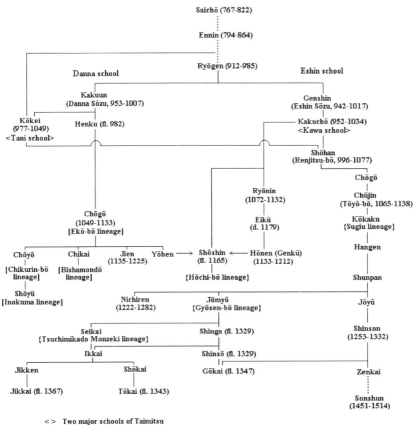

Abbreviated Lineage Chart of Medieval Tendai

Saichō (767-822)

Ennin (794-864)

Ryōgen (912-985)

Danna school   Eshin school

Kakuun
(Danna Sōzu, 953-1007)

Genshin
(Eshin Sōzu, 942-1017)

Kōkei
(977-1049)
<Tani school>

Henku (fl. 982)

Kakuchō (952-1034)
<Kawa school>

Shōhan
(Renjitsu-bō, 996-1077)

Chōgō

Ryōnin
(1072-1132)

Chūjin
(Tōyō-bō, 1065-1138)

Chōgō
(1049-1133)
[Ekō-bō lineage]

Eikū
(d. 1179)

Kōkaku
{Sugiu lineage}

Hangen

Chōyō
|
[Chikurin-bō
lineage]

Chikai
|
[Bishamondō
lineage]

Jien
(1135-1225)

Yōben ⟶ Shōshin ⟵ Hōnen (Genkū)
(fl. 1165)   (1133-1212)
{Hōchi-bō lineage}

Shoyu
[Inokuma lineage]

Nichiren
(1222-1282)

Jōmyō
{Gyōsen-bō lineage}

Shunpan

Jōyū

Seikai
{Tsuchimikado Monzeki lineage}

Shinga (fl. 1329)

Shinson
(1253-1332)

Ikkai

Shinsō (fl. 1329)

Jikken

Shōkai

Gōkai (fl. 1347)

Zenkai

Jikkai (fl. 1367)

Tōkai (fl. 1343)

Sonshun
(1451-1514)

< >   Two major schools of Taimitsu
{ }   Four major Eshin lineages
[ ]   Four major Danna lineages

Based on *Tendai hongaku ron*, pp. 594-95.

common origin, on the other, as diverse lineages sought to legitimize themselves by tracing their descent back to the same few patriarchs, such as Saichō, Ennin, Enchin, and Genshin.

Origins of the Medieval Tendai Lineages

How, then, did the Eshin and Danna schools, along with their sublineages, come into being? This section will consider the broad religious, institutional, and social factors that contributed to the emergence of these lineages, as well as the doctrinal resources within Tendai Buddhism upon which they drew in formulating their transmissions.

Schools of Esoteric Ritual

Perhaps the major influence contributing to the eventual emergence of medieval Tendai *kuden* lineages was the formation from the mid-Heian period, within both Tendai and Shingon institutions, of rival lineages transmitting secret Mikkyō rituals *(himitsu shuhō)*. As mentioned in chapter 1, esoteric ritual performance was highly valued for its perceived apotropaic effects and had early on been sponsored by the court for the health of the emperor, the protection of the country, sufficient rainfall and good harvests, safe delivery for imperial consorts, and so forth. An imperial edict dating from the early tenth century prohibited private sponsorship of such rituals, suggesting that the court sought to monopolize the sacred powers that they were believed to control.[54] However, such efforts proved largely ineffective. With the breakdown of the Ritsuryō system of centralized land rule and the rise of powerful factions among the aristocracy competing for control of private estates, *shuhō* were increasingly sponsored by individual nobles, a trend that reached its height in the Insei period. The performance of these rites served to cement ties between individual master-disciple lineages of Mikkyō ritual specialists and specific factions among the ruling elites and thus served as a thaumaturgical support for what Kuroda Toshio has called the *kenmon taisei*—the system of shifting alliances among the parties of the emperor, the retired emperor, noble families, temple-shrine complexes, and eventually warriors—that formed the dominant power structure of the medieval period. Hayami Tasuku notes two key developments in the *shuhō* of the eleventh and twelfth centuries: (1) a growing elaborateness and complexity of ritual performance, seen specifically in an increase in the number of altars employed, suggesting both a quantitative approach to ritual efficacy and competition in economic outlay for the sponsoring of *shuhō;* and (2) striking innovation, seen both in the introduction of noncanonical iconic forms and in an expansion of the purposes for which such rituals were employed, including the defeat of enemies, birth of male heirs, prolonging of life, success in love, and other personal aims.[55] In their competition for the patronage of nobles seeking their aid, adepts of the various lineages sought to emphasize the uniqueness of their own rites and to keep them secret from outsiders.

Lines of transmission multiplied, and by the Insei period there are said to have been no fewer than thirteen lineages of Taimitsu *shuhō*. These were paralleled by twelve or, by some accounts, thirty-six lineages of Tōmitsu *shuhō*.[56] The differences among these schools were not chiefly of doctrine but of concrete ritual forms *(jisō)*, such as the mūdras, mantras, and other secret formulas *(hihō)* used in esoteric rituals.[57]

What direction the altar should face, what deity should be enshrined as the object of worship *(honzon)* and what form it should take, what mantras or dharani should be recited and how many times, what offerings made, and so forth all came under the category of *jisō;* on their proper performance, the efficacy of the ritual was thought to depend. Such matters readily lent themselves to construction as secret knowledge and were kept hidden and transmitted orally and in private from master to disciple.

These lineages of Mikkyō ritual performance thus influenced to a great degree the rise of what might be termed a medieval culture of secret transmission. Similar patterns of master-to-disciple secret transmission appear to have been a widespread development in the religious world of the Insei period.[58] Knowledge, as well as land, wealth, and political power, was becoming privatized. For example, this period witnessed the emergence of hereditary schools of poetry *(waka no ie)*, such as the Rokujō school that began with Fujiwara no Akisue (1055–1123) and the Mikohidari school that produced such luminaries as Fujiwara no Shunzei and his son Teika.[59] This phenomenon was in turn related to the rise of the idea of *michi,* or "Way"—the pursuit, as a vocation, of some specialized art or knowledge that was transmitted through a lineage, from father to son, or master to disciple.[60] Over the course of the medieval period, secret initiation and lineal transmission became common practice in all schools of Buddhism, including the "new" Zen and Pure Land traditions, as well as in Shugendō (mountain asceticism), Onmyōdō (yin-yang divination), and Yoshida Shintō. The practice of secret transmission also developed in the cultural arts, including poetry, calligraphy, the Nō drama, *biwa* recitation, flower-arranging, tea ceremony; in the martial arts; and in the crafts and manufacturing arts. In short, this became the normative mode of transmitting knowledge in premodern Japan.

A key figure in the development of early medieval Tendai esoteric ritual was the monk Kōkei or Kōgyō (977–1049), also known as Ikegami Ajari or Tani Ajari and regarded as founder of the Tani school of Taimitsu practice.[61] On Mt. Hiei, Kōkei studied Taimitsu ritual with Amidabō Shōshin, who also taught Genshin's disciple Kakuun. In the Chōhō era (999–1004), he went to Chinzei (Kyushu) and studied Tōmitsu ritual with the *ācārya* Keiun of the Tōji, from whom he also received Shingon esoteric *kanjō* or initiation. Later in life he retired to Ikegami in Tanba, eventually returning to Hiei before his death. Many of the distinctive forms of Taimitsu *shuhō* took form in Kōkei's time. While not the first Tendai monk to receive Shingon *kanjō*, Kōkei was innovative in incorporating Shingon ritual forms *(jisō)* into those of Tendai Mikkyō and developing a Taimitsu ritual system. He transmitted his ritual teach-

ings orally to his disciples, of whom he had more than thirty, and his influence is said to have extended to most of Mt. Hiei. His verbal teachings on esoteric ritual were recorded over a fifteen-year period by his
leading disciple Chōen (1016–1081) as the *Shijūjō-ketsu* (Determinations
in forty fascicles). One version of the text says that it is to be "hidden
deep in the palm, secretly stored at the right hand of one's seat," indicating the conventions of secrecy surrounding the transmission of
recorded oral teachings in Taimitsu lineages.[62] Kōkei was in fact a pioneer in the development of secret oral transmission.

The emphasis in influential Taimitsu lineages on the authority of secret master-disciple transmission no doubt helped to set the pattern for
later Tendai *kuden* transmission in the medieval Tendai Eshin and Danna
schools. Clearly these schools have roots in the medieval culture of secret transmission that developed within Mikkyō lineages generally. However, they may also have some more specific connection to Kōkei's time.
Kōkei is known as the founder of the Tani school of Taimitsu *shuhō,* "tani"
probably being an abbreviation of "Minamidani," one of the valleys of
the Eastern pagoda precinct where he lived. Genshin's disciple Kakuchō,
a contemporary of Kōkei, is said to have been the founder of the Kawa
school of Taimitsu, "kawa" being short for Yokawa where Kakuchō lived.
Rival Taimitsu lineages tended to be based in differing areas of Mt. Hiei—
the "three pagodas and sixteen valleys"—and the possibility of a geographical connection between the Yokawa-based Kawa school, and the
Eastern Pagoda–based Tani school, of Taimitsu, and the Eshin and
Danna schools, respectively, has already been noted. Other divisions
within Taimitsu may underlie many of the splits within the Eshin and
Danna schools, as many Eshin and Danna scholars were also Taimitsu
ritualists.[63] Moroever, one of Kōkei's students, Renjitsu-bō Shōhan
(996–1077), who was also a disciple of Genshin's disciple Kakuchō, figures prominently in medieval *kuden* literature as the source of specific
Eshin transmissions. Oral transmissions related to original enlightenment ideas may in fact have begun around Shōhan's time.[64] Thus, even
if the Eshin and Danna schools cannot, as their origin myth would have
it, be traced to Ryōgen's disciples Genshin (Eshin Sōzu) and Kakuun
(Danna Sōjō), they may have roots two generations later, in the time of
Kōkei's disciple Shōhan.

Aristocraticization and the Social Basis of Monastic Lineages

Rival lineages of Mikkyō ritual, and later *kuden* lineages such as the
Eshin and Danna schools and their subbranches, were also grounded in
hereditary factions among the nobility that were transplanted into the
clerical world as increasing numbers of aristocrats took holy orders from
the mid-Heian period on.[65] Based on documents from the Enryakuji and
the Kōfukuji, the most powerful temple-shrine complex in Nara, histo-

rian Hirata Toshiharu investigated the family background of monks known to have held the position of *zasu* of the Enryakuji or *bettō* (chief abbot) of the Kōfukuji, or who figured prominently in the annual court-sponsored lectures on the sūtras *(sandai-e)*. He found that from 782 to 990, 97 percent of such monks were of common origins *(shomin)*, but between 991 to 1069, this figure had fallen to 52 percent, and from 1070 to 1190, to only 10 percent.[66] Despite repeated instances of protest, the traditional monastic hierarchy based solely on length of time since ordination gave way to a hierarchy of pedigree as commoners were increasingly excluded from high clerical positions.[67]

On Mt. Hiei, the beginnings of this trend can be traced to the relationship between Ryōgen or Jie Daishi, who became the eighteenth *zasu* and "restorer" of Mt. Hiei, and Fujiwara no Morosuke (908–960), regarded as the ancestor of the powerful Kujō subbranch of the northern Fujiwara house. Morosuke sought Ryōgen's support as ritual specialist *(kitōsō)*, who would offer prayer rituals for the prosperity and success of himself and his descendants. Ryōgen, who had started out as a talented and ambitious young cleric albeit lacking in connections, rose to prominence through the patronage of Morosuke and his sons. With generous Fujiwara donations, Ryōgen effected the restoration of Mt. Hiei and established his own community of monks at the Yokawa precinct, where Morosuke financed the building of a Hokke Zanmai-dō, or hall for *Lotus*-based ritual practice. Eventually he would achieve the supreme position of *zasu*. To cement the understanding between them and ensure continued ritual support from Ryōgen and the Yokawa community, Morosuke sent his son Jinzen (943–990) to be Ryōgen's disciple. After Ryōgen's death, Jinzen succeeded Ryōgen as *zasu*. As though in testimony to the success of Ryōgen's thaumaturgical powers, Morosuke's descendants monopolized most major court offices for the next two hundred years.[68]

The Ryōgen-Morosuke-Jinzen connection set the pattern for the subsequent "aristocraticization" of Mt. Hiei, as nobles began to join the clergy in growing numbers. Many established personal temples on the mountain, which were supported by private estates or *shōen*. These estates were donated to them by the patron families whom they served as ritual specialists and with whom they maintained close ties. Hereditary transmission of the regency and of other court offices was paralleled on Mt. Hiei by the transmission from master to disciple—typically of the same family—of clerical position, temple buildings, *shōen*, texts, ritual implements, and other wealth held by individual temples. As an example, one may take Jinzen's lodging temple, the Myōkōin. On his death in 990, Jinzen bequeathed to the next Myōkōin abbot, also of the same Kujō house, eleven estates donated to him by his father Morosuke and three affiliated *betsuin* or detached cloisters that were under Myōkōin administration. The Myōkōin became the central administrative unit of the Yokawa and by 1063 boasted twenty-two *betsuin*. Along with its portfolio of estates, it was passed down through seven generations of Kujō family members and then transmitted to the Ichijō Fujiwara subbranch for another seven.[69]

By the Insei of the retired emperor Shirakawa (retired 1086–1129), few notices can be found of prominent Tendai monks from commoner families; most were men of at least the provincial administrator *(zuryō)* class or above. The position of *zasu* was held exclusively by men of the fifth court rank or higher, and, of eight *zasu* who held office during this period, four came from the regental family *(sekkanke)*.[70] Having sons well placed among the clergy was considered not only a source of religious merit for one's family but also an effective strategy for securing influence within the increasingly powerful temple-shrine complexes. This was particularly evident in the case of the *hōshinnō*, or princely abbots, a title first bestowed by Retired Emperor Shirakawa on his son Kakugyō in 1099. From Shirakawa on, retired emperors placed imperial princes as ranking abbots at the Enryakuji, Onjōji, and other major temple-shrine complexes in an effort to gain some control over these institutions and their armed forces.[71] The first *hōshinnō* at the Enryakuji was Saiun, son of Emperor Horikawa, appointed *zasu* in 1156 by Retired Emperor Goshirakawa. From the Insei of Retired Emperor Toba (retired 1129–1156), virtually all *zasu* were imperial princes.

Since the time of the fourth *zasu* Anne, who assumed this position in 864, the *zasu* had been appointed by the emperor;[72] he then served as a liaison between the imperial court and the Enryakuji clergy. But with the emergence of rival factions accompanying the privatization of power in the latter Heian, the *zasu*'s influence as the central figure of a unified Mt. Hiei declined. In contrast, the emerging institution of *hōshinnō*—one of whom often also doubled as *zasu*—allowed for multiple, competing connections between nobility and clergy.[73] Princely and other aristocratic abbots monopolized the highest clerical ranks and lived in special cloisters known as *monzeki*, a term also denoting the lineage of such a cloister. Five *monzeki* were established on Mt. Hiei.[74] They maintained affiliated residences on the outskirts of the capital *(sato-bō)*, where the *monzeki* abbot would stay when his ritual services were required at court; eventually, the *monzeki* cloisters transferred their location off-mountain to these *sato-bō*. Over time, the majority of the Enryakuji monks came to be organized under the leadership of one or another of the rival *monzeki*. Two in particular require mention here. The Shōren-in *monzeki*, established as the residence of the forty-eighth *zasu* Gyōgen (1093–1152), was originally located in the Eastern pagoda precinct but moved in the mid-twelfth century to Awataguchi at the Sanjō-Shirakawa intersection of the capital. Jien (1155–1222)—younger brother of the regent Kujō Kanezane, leading poet, author of the famous interpretation of Japanese history *Gukanshō,* and four-time *zasu* of the Enryakuji— was its third abbot. The major rival to the Shōren-in *monzeki* lineage was the Kajii *monzeki,* also known as the Nashimoto or Sanzen-in *monzeki.* Established during the tenure of the thirty-second *zasu* Myōkai, who held office from 1053–1070, it was originally located in the same area of the Eastern Pagoda precinct as the Shōren-in but later moved to the Ōhara on the outskirts of Kyoto. From the Insei of Retired Emperor Toba, the position of *zasu* was virtually monopolized by these two *monzeki* lineages, who engaged in frequent disputes over their respective candidates.[75]

Monzeki lineages tended to be identified with particular branches of Taimitsu *shuhō;* the Shōren-in transmitted the Sanmai lineage, and the Sanzen-in, the Nashimoto lineage, both rival branches of the Tani school of Taimitsu.[76] Specific texts were also part of individual *monzeki* transmissions, such as the 184-fascicle *Mon'yōki,* a compendium of Tendai ceremony and ritual passed handed down by the Shōren'in.[77] Nor were ritual, texts, and clerical office the only components of master-disciple transmission within the noble cloisters. Building upon the pattern seen in Jinzen's transmission of the Myōkōin, *monzeki* remained economically independent of the central Enryakuji administration; their vast estate portfolios were transferred from one *monzeki* abbot to his successor, attendant only upon the approval of the imperial court.[78] *Monzeki* wealth was poured into sūtra copying and the production of Buddhist icons, ritual implements, and adornments for practice halls, achieving a high level of religious art.[79] By the mid-Muromachi period, Tendai *monzeki* would become centers for the practice of other artistic and cultural traditions, including poetry and tea ceremony.[80] The Shōren-in transmitted the Shōren-in or Awataguchi school of calligraphy, said to have begun in the early fourteenth century with the abbot Son'en (1298–1356), the sixth son of Emperor Fushimi.[81]

The secret *kuden* transmissions of the Eshin and Danna schools, associated with original enlightenment thought, may be seen as part of a larger social picture, crossing lay-clerical lines and based on the privatizing by influential houses of land, political power, knowledge, and the arts that began in the latter Heian period. Within the large temple-shrine complexes, rival lineages developed as members of competing aristocratic factions took clerical orders and established themselves in private cloisters. A given lineage would often be based at a specific cloister and draw its members from the same aristocratic family. In time these rival lineages developed their own doctrinal and ritual characteristics. Traditions of practice and doctrinal interpretation, clerical ranks, estate holdings, texts, and ritual implements were all handed down within these master-disciple lineages, paralleling the transfer of worldly wealth, court rank, and specialized knowledge from father to son in aristocratic families.

The transplanting of aristocratic factions into the clerical world thus provided the "social basis" for medieval Tendai *kuden* lineages, as Nakanishi Zuikō has pointed out. Nakanishi has additionally drawn attention to a possible connection between the medieval Tendai *kuden* tradition and the aristocraticization of Mt. Hiei, in the transmission via noble houses of precedents and ancient customs surrounding the ceremonies of the court. Nakanishi draws here on Takeuchi Rizō's study of the records of *kuden* (oral transmissions) and *kyōmei* (instructions) concerning court ritual that were transmitted in certain families, known as *denke*.[82] Takeuchi traces the origin of such transmission to the time of the courtier Fujiwara no Mototsune (836–891). As he had served five emperors and held the posts of both regent *(sesshō)* and chancellor *(kanpaku),* Mototsune's knowledge of court protocol was considered authoritative. His pronouncements were compiled by his son Tadahira (880–949), initiating the forms of *kuden* and *kyōmei,* and were transmitted by Tadahira's sons, Saneyori and Morosuke (Ryōgen's patron), in two distinct *kuden* lineages, the Ono-no-miya and the Kujō, respectively. In time these transmissions of court ritual and precedent were written down, rival lineages emerged, and secret transmissions were produced. Belonging to the line of succession in a "transmission house" *(denke),* a family that transmitted *kuden,* or in a "diary house" *(nikki no ie),* a family in which successive generations of fathers and sons had kept and passed on diaries of public life and official ceremony, gave one a respected voice in court affairs.[83] This respect for the authority of *kuden,* Nakanishi suggests, was introduced into the Tendai monastic world by the nobles who filled its ranks in the latter Heian. The development among these noble houses of rival lineages of secret transmissions had no doubt itself been shaped by the transmissions of esoteric ritual. The two can be seen as parallel developments born of a shared social context: the *kenmon taisei,* or system of joint governance by competing influential parties that took shape in the latter Heian period. The *kuden* transmissions of the Eshin and Danna schools represent a slightly later development within this shared milieu.

Roots in Tendai Doctrinal Examination and Debate

The culture of secret transmission, shaped by the development of Mikkyō rival lineages and emerging within the social milieu of the privatization of power by influential houses, was common throughout the Buddhist world of early medieval Japan. The Eshin and Danna *kuden* schools of medieval Tendai were firmly embedded within this shared culture. However, they also drew on sources that were particular to the Tendai tradition. One of these was the distinctive Tendai educational system by which monks were trained and qualified in doctrinal studies through formal debate *(rongi).*[84]

Buddhist debate itself was by no means unique to Tendai but had formed a standard feature of state-sponsored Buddhist ceremonies since the Nara period. It was integral to the "three great assemblies" of the Nara schools *(sandai-e)* held annually for the sake of the country's welfare: the Yuima-e, the Misai-e (or Gosai-e), and the Saishō-e.[85] Debate was also incorporated into the ceremonial series of eight lectures on the eight scrolls of the *Lotus Sūtra* (Hokke Hakkō), often performed as memorial services and sponsored by the imperial family or other aristocrats, that became popular in the early Heian period.[86] The exposition of doctrine performed on these occasions was not merely delivered in lectures, but developed through question-and-answer form. The lecturer *(kōji)* would be questioned by an interlocuter *(monja)* and have to respond in defense of his interpretation; his arguments would then be evaluated by a judge *(shōgisha)*. Since lecturers and interlocuters were often chosen from different schools, Buddhist debates provided forums for sectarian rivalry and thus assumed the aspect of competition. Skill in debate provided an avenue by which individual monks could win recognition, patronage, and advancement. Ryōgen, for example, rose to prominence following a brilliant performance in the court-sponsored Ōwa debate of 963 between the Tendai and Hossō schools.[87] The assemblies where these debates took place tended to be lavish ceremonial affairs and thus afforded their sponsors an opportunity to display their wealth and prestige. For attending nobles, they provided entertainment and aesthetic pleasure as well as edification, and in the case of debates financed by the court, such as the three great assemblies, they also worked to reinforce the close ties between the imperial court and leading temples.[88]

Ryōgen, shortly after his appointment as Enryaku-ji *zasu* in 966, lent Buddhist debate yet another dimension, by institutionalizing debate-style examinations *(ryūgi)* as part of the system of doctrinal training on Mt. Hiei.[89] In so doing, he sought to establish a system for the recognition and qualification of Tendai monks independent of the court-sponsored assemblies such as the Yuima-e, to which Tendai representatives were infrequently appointed. He also sought to foster the study of Tendai exoteric studies and provide public standards of doctrinal mastery as a basis for determining clerical advancement. This was in part to counter the factionalism developing with the proliferation of secret esoteric lineages in which the master alone would evaluate and reward a disciple's attainments.[90] As defined by Ryōgen, the Tendai examination was to be a "debate on broad learning" *(kōgaku ryūgi),* embracing not only Tendai doctrine but Buddhism in general. It was held regularly following the two major lecture assemblies on the *Lotus Sūtra* conducted on Mt. Hiei: the Minazuki-e Hokke Dai-e held in the sixth month and the Shimotsuki-e Hokke Dai-e held in the eleventh month and commemorating Saichō and Chih-i, respectively. After Ryōgen's time, the focus of Tendai debate shifted still further away from doctrinal sparring with other schools and

competition for aristocratic patronage to an internal endeavor of training Tendai monks. A novice scholar-monk's training was conducted at
the specific temple or cloister where he was affiliated, and focused on
abhidharma, Tendai studies, and other basics.[91] Learning was regularly
tested in public debate that formed a major feature of the religious assemblies *(kō)* held in the various valley or *tani* units of the mountain. For
example, at Mudōjidani of the Eastern Pagoda precinct, monks from the
second through twentieth year of their postordination training were required to attend three such assemblies monthly: (1) the Sōō Kashō-kō,
held on the third day of each month in commemoration of Sōō (831–
918), who is said to have initiated the *kaihōgyō* walking meditation of Mt.
Hiei; the examination at this assembly was on Tendai doctrine; (2) the
Dengyo Daishi-kō, held on the fourth day of the month in commemoration of Saichō, where an examination took place on *abhidharma* studies; and (3) the Sannō Gongen-kō, held on the sixteenth day of the
month to honor the Sannō guardian deities of Mt. Hiei, where examination was conducted on a chapter of the *Lotus Sūtra.*[92] Monks of more
than twenty years' standing took part in their own series of debates, which
focused on the *Lotus Sūtra* and the works of T'ien-t'ai founder Chih-i:
the Jie Daishi-kō, held on the eighteenth of each month to commemorate Ryōgen; the Jichin Kashō-kō, held on the twenty-fifth of each month
to commemorate Jien; and the Bishamon-kō, held each month on the
twenty-eighth.[93] Different valleys on the mountain developed similar systems. In the course of the examinations, both candidates and their examiners were required to establish an argument *(dōri)* and cite proof texts
(monshō) in its support. Topics of debate and examination fell into three
general categories: essential doctrines of the Tendai school *(shūyō),*
points of difference with other school *(gika),* and miscellaneous topics
(mon'yō).

Debates were also held in which monks representing all the valleys
of a given pagoda precinct—five valleys each belonging to the Eastern
and Western pagodas and six valleys belonging to Yokawa—participated.
In the Eastern and Western pagoda precincts, younger monks took part
in the Goji-kō (Assembly of the five periods), which entailed a series of
debates, six daily for the first seven days of the fourth month, on the
teachings of the five periods into which the T'ien-t'ai/Tendai classification system divides the sūtras: the Āgama, *Avataṃsaka, vaipulya, prajñā,* and *Lotus/Nirvāṇa* periods. Older monks took part in similar assemblies in which daily lectures on the successive chapters of the *Lotus
Sūtra* were followed by debate. These were the Nijū Hakkō of the Western Pagoda, covering the twenty-eight chapters of the sūtra, and the
Sanjū-kō of the Eastern pagoda, covering the twenty-eight chapters plus
the *Wu-liang-i ching* (Sūtra of unfathomable meanings) and *Fo-shuo kuan
P'u-hsien P'u-sa hsing-fa ching* (Sūtra of the Buddha's preaching on the

method of contemplating Bodhisattva Samantabhadra), the opening and concluding scriptures to the *Lotus.* In contrast, the Yokawa precinct employed a distinctive system. Young monks took part in the Shiki-kō (four seasonal assemblies), in which lectures were given on the *Nirvāṇa Sūtra* in spring, the *Hua-yen ching* in summer, the *Lotus* in fall, and the *Ta-chi-ching* (Great collection of sūtras) in the winter.[94] Examinations were held at spring and summer assemblies, two candidates participating at each. More seasoned monks took part in the Gansan Gohakkō or Gansan-e, a Hokke Hakkō or series of eight lectures on the eight rolls of the *Lotus,* two held daily for the first four days of the year. In 1227 imperial permission was granted to increase the number of monks participating in the Gansan-e to twenty, and monks from the Eastern and Western pagoda precincts began to take part.[95] The Eastern and Western Pagoda precincts also sponsored Kangakkō (assemblies for encouraging learning) in which experienced representatives from the entire mountain participated. These were major affairs; the Kangakkō of the Eastern Pagoda took place over the course of six days with as many as a hundred persons participating, and that of the Western Pagoda was conducted on a comparable scale. The Kangakkō of the Eastern Pagoda was funded by income from the Fujishima-shō, an estate in Echizen donated to Mt. Hiei by Minamoto no Yoritomo and used by the *zasu* Jien to promote learning via the Kangakkō.[96] Income from other estates was similarly earmarked for support of other assemblies: the Kangakkō of the Western Pagoda was funded by revenues from the Kurita-shō in Ōmi,[97] and the Yokawa Shiki-kō, by income from twenty-four *chō* of land designated for that purpose by Ryōgen and his successor Jinzen.[98]

The most important examinations on Mt. Hiei, however, were the Minazuki-e and the Shimozuki-e, held in the sixth and eleventh months, respectively. These assemblies, attended by representatives of the court, involved morning lectures on the *Lotus Sūtra* delivered by the most seasoned scholars *(ikō),* who then served in the afternoon as examiners for the "examinations on broad learning." Only successful veterans of examinations at the valley and pagoda precinct levels could participate as candidates *(rissha* or *ryūgisha).* Of those judged victorious, some remained on the mountain to pursue their studies and achieve higher scholarly rank, perhaps aspiring to the position of *tandai,* or judge, of the *kōgaku ryūgi.* Others left to become instructors in the many Tendai seminaries *(dangisho)* that began to develop in eastern Japan during the Kamakura period.

Debate as a mode of doctrinal training and examination was thus central to the practice of Tendai scholar-monks. Those preparing as candidates often made notes of interpretations of particular debate topics on which they might be examined. With the division of Mt. Hiei in the latter Heian period into quasi-independent monastic factions based in ge-

ographically distinct valleys and pagoda precincts, different lineages began to develop and transmit distinct interpretations of debate topics. The
emergence of the Eshin and Danna *kuden* may possibly have roots in divergent interpretations of debate topics among monks affiliated with different geographical areas of the mountain.[99] Tendai literature related
to debate hints occasionally at a dual transmission of debate topic interpretations from Ryōgen through his disciples Genshin and Kakuun
in a manner that parallels the origin myths of the Eshin and Danna
schools. An example can be found in the *Shūen shū* and *Shūman shū*, medieval Tendai collections of oral transmissions on roughly a hundred
shūyō or debate topics concerning Tendai doctrine. Both purport to have
originated with Ryōgen, who conferred the *Shūen shū* and *Shūman shū*
upon his two leading disciples, Eshin Sōzu Genshin and Danna Sōzu
Kakuun, respectively; the two collections were then allegedly transmitted through Genshin's and Kakuun's respective lines.[100] Similarly, the
Hokke ryakugi kenmon, attributed to Chūjin (1065–1138) but probably dating from the latter part of the Kamakura period, tells of a tradition of
doctrinal differences that first emerged during a debate at the Ōhara
Shōrin-in between Kakuchō and Henku, the two leading disciples of Genshin and Kakuun, respectively.[101]

Also suggestive of a connection between the Tendai debate tradition
and the Eshin and Danna *kuden* transmissions is the fact that a number
of the late Heian and Kamakura period figures who figure prominently
in Eshin and Danna *kuden* texts are known to have been active in debate.[102] The earlier-mentioned Renjitsu-bō Shōhan, thirty-third *zasu* of
Mt. Hiei and a disciple of both Genshin's disciple Kakuchō and the esoteric master Kōkei, was the author of two *shiki* or personal commentaries on debate topics. Tōyō-bō Chūjin, putative author of the *Kankō
ruijū* and other important Eshin *kuden* texts, served as *kōji* at the Saishō-
kō in 1121 and as examiner *(shōgisha)* at the Saishō-e in 1132. Shunpan
(fl. mid-thirteenth century), a major scholar of the Eshin Sugiu lineage,
served as *tandai* or judge of the "examination on broad learning" at Mt.
Hiei, and his doctrinal decisions made in this capacity are recorded in
Tendai debate texts.[103] Jōmyō, a disciple of Shunpan and regarded as
the founder of the Gyōsen-bō subbranch of the Eshin lineage, is considered to be the author of a major collection of commentaries on debate topics, the *Tendai hyakudai jizai-bō.*

A number of Eshin and Danna oral transmissions were produced on
traditional debate topics, on which they purport to deliver a secret interpretation from the standpoint of original enlightenment. There may
be a distinction to be drawn between transmissions concerning debate
topics, which were stated publicly in examinations, and the *kuden hōmon,*
which were transmitted secretly.[104] Nonetheless, there does appear to
have been a close association between debate topics and orally trans-

mitted doctrines. Secret oral transmissions concerning debate topics may have begun after the debate system was well established and its topics formalized.[105] In any event, it seems clear that Eshin and Danna lineages, as well as their subbranches, identified themselves at least partially in terms of their distinctive interpretation of traditional debate topics. Not only were interpretations differentiated among lineages, but so were some outward conventions. For example, the Danna lineages of the north and west valleys of the Eastern Pagoda precinct made a point of using different Chinese characters, respectively, to write the phrase *kokoro ikan* (What is the meaning?) in their debate texts. Different lineages also adopted distinctive pronunciations of Buddhist technical terms.[106]

The Reinvention of Saichō's Heritage

Lastly, the Eshin and Danna schools discovered, or one might say invented, a basis for their transmissions in the writings of the Japanese Tendai founder Saichō. As explained above, these lineages claimed that their transmissions had been handed down from Hui-ssu and Chih-i through Tao-sui and Hsing-man to Saichō, but there is little evidence that secret oral transmissions played a significant role in Chinese T'ien-t'ai or early Japanese Tendai. Chih-i's *Mo-ho chih-kuan* occasionally mentions the need for "verbal decisions" (*k'ou-chüeh, kuketsu*) to be conveyed by the master to disciple with respect to meditative practice.[107] Chan-jan's commentary on the *Chih-kuan* also criticizes a faction within the T'ien-t'ai school that evidently held that some "essential of mind" was conveyed verbally from master to disciple and apart from texts, thus suggesting that secret oral transmission was in fact practiced to some extent.[108] Saichō's authenticated works contain two references to oral transmission: The *Kenkai ron* says that Tao-sui taught him "the threefold contemplation in a single mind, transmitted in one phrase,"[109] and the *Shugo kokkai shō* states, "The meaning of [the analogy of] the perfect interfusion of the mirror and its images cannot be understood unless it is conveyed verbally. Truly there is reason for the transmission from master to disciple!"[110] However, as Hazama Jikō has pointed out, in the main, references to oral transmission in the earlier T'ien-t'ai/Tendai tradition simply indicate the importance of verbal explanation to supplement written texts and do not represent instances of secret transmission.[111] There is no evidence directly connecting the medieval *kuden* tradition to similar practices in Saichō's time.

Nevertheless, the participants in that tradition saw themselves as upholding, elaborating, and transmitting a Dharma heritage received in a direct line from Saichō. This putative heritage was grounded in the two statements from Saichō's writings just cited, concerning the "threefold contemplation in a single mind, transmitted in one phrase" (*isshin sangan dennō ichigon*) and the "perfect interfusion of the mirror and its im-

ages" *(kyōzō en'yū)*. These two phrases were "reinvented" as the substance
of an ancient transmission that Saichō had received in China. According to the Kamakura period *kuden* collection *Kawataya bōshō jūkutsū*
(Nineteen main and subsidiary articles of Kawataya):

> This Dharma [of Chih-i's inner enlightenment] is extremely profound.
> Therefore, when Chang-an [Kuan-ting] recorded it, he did not [fully]
> express its meaning. The teachers of north and south expounded it
> but did not grasp its heart. But when Sange [Daishi, i.e., Saichō] was
> in T'ang [China], the threefold contemplation in a single mind trans-
> mitted in one phrase, and the verbal decision concerning the perfect
> interfusion of the mirror and its images, were transferred to him. Thus,
> without verbal decisions, among later scholars mired in delusion, who
> could readily understand it?[112]

Numerous medieval Tendai *kuden* purport to transmit and explicate the
meaning of Saichō's statements, which also became the basis of meditative and ritual practices. Ōkubo Ryōjun has even suggested that the
origins of Eshin and Danna *kuden hōmon* may be understood not merely
in the broad terms of the rise of *hongaku* thought or Mikkyō influence
on Tendai exoteric teachings, but with respect to the concrete influence
of these two phrases.[113]

The "threefold contemplation in a single mind" *(isshin sangan)*, to be
discussed in greater detail in the next chapter, is taught in Chih-i's meditation manual *Mo-ho chih-kuan* (Great calming and contemplation). Its
aim is to perceive, through contemplation of the thought-moment, that
all phenomena manifest the three truths of emptiness, conventional existence, and the middle, that is, being simultaneously both empty and
provisionally existing. In the medieval Tendai tradition, the threefold
contemplation refers not only to the method of introspective meditation taught by Chih-i, but to the inherent nature of reality: "As for the
threefold contemplation in a single mind [transmitted] in one phrase,
it is originally unborn, separated from causality, constantly abiding without perishing, pervading everywhere."[114] When Saichō wrote that Tao-
sui had conveyed to him the threefold contemplation "in one phrase,"
he probably meant that the Chinese master's explanation had been
brief.[115] However, a number of medieval Tendai *kuden* purport to transmit the actual content of the "one phrase," which undergoes extensive
elaboration as the tradition develops. The great range of interpretations
that existed even from an early date is suggested by the *Shuzenji-ketsu*
([Doctrinal] decisions of Hsiu-ch'an-ssu), a text attributed to Saichō and
probably dating somewhere from the late Heian through mid-Kamakura
periods. The *Shuzenji-ketsu* devotes its entire first fascicle to the threefold
contemplation in a single mind, discussing it under the three perspectives of teaching, practice, and realization. "Teaching" is discussed in

terms of three categories: the threefold contemplation as incompletely set forth in the provisional teachings; the threefold contemplation of "subtle essence" *(myōtai no isshin sangan)*—that is, of the perfect inter-fusion of the three truths found in the *Lotus Sūtra;* and the threefold contemplation as explained in the T'ien-t'ai commentaries. These in turn have subcategories: for example, the threefold contemplation in terms of "subtle essence" is divided into the threefold contemplation in terms of one's mind alone, concrete phenomena, the true aspect, and original enlightenment.[116] The section on "practice" develops the claim that the threefold contemplation may be cultivated with respect to dif-ferent objects. Thus the T'ien-t'ai precursor Hui-wen (d.u.), teacher of Hui-ssu, is said to have practiced the threefold contemplation in terms of "production through causes and conditions" *(innenshō no isshin san-gan);* Chih-i's teacher Hui-ssu transmitted the threefold contemplation in terms of the single phrase "unbornness of the one mind" *(isshin fushō no ichigon);* and Chih-i himself, the threefold contemplation of the "non-duality of the object [of contemplation] and wisdom [of the contem-plating mind]" *(kyōchi funi no isshin sangan).* Moreover, while practicing this meditation on Mt. Ta-su, Chih-i received directly from Śākyamuni the threefold contemplation in the single phrase "nonduality of quies-cence and illumination" *(jakushō funi no ichigon);* and his disciple Kuan-ting cultivated the threefold contemplation of "the enlightened work-ings of birth and death" *(shōji kakuyō no isshin sangan).*[117] Appended to the "Realization" section of the *Shuzenji-ketsu's* discussion are an addi-tional fourteen kinds of "threefold contemplation in a single mind."[118]

Interpretations of this contemplation's transmission "in one phrase" became a standard feature of later systematizations of the *kuden hōmon.* The *Ichijō shō,* dating from around the early fourteenth century, em-phasizes the single phrase "object [of contemplation] and wisdom [of the contemplating mind]" *(kyōchi no ichigon).* However, it notes that, due to the infinite varieties of human capacity, the "one phrase" is not fixed but can vary according to circumstances. It also adds as "a secret matter of this school" that prior to such distinctions in capacity and the arising of appropriate verbal formulations is "the one phrase that is the letter A" *(aji no ichigon)*—a clear instance of esoteric appropriations.[119] The *Nijō shō kenmon* of Sonshun, compiled in 1501, lists various interpretations of the "one phrase" transmitting the threefold contemplation, including "identity with the middle" *(sokuchū no ichigon),* "compassion" *(jihi no ichigon),* "object and wisdom" *(kyōchi no ichigon),* "birth and death" *(shōji no ichigon),* "no-self" *(muga no ichigon),* "calming and contemplation" *(shikan no ichigon),* "Wonderful Dharma" *(myōhō no ichigon),* "mind es-sentials" *(shin'yō no ichigon),* "innate and self-luminous" *(tenjin dokurō no ichigon),* "ultimate equality from beginning to end" *(honmatsu kukyō-tō no ichigon),* "contemplation of the mind" *(kanjin no ichigon),* "quiescence and illumination" *(jakushō no ichigon),* and, prior to all these, the originally inherent single phrase, the letter A.[120]

Such interpretations of "the threefold contemplation" are central to a great many medieval Tendai doctrinal *kuden* texts. In *The Tale of the Heike,* when the Enryakuji *zasu* Meiun incurs the anger of the retired emperor Goshirakawa and is sent into exile, the monk Chōken accompanies him partway:

> Moved by his concern, Meiun transmitted to him the threefold contemplation in a single mind, which he had kept secret for many years. That doctrine, expounded by the Buddha and gradually handed on ever since the time of the monk Memyō [Aśvaghoṣa] of Vārāṇasī and the bodhisattva Ryūju [Nāgārjuna] of Southern India, was taught to Chōken that day in gratitude for his sympathy. Awesome, indeed, must Chōken's sentiments have been as he journeyed back toward the capital.[121]

This passage suggests that Meiun conferred upon Chōken not the "threefold contemplation" as a meditation method set forth in the *Mo-ho chih-kuan,* which would have been publicly accessible, but one of the many secret understandings of this doctrine that formed the core of the medieval Tendai *kuden hōmon.*

The "perfect interfusion of the mirror and its images," the second of Saichō's two references to oral transmission, represents a variation on the same teaching, this analogy having been used by Chih-i to illustrate that the three truths are perfectly integrated and inseparable.[122] Here one must imagine not a glass mirror, but one made of bronze or some other metal, polished to form a reflecting surface. The luminous, reflecting quality of the mirror represents emptiness; the images reflected in it represent conditioned, provisional existence; and the mirror itself represents the middle. These three are always inseparable and simultaneous, three aspects of one reality. Transmissions concerning "the mirror and its images" occur in early *kirikami* collections, such as the *Tendai Hokkeshū gozu hōmon yōsan* attributed to Saichō and the *Koshinjū ki* attributed to Kakuchō.[123] A tradition developed that Saichō had received the transmission of an actual mirror in China, or that Enchin, when he journeyed there, had received two.[124] Medieval Tendai texts also contain descriptions of meditative practices and initiation rituals that prescribe the use of mirrors as visible metaphors for realizing or conveying the nonduality and interpenetration of the dharmas. The *Shuzenki-ketsu,* for example, gives instructions for a method of practicing the threefold contemplation in a single mind, in which one sits facing a Buddha image arranged so that both the image and the practitioner are simultaneously reflected in a mirror, as an aid to realizing that "living beings" and "the Buddha" are one essence.[125] Some Eshin *kuden* texts instructed that two mirrors are to be hung on the east and west walls, respectively, of the practice hall, so that reflections of both the practitioner and the Buddha image positioned between them are endlessly replicated; in this way, the presence of the three thousand realms (i.e., all dharmas) in a single thought-moment can be clearly realized.[126] A text of the Danna school *genshi kanjō* ritual—an initiation *(kanjō)* into the "profound purport" *(genshi)* of the threefold contemplation—mentions two mirrors: a round silver mirror and an octagonal bronze one, presented to Chih-i by Emperor Yang of the Sui and the deity of Mt. T'ien-t'ai, respectively. Such mirrors are to be employed in the ritual, the round one held in the right hand and the octagonal one in the left, to convey the teachings of nonduality.[127] Similar use of a round and an octagonal mirror is described in texts outlining the precept initiation *(kai kanjō)* of the Kurodani precept lineage, which transmitted the "perfect and sudden precepts" *(endon kai),* of which more will be said later. Here the round and octagonal mirrors represent, respectively, the primary and secondary textual ground of the precepts, that is, the *Lotus Sūtra* and the *Fan-wang ching.*[128] This ritual probably developed out of the *genshi kanjō*. Mirrors were also employed in the *kimyodan kanjō,* another Danna initiation ritual. Mirror analogies have a long history in Buddhist philosophical texts,[129] while actual mirrors have been used throughout Asia for divination and other shamanistic purposes. In Japan they were employed as *goshintai* or sacred objects onto which the *kami* might descend and dwell. Though such connections have yet to be fully explored, the transmission concerning "the perfect interfusion of the mirror and its images" as well as the use of actual mirrors in medieval Tendai ritual and meditative practices are clearly linked to these broader traditions.

While the medieval Tendai *kuden* tradition cannot be traced back to Saichō, his "reinvented heritage"—centering on the threefold contemplation in a single mind and the analogy of the mirror and its images— was absolutely central to it and formed the basis of entire systems of medieval Tendai doctrine and practice.

Other Lineages: Chroniclers, Precept Keepers, and Shōmyō Chanters

Above we have seen how the formation of the Eshin and Danna schools and their subbranches—the main doctrinal lineages of medieval Tendai—was influenced by the earlier emergence of lineages of secret esoteric *shuhō,* and how this process of lineage formation was grounded socially and politically in the privatization of power among competing factions of the aristocracy. We have also outlined how, in addition to these more general trends, Eshin and Danna transmissions were shaped by their reliance on elements specific to the Tendai tradition, such as the system of debate-style examination and key passages in Saichō's teachings, as a basis for their transmissions. This section will look briefly at other, often overlapping Tendai lineages that transmitted other sorts of teachings, but which were also informed by ideas of original enlightenment. Three examples of such lineages will be considered: those of the chroniclers, the precept-keepers, and the chanters of *shōmyō*.[130]

"Chroniclers" *(kike)* were those who studied, interpreted, and transmitted the "records" or "documents" *(kiroku)* of Mt. Hiei.[131] According to the massive *kike* compendium *Keiran shūyō shū* (introduction dated 1318) compiled by Kōsō, such documents fell into four categories: exoteric teachings *(ken)*, esoteric teachings *(mitsu)*, precepts *(kai)*, and records *(ki)*, each of which had an accompanying *kanjō* (Skt. *abhiṣeka*) or initiation ritual.[132] Thus, in a broad sense, all the documents of Mt. Hiei counted as *kiroku*. The activity of the *kike*, however, seems to have focused on transmissions of the fourth category, which was subdivided into six areas: (1) the sacred boundaries *(kekkai)* or divisions within the precincts of Mt. Hiei; (2) the halls and temples of the mountain and the Buddha images enshrined there; (3) manifestations of the protective deities; (4) the tradition of nation protection; (5) rituals; and (6) regulations, observances, and practices of the monks. In short, the chroniclers recorded the traditions of the mountain. But they were far more than mere recorders of facts. They also produced and transmitted *kuden* concerning these traditions, which gave mystical interpretations decoding the geographic features, temples and halls, deities, rituals, and so forth of Mt. Hiei as the numinous embodiments of the realm of truth expressed in Tendai doctrine. The *Kuin bukkaku shō*, a collection of the Kajii lineage of chroniclers compiled between 1324 and 1383, correlates the six divisions in the documents to four lines in an "abbreviated verse" describing the mission of the Enryakuji:

> Preserve the three treasures.
> Dim the radiance and appear in this world.
> Purify the Buddha land.
> Benefit all living beings.[133]

To interpret and transmit the records concerning the Buddha images, the rituals, and the activities of the monks of Mt. Hiei corresponds to preserving the three treasures of the Buddha, the Dharma, and the sangha, respectively. To interpret and transmit the records concerning the *kami* corresponds to "dim the radiance and appear in this world," a phrase referring to the idea that *kami* are the local and therefore more accessible manifestations of Buddhas and bodhisattvas. Similarly, transmissions concerning the sacred precincts of Mt. Hiei correspond to "purifying the Buddha land," and those concerning nation-protection to "benefiting all living beings." Thus the interpretive work and transmissions of the *kike* were seen as bodhisattva practice and preservation of the original mission of Mt. Hiei.[134]

There were also said to be six divisions in the *kike* transmissions according to the degree of secrecy required in their handling, ranging from those that could be cited openly to those that had to be transmitted orally or could be revealed only by a master on his deathbed to one chosen disciple.[135] Hazama Jikō has suggested that while the former correspond to "records" in the conventional sense, the latter are mystical transmissions. To cite his example, transmissions about the origins of the three pagoda precincts would be ordinary records, but to interpret them as embodying the three groups of pure precepts inherent in the precept repository of the one mind would be a mystical transmission.[136] This latter mode of interpretation is called *kanjin*-style interpretation or "interpretation from the standpoint of the contemplation of the mind" and will be discussed in the next chapter.

The thrust of many of these transmissions was to present the features of Mt. Hiei as manifesting the realm of original enlightenment and the physical embodiment of Tendai doctrine. For example:

> An oral transmission states: Ascending the mountain is proceeding from cause to effect [i.e., from the state of an unenlightened practitioner to that of the Buddha]; it is "upwardly seeking bodhi," the intent of the trace teaching. Descending the mountain toward Sakamoto is proceeding from effect to cause [i.e., original enlightenment manifesting itself in the phenomenal world] and the dharmas arising in accordance with conditions, the heart of the origin teaching. Our ascending and descending the mountain is the unproduced subtle practice of the original ground and plants great wholesome roots without our knowing or realizing.[137]

To produce and transmit such *kuden* involved contemplation and cognition of the phenomenal world—specifically, the features of Mt. Hiei—as the embodiment of original enlightenment. Interpretations of this kind were linked to the mandalization of space and the identification of specific sites with pure lands; for example, the identification of Mt. Hiei's three pagoda precincts with the Vajra, Matrix, and Soshitsuji realms, found in a number of *kike* texts. It also contributed to the development of the *kaihōgyō* walking meditation, a form of mountain asceticism unique to Mt. Hiei, in which the practitioner who traverses the routes circling mountain participates in its sacrality as geographic mandala, revering its sacred sites and the deities who abide therein.[138]

Kike were also instrumental in the emergence of the cult of Sannō Shintō, which grew up around the Hie shrine complex located at the eastern foot of Mt. Hiei.[139] These shrines were organized in three groups and devoted to seven *kami*, regarded as the local manifestations *(suijaku)* of specific buddhas and bodhisattvas. For example, the Buddhas enshrined in the main temples of each of the three pagoda precincts—

Yakushi (Skt. *Bhaiṣajyaguru*) in the Ichijō Shikan-in of the Eastern Pagoda precinct; Śākyamuni in the Hokke Hōtōin of the Western Pagoda
precinct; and Amida, enshrined in the Shuryōgon-in of Yokawa—were
assigned local forms as the *kami* of the Eastern Shrine, the Western
Shrine, and the Usa shrine—the core of the Hie complex—respectively.
By the late Heian and Kamakura periods, these *kami* together with their
Buddha-counterparts came to be referred to under the single rubric
Sannō (mountain king), a name originally denoting the protective deities of Mt. T'ien-t'ai in China. *Kike* documents, as well as those of other
lineages, interpret Sannō as an embodiment of Tendai teachings.[140] Even
the characters of the name "Sannō"—*san* written with three vertical
strokes and one horizontal one, and *ō*, with three horizontal strokes and
one vertical one—were seen as hierophanies of the threefold contemplation in a single mind, an interpretation well established by the mid-
Kamakura period.[141]

Like those of the Eshin and Danna lineages, *kike* transmissions were
retrospectively attributed to great Tendai masters of the past. Their fundamental texts were said to be the "twenty volumes of the three sages
and two teachers," the "three sages" being Saichō, Ennin, and Enchin,
and the two teachers, Annen and Ryōgen.[142] In fact, the tradition did
not originate until much later. An important figure in medieval accounts
of the tradition is Kenshin (1131–1192), putative author of the *Sange
yōryakki* (Abbreviated record of the essentials of the mountain school),
a representative *kike* text. Whether the *kike* had actually emerged by Kenshin's time, however, is problematic.[143] With Kenshin's two disciples
Ninkai and Ninzen, his lineage is said to have split in two, forming the
Daitōmon and Kajii lines, respectively. The Kajii, a *monzeki* line, was the
dominant one, to the point that the *kike* tradition is largely identified
with the Kajii lineage. The Kajii chroniclers also belonged to the Danna
school. The Daitōmon had some Eshin connections, but *kike* are for the
most part regarded as a Danna development.[144] *Kike* transmissions seem
to have been systematized by Gigen (c. 1289–1351) and his disciple Kōsō
(or Kōshū) (1276–1350), compiler of the *Keiran shūyō shū*. The literary
activities of these men mark the pinnacle of *kike* achievements.

Another noteworthy lineage to develop on Mt. Hiei during the Kamakura period was the *kaike* or precept lineage, based at Kurodani in
the vicinity of the Western Pagoda.[145] Unlike the Eshin teachers, who,
as we shall see, regarded "mind contemplation" *(kanjin)* or "calming
and contemplation" *(shikan)* as representing the ultimate truth of Buddhism, the *kaike* held the "perfect and sudden precepts" *(endonkai)* to
be central, supreme, and all-encompassing. The term "perfect and sudden precepts," now a standard way of referring to the Tendai bodhisattva precepts, came into use in the Kamakura period to indicate a
formless precept-essence conferred during ordination and reflected a

tendency to understand the bodhisattva precepts in terms of the underlying spirit of the *Lotus Sūtra,* rather than as a set of ten major and forty-eight minor rules set forth in the *Fan-wang ching.*[146] The *kaike* lineage, however, sought also to revive actual observance of the precepts as standards governing conduct. The term *kaike* appears from around the time of Ejin (d. 1289?), who is regarded as the *kaike* founder. Ejin appears to have received Eshin, Danna, and precept transmissions.[147] He traced his precept lineage through Eikū, a disciple of Ryōnin, famous as the itinerant teacher of the *yūzū* or all-pervading *nembutsu.* Eikū had lived at Kurodani, where he had numbered Hōnen among his disciples. From Hōnen, Eikū's precept lineage passed to Shinkū and then to Tankū, both Tendai monks who also studied the Pure Land teachings.[148] Ejin received the transmission of this lineage from Tankū. He sought to revive strict observance of the precepts and also vowed to remain on Mt. Hiei for twelve years without interruption, reviving a practice Saichō had initiated for the training of monks but that had long since been allowed to lapse. Ejin abandoned the coarse white silk robes that had become standard garb for the monks of Mt. Hiei since Ryōgen's time and donned instead the *ritsu-e* or black robes of a *vinaya* master. Criticized for violating the usages of the mountain, he eventually left Hiei and established Shinkurodani (new Kurodani) in the vicinity of Shirakawa in the capital.[149] However, his disciples were able to reestablish themselves at Kurodani and at the Shinzōji in the Eastern Pagoda precinct.

Among the most important of Ejin's successors was Kōen (1262/1263–1317), a disciple of Ejin's disciple Egi. His career is recounted in the *Denshin Kashō den,* attributed to the chronicler Kōsō.[150] In 1305 Kōen began a twelve-year term of uninterrupted residence on Mt. Hiei, vowing to uphold and spread the perfect precepts. During this time he appears to have devoted himself to intense practice. In 1310, at the Shinzōji, he revived the long-defunct institution of the summer retreat *(ango)* together with four disciples. From 1311 to 1314 he conducted with others a thousand-day uninterrupted *goma* or fire-offering ritual and is also said to have practiced seated meditation for two periods each day and contemplation coupled with recitation *(nenju)* for three.[151]

From Kōen's time, close connections developed between the Kurodani precept lineage and the Kajii lineage of chroniclers. In 1309 the chronicler Gigen added his signature to Kōen's vow to uphold the precepts, "without regard for slander or persecution," suggesting that Kōen, like Ejin before him, had become a target of criticism.[152] Kōsō, who is famous among the chroniclers as the compiler of the monumental *Keiran shūyō shū,* was one of Kōen's disciples and received a number of *kike* transmissions from Gigen.[153] Kōen's disciple Echin (or Enkan), who was based at the Hosshōji in the capital, was an ardent supporter of Godaigo and may have been instrumental in the compilation of the chronicle *Taiheiki*. With Echin, the activities of the lineage took on the character of an independent revival movement.[154]

As noted in the first chapter, Saichō understood the bodhisattva precepts as expressions of innate Buddha nature. Immanentalist understandings of the precepts were also developed by later teachers, such as Annen. For the *kaike*, the precepts were to be understood in terms of original enlightenment. The *Isshin myōkai shō* (On the single-mind subtle precepts), written in 1266 and thought to be the work of Ejin, reads as follows:

> The Mahāyāna precepts have beginningless and originally inherent unchanging suchness as their precept-essence *(kaitai)*. Although this suchness is endowed with the ten realms [from hell to Buddhahood], those beings of the nine [unenlightened] realms have yet to manifest [Buddhahood]; therefore, they launch practice and aspire to realize the Buddha realm. This practice represents the acquired enlightenment *(shikaku)* latent within original enlightenment. Because practice is rooted in [original] nature, it is called the beginningless and originally inherent practice. . . . Thus the Buddha realm is the essence of the precepts, and the nine realms, the practice of the precepts. . . . [Alternatively,] the single thought-moment is the precept-essence, and the three thousand realms [i.e., all dharmas], the practice of the precepts.[155]

In some *kaike* texts, such as Kōen's *Endonkai hiketsu yōshū* (Essentials of the secret determinations concerning the perfect and sudden precepts), receiving the precepts is presented as the sole way of the immediate realization of Buddhahood. Here the precepts are contrasted with calming and contemplation *(shikan)*, which is relegated to the status of a gradual, and therefore lesser, teaching:

> The intent of calming and contemplation, etc. is that by encountering a good teacher or the scriptural rolls, one understands that one's own person is Buddha, and on the basis of this subtle understanding, one establishes subtle practice, awakens wisdom, and severs delusion, becoming a Buddha and attaining the Way. But the intent of the *kaike* [transmission] is that because receiving the precepts with faith is the realization of Buddhahood, one does not establish [the sequence of] understanding, practice, and realization.[156]

Such immanentalist interpretations might seem to suggest that since the precepts are inherent, there is no special need to observe them as specific rules of conduct, or that, having received them, no further practice would be necessary. And yet Ejin and Kōen explicitly upheld the ten major and forty-eight minor bodhisattva precepts.[157] While the very arduousness of *kaike* practice may have set these men apart from many of the monks of Mt. Hiei and thus made them nonrepresentative, their example suggests the danger of assuming that rhetoric of original enlightenment or of sudden realization implied a denial of the need for practice.

Yet another type of lineage to transmit ideas related to *hongaku* thought was that of the performers of *shōmyō*, or Buddhist vocal music. Originating in India, *shōmyō* in medieval Japan comprised several types, including hymns of praise for the Buddha in transliterated Sanskrit; hymns in Chinese, including both translations of Sanskrit and those newly composed in China; singing of *gāthās*, or verses from sūtras; sung forms of the *nembutsu*, such as the *inzei* or "prolonged voice" *nenbutsu* established on Mt. Wu-t'ai and introduced from China by Ennin in the ninth century; chanting of the names of the Buddhas, set to music and performed at religious ceremonies; and hymns of praise composed in Japanese *(wasan)*.[158] *Shōmyō* was performed during public Buddhist assemblies *(hōe)* and also during some secret Mikkyō initiation rites: Annen had specified that during the ceremony of initiation, certain melodies were to accompany the offering of incense, flowers, lights, and food offerings, respectively, and that these melodies were equivalent to secret mantras and mūdras.[159] Tendai *shōmyō* was systematized by Ryōnin (1072–1132), also known as the founder of the "all-pervading *nenbutsu*" or *yūzū nenbutsu* movement. Ryōnin studied both Sanskrit and Chinese, as well as esoteric and exoteric, forms of *shōmyō*. The Ōhara *bessho*, where he had retired while still in his 20s, became a center of *shōmyō* practice, and Ryōnin himself is regarded as the founder of the Ōhara lineage of *shōmyō*. *Shōmyō* lineages were also retrospectively created linking Ryōnin and his disciples to a line traceable to Ennin.[160] Ryōnin's Ōhara lineage soon divided into two, the Raigō-in and the Shōrin-in. Other *shōmyō* divisions formed among the later followers of Ryōnin, in the pattern of lineage branching common in this period.

Shōmyo is built around five basic tones, which early on were equated under Mikkyō influence with the five wisdom Buddhas, the five elements, the five directions, and so forth.[161] The doctrinal supports of *shōmyō* practice owe much to Kūkai's teaching that "voices and letters are precisely the true aspect" *(shōji soku jissō)* and to esoteric notions that all sounds—the human voice included—are the preaching of the Dharma body. In the late Heian and Kamakura periods, however, these ideas came to be understood in a very literal way: to believe in the five tones as the direct preaching of the five Buddhas was to realize Buddhahood in the chanting of *shōmyō (shōmyō jōbutsu);* the voice chanting the tones was itself to be revered as the Buddha's voice. Hazama Jikō has suggested that the development of a distinct doctrine surrounding *shōmyō* that equated it with the realization of Buddhahood reflects the influence of *hongaku* thought, which sees concrete phenomena as embodying true reality.[162]

Original enlightenment thought, in short, was not limited to transmissions concerning doctrine but informed those concerning the temples, icons, deities, and practices of Mt. Hiei; the bodhisattva precepts; and Buddhist vocal music. Virtually all forms of medieval Tendai secret transmissions were grounded in the assumption of original enlightenment. It was this, in fact, that lent them their potency as secret transmissions: In each case, the ultimate "secret" is that a particular set of forms, actions, or whatever the specific content of the transmission, is in itself the expression of innate enlightenment. The clear presence of *hongaku* ideas in transmissions associated with *kaihōgyō*, rites directed toward the *kami*, precept observance, and the chanting of hymns also raises serious questions about the claim that original enlightenment thought represents a theory divorced from practice.

"Exoteric" Initiation Rituals

Before considering the dynamics of secret transmission in specific lineages, one more element needs to be addressed: the distinctive initiation rituals *(kanjō,* Skt. *abhiṣeka)* developed within the various medieval Tendai lineages for the transfer of secret teachings from master to disciple. These are sometimes collectively termed "exoteric initiations" *(kengyō kanjō)* to distinguish them from the rites of initiation used in Taimitsu proper; however, many of the forms employed, as well as the notion of *kanjō* itself, clearly derive from Mikkyō. These rituals appear to have begun in the Kamakura period and developed rapidly after about 1300, in conjunction with a notable increase in the production of *kuden* literature.[163] They may have served as a control on transmission, that is, to check the possibility of careless dissemination and commercialization of *kuden.*[164] At the same time, they worked to support the authority of lineage and of the persons receiving them. Such rituals not only served to initiate disciples into teachings or practices informed by notions of original enlightenment, but frequently embodied *hongaku* ideas in their symbolism and structure.

The *Genshi Kanjō* and *Kimyōdan Kanjō*

Perhaps the earliest of these exoteric initiations was the *genshi kanjō* (or in some texts, *kanjō genshi*), a distinctive ritual of the Danna school.[165] *Genshi* here means "profound purport" or "profound essence" and refers to the essence of Chih-i's enlightenment said to have been transmitted in a direct line to Saichō. After the initiate had prepared through a week of purificatory disciplines, including sūtra chanting and *Lotus-*

based rites of repentance *(Hokke senpō)*, the ritual began at sundown on an auspicious day and was completed in a single night. It began outside the practice hall *(dōjō)* with the teacher's conveying to the disciple a number of *injin* or articles of transmission. While eventually these numbered fifteen, seventeen, or more, they at first seem to have consisted of five articles *(goka sōden)*, which remained central to later, more elaborate transmissions.[166] The first, the Tendai *kanjō genshi*, is said to represent Chih-i's teaching—with Saichō's commentary—on the threefold contemplation in a single mind, that was transmitted to Saichō by Tao-sui "in a single phrase."[167] It is also called the "transmission of the stone stūpa," based on the tradition that Chih-i made two copies of this document: one he gave to his disciple Kuan-ting, and the other, at Chih-i's request, was interred with his remains in a stone stūpa. Kuan-ting's copy was handed down through the T'ien-t'ai lineage to Tao-sui, who, finding no one worthy to receive it, committed it, too, to the stone stūpa. On Saichō's arrival, Tao-sui realized the Japanese monk's ability and retrieved the transmission to pass on to him.[168] The second transmission, the "transmission of three phrases" *(sanku kuketsu)*, concerns three phrases comprising the name and title by which Saichō designates the Buddha of the *Lotus Sūtra*: "[Lord of] the Land of Ever-Tranquil Light, the truth that is the cardinal meaning" *(jō jakkōdo daiichigi tai)*, "[the Buddha of] the Pure Land of Eagle Peak, who realized enlightenment in the remote past *(ryōzen jōdo kuon jitsujō)*, and "Lord Śākyamuni within the stūpa of [the Buddha] Many Jewels" *(tahō tatchū Ōmuni seson)*.[169] In the transmission, these three phrases are said to express the meaning of the teaching conveyed to Saichō by Tao-sui and are respectively correlated with the three truths of the middle, emptiness, and conventional existence and the three "bodies" of the Buddha: the Dharma body (Jpn. *hosshin, dharma-kāya*), the truth realized by the Buddha, conceived as a body; the recompense body *(hōjin, saṃbhoga-kāya)*, or the wisdom achieved by the Buddha through practice, also conceived as a body; and the manifested body *(ōjin, nirmāṇa-kāya)*, the physical body with which the Buddha appears in the world. The three bodies of the Buddha represent an important concept in medieval *kuden* literature and were considered as inseparably related to the threefold contemplation in a single mind: where the "threefold contemplation" represents "cause" or practice for realizing the three truths, the threefold body of the Buddha represents the enlightenment achieved as the fruit or "effect" of that realization. The third and fourth transmissions, called "the transmission of the threefold contemplation in a single mind" *(isshin sangan den)* and "the record of the threefold contemplation in a single mind" *(isshin sangan ki)*, were said to be teachings on the threefold contemplation composed by Ryōgen and Kakuun, respectively. The fifth and last transmission is the "oral decisions concerning the perfect interfusion of the mirror and its images" *(kyōzō en'yū kuketsu)*, which, as mentioned above, is an analogy for the perfect interfusion of the three truths. Transmission of these five articles is attested from the latter part of the thirteenth century, specifically from the time of the monk Kyōyū (c. 1257–1289) and his teacher Jōsen of the Ekō-bō lineage of the Danna school.[170] Having received these articles, the disciple pronounces a vow to uphold the teaching transmitted in the ritual and calls down upon himself the punishment of the patriarchs who have handed down the transmission and the deities who protect it, should he violate his oath.

Master and disciple then enter the *dōjō*, where a series of icons are enshrined. At some point, the deity Matarajin was adopted as the main object of worship *(honzon)* of the ritual.[171] Matarajin was said to protect the practice of the "constantly walking samādhi" *(jōgyō zanmai)* and the halls *(jōgyōdō)* where it was practiced.[172] Possibly because Amida is the object of worship of the constantly walking samādhi, Matarajin came to be viewed as a manifestation of Amida. In the *genshi kanjō* ritual, he is often depicted, below the seven stars of the big dipper, with a drum and flanked by two dancing boys holding, respectively, shoots of ginger and bamboo. The symbolism of these and other icons employed in the ritual was elaborated endlessly in terms of Tendai doctrine. For example, the Matarajin triad was said to represent the three truths, or the oneness of the three truths and the three poisons of greed, hatred and folly, thus demonstrating the ultimate nonduality of the Buddha's original enlightenment and the ordinary deluded state. The bamboo and ginger stalks held by Matarajin's attendants—as well as actual bamboo and ginger used as offerings during the ritual—were said to represent sharp and dull faculties, as well as the object of meditation *(kyō)* and the wisdom to realize it *(chi)*; alternatively, ginger—thought to produce dullness in those who ate it—was said to represent the nature of the three poisons; or the bamboo's hollowness, to represent emptiness; its constant greenness, the middle; its joints, conventional existence; and so forth.[173] As time passed, the iconography and actions of the ritual grew increasingly complex. Banners were hung in the eight directions and a number of subsidiary *honzon* were enshrined, including the Buddhas Śākyamuni and Many Jewels; the bodhisattvas Monju (Mañjuśrī), Fugen (Samantabhadra) and Kannon (Avalokiteśvara); representations of the Sannō shrines; portraits of the great T'ien-t'ai/Tendai patriarchs; and calligraphic representations of the twelve-link chain of dependent origination and the ten realms of existence. Master and disciple circumambulate the hall, the master preceding in order to illustrate the principle of proceeding from "cause" or practice to "effect" or enlightenment *(jūin shika)*. Before the *honzon*, both perform bows and recite appropriate formulas. In some versions of the ritual, the master poses Zen-style *kōan* to the initiate. Central to the proceedings is his explanation of the secret meanings of the initiation, including the signficance of the Matarajin triad interpreted in terms of the three truths. After the two leave and reenter the hall, the disciple is instructed in a secret mūdra said to have been transmitted from Chih-i. The master now bows three times to the disciple, expressing the principle of "preceding from effect to cause" (*jūka kōin*), reveals to him the meaning of the secret transmissions, and confers on him a certificate of initiation. Eventually, the *genshi kanjō* was combined with another, later Danna ritual, the *kimyōdan kanjō*, to form the still more complex *genshi kimyōdan kanjō*.[174]

The *kimyōdan kanjō* takes place in three phases. The initial phase, conducted outside the *dōjō*, marks the transition from the *genshi* to *kimyōdan kanjō*; again offerings are made to Matarajin. In the second phase, however, which occurs inside the *dōjō*, the object of worship is Amida. Two mirrors are placed above the altar, and offerings of rice cakes and fruit are arranged in groups of three threes, representing the nine grades of birth in the Pure Land. Again, *kōan* are posed and secret teachings are conferred.

"This initiation," says one text, "is truly the ultimate for arriving at the sole great matter of birth and death and returning to the original source of the one mind."[175] This "return to the original source" is understood as realizing the threefold contemplation in a single mind and manifesting oneself as the triple-bodied Tathâgata of original enlightenment. In this second phase of the ritual, the initiate is led blindfolded into the *dōjō* and made to sit before the altar. He is instructed to contemplate his breath as Amida:

> On entering the place of practice, [the initate] should be taught that the breath inhaled through the nose and mouth is Amida's coming to welcome the devotee (*raigō*), and the exhaled [breath], the going to the Pure Land (*ōjō*). He should think that the breath exhaled and inhaled through the nostrils is [Amida's attendant bodhisattvas,] Kannon and Seishi; the breath exhaled and inhaled through the mouth is the Tathâgata Amida. When he grasps this, then at each moment, he is welcomed by the Buddha, and, at each moment, goes to the Pure Land.[176]

The initiate is then given a *kōan* about the "threefold contemplation of the unattainable object" (*fushikyō no isshin sangan*). If he cannot answer, he is instructed that this refers to the Pure Land lying many world spheres away to the West. Then he is asked about the "threefold contemplation of the attainable object" (*shikyō no isshin sangan*). At this point, the blindfold is removed, and he is instructed that the "threefold contemplation of the attainable object" is the identity of Amida and the practitioner, manifested in the ritual now being conducted before Amida's image; the Pure Land is right here. The identification of Amida with the breath links the *kimyōdan* ritual to broader streams of esoteric *nenbutsu* thought and practice interpreting Amida as the breath of life, which had developed earlier in medieval Tendai, Shingon, and Pure Land lineages.[177] In the final part of this phase, the two mirrors are taken up to illustrate for the initiate the fusion of the true aspect of reality as object of contemplation *(kyō)* with the wisdom to understand it *(chi),* an act drawing on the tradition of "the perfect interfusion of the mirror and its images" central to many medieval Tendai *kuden.*

The *kimyōdan* or final phase, conducted outside the *dōjō,* is a dawn ritual begun once the morning star has appeared. A large mirror is placed on a round altar. The master stands on the altar's west side facing east, and the initiate, on the south side facing north. After conferring secret transmissions, he takes up the mirror to reflect the seven stars of the big dipper and then has the disciple do likewise. According to some *kimyōdan* texts, the spirits of seven stars were thought to descend and animate the union of male and female sexual fluids at conception, and return to the heavens at the time of the individual's death.[178] This represents an assimilation to the *kimyōdan* initiation of the cult of the seven stars, as well as an appropriation of popular Taoist elements to express the ideas of "arriving at the sole great matter of birth and death" and "returning to the ultimate source of the one mind."[179]

The *genshi* and *kimyōdan* initiation rituals were conducted sequentially and linked through the grammar of paired doctrinal concepts. They take as their respective *honzon* the local manifestation as *kami* (Matarajin) and the Buddha who is its original ground (Amida). They were also regarded as embodying, respectively, the two aspects of "cause" or practice (i.e., the threefold contemplation) and "effect" or realization (the reality of the triple-bodied Tathâgata that is thereby manifested).[180]

In time, the *genshi kimyōdan kanjō* came to be associated with tantric sexual elements, and it is often described today as a Tendai equivalent of the practices of the so-called Tachikawa school of Shingon.[181] The *kimyōdan* component in particular was intepreted in left-handed tantric terms; the "original source of life" associated with the seven stars was identified with the male and female sexual fluids, and the inhaling and exhaling of the breath-as-Amida, with the rhythm of sexual intercourse. In addition, the *honzon* formed by the Matarajin triad was understood to represent the three poisons and the dance of saṃsāra; Matarajin's two attendants also came to be associated with sexual desire and "the dance of male and female." Reikū, a leader of the the Anraku *vinaya* revival movement that rose to prominence on Mt. Hiei during the Edo period, denounced the *genshi kimyōdan kanjō* in his 1689 work *Byakuja hen* (or *Hekija hen*) as a corrupt ritual transmitted by licentious and dissolute monks. Reikū's opposition put an end to performance of the ritual. Probably because of his criticism, the *genshi kimyōdan kanjō* has since the modern period acquired the reputation of a decadent rite performed for the fulfillment of worldly desires. Over and against this view, Hazama Jikō has argued that this ritual stands squarely within the traditional Tendai synthesis of exoteric teachings, esoteric teachings, Zen, and precepts, and deserves attention in particular for its place in Tendai Pure Land thought and practice.[182] Its significance to our purpose here, especially in its early form as *genshi kanjō*, is as a prominent example of the "exoteric initiations" that mediated the transmission of secret teachings in medieval Tendai *kuden* lineages.

The *Kai Kanjō*

Another important exoteric initiation ritual, also associated with the Danna school, is the *kanjō jukai* of the Kurodani *kaike* lineage, a ritual said to transmit the ultimate secret meaning of the perfect precepts. It eventually came to be called *kai kanjō* or *jūjukai kanjō*, indicating that the initiation *(kanjō)* was performed as a separate "level" *(jū)* over and above the conferring of the precepts. Scholars now generally agree that it existed from the time of Ejin, regarded as the *kaike* founder, although whether or not Ejin initiated it remains unclear.[183] Kōen's biography records that he received this *kanjō* in 1307 from his teacher Egi, Ejin's disciple.[184] In 1316, the year before his death, Kōen compiled the *Enkai jūroku chō* (Sixteen articles on the perfect precepts), the first written description of the ritual.[185] Kōen's disciple Echin (or Enkan) had two prominent disciples, Kōsō—who also figures in the Kajii *kike* lineage—and Iken. With these two, transmission of the *kai kanjō* branched into two, Kōsō's Gannōji line and Iken's Hosshōji line. The Gannōji transmission eventually died out, but *kai kanjō* is still conducted today at the Saikyōji in Ōtsu, head temple of the Shinsei branch of Tendai, which has incorporated the Hosshōji transmission.[186]

Like the *genshi kanjō* transmissions with their associated tradition of the "stone stūpa transmission," the *kai kanjō* developed an origin myth for its *kuden*. *Kaike* texts tell how, when Saichō first ascended Mt. Hiei, he was approached by Brahmā and Indra in human form. These deities presented him, respectively, with a box and an eight-pronged key. The box contained a document related to the essence of the perfect precepts. Determined to transmit them, Saichō went to China and was instructed by Tao-sui in the bodhisattva precepts.[187]

The *kai kanjō* consists of three parts: conferral of the precepts, of *kanjō*, and of secret teachings. According to Kōen's *Enkai jūroku chō*, the first part is conducted according to the ordinary procedures for conferring the precepts. The second and third parts of the ritual, however, are conducted "according to the order of the Dharma auditing on Sacred [Eagle] Peak." The second part (*denju dan*, literally "platform of transmission") corresponds to the trace teaching and to the perspective of acquired enlightenment. The master occupies a raised seat and the disciple a lower one, reflecting the logic of the *shikaku* view that one "precedes from cause [practice] to arrive at effect [enlightenment]" *(jūin shika)* and that "cause is shallow and effect, profound" *(inga senjin)*. However, the third part of the *kai kanjō*—the *shōkaku dan* or "platform of right enlightenment"—corresponds to the origin teaching and to original enlightenment. Here master and disciple share the same seat and are of equal status, like the two Buddhas Śākyamuni and Many Jewels in the jeweled stūpa.[188] Kōen explains that the transmission of the jeweled stūpa does not, in the *kaike* reading, have the meaning of a sequential line of transmission, as from Śākyamuni to Kāśyapa, and so on. In accordance with the teaching that "the assembly on Sacred [Eagle] Peak is solemnly present and has not yet dispersed," in the context of the *kai kanjō*, master and disciple are manifested as the Buddhas Śākyamuni and Many Jewels, and the mythic time when the *Lotus Sūtra* was expounded is re-created in the present moment.[189] A similar understanding appears to underlie the *kanjō* rituals of other medieval Tendai *kuden* lineages as well. It is almost certainly connected to esoteric ideas about realizing union with the cosmic Buddha in the act of ritual practice, and it is also related to the nonlinear, nonsequential nature of *hongaku* ideas.

"In the precept lineage [*kaike*]," Kōen writes, "the profound ultimate is transferred by means of concrete ritual forms *(jisō)*."[190] The most distinctive ritual form of the *kai kanjō* is its elaborations of the mūdra of the palms placed together *(gasshō)*. This mūdra, says Kōen, was performed by Śākyamuni and Many Jewels in the jeweled stūpa and represents the fusion of the object of contemplation and the wisdom that realizes it *(kyōchi myōgō)*, as well as the supramundane truth and the worldly truth being a single suchness *(shinzoku ichinyo)*. Cause and effect, dependent and primary recompense, the single thought-moment and the three thousand realms, yin and yang—all dharmas are encompassed in the gesture of *gasshō*, which is called the "mūdra of the true aspect" *(jissō no in)*.[191] The *Enkai jūroku chō* elaborates three kinds of *gasshō* corresponding to the "three kinds of *Lotus Sūtra*," the classification of the Buddha's teachings employed by Saichō to subsume them within the One Vehicle.[192] Later forms of *kai kanjō* develop more complex variations of the *gasshō* mūdra with more elaborate doctrinal significations.[193] Another ritual form employed in *kai kanjō*, as in other medieval Tendai *kanjō*, was mirrors, used to convey the perfect interfusion of the three truths. *Kai kanjō* specifically required a round mirror, representing the *Lotus Sūtra*, and an octagonal mirror, representing the *Fan-wang ching*, regarded as the primary and secondary textual bases for the bodhisattva precepts. Other significations of the mirrors were also elaborated, for example: "The round mirror is the mirror of the Wonderful Dharma *(myōhō)*. The octagonal mirror is the mirror of the lotus blossom *(renge)*. Their fusion is the word 'sūtra' *(kyō)*. The title [of the *Lotus Sūtra, Myōhō-renge-kyō*] is understood as the threefold contemplation in a single mind. This is also the threefold contemplation of the secret store of the precept lineage."[194]

In his discussion of the *kai kanjō* ritual, Shikii Shūjō suggests that it is informed by ideas of the phenomenal as embodying ultimate reality *(sokuji nishin)*, which is characteristic of *hongaku* thought. The precept essence—the Buddha nature or true aspect of the dharmas—is grasped not through discursive explanation, but through the concrete forms and gestures of the ritual.[195] Thus these forms are not "merely" symbolic but are seen as embodying or identified with the realities they represent. Shikii's observations hold true for other medieval Tendai initiation rituals as well. The notion of "transmission through concrete forms" is grounded in Mikkyō and also in *hongaku* notions that there is no true reality apart from the concrete phenomena of this world.

Other Initiation Rituals

A number of additional exoteric *kanjō* have been identified. Chroniclers *(kike)* conducted the *wakō dojin kanjō* (initiation [into the transmission concerning the deities who] dim their light and mingle with the dust of the world), an initiation into the secrets of the cult of Sannō Shinto.[196] There was also the *Tendai Eshin-ryū gojū sōden kanjō* (initiation into the fivefold transmission of the Tendai Eshin school), "Eshin-ryū" here referring not the medieval Eshin *kuden* lineage but to the stream of Tendai Pure Land thought deriving from Genshin. The transmissions conferred in this *kanjō* unite the perfect precepts, Tendai-*Lotus* teachings, and esoteric *nenbutsu*, while the ritual itself shares elements with the *genshi kimyōdan kanjō* and *kai kanjō*.[197] While the *kanjō* mentioned thus far were for the most part associated with the Danna school, Eshin lineages developed similar initiation rituals. These included the "ritual of the jeweled stūpa" *(hōtō gyōhōshiki)* and the "ritual of realizing Buddhahood in this very body" *(sokushin jōbutsu gyōhōshiki)*.[198] Eshin rituals, however, have yet to be studied in detail.

All these initiation rituals served to reinforce the authority of lineage, emphasize secrecy, and act as a control on transmission. They were also part of a larger context, in the development during the medieval period of esoteric-style initation rituals in *waka*, music, calligraphy, and other forms of learning and the arts. Here, it is of significance to note that, in light of their underlying logic that ultimate reality is embodied in concrete ritual forms *(jisō)*, they amounted to performances of the nonduality of the Buddha and the beings which is the major premise of *hongaku* thought. That is to say, ideas of original enlightenment were not only transmitted through these initiation rites but embodied in their structure, iconography, and ritual gestures.

The Politics of Secret Transmission

This section will examine the dynamics of ritualized secret transmission
and how it served to establish and preserve the authority of lineage. It
will consider the competing ways in which lineage was defined within
the aristocratic Tendai lineages of the capital, and the challenge to that
authority mounted by Tendai monks of the eastern Kantō provinces,
which began to emerge around the mid- to late Kamakura period as a
very differently constituted and rival locus of medieval Tendai activity.

Since it is often around the cracks and stress points that strategies of
legitimation become most apparent, it will be useful to begin by considering three differing accounts of a lawsuit in the late Kamakura period between the supporters of two rival claimants to the succession of
a Tendai lineage. Since these accounts were not compiled until the Muromachi period, well after the events they purport to describe, their historical accuracy is problematic at best. They are, however, nonetheless
illuminating in that they suggest the various strategies by which the authority constituted by secret transmission was defined.

The story begins in the latter thirteenth century with Awataguchi
Jōmyō, a son of the noble Fujiwara no Sukeyoshi and the current patriarch of the Sugiu lineage, regarded as the main line of the Tendai Eshin school. Jōmyō was fourth in a Dharma lineage that had passed from
father to son. The Sugiu line begins with Kōkaku, regarded as the
founder of the lineage and a disciple of the forty-sixth *zasu* of the Enryakuji, Chūjin (1065–1138). From Kōkaku the line of transmission
passed to his son Hangen, to Hangen's son Shunpan, and to Shunpan's
son Jōmyō. Jōmyō is considered the founder of a new lineage, the Gyōsen-
bō, which passed from him to his son-in-law Shinga and then continued
from father to son down to Shinga's great-grandson Shin'yū.[199] According to the *Nijō shō kenmon* of Sonshun, compiled in 1501, Jōmyō's only
grown child was a daughter, so he took the monk Shinga as his son-in-
law and transmitted the line to him. However, Jōmyō did have a very
young son, Jōhan. Jōmyō appointed the monk Isen to be Jōhan's guardian, and on his deathbed gave him a transfer document for Jōhan,
though the boy was only seven at the time. This led to a dispute between
the supporters of Shinga and of Jōhan over who was Jōmyō's legitimate
successor. Eventually the case was submitted to court. Jōhan's guardian
Isen is said to have pressed his claim as follows:

> The lineage of this school has for generations been transmitted con-
> tinuously from father to son. We understand the transmission of lin-
> eage (*kechimyaku sōjō*) to mean transmission that follows the bloodline.
> Thus, if not to one's own flesh and bone, there should be no trans-
> mission. Jōhan was Jōmyō's true son. Because he was his most beloved

true son, day and night he followed [Jōmyō], who conferred upon him the secret doctrines. Although he is young, the transmission of the perfect and sudden teaching should not depend on the length of time [the recipient has spent in study].[200]

Shinga's advocate, his disciple Shinsō, countered that the essentials of the Tendai school required sustained effort to master and could not be acquired in a short time; moreover, the Dharma transmission is conferred from mind to mind *(ishin denshin)* and depends on the disciple having achieved an enlightenment equal to his teacher's. This argument was accepted, and in addition, Shinga was able to produce a document of succession *(kechimyaku)* that Jōhan's side did not have.[201] The verdict named Shinga the legitimate successor. Jōhan ultimately found it hard to remain in the vicinity of the capital and ended up as the head of instruction *(gakutō)* at a temple in Bizen Province.

This version of the dispute—Sonshun's *Nijō shō kenmon*—depicts the controversy as chiefly a conflict between two ways of defining the criterion of legitimate Dharma succession: blood lineage versus enlightened understanding. The adopted Shinga himself went on to initiate a new line of father-to-son transmission—the Gyōsen-bō lineage—that continued down to his great grandson, Shin'yū. This account was compiled by his successors. Thus, while it appears to be critical of father-to-son transmission, it can also be read as a retrospective attempt at self-legitimation on the part of Shinga's lineage, which lacked the claim to Jōmyō's bloodline, over and against that of Jōhan, which possessed it.[202]

"Transmission to one's own son" *(jisshi sōzoku)* was by no means uncommon, blood sons being indicated by the term "true disciple" *(shin-tei* or *shin deshi)* in lineage charts.[203] Shinran has sometimes been celebrated as the first Japanese Buddhist monk to take a wife openly, but de facto clerical marriage is attested since the Nara period and was widespread by the late Heian: "Those who hide it are saints; those who don't do it are Buddhas," the retired emperor Goshirakawa is said to have remarked.[204] For monks to marry or amass property was a violation of the Ritsuryō code, yet the right of their wives and children to inherit had been legally recognized since the ninth century, suggesting that the practice was far from uncommon.[205] By the latter Heian period, such practices were being assimilated to the institution of the master-disciple lineage. Early examples of father-to-son transfer of temple administrative positions can be found by the late eleventh and twelfth centuries, becoming established custom by the mid-Kamakura period.[206] *Jisshi sōzoku* was also practiced among lineages of scholar monks, such as those of the Eshin and Danna schools, as the above example of the Sugiu lineage indicates.

Dharma transmission within the bloodline depended on a second type of clerical establishment that grew up on the periphery of temple-shrine complexes. Mt. Hiei and other religious institutions of its kind were strictly gendered space, ringed by sacred boundaries *(kekkai)* that women were not allowed to pass. However, clerics came to maintain wives and families in the numerous *sato-bō* located below the mountain in the gate town of Sakamoto or in the capital. The unofficial though doubtless critical role of women in maintaining these clerical "houses" has only begun to be investigated.[207]

Within clerical lineages practicing *jisshi sōzoku*, the dual relationships of master and disciple, and father and son, seem to have enhanced one another's authority, and it is sometimes difficult to say which was deemed fundamental. Kuroda Toshio, pointing to the medieval usage of the term "true disciple" *(shintei)* to designate Dharma heirs who were biological sons, suggests that the master-disciple relationship remained the organizing principle within such lines.[208] On the other hand, Nishiguchi Junko has called attention to lineages, such as that of the Agui school of *shōdō* preaching, which were represented as a long line of father-to-son blood transmission but actually included the occasional adopted son, nephew, or other anomaly.[209] That they were nonetheless represented as pure *jisshi sōzoku* lineages suggests that the father-son relation was seen as carrying authority, even in a monastic context.

"Transmission to one's own son" has sometimes been cited as indicative of the "corruption" in medieval Tendai encouraged by "world-affirming" *hongaku* thought. Undeniably, it represents a departure from the monastic ideal, but that ideal had long since been compromised by a number of factors unrelated to *hongaku* doctrine, including the unforeseen consequences of Saichō's use of the bodhisattva precepts for ordination; esoteric interpretations of the precepts that stressed the primacy of an underlying Mahāyāna spirit and deemphasized the importance of specific rules of conduct; and modifications of clerical life to accommodate the nobility, who took orders in increasing numbers. By the Insei period, monastic norms were being further undermined by rhetoric about the impossibility of keeping precepts in the Final Dharma age *(mappō)* as well as corollary claims about the possibility of salvation for "evil men" *(akunin)*. However, the major factor in the development of father-to-son transmission was doubtlessly the monopolization of high clerical offices by the sons of noble families discussed above. Even where father-son transmission was not involved, master and disciple were frequently blood relatives, as young sons of the aristocracy destined for the clergy were often ordained and educated under the guidance of monks from the same family. Thus clerical ranks, temples, and the estates attached to them could be kept within the family. The institution of *jisshi sōzoku* was due less to the influence of world-affirming *hongaku* thought than to the extension into the clerical world of the kind of family-based privatization of authority that characterized the early medieval period.

A second, variant account of the dispute over the succession to the Sugiu lineage occurs in a source external to the Tendai school, in a document of the Fuji lineage of the Nichiren Hokkeshū, recording the oral teachings of Nichiu (1409–1482), ninth abbot of the main Fuji temple, the Taisekiji, and probably dates from slightly earlier than the *Nijō shō kenmon*. According to this account, Jōhan was Jōmyō's nephew, rather than his son, so the issue of father-to-son transmission does not arise; the dispute is presented with a different emphasis. In this version, Jōhan's advocate argued the legitimacy of his succession on the grounds that Jōhan had received a transfer document from Jōmyō while Shinga had not. Shinga's representative countered that the essence of the Tendai transmission is mind to mind and not based on what is committed to writing. This argument silenced Jōhan's representative, and the decision was made in favor of Shinga. This account, however, sharply criticizes the verdict for setting aside the evidence of the transfer document. Jōhan's advocate *should* have argued that Jōhan had received both the mind-to-mind transmission *and* the transfer document, which Shinga had not. Thus, says the text, Shinga stole the succession of the Buddha-Dharma, and the legitimate Tendai lineage was cut off.[210]

This version seems to suggest that master-disciple transmission is to be legitimized in quasi-legalistic terms: insight shared with the master is essential, but possession of a transfer document is not to be dismissed. However, the defining of master-disciple transmission in terms of legalistic documents also carried the potential for abuse, as becomes clear in what may be yet a third version of these events. This account, which occurs in the *Isshin sangan kanjin sūken* (Investigation into the pivotal points of the threefold contemplation and the contemplation of the mind) and is probably considerably earlier than the other two, purports to describe events that occurred in the late Kamakura period in the Bishamondō lineage of the Tendai Danna school.[211] According to this text, on his deathbed the master Kyōkai (b. 1207) promised to make his disciple Kanryū his successor. However, because Kanryū was still a child, Kyōkai appointed Isen as his guardian in religious matters (*shintai*), and Jitsugen (or Jisshin), in those concerning worldly affairs (*zokutai*). However, Kanryū died shortly thereafter, and Jitsugen stole the transfer document that had been given to him, posing successfully as the true successor. On the other hand, Isen, who possessed the deeper understanding, lacked such a document; thus people said that he had never received Kyōkai's transmission, and eventually he had to leave for the provinces.

This account at first appears unrelated to the other two, involving people with different names and occurring in a different, rival lineage. However, all three versions concern succession disputes triggered by prob-

lems arising from transmission to a disciple not yet of age, and the first
and third versions, in the *Nijō shō kenmon* and the *Isshin sangan kanjin
sūken,* involve a guardian named Isen. Ōkubō Ryōjun, who has analyzed
these two accounts in detail, finds reason to question the accuracy of
both: the historical Jōhan does not appear to have ended his life in Bizen
Province, and the historical Kanryū did not die young. Ōkubō points
out, however, that both accounts similarly appropriate Isen, who appears
to have been a formidable Tendai scholar of his time with both Eshin
and Danna connections.[212]

For purposes of this study, the value of such accounts lies not in their
factual accuracy, but in what they reveal about various strategies for legitimizing succession in medieval Tendai lineages and the potential problems these strategies entailed. A disciple's understanding—an enlightenment shared with his teacher—was clearly considered important, but
insufficient in itself. One imagines that, used as a sole criterion, it could
open the door to false or inflated claims of personal insight and prove
especially dangerous in a context where teachings were supposed to be
transmitted orally and in secret. Hence the need for additional, externally verifiable criteria, such as the possession of legalistic transfer documents or the fact of being one's teacher's blood son. It would be a mis-
take, however, to regard these as "mere" external forms subordinate to
inner understanding. Transmissions were understood not only in terms
of the disciple's mastery of a body of knowledge, but as conferring the
same kind of magical empowerment as esoteric initiation. Thus, com-
pliance with conventions of succession, such as the issuing of a transfer
document, was—like adherence to the proper forms of an initiation
ritual—deemed essential for authentic Dharma transmission to take
place. At the same time, there was awareness that relying only on these
externally verifiable criteria without regard for a disciple's insight was
also open to abuse: a biological son might be incapable, and a transfer
document could have been forged or stolen.

However defined—whether by blood succession, possession of transfer documents, or mind-to-mind transmission—the authority of master-
disciple lineages was maintained by exclusion. We see this in the elaborate conventions of secrecy that surrounded these transmissions, binding
both conferer and recipient. Many oral transmission texts warn in the
most fearsome terms against careless disclosure of their contents. The
Juketsu entaragishū tōketsu, an early collection of transmissions attributed
to Ennin, which Hōchi-bō Shōshin criticized as apocryphal, admonishes
that it is never to be passed on to unqualified persons, "not even for a
thousand in gold."[213] The *Sanjū shika no kotogaki,* an important *kirikami*
collection, reads, "Even if it should cost your life, do not confer this [in-
appropriately]. . . . If there is no one qualified to receive it, this transmission should be buried in the depths of a wall."[214] As the tradition devel-

oped, it appears that those initiated into a particular lineage sometimes signed pledges or contracts binding them to secrecy.[215] In a pledge inscribed in 1285, the monk Endon-bō Songai (1253–1332) from a Kantō branch of the Eshin school, of whom more will be said below, vows not to share the transmission he has received with more than one chosen disciple and calls upon the Three Jewels and all deities of heaven and earth to visit punishment upon him should he break his oath.[216] A much later, Edo period text (1650), a surviving contract of the Ekō-bō lineage of the Danna school, similarly binds the recipient of a text setting forth the secret protocols of the *genshi* initiation ritual. He is not to depart from the way of master and disciple in this life or the next. He must not pass on the transmission to an unqualified disciple. He is not to use the doctrine of his own lineage to supplement that of another; even if he receives the transmission of another lineage, he is never to regard it as primary and his own as subordinate. Should he arouse insurmountable doubts about the teaching of his own lineage, he is to return the text and never speak of the doctrines of the lineage. Should he have no qualified disciples, he is to return the text, and should this be impossible, he is to burn it. Moreover, he must ensure that any disciple to whom he transmits the teachings must agree to the same conditions. Lastly, he invokes upon himself the wrath of the Sannō deity should the contract be violated.[217]

It is worth noting in this context that the major writings of Hōnen and Nichiren also warn that their content is to be kept secret. Hōnen's *Senchaku hongan nenbutsu shū* (Collection [of passages] on the *nenbutsu* chosen exclusively in the Original Vow) concludes: "I beg that after reading [this work], you will bury it in the depths of a wall and not leave it [exposed] before a window. This is so that people who slander the Dharma will not fall into the evil paths."[218] Nichiren's cover letter to his *Kanjin honzon shō* (On the contemplation of the mind and the object of worship) admonishes the recipient: "Keep this secret. Perhaps you may show it to someone of unsurpassed resolve. . . . But even if you show it to others, three or four persons should not sit and read it together."[219] Such warnings serve to suggest that the works they accompany are radical and profound; probably they were also intended to guard against both misunderstanding on the part of immature followers and persecution from a religious establishment that would likely regard the writings in question as heterodox. At the same time, however, it is possible that such admonitions also reflect the medieval Tendai convention of secret transmission, to which both Hōnen and Nichiren would have been exposed during their training on Mt. Hiei.

Corollary to such conventions of secrecy was the rhetoric of "transmission to a single person" *(yuiju ichinin)*, the master's private initiation of a chosen disciple in which others were not permitted to participate.

Sonshun's *Nijō shō kenmon* reads, "Since the master of Mt. Hiei [Saichō] first received this transmission in another country, it has been handed down only to one person [in sequence]. Others are not permitted to listen together. This is because it is patterned after what the esoteric teachings call the conferring of initiation."[220] Dharma transmission was often depicted as a body of secret teachings passed in a single line from one person to another and never revealed to outsiders. In reality, however, the picture was far more complex. An individual monk might receive transmissions from more than one lineage, and a master might confer secret teachings upon more than one disciple. The situation is illuminated by a distinction that Kamikawa Michio has drawn between *inge,* or master-disciple lineages confined to a particular cloister *(in),* which involved the transmission of the cloister's incumbency, including its wealth and property, and were indeed transmissions to a single person; and *monryū,* or master-disciple lineages transmitting secret teachings on ritual or doctrine, such as the lineages of Taimitsu *shuhō,* or the Eshin and Danna schools and their sublineages. A *monryū* lineage, while sometimes based at a particular cloister, was not confined to it and could include disciples from other cloisters within the temple complex, or even from other temples.[221] As seen by the examples of men like Kōsō or Gigen, who had affiliations to the Danna school, the Kajii *kike* lineage and the Kurodani *kaike* lineage, one individual could receive transmissions from more than one *monryū.* Thus, despite rhetoric of maintaining secrecy within lineages, inevitably, elements from the transmissions of one lineage were incorporated into those of another. For example, Ōkubo Ryōjun has uncovered ample evidence of such exchange between Eshin and Danna lineages in matters of both doctrine and ritual; certain individuals received transmissions from both schools, and a number of *kuden* texts contain both Eshin and Danna transmissions. This tendency toward "mixed transmission," Ōkubo says, increased from the fourteenth century on.[222]

While the ideal of "transmission to a single person" was not always implemented in practice, such rhetoric itself was part of a larger pattern of defining lineage and transmission in exclusive terms. Secret teachings, Mikkyō-esque initiation rituals, and one-to-one or even father-to-son transmission all served to contain *kuden* and the authority they carried within the closed nexus of noble lineages. Was this system in any way vulnerable to penetration or usurpation by outsiders?

Here one should note the warnings in transmission texts that they are not to be passed on inappropriately, "not even for a thousand in gold." It is rare to find prohibitions against nonexistent conduct, and in fact there is evidence that master-disciple transmissions sometimes involved some form of financial transaction. Hazama Jikō has linked such transactions to the conventions observed in Mikkyō initiation rituals, where the recipient was often expected to defray the cost of erecting the altar and conducting the rite.[223] Such transactions were open to various interpretations. The *Keiran shūyō shū* defends them as offerings made for the Dharma's sake. Saichō himself is represented as having established a precedent by offering a hundred *ryō* of gold to the Kuo-ch'ing-ssu in China, in exchange for the transmission of T'ien-t'ai texts. The *Keiran shūyō shū* likens such donations to the dragon girl offering the Buddha a priceless gem or Hui-k'o presenting his severed arm to Bodhidharma; Dharma transmissions are to be "purchased according to one's ability."[224] Less charitable readings represent these transactions as a sort of crude commercialism. For example, the *Risshōkan jō* attributed to Nichiren criticizes Tendai monks who "produce some writing at their whim and put it in a brocade bag and hang it around their necks, or bury it in the bottom of a box and sell it for a high price. In this way, false doctrines have spread throughout the country, and the Buddha-Dharma of Tendai has been destroyed."[225] This passage has often been quoted by modern scholars to bolster a view of the new Kamakura Buddhist leaders as reformers reacting against the "corruption" of medieval Tendai institutions. Nichiren, a strong critic of the Tendai institutions of his day (or one of his disciples, if the *Risshōkan jō* is apocryphal), may not have been the most disinterested of observers, but commercialization of *kuden* may well have occurred to some extent.

In most cases, however, financial transactions accompanying transmission were probably pragmatic arrangements occupying some middle ground between the extremes of selfless Dharma offerings and crass "buying and selling." Initiates staying at a teacher's cloister or lodging temple needed to pay their keep, and ritual performance in general could be a major source of temple income. Yet, however construed, the transfer of wealth at the time of transmission represented a potential weak link in the ritually controlled system of closed aristocratic lineages. Here let us consider three accounts of wealth changing hands on such occasions that suggest this argument. Here again, the accounts are after the fact; their value lies not in the historical accuracy of their details but in what they suggest about the exclusive system of secret transmission.

The first, from a Kamakura collection of the Tendai Danna school, tells of a monk from Hitachi in the eastern part of Japan who came up to Mt. Hiei seeking the transmission of secret teachings concerning a particular *sandai,* a topic for examination or debate. The *kōgaku ryūgi* or debate-style "examinations on broad learning" were important avenues of clerical advancement and in theory open to any Tendai monk; in practice, however, from the Insei period, it had become increasingly difficult for those outside the noble lineages of the capital to acquire the knowledge and experience needed to participate.[226] The monk from Hitachi "went once [to Mt. Hiei] and even twice, but was not permitted [to receive the transmission]. The third time, he was felt to be a person of profundity and it was entrusted to him. At that time, this monk presented many treasures, and the cardinal meaning of the transmission was expounded for him."[227]

The next two accounts concern disciples of Shinson, a monk from a subsidiary branch of the Eshin Sugiu lineage who, in the mid-thirteenth century, had settled in a place called Kawataya in Musashi Province in the east, where he founded a small Tendai *dangisho* or seminary under the patronage of the local overlord *(ryōshu)*.[228] The first narrative centers on one Kōkai, represented as one of the less capable of Shinson's leading disciples: for every ten parts Shinson expounded, Kōkai understood seven.[229] It tells how Kōkai goes up to Mt. Hiei and receives instruction from Awataguchi Jōmyō, the patriarch of the Eshin school. This account was compiled by Tendai monks from eastern Japan and suggests a certain tongue-in-cheek irreverence in its description of ritual transmission as practiced on Mt. Hiei:

> Because it was his first time staying on the mountain, Kōkai presented [Jōmyō's disciple] Seikai of the Shōrin-bō with thirty *kan* in fees. At that time, they had sake and also entertainment. Seikai said, "If Kōkai can drink a lot of this sake, I'll give him transmission texts as a present." Kōkai drank fully sixteen cups, and texts amounting to ninety-two fascicles were presented to him. Seikai said, "Because these are profoundly secret, sacred teachings, it is hard to let them go down to the countryside *(inaka)*. But because of your sincerity, I will do so."[230]

In the narrative, Kōkai's story serves as a prelude to that of Endon-bō Songai (1253–1332), a native of Adachi in Musashi Province and Shinson's leading disciple. For every ten parts that Shinson preached, we are told, Songai understood twelve or thirteen. At the point in the narrative when Kōkai comes back to the Kantō from Mt. Hiei with his secret texts, Songai asks to see them. Kōkai replies, "If you become my disciple, there can be no objection." Songai reflects, "It would be a shame to become the disciple of a man inferior to myself" and decides to wait for a chance to receive direct instruction on Mt. Hiei. An opportunity eventually materializes through the patronage of a local landholder. Songai arrives in the capital in style, escorted by four young male attendants and sixteen horsemen and with more than a thousand *kan* for his expenses. Depending upon the account, Songai made a total of three, six, or seven trips to Mt. Hiei, receiving instruction chiefly from Shinga (the victor in the earlier-mentioned lawsuit) in both commentarial and debate literature. On his third (or fourth) trip, he is said to have contributed more than three hundred (or four hundred) *kan* to the repair of Shinga's cloister, the Jōraku-in in Kyoto. Shinga then recognized him as a person of unusual resolve and formally transferred to him the seven great matters that form the innermost secret teachings of the Eshin school.[231]

From the perspective of Mt. Hiei, the monk from Hitachi, Kōkai, and Songai were outsiders. They were not of the nobility, and they came from eastern Japan, an area looked down upon by educated persons of the imperial capital as a cultural backwater. Although the stories about them may in part be retrospective constructions and thus not reliable in their details, their recurring elements—such as the theme of multiple trips to Mt. Hiei made as a proof of sincerity—suggest how difficult it was for obscure monks from the Kantō provinces to gain the imprimatur of ritual transmission from teachers affiliated with the great religious center near the imperial capital. These narratives also suggest that sizable cash donations, originating with their warrior patrons, substantially helped them to accomplish this.

Nothing further is known of the monk from Hitachi or of Shinson's lesser disciple, Kōkai. Songai, however, parlayed the legitimation conferred upon him via Shinga's transmission into a remarkable career as a scholar, teacher, and institution builder. The *dangisho* or seminary that he established at Senba in Musashi Province became central to a network of Tendai temples that grew up in the Kantō during the late Kamakura and Muromachi periods. Around Songai, his successors, and the temples they established there crystallized a second medieval Tendai tradition—the Tendai of the east—which was also an important locus in the development of original enlightenment doctrine and the production of *kuden hōmon*. Thus, in conferring its secret transmission upon Songai—and presumably, others like him—the aristocratic Eshin Sugiu lineage of the capital unwittingly legitimized someone who would help establish a formidable rival institution. Having received this transmission, Songai also acquired its authority and legitimation. However, he also seems to have modified that authority and legitimation in terms of his own Kantō-based social, economic, and political nexus. According to his biography, for the sake of spreading the Dharma, Songai chose deliberately to flout the convention of transmission to a single disciple, to which he had earlier pledged himself. "Even if I myself should fall into hell for breaking my vow, it is better that the Dharma should long prosper. I will choose one person from each of the sixty-six provinces [of Japan] and confer [this Dharma] upon him."[232] Whatever its historicity, this element in the narrative points to increased accessibility of learning at Senba and other eastern Tendai *dangisho*. Conventions of secret transmission and elaborate initiation rituals were maintained, but transmission to a single disciple was not emphasized, nor was lineal transmission confined within families. As we will see in chapter 7, transmissions were sometimes even conferred upon persons not primarily affiliated with Tendai, such as scholar-monks of the Nichiren sect.

Tendai secret transmissions constituted a kind of territory, in the sense of the field of authority or legitimation that they conferred. How that territory was defined, however, was determined by the varying social and economic contexts in which the transmission was conducted. Within the aristocratic lineages of the capital, this territory was defined by various exclusionary containment strategies—such as one-to-one or father-son transmission—and was often construed as property, to be kept within the "family," whether real or constructed. In contrast, in eastern Japan, with the fresh opportunities afforded by warrior patronage, the territory constituted by ritual transmission was linked to an emphasis on expansion, as new Tendai institutions sought to become established and extend their influence.

Tendai in the Kantō

The Kamakura period was a time of expansion into the Kantō. Improvements in farming techniques brought previously infertile land under cultivation, resulting in increased harvests. Peasants, artists, craftsmen, and other people of all classes migrated east to share in the new wealth, as did shrine priests and Buddhist monks, seeking new territory to proselytize as well as the opportunity of patronage by the Kamakura *bakufu* and other powerful warrior families. Nichiren, writing in 1275, comments sarcastically on the number of Mikkyō ritualists from Tōji, Mt. Hiei, Onjōji, and the Nara temples as well as other monks who "come down to the Kantō and bow their heads, bend their knees, and in one way or another win the hearts of warriors, becoming abbots or other officials of temples and monasteries."[233] A growing Tendai presence in the east eventually gave rise, within that tradition, to a distinction between the Tendai of the capital (*miyako* Tendai) and eastern or provincial Tendai (Kantō Tendai, *inaka* Tendai).

Extant Tendai documents of the premodern period tend to stress the activities of Eshin monks in the Kantō. Shinson, Songai's first teacher, is traditionally said to have first brought the Eshin doctrine to eastern Japan, when he established himself at Kawataya in Musashi and lectured there on the *Mo-ho chih-kuan* in the Kangen era (1243–1247). However, modern scholarship has established that both Eshin and Danna lineages were active in the Kantō, and that Tendai monks had begun to come east to Kamakura well before Shinson's time.[234] The Kamakura history *Azuma kagami* (Mirror of the east) mentions two monks, Jōhen and Jōren, who preached in Kamakura on 3/23/1215 on the *Lotus* and Pure Land teachings; Hazama Jikō has identified these men as belonging to the Eshin school.[235] Among Tendai monks who came to Kamakura to preach were some who were well known as scholars and teachers, such as Seikaku (or Shōkaku, 1167–1235), fourth in the line of succession to the

Agui lineage of *shōdō* preaching, who was also a teacher of the Chikurin-bō lineage of the Danna school and had served as *tandai* or judge of the Tendai *kōgaku ryūgi* or "examination on broad learning." Seikaku is known to have preached in Kamakura in 1227.[236] Monks from Mt. Hiei not only preached but also acted as *kusō* (monks in service to a deity) at the Tsurugaoka Hachiman shrine, though they were outnumbered there by other Tendai monks from the Onjōji, which had formed close ties with the Minamoto, and, to a lesser extent, by Shingon monks from the Tōji in the imperial capital.[237]

In time, Tendai monks established numerous temples and also *dangisho*—seminaries, or centers for doctrinal study—in eastern Japan.[238] Sixty-one Tendai *dangisho* have been identified to date, thirty-eight of them in the eight Kantō provinces.[239] The oldest of these were established in the Kamakura period, many more being built in the Muromachi. With a few exceptions, Tendai *dangisho* in the east did not transmit Taimitsu *shuhō*.[240] Rather, they emphasized traditional Tendai studies, educating monks through a rigorous program of debate-style doctrinal training paralleling that of Mt. Hiei. Some in fact studied with the aspiration of ascending Mt. Hiei to undergo the "examination in broad learning."[241] Most Tendai *dangisho* and other Tendai temples in the Kanto installed the *kami* of the Hie shrines, thus transplanting the Sannō cult of Mt. Hiei to eastern Japan. At the *dangisho*, debates were regularly held in honor of these *kami*, based on the tradition that Ryōgen, reviver and systematizer of the examination by debate system, had had debates conducted for this purpose in the precincts of the Hie Sannō shrine complex.[242] In the late medieval period, in addition to their emphasis on debate training, *dangisho* became important centers of *jikidan*, a form of popular preaching on the *Lotus Sūtra*.[243]

Probably the most prosperous and influential of the eastern Tendai *dangisho* was Songai's Senba *dangisho*, located at the Hoshino-san Muryōjuji (now the Kita-in) at Senba in Kawagoe in Musashi Province. The site of this temple was said to have been opened by a hermit named Senbō, and the temple itself, to have been constructed by Ennin in 830. Destroyed by fire in the Genkyū era (1204–1205), it was restored in 1296 by Songai, who established a *dangisho* there at the Butsuzō-bō. The Butsuzō-bō (later the kita-in) was one of the three main cloisters to be established at the Muryōjuji. Eventually, *dangisho* would be founded at the other two—the Butsuji-bō (also Butsuji-in or Butchi-in) and the Jizō-bō—as well. Collectively these Senba *dangisho* transmitted the Eshin teachings and were extremely influential in the dissemination of Tendai in the east. An edict said to have been issued by Emperor Go-Nijō in 1301 names the Butsuji-in as the head temple of all Tendai temples in the Kantō. While this edict is very likely a later forgery, it does point to the growing importance of Senba as a center of eastern Tendai.[244] The Senba *dangisho* became central to a network of similar Tendai institutions in the Kantō, forming the basis for later main temple–branch temple relations in the Edo period. Songai had four major disciples: Kankai, Zenkai, Seikai, and Gōkai. Kankai succeeded to the Butsuzō-bō; Zenkai established a *dangisho* at the Butsuji-bō; Seikai established a *dangisho* at the Shūkōji in Naganuma in Shimotsuke Province with the support of the local lord, Naganuma Gorō Munemitsu; and Gōkai founded yet another, the Kanasana *dangisho*, at the Daikōfushōji in Musashi Province.[245] Songai's line thus became instrumental in the dissemination of medieval Tendai Buddhism, including ideas of original enlightenment, in eastern Japan.

Though little is known about the economics of Tendai *dangisho*, they appear to have been supported by local warrior patronage. *Dangisho* tended to be located near major highways and provincial centers of government[246] and evidently maintained connections with other *dangisho* and with Mt. Hiei. Scholar-monks traveled from one to another, studying and transcribing texts. *Dangisho* were sites of tremendous production of documents, especially of *kuden hōmon* and texts related to doctrinal debate. When Oda Nobunaga razed Mt. Hiei in 1571, its archives were replenished by drawing on those of the Kantō *dangisho*. This task was accomplished largely through the efforts of the Tendai monk Tenkai (1536–1643), known chiefly for his role in establishing the shrine to Tokugawa Ieyasu at Nikkō.[247]

Thus there grew up in the east a rival locus of the medieval Tendai tradition, drawing its monks from a different social stratum and supported by a different kind of economic base from the aristocratic Tendai of the capital. Here in the east were produced several of the major later commentaries on the *kuden hōmon*. In time, Kantō Tendai monks also developed distinctive doctrinal positions, different from those of "the mountain" and often said to have originated with Songai. Intellectual exchange, as well as tensions, between the Tendai of the capital and of the Kantō tradition form yet another dimension of the medieval context in which ideas of original enlightenment were elaborated.

Conclusion

Medieval Tendai *hongaku* thought developed within a culture of secret transmission that began to emerge in the latter Heian period. Institutionally, this culture was the product of the *monryū*, or lineages of scholar-monks originally based at individual cloisters or associated with distinct geographical divisions of Mt. Hiei. Secret transmission in general found its model in the transmission of esoteric rites, by which Taimitsu lineages competed for aristocratic patronage, and which served as the thaumaturgical support for the *kenmon taisei*, the system by which governance was shared among "influential houses" or ruling elites. Politically, socially, and economically, the culture of secret transmission was grounded in the privatization of land and power by these *kenmon,* in the aristocraticization of the clergy, and in the consequent transplanting of noble factions into the world of the temple-shrine complexes. Its distinctive features included the primacy of the bond between master and disciple, sometimes reinforced by blood ties; Mikkyō-esque initiation rites; and secret transmissions that, even when written down, continued to be called *kuden,* emphasizing their origins in private explanation given by the teacher to his chosen disciple, which others were not permitted to hear. Such conventions of secret transmission became normative for the dissemination of knowledge—not only in religious matters but in court ceremony, literature, the visual and performing arts, and many crafts—throughout the medieval period.

Embedded in this culture of secret transmission, ideas of original enlightenment were transmitted not only as doctrinal formulations, as in many Eshin and Danna *kuden,* but in transmissions concerning the cult of the Sannō shrines, the sacred geography of Mt. Hiei, the *kaihōgyō* ascetic practice, the secret meaning of the sudden and perfect precepts, and *shōmyō* chanting. Such ideas were also embodied in the symbolic iconography and ritual gestures of *kanjō* or initiation rites that safeguarded exclusivity of transmission. When joined to conventions of secrecy, the original enlightenment perspective was in large measure what endowed secret transmissions with their power. Its logic of concrete forms being identical with true reality *(sokuji nishin)* enabled the assertion that the given practices, rituals, observances, or doctrinal formulations transmitted by a given lineage were in themselves the embodiment of original enlightenment, and that the realization of such enlightenment lay in correctly receiving and upholding these transmissions.

Two points relative to the broader issues of this study arise in connection with the present chapter's discussion of Tendai secret transmission. First, it is startling to note how innovative the culture of secret transmission really was. This culture did not exist in the time of the patriarchs Saichō or Ryōgen but emerged only in symbiotic relation with the distinctive economic, social, and political developments of the medieval period. The proliferation of private lineages specializing in Taimitsu *shuhō,* practices associated with shrines and sacred geography, precepts, Buddhist hymns, doctrinal interpretation, and other aspects of the Tendai tradition gave rise to a wealth of rituals, practices, and interpretations and resulted in a staggering production of texts recording and interpreting *kuden* concerning them. While carefully legitimized as secret transmissions originating with remote patriarchs, these were in fact new developments. Expansion into the Kantō also gave rise to a competing Tendai tradition in the east whose social and economic foundations, institutions, and doctrines differed in key respects from those of Mt. Hiei,

Onjōji, and other Tendai centers in the region of the imperial capital. All this distinguishes medieval Tendai from the Tendai of the early Heian period and makes it, in effect, a "new Buddhism." This new medieval Tendai began to emerge somewhat before, and then developed coevally with, the so-called new Kamakura Buddhism. By no means was this a period of Tendai instititutional vitiation or loss of intellectual creativity. The burgeoning of new forms of practice, ritual, doctrine, and modes of transmission that it encompassed fundamentally challenges the received picture of medieval Tendai as a static, moribund "old Buddhist" tradition, against which a handful of individuals such as Hōnen, Shinran, Dōgen, and Nichiren initiated movements for reform.

Second, we can now begin to assess the suggestion, made by Kuroda Toshio and others, that original enlightenment typified *kenmitsu* Buddhism and was thus part of the ideology that supported the medieval ruling elites. In that it was expressed through and lent potency to secret transmissions, it did indeed legitimize the authority of aristocratic clerical lineages. This is not to suggest that the *hongaku* doctrine is inherently elitist, but simply to observe that it was contained, mediated, and appropriated by exclusivistic and elite lineage structures. In a different sort of institutional setting, its power of legitimization might work very differently. It is not clear, moreover, how original enlightenment thought in and of itself would have served as an ideology for other ruling elites, such as the court, lay aristocrats, or powerful warriors. The Tendai *dangisho* of eastern Japan raise a further question. As noted above, these institutions formed an important locus for the development of *hongaku* doctrine, yet many of them did not transmit Taimitsu ritual or provide Taimitsu ritual services. Thus it remains unclear whether they should even be considered part of *kenmitsu* Buddhism—in fact, how far the model of the *kenmitsu taisei* may apply to eastern Japan remains to be determined.[248] The relation of original enlightenment discourse to both the *kenmitsu* system and broader issues of power in the medieval period will require further investigation.

Above I have sought to demonstrate that medieval Tendai original enlightenment thought—or discourse, if one prefers—was not a disembodied philosophical exercise but deeply embedded in institutional settings emphasizing lineage and secret transmission, as well as in specific practices and rituals. However, it has come to be categorized as "thought" in part precisely because of its highly developed intellectual and doctrinal aspects. It is to these that we now turn.

Chapter Four

Hermeneutics, Doctrine, and "Mind-Contemplation"

MUCH OF THE MODERN scholarship on Kamakura Buddhism presents us with an implicit paradox. Hōnen, Shinran, and other founders of the new Buddhist movements are widely acknowledged to have possessed a broad and sophisticated understanding of Buddhist doctrine, presumably acquired during their early years of training on Mt. Hiei. And yet, according to received scholarly opinion, Mt. Hiei had by that time already slipped into serious intellectual decline. Ōsumi Kazuo indirectly addresses this paradox when he suggests that the originators of the new Kamakura Buddhist movements had "studied on Mt. Hiei while it was still in the twilight of its doctrinal heyday, a time when priests in training might devote ten or twenty years to study."[1] There was by implication still enough "light" available that a deeply motivated person like Hōnen or Shinran could acquire a mastery of doctrine. Other scholars, however, have suggested that a serious fall in intellectual standards had already occurred within Tendai Buddhism from as early as the latter Heian period. Inoue Mitsuada lists "decline in scholarship" as a defining characteristic of Tendai during the early Insei period, citing evidence that Buddhist logic *(inmyō)* had been dropped from the Tendai curriculum by the latter eleventh century, as well as a six-article statement issued by the Enryakuji in 1131 condemning monks who sought to take part in the "examination on broad learning" or who aspired to the rank of *ajari* (Skt. *ācārya*), or master of esoteric teachings, without adequate study or training.[2] The presumed decline in Tendai intellectual endeavors is frequently said to have resulted from the armed strife and political upheaval of the late Heian and early Kamakura periods, and to have been aggravated by monastic factionalism with its accompanying emphasis, upheld throughout the medieval period, on secret *kuden* transmissions not subject to public verification and on the subjective, *kanjin* style of interpretation that valued personally derived meanings over fidelity to texts.[3]

Often cited as symptomatic of the alleged decline in medieval Tendai scholarship are the apparent errors occurring in *kuden* texts concerning the known facts of Saichō's biography. Saichō sailed for China in the twentieth year of the Chen-yüan era by the Chinese calendar (Enryaku 23 in Japan, or 804) and returned the following year. However, according to the *Shuzenji-ketsu,* a *kuden* collection of the late Heian or Kamakura period, Saichō received a transmission from his Chinese teacher Tao-sui on the third day of the sixth month of Chen-yüan 24.[4] In fact there was no such year; the era name was changed to Yung-chen in 805. And even if the date Chen-yüan 24 (which occurs twice in the *Shuzenji-ketsu*) were a transcription error for the proper year, Chen-yüan 21, Saichō had already left China in the fifth month and so could not possibly have received a transmission from Tao-sui in the sixth. The *Kankō ruijū* similarly has Saichō receiving secret texts from Tao-sui in the sixth month of Chen-yüan 21, when he was already en route home to Japan.[5] Dates equally at variance with the known chronology of Saichō's journey to China occur routinely in the medieval Tendai *kuden* literature.[6] As discussed in the preceding chapter, medieval Tendai lineages constructed an identity for themselves as the inheritors, interpreters, and transmitters of a Dharma that Saichō, founder of the Japanese Tendai tradition, had received in China from Tao-sui. Why then did their *kuden* texts consistently alter the received facts of that encounter? The standard explanation for these alterations has been to regard them as errors attributable to the lamentably reduced state of Tendai scholarship.[7]

Here and there, a very few voices have questioned this received picture of pervasive intellectual decay. One example is Nakanishi Zuikō, who has called attention to Nanbokuchō- and Muromachi-period Tendai texts stressing the importance of a prospective initiate's qualifications. The *Shokoku ikken hijiri monogatari,* dated 1387, says that transmission should be made only to a disciple who has thoroughly trained in study and practice of both exoteric and esoteric teachings.[8] The *Shikan shin'yō* says that transmission should not be made to a disciple who has not trained under the master for twelve years, even if he is a person of ability.[9] Citing such references, Nakanishi questions longstanding scholarly opinion about the *kuden* tradition as representing a decline in Tendai Buddhist scholarship.

Another such voice is that of Hanano Michiaki. Hanano suggests that the misdating of Saichō's transmissions from Tao-sui is so obvious and consistent throughout the medieval Tendai *kuden* literature that it may well have been done deliberately and have carried tacit significance, perhaps serving to distinguish these medieval transmission texts from Saichō's authentic writings. He also speculates: "They [the producers of *kuden*] were people who emphasized *kanjin*-style interpretation. Transcending the rational, scholarly realm that distinguishes authentic from apocryphal, they moved in the non-rational realm of religious experience. Probably they were in the same psychological state as those who produced the *Lotus Sūtra* and other Mahāyāna scriptures."[10]

We have no access today to the minds of those who compiled either the Mahāyāna sūtras or the medieval Japanese Tendai *kuden* literature, though some Mahāyāna sūtras may indeed have been inspired by intense meditative states in which people experienced themselves as being in the Buddha's presence and hearing his preaching.[11] Nonetheless, as shall be discussed below, Hanano makes a vital point in insisting that the *kanjin* mode of interpretation be considered in terms other than the putative decay of traditional Tendai scholarship.

All this begs the question: Was there indeed a massive decline in the standards of Tendai doctrinal study during the medieval period? Very real changes occurred in the mode and direction of Tendai scholarship during this era, but these cannot always be read as unambiguous evidence for decline. We have already noted Inoue Mitsusada's observance that Buddhist logic was dropped from the Tendai curriculum around the Insei period, but it is open to question whether this represented a lowering of scholarly standards, as Inoue suggests, or simply reflected a shift in the orientation of Tendai studies, as debate became a matter of internal doctrinal training rather than competition with other schools.[12] Interest definitely waned in the exegesis of complete texts: Jōsan (b. 997) of the Iimurodani of the Yokawa, Shōkaku-bō Dōsui (d. 1157), and Hōchi-bō Shōshin, all of whom wrote thorough commentaries on Chih-i's major works, were marked exceptions this regard.[13] This disinclination to explicate complete texts may also reflect a shift of focus within the medieval Tendai examination system. Paul Groner writes:

> Instead of reading T'ien-t'ai Chinese texts as wholes and writing commentaries on the entire text, Japanese Tendai thinkers would often take Chinese doctrines out of context and juxtapose them with passages from other texts, or consider them from the perspective of a particular problem that interested them. Texts by Chih-i and Chan-jan, for example, were used in arguments on topics that were seldom or never discussed in China. New doctrinal interpretations arose. For example, *sokushin jōbutsu* (the realization of Buddhahood with this very body) and *sōmoku jōbutsu* (the realization of Buddhahood by trees and grasses) were not major topics in Chinese T'ien-t'ai doctrine, but became so in the Japanese Tendai examination system.[14]

Thus there is room to see this particular development not as a decline in orthodox modes of exegesis, but as a creative reformulation of doctrinal issues in response to institutional change.

As the medieval period progressed, the Tendai examination system became increasingly formalized, especially after examination topics were standardized and debate manuals began to be produced. Nonetheless, the immense volume of debate literature produced both by the "Tendai of the capital" and at Tendai *dangisho* in the Kantō argues that it continued to be treated as a serious intellectual endeavor. Doctrinal studies in medieval Tendai differed in approach and content from what they had been during the so-called golden age of Ryōgen, Genshin, and Kakuun. However, to dismiss this as scholarly desuitude is to overlook new and significant developments. As a way of understanding some of these developments, this chapter will first consider the distinctive *kanjin*-style hermeneutical approach that characterized much of the Tendai *kuden* literature and then turn to specific Tendai doctrinal systems of the medieval period, within which ideas of original enlightenment were formulated.

The Hermeneutics of "Mind-Contemplation"

The *kanjin*-style interpretative mode found in many medieval *kuden* texts aims at retrieving hidden meanings held to embody the most profound insights of religious liberation. Such hidden meanings, it was thought, could be accessed only by those with enlightened insight and transmitted only to the properly initiated; they were not part of common doctrinal understanding. This mode of interpretation has been characterized by modern scholars as undermining orthodox doctrinal understanding by encouraging the proliferation of arbitrary, private readings. As noted above, it is often cited as evidence for an alleged decline of learning in medieval Tendai, and the term used for it in modern Japanese scholarship—*kanjin-shugi* (literally, "*kanjin*-ism") frequently carries pejorative overtones. In large measure, this dismissal may be traced to a profound epistemological gap that separates the way scholars read texts today from the way they were read by scholar-monks of the medieval period. Something very like the *kanjin* mode of interpretation still persists in certain quarters, for example, in the folk etymologies of new religious movements. Okada Kōtama (1901–1974), founder of the new religion Sūkyō Mahikari, placed great emphasis on what he termed "spiritual word studies" *(kotodama-gaku);* when he interpreted the word "scholarship" *(gakumon)* as really meaning "the suffering of self" *(ga-kumon),* or egotism, he was engaging in *kanjin*-style hermeneutics.[15] But a long time has passed since scholars have deemed this a legitimate way to read texts; indeed, the entire way of seeing the world that underlies and supports this mode of interpretation has become quite foreign to us. Nevertheless, some effort at appreciating it is necessary, to understand both medieval Tendai thought and medieval Japanese culture more generally. What follows represents such an attempt.

Background in Chih-i's Thought

In the T'ien-t'ai/Tendai tradition, *kuan-hsin* or *kanjin* (literally, the "contemplation of the mind") generally denotes meditative practices, in contrast to doctrinal study *(chiao-hsiang, kyōsō)*. The choice of "the mind" as the object of contemplation is grounded in a passage of the *Hua-yen ching*: "The mind, the Buddha, and all living beings: these three are without distinction."[16] Chih-i reasoned that, for novice practitioners, the "Buddha" as an object of contemplation would be too deep, while "living beings" would be too broad. Contemplating one's own mind, however, is easy.[17]

However, in his commentary *Fa-hua wen-chü* (Words and phrases of the *Lotus Sūtra*), Chih-i uses the term *kanjin* in a somewhat different sense as the last of the "four modes of interpretation" *(ssu-shih, shishaku)*, a four-part hermeneutical guideline for interpreting the "words and phrases" of the *Lotus Sūtra*. The first is to see the sūtra's words and phrases in terms of "causes and conditions" *(yin-yüan, innen)*—that is, how they represent the Buddha's response to the specific receptivity of his hearers. The second, "correlation with teachings" *(yüeh-chiao, yakkyō)*, is to understand them in terms of each of the "four teachings of conversion"—the categories into which Chih-i analyzed the Buddhist teachings.[18] The third, *pen-chi* or *honjaku*, is to understand them from the two viewpoints of the "trace teaching" and the "origin teaching," the two exegetical divisions into which Chih-i analyzed the *Lotus Sūtra*. Fourth, having grasped the meaning of a particular word or phrase from these three doctrinal perspectives, one then internalizes it, contemplating its meaning with respect to one's own mind.[19] In this case, the "words and phrases" of the *Lotus Sūtra* are understood as referring not to abstract or external events, but to the practitioner's own contemplation and insight. For example, in the *kanjin* reading of the sūtra's opening passage, "Thus have I heard at one time" the word "I" *(wo, ga)* is interpreted as follows: "The dharmas produced by dependent origination prove, on contemplation, to be at once empty, conventionally existent, and the middle. 'Empty' means that self *(wo)* is without self. 'Conventionally existent' means that self is distinguished [from other]. 'The middle' means the true and subtle self."[20] The words "at one time" are interpreted in this way: "To contemplate the mind as first empty, then conventionally existent, and then as the middle is the sequential mind-contemplation. To contemplate the mind as simultaneously empty, conventionally existent, and the middle is the perfect and subtle mind-contemplation."[21] In these instances, words and phrases of the *Lotus* are taken as revealing the threefold contemplation and discernment. In other *kanjin* interpretations from the *Wen-chü,* the sūtra's imagery is internalized as an expression of meditative insight. For example, the stūpa of the Buddha Many Jewels emerging from beneath the earth and rising into the air indicates breaking through the mind-ground of ignorance to dwell in the emptiness that is the supreme meaning; Śākyamuni's three acts of purifying myriads of millions of world spheres means that one purifies oneself of the three categories of delusion, and so on.[22] Through this "interpretation from the standpoint of mind-contemplation" *(kuan-hsin-shih, kanjin-shaku)* the meaning of a text is taken into oneself and personally appropriated.

Kanjin-style interpretations in medieval Tendai texts draw on this tradition of *kuan-hsin-shih* in the works of Chih-i but are more than a simple extension of it.[23] They assimilate Chih-i's method to a medieval Japanese episteme shaped by nativistic, Taoist, esoteric Buddhist, and other elements and to a very specific doctrinal agenda, one informed by the premise of original enlightenment. This kind of interpretation is to be found throughout medieval Japanese thought and culture and is by no means confined to the Tendai tradition, but our focus here will be on its use in Tendai texts. What all *kanjin*-style readings have in common is that, from a modern perspective, they are not *exegesis,* the "reading out" from a text to determine its meaning, though the medieval thinkers who produced them may often have understood what they were doing as uncovering the text's true purport. Rather, they are a deliberate *eisegesis* or "reading in" that reconfigures the text in support of a prior insight or philosophical position—in this case, that of original enlightenment. It is this prior insight or position, and not the text itself, that forms the basis of interpretation. Not only written texts were interpreted in this way but also geography, institutions, the human body, and other aspects of the phenemonal world. *Kanjin*-style readings employ a variety of interpretive devices, including sophisticated kinds of word play and magical associations. Here we will consider some of the more common interpretive devices found in such readings in the medieval Tendai *kuden* literature.

Invention and Rearrangement of Sources

Lacking appropriate proof texts to support a given proposition, the producers of medieval *kuden* sometimes simply invented them. Tendai oral transmission texts routinely cite fictitious sūtras and commentaries, or attribute to actually existing works both passages and doctrinal categories that they do not in fact contain. Paul Groner has analyzed the use of fictive sources in the *Kankō ruijū,* which dates probably from the latter Kamakura period.[24] The *Kankō ruijū* purports to be a commentary on the *Hsin-yao* (Essentials of mind), said to record the transmission that Hui-ssu and Chih-i received from Śākyamuni on Eagle Peak; this *Hsin-yao* is said to have provided the basis for Chih-i's *Mo-ho chih-kuan.* There is in fact a work called *Hsin-yao,* or rather *Shin'yō,* as it appears to be a

Japanese production.[25] It consists of passages excerpted from fascicles 1 and 6 of the *Mo-ho chih-kuan* that stress the inherence of suchness in all things, thus suggesting that this emphasis, rather than the *Chih-kuan*'s detailed instructions on meditative practice, is what represents its heart.[26] The *Kankō ruijū* also cites the *Naishō denbō-ketsu* (Decisions on the transmission of inner enlightenment) and a "record concerning the three transmissions of teaching, practice, and realization," both fictive works attributed to Saichō. It also cites several nonexistent passages from the *Nieh-p'an ching (Nirvāṇa-sūtra)*. Groner's analysis suggests that this interpretive approach was by no means the result of ignorance of source materials; nor does the modern idea of forgery, with its connotation of deliberate deceit, seem to apply here. It was simply that the compilers of such texts were guided by a hermeneutical principle of fidelity, not to a received body of classic texts, but to a particular premise or insight said to be grounded in "mind-contemplation"—namely, the premise of original enlightenment.

Word Play

Kanjin-style readings frequently employ elaborate forms of word play. One common device is the creative "breakdown" *(yomikudashi)* of a text written in literary Chinese text to produce a Japanese reading unrelated to, or even at odds with, the sense of the Chinese original. Syntactical markers and phonetic syllables indicating grammatical inflection were often added to a Chinese text so that it could be read in Japanese word order. Most Chinese characters are not in themselves nouns, verbs, or modifiers but function as such according to their syntactical placement; thus the creative use of such indicators can rearrange, even subvert, the Chinese text to produce a Japanese reading radically different in meaning from the original yet still technically "faithful" to it in the sense that every character is preserved and accounted for. Thus the text is made in effect to testify against itself; its authority as a classic document is appropriated to legitimate an interpretation quite different from what it actually says.

This device could potentially be used in the service of any doctrinal or polemical agenda, and some famous examples come from outside the Tendai tradition. It is well known how Dōgen restructured the passage from the *Ta-pan-nieh-p'an ching (Mahā-parinirvāṇa-sūtra)*, "All sentient beings without exception have the Buddha nature," to read, "All sentient beings, i.e., all existents, are the Buddha nature," playing on a double meaning of the character *u* ("to have" and "existents") in order to deny the idea of Buddhahood as a reified, unchanging substrate and to identify it with the flux of impermanent phenomena.[27] Shinran reread the phrase "transfers his merit with sincere mind" *(shishin ekō)* in Amida's eighteenth vow as given in the *Wu-liang-shou ching* (Sūtra of [the Buddha of] immeasurable life), adding to it the honorific verb *shitamaeri,* which changes the subject of the phrase from the believer seeking birth in the Pure Land to Amida himself; in this way, he made the vow consistent with his emphasis on absolute Other-Power *(tariki),* the doctrine that salvation comes not from the believer's efforts but wholly from Amida.[28] Or to give another example, it is said that during the Ōwa debate of 963, when Ryōgen debated the Hossō monk Chūzan on the issue of whether or not all beings have the Buddha nature, he cited, in support of the affirmative side, the passage from the *Lotus Sūtra* "*mu ichi fu jōbutsu,*" which he read straightforwardly as "[Among those who hear this Dharma,] there is not one who shall not attain Buddhahood" *(ichi toshite jōbutsu sezaru wa nashi).* Chūzan, however, argued that the passage should be construed as "one without [the nature of enlightenment] shall not attain Buddhahood" *(mu no ichi wa jōbutsu sezu),* thus inverting the universalist message of the passage in question to support the Hossō position that certain persons are not capable of realizing Buddhahood.[29] This device is also found in medieval transmission literature, where it is often deployed to stress notions of original enlightenment. For example, the phrase *sōmoku jōbutsu*—"grasses and trees realizing Buddhahood" is reconstructed to read "the Buddha who becomes even grasses and trees" *(kusa ni mo ki ni mo naru hotoke)* to show that plants and trees do not undergo transformation and "realize" Buddhahood but, just as they are, manifest the cosmic Tathâgata who is original enlightenment.[30]

Another form of word play used in producing *kanjin*-style readings involves assigning phonetic readings to one or more Chinese characters that alter their conventional meaning. For example, *kuon,* literally the "remote past" when Śākyamuni of the *Lotus Sūtra* is said to have first attained Buddhahood, is assigned such alternative readings as *tsukurowazu* (unadorned) or *moto no mama* (as it is originally); in this way, the Buddha's attainment in the remote past is transformed into a metaphor for the enlightenment originally inherent in all ordinary worldlings.[31]

Correspondence and Association

Another, extremely frequent device used in the production of *kanjin*-style readings draws correspondences between two unrelated or even opposing categories in order to suggest an ontological identity. A very common form of such interpretation by association is numerical correspondence, in which two or more categories are identified by virtue of possessing the same number of elements. A widespread instance of numerical correspondence, rooted in Chinese thought and developed in esoteric Buddhism, involves correlations of fives: the five elements (wood, fire, earth, metal, and water) are equated with the five directions (east, south, center, west, and north); the five planets; the five virtues (benevolence, propriety, good faith, righteousness, and wisdom); the five

colors; the major five organs of the human body; and so forth.[32] In esoteric Buddhism, these pentads are further equated with the five great elements (earth, water, fire, wind, and space) and the five Buddhas, and
in medieval Tendai, they are assimilated to the five tones used in *shōmyō*
chanting or to the five characters *myō-hō-ren-ge-kyō* that comprise the title
of the *Lotus Sūtra*. Such associations reflect underlying assumptions about
the oneness of microcosm and macrocosm, and—when assimilated to
the episteme informed by esoteric Buddhism—about all phenomena as
nondual manifestations of the cosmic Buddha, Mahāvairocana or
Dainichi. Such an understanding of the world, assuming an inner unity
endlessly refracted in each of its elements, was by no means limited to
medieval Japan. A number of scholars have written on the episteme of
medieval Europe, in which the world was seen in totalistic fashion as a
system of hidden correspondences, upon whose proper recognition and
identification rested the practice of such arts as astrology, divination,
and magic. Carolly Erickson has written of the "holistic and multidi-
mensional reality of the middle ages," characterized by "a perception of
ideas and events in terms of an all-encompassing design."[33] George
Conger has broadly surveyed philosophical theories of microcosm and
macrocosm that developed in the Mediterranean and Atlantic regions,
finding that they may include "expressions of either metaphysical, religious, ethical, noetic or aesthetic interests; or, as most often occurs, may
combine something of several or all of these."[34] Also relevant to the medieval Japanese case is Michel Foucault's notion of "resemblance" as "that
[which] organized the play of symbols, made possible knowledge of
things visible and invisible, and controlled the art of representing them"
in the episteme that prevailed in Europe up to the end of the sixteenth
century.[35]

The *kanjin*-style readings found in medieval Tendai texts and in other
kuden literature are grounded in this general medieval Japanese episteme, which was informed by traditions concerning the *kami,* Taoism,
and especially esoteric Buddhism, and which saw all things as expressions of a single all-pervasive reality, their essential unity being expressed
in infinite correspondences and isomorphisms. However, *kanjin*-style
readings usually have a more specific agenda. Since all things are seen
as nondual and interpenetrating, anything could in theory be equated
with anything else; however, the choice of correspondences in these interpretations is by no means arbitrary but serves particular philosophical and ideological commitments. To equate, for example, the three
poisons of greed, hatred, and folly with the three bodies of the Buddha,
or the seven orifices in the human head with the seven precious sub-
stances that compose the stūpa of the Buddha Many Jewels, is not simply to make statements about nonduality. These are more pointed claims
that ordinary deluded persons are Buddhas inherently. The equation

of the three characters of the name *A-mi-da* with the threefold truth of
emptiness, conventional existence, and the middle *(Amida santai-setsu)*
not only argues the identity of the Tendai *Lotus* and Pure Land traditions but also assimilates devotion to Amida Buddha within a distinctively Tendai doctrinal framework.[36] One also sees this device of resemblance used in *honji-suijaku* combinations of Buddhist and Shinto
elements, for example, in the Sannō cult, where the two characters in
the name Sannō (Mountain King), written respectively with three vertical strokes and one horizontal stroke *(san),* and three horizontal
strokes and one vertical stroke *(ō),* are said to reveal the threefold contemplation in a single mind. Allan Grapard has pointed out that such
associations were used to equate local deities *(kami* or *gongen)* with corresponding Buddhas and bodhisattvas, and he suggests that identifying
such correspondences and transmitting knowledge of them may have
been seen as a magically potent act: "The fact that these oral transmissions were given in the context of specific rituals and in absolute secrecy,
and only between a master and his son, shows that decoding or transmitting techniques of interpretation leading to a knowledge of liberating character was regarded as a mystical activity surrounded by danger
and power; this may explain why it was ritualized."[37] This important suggestion has relevance not only to associations of Buddhas and *kami,* but
to a broad range of medieval *kanjin*-style interpretations. Through linguistic association and word play, not only Buddhas, bodhisattvas, and
kami, but Taoist and other deities, *yin-yang* notions, and the specifics of
any doctrinal or ritual system, or of any art or discipline, could be correlated; hidden associations and identities could be discerned; secret
kuden explicating them could be produced; and individual lineages legitimized. The *kanjin* mode of interpretation was in fact inseparable
from the culture of secret transmission that characterized Japan's medieval period.

In addition to the numerical correspondences just mentioned, the
kanjin repertoire also included correspondences of form, or isomorphisms, in which some aspect of the visible world, such as features of
the human body, were read as the embodied realities of mental representations having a similar "shape." Thus the inhaled breath was seen
as the coming of Amida to welcome the practitioner, and the exhaled
breath, as going to the Pure Land. Correspondences might be both numerical and formal; the placing of the ten fingers together in the *gasshō*
gesture was seen as the mutual inclusion of the ten dharma realms and
the true aspect of reality. The landscape—natural and institutional—
provided another important locus for the productions of *kanjin*-style
readings, which were important in the construction and articulation of
sacred geography. Mt. Hiei inspired a number of such readings. In *kike*
documents, the three pagoda precincts were for example associated with

the realms depicted in esoteric mandalas and with the threefold contemplation: the Eastern Pagoda precinct with the Vajra-Realm mandala and the contemplation of the middle; the Western Pagoda precinct with the Matrix-Realm mandala and the contemplation of conventional existence; and Yokawa, with the realm of the *Su-hsi-ti ching (Susiddhikara-sūtra)* and the contemplation of emptiness. These were only the beginning of the complex doctrinal associations mapped onto the features of the mountain.

It is in connection with sacred geography that the political and ideological character of certain *kanjin*-style readings becomes most obvious. In a commentary on Chih-i's *Fa-hua wen chü* (Words and phrases of the *Lotus*), Sonshun (1451–1514), a Tendai scholar-monk of the Kantō E-shin tradition, writes concerning Gṛdhrakūṭa (Eagle or Vulture Peak), the mountain where the *Lotus Sūtra* was said to have been preached:

> [As for the tradition that] all Buddhas of the three time periods invariably dwell on this mountain when they expound the *Lotus Sūtra:* This mountain lies to the northeast of Rājagṛha [the capital of Magadha]. Because the *Lotus Sūtra* expounds the essential [teaching] that the worldly truth constantly abides, the *Lotus* is expounded in the direction of the demon gate, and prayers are offered [there] for the well-being of the Son of Heaven, so that the country may be at peace and the people happy. For this reason, [the temples on] Mt. T'ien-t'ai in the land of the T'ang and on Mt. Hiei in Japan were erected to the northeast of the ruler's palace and revered as places of practice for the protection of the nation. . . . Those monks who dwell on Mt. Hiei even for a time should be understood as the assembly who hears the Dharma on Sacred [Eagle] Peak.[38]

Here Sacred Eagle Peak, Mt. T'ien-t'ai, and Mt. Hiei are identified by virtue of all lying in a common direction, namely, northeast of the capital, and in a position to block the malevolent influences thought to originate from that direction. The equation of Mt. Hiei with the site of the *Lotus Sūtra*'s preaching is used to legitimize its authority as the major cultic center for rituals of nation protection.

In an episteme where all things are seen as manifesting the same nondual reality and all phenomena as inherently enlightened, any place could in theory be the site of the *Lotus Sūtra*'s preaching. However, *kanjin*-style interpretations such as the one just quoted serve to "localize" notions of original enlightenment and assimilate them to the authority of a particular lineage or tradition. This was an important way in which *hongaku* ideas were appropriated to legitimize the transmissions of particular lineages. Such readings would have been inherently unstable, however, in that the potential was always present for groups with conflicting interests to challenge them by drawing new sets of correspondences.

Reversal

"Reversal" may be seen as a subset of correspondence and association; it denotes a case where the identification of two elements functions to invert their conventional meanings. The logic of original enlightenment itself entails precisely this sort of reversal. It proceeds not from cause (practice) to effect (realization) but from effect to cause. Thus it inverts conventional notions of enlightenment as a linear process of cultivation culminating in eventual realization; rather, enlightenment is held to be inherent, and it is only when based upon this insight that cultivation is considered meaningful. Cultivation then becomes the expression of original enlightenment. It is because of this reversal of conventional perspective that original enlightenment thought has been referred to as representing a "Copernican revolution."[39] Reversal as an interpretive technique recapitulates this fundamental reversal at the heart of the notion of original enlightenment.

For an example, let us turn again to Sonshun's discussion of "Mt. Gṛdhrakūṭa" in his commentary on the *Wen-chü*. In the following passage, he strives to reconcile the tension between two traditional Tendai readings: one holding that "wherever the *Lotus Sūtra* is preached is the pure land"; the other maintaining that Eagle or Vulture Peak in India, where the *Lotus Sūtra* is said to have been preached, takes its name from the presence of many vultures who fed off corpses abandoned in a nearby charnel ground.[40]

> In this world, a pure place *(kiyoki tokoro)* is called a pure land *(jōdo)*. Such a pure place is [precisely] a charnel ground *(sanmaijo)*. The reason is: Within the worlds of the trichiliocosm, there is not an inch of space without its owner; thus there are sure to be attachments. But since a charnel ground is a place where the dead are abandoned, its inhabitants do not give rise to hopes nor do they form attachments; thus it should certainly be called a pure land. . . . [W]hen one dies and is abandoned in an open field, if burned in flames, he feels no pain, and if buried in the earth, he does not fear. He does not shun the rain and dew, nor lament the frost and snow. Separated from all things, without sufferings or pleasures—this is the great peace and happiness. It is the true realization of Buddhahood. This is precisely why a Tendai interpretation holds that to become white bones is to see the Dharma nature. . . . When one does not know this, the fruit of Buddhahood is far away, [for such a person] seeks the Dharma apart from the mind.[41]

In the Buddhist tradition of South Asia, meditation performed in a charnel ground was sometimes recommended to awaken the realization of impermanence and to undercut attachment to the body.[42] In Japan as well, the grosser aspects of physical decay were invoked to inspire loathing for this impure world and aspiration for the pure land, where impermanence is transcended. Notions of pollution and of the malevolence of the unhappy dead no doubt infused those places where the dead were abandoned with a particular sense of horror and revulsion. The identification in Sonshun's text of the pure land with a charnel ground dramatically reverses the conventional connotations of both. There is also a playful note in his equation of pure lands and graveyards by virtue of the fact that they are both places of "nonattachment." It may be that the production of *kanjin*-style readings—in addition to being a magically dangerous act—was also in a sense a game, one demanding a high degree of skill in identifying and establishing those precise sets of correspondences that would support a particular vision of reality, doctrinal position, or ideological claim.

When used in combination, the various forms of *kanjin*-style interpretation could produce readings of astonishing complexity and ingenuity. Here is part of a long passage, from a different portion of the same text, arguing the so-called reverse-*honji suijaku* position that elevates *kami* above Buddhas. In so doing, it makes use of virtually all the hermeneutical devices discussed above:

> When our original teacher [Saichō] interpreted the top and bottom of our mountain [Hiei] in terms of the distinction of original ground *(honji)* and manifested traces *(suijaku),* he identified Sakamoto as the original ground and the sacred peak as the manifested trace. Thus he made the interpretation that the origin is below, and the trace, above. That is to say, the erection of the ordination platform among the Buddhist halls at the summit, establishing the distinction between upholding and violating [the precepts] and enjoining strict observance of the sevenfold sacred boundaries *(kekkai),* expresses the realization of the way according to [the principle of] acquired enlightenment *(shikaku),* by which one moves from [the stage of] virtual enlightenment *(tōgaku)* to that of wondrous enlightenment *(myōkaku).*[43] Thus it corresponds to the trace standing above. But the mingling of clergy and laity, men and women, as they visit the seven [Hie] shrines established beneath the trees [at the mountain's foot] expresses the realization of the way by moving from virtual enlightenment to identity [with the Buddha] in principle *(ri-soku);* thus it corresponds to the origin standing below. In the final analysis, Buddhas achieve the way by acquired enlightenment; thus they are regarded as traces. *Kami* convert and teach by virtue of original enlightenment; thus they are called "original ground."

There are four reasons why *kami* correspond to original enlightenment. First, when one visits a shrine, one offers water, and when one visits a Buddha, one offers hot water.[44] In other words, the *kami* cor-

respond to *yin* and have water as their essence. Water here corresponds
to original enlightenment. The Buddhas correspond to *yang* and have
fire as their essence. Hot water is a transformation of water; thus it corresponds to acquired enlightenment. Once the originally undifferentiated *yin* and *yang* have separated, *yin* here becomes the seminal
essence and manifests the function of *yang;* thus *kami* are the origin
and Buddhas, the manifest traces. . . .[45]

Third, when one learns the symbols *(sanmaya)* of the three countries, Japan is represented by a single-pronged vajra and is called the
land of the *kami (shinkoku).* China is designated by a three-pronged vajra. India is customarily called the land of the Buddha [and is represented by a five-pronged vajra]. The five- and three-pronged vajras originally derive from the single-pronged vajra; thus the *kami* are equated
with original enlightenment. . . .

Fourth, the character *kami* is read as "spirit" *(tamashii).* This word
expresses the origin that gives rise to the myriad things. This is to be
kept secret.[46]

The initial effect of such passages is so dizzying that it is small wonder so many modern scholars have dismissed their interpretations as "arbitrary." But closer examination reveals an elaborate internal logic, based
on the assumption that correspondences of number and form reveal a
fundamental identity. The altitudinal distinction between the ordination
platform at Hiei's summit and the gate town of Sakamoto at its foot; the
strictly gendered space within the sacred boundaries versus the mingling
of the sexes at the Hie shrine precincts; the directional "shape" of contrasting doctrines, such as the linear ascent implied by acquired enlightenment versus the nonlinear reversal of original enlightenment; the
differences in devotional action directed toward Buddhas and *kami;* the
movements of *yin* and *yang;* and the shape of ritual implements are all
adduced as evidence that the *kami* are the origin and the Buddhas, their
manifest traces. Today this does not impress us as an argument, because
we do not accept its premise, namely, that of a holistic universe whose
hidden meanings can be decoded by the proper identification of correspondences and isomorphisms. But this way of thinking was central
not only to Tendai *kuden,* but also to the Japanese medieval episteme
and to the culture of secret transmission.

Above we have indicated three ways, by no means mutually exclusive,
in which the *kanjin* mode of interpretation may have been understood
by its producers. First, in keeping with its roots in traditional T'ien-t'ai
hermeneutics, it was probably considered a form of meditative discernment, in that it entailed cultivating a particular way of seeing and experiencing the world, such that correspondences of geographical shapes,
words and names, ritual forms, bodily activities, indeed all phenomena,

were cognized as expressing the reality of Tendai doctrines, most particularly, the truth of original enlightenment. Second, as Grapard has noted, it was perhaps a magically potent and therefore even dangerous act, of identifying and bringing to light secret correspondences thought to reveal the true nature of reality. Because the knowledge of these hidden meanings was held to be liberating and empowering, it had to be contained by rituals of initiation and conventions of secret transmission exclusively to qualified persons. And third, in light of the playful character of many *kanjin*-style readings, it appears to have had the character of a game, albeit a deeply serious one. Players of this game would have sought to excel in establishing those readings and associations that would support their particular doctrinal stance. One imagines that especially clever word plays, associations, combinations, and reversals gave scope to individual creativity and afforded no small intellectual enjoyment, even entertainment, to both the producers and transmitters of *kuden*.

In any event, it is clear that *kanjin*-style interpretation was by no means arbitrary. Modern criticisms of *kanjin-shugi* as subjective and unrelated to the texts it purports to interpret have failed to grasp that this was precisely the point: It was a hermeneutics grounded in a particular insight or *a priori* position believed to carry greater authority than the literal or surface meaning of the text. Nonetheless, to be effective, the *kanjin* mode of interpretation would have had to depend on more conventional doctrinal studies. One must know doctrines and texts before one can rearrange and reinterpret them; traditional doctrinal study was thus necessary to acquire the resources with which the game of *kanjin*-style intepretation, so to speak, was played. Moreover, many *kanjin*-style readings rely for their impact on the fact that they undercut or reverse conventional understandings. Dōgen's assertion that "all sentient beings are the Buddha nature" seems radical and impressive precisely because of its contrast with the more traditional reading that it implicitly critiques. The perception of the inhaled breath as the coming of Amida is compelling precisely because it is in tension with more "common-sense" ideas about Amida Buddha as presiding over a remote pure land in the West and descending to welcome the believer at death. Thus, both the production and appreciation of interpretations in the *kanjin* mode would have depended on a knowledge of "orthodox" readings. Without the check imposed by publicly accessible documents and some general consensus as to their meaning, there would be little for *kanjin*-style hermeneutics to operate upon, and it would quickly degenerate into a series of arbitrary assertions. Perhaps this did in fact occur at some junctures. Nevertheless, it would seem that the magical, creative, and exuberant *kanjin*-style readings of the medieval *kuden* coexisted and interacted with more sober, exegetical modes of scholarship and doctrinal study.[47]

Doctrinal Formulations

Against the view of the medieval period as an era of Tendai scholarly decline, one must point out that during this time, entire new doctrinal systems were formulated, reorganizing Tendai thought from the standpoint
of original enlightenment. The remainder of this chapter will consider
two such systems, both of the Eshin school, whose teachings seem to have
been more formally organized—or at least more extensively studied—
than those of the Danna school. We will look first at the "fourfold rise
and fall," a new doctrinal classification, and then at the "threefold seven
great matters," which systematizes Eshin doctrine and practice.

Doctrinal Classification: The Fourfold Rise and Fall

As discussed in chapter 1, the comparative, usually hierarchical
classifications of the Buddhist teachings known as *kyōsō hanjaku* or simply *kyōhan* are one means by which individual schools position themselves
vis-à-vis the larger Buddhist tradition and by which they seek to legitimize
their claims to uniqueness and authority. A particular school's *kyōhan*
serves as an index to the ideas it defines as most important and consti-
tutive of its identity. Teachers who initiated new Buddhist movements
have often formulated new *kyōhan*, as Hōnen and Nichiren did. New
kyōhan may also emerge when an existing school is undergoing self-
redefinition, as we see in the theoretical systematization of Taimitsu
worked out by Ennin, Enchin, and Annen in the first part of the Heian
period. From about the latter half of the thirteenth century, a new doctrinal classification emerged within medieval Tendai, specifically within
the Eshin school. Known as the *shijū kōhai* or "fourfold rise and fall," it
served to legitimate and encourage a growing emphasis on both *hongaku*
thought and *kanjin*-style hermeneutics.

The four category divisions that comprise the "fourfold rise and fall"
are (1) the pre–*Lotus Sūtra* teachings *(nizen)*, a category based on the traditional T'ien-t'ai/Tendai schema that assigns the *Lotus* to the final
preaching period of the Buddha's life; (2) the "trace teaching" *(shakumon)*, or first fourteen chapters of the *Lotus Sūtra*, which take the form
of preaching by the historical Śākyamuni, who is later revealed to be a
"trace" *(suikjaku)* manifested by the original Buddha; (3) the "origin
teaching" *(honmon)*, the latter fourteen chapters of the *Lotus Sūtra*, which
take the form of preaching by the Buddha in his original ground *(honji)*,
that is, as the original Buddha *(honbutsu)* who reveals himself to have been
enlightened since the inconceivably remote past; and (4) "mind-contemplation" or "mind-discernment" *(kanjin)*, a term used in this case with
a wide range of meanings, denoting not only formal contemplative practice but also the insight thereby achieved, as well as an original ground
prior to all verbal and conceptual distinctions. "Rise and fall" is an in-

dication of relative superiority, as in "when the trace teaching rises, the pre–*Lotus Sūtra* teachings fall." The system thus comprises four categories of increasing superiority; each becomes "true" with the respect to the category preceding it, which is then superseded and relativized as "provisional." The four category names derive from Chih-i's *Fa-hua hsüan-i*, where the meaning of "wondrous" or "subtle" *(miao, myō)*, the first character in the *Lotus Sūtra*'s title, is discussed in terms of the teachings of expedient means, the trace teaching, the origin teaching, and the contemplation of the mind.[48] However, in Chih-i's works, these four categories do not represent a hierarchical ranking of teachings.

The fourfold rise and fall is first clearly set forth in the *Hokke ryakugi kenmon* (Notes on the abbreviated meaning of the *Lotus Sūtra*) and in the *Kankō ruijū*, two related works both attributed to Chūjin (1065–1138), forty-sixth *zasu* of Mt. Hiei and the teacher of Kōkaku, regarded as the founder of the Sugiu line of the Eshin school. However, since both texts cite the teachings of Jōmyō (fl. mid-13th cent.), fourth in the line of succession after Chūjin, they were probably compiled during or somewhat after his time.[49] The *Ryakugi kenmon* outlines the fourfold rise and fall as follows: "When the great teaching of *shakumon* rises, the great teachings prior to the *Lotus Sūtra* are superseded. When the great teaching of *honmon* rises, the great teaching of *shakumon* is superseded. And when the great teaching of *kanjin* rises, the great teaching of *honmon* is superseded."[50] These three steps in which a subsequent teaching supersedes and relativizes the preceding one each reflect a distinctive trend in the development of medieval Tendai thought.[51]

1. "When the great teaching of *shakumon* rises, the great teachings prior to the *Lotus Sūtra* are superseded." This step assumes a sharp discontinuity between the *Lotus Sūtra* and other Buddhist teachings. Again, as discussed in chapter 1, throughout its history the T'ien-t'ai/Tendai tradition has developed a dual strategy for asserting the unique position of its basic scripture. One has been to stress the *centrality* of the *Lotus;* this is a strategy of subsumption and appropriation, in which the *Lotus* is said to open and integrate *(kaie)* all other teachings within itself. The other has been to insist on the *superiority* of the *Lotus;* this is a strategy of comparison and sometimes confrontation, in which the greater merits of the *Lotus* are argued over and against other scriptures.[52] Usually the two approaches have coexisted, one being stressed over the other as the occasion demanded. In the recorded teachings of the T'ien-t'ai founder Chih-i, the perfect teaching as embodied in the *Lotus Sūtra (Hokke no en)* and the perfect teaching embodied in the preceding teachings *(nizen no en)* are not radically distinguished.[53] The perfect teaching of the *Lotus Sūtra* is said to have the function of integrating all other teachings within itself, while the perfect teaching found within the pre–*Lotus Sūtra* teachings does not; otherwise, there is no essential difference. However, in

later developments of T'ien-t-'ai thought, the supreme position of the *Lotus Sūtra* was increasingly emphasized. This tendency can be seen, for example, in the works of sixth patriarch Chan-jan, in his efforts to make clear the position of T'ien-t'ai vis-à-vis the increasingly influential tradition of Hua-yen. It is even clearer in the case of Saichō, who faced the challenge of establishing and winning imperial support for a new Buddhist school in the face of opposition from the older schools of Nara. As we have seen, while including precepts, meditation, and esoteric teachings within the framework of Tendai, Saichō at the same time insisted strongly on the superiority of the *Lotus*. His *Hokke shūku* elaborates ten points by which he claimed the *Lotus* surpassed all others; he also argued that only this sūtra was suited to the faculties of the Japanese. Arguments for the superior status of the *Lotus* reached new levels with the development of Taimitsu thought. Enchin (814–891) sharply distinguished between the perfect teaching as embodied in the *Lotus Sūtra* and the perfect teaching as found in the sūtras prior to the *Lotus,* holding that only the former was identical to the secret esoteric teachings. Enchin is also associated with the doctrine that "the *Lotus* transcends the eight" *(Hokke chōhachi),* a claim that the *Lotus Sūtra* stands above the eight categories into which traditional T'ien-t'ai/Tendai thought divides the Buddhist teachings. *Chōhachi* thought gained considerable influence within Tendai in the late Heian and Kamakura periods and may well have influenced the emergence of single-practice rhetoric in the new Kamakura Buddhist movements.[54] The first step of the fourfold rise and fall reflects this influence.

2. "When the great teaching of *honmon* rises, the great teaching of *shakumon* is superseded." Just as the *Lotus Sūtra* is considered to be essentially different from and superior to all other sūtras, so the origin teaching, or second fourteen chapters of the *Lotus,* is distinguished from and set above the trace teaching, or first fourteen chapters. The distinction between the trace and origin teachings was originally drawn for purely exegetical purposes, and their chief difference was seen as that of the status of the Buddha who preaches them: the trace teaching is preached by Śākyamuni in his transient aspect as a Buddha who first attained enlightenment in this lifetime, and the origin teaching, by Śākyamuni in his true aspect as the Buddha enlightened since the inconceivably remote past. The terms "trace" and "origin" were first used by Seng-chao (384–414), a disciple of the *Lotus Sūtra*'s famed translator, Kumārajīva, in interpreting the relationship between skillful means and enlightened wisdom in his commentary on the *Vimalakīrti-nirdeśa.* Seng-chao concludes that trace and origin are "inconceivably one" *(fushigi ichi).*[55] Chih-i adopted these terms to denote two divisions within the *Lotus Sūtra,* elaborating six points of difference between them.[56] The key distinction for him was the Buddha's "lifespan," that is, how long had

passed since the Buddha's first attainment of the Way. He saw the origin teaching as differing from all other sūtras in that it alone reveals the Buddha's original attainment in the remotest past. Nonetheless, the trace and origin teachings were for Chih-i always of a single Dharma-essence and "inconceivably one."

In Japanese Tendai, however, a need to reconcile the *Lotus Sūtra* with the esoteric teachings led to growing emphasis on the origin section of the sūtra, giving rise to a distinctive "*honmon* thought."[57] Where the Buddha of the trace teaching is a finite existence, the Buddha of the origin teaching, enlightened since inconceivable kalpas ago, was readily assimilated to notions of the cosmic Buddha, Mahāvairocana or Dainichi. The identification of Śākyamuni with the cosmic Buddha is clearly reflected in the medieval Tendai *kuden:* Śākyamuni's revelation of his first attainment of enlightenment in the distant past *(ji kempon)* as described in the "Fathoming the Lifespan" chapter of the *Lotus* is interpreted as a metaphor for originally inherent enlightenment in all beings *(ri kenpon).*

In Eshin and Danna transmissions, origin and trace teachings are held to represent essentially different principles, and the origin teaching is clearly superior.[58] Various transmission texts give different, often doctrinally complex, descriptions of the differences between the two sections of the *Lotus Sūtra.*[59] For example, it is said that the trace teaching maintains the perspective of acquired enlightenment while the origin teaching reveals that of original enlightenment; that the trace teaching adopts a static view of suchness as an unchanging principle *(fuhen shinnyo no ri),* and the origin teaching, a dynamic view of suchness as wisdom that accords with conditions *(zuien shinnyo no chi);* that the trace teaching holds the position that delusions are to be extirpated, and the origin section, that they are always inherent; that the trace teaching sets forth the view of moving from cause, or practice, to arrive at effect, or enlightenment *(jūin shika),* and the origin teaching, the view of proceeding from effect to cause *(jūka kōin);* and so forth. One of the most fundamental distinctions drawn between the two divisions of the *Lotus Sūtra* in medieval Tendai thought associates the trace teaching with abstract principle *(ri),* and the origin teaching, with concrete actuality *(ji).* This has some basis in continental T'ien-t'ai, where "principle" refers to the "true aspect of the dharmas" set forth in the trace teaching, and "actuality," to Śākyamuni's revelation of his first attainment of the Way in the remote past.[60] However, medieval Tendai develops this distinction much further. The "actuality" set forth in the origin teaching, equated with the revelation of Buddha's original enlightenment, is extended to include grass, trees, and all phenomena of this world, which are absolutized by being identified with the originally enlightened Buddha.

Two major points seem to be at stake here in the origin teaching/trace teaching distinction as interpreted in medieval Tendai doctrine. One is a clear preference for concrete realities over transcendent abstractions: There is no truth behind, or above, or underlying actual phenomena; truth is what one sees with one's own eyes. The other is a differentiation and hierarchical arrangement of two approaches to practice and enlightenment. The first, that of proceding linearly toward enlightenment as a remote goal by extirpating delusion and cultivating virtue, is relegated to the trace teaching and termed inferior; the second, that of realizing that enlightenment is inherent from the outset, is identified with the origin teaching and deemed superior.

3. "When the great teaching of *kanjin* rises, the great teaching of *honmon* is superseded." The first three elements in the fourfold rise and fall— the pre–*Lotus Sūtra* teachings, together with the trace and origin teachings that comprise the *Lotus Sūtra* itself—form the body of Buddhist doctrinal teachings *(chiao-hsiang, kyōsō)*. Chih-i balanced the study of doctrinal teachings with meditative disciplines *(kuan-hsin, kanjin)*, holding both to be essential to liberation. What was expounded in the text and what was realized in meditation he deemed to be the same truth, the only difference being whether one grasped it conceptually or realized it intuitively. In the fourfold rise and fall, however, these two categories become part of a hierarchical classification of teachings, and the "contemplation of the mind" is elevated to the supreme position. "The contemplation of the mind" or *kanjin* in this medieval Tendai context refers less frequently to a specific method of meditation than to the insight of original enlightenment, considered as an a priori ground. This *kanjin* is prior to the distinction of origin and trace teachings *(honjaku mibun)* or of subject and object, "before the arising of a single thought," and is said to be "innate and self-luminous" *(tenjin dokurō)*. (The phrase "innate and self-luminous is taken from Kuan-ting's preface to the *Mo-ho chih-kuan,* where it is used to suggest that Chih-i's teaching of "calming and contemplation" was born of his innate wisdom and not acquired from a teacher.[61] In medieval Tendai *kuden* texts, however, it is often used to mark a *kanjin*-style reading or interpretation from the standpoint of original enlightenment.)

Chih-i's specific contemplation methods—such as the threefold contemplation or the contemplation of a single thought-moment being three thousand realms—have their textual basis in the trace teaching, specifically, in the chapter on Skillful Means.[62] In Japan, however, with the rise of Taimitsu and the accompanying tendency to emphasize the origin teaching, "mind-contemplation" or "mind-discernment" *(kanjin)* or "calming and contemplation" *(shikan)*—terms employed to mean not simply meditative practices but the essence of Tendai *Lotus* studies[63]— came to be associated with the origin teaching. This association is evident by the late Heian.[64] Specific meditation methods in which a contemplating subject brings the illumination of a focused mind to bear upon analysis of an object were regarded as linear in approach, "moving from cause to effect"; they were termed "contemplation of principle" *(rikan)* and associated with the trace teaching. In contrast, the "contemplation of the mind" associated with the origin teaching was termed "contemplation of actuality" *(jikan)* and simply denoted the insight that all things, just as they are, are the Buddha of original enlightenment. This contemplation was considered nonlinear, "moving from effect to cause," and was often associated with "a single moment's faith and understanding" *(ichinen shinge).*[65] Traditionally said to represent the first step of the Way, in medieval Tendai thought, "a single moment's faith and understanding" is often held to encompass the Way in its entirety. Hazama Jikō, collating from a number of *kuden* texts, offers the following description of this contemplation:

> The green of willows and the red of cherry blossoms are precisely the form of the naturally inherent and self-luminous [contemplation]; the three thousand realms comprised by all phenomena of the universe, just as they are, are the primordial Buddha of original enlightenment and the behavior of the original enlightenment of that [Buddha's] self-enjoyment body. . . . In this meditation, apart from seeing mountains as mountains and rivers as rivers, there is no separate state one needs to enter. Not only is this precisely the realm of the Tathâgata's self-enjoyment body, but, because it is the original naturalness of the Dharma, apart from the moment of self-awakening, there is no fruit to be obtained and no practice to be cultivated. Simply, after the moment of self-awakening, striving to actualize the content of this originally inherent virtue of enlightenment is the whole of daily life; this is the sequence of "preceding from effect to cause."[66]

Once associated with the origin teaching, the "contemplation of the mind" was then elevated beyond it. While individual Tendai *kuden* texts differ on this issue, there was an increasing tendency to see *kanjin* not as meditative insight that illuminates the sūtra text, but as an originally inherent reality that is prior to it. This move was especially pronounced in the doctrinal interpretations emanating from the Senba *dangisho* at Kawagoe in Musashi, where it became known as the doctrine of *shikan shō Hokke* or "calming and contemplation surpasses the *Lotus*." Some Senba texts insist that *kanjin* is independent of the sūtra and even define "the contemplation of the mind" as constituting a distinct lineage or school *(shū):* the textual tradition represented by classical *Lotus Sūtra* commentaries constitutes the Hokkeshū, while the "contemplation of the mind" transmitted from master to disciple in the *kuden* tradition represents the Tendaishū.[67] Since *kanjin* had already become identified with the origin teaching, the question arises as to why it was deemed necessary to establish it as a separate, superior category. However, the posit-

ing of *kanjin* as the highest stage of doctrinal classification, distinct from
and "above" the sūtra text, would have served to legitimate the secret,
kanjin-style readings discussed above.

The origins of the fourfold rise and fall are not altogether certain.
Some scholars, notably Tamura Yoshirō, have argued that the establishment of "mind contemplation" as a separate category superior even to
the text of the *Lotus Sūtra* reflects the influence of the "sudden enlightenment" Ch'an (Jpn. Zen) tradition introduced from Sung China in the
mid-Kamakura period. Tamura suggests a connection, first, with the
"worldless Zen" of Dainichi Nōnin, founder of Darumashū and, more
particularly, with the prominent Zen teacher and abbot of the Tōfukuji,
Enni (a.k.a. Bennen or Shōichi Kokushi, 1202–1280).[68] According to the
Genkō shakusho compiled in 1322, Jōmyō, regarded as the founder of
the Gyōsen-bō branch of the Sugiu lineage of the Eshin school, studied
Zen with Enni.[69] Bennen himself is said to have described the "contemplation of the mind" as surpassing the origin and trace teachings that
comprise the *Lotus Sūtra*.[70] Some later Eshin commentaries explicitly
identify *shikan* of the Tendaishū with the Zen tradition's "separate transmission outside the scriptures."[71] The *Risshōkan jō*, attributed to Nichiren,
also points to a connection—negatively evaluated—between "wordless"
Zen and medieval Tendai ideas about *kanjin* as independent of the sūtra text: "If *shikan* is not grounded in the *Lotus Sūtra*, then the Tendai
shikan becomes equivalent to the Daruma[shū]'s diabolical and false
teaching of a separate transmission outside the scriptures."[72]

While there is evidence of Zen influence on medieval Tendai notions
of *kanjin* as surpassing even the *Lotus Sūtra*, we may parenthetically note
that the compilers of the Tendai *kuden* texts seem not to have made so
fervent a commitment as their Zen counterparts to the rhetoric of wordless transmission. The *Kankō ruijū* contains a transmission titled "written words are not [merely] written words; language is liberation," which
criticizes the extremes of both attachment to, and denial of the validity
of, written texts.[73] The *Zōda shō*, a Muromachi period *kuden* collection,
also rejects the dictum of "no reliance on words and letters."[74] The fourfold rise and fall in particular, and medieval Tendai thought in general,
position the *Lotus Sūtra* as mediating between conceptual and noncon-
ceptual understanding. It is only by encountering the words of the sūtra, or hearing its teaching that "all dharmas are the Buddha-Dharma,"
that the ineffable, "naturally inherent and self-luminous" enlightenment
known as *kanjin* can be accessed.

In addition to the influence of Southern Ch'an, the fourfold rise and
fall may have roots in the tradition of contemplative Pure Land practices
that developed within Tendai during the Heian period and that stress
the nonduality of Amida Buddha and the practitioner. A medieval
Tendai Pure Land text known as the *Jigyō nenbutsu mondō* (Questions and

answers on the *nenbutsu* as self-practice), retrospectively attributed to Genshin, discusses the karmic bonds between Amida and the beings of this Sahā world from four perspectives, distinguished as the "four kinds of Amida": (1) Amida of the pre–*Lotus Sūtra* teachings, who in the past, as a king, launched his bodhisattva practice under the Buddha Jewel Store (Ratnagarbha, Hōzō); (2) Amida of the trace teaching of the *Lotus Sūtra,* who is described, in chapter 7 of the sūtra, as one of sixteen princes who renounced the world to follow the teachings of their father, the Buddha Victorious through Great Penetrating Wisdom, and who are now preaching in the lands of the eight quarters; (3) Amida of the origin teaching, who is identified with Śākyamuni as the Buddha who first realized enlightenment in the remote past and has been preaching here in this world ever since; and (4) Amida of mind-contemplation *(kanjin),* who is identified with the ninth consciousness of all living beings and with the Dharma body.[75] Here "Amida" is interpreted in terms of the same four categories that comprise the *shijū kōhai.* The dating of the *Jigyō nenbutsu mondō* is not certain, nor is the extent to which ideas about the "four kinds of the Amida" circulated. Still, there may be a connection between the ideas expressed in this text and the later development of the Eshin comparative classification of the "fourfold rise and fall."[76]

Another possible inspiration for this new doctrinal classification scheme may have come from the Tendai system of debate-style doctrinal training. Ozaki Kōjin suggests that the "fourfold rise and fall" was influenced by a form used in debate, in which a particular topic would be explicated sequentially in terms of the same four categories: the pre–*Lotus Sūtra* teachings, the trace teaching, the origin teaching, and the contemplation of the mind.[77] Still another possibility, suggested Shigyō Kaishū, is that the fourfold rise and fall grew out of a *kenmitsu* synthesis of Mikkyō and traditional T'ien-t'ai/Tendai studies, in which the "esoteric" side was accorded superior status. Viewed from this standpoint, *kanjin* or mind-contemplation represents the timeless enlightenment of the original Buddha transmitted directly to Chih-i on Sacred Eagle Peak and corresponds to the "esoteric teachings," while the other three categories represent the historically conditioned, textually based doctrines expounded in accord with their listeners' capacity, and thus correspond to "exoteric teachings."[78]

Whatever its sources, the doctrinal classification the fourfold rise and fall clearly served to legitimize the medieval Tendai *kuden* tradition, as Sueki Fumihiko has pointed out.[79] In particular, establishing the category of *kanjin* as independent of and superior to the sūtra text was logically consistent in the context of a tradition that grounded its authority not on publicly accessible documents such as sūtras and commentaries, but on the transmission of secret interpretations handed down within relatively closed lineages.

The "Threefold Seven Great Matters"

As *kuden* transmissions on particular topics developed in both Eshin and Danna lineages, they began to be codified as "great matters" *(daiji)* and organized into systems. Danna *kuden* texts elaborate two, three, five, or seven or more such articles of transmission.[80] The five articles of transmission conferred in the Danna *genshi kanjō* ritual were discussed in the preceding chapter. In the Eshin school, orally transmitted doctrines *(kuden hōmon)* were eventually systematized as the "threefold seven great matters" *(sanjū shichika no daiji)*. These seven "great matters" are subdivided into two groups: the four broad categories of transmission and the three abbreviated transmissions. The four broad categories of transmission *(kōden shika)*, also called the four essential phrases of transmission *(denbō yōge no shika)*, are: (1) the threefold contemplation in a single mind *(isshin sangan)*; (2) the meaning of the mind and its objects *(shinkyōgi)*; (3) the essentials of calming and contemplation *(shikan taishi)*; and (4) the deep meaning of the *Lotus Sūtra (Hokke jingi)*. The three abbreviated transmissions *(ryakuden sanka no daiji)* are elaborations on the fourth of the broad categories, "the deep meaning of the *Lotus Sūtra*," and consist of: (1) the triple-bodied Tathâgata of the perfect teaching *(engyō sanjin)*; (2) the significance of the Land of Ever-Tranquil Light *(jō jakkōdo gi)*; and (3) the causality of the *Lotus (Hokke inga)*.

This system was formulated over a considerable period of time, probably beginning around the latter part of the thirteenth century and continuing into the Nanbokuchō and Muromachi periods.[81] The names of the four broad categories first appear in the *Tendai Hokkeshū denbōge* (Verses of Dharma transmission of the Tendai-*Lotus* lineage), a work attributed to Saichō that was probably composed by about 1100.[82] They are elaborated in the *Shuzenji-ketsu*, a text whose date has been hotly disputed but which was probably compiled somewhere between the late Heian and mid-Kamakura periods. However, the explanations of the four broad categories given in the *Shuzenji-ketsu* differ from those of later texts, and the three abbreviated categories, while enumerated, are not explained. The first text to present the seven great matters in their eventual form, and explicitly to identify them with the Eshin school, is the *Eshin-ryū naishō sōjō hōmon shū* (Collection of doctrines of the transmission of the inner enlightenment of the Eshin school), more conveniently known as the *Ichijō shō* or "one-fascicle writing." It was compiled by Shinsō (fl. 1329), a disciple of Shinga, who was a disciple of Jōmyō (fl. late 13th cent.), regarded as the founder of the Gyōsen-bō lineage of the Eshin school. According to Shinsō's colophon, the work was first drafted by Jōmyō's teacher Shunpan, recording the secret oral teachings handed down from Chūjin (1065–1138), which Shunpan had presented to Emperor Gosaga.[83] (The transmission from Chūjin, Shunpan's authorship, and his presentation to the throne are all open to question, though Gosaga's connections with eminent Tendai clerics are well attested.[84]) Extant commentaries on the seven great matters were compiled by monks of both Mt. Hiei and of the Kantō, but all traced their lineage to Jōmyō, especially through his disciple Shinga.[85] Hazama Jikō has therefore suggested that Jōmyō and his disciples, especially Shinga, were central to the system's development.[86]

To give a sense of the system, we will briefly outline the seven categories, including both their origins in earlier T'ien-t'ai/Tendai sources and their interpretation in Eshin-school commentaries, focusing on the earliest, Shinsō's *Ichijō shō.*

The Four Broad Categories of Transmission

The first category, the "threefold contemplation in a single mind" *(isshin sangan),* is, as noted earlier, the contemplation for discerning the three truths of emptiness *(kūtai),* conventional existence *(ketai),* and the middle *(chūtai).* The three truths are central to Chih-i's *Fa-hua hsüan-i,* his commentary on the meaning of the *Lotus Sūtra,* and the threefold contemplation is developed in his meditation treatise *Mo-ho chih-kuan;* together they form the "deep structure" underlying the entire T'ien-t'ai system of doctrinal study and meditation.[87]

The *Mo-ho chih-kuan* explains the "threefold" aspect of this contemplation as follows.[88] First is "entering [the insight of] emptiness from the [viewpoint of] the conventional"; that is, one contemplates the conditioned, dependent nature of all phenomena, which are without permanence or self-essence. From the perspective of this insight, all categories, hierarchies, and boundaries are collapsed; it is a discernment of ultimate equality. The discernment of all phenomena as empty frees one from attachment to desires and intellectual constructs and is said to correspond to the insight of arhats and bodhisattvas of the Tripiṭaka and shared teachings.[89] Next is "entering [insight into] the conventional from [the discernment of] emptiness." Having discerned the nonsubstantial, contingent nature of things, one cognizes their provisional existence as phenomena arising through dependent origination and is thus able to act in the world in a soteriologically effective way. This discernment reestablishes categories and distinctions, but without biased attachment or false essentializing; it is said to correspond to the wisdom of bodhisattvas of the separate teaching. Last is the "contemplation of the Middle Way that is the supreme meaning." Here one contemplates phenomena as both empty and provisionally existing, discerning both aspects simultaneously. This is said to correspond to the wisdom of the Buddha and of the perfect teaching. This progression through the three contemplations of emptiness, conventional existence, and the middle described here is called the "sequential threefold contemplation" *(tz'u-*

ti san-kuan, shidai sangan). However, Chih-i defines as superior the contemplation in which all three truths are discerned simultaneously; this is the "perfect and immediate calming and contemplation" *(yüan-tun chih-kuan, endon shikan).*

As we have seen, the threefold contemplation in a single mind, considered as Chih-i's inner enlightenment and the substance of Tao-sui's transmission to Saichō, is central to the medieval Tendai *kuden* tradition. Its importance is indicated by its position as the first of the seven great matters. The *Ichijō shō* and other commentaries discuss it in terms of the two nondual aspects of object and subject: that is, that which is to be contemplated, "the threefold truth in a single mind, which is object" *(kyō no isshin santai)* and that which contemplates, the "threefold contemplation in a single mind, which is wisdom" *(chi no isshin sangan).* As with subsequent "great matters," the threefold contemplation is explained first in terms of its meaning in classical T'ien-t'ai texts and then given a characteristically *hongaku* or *kanjin*-style reading. From the latter perspective, the threefold contemplation is not a meditation method but the originally inherent nature of reality:

> Everything from our own speech to the sound of the waves rising or the wind blowing is the threefold contemplation in a single mind, the originally inherent three thousands realms [i.e., all dharmas]. There is nothing to cultivate and nothing to attain. . . . The forms of all things exerting their functions and arising in dependence upon conditions, is, without transformation, the threefold contemplation in its totality.[90]

The second transmission, that of "the meaning of the mind and its objects," concerns the single thought-moment comprising three thousand realms *(ichinen sanzen),* Chih-i's complex, architectonic model for the mutual inclusion of the dharmas and the nonduality of the mind and the phenomenal world.[91] In the seventh chapter of the *Mo-ho chih-chuan,* Chih-i sets forth ten modes of contemplation, ranging from subtle to coarse. The first and most fundamental, "contemplating the realm of the inconceivable" *(kuan pu-k'o-ssu-i ching, kan fukashigi kyō),* is to discern that the present object of contemplation is identical with the true aspect of reality, that is, the threefold truth.[92] This is the portion of the text that sets forth the "single thought-moment comprising three thousand realms." Since explanations of this concept in English sources are few, and since it is important not only in the medieval Tendai context but to the discussion in chapter 6 of Nichiren's thought, it is worth presenting here in some detail.[93]

The "single thought-moment" indicates the briefest possible instant in the thoughts of ordinary worldings that arise from one moment to the next, while the "three thousand realms" indicates the whole of phenomenal reality. In explaining the structure of "one mind" being "three thousand realms," Chih-i says:

> Now one mind comprises ten dharma realms, but each dharma realm also comprises ten dharma realms, giving a hundred dharma realms. One realm comprises thirty kinds of realms, hence a hundred dharma realms comprise three thousand kinds of realms. These three thousand are contained in a fleeting moment of thought. Where there is no mind, that is the end of the matter; but if mind comes into being to the slightest degree whatsoever, it immediately contains the three thousand.[94]

Although each "thought-moment" is here said to "contain" the three thousand realms, Chih-i is careful to make clear that, in his system, the mind is not prior to dharmas:

> One may say neither that the one mind is prior and all dharmas posterior nor that all dharmas are prior and the one mind posterior. . . . If one derives all dharmas from the one mind, this is a vertical relationship. If the mind all at once contains all dharmas, this is a horizontal relationship. Neither vertical nor horizontal will do. All one can say is that the mind is all dharmas, and all dharmas are the mind. Therefore the relationship is neither vertical nor horizontal, neither the same nor different. It is obscure, subtle and profound in the extreme. Knowledge cannot know it, nor can words speak it. Herein lies the reason for its being called "the realm of the inconceivable."[95]

As noted in chapter 1, this mutual encompassing of the mind and all dharmas marks an important difference between Chih-i's thought and that of Hua-yen and other forms of Mahāyāna in which the dharmas are said to arise from the one mind.

Chih-i begins by noting that the mind comprises "ten dharma realms." These ten realms (*jikkai*) refer to the ten categories of living beings: hell-dwellers, hungry ghosts, asura demons, humans, gods, voice-hearers, condition-perceivers, bodhisattvas, and Buddhas.[96] While these ten are ranged hierarchically from the viewpoint of provisional existence, from the viewpoint of emptiness, they lack independent self-nature and therefore copenetrate, thus making "a hundred dharma realms." The mutual encompassing or copenetration of the ten realms (*jikkai gogu*) collapses any ontological distinction between the Buddha and the beings, implying that the nine realms of unenlightened beings possess the Buddha nature inherently, while the Buddha possesses the nine realms of unenlightened beings. The mutual inclusion of the ten realms represents an important characteristic of Chih-i's thought: there is no original "pure mind"; good and evil are always nondual and mutually possessed. The most depraved *icchantika* is endowed the Buddha realm, while the Buddha is still latently endowed with the realms of unenlightened beings. This would eventually give rise to the controversial T'ien-t'ai doctrine of "inherent evil not being extirpated" even in the mind of the Buddha.[97]

Each of the ten realms further possesses the ten suchnesses *(jūnyoze)* that constitute the "true aspect of the dharmas" as set forth in the following passage of the *Lotus Sūtra:*

> Only a Buddha and a Buddha together can fathom the true aspect of the dharmas, that is to say, the suchness of their characteristics, the suchness of their nature, the suchness of their essence, the suchness of their power, the suchness of their activity, the suchness of their causes, the suchness of their conditions, the suchness of their effects, the suchness of their recompenses and the suchness of their ultimate equality from beginning to end.[98]

Chih-i explains these ten suchnesses as follows:

> "Characteristics" has its point of reference externally. What can be distinguished by being seen is called "characteristics." Nature has its point of reference internally. That which intrinsically belongs to oneself and does not change is called "nature." That which is the central quality [of something] is called "essence." The ability to influence is called "power." That which constructs is called "activity." Repetitive causes are called "causes" [i.e., karma]. Auxilliary causes are called "conditions." Repetitive results are called "effects." Retributive effects are called "recompenses." The first, "characteristics," is called the "beginning"; the ninth, "recompense," is called the "end"; and the place to which they belong is "ultimately equal."[99]

Each of the ten realms contains the ten suchnesses.[100] The ten dharma realms, interpenetrating to form a hundred realms that each simultaneously possesses the ten suchnesses, comprise the thousand suchnesses.

Moreover, each of the ten dharma realms may be understood in terms of the three realms *(san seken):* the realm of the five *skandhas* or aggregates, the realm of sentient beings, and the realm of the land.[101] The "realm of the five *skandhas*" represents an analysis of the sentient being in terms of its psychosomatic constituents: forms, perceptions, conceptions, volitions, and consciousness. The "realm of living beings" views the living being as an independent existent that can be said to belong to one or another of the ten dharma realms. The "realm of the land" is the objective realm in which the beings dwell. Because each of the ten dharma realms, which embodies the ten suchnesses, can also be understood in terms of these three categories, Chih-i says, "One realm comprises thirty kinds of realms." Thus, the ten dharma realms, copenetrating, yield a hundred realms; multiplied times the ten suchnesses they yield a thousand suchnesses; and multiplied times the three realms they equal three thousand realms.

The number three thousand is itself arbitrary; the point is that "all of reality is an integrated, interdependent unity," as Paul Swanson puts it.[102] The concept of the "three thousand realms in a single thought-moment" is not, however, merely an analysis of the structure of reality. It is the "realm of the inconceivable" to be discerned in meditation by the practitioner, who in so doing realizes one's own identity with the totality of all that is. Kanno Hiroshi, in an essay on *ichinen sanzen*, lists five soteriological implications of this concept.[103] (1) By virtue of the ten suchnesses, which constitute "the true aspect of the dharmas," all beings in the hierarchy of the ten dharma realms, from hell-dwellers at the bottom to Buddhas at the top, are shown to have a common ontological structure, upon which the mutual inclusion of the ten realms can be asserted. Thus the *ichinen sanzen* concept structurally clarifies the basis upon which deluded beings can realize Buddhahood. Specifically, because the Buddha realm is inherent in the human realm, ordinary worldlings can potentially become Buddhas. (2) As a corollary, the ontological equality of all beings is established, whatever their place in the hierarchy of the ten dharma realms. (3) Just as the Buddha realm is contained even in the hell realm, so the hell realm is contained even in the realm of Buddha. This undergirds the claim that the Tathâgata still possesses the nature of evil innately and thus clarifies the basis of the Buddha's compassion, upon which his salvation of evil beings can become reality. (4) The subjective individual and the objective dharma realm are shown to be nondual; hell-dwellers live in hells, Buddhas in Buddha lands, and so on. Thus, potentially, the individual's realization of Buddhahood can transform the outer world. As will be noted in chapter 6, this implication of the *ichinen sanzen* concept undergoes particular development in the teaching of Nichiren. And (5) all existential possibilities, from the utmost suffering of the hells to the Buddha's liberation, are implicit in the present thought-moment of the ordinary person; thus all potential is located within the individual.

In the *Ichijō shō* and other Eshin commentaries of the medieval Tendai tradition, the "single thought-moment being three thousand realms" is characterized from an immanentalist standpoint as the "original principle that is innate and self-luminous" *(tenjin dokurō naru honri no ichinen sanzen)*. As noted above, this phrase marks the introduction of a secret interpretation made from standpoint of original enlightenment. In this *kanjin*-style reading, the "single thought-moment being three thousand realms" is the moment of the "first thought" when "[the thought of] plum blossoms arises and plum blossoms appear, [the thought of] cherry blossoms arises and cherry blossoms appear"—the inseparability and simultaneous arising of the mind and the phenomenal world. "Apart from

the continuous arising of the present thought-moment, there is no practice to cultivate. The true essence of this thought that now arises, just as
it is, manifests direct realization of dharma realm."[104]

These first two of the four broad categories, the transmissions concerning the "threefold contemplation in a single mind" and "the mind
and its objects," may be said to encapsulate the two fundamental T'ien-
t'ai/Tendai teachings on meditation, reformulated from the standpoint
of original enlightenment.

The third transmission, that of "the essentials of calming and contemplation," is said to represent the gist of Chih-i's great meditation treatise, the *Mo-ho chih-kuan* (The great calming and contemplation). The
Ichijō shō and other Eshin *kuden* commentaries consider the "essentials"
of this work under two aspects: essence *(shūshi)* and teachings *(shūkyō)*.
"Essence" is the "innate and self-luminous calming and contemplation";
it denotes the mind prior to words and concepts and to the distinctions
of delusion and enlightenment, practice and attainment, self and other,
and so forth. "Teachings" refers to the textual tradition. In terms of transmission, the textual tradition passed sequentially from master to disciple is called the Hokkeshū, but the transmission of the *shikan* that Chih-i
"practiced within his own mind" is direct and intuitive and is called the
Tendaishū.[105]

"The essentials of calming and contemplation" represents one of those
instances in which concern for differences in human ability finds its way
into original enlightenment discourse. "Calming and contemplation" is
equated with original enlightenment and thus can have no levels or
grades, but individual capacity is not equal. Persons of superior faculties
are said to realize that "a single thought-moment is the dharma realm"
(ichinen hokkai) on merely encountering the preface to the *Mo-ho chih-
kuan*. Those of intermediate faculties can do so through the five lesser
chapters that comprise the initial "Ta-i" or "Synopsis" chapter of this
work: Arousing the Great Thought, Engaging in the Great Practice, Manifesting the Great Results, Rending the Great Net, and Returning to the
Great Abode.[106] Those of lesser capacity can realize enlightenment
through the entire *Mo-ho chih-kuan*. In the course of this discussion, all
the subheadings of Chih-i's "Synopsis" chapter are given *kanjin*-style interpretations from the standpoint of original enlightenment. For example,
the literal meaning of "Arousing the Great Thought"—producing the
bodhicitta or aspiration for enlightenment—is given an esoteric reading
as "believing that the myriad dharmas are the single unborn"; "Engaging in the Great Practice" means that the room one lives in is the splen-
didly adorned practice hall where the entire dharma realm performs the
four types of *samādhi*, and so forth.[107] Of the three kinds of "calming and
contemplation" set forth in the *Mo-ho chih-kuan*—"gradual," "indeterminate" (i.e., a combination of gradual and sudden methods employed

according to circumstances), and "perfect and sudden"—the first two are rejected as "not the fundamental interpretation of this school." The perfect and sudden *shikan* itself is interpreted as "nonduality" and "the dharma realm."[108]

Just as the third transmission is said to encompass the essentials of the *Mo-ho chih-kuan,* the fourth, "the deep meaning of the *Lotus Sūtra,*" is said to convey the essentials of Chih-i's *Fa-hua hsüan-i* (Profound meaning of the *Lotus Sūtra*). This transmission concerns the "five profound principles" *(gojū gengi)* in which terms the *Lotus Sūtra* is analyzed in Chih-i's *Hsüan-i:* name, essence, gist, function, and teachings.[109] In the *Ichijō shō* and similar texts, *"Lotus Sūtra"* is taken in its ultimate sense to refer not to a scriptural text, but to the perfectly interpenetrating dharma realm in its totality, and the "five profound principles" are interpreted as attributes of the dharma realm.[110] For example, its "name" is conventional truth *(saṃvṛti-satya, zokutai),* its "essence" is the principle of the true aspect, and so forth. This transmission draws on Saichō's concept of the "three kinds of *Lotus Sūtra*" *(sanshu Hokke),* discussed in chapter 1, which it explains in this fashion: the "fundamental *Lotus Sūtra*" indicates the primordial origin, prior to the advent and preaching of the Buddha; the various teachings of the Buddha's lifetime, Hīnayāna and Mahāyāna, true and provisional, are the "hidden and secret *Lotus Sūtra*"; and the *Lotus Sūtra* that represents the fifth period in the Buddha's preaching life and integrates all earlier teachings is the "explicitly preached *Lotus Sūtra.*" Thus all truth, whether prior to words or formally articulated, and of whatever sūtra, is subsumed within "the *Lotus Sūtra.*"

The *Ichijō shō* also includes in this transmission a discussion of the "*Lotus* precepts," which are given a strongly immanentalist, *kanjin*-style reading. "Keeping the precepts means dwelling securely in the dharma realm and manifesting [the realization] that this [present] body is originally inherent and constantly abiding. Not [thus] dwelling securely is called breaking the precepts." As for the three groups of pure precepts *(sanju jōkai),* those for the prevention of evil are "each of the myriad dharmas as it is, which is the total aspect of meditation and wisdom"; those for the promotion of good are "the functions of the myriad dharmas: the wind blowing and scattering blossoms, smoke rising, and incense perfuming"; and those for the salvation of sentient beings comprise such matters as "clothes warding off cold and food prolonging life, naturally benefitting living beings."[111]

Since the last two of the four broad transmissions concern, respectively, the *Mo-ho chih-kuan* and the *Fa-hua hsüan-i,* the question arises as to why there is no transmission concerning the third of Chih-i's three major works, the *Fa-hua wen-chü* (Words and phrases of the *Lotus Sūtra*). Some Eshin texts clarify this by saying that the *Chih-kuan* represents the Dharma that Chih-i practiced in his own mind, and the *Hsüan-i* likewise represents the Buddha's inner enlightenment. The *Wen-chü,* however, deals with the specific words and phrases of the sūtra, which are accommodated teachings. However, were the *Wen-chū* to be read from the perspective of the Buddha's true intention, his innermost enlightenment, it would then come under the transmission concerning "the deep meaning of the *Lotus.*"[112]

The four broad categories of transmission discussed above may be said to encapsulate the entire T'ien-t'ai/Tendai system of doctrine and meditation, reinterpreted from a *hongaku* perspective. They deal, from four different perspectives, with the same concept: the total and perfect identity of the single thought-moment with the cosmos or dharma realm, a reality cognized as empty, conventionally existing, and both simultaneously. This reality is held to be the essence of Chih-i's inner enlightenment, the deepest meaning of the *Lotus Sūtra,* and the truth to be accessed by the practitioner. As Hazama Jikō has pointed out, the "threefold contemplation" provides the unifying structure for the entire system.[113] A later Eshin text makes this point by applying a *kanjin*-style reading using numerical correspondence to the four categories. The "threefold contemplation in a single mind" is equated with emptiness; "the meaning of the mind and its objects," with conventional existence; the "essentials of calming and contemplation" with the middle; and the "deep meaning of the *Lotus,*" with the threefold contemplation as the totality of the single mind or thought-moment, thus showing the centrality of *isshin sangan* to the four broad transmissions.[114]

The Three Abbreviated Transmissions

The three abbreviated transmissions *(ryakuden sanka no daiji)* represent elaborations on the fourth of the broad categories, the "deep meaning of the *Lotus Sūtra.*" They are as follows:

The transmission concerning "the three bodies of the perfect teaching" *(engyō sanjin)* clarifies the Buddha of the "Fathoming the Lifespan" chapter of the *Lotus Sūtra.* This Buddha is said to possess all three kinds of Buddha body *(trikāya, sanjin):* the manifested body *(nirmāṇa-kāya, ōjin),* or physical person of the Buddha who appears in this world; the recompense body *(saṃbhoga-kāya, hōjin),* or the wisdom the Buddha has attained through practice, conceived of as a subtle "body"; and the Dharma body *(dharma-kāya, hosshin),* or the Buddha as personification of ultimate truth. These three "bodies" originally represented attempts to organize different concepts of the Buddha, or to explain the differences among various Buddhas appearing in the sūtras.[115] For example, Śākyamuni who appeared in this world was considered a Buddha in the manifested-body aspect; Amitābha, a Buddha in the recompense-body aspect; and Mahāvairocana, a Buddha in the Dharma-body aspect. Chih-i, however, interpreted these three bodies as the attributes of a single, original Buddha, the Śākyamuni of the sixteenth chapter of the *Lotus Sūtra,* enlightened since countless dust-particle kalpas ago. For Chih-i, the unity of the three was mediated by the recompense body, which he saw as central.[116]

As discussed in chapter 1, with the development of Japanese Taimitsu thought, Chih-i's triple-bodied Buddha of the *Lotus Sūtra* came increasingly to be identified with the timeless cosmic Buddha Mahāvairocana or Dainichi, whose thoughts, speech, and body are all phenomena. In this process, the Buddha of the *Lotus* progressively lost his individual character as Śākyamuni who had once cultivated bodhisattva practice over innumerable lifetimes and finally achieved Buddhahood in the remote past and was transformed into a personification of ultimate reality, timeless and omnipresent. In medieval Tendai texts, the triple-bodied Tathāgata of the *Lotus Sūtra* is typically referred to as "spontaneous" or "unproduced" *(musa sanjin).* The term *musa* in Chinese T'ien-t'ai texts originally designated "ultimate reality that is beyond conceptualization and verbal distinctions."[117] In the medieval Japanese Tendai tradition, it assumed the additional connotations of "natural" or "just as it is"—in short, a synonym for original enlightenment.[118] The term "unproduced triple-bodied [Tathāgata]" appears to have been coined by Saichō, though he employed it in a sense different from its usage in the later Tendai *kuden* literature.[119] There, in the expanded sense of *musa,* it is employed to mean the originally inherent Buddha who is prior to the distinction between practice and awakening, delusion and enlightenment. The *Ichijō shō* cites an apocryphal transmission from Saichō to the effect that this Buddha "transcends august features" *(shussongyō);* the ordinary aspects of life, such as "wearing clothes and using fans," is his true form. "All beings of the ten realms, including us ordinary worldlings, are the unproduced triple-bodied Tathāgata in his original ground."[120] The so-called eight aspects of a Buddha's life—being born in the Tuṣita heaven, descending from the Tuṣita heaven, entering the womb, leaving the womb, renouncing the world, subduing Māra, attaining the Way, turning the Dharma wheel and entering nirvāṇa—are interpreted as "the totality of the beings of the ten worlds being born, abiding, changing, and perishing, dying in one place and being born in another."[121]

The transmission concerning "the meaning of the Land of Ever-Tranquil Light" concerns the realm that the unproduced triple-bodied Tathāgata inhabits. The "Land of Ever-Tranquil Light" originally denoted one of the four kinds of lands enumerated by Chih-i: (1) lands where ordinary persons and sages dwell together, as in this Sahā world; (2) provisional lands, inhabited by persons of the two vehicles who have eradicated the delusions of intellectual views and emotional attachments *(chien-ssu-huo, kenji-waku)* but not the remaining two of the three categories of delusion; (3) lands of actual reward, inhabited by bodhisattvas who have to a certain extent realized the Middle Way; and (4) the Land of Ever-

Tranquil Light, presided over by the Buddha in his self-enjoyment body.[122] The *Ichijō shō* and other Tendai *kuden* texts discuss this land under the two aspects of principle *(ri)* and actuality *(ji)*. The Land of Ever-Tranquil Light in terms of principle designates that which is prior to the arising of the single thought-moment, before the "myriad things" have been differentiated, while the land of Ever-Tranquil Light in terms of concrete actuality denotes the differentiated three thousand realms that comprise the phenomenal world in its entirety. This land—like the Buddha who inhabits it and with whom it is nondual—is omnipresent and originally inherent. The other three kinds of land reduce to this one; the four categories are established only in response to differences in the intellectual constructs to which people are attached.[123] This transmission typifies the "antitranscendent" rhetorical stance found in one strand of medieval Tendai literature, which identifies the immediate, visible world with ultimate reality and dismisses teachings about other realms as mere expedients.

The last "great matter" is the "causality of the *Lotus.*" Conventionally, "cause" refers to the practice for attaining enlightenment, or those who are at the stage of practice, while "effect" denotes the enlightenment that is attained, or the Buddha who has attained it. Here, however, since the "cause" and "effect" in question are those of the unproduced triple-bodied Tathâgata, they are simultaneous and originally inherent. Or in other words, "cause" (living beings of the nine realms) and "effect" (the Buddha) copenetrate and are mutually encompassing; the three thousand realms represent the forms of this causality. This is called the "causality of the lotus" by analogy to the lotus plant, which is said to bear blossoms and seed pods simultaneously. In a typical *kanjin*-style reversal, the name "lotus blossom" *(renge)*, denoting the simultaneity of cause and effect, is said to have existed since the beginningless past and was only at some later point applied to the flowering plant known by this name.[124] The "causality of the lotus" is identified with the dharma realm and specifically with the body of the ordinary worldling, drawing on the widespread notion that the lobes of the heart in the human breast resemble the eight-petalled lotus of the central court of the Matrix-Realm mandala.[125]

The three abbreviated transmissions are really different perspectives on the same thing: the triple-bodied Buddha of the perfect teaching. This Buddha himself, the land he inhabits, and his cause and effect are all explained as the perfectly interpenetrating dharma realm just as it is, fully present in and identified with a single moment of thought. This is in essence the same vision of reality elaborated by the four broad transmissions. However, where the four broad transmissions focus on a single mind being the dharma realm in terms of "cause"—the threefold contemplation—the three abbreviated transmissions present this reality from the standpoint of "effect"—the enlightenment accessed thereby. However, as "cause" and "effect" are regarded as simultaneous, the two are mutually identified. Thus the entire system of the "seven great matters" can be seen as exfoliating from the threefold contemplation in a single mind.[126] This is true of Chih-i's system of doctrine and meditation as well; here, however, the received T'ien-t'ai tradition is reinterpreted from a *hongaku* perspective. Over time, transmissions of the seven great matters became increasingly complex, additional layers of interpretation and commentary being added to each category.

The seven great matters are said to be "threefold" *(sanjū)* because they eventually came to be transmitted under the three aspects of teaching *(kyō)*, practice *(gyō)*, and realization *(shō)*.[127] In other words, as "teaching," they represent topics of doctrinal study; as "practice," objects of contemplation; and as "realization," the content of insight. As the tradition developed, separate initiation rituals were conducted for transmitting each of the three "folds,"[128] and distinct bodies of transmission literature grew up around, or came to be assigned to, the two categories of "teaching" or "practice." Transmissions belonging to the "practice" category were said to represent the "teaching [revealed] within the [jeweled] stūpa" *(tatchū hōmon)* that emerges from beneath the earth in chapter 11 of the *Lotus Sūtra;* both these transmissions and the rituals for conferring them were linked to identification of the jeweled stūpa of the Buddha Many Jewels with the dharma realm, and the understanding of the Buddha's preaching on Eagle Peak as timelessly and universally occurring. The "realization" category by definition cannot be expressed in words, and its transmission consisted simply of a certificate of transmission bestowed upon the initiate, placing him within the lineage beginning with Śākyamuni who preaches the truth that is the supreme meaning in the Pure Land of Eagle Peak.[129] The development of the "practice" category of transmission texts seems to have occurred in Kantō Eshin lineages, and transmission of the seven great matters in terms of three "folds" may possibly have been restricted to eastern Japan.[130]

"Teaching, practice, and realization" were of course not new categories. Chih-i had proposed them as three aspects of the term "vehicle."[131] They had also long been used in connection with eschatological notions of a three-stage process of Buddhist decline: in the age of the True Dharma *(shōbō)*, the teaching flourishes, people practice and achieve realization; in the age of the Semblance Dharma *(zōhō)*, teaching and practice remain but realization is no longer achieved; and by the Final Dharma age, only the teaching remains, there is neither authentic practice nor realization.[132] It is in fact characteristic of the medieval Tendai *kuden hōmon* that, rather than inventing new categories, they employed existing ones in creative ways. It has also been suggested that Shinran, while staying in Hitachi, may have taken these three categories from Kantō Tendai sources and incorporated them into the structure of his *Kyōgyōshinshō* (Teaching, practice, faith, and realization).[133]

In this connection, it is worth noting that the system of transmissions concerning the "seven great matters" encompasses both "orthodox," text-based readings as well as *kanjin*-style interpretations. Collections of *kuden hōmon* like the *Ichijō shō* in fact assume a considerable knowledge of fundamental T'ien-t'ai texts such as the *Fa-hua hsüan-i* and *Mo-ho chih-kuan;* without such knowledge, they would scarcely be comprehensible. This supports the suggestion, made earlier in this chapter, that the *kanjin* hermeneutical mode did not wholly supplant, but was in fact dependent on, a more traditional manner of doctrinal and textual understanding. Rather than representing a rejection of orthodox, textual knowledge, *kanjin*-style interpretations purported to present a deeper, estericized reading of this knowledge, reoriented from the "ultimate" perspective of original enlightenment.

Conclusion

Two key issues emerge from the above discussion of medieval Tendai hermeneutics and doctrine. One is the centrality of "mind-contemplation" or *kanjin,* whether understood as contemplative practice; as meditative insight or discernment; as a particular mode of interpretation; or as an originally inherent reality prior to conceptions and verbalizations, which both meditative discernment and *kanjin*-style interpretation were believed to reveal. The practice of hermeneutics in the *kanjin* mode generated the distinct content of transmissions particular to individual lineages. Exegetical readings, in that they follow from texts in the public domain, do not lend themselves to the status of "secret knowledge." *Kanjin*-style readings, on the other hand, underlay the privatizing of knowledge claims made by closed, independent lineages and thus supported the entire culture of secret transmission discussed in the preceding chapter. Hermeneutical practice in the *kanjin* mode was in turn legitimized by the new doctrinal classification of the fourfold rise and fall, which not only accommodated but privileged it. The establishment of *kanjin* as the highest category of doctrinal classification validated, and raised above orthodox exegetical understandings, subjective insights into the realm of original enlightenment, which was held to be both deeper than, and prior to, written texts. With *kanjin*-style readings thus valorized, the entire system of Tendai doctrine and practice was reformulated to include them, for example, in intricate schema such as the threefold seven great matters comprising the *kuden hōmon* of the Eshin school. Medieval Tendai hermeneutics and doctrine were nothing less than a reworking in its entirety of the received T'ien-t'ai/Tendai tradition from perspective of original enlightenment.

All this, in turn, demands that we rethink the alleged decline of scholarship said to have characterized medieval Tendai. Taking place as it did within an institutional structure of relatively closed lineages, much of medieval Tendai intellectual activity was exclusivistic and thus not compatible with abstract (and often ahistorical) ideals of universal Dharma access; nor, being grounded in the holistic assumptions of a radically different episteme, was its *kanjin*-style hermeneutic what we understand as scholarship today. It differed from the learning of Tendai Buddhism in both the early Heian and the modern period in that it emphatically relegated the exegetical mode to second place and took as its interpretive basis a premise—that of original enlightenment—external to the received tradition, which was then read back into its classic texts. Nonetheless, medieval Tendai scholarship had its own rules, logic, and standards and exhibited a great deal of creativity, all of which has been obscured by the modern academic rhetoric about scholarly decline. A fuller understanding of the intellectual bases of the *kuden* tradition is essential to an accurate understanding not only of medieval Tendai, but, more broadly, of high culture in Japan's medieval period.

Chapter Five

Tendai Hongaku *Thought and the New Kamakura Buddhism: A Reappraisal*

HAVING OUTLINED the institutional setting of competing lineages from which medieval Tendai original enlightenment thought emerged, the culture of secret transmission within which it developed, and the hermeneutical modes and doctrinal systems by which it was elaborated, it is now appropriate to return to the question of its relation to the teachings of the so-called new Kamakura Buddhism. First, however, two questions remained to be addressed. As discussed in chapter 2, Tendai original enlightenment thought has been widely understood by modern scholars as an absolute affirmation of the phenomenal world that in effect denied the necessity of Buddhist practice and legitimated evil conduct. And as a corollary, the new Kamakura Buddhist movements are said to have arisen, at least in part, as a corrective to this trend. But is this characterization accurate? The first part of this chapter will consider the questions of the relation of *hongaku* thought to Buddhist practice and to the problem of evil through a close examination of specific Tendai texts produced slightly before or during the time when the leaders of the new Kamakura Buddhism were active. Its second part will offer a reconsideration of the relation between medieval Tendai original enlightenment thought and the doctrines of the new Kamakura Buddhism.

Practice, Realization, and Original Enlightenment

Basic to Tendai *hongaku* thought is the premise that all persons—all phenomena—are Buddha inherently. We have already seen that the most profound standpoint of *kanjin* or "mind-contemplation" is equated with a perspective from which cause and effect are originally inherent, where there is "nothing to cultivate and nothing to attain." Did this discourse then deny the need for Buddhist disciplines? One can isolate passages from within the *kuden* literature that would certainly appear to support such a claim:

> There is no meditation method to be cultivated. Walking, standing, sitting, and lying down are themselves the essence of calming and contemplation *(shikan)*.[1]

> Apart from the continuous arising of the present thought-moment, there is no practice to cultivate. The true essence of the thought that now arises, just as it is, manifests direct realization of the dharma realm.[2]

However, the relationship of practice and original enlightenment is an exceedingly complex issue and merits more detailed examination. In addressing it, we will consider relevant portions from three medieval Tendai texts, all dating from the late Heian or Kamakura periods, which participate in *hongaku* discourse and whose arguments are in many ways representative of a larger body of such literature.

The Contemplation of Suchness

First is the *Shinnyo kan* (The contemplation of suchness), which develops ideas of original enlightenment within the context of late Heian Tendai Pure Land thought.[3] The *Shinnyo kan* is not a *kuden* text but rather a long essay, belonging to that strand of early original enlightenment literature interpreting Pure Land thought from a *hongaku* perspective. Retrospectively attributed to the great Tendai Pure Land teacher Genshin (942–1017), it was almost certainly written at some point during the twelfth century.[4] Unlike most of the *kuden* literature, which is composed in literary Chinese *(kanbun)*, the *Shinnyo kan* is written in Japanese, with a mixed style of Chinese characters and the Japanese phonetic syllabary, and with phonetic indicators *(furigana)* provided for the characters.[5] Certain portions of its content suggest that it was intended for an educated lay reader. The fact that it is cited in two external sources from the late twelfth/early thirteenth century—the *setsuwa* collection *Hōbutsu shū* (A collection of treasures) and Hōnen's *Hyaku shijūgokajō mondō* (One hundred forty-five questions and answers)—indicate that it had circulated to a certain extent. This in turn would suggest that, while specific *kuden* doctrines may have been kept secret, ideas of about original enlightenment had by this time spread well beyond the monastic context.

The theme of the *Shinnyo kan* is the immediate realization of Buddhahood by awakening to the universal reality of suchness (Jpn. *shinnyo*, Skt. *tathatā*) or—as the text alternatively phrases it—"suchness that is original enlightenment" *(hongaku shinnyo)*. The term "suchness" is equated in this text with the true aspect *(jissō)*, the dharma realm *(hokkai, dharma-dhātu)*, the Dharma body *(hosshin, dharma-kāya)*, the Dharma nature *(hosshō, dharmatā)*, the Tathâgata *(nyorai)*, and the cardinal meaning *(daiichi gi).*[6] "Suchness" is not an ontological substrate but all things being empty and thus mutually encompassing:

> If you wish to realize Buddhahood quickly or be born in the Pure Land without fail, you must think that your own mind is precisely the principle of suchness. If you think that suchness, which pervades the dharma realm, is your own person, you are at once equivalent to the dharma realm; do not think there is anything outside this. When one is enlightened, all Buddhas and all bodhisattvas of the ten directions of the dharma realm dwell within one's own person. . . . Moreover, the *Lotus Sūtra* and all the eighty thousand dharma repositories that compose the twelve kinds of sūtras, as well as the myriad practices conducted by all Buddhas and bodhisattvas while at the causal stage, the myriad virtues they achieved as a result, and the boundless merit they achieved through practice for their own enjoyment and for teaching others— what is there that is not within oneself?
>
> . . . Because one contemplates suchness, one can quickly realize even Buddhahood, which is difficult to attain. How much more so is one certain beyond doubt to achieve birth in [the Pure Land of] Utmost Bliss, which is easy![7]

Parenthetically, it is worth noting that while the *Shinnyo kan* argues for both the identity of the believer with Amida and the immanence of the Pure Land in this world, its author evidently found no difficulty in speaking of "birth in the Pure Land" as a real event. The last chapter mentioned the "antitranscendent" stance of some medieval Tendai literature, which dismisses notions about other realms as merely provisional or metaphoric. However, one also finds writings such as this one, which endorse both immanentalist and literal understandings of the Pure Land. As a further example, one can point to this passage in the *Jigyō nenbutsu mondō* (Questions and answers on the *nenbutsu* as self-practice), another text belonging to the Pure Land strand of Tendai *hongaku* literature:

> Even though one knows Amida Buddha to be one's own mind, one forms a relationship with Amida Buddha of the west and in this way manifests the Amida who is one's own mind. Thus, those who say that one should not contemplate the west because Amida is one's own mind commit a grave error. Generally speaking, they fail to understand the intent of all Buddhas. Those who practice the four kinds of *samādhi* know that Amida is the mind, but nonetheless they take Amida as their object of worship *(honzon)*. As for direction, one should by all means face the west.[8]

Such passages suggest that "immanentalist" and "dualistic" modes of Pure Land thought may not always have been seen as contradictory. Though one stance was at times posited against the other for polemical purposes, in practice, they often appear to have coexisted.

In the discernment of suchness, all distinctions collapse:

> What we call the principle of suchness pervades the dharma realm; there is no place where it does not reach. Though the dharmas in number are incalculable and boundless, none is separate from the principle of suchness. Moreover, because the myriad dharmas interpenetrate to form the whole, we speak of the principle of all dharmas being a single suchness. This being the case, the worldly passions are none other than enlightenment; birth and death are precisely the Dharma body; and our evil karma is precisely liberation. . . . Moreover, of all insentient beings, the grasses and trees, mountains and rivers, the great ocean and the empty sky—there is none that is not suchness. Because all these are suchness, they are all Buddha. Suchness is the real Buddha. It is clear in the *Lotus Sūtra* that the Buddha taught that the bodies and minds of all of us, living beings, are precisely suchness.[9]

This collapsing of dualities corresponds to what Tamura Yoshirō explains as the first philosophical move that constitutes original enlightenment thought, in which all things, being seen as empty of independent self-nature (or in this text, as identical to suchness), are revealed as nondifferentiated and mutually encompassing. This is a view that, in Ruben Habito's words, regards "self as Buddha, everything as Buddha."[10] However, according to the *Shinnyo kan,* the realization of one's identity with the Buddha is by no means a given; one can, in fact, obstruct this realization for countless kalpas, simply by disbelieving it:

> If one does not believe [in the identity of oneself with suchness], that person slanders all Buddhas of the ten directions and three periods of time, [because] the Buddhas of the ten directions, as well as the *Lotus Sūtra,* all make suchness their essence. The "Parable" chapter expounds the karmic retribution for the sin of slandering the *Lotus Sūtra,* saying: "Such a person, at life's end, shall enter the Avīci hell, where he shall fulfill one kalpa. When the kalpa is exhausted, he shall be reborn there, transmigrating in this way for kalpas without end."[11]

This is followed by a gruesome description of the eight major hells, of which the Avīci Hell, the hell without respite, is the most horrifying. This appears to have been inspired by the opening chapter of Genshin's famous treatise *Ōjō yōshū* (Essentials of birth in the Pure Land), which describes the six realms of transmigration that are to be shunned in favor of aspiration to Amida's Pure Land, devoting particular attention to the hells. The *Shinnyo kan* remarks: "How awesome! Whether we fall into the Avīci hell or are born in the land of Utmost Bliss depends solely on our [attitude of] mind in this lifetime. We ourselves are precisely suchness. One who does not believe this will surely fall into hell. But one who believes it deeply without doubting will be reborn in [the pure land of] Utmost Bliss."[12] Salvation thus hinges on this all-important condition of whether one does or does not believe that "oneself is precisely suchness." In comparison, the negative soteriological impact of ordinary misdeeds is seen as insignificant:

> From today on, knowing that your own mind is itself suchness, evil
> karma and defilements will not be hindrances; fame and profit will
> instead become nourishment for the fruition of Buddha[hood] and
> bodhi. Even if you should violate the precepts without shame or be neg-
> ligent and idle [in religious observances], so long as you always con-
> template suchness and never forget to do so, you should never think
> that evil karma or defilements will obstruct your birth in the Pure Land
> of Utmost Bliss.[13]

Such emphasis on the overriding importance of faith has much in common with the teachings of Hōnen, Shinran, and Nichiren, who also taught that it is faith, not virtuous deeds or the eradication of defilements, that brings about one's salvation. One should note here, however, that to "always contemplate suchness and never forget to do so" would in fact require considerable exertion and commitment; to an extent, the text thus undercuts its own "legitimizing" of negligence.

Failure to know oneself as suchness is presented not only as the sole evil that obstructs liberation, but as the root of the entire samsaric process:

> Originally, in the principle that is the single truth of suchness, there are
> no distinctions of the nine realms [from hell-dwellers through bo-
> dhisattvas]. The first thought with which one turns one's back on this
> original enlightenment, which is the principle of suchness, and arouses
> the delusion of the realms of transmigration, creates the realms of trans-
> migration. According to the teachings of the Lotus Sūtra, when one knows
> that oneself is precisely suchness, that very thought creates the Buddha-
> realm. . . . Up until today, because we have not known that we ourselves
> are precisely suchness, we have been deluded beings transmigrating
> in the realm of birth and death for lifetime after lifetime without hope
> of exhausting it. But now, learning from a teacher or from the teach-
> ings of the scriptural rolls that we are precisely suchness, we awake from
> the sleep of ignorance, and the dream of delusive thoughts comes to
> an end. Awaking from the dream of delusive thoughts of the nine worlds,
> we return to original enlightenment, the principle of suchness.[14]

This passage reflects the incorporation into Tendai thought of Hua-yen/Kegon thinking about an originally pure mind that, coming into contact with the defilements, produces the differentiated samsaric realm. As discussed in chapter 1, this is quite different from the orthodox T'ien-t'ai position, which holds that the mind and the dharmas are always mutually inclusive, and that the nonduality of good and evil is the true aspect of reality.

To realize that "oneself is precisely suchness" by implication transforms ordinary life, infusing even mundane acts with hitherto unsuspected meaning:

> You should know that suchness is to be contemplated with respect to all things. Clergy and laiety, men and women—all should contemplate in this way. When you provide for your wife, children, and retainers, or even feed oxen, horses, and the others of the six kinds of domestic animals, because the myriad things are all suchness, if you think that they are precisely suchness, you have in effect made offerings to all Buddhas and bodhisattvas of the ten directions and to all living beings, without a single exception. . . . And this is not only true of offerings made to others. Because we ourselves are precisely suchness, one's own person includes all Buddhas and bodhisattvas of the ten directions and three time periods and is endowed with the hundred realms, thousand suchnesses, and the three thousand realms, lacking none. Thus, when you eat while carrying out this contemplation, the merit of the *pāramitā* of giving at once fills the dharma realm, and because one practice is equivalent to all practices, the single practice of the perfection of giving contains the other *pāramitās*. And because cause and effect are nondual, all practices, which represent the causal stage, are simultaneously the myriad virtues of the stage of realization.[15]

When performed on the basis of the contemplation that all things, by virtue of their mutual inclusion, are suchness, even the simplest act of daily life, such as eating, is the Buddha's conduct. The passage as a whole suggests not only that the *Shinnyo kan* may have been intended for a lay reader, but also that *hongaku* thought was not necessarily an "ideology of ruling elites": it could also be assimilated to more egalitarian positions. Its use in the passage above, for example, suggests that liberation is fully accessible to anyone who "contemplates suchness," even outside the monastic setting.

Contemplating all things as suchness while in the midst of daily activities may actually have been carried out in the early Kamakura period as a form of lay practice. As Sueki Fumihiko has pointed out, the *setsuwa* collection *Hōbutsu shū*, explicitly citing the *Shinnyo kan*, advises:

> When you eat, visualize [this act] as making offerings to the thirty-seven honored ones, and when you feed others, form the thought that

you are, upwardly, making offerings to the Buddhas of the ten directions and three periods of time, and downwardly, giving alms to hell-
dwellers, hungry ghosts, and those in the animal realm. And you
should likewise form this thought when you feed your servants and
retainers, or give food to horses and cattle, birds and beasts. For lay
people, men and women engaged in public and private affairs, what
practice could possibly be superior?[16]

Sueki suggests that this should probably be regarded as a habitual attitude of mind to be cultivated, rather than a formal meditation method,
although the distinction is not necessarily clear-cut. In any event, we find
here another similarity to the ideas of the new Kamakura Buddhist
thinkers in that all forms of good practices and their resulting virtues
are held to be contained in a single kind of action. Here that single kind
of action is not a specific form of practice, such as chanting the *nenbutsu*
or the *daimoku,* but any act performed with a specified attitude, that is,
the contemplation of all things as suchness. When informed by this habit
of mind, any action can become Buddhist practice.

The undercutting of dualities in this text also collapses the linear
distinctions of past, present, and future into the immediate moment,
so that practice and realization occur simultaneously in the instant of
cognizing—or even having faith in—one's identity with suchness. Such
a view is of course at odds with traditional notions of the Buddhist path
as requiring cultivation over many lifetimes. The *Shinnyo kan* poses the
contrast in such a way as to suggest that conventional, linear notions of
the path are in fact delusive constructs arising from ignorance of suchness, and any enlightenment said to be attained thereby is dismissed as
illusory:

While we did not yet know that we ourselves are precisely suchness, we
have thought that the Buddha and ourselves differed greatly and were
widely separated. The reason is that we are ordinary worldlings who
have not yet extirpated delusions, while the Buddha, throughout countless kalpas, carried out difficult and painful practices, both for his own
self-cultivation and to teach others, and is fully possessed of unfathomable merits. Of the Buddha's six perfections and myriad practices,
what merit do we possess? Not even in this lifetime have we broken
our bones and thrown away our lives [for the Dharma's sake], let alone
for countless kalpas! Rather, because it has been our habit from the
beginningless past, we value only worldly fame and profit, aspiring to
this estate or that temple or shrine; hastening in pursuit of the world's
pleasures and prosperity, we have not sustained our aspiration for birth
in [the land of] Utmost Bliss, or, more importantly, for Buddhahood
and *bodhi*. Having spent this life in vain, in our next life, we are certain
to sink into the depths of the three evil paths—so we have thought,

but this was merely the deluded mind at a time when we did not yet know the contemplation of suchness.[17]

> Bodhisattvas of the provisional teachings, ignorant of the contemplation of suchness, for countless kalpas carried out difficult and painful practices, not begrudging bodily life, and thus attained Buddhahood. But it was not real Buddhahood, only a provisional fruit obtained in a dream. Those who know the contemplation of suchness become Buddhas in an instant.[18]

Thus, while the contemplation of suchness is presented on one level as an easy and accessible practice, on another, it is said to be the only true way of realizing Buddhahood. This, too, represents a point of similarity with the single-practice rhetoric of the new Pure Land and Nichiren movements: the single practice, whether the *nenbutsu* or the *daimoku,* is touted as both universally accessible *and* the only true vehicle of liberation.

The text anticipates a number of objections:

> Someone asks: "I do not understand how we can all be Buddhas, without distinction. As I have maintained from the outset, a Buddha is regarded with unceasing reverence in the world and honored with the title of "Buddha" because he possesses the thirty-two marks and because his supernatural powers and wisdom surpass those of all others. And other people in the world are accustomed to think so, too. You are the only one who maintains that even dogs, birds, ants and mole crickets are all Buddhas. Who could believe it? . . . Even if you call yourself a Buddha, you do not possess the thirty-two marks, nor have you acquired supernatural powers. Arousing surpassing arrogance, you call it the Buddha wisdom.[19]

The *Shinnyo kan* addresses this issue in terms of the six identities *(liu chi, rokusoku)* or stages of practice of the perfect teaching enumerated in the *Mo-ho chih-kuan.*[20]

1. Identity in principle *(ri-soku),* the stage of the ordinary worldling. Though persons at this stage have yet to encounter the Dharma, their every thought is nonetheless ontologically identical to the ultimate principle of the threefold truth.
2. Verbal identity *(myōji-soku),* the stage where one encounters a teacher or the sūtra text and reaches the verbal understanding that all dharmas are the Buddha-Dharma. This represents the initial stage of practice.
3. Identity of meditative practice *(kangyō-soku),* the stage at which one's contemplative wisdom accords with one's intellectual understanding, and one's actions match one's words.

4. Identity of resemblance *(sōji-soku)*, at which stage one achieves wisdom that resembles true enlightenment.
5. Identity of partial realization of truth *(bunshin-soku)*, at which stage one increasingly eradicates delusion and manifests wisdom.
6. Ultimate identity *(kukyō-soku)*, the full enlightenment of Buddhahood.

"Identity" in each case indicates that although a difference exists in the level of cultivation, no ontological distinction is made. The *Shinnyo kan* states:

> We have already heard the name of the threefold truth and understood that we, ourselves, are precisely suchness. If we position this in terms of the six identities, it corresponds to the stage of verbal identity. . . . It is Buddhas [at the stages] of [identity of] partial realization and ultimate [identity] who possess the major distinguishing marks and minor excellent characteristics, as well as the freedom of supernatural powers. You revere only the physical marks and supernatural powers and disdain the merits of the inner awakening and the originally inherent nature of principle. This is the extremity of foolishness and ignorance.[21]

This discussion may be understood in the context of an ongoing interpretive effort by Japanese Tendai monks, beginning from Saichō's time, to locate the realization of Buddhahood in this very body at increasingly lower stages of the path.[22] Though the claim for enlightenment at the stage of verbal identity *(myōji-soku)*—the very first stage of practice—can occasionally be found earlier, it becomes a recurring feature of medieval Tendai *hongaku*-related texts.[23]

The *Shinnyo kan* is careful to account for possible disjunctures between its rhetoric of immediately realizing enlightenment on hearing that all is suchness, and the reality of what many people were likely to experience. It does so by reference to the issue of human capacity, a matter of great concern to Buddhists in the late Heian and Kamakura periods:

> Beings of the sharpest faculties, like the dragon girl, discern that they themselves are precisely suchness, and in an instant become Buddhas. Beings of dull faculties may discern at one moment that they are precisely suchness, but at the next moment, because it has been their way since time without beginning, on seeing forms or hearing voices, their mind moves in accordance with external objects. Meeting objects that are pleasing, it arouses the defilement of greed; meeting objects that are not pleasing, it arouses the defilement of anger. . . . In accordance with the distinction of superior and inferior faculties, there exists the inequality of sooner or later in the perfection of contemplative practice. Thus there are those who can manifest enlightenment

in a day, two days, a month, two months, or a year, and those who require a lifetime.[24]

Thus, though all are Buddhas inherently, some may take time to achieve and sustain that realization. Toward that end, the *Shinnyo kan* acknowledges the need for, and even encourages, continued practice:

> Since we have just now begun the contemplation of suchness, we are pulled by conditions, and in the face of circumstances, it is easy to retreat and hard to continue. By what useful expedient may one put a stop to the delusive thoughts to which we have been accustomed since the outset and manifest the true principle of suchness? First, one should cultivate the contemplation of emptiness [of the dharmas], loosening one's attachment to saṃsāra so as to manifest in oneself the principle of suchness.[25]

In addition to the contemplation of emptiness *(kūkan)*, the invocational *nenbutsu* is recommended, though it must be based on knowing the nonduality of oneself with Amida and all other Buddhas.[26] The practitioner is also urged to contemplate oneself as suchness "night and day, walking, standing, sitting and lying down, without forgetting" and, with this understanding, to "say the *nenbutsu* and recite the sūtra, transferring the merit [from such acts] to all beings."[27] In this text, at least, the premise that all beings are originally Buddhas does not lead to a denial of the need for practice.

Sanjū shika no kotogaki

The *Sanjū shika no kotogaki* (Notes on thirty-four articles, hereafter referred to as the *Kotogaki*) is an oral transmission text of the Eshin school.[28] This text, it will be recalled, was regarded by Tamura Yoshirō as a watershed work, in which all the concepts of mature *hongaku* thought were present, although not yet systematized.[29] Like most of the *kuden* literature, the *Kotogaki* was clearly intended for a monastic readership, being written in literary Chinese *(kanbun)* and assuming a sophisticated knowledge of Tendai technical vocabulary. As its title suggests, it consists of thirty-four transmissions, probably originally separate *kirikami*. Its colophon claims that it records the secret essentials of the school and warns sternly against revealing its content: "Even if it should cost your life, do not confer this [inappropriately]. Being that it is the profound Dharma, if such were to happen, both master and disciple would fall into hell. . . . If there is no one qualified to receive it, this transmission should be buried in the depths of a wall."[30]

According to the same colophon, the teachings contained in *Kotogaki* had been transmitted orally from master to disciple and were committed to writing by Kōkaku (fl. c. 1150), said to be fifth in the line of succession after Genshin. Kōkaku, later regarded at the originator of the

Sugiu line of the Eshin school, was a ranking Tendai prelate and son of
the poet Fujiwara no Mototoshi (1056–1142).[31] A variant, probably somewhat later edition of the *Kotogaki* is known as the *Makura sōshi* (Pillow
book) and is attributed to Genshin himself.[32] With the exception of Tamura Yoshirō, who places it around 1250, most scholars date the *Kotogaki*
from the late Heian period.[33]

While the *Kotogaki* consists of separate transmissions, these have enough
consistency to give the work a coherent philosophical position. Before
addressing the implications of this text for practice and realization, this
philosophical position will be examined in some detail.

The *Shinnyo kan,* as noted above, may be seen as illustrating the first
of the two philosophical moves into which Tamura Yoshirō analyzes the
structure of original enlightenment thought. That is, it emphasizes the
dissolution of distinctions, based on the insight that all phenomena are
without independent ontological status: self and other, delusion and enlightenment, subject and object, are all equally "suchness." The *Kotogaki,*
on the other hand, serves better to illustrate what Tamura has described
as the subsequent move, in which the distinction between the nondifferentiated, equal aspect of things, and their individuated, phenomenal
aspect, is itself negated. This creates the "reverse move" in which individual concrete phenomena, just as they are, are "affirmed" as the manifestations of nondual reality. The *Kotogaki* speaks of these two perspectives in terms of "principle" and "actuality":

> You should understand carefully what is meant by principle *(ri)* and
> by concrete actuality *(ji).* "Principle" means that, although the dhar-
> mas have distinctions, because they are all suchness, they are resolved
> in the one. . . . With respect to principle, there are no distinctions what-
> soever; the myriad dharmas are dissolved. But with respect to actual-
> ity, the myriad dharmas are not dissolved; they remain constant in
> themselves.[34]

"Principle" is subsequently equated with the trace teaching *(shakumon)*
of the *Lotus Sūtra,* which is said to resolve all dharmas into the true aspect; "concrete actuality" is associated with the origin teaching *(honmon),*
which is said to establish each individual phenomenon in itself as absolute. Ultimately, however, any duality between the two perspectives is
denied. In Chih-i's thought, the Buddha of the trace teaching is likened
to the reflection of the moon on water, while the Buddha of the origin
teaching is likened to the moon in the sky.[35] The *Kotogaki,* however, in a
transmission on the "ever-equal three bodies," collapses this metaphor
and denies the distinction between the two kinds of Buddhas:

> To see the Buddha in his manifested trace *(suijaku-butsu)* is to see the
> Buddha in his original ground *(honji-butsu).* To see the moon in the
> water is to see the moon in the sky. Ignorant people do not know

this. . . . One does not see in the water a reflected moon; one directly
sees the moon in the sky. It is the same with the trace teaching. There
is no separate, manifested trace Buddha. There is only the original
Buddha.[36]

The phenomenal world is not a reflection or projection of a prior, more
"true" reality but is itself the ultimate reality. The *Kotogaki* clarifies its emphasis on the concrete and the phenomenal by privileging the "conventionally existent" among the three truths of emptiness, conventional
existence, and the middle:

> From the standpoint of nonduality, there is no hierarchy whatsoever
> among the three truths, because one truth encompasses three truths,
> and the three truths are implicit in one. But from the standpoint of
> duality, the truth of conventional existence is superior, while those of
> emptiness and the middle are inferior. The truth of conventional ex-
> istence is the realm before our eyes, the myriad phenomena, the body
> of what is originally unborn. . . . Emptiness and the middle are the
> adornments of conventional existence.[37]

Not only is the "conventionally existing" privileged, but its ordinary pejorative associations with change and decay are radically undercut:

> In the various teachings [other than the *Lotus*], "conventionally ex-
> isting" is taken to mean that while the myriad phenomena exist in
> infinite variety, because they all are formed by a temporary union [of
> dharmas] depending on causes and conditions, they exist provision-
> ally. In no way do they constantly abide. Our school's understanding
> of "conventionally existent" is not like this. Because all phenomena
> constantly abide, the conventionally existent constantly abides. Because
> the water constantly abides, the waves constantly abide. Because the
> Dharma body constantly abides, the conventionally existent constantly
> abides.[38]

The expression "constantly abiding" (*jōjū*), sometimes translated less
literally as "eternal," derives from a passage in Kumārajīva's translation
of the *Lotus Sūtra:* "The dharmas dwell in a Dharma-position / and the
worldly aspect constantly abides" (*zehō jū hōi, seken sō jōjū*).[39] This passage,
widely cited in medieval Tendai *kuden* literature, is also the source of the
term "Dharma-position" (*hōi*), the whole of nondual reality manifested
in one spatio-temporal particularity just as it is.[40] While better known
from Dōgen's writings, the concept of "dwelling in a Dharma-position"
was actually developed earlier in medieval Tendai *kuden* texts.

The "constant abiding of the phenomenal world" is not, as it might
at first appear to be, a flat denial of Buddhist notions of impermanence.
A transmission from the *Kotogaki* entitled "birth-and-death is precisely
nirvāṇa" reads:

As for the meaning of birth and death being precisely nirvāṇa: people ordinarily think of nirvāṇa as not dying in one place and being
born in another, an unchanging, fixed, and motionless state. But such
is in no way the case. They think so because they have not yet grasped
the teaching that the worldly aspect constantly abides. "Constantly
abides" here does not mean being fixed and immobile. "The worldly
[aspect]" has the meanings of impermanence and distinctions. Impermanence, while being impermanence, constantly abides and is not
lost. Distinctions, while being distinctions, constantly abide and are not
lost. Not to grasp this is to fall into a partial view. To illustrate, though
waves move, the movement continues constantly from past to present
to future. There is no beginning to this movement and no end. . . . Because the ten realms are originally inherent from the outset, even
though one dies in one place and is reborn in another, one never leaves
the ten realms.[41]

Nirvāṇa does not transcend the realm of saṃsāra but is inseparable
from it. Saṃsāra, just as it is, in all its particularity and flux, is affirmed
as ever-present. The *Kotogaki* gives several instances in which phenomenal distinctions "constantly abide and are not lost." One of the most remarkable of these concerns the doctrine that grasses and trees realize
or attain Buddhahood *(sōmoku jōbutsu)*. As discussed in chapter 1, this
doctrine emerged within early Heian Tendai as a distinctive development
of earlier T'ien-t'ai thought, especially that of Chan-jan, concerning the
potential for Buddhahood in nonsentient beings. The attainment of Buddhahood by grasses and trees was a frequent topic in the Tendai system
of examination and debate.[42] The following section from the *Kotogaki*
may represent an instance of a secret transmission, informed by the
premise of orignal enlightenment, concerning a standard debate topic.
The relevant section of the text begins by referring to the traditional
T'ien-t'ai position on the subject, which is that grasses and trees become
Buddhas by virtue of the nonduality of the living subject (i.e., primary
[karmic] recompense, *shōhō*) and its environment (dependent recompense, *ehō*). When a sentient being (subject) attains Buddhahood, so do
grasses and trees (environment). However, this is dismissed as "the conventional view":

> Now our understanding is that grasses and trees do *not* attain Bud-
> dhahood. This is a profound interpretation. Why? Grasses and trees
> represent dependent recompense, while living beings represent pri-
> mary recompense. Dependent recompense, *qua* dependent recom-
> pense, displays the virtues of the ten realms. Primary recompense, *qua*
> primary recompense, displays the virtues of subjects [of the ten
> realms]. If grasses and trees attained Buddhahood, dependent rec-
> ompense would decrease; there would be a diminution of the container

worlds of the trichiliocosm. Thus, the expression "attainment of Buddhahood by grasses and trees" appears remarkable but is in fact shallow. And the same is true of other cases. The Buddhahood of the hells, the Buddhahood of the hungry ghosts, on up to the Buddhahood of the bodhisattva realm, is in each case the same. Because they display the dharmas inherent to them without discarding their identity, they benefit the dharma realm. If they transformed their original status, there would remain only the Buddha realm. The constantly abiding ten worlds do not change. Grasses and trees constantly abide. The beings also constantly abide, and the five *skandhas* also constantly abide. You should ponder this well.[43]

The text goes on to explain that the doctrine of grasses and trees attaining Buddhahood is asserted to counter those who claim that insentient beings lack the Buddha nature, probably a reference to Hossō scholars such as Tokuitsu, with whom Saichō debated. However, this does not mean that grasses and trees change their insentient state and become sentient. While being insentient, just as they are, they are Buddha. This argument is structurally similar to the famous opening passage of Dōgen's "Genjō kōan" (The *kōan* realized in reality): "When all dharmas are the Buddha-Dharma, there are illusion and enlightenment, practice, birth, death, buddhas, and sentient beings."[44] The Buddha-Dharma transcends even the distinction between identity and difference; this discernment produces the "reverse move" of which Tamura Yoshirō has written, in which diverse phenomena, sentient and insentient, enlightened and deluded, are seen, just as they are, as expressions of nondual reality.

In his discussion of the *Kotogaki,* Sueki Fumihiko calls attention to a structure recurring throughout the text that he terms "A is A and none other than A" as the way in which this particular text expresses the notion that "A is in itself Buddha." Sueki terms this structure "self-consistency" or "self-identity" (*jiko dōisshō,* literally, "of the same nature as itself").[45] Insentient plants do not "become" Buddha, nor do they change into sentient beings. Grasses and trees, while retaining their own nature as grasses and trees, are Buddha. This, too, finds a corollary in Dōgen's idea of the "total exertion of a single thing" *(ippō gūjin),* in which a particular phenomenon, action, or event is discerned, not in a dualistic sense that would relativize it vis-à-vis other events as superior or inferior, before or after, cause or effect, but as the total embodiment of nondual reality in the present moment.[46]

From the perspective that "A is A and none other than A," the *Kotogaki* repudiates even the idea of "attaining" Buddhahood:

> In ordinary debate it is stated that "attaining Buddhahood" implies
> that the nine realms decrease and the Buddha realm increases. The

understanding of our school is completely different. [Ours is] the contemplation and understanding that the ten realms from the outset constantly abide. . . . The provisional teachings do not reveal the constant abiding of the ten realms; thus they teach that the beings change and achieve the Buddha body. But the meaning of the perfect teaching is not that the beings change and become Buddhas. It is the realization that the beings as beings, and the Buddha realm as the Buddha realm, both constantly abide. There is nothing to choose or reject, and therefore, no increasing or decreasing.[47]

Note that, according to the *Kotogaki,* the distinctions of the ten realms are originally inherent and not, as the *Shinnyo kan* asserts, a false discrimination produced when an originally pure mind comes in contact with the defilements. As this contrast illustrates, the single category "original enlightenment thought" is not necessarily internally consistent but can encompass a variety of doctrinal positions.

In this text, there is no motion up or down the hierarchy of the ten realms, and no transformation from one state to another. Indeed, there is no attaining Buddhahood at all; all things are Buddha from the outset. Not only are the ontological distinctions among the ten realms said to "constantly abide," but so are the defilements. As in the *Shinnyo kan,* the aim presented in the *Kotogaki* is not to eradicate defilements but to realize that the defilements, as defilements, are none other than enlightenment. "Our deluded thoughts that continue from moment to moment are entirely the wisdom according with *prajñā.* They are called *prajñā* not because one transforms them [into wisdom], but because one knows nonduality and equality."[48] And just as all dharmas "constantly abide" and are the "true aspect of liberation," so all actions represent Buddhist practice:

> The *Lotus Sūtra* is the all-encompassing body of the dharmas, and living beings are likewise the all-encompassing body of the dharmas. "Contemplating the mind" does not necessarily entail shutting oneself in a room and achieving quiescent illumination. Of all [activities of] the four postures, [walking, standing, sitting, and lying down,] there is none that is not subtle contemplation.[49]

This would indeed seem to deny the necessity for any particular form of practice and to affirm absolutely the identity of the ordinary worldling with the Buddha. A careful reading, however, reveals that the claims about deluded thoughts being *prajñā* and all activities being subtle contemplation are premised upon a particular insight or understanding that lies at the heart of this text. Like the *Shinnyo kan,* but with greater doctrinal sophistication, the *Kotogaki* explains this in terms of the six identities:

Question: At what point do we speak of attaining wondrous awakening *(myōkaku)*?

Answer: The attainment of wondrous awakening lies in the single thought-moment of the mind of [a person at the stage of] identity in principle. . . . The undifferentiated dharma realm, which is from the outset constantly abiding and without transformation, is called "wondrous awakening" and is [also] called "[the Pure Land of] Tranquil Light." Thus, although there are distinctions to be made in the stages above that of identity in principle, this is no more than arguing endlessly the virtues [already inherent] within the stage of identity in principle.[50]

Thus perfect enlightenment is said to be fully present in each thought of an ordinary deluded person, even prior to practice. Nonetheless, there is still a vital epistemological distinction to be made between such a person and a Buddha. The text immediately continues:

The day that one does not know this, the Tathâgata is apart from oneself. The day that one knows it, all is oneself. . . . This is called "returning to and becoming identical with original enlightenment" *(gendō hongaku).*[51]

This "knowing" is identified in another section of the text with the stage of verbal identity, which is the initial stage of practice:

At the stage of verbal identity, one encounters a teacher and hears the Dharma of the sudden and ultimate [teaching], and understands on the spot that the self is precisely Buddha. There being nothing else to seek, one dwells in the undifferentiated great wisdom. Understanding, practice, and enlightenment are simultaneous; in the space of a moment one achieves realization, like turning over the hand.[52]

As in the *Shinnyo kan,* this instantaneous achievement of realization is contrasted with linear models of cultivation over time and found to be superior:

[According to the provisional teachings,] delusion and enlightenment are separate. One must first extirpate delusion and then enter enlightenment; thus one does not enter the stage [of enlightenment] from the outset. But in the perfect and sudden teaching, practice—that is, hearing the teaching, contemplating it, and cultivation—is simultaneous with enlightenment. One does not move from one stage to another. The time of encountering the teaching is precisely [the time of] realization. All practices and good deeds are skillful means subsequent to the fruit [of enlightenment].[53]

206 THE WORLD OF MEDIEVAL TENDAI

"Skillful means subsequent to the fruit" is one of the *Kotogaki*'s very few comments on the subject of ongoing practice. This is probably because the entire focus of this text is on the single moment of realization, which is equated with the stage of verbal identity. Not only does that moment contain the whole of the path, but it is only at that moment—on encountering and grasping the teaching of nonduality—that the inherence of Buddhahood prior to practice can be cognized:

> The various stages are different names for one stage. This is the inconceivable nature of [the Dharma transmitted by] the lineage of the perfect teaching *(enke)*. Once one hears and understands the name of the perfectly interpenetrating threefold truth, there is nothing else to seek, nothing to choose or reject. Dwelling in the nondifferentiated dharma realm, why should one seek various stages? . . . However, the existence of the Buddhahood, or wondrous awakening, at the stage of identity in principle *is a mere doctrinal teaching*. In reality, it is after achieving the stage of verbal identity that one understands a portion of Buddhahood to be present at the stage of identity in principle. (emphasis added)[54]

All persons may be Buddhas inherently, even prior to practice, but it is only on encountering and understanding the teaching that one can "look back," as it were, from the stage of verbal identity and realize this to be so.

Sueki Fumihiko finds a contradiction between the "A is none other than A" principle of self-consistency that recurs throughout the *Kotogaki* and the transformation of understanding involved in the shift from the stage of identity in principle to that of verbal identity. The claim that plants and trees, without transformation, are Buddhas, or that defilements, as defilements, are enlightenment, seems to follow a different logic than does the assertion that original enlightenment is realized only on hearing and understanding that "all dharmas are the Buddha-Dharma." However, if one were fully and actually enlightened in every sense prior to encountering the teaching, Buddhism would lose its *raison d'être*. Sueki accordingly suggests that the emphasis on realizing original enlightenment at the stage of verbal identity represents a sort of last-ditch attempt to preserve the most minimal significance of religion.[55] It is true that, in *hongaku* discourse, the difference between realizing or not realizing the fact of original enlightenment is the only distinction drawn between ordinary worldlings and Tathâgatas and, by implication, represents the only reason for Buddhism to exist. However, this distinction appears to have been seen by medieval Tendai thinkers as a soteriologically significant gap, toward whose resolution all religious efforts were directed. If it is only in the moment of realization that one perceives "A, without changing its nature as A, to be precisely Buddha," then it is only in that moment that it becomes experientially true. Thus it seems altogether likely that statements about defilements being enlightenment should be understood as articulated from the standpoint of the insight represented by the stage of verbal identity. The *Kotogaki* assumes a greater coherence when read in this way.

One more feature of this text must be addressed before proceeding, as it represents an important strand of *hongaku* discourse more generally. This is the *Kotogaki*'s rejection of linear time. We have already seen how hearing the Dharma, cultivating practice, and achieving realization— conventionally thought of as a process occuring over time—is collapsed into a single moment of insight in which one realizes that one has been enlightened all along. The *Kotogaki* routinely collapses past and future into a timeless and "constantly abiding" present; specific events are re-constructed, not as unique moments within a temporal stream, but as "beginningless" and ever present. For example, in the sixteenth or "Fath-oming the Lifespan of the Tathâgata" chapter of the *Lotus Sūtra*, Śākya-muni Buddha is said to have first attained enlightenment at a point in the inconceivably remote past called *gohyaku jindengō*.[56] The *Kotogaki* dis-misses this as a "provisional explanation" *(kesetsu)* designed to "benefit the beings" and "awaken faith" in accordance with their capacity. "With respect to the principle of the *tathâgata-garbha,* one can from the outset speak neither of attaining nor nonattaining, [for] there is no distinction of beginning, middle, or end. How can one dispute [whether the Bud-dha first achieved enlightenment in] the remote past or [in] the pres-ent time?" The text continues:

> The true aspect is originally without beginning, middle, or end, for the three thousand realms constantly abide and are inherent originally. The Buddha who first attained enlightenment in this world may seem to have first appeared today, but the true aspect that he realized was not realized now for the first time, nor was it realized [for the first time] in the past. It is not within the three time periods, nor does it tran-scend them.[57]

The *Makura sōshi,* a later redaction of the *Kotogaki,* adds this analogy:

> The sun and moon of the remote past, the sun and moon of today, and the sun and moon of the future are all the same sun and moon. Ignorant persons think that a different sun and moon have appeared today for the first time.[58]

Chapter 16 of the *Lotus* is here given a reinterpretation that recurs throughout medieval Tendai texts: The Buddha's declaration that he first attained Buddhahood at a point in the remote past is taken not as a rev-elation of one individual's actual attainment *(ji kenpon)* but as a metaphor revealing the enlightenment that, in principle, originally inheres in all *(rikenpon)*.[59]

Similarly reconstructed is the notion of a "first moment" *(ganjō)* when an originally pure mind gives rise to delusion, or when one first encounters the teaching and achieves realization:

> In the constantly abiding nature, there is no before and after, and therefore, no beginning of delusion. Thus what is called the "first thought" *(ganjō no ichinen)* is a constantly abiding and unchanging thought-moment. Our thoughts that arise from past to present to future are all the same thought-moment. Just as, in the waves of the great sea, yesterday's waves and today's waves are both the same essence, so the thoughts of past, present, and future are all the same thought-moment. The thought-moment that arises now when one encounters the teaching is the entirety of the dharma realm, the constantly abiding thought-moment. The "first thought-moment" is knowing that the three time periods are a single time period, good and evil are nondual, and wrong and right are a single suchness.[60]

Here the stage of verbal identity, the moment at which one understands through the sūtra's teachings or the words of a teacher that "all dharmas are the Buddha-Dharma," is reconstituted not as one moment in the flow of time but as a moment in which all time is contained. The analogy of the waves may represent a deliberate subversion of the famous metaphor from the *Awakening of Faith,* in which the originally smooth surface of the water (mind) produces waves when agitated by the wind (ignorance); when the wind subsides, the waves cease.[61] In the *Kotogaki,* the waves always have been and always will be.

It is an oddly static landscape that emerges from this text, undisturbed by unique temporal events, frozen in a single luminous moment of understanding. The moon of yesterday shines unchanged today and tomorrow; the waves of today are no different from those of yesterday. Nothing moves; plants and trees do not "become" sentient, deluded beings do not "become" Buddhas. The realms of delusion do not decrease, the Buddha realm does not increase; everything "constantly abides," remaining in its "Dharma-position" and manifesting originally inherent enlightenment "without change of original status." Where change cannot be denied, it is contained and domesticated within the framework of a perfectly integrated and inherently enlightened "dharma realm." Impermanence "constantly abides": one may "die here and be born there," but one will never leave the ten realms. It is as though the world is envisioned as a mandala. The hell dwellers, demons, gods, ordinary humans, sages, and Buddhas; the deluded and the awakened; the sentient and the nonsentient; each occupy their proper place in the design of an enlightened cosmos. Without each particular existent dwelling in its "Dharma-position," the design of mandala could not exist. The practitioner may "traverse" the mandala in meditation from one structural component to another, but the relative positions among the individual components are unchanging.[62] This represents yet another way in which original enlightenment thought reflects ongoing efforts to reinterpret traditional T'ien-t'ai doctrines through an esotericized sensibility and mode of cognition.

Shuzenji-ketsu

The *Shuzenji-ketsu* ([Doctrinal] decisions of Hsiu-ch'an-ssu), a work in four fascicles, presents itself as Saichō's record of transmissions he received in China, especially from master Tao-sui of the temple Hsiu-ch'an-ssu on Mt. T'ien-t'ai.[63] As mentioned in chapter 4, it represents an early stage in the systematization of the "threefold seven great matters" of the Eshin doctrinal system. Attempts at dating the *Shuzenji-ketsu* have been complicated by references in the text to chanting the *daimoku* or title of the *Lotus Sūtra,* a practice that has traditionally been associated with Nichiren. For example, it has been argued that *Shuzenji-ketsu* represents a Tendai appropriation of a Nichiren Buddhist practice, or conversely, that it was a forgery on the part of Nichiren's later disciples attempting to legitimate the *daimoku* practice he had taught by connecting it with Saichō.[64] However, as Takagi Yutaka has established, the *daimoku* was being chanted before Nichiren's time, although it was not widespread and lacked a systematized doctrinal foundation.[65] Thus there is no reason to assume the *Shuzenji-ketsu* must postdate him. Nonetheless, scholarly opinion on the dating of this text remains divided, with suggestions ranging from the Insei period through the latter half of the thirteenth century.[66]

The following discussion will focus primarily on the first fascicle of the text, which discusses the "threefold contemplation in a single mind" from the three perspectives of "teaching," "practice," and "realization." As noted in the preceding chapter, this threefold categorization would later become a standard feature of Eshin-school transmissions. The "teaching" section treats the threefold contemplation from a variety of doctrinal perspectives, which will not detain us here. The second, "practice" section is subdivided into four categories: (1) fundamental understanding of the threefold contemplation *(honge no isshin sangan);* (2) practice for specific times *(betsuji no isshin sangan);* (3) practice for ordinary times *(jōyō no isshin sangan);* and (4) practice for one's final moments *(rinjū no isshin sangan).* Concerning "fundamental understanding," the text reads:

> The practitioner of calming and contemplation should first establish the fundamental understanding. Each dharma, down to the smallest particle of dust, is simultaneously empty, conventionally existing, and

the middle, completely separated from deluded thoughts. When the subtle principle of the threefold contemplation is [thus] illuminated, there is nothing to practice and nothing to realize. At the time of practice and realization, how can one dispute over now [attaining enlightenment] versus [being enlightened] originally?[67]

It soon becomes clear, however, that the fundamental understanding, wherein there is "nothing to practice and nothing to realize," is intended not to deny the need for practice but to inform its concrete methods, which are described in the next three categories of "practice."

As scholars have long noted, these three categories of practice—for specific times, for ordinary times, and for the moment of death—suggest the influence of Genshin's *Ōjō yōshū*, which establishes a similar division.[68] However, in contrast to Genshin's text, which emphasizes the Pure Land strand of Tendai teachings, the *Shuzenji-ketsu* draws heavily on the *Lotus Sūtra*, Chih-i's *Mo-ho chih-kuan*, and Taimitsu thought and practice. In the *Shuzenji-ketsu*, "practice for specific times" involves formal secluded meditation for periods of seven, twenty-one, or a hundred days. A square hut is to be erected in a secluded place. Inside, icons are to be enshrined in each of the four directions: Śākyamuni to the north, Amida to the west, Kannon (Avalokiteśvara) to the south, and Monjushiri (Mañjuśrī) to the east. (This in effect creates a mandala, with the practitioner in the center occupying the central position of Mahāvairocana).[69] The practitioner sits facing Amida. Near each icon, a mirror is to be placed so that it simultaneously reflects both the icon and the practitioner. After offering flowers and incense, the practitioner is to assume the half-lotus posture and meditate for three periods (that is, six hours) in the morning and in the evening. In the case of a session lasting seven days:

> On the first day, one should practice the contemplation of Buddhas and living beings being a single suchness. Since the mind is the essence of all dharmas, living beings and the Buddha are all encompassed in a single mind. How could they be separate entities? The object of worship and the practitioner both appear in the same mirror because the beings and the Buddha are nondual. If the beings and the Buddha were truly separate, how could they appear in the same mirror? . . . The practitioner's three categories of action [i.e., body, speech, and mind] are in no way separate from those of the object of worship. The person of the practitioner who contemplates this is the subtle body of the sea of [wondrous] effects, forever released from the form of a deluded person.[70]

Chih-i's analogy of the mirror, by which he illustrated the threefold truth, is here employed as an aid to meditation through the use of actual mirrors. Also evident is the influence of esoteric notions of the three mysteries: the union of the body, speech, and mind of the practitioner with those of the cosmic Buddha in the act of esoteric ritual.

For the next three days, the practitioner is instructed continuously to arouse great doubt about the practice of *shikan* in the course of his meditation. For example, one should think, "How can we, in a single thought, achieve the threefold contemplation? Even having encountered a teacher or the sūtra rolls and understood [the principle of] the three-fold contemplation in a single mind, without some correspondence to actuality, this principle is hard to understand." For the last three days, one practices the threefold contemplation straightforwardly.

A single mind itself, having neither name nor form, corresponds to emptiness. Yet while having neither name nor form, the mind arises continuously from one thought to the next; this corresponds to con-ventional existence. And the essence of the mind is the Middle Way. The essence of the mirror is [likewise] the Middle Way. The [reflected] image of the being [i.e., the practitioner] is conventional existence, and the [reflected] image of the Buddha is emptiness. The perfect in-terpenetration of the mirror and its images is precisely the actual proof of the threefold contemplation in a single mind.[71]

Here the dialectical structure of the threefold truth is replicated in the sequence of the meditation, in which the practitioner first affirms, then questions, and then reaffirms the nonduality of the Buddha and himself, aided by the mirrors and their reflections as visual representa-tions of the threefold truth. According to the *Shuzenji-ketsu,* this medi-tation can be undertaken for a variety of purposes: to achieve liberation from saṃsāra, or for the sake of prolonging life, or to transfer merit to specific persons or to all beings generally. Whatever the practitioner's aim, on entering the place of practice, he is to invoke the aid of all Bud-dhas and bodhisattvas in carrying out his meditation.

In contrast to "practice for specific times," where a period of days, weeks, or months is set aside for concentrated contemplative and ritual discipline, the third category, the threefold contemplation for ordinary times, can be practiced at any time. It is a formless meditation to be car-ried out in the midst of daily activities:

Walking, standing, sitting, or lying down, one should always practice the threefold contemplation in a single mind. Taking the previous thought-moment as the object [of contemplation], one contemplates it with the next thought-moment. If evil thoughts continue [unexam-ined] from one moment to the next, one will give up and fall into the three evil paths. Even if evil thoughts should arise, if they do not con-tinue [unexamined but instead are observed in contemplation], then the evil thought of the moment before is the subtle embodiment of the simultaneous threefold truth.[72]

This in fact corresponds precisely to the practice of "cultivating [samādhi] wherever the mind is directed" *(sui-tzu-i, zuijii),* which Chih-i included under the category of the "neither walking nor sitting samādhi" *(fei-hsing fei-tso san-mei, higyō hiza zanmai),* the last of the four kinds of samādhi taught in his *Mo-ho chih-kuan.*[73]

The fourth and final category in the section on the threefold contemplation in terms of practice is practice for the moment of death *(rinjū):*

> The practice of this [deathbed] rite does not resemble the form of meditation for ordinary times. When one faces his end and the pain of dissolution comes upon him suddenly and wracks his body, his spiritual faculties are blunted, so that he is unable to discern things clearly. What will your learning in ordinary times avail you, if in your dying moments you fail to carry out the practice essential for liberation? Therefore, at this stage, you should practice the threefold contemplation in a single mind as encompassed in the Dharma container *(hōgu).* The "threefold contemplation in a single mind as encompassed in the Dharma container" is precisely Myōhō-renge-kyō. . . . At the time of death, one should chant Namu-myōhō-renge-kyō. Through the workings of the three powers of the Wonderful Dharma [i.e., the powers of the Dharma, the Buddha, and faith], one shall at once attain enlightened wisdom and not receive a body bound by birth and death.[74]

The premise of original enlightenment, it should be noted, does not preclude relying on the superior powers of the Buddha and the Dharma in negotiating the dangerous transition of the last moment.

Having set forth these four categories of practice, the *Shuzenji-ketsu* then poses the following question, crucial to the relation of practice and original enlightenment:

> Question: If we go by the original intent of the *Chih-kuan,* sentient beings and the Buddha are from the outset nondual; there is no aspect of delusion or enlightenment. Why do you now separately confer such contemplative practices that are of inferior form [i.e., in presuming a duality of delusion and enlightenment that is to be bridged]?

> Answer: The intent of the *Mo-ho chih-kuan* is that concrete phenomena are precisely the realm of truth and that existence and nonexistence are nondual. Thus the three contemplations clarified above, for specific times, ordinary times, etc., are precisely the forms of the non-

duality of sentient beings and the Buddha. If you postulate apart from these a practice of the nonduality of sentient beings and the Buddha— the original intent of the *Chih-kuan*—it is not to be found. . . . [D]welling in the original mind that is without aspect, one returns to and becomes identical with that which has form. This is the actual practice for realizing the Buddha's enlightenment.[75]

Practice, in other words, is not to be seen as the inferior element in a dualistic hierarchy of means and end, but is itself the exemplary expression of the original enlightenment in which the Buddha and the beings are nondual. The compiler(s) of the text seem here to have anticipated the possibility that notions of nondual original enlightenment could be seen as canceling the need for concrete practices, and to have unambiguously rejected it.

Lastly, the threefold contemplation in a single mind is discussed in terms of "realization." This section reads in part: "As for the threefold contemplation from the perspective of realization: Since [this contemplation] is originally inherent, there is no need to practice anything. One need not fear evil thoughts nor rejoice in good ones, because both are originally endowed with the threefold contemplation."[76]

The location of this statement in the section on "realization" is significant. It is only here, from the "Buddha-eye view," so to speak, of one who has already realized original enlightenment, that ordinary thoughts can be equated with meditation. From the standpoint of "practice," specific forms of discipline are still required.

Like the *Shinnyo kan,* the *Shuzenji-ketsu* qualifies its claims for the full realization of enlightenment at the stage of verbal identity by attention to the problem of differences in individual human capacity. One example occurs in a section on "the essentials of calming and contemplation," in a discussion of the meaning of "engaging in the great practice," the title of the second lesser chapter of the first chapter, "Synopsis," of the *Mo-ho chih-kuan.*[77] One interpretation given is that to "engage in the great practice" is simply to sustain the understanding, achieved at the stage of verbal identity, that "all dharmas are the Buddha-Dharma." Another is that, on the basis of such understanding, all thoughts—good, evil, and neutral—become "subtle practice." However, this interpretation is qualified as pertaining only to people of superior faculties. This qualification obtains all the more in the case of a third interpretation, namely, that understanding and practice are nondual: "[I]n the understanding that accompanies [the stage of] verbal [identity], beneath the words, verbal categories are obliterated, and enlightenment is opened all at once. These are people for whom understanding is precisely practice and realization; their capacity is that of the most superior keen faculties."[78] Thus the achievement of full enlightenment at the stage of verbal identity is presented as a theoretical possibility, but one limited only to the most capable.

What, then, of persons with dull faculties? This issue is raised in the section on the "deep meaning of the *Lotus Sūtra*," in a discussion of "name," the first of the five profound principles of the *Lotus* enumerated in the *Fa-hua hsüan-i*. The text purports to reproduce a reply from the abbot of Fo-lin-ssu (Hsing-man) in response to a question from Saichō as to "why, though we may earnestly believe and chant the Wonderful [Dharma] with delight, do we not realize the fruit of Buddhahood?"[79] Hsing-man responds in part that those of keen faculties can, with a single utterance of the sūtra's name, transform their accumulated delusions into the three virtues of the Dharma body, *prajñā*, and liberation. However, in case of those of dull faculties, their physical and mental constituents *(skandhas)* have been produced by evil deeds in prior lives, so this transformation does not occur at once. Nevertheless, at the time of death, such people invariably attain the subtle body of the Dharma nature and can travel freely among the Buddha lands to benefit sentient beings: "Since all of you [such persons] already chant the name of the Wonderful Dharma, you will form the assembly beneath the dragon blossom tree at the dawn [of Maitreya's advent] and increase the bright virtue of the *Lotus;* repaying your debt from the past, you will preach the *Lotus* for others' sake."[80] Since the wording of this passage places Saichō himself among "those with dull faculties," one would assume that most people were thought to come under this category. However, continued practice is not always associated in the *Shuzenji-ketsu* with inferior capacity. Although the theme is not developed, the *Shuzenji-ketsu* twice refers to a form of the threefold contemplation in a single mind in which a person of superior faculties, having realized enlightenment, continues always to practice "for the pleasure of contemplation" *(yukan)*.[81]

General Reflections

In purely quantitative terms, the *Shinnyo kan, Sanjū shika no kotogaki,* and *Shuzenji-ketsu* comprise only a fraction of the vast body of medieval Tendai literature. Nonetheless, they are key texts, embodying themes that were being widely elaborated within the medieval Tendai milieu. The *Shinnyo kan,* attributed to Genshin, represents the Pure Land strand of *hongaku* thought, which, as noted in chapter 1, may well be one of the earliest forms of Tendai original enlightenment discourse. The *Sanjū shika no kotogaki* develops important issues discussed widely in the *kuden* literature; for Tamura Yoshirō, it embodied the full emergence of *hongaku* thought, in which all its distinctive attributes were fully present. And the *Shuzenji-ketsu,* as noted in the preceding chapter, appears to have been seminal in the formation of the "threefold seven great matters" that systematize the transmissions of the Eshin school. Thus, especially when considered together, these three texts may be said to argue the need for a more contextualized and nuanced understanding of the relationship between practice and original enlightenment in medieval Tendai thought more generally. As we have seen, they do in fact refer to Buddhist practice, including various contemplations, both formless contemplations and contemplations having form; sūtra recitation; chanting of the *nenbutsu* or the *daimoku;* invoking the aid of Buddhas and bodhisattvas; and also deathbed observances. The presence of such clear textual references to ritual and contemplative practices in medieval Tendai texts represents an obvious but nonetheless compelling reason to question the common assertion that *hongaku* thought represented a denial of the need for practice. How, then, was the relationship between practice and original enlightenment understood? While it would be premature to draw definitive conclusions, certain preliminary suggestions can be made.

First, the examples discussed above suggest that claims about the original enlightenment of ordinary worldlings were not advanced in a naive or simplistic fashion, but hinged on the crucial qualification of faith and insight. *Hongaku* discourse may in one sense be seen as a rhetorical stance grounded in a philosophical commitment to collapsing any sort of distance between ultimate reality and the quotidian world, or between the Buddha and ordinary worldlings. How closely this ideal of "absolute" nonduality is approached becomes the standard for its own claim to superiority over other doctrinal positions. Medieval Tendai *hongaku* discourse shared with the larger Mahāyāna tradition a denial of any ontological distinction between saṃsāra and nirvāṇa, or between conventional and ultimate truth, but presented itself as more fully representing this nondual reality than any other tradition and therefore more profound. Over and against all lesser teachings, which are associated with the position that liberative insight into nonduality is realized by eradicating the defilements and thus relegated to the category of "acquired enlightenment" *(shikaku)*—medieval Japanese *hongaku* doctrine maintains that the defilements, *without transformation,* are liberation—the position of original enlightenment. Yet even in this self-allegedly most nondualistic of all Buddhist intellectual traditions, there remains an opposition, tension, or disjuncture—epistemological and experiential—between the state of realizing original enlightenment and the state of not realizing it. In the vocabulary of the *Shinnyo kan,* one who "believes deeply" in one's identity with suchness realizes original enlightenment; one who disbelieves remains bound to samsaric suffering.

Shimaji Daitō, the first modern scholar of Tendai *hongaku* thought, wrote that acquired enlightenment is a doctrine of many insights and many delusions, but original enlightenment is a doctrine of one insight and one delusion.[82] The one insight is discerning, or believing, that "all dharmas are the Buddha-Dharma"; the one delusion is failure to discern it. The gap between the two is articulated in Tendai terms as the distinction between the stage of identity in principle, where one does not yet know that "all dharmas are the Buddha-Dharma," and the stage of verbal identity, where one encounters this teaching, takes faith in it, and discerns its truth for oneself. Judged against more elaborate, linear *mārga* schemes—such as the fifty-two stages of the path elaborated in traditional T'ien-t'ai thought—this distinction may appear to be a very slender one. However, according to medieval Tendai texts such as those considered above, it is no less than the difference between bondage and liberation. As seen in the *Shinnyo kan,* radical claims are made for the transformative power of the single moment's faith and understanding *(ichinen shinge)* achieved at the stage of verbal identity: fame and profit, no longer delusive, becomes the "nourishment" of enlightened wisdom; providing for one's dependents becomes an act of making offerings to all Buddhas and bodhisattvas of the universe. Informed by insight into nonduality, all one's actions, however mundane, are the actions of original enlightenment.

Second, in this light, it becomes clear that statements about there being "nothing to practice and nothing to realize" do not represent the stage of identity in principle, that is, what ordinary worldlings experience prior to practice. In the scheme of "teaching, practice, and realization," they articulate the standpoint of "realization," that is, the perspective of one presumed to have insight into nondual original enlightenment, and not that of one lacking such insight. It is only after encountering the teaching and realizing that "all dharmas are the Buddha-Dharma" that one is said to be able to "look back" and understand that one has been enlightened all along; before that, the Buddhahood of ordinary worldlings is "a mere doctrinal teaching." To say that "walking, standing, sitting, and lying down are themselves the essence of calming and contemplation" is thus to express the insight of one awakened to original nonduality, not to deny the necessity of practice. Such statements would have served as a guide to contemplation, in indicating the nature of what is to be realized, and also to deny purely instrumental understandings of practice as a means undertaken to achieve a particular end. In the *hongaku* discourse, specific practices are redefined in nonlinear fashion as "precisely the form of the nonduality of the Buddha and the beings"—not the cause leading to enlightenment, but the expression of enlightenment itself.

Third, although full realization of enlightenment at the stage of verbal identity is presented as a theoretical possibility, there is a concomitant awareness that some persons, perhaps even most persons, are not able easily to achieve or sustain such realization. Beings of keen facul-

ties discern their identity with suchness and become Buddhas in an instant, but those of lesser faculties may discern it at one moment, only to
lapse into delusion at the next; or they may not realize enlightenment
until life's last moment. Thus, practitioners are encouraged to cultivate
the contemplation of emptiness, the contemplation of suchness, to recite sūtras or recite the *nenbutsu* or the *daimoku,* and so forth. Such ac-
knowledgments of the difficulty of achieving or sustaining insight into
nondual reality betray the rhetorical nature of claims that all beings are
enlightened from the outset. *Hongaku* discourse aimed at promoting a
particular reimagining of Buddhist practice and liberation in a nonlinear, nondual, and even mandalic fashion, but not at naively dispensing
with practice altogether.

Fourth, the rhetoric of absolute nonduality existed in combination
with, and was modified by, other elements that did not necessarily cohere with it logically. Judging solely from the evidence of the three texts
cited above, these included aspiration to the Pure Land, merit transfer-
ence, the possibility of invoking the power of Buddhas and bodhisattvas,
the coming of Maitreya in a future age, and the need ritually to mediate the moment of death. *Hongaku* thought is best understood not as a
tightly organized philosophical system that rejected inconsistent elements, but as a broad perspective from which the entirety of the received
Tendai tradition could potentially be reinterpreted in immanentalist
terms. Like traditional doctrines, the various forms of Buddhist practice
were not excluded or abandoned as inconsistent with the *hongaku* perspective but refigured, sometimes rather incompletely, in its light.

All this calls into serious question the assumption that medieval
Tendai original enlightenment discourse can be accurately understood
as a denial of the necessity for Buddhist practice. And if Tendai original enlightenment discourse did not entail a denial of practice, then it
is equally inappropriate to characterize the new Kamakura Buddhist
movements as attempts to restore the primacy of practice, over and
against a decadent Tendai tradition that had supposedly abandoned it.
This longstanding though problematic characterization may stem not
only from assumptions about "old" and "new" Buddhism, but also, at
least in part, from insufficient attention to differences in textual genre
and institutional context. One reason why many medieval *kuden* texts
do not give detailed instructions for practice is that they are not ritual
or meditation manuals but are instead concerned primarily with doctrinal interpretation; thus there is no particular reason why they should
explicate practice.[83] Moreover, they were intended for monks and were
transmitted within an established clerical context in which separate instruction in practice, ritual, and so forth may have well been assumed.
The founders of the new Kamakura movements, on the other hand,
were striving to establish religious communities *de novo* and to promote

new forms of practice—or more precisely, new interpretations of a particular existing practice that had been singled out and redefined in an exclusivistic light. Many of their extant works accordingly take the form of explanation and exhortation to individual converts, or to their disciples as a group, about the proper forms of practice and the attitudes that should underly them. Thus we find several reasons why the writings of the Kamakura founders may on the whole stress practice more than do medieval Tendai *kuden* texts, without necessarily assuming that they were restoring an essential part of Buddhism which their Tendai counterparts had allowed to lapse.

Original Enlightenment and the Question of Evil

Now let us turn to the charge that original enlightenment thought, in its extreme emphasis on nonduality, represented an uncritical "world affirmation" that in effect legitimized evil conduct. Certain passages in some medieval Tendai writings do indeed suggest that the doctrine would have been susceptible to this interpretation, such as this statement from the *Shuzenji-ketsu:*

> If someone should come to you and ask, "What is the inner enlightenment of calming and contemplation *(shikan)*?" you should inquire in return: "What is your chief occupation?" If the response should be, "My lifelong occupation has been killing living beings," then you should immediately explain that killing living beings is the inner enlightenment of calming and contemplation. Apart from our wrong thoughts from one moment to the next, what other [object of] contemplation could there be?[84]

Close reading, however, shows that such statements are often carefully qualified by their context. To explore this issue, let us consider the doctrine that "karma (i.e., volitional action) is precisely liberation" *(gō soku gedatsu)* discussed in a number of medieval Tendai texts. It is treated at some length in a transmission of this heading included in the *Sanjū shika no kotogaki*, which reads in part:

> Question: Does "karma is precisely liberation" mean that deluded action, without transformation of its essence, is itself liberation? Or does it mean that liberation follows upon the transformation of deluded action?

> Answer: According to the interpretation of our school, being originally nondual in essence is called "identity" *(soku)*. . . . When one knows the doctrine of the perfectly interpenetrating true aspect, deluded action in its essence is endowed with all dharmas; thus it is not merely deluded action but the perfect interpenetration of the dharma realm

in its entirety. A hawk seizing a bird is, without transformation of its essence, precisely the true aspect of liberation. A fierce dog pursuing a beast is, without transformation, precisely the true aspect of libera-tion. And all other sorts of actions should be understood in light of these examples. The point is to understand the constant abiding of the dharmas. "Constant abiding" means that the dharmas perfectly in-terpenetrate and none is lacking. One should simply sweep aside all partial views and dwell in the undifferentiated true aspect. One who does not dwell in understanding of the undifferentiated dharma realm has not yet grasped the meaning of karma being precisely lib-eration. One who has understood it should not further publicize this oral transmission.[85]

Here the assertion that "karma is liberation" represents a specific for-mulation of the broader idea that the dharmas, being empty, are mutu-ally encompassing. Thus it can only be grasped on the basis of insight into the nondual nature of reality. "Karma is precisely liberation," in other words, is an ontological, not a moral, statement. However, the text seems to reflect an awareness of the potential dangers of such a doctrine, in its admonishment against making it public. A similar awareness is also evident in a passage from the first fascicle of the *Kankō ruijū*, which warns that this is a doctrine for advanced practitioners:

In the case of the good and the neutral, there can be no objection. But if the essence of evil is [the same as] that of calming and con-templation, then this leads to the wrong view that one is free to com-mit evil at will. How do you reply? . . .

Answer: This is a matter of prime importance. According to Tao-sui's interpretation, "In accordance with people's capacity, there is in-struction for those who are novices and instruction for those who are advanced. . . . When one instructs those at the novice stage, one should not teach that evil can be taken as the essence of calming and contemplation, as that would increase deluded views. But when in-structing those who are advanced, [one may reveal that] the essence of the deluded mind is precisely calming and contemplation." This is the meaning of Master Kuan-ting's statement, where he writes, "Do not expound the reconciling of dichotomies to evil persons."[86]

As Paul Groner points out, this passage reflects Chih-i's admonitions that beginners should not be encouraged in the meditation on evil, a variant of the "neither walking nor sitting samādhi" in which evil thoughts—those stemming from greed, immorality, anger, laziness, mental distrac-tion, and stupidity—are taken as the object of contemplation for dis-cerning the threefold truth.[87]

Another passage of the *Kankō ruijū*, this one from the second fascicle, explictly addresses the moral implications of the teaching that "evil karma is precisely liberation":

> Question: To press you again, this is still difficult to conceive. Even if it should be the true purport of the perfect and sudden [teaching], how am I to understand that the essence of evil karma is the same as the wondrous essence of liberation? If so, is the practitioner of calming and contemplation able to commit evil deeds such as killing or theft without fear, according to whim?

> Answer: I will answer you from the standpoint of my original premise. Karma has as its essence the three thousand realms and three truths, and is lacking in none of them. Therefore it is said that karma is precisely liberation. But as for whether the practitioner of calming and contemplation can commit evil deeds at whim: Absolutely not. There are several arguments to be made here. First, karma and liberation are [in terms of their essence] both the ungraspable, inconceivable naturalness of the Dharma. This is called karma being precisely liberation. This being the case, how could [a person who has realized this] fall into a one-sided emotion and commit evil deeds? (This is the first point.) Moreover, evil karma is endowed with the three thousand realms, and liberation is also endowed with the three thousand realms. Therefore, "karma being precisely liberation" means that self and other are nondual and that all dharmas are of a single nature, which is without self. At this time [of so realizing], how could one entertain separate discriminations of this and that, and so commit evil deeds? (This is the second point.) However, if, returning [to the realm of daily affairs] from the inner enlightenment of calming and contemplation, one were to commit evil deeds without selfish intent (*musa*) in accordance with circumstances (*nin'un*), there could still be no difference [between karma and liberation]. This is what is meant by Kannon appearing as a fisherman and killing all sorts of water creatures.[88]

Here, a person with insight into the nonduality of self and other is said to be incapable of arousing the discriminative passions that lead to deliberate commission of evil. Nevertheless, the text acknowledges that such a person might still do evil without deliberate or egoistic intent, as the result of destiny, and that such unavoidable misdeeds would not obstruct that person's liberation. This is remarkably similar to Shinran's argument that one who has placed faith in Amida will not do evil in a calculated fashion but might do so as a result of past karma, in which case such deeds would not obstruct that person's birth in the Pure Land.[89] The references in such passages to persons whose "lifelong occupation is killing living beings," to "a hawk seizing a bird," and to the bodhisattva Kannon (Skt. Avalokiteśvara) appearing as a fisherman link this strand of original enlightenment discourse to larger concerns of late Heian and early Kamakura periods about the salvation of "evil persons" *(akunin ōjō).*[90] This rather complex category included those who, due to inborn karmic hindrances, were unable to practice meditation, or who, because of karmic circumstances, were forced to violate Buddhist precepts, especially the prohibition against taking life. While hunters and fishermen are often cited as the prototypes of *akunin*, with the rise of *bushi* power, such concerns were increasingly focused upon warriors. The warrior was fast emerging as a major social force, but his professional obligation to engage in killing—of animals in the hunt, as a form of war training, and of men on the battlefield—presented unique soteriological problems.

Earlier sections of this chapter considered passages in the medieval Tendai *kuden* literature, such as: "There is no meditation method to be cultivated. Walking, standing, sitting, and lying down are themselves the essence of calming and contemplation"; the suggestion was made that such statements are articulated from the perspective of someone who has realized nondual original enlightenment and are not intended as a denial of the need for Buddhist practice. The assertion that "evil karma is liberation" clearly follows the same logic. It is a statement about the nondual nature of reality and is experientially meaningful only in the case of someone who has realized that nonduality; it is not an endorsement of misconduct. However, in warning that it be kept secret and given only to advanced practitioners, the compilers of these texts seem to have recognized that "evil karma is precisely liberation" and similar ideas related to original enlightenment thought were open to abuse. On the other hand, it must be acknowledged that original enlightenment thought by itself provides little basis for making moral judgments or for resisting evil, and the message of nonduality is easily misunderstood (or misappropriated) as an excuse for wrongdoing. Evidence suggests that some individuals did in fact so abuse it. Mujū Ichien (a.k.a. Dōgyō, 1226–1312) complains about monks who, without having "penetrated the mind-ground of original enlightenment" or discerned "the true intent of the Buddha-Dharma," pervert tantric teachings out of worldly attachment:

> [Such] teachers with evil views, lacking wisdom and aspiration for the Way, have appeared in great numbers. They distort such phrases as "all dharmas are the true aspect" or "all is the Buddha-Dharma," or such terms as "the defilements are *bodhi*, saṃsāra is nirvāṇa." Knowing nothing of how teachings should accord with people's capacity, or of the distinction between understanding and practice, they equate male and female with the two realms [i.e., the Diamond and the Matrix] of Dainichi

Nyorai, and their sexual intercourse, with the union of principle and wisdom. Thus they teach that impure acts are the secret practice of the esoteric teachings. Unable to abandon their evil and perverted views, they will incur the wrath of all heavenly deities.[91]

This passage has echoes of contemporaneous criticisms of the so-called Tachikawa school of Shingon, which allegedly advocated sexual intercourse as the path of liberation.[92] Although Mujū seems to have been speaking primarily of teachers within Shingon, his own sectarian affiliation, one can readily imagine that "nondual" doctrines of other schools, including Tendai *hongaku* thought, were similarly misappropriated by some individuals to legitimate immorality or wrongdoing.

More questionable is the modern scholarly tendency to associate original enlightenment thought with an overall decline in standards of monastic conduct in Tendai institutions, in such fashion that the *hongaku* doctrine is seen as expressing, even legitimizing, widespread clerical corruption and wrongdoing. Two such suggestions may be mentioned here for purposes of discussion. One, advanced by historian Akamatsu Toshihide, proposes that original enlightenment thought underlay the violent activities of armed monks. Akamatsu draws here on a particular incident of clerical violence as recounted in *Heike monogatari* (The tale of the Heike), the epic account of events surrounding the fall of the Taira clan and the victory of the Minamoto. At the funeral of Emperor Nijō in 1165, a dispute broke out between monks of the Enryakuji and the Kōfukuji over precedence in the ritual. The conflict escalated, and armed monks of the Kōfukuji razed a number of Tendai buildings. Enryakuji monks retaliated by burning the Kiyomizudera, a branch temple of the Kōfukuji in the eastern part of the capital.[93] Drawing on the literary scholarship of Yamashita Hiroaki, Akamatsu notes that, according to several early versions of the *Heike,* probably compiled in the thirteenth century, when the armed monks from the Enryaku-ji torched the Kannon Hall of the Kiyomizudera, their leader recited the following verse:

zaigō moto yori shou nashi	Sinful deeds are from the outset without substance.
mōsō tendō yori okoru	They arise from deluded thoughts and perversions.
shinshō moto kiyokereba	Because the mind-nature is originally pure,
shujō sokubutsu nari	sentient beings are precisely Buddha.

Akamatsu notes that this same verse also appears in an early version of Shinran's *Shōzōmatsu wasan* (Japanese hymns on the True, Semblance, and Final Dharma ages). However, late in life, Shinran revised it to read:

zaigō moto yori katachi nashi	Sinful deeds are from the outset without form,
mōsō tendō no naseru nari	produced by deluded thoughts and perversions.
shinshō moto yori kiyokeredo	But although the mind-nature is originally pure,
kono yo wa makoto no hito zo naki[94]	there is no sincere person in this world.

On this basis, Akamatsu suggests that prevalent ideas of original enlightenment informed the creed *(shinjō)* of warrior monks and provided doctrinal support for their activities, obviating any need on their part to reflect upon or repent their violent deeds. In contrast, founders of the new Kamakura Buddhism, such as Shinran, while appreciating the philosophical nondualism of original enlightenment thought, recognized its moral dangers and revised it accordingly.[95]

Akamatsu's suggestion is an intriguing one, but it rests on a single literary source, the *Heike,* which was compiled several decades after the incident in question. While the author(s) of this particular episode imply that *hongaku* doctrine could be seen as legitimating monastic violence, it remains unclear whether in fact this doctrine was so used historically. Recent scholarship has come to view the activities of warrior monks less as indications of secularization and decadence within the Buddhist world than in terms of the factional rivalries inherent in the system of shared rule *(kenmon taisei),* whereby major shrine-temples such as the Enryakuji had to rely on their own resources to defend their assets and privileges.[96] Further evidence is necessary to determine whether warrior monks even thought their actions required a particular doctrinal justification beyond the need to "protect the Dharma"—which would have been identified with the interests of their particular religious institution.

Another such interpretation sees Tendai *hongaku* thought as reflecting and legitimizing a trend toward escapism or even cynical indifference on the part of elite clerics with respect to the sufferings of their time. This opinion has been forcefully expressed by Nishi Giyū. The Insei period, in Nishi's view, was one of the most disastrous in Japanese history, punctuated by floods, epidemics, famines, devastating storms, the Genpei War, and the depredations of monastic armies, including infighting on Mt. Hiei. Those who, in the face of such misery, could assert the innate enlightenment of the phenomenal world

> not only did not see things as they were, but remained ignorant, or pretended not to know. Moreover, they shut their eyes to the internal

state of affairs on Mt. Hiei, where they themselves lived, and seem not to have reflected upon or to have had the slightest awareness of their own implication in these matters. If we assume that they were aware of all this and yet still proclaimed that the Sahā world is the Pure Land and that the defilements are enlightenment, then surely their thought was no more than a meaningless play of rhetoric, a product of the fantasies of heartless men vainly addicted to illusory word games in the ivory tower of their temples, far removed from the common people and the society around them, with respect to whom their thought was blind. In light of the bodhisattva path of the Mahāyāna, theirs was in any event a complacent thought, utterly lacking in compassion, truly nothing more than an abstract game of some naturalist heresy, without moral precepts or shame.[97]

Since the authors of most Tendai *kuden* texts written before the fourteenth century cannot be identified, it is difficult to make conclusive statements about them. Nonetheless, one can probably dismiss outright the possibility that they were ignorant of events in the larger world. Investigation of the men whose names compose the major Tendai *kuden* lineages reveals many of them to have been ranking nobles who maintained ties with their families, conducted religious rituals for the court, and in many cases resided primarily not on Mt. Hiei at all, but in cloisters in or near the capital.[98] Ironically, it is Hōchi-bō Shōshin, a harsh critic of the *hongaku* doctrine, who better fits the notion of an ivory-tower scholar. According to tradition, Shōshin was so absorbed in his doctrinal studies that he knew nothing about the fighting between the Taira and the Minamoto.[99]

Should one then follow Nishi and assume that, being well aware of the social upheavals of their day, the late Heian Tendai scholars engaged in the development of original enlightenment doctrine were callous men who could cynically assert, in the face of natural disasters and violent social unrest, that all beings are enlightened and this world is the pure land? Here again, further evidence is necessary. Although it would remain equally unsubstantiated, one could in fact make the opposite argument: that *hongaku* thought in the late Heian represented not callous indifference, but a creative response to the uncertainties and upheavals of the times. The late Heian period was characterized, at least among the nobility, by an acute sense of degenerative historical change. One manifestation of this awareness was competing discourses about *mappō* and what it meant to be living in an evil age. Political events, most notably the rise of warrior power, fed aristocratic convictions that the times were in decline. The *Gukanshō*, the first Japanese work to propose a theory of history written by the Tendai *zasu* Jien (1155–1225), outlines successive stages of decay. Yet this same period saw the rise of original enlightenment ideas, which characterize liberation as immanent from the outset, timeless, and "constantly abiding."

The above discussion of the *Sanjū shika no kotogaki* identified, as one strand of *hongaku* rhetoric, the denial of linear time and the domestication of change. The idea that the worldly aspect "constantly abides," that all things "dwell in their Dharma-position" and are enlightened "without change of original status," recurs throughout the medieval Tendai *kuden* literature. So does an emphasis on a single moment of insight as the collapsing of past, present, and future into a timeless "now." On one hand, as suggested above, all this can be seen as a "mandalization" of space and time, reflecting the influence of Mikkyō on traditional Tendai thought. However, in the late Heian context, this mandalic world view might also have represented an attempt to interpret change and impermanence in ways that drained them of terror and apparent randomness by assimilating them to some originally inherent structure of reality. This suggests itself as a possible reading, for example, of the following passages, both from late Heian-period *kuden* collections:

The Dharma-essence of the threefold world has no beginning, nor does it perish. The Buddha, for the beings' sake [i.e., as an expedient], said that it is like a burning house. In other words, principle *(ri)* is always equal. Because it is always equal, [things] always dwell in their Dharma-position. Concrete phenomena *(ji)* always entail distinctions. Because they always entail distinctions, they arise in accordance with conditions. The always equal is precisely the always differentiated; the always differentiated is precisely the always equal.[100]

Unproduced birth and death are originally without beginning or end. Being and nothingness, viewed in terms of the principle of the perfect [teaching], are neither permanence nor annihilation. You should contemplate this well, and not fear saṃsāra. Saṃsāra is originally pleasurable. It is only because people are deluded that they view it as suffering.[101]

Attempts to reconstitute the unpredictable flux of events as "inherently enlightened" and "constantly abiding" could have served as attempts to cope with what were seen as inexorable, degenerative historical processes, such as the idea of *mappō* and the shift of power from court aristocrats to warriors. Hayami Tasuku has voiced a similar opinion:

The idea [of original enlightenment], which sought to affirm even the ceaselessly changing phenomena of the time of *mappō* as expressions of a constantly abiding and absolute truth, can be said to have been grounded in recognition of the realities of the Insei period as a time coinciding with the arrival of the Final Dharma age, and to have aimed at positively overcoming its dangers.[102]

Should Hayami be correct, then original enlightenment discourse at this particular historical moment may be understood not as condoning the violence and misery of the period, but as an effort to make sense of them.

In short, it is very difficult in the present state of scholarship to establish what connections existed, if indeed there were direct connections, between the rise of *hongaku* thought in the latter Heian and early Kamakura periods, and decline in standards of monastic behavior. *Hongaku* thought may have contributed to an atmosphere in which strict observance of the Buddhist precepts and rules of monastic conduct was not valued, as Taira Masayuki has suggested[103]—though one must also take account of those monks of the Kurodani precept lineage, such Ejin and Kōen, who sought to revive the literal practice of the precepts even while interpreting them from a *hongaku* perspective. The conduct of ranking clerics of the Enryakuji and other major temple-shrine complexes did indeed often run counter to normative monastic ideals, and ideas of original enlightenment may have been used to rationalize such departures. However, the abandoning by many prelates of strict observance of the precepts and monastic regulations—including the prohibitions against sexual activity, amassing wealth, maintaining worldly rank, taking up arms—must be assessed not merely in contrast to idealized images of how Buddhist monks "should" behave, but in terms of the changing economic, social, and political roles of temple-shrine complexes, as they emerged as one of the powerful parties *(kenmon)* in the medieval system of shared rule. Such a reassessment must also inevitably revise understanding of the medieval *hongaku* discourse.

This is not to deny that original enlightenment thought can be morally ambiguous. On an individual level, it undoubtedly was misused to rationalize wrongdoing, at least upon occasion. While the compilers of Tendai *kuden* texts clearly recognized this danger and warned against it, there is, as noted above, little in original enlightenment thought per se that could serve to check such misappropriation. Its potential danger, both for these producers of medieval *kuden* and for modern critics of the doctrine, lies in its extreme emphasis on nonduality, which can acknowledge even deluded thoughts and sinful deeds as the expressions of original enlightenment. However, one also finds contemporaneous instances of misdeeds being rationalized in the name of a doctrine often described as *dualistic*—namely, the exclusive *nenbutsu* of Hōnen and his followers. As is well known, Hōnen, Shinran, and others taught that the evil one does unavoidably, for example, because of past karma, cannot obstruct the salvific workings of Amida's compassionate vow. Indeed, it is precisely "evil persons," unable to perform difficult Buddhist disciplines or to uphold the precepts through their own efforts, who are the special object of the original vow *(akunin shōki).*[104] On the part of followers, this was sometimes misunderstood as a form of "licensed evil" (*zōaku muge*).[105] Hōnen at one point found it necessary to admonish his adherents to "refrain from saying that there is no practice of the clerical precepts in the *nenbutsu* path, from avidly encouraging sexual indulgences, liquor, or meat eating, . . . and from teaching that those who rely on Amida's principal vow have no reason to fear committing evil."[106] Shinran, similarly, had to admonish against using Amida's compassion for the wicked as an excuse for willful wrongdoing: "It is admirable to believe that Amida's vow is for the person overwhelmed by evil inclinations. But to encourage falsehoods intentionally in one's heart, or in word or deed, simply because the vow is for the evil person, is not what we call the Pure Land teachings."[107]

Nevertheless, morally problematic though the *akunin shōki* doctrine may have been, its intent was not to rationalize or encourage evil, but to alleviate anxieties about retribution for the evil one cannot avoid committing. Behind it lay the fears of hell and the consequent attraction to karma-transcending "theories of salvation" that characterized much of Buddhist thought during this period.[108] It is in this same light that we should understand some of the more ethically disturbing passages in the *hongaku* literature, such as the *Shuzenji-ketsu*'s statement that those whose profession is killing should take killing as their meditation, or the *Kankō ruijū*'s claim that one who has awakened to innate enlightenment cannot be hindered by the wrong he commits without selfish intent as a result of karmic circumstances. The comparison with the exclusive *nenbutsu* is instructive here, in that it suggests that the moral ambiguity of medieval Tendai texts should be seen not as a problem unique to nondual *hongaku* doctrine, but as embedded in larger intellectual concerns of the age. Pure Land claims that human shortcomings cannot obstruct the workings of Amida's compassion were, at least in part, responses to fears about the difficulty of achieving salvation in a degenerate age when all are sinful and burdened by evil karma. Though it represents a very different sort of doctrine, *hongaku* thought in the late Heian and early Kamakura periods may have worked in a similar way. The idea of original enlightenment would have given assurance of salvation in an era widely seen as soteriologically unfavorable, offering an enlightenment that was unobstructable because it was innate from the outset.

It is common in modern scholarship, however, that Hōnen's and Shinran's teachings about evil deeds not obstructing one's salvation are viewed as compassionate attempts to extend liberation to the sinful, while medieval Tendai texts that make similar arguments have been characterized as dangerous endorsements of wrongdoing. Even Tamura Yoshirō, who argued that Shinran had been strongly influenced by ideas of original enlightenment, wrote that in Shinran's case, nondual *hongaku* ideas are "not brandished in the abstract" but mediated by the "existential depths" of Shinran's keen awareness of human sinfulness and limitation.[109] Here again, one must ask to what extent this apparent distinction is the product of differences in the sort of texts available. In comparison to the author(s) of any given Tendai *kuden* text, a great deal is known about Shinran as a person. Personal letters from him survive, including confessional statements and expressions of dismay about followers who took the doctrine of Amida's compassion for the sinful as an excuse for misconduct. The Tendai *kuden* texts are in contrast an impersonal genre. One cannot conclude, therefore, that their compilers considered notions of nonduality only in the abstract or had no sense of the existential implications of their teachings. In addition, it is clear that new Kamakura Buddhist teachings about Amida saving even (or especially) the wicked, or faith in the *Lotus Sūtra* protecting the believer from the consequences of worldly misdeeds, were complemented in early Pure Land and Nichiren confraternities by Confucian and other forms of social morality, and in no way constituted the whole of followers' ethical frameworks.[110] Tendai *hongaku*-related writings of the same period, however, are much more difficult to contextualize. We know very little about who wrote them or under what cirucmstances, or about what role(s) they played in the lives of those who transmitted them. Thus it has perhaps been too easy to read them in the abstract as "uncritical affirmations" of evil.

Tendai Hongaku Thought and the New Kamakura Buddhism: A Shared Paradigm

The models by which medieval Tendai original enlightenment thought and the doctrines of the new Kamakura Buddhism have been contrasted tend to see the latter as reacting against, purifying, or correcting the alleged tendencies of *hongaku* discourse to deny the need for Buddhist practice, legitimate misconduct, and aggravate institutional decay. Such models not only privilege the new Kamakura movements but, as discussed above, rest on some questionable assumptions about medieval Tendai. Is there, then, another perspective from which the relation of the two can be more fruitfully considered?

Before proposing anything in the nature of an alternative model, it is vital to stress the complexity of the picture. Neither medieval Tendai original enlightenment discourse nor the teachings of the new Kamakura Buddhism were discrete, monolithic entities; neither were their institutional, social, and ritual contexts. Mutual influences, borrowings, and confrontations can be found between various strands of medieval Tendai and different lineages of Pure Land, Zen, and Nichiren Buddhism—to say nothing of influences from other Buddhist and non-Buddhist traditions. These interactions changed over time and show regional differences, most notably between the area of the capital and eastern Japan.

The suggestion of chronological sequence implied in the categories of "old" and "new" Buddhism must also be revised with respect to both original enlightenment thought and medieval Tendai as a whole. Although the beginnings of *hongaku* discourse somewhat predate the founders of the new Kamakura movements, the latter did not emerge from a fixed and static "old" Tendai Buddhism. The *hongaku*-dominated medieval Tendai tradition and the new Kamakura Buddhist movements are to a great degree synchronous, both undergoing their formation and early development roughly from the late twelfth through early fourteenth centuries. In this sense, both can be considered part of "new Buddhism."

Since the new movements drew upon preexisting elements of Tendai doctrine and practice, continuities are to be found. On the other hand, as Kuroda Toshio and others have stressed, the new movements stood in ideological, social, and political tension vis-à-vis the parent institution: Tendai representing the *kenmitsu* Buddhism that constituted much of established religion, and the new movements representing the *itan,* or marginal heterodoxies. Thus it is no surprise to find both continuities and disjunctures between them.

What is striking is that within approximately the same time frame— the Kamakura period—they were both engaged in elaborating a constellation of very similar ideas about enlightenment or salvation. Together— Tendai in the center of the religious establishment and the new schools on the peripheries—they may be seen as participating in the articulation of an emerging paradigm of Buddhist liberation.[111] Tracing this shared paradigm or constellation of ideas thus throws into relief some of the major religious concerns of the period. While subject to numerous local variations, it may be broadly sketched in terms of the following interrelated characteristics. These may be understood as constituting a general framework, which was fleshed out with the specific doctrines, religious symbols, and mythic visions of the various Tendai lineages and of the new Tendai-derived Buddhist movements.

Nonlinearity

On a rhetorical level, the pursuit of salvation as a remote goal requiring a long process of effort is denied; liberation is said to occur in a single moment. Medieval Tendai writings often identify this liberative moment in terms of the stage of verbal identity, in which one realizes that "all dharmas are the Buddha-Dharma." This moment is characterized somewhat differently according to the text. The *Shinnyo kan* presents it as a moment of insight (or faith) that can be gained, lost, and regained; the *Sanjū shika no kotogaki* focuses on the structure of this moment in and of itself, as an instant in which all distinctions of past, present, and future collapse in a constantly abiding "now." Conventional ideas about achieving Buddhahood as the culmination of a linear process of cultivation are typically relegated to the status of expedients or inferior views:

> In the provisional teachings established in accordance with their hearers' capacity, cultivation culminating in enlightenment requires immeasurable kalpas. But from the standpoint of the *Lotus Sūtra,* the treasury of profound secrets, manifesting the Dharma-body Buddha who is [one's own] mind occurs in the space of a moment. . . . One who awakes to the Buddha essence of the mind-nature achieves realization instantaneously.[112]

The notion of salvation or liberation in a single moment also occurs in the teachings of the new movements. It is related to the "single-recitation doctrine" *(ichinen gi)* of Hōnen's disciple Kōsai (1163–1247), who taught that when a single *nenbutsu* is uttered with faith, the mind of the Buddha and the mind of the practitioner are united, assuring one's birth in the Pure Land.[113] Shinran stressed the moment when, casting off all reliance on self-effort, one is seized by the compassionate workings of Amida's Vow, never to be let go, and dwells in "the company of the truly settled" *(shōjōju).* Dōgen emphasized not one specific moment in the course of a lifetime, but the "absolute now" *(nikon)* in which practice and enlightenment are inseparable. Nichiren, too, held that Buddhahood is accessed in the moment of embracing in the *Lotus Sūtra:*

> As life does not go beyond the moment, the Buddha expounded the blessings that come from a single moment of rejoicing [on hearing the *Lotus Sūtra*]. If two or three moments were required, this could no longer be called the original vow of the Buddha of great undifferentiating wisdom, the single vehicle of the teaching of immediate enlightenment that enables all beings to attain Buddhahood.[114]

The rhetoric of the soteric potential of a single moment works to suggest the direct accessibility of salvation or liberation by undercutting a perceived distance between ordinary deluded consciousness and the Buddha's enlightened state. It does not negate the importance of continued faith or effort, but that continuation is characterized, to borrow Dōgen's phrase, as "practice on the basis of realization";[115] or in the words of the *Sanjū shika no kotogaki,* as "skillful means subsequent to the fruit [of enlightenment]";[116] or, in Shinran's thought, as the *nenbutsu* recited in gratitude for a salvation that is already assured. Ongoing devotion is characterized, not as progress aiming toward a future goal, but as the confirmation and deepening of a liberation that in some sense is already present.[117] This reimagining of liberation in "nonlinear" terms as accessible in the present moment, rather than as the culmination of a long period of striving, has roots in Mikkyō teachings concerning the three mysteries, in which the identity of the mind, speech, and body of the

adept with those of the cosmic Buddha Dainichi is realized and manifested in the act of esoteric practice.

Single Condition

Because it is seen as directly accessible in a single moment and not as
the result of a linear process of cultivation, liberation or salvation is said
to depend not on a variety of good acts, but on one factor alone. In the
case of original enlightenment thought, the determining factor is held
to be whether or not one discerns the truth of nonduality: "One who
knows this is called a sage; one deluded to this principle is called an ordinary worldling."[118] Or, as in the case of the *Shinnyo kan*, faith, rather
than discernment, may be seen as the decisive condition: "We ourselves
are precisely suchness. One who does not believe this will surely fall into
hell. But one who believes it deeply without doubting will be born in
[the pure land of] Utmost Bliss."[119] In the new Kamakura Buddhist movements, the single condition on which liberation was thought to depend
was often construed as a single form of practice or single object of devotion, as in Hōnen's exclusive practice of the *nenbutsu*, Dōgen's "*zazen*-
only," and Nichiren's exclusive devotion to the *Lotus Sūtra*. Sometimes
the rhetoric of a single condition is expressed negatively, in terms of a
single evil that alone can obstruct one's salvation. Thus the author(s) of
the *Shinnyo kan* condemns failure to believe in one's identity with suchness as the cause for falling into hell; Shinran warns against "calculation"
(hakarai), or the persistent tendency to rely egotistically on one's own efforts for achieving salvation; and Nichiren denounces "slander of the
Dharma," or disbelief in the *Lotus Sūtra*.

This emphasis on a single condition provides an example of how similar conceptual structures were appropriated in ideologically different
ways. As some historians of the *kenmitsu taisei* have pointed out, the exclusive commitment to a single form of practice found in the new Kamakura Buddhist movements was potentially subversive.[120] Advocacy of
a single practice as the sole vehicle of liberation in effect denied the validity of all the rites and observances of the leading cultic centers that
provided thaumaturgical support for the ruling elites, and instead established a single, transcendent source of religious authority. Thus the
single-practice stance embodied an element of political critique. In contrast, in Tendai *hongaku* discourse, liberation is held to depend on a particular insight or attitude, rather than on commitment to a specific form
of practice; thus it did not challenge devotion to the cults of particular
Buddhas, bodhisattvas or *kami* that supported the authority of local rule.
Both Tendai *hongaku* thought and the doctrines of the new Kamakura
schools are structurally similar, however, in seeing salvation as dependent on one factor, rather than a plurality of factors.

Why the notion of single practice—or, more broadly speaking, of a

single condition on which salvation depends—appeared at this particular historical juncture has yet to be thoroughly explained. The formation of rival lineages within Tendai, each claiming unique possession
of the most profound, secret Dharma, may well have fostered this
trend.[121] Some scholars have suggested roots in the practices of certain
hijiri ("holy men" outside the monastic establishment) and *jikyōsha* (devotees of the *Lotus Sūtra,* including lay practitioners as well as *hijiri*) who,
though without developing a rhetoric of exclusive commitment, nevertheless relied solely on the *nenbutsu* or the *Lotus* for their personal
salvation.[122] Another theory is that the single-practice orientation had
roots in the activities of the *dōshū,* or lower-ranking monks whose function in the major temple-shrine complexes was to perform routine contemplative or ritual practices, such as seated meditation or chanting of
the *nenbutsu.*[123] Intellectual trends played a role as well. Hazama Jikō
notes that, within the Tendai tradition, side by side with inclusive readings in which all practices are seen as the practice of the one vehicle,
there have existed exclusive, hierarchical readings that elevate one
teaching or practice above others and assert its superiority, as seen, for
example, in Saichō's subordination of "Hīnayāna" precepts to Mahāyāna; in Taimitsu thought, which identified the one vehicle with the esoteric teachings and ranked it above exoteric, three-vehicle teachings;
or in Genshin's advocacy of the Pure Land path as uniquely efficacious
for ignorant persons of the Final Dharma age. The trend toward hierarchical arrangement of teachings in which a particular form is held to
surpass all others was, in Hazama's view, especially prominent in the medieval Tendai emphasis on private, *kanjin*-style readings as revelatory of
the most profound truth; it was this structure, he argues, that influenced
Hōnen and Nichiren in their commitment to a single practice.[124] At the
same time, the single-practice orientation may also have been a response
to the perceived soteriological uncertainties of the age. If salvation depended on the performance of various kinds of good acts, then one
might never be confident of being able to perform them all. However,
if salvation depended on only one condition, then in fulfilling it, one
could feel reassured.

All-inclusiveness

Because liberation is said to be directly accessed in the moment and
thus can depend on only one factor, both the moment of liberation and
the factor on which it depends—whether defined as faith, insight, or exclusive commitment to a single form of practice—are typically said to
contain the whole of enlightenment. Thus what had traditionally been
regarded merely as an initial step toward enlightenment—faith, the stage
of verbal identity, or a simple act of practice—is now said to encompass
the entire path. The way in which medieval Tendai *hongaku* thought col-

lapses the stages of the path into the initial stage, that of verbal identity, has already been discussed. Nichiren, too, emphasized only the stage of verbal identity, which he equated with faith in the *Lotus Sūtra,* and held that Buddhahood is inherent in the act of chanting the *daimoku.*[125] Shinran similarly wrote that faith was equivalent to the Dharma-nature and rendered one "equal to Tathâgatas."[126] In like manner, the single practices are said to encompass all virtues. For Hōnen, the *nenbutsu* contains Amida's three bodies, ten powers, and four fearlessnesses,[127] while for Nichiren, the *daimoku* contains all of the eternal Śākyamuni's causal practices and their resulting fruits.[128] The self-sufficiency of faith or the first stage of practice is probably indebted to the Pure Land thought that developed within Tendai, and, more remotely, to early Mikkyō-influenced Tendai developments in the concept of "realizing Buddhahood with this very body" *(sokushin jōbutsu),* which sought to locate this attainment at increasingly lower stages of the path. The idea that all merit can be completely contained within a single act or moment's motion of the mind also can be traced to the great Mahāyāna philosophical systems—both T'ien-t'ai and Hua-yen—setting forth the mutual encompassing or interpenetration of the dharmas, as well as esoteric notions that inconceivable powers may be encapsulated in the "container" of a mantra.

Denial of the Obstructive Power of Evil Karma

The causal connection between morality and salvation is relaxed, in that liberation is no longer directly tied to the eradication of sin or the production of merit. This idea finds expression in *hongaku*-related claims that enlightenment does not depend on the eradication of defilements, in the discourse of *akunin ōjō,* or the salvation of evil persons, and in Pure Land teachings that evil karma cannot obstruct the workings of Amida's Vow. Nichiren, too, taught that those who have faith in the *Lotus Sūtra* and chant the *daimoku* will not be dragged down into the lower realms of transmigration by ordinary worldly misdeeds.[129] As a corollary, it is sometimes suggested that the person of true faith (or insight) will not do evil gratuitously. The *Kankō ruijū,* as noted above, asserts that one who has realized that "self and other are nondual and that all dharmas are of a single nature, which is without self" will not "entertain separate discriminations of this and that, and so commit evil deeds."[130] Shinran writes that although evil will not obstruct one's birth in the Pure Land, "When people come to have faith in the Buddha deep in their heart, they genuinely renounce this life, they lament their transmigration in saṃsāra. . . . If these people truly desire not to commit the evil deeds that they may be inclined to do, it is an indication of their renunciation of this world."[131] Nichiren similarly claims that "one who chants [the *daimoku*] as the *Lotus Sūtra* teaches will not have a crooked mind."[132]

Such ideas were of course open to antinomian readings. Over the course of time, in becoming orthodoxy, they have also helped undermine the religious resources of Japanese Buddhist individuals and communities— "new" and "old" alike—to take moral stands in opposition to the status quo. However, in their original historical context, they may well have served to give hope of salvation in an age widely seen as degenerate and sinful. They may also have represented a reaction against the fears of rebirth in the hells and near-obsessive emphasis on merit accumulation that characterized much of late Heian aristocratic religion.[133]

The high tolerance for moral ambiguity and the denial of the obstructive power of evil karma seen in this paradigm also have older roots in the early Japanese Buddhist tradition. These include Tendai adoption of the bodhisattva precepts, which stress the underlying spirit of one's actions, rather than specific forms of conduct; Mikkyō-esque interpretations of the precepts, such as Annen's, which treat ordination as a form of esoteric initiation establishing an indissoluble bond with the Dharma and a guarantee of Buddhahood, rather than as conferring a set of moral precepts; and the accommodation, from the mid-Heian period on, of clerical life to suit the preferences of the aristocrats who joined it in growing numbers. More remotely yet, one notes connections with pan-Asian beliefs that the compassion of Buddhas and bodhisattvas can transcend a strictly mathematical calculation of good and evil. Kannon, it is said, will deliver from shackles anyone who calls on the bodhisattva's name— "whether guilty or guiltless."[134]

In speaking of this constellation of ideas as a new paradigm of Buddhist liberation that emerged in the early medieval period, several qualifications are in order. First, this paradigm by no means encompasses the whole of Kamakura Buddhism but refers only to medieval Tendai and the new movements that emerged from it. Competing models were certainly available. Whether, and to what extent, this schema is useful in explaining other Buddhist developments of the times remains a subject for further study. The *vinaya* revival movements that appeared from within the Nara schools, for example, may represent a different understanding of practice and enlightenment. Second, this conceptual structure represents the level of formal doctrine and rhetoric. On the ground level, so to speak, it did not exist nearly as neatly as presented here but was combined with and modified by other, not necessarily logically related, elements, such as specific rules of conduct for followers, miscellaneous forms of merit accumulation, and apotropaic rituals. Nor were all of the component concepts of the structure always equally stressed by all thinkers and texts that participated in the paradigm. Hōnen, for example, places less emphasis on the "nonlinear" aspect of salvation as accessed in a single moment than do other Kamakura teachers, though it is not absent from his thought. Lastly, as noted in the above discussion, none of the components was new; all had precedents both in continental Mahāyāna thought and practice and in specific developments in the earlier Japanese Buddhist tradition. What is significant is the way these characteristics came together in the late Heian and early Kamakura periods to form a new way of imagining Buddhist liberation. In its various forms, this new model became extremely widespread, cutting across the division known as "old" and "new" Buddhism. It was encoded in highly technical language in secret *kuden* texts transmitted by nobly born Tendai prelates and preached openly in more accessible forms to lay people of a spectrum of social classes. By the late Kamakura period, it had achieved the status of an orthodoxy—not the only orthodoxy, to be sure, but an extremely important one.

To suggest that Tendai original enlightenment thought and the new Kamakura Buddhism both reflected and contributed to a shared, emergent paradigm of immediate, "nonlinear" Buddhahood is in no way to collapse important distinctions in their doctrines, nor to deny significant variations in their organizational structure and forms of practice or the very real political and socioeconomic differences between them. Nevertheless, the formative period of *hongaku* thought and the emergence of the new Kamakura movements occupied roughly the same time frame, and the two reflect certain shared concerns. Because neither was monolithic, because the interactions between them were complex, and because they developed coevally, there are limitations in trying to understand Tendai *hongaku* discourse as a given to which the doctrines of the new Kamakura movements then responded. Rather, in terms of their intellectual content, it is more fruitful to see both as varied, ongoing, and often interacting efforts to elaborate—within their differing social and institutional contexts—a shared structure of ideas about salvation that was distinctively characteristic of the medieval period.

The second chapter of this study outlined three theories about the relation of the new Kamakura Buddhist movements to the medieval Tendai tradition, terming them "Tendai as matrix," "the radical break," and "dialectical emergence." Each offers a useful perspective. As the "matrix" theory underscores, the new movements did, undeniably, emerge from within a medieval Tendai tradition dominated by original enlightenment thought, a tradition with which they exhibit continuities. Yet at the same time they also represent significant divergences, institutionally, ritually, and intellectually, a point stressed by the "radical break" theory. The dialectical model has validity, too, in that later forms of Kamakura new Buddhism, such as the teachings of Shinran and Nichiren, can be seen as synthesizing elements from both the parent, Tendai tradition and the exclusive *nenbutsu* teachings of Hōnen. The objection to all three models lies in their shared, evolutionary assumption that the new movements can be understood as rectifications, purifications, or refinements of a "corrupt" medieval Tendai whose emphasis on original enlightenment thought denied the need for practice and served to legitimate immoral conduct. As discussed above, original enlightenment doctrine did not entail an abandoning of Buddhist practice; thus the new movements cannot accurately be seen as restoring it. Similarly, issues that were problematic in medieval Tendai *hongaku* thought, such as its high tolerance for moral ambiguity, remain problematic in the teachings of the new Buddhist movements. In abandoning both such hierarchical valorizing of "new" over "old" Buddhism and also notions of a static, monolithic Tendai over and against which the new movements arose, a fourth theory of the relation between the two may be proposed. This would be termed the "interactive theory." Such a theory would take into account the continuities, exchanges, appropriations, tensions, and conflicts occurring between Tendai and the new movements, not merely at the moment the new movements arose, but over the course of the Kamakura and Muromachi periods. It would also pay attention to change within both Tendai and the new movements. Such an approach will be illustrated in chapter 7, in discussing the intellectual exchange and mutual influence occurring between Tendai and Nichiren Buddhist institutions in late medieval times.

What the new Buddhist movements of the Kamakura period appropriated intellectually from their parent, Tendai tradition is best understood, not as a uniform "original enlightenment thought," but as a particular model or paradigm for reimagining liberation, of which original enlightenment thought itself represents one variation. The new movements reformulated this paradigm in a number of ways and with the specific coloration of their own religious visions and forms of practice. At the same time, this model continued to undergo further elaboration in Tendai. Because it was understood by those who embraced it as a way of representing enlightenment that was superior to older, linear models, it was employed both by the new movements and by medieval Tendai lineages to legitimate their claims to religious authority.

Part Three

Nichiren and His Successors

Chapter Six

Nichiren and the New Paradigm

How was this new, "nonlinear" paradigm of liberation appropriated and developed in the teachings of the new Kamakura Buddhist movements? For an example, we turn now to Nichiren (1222–1282) and his doctrine of exclusive devotion to the *Lotus Sūtra*. One could also fruitfully pursue this question by investigating the ideas of Shinran, Dōgen, or others among the teachers of the New Buddhism. Nonetheless, for a number of reasons, Nichiren's thought is particularly useful for illustrating the thesis that both medieval Tendai and the new Buddhist movements of the Kamakura period participated in developing a common paradigm of liberation. First, because Nichiren drew on the same tradition and vocabulary of *Lotus Sūtra* studies as did medieval Tendai, he serves as a convenient choice. Second, as noted in chapter 1, the first challenge to the notion of original enlightenment thought as the "womb" or matrix of the new Kamakura Buddhism originated in the realm of Nichirenshū sectarian studies, when Asai Yōrin questioned the authenticity of writings attributed to Nichiren that deal with *hongaku* thought. Such writings, Asai claimed, were Muromachi-period forgeries made by later disciples who had fallen under the spell of the dominant Tendai *hongaku* discourse, a discourse that Nichiren himself had rejected. Given this early importance of Nichiren's case in shaping scholarly argument about the relationship of medieval Tendai and the new Kamakura Buddhism, it is appropriate to return to Nichiren, and to his later followers, in reevaluating that relationship.[1] This chapter will consider how the new paradigm of liberation was appropriated, modified, and elaborated in Nichiren's teachings. The next chapter will discuss how his later followers then assimilated *hongaku* doctrine and other elements of medieval Tendai thought to a distinctively Nichiren Buddhist interpretive frame.

Up until now, the issue of Nichiren's relation to medieval Tendai has often been cast in terms of whether or not, or to what extent, he was

239

influenced by ideas of original enlightenment. However, there are significant limitations to framing the question in this way. First, as noted, it is mediated by problematic texts. A number of writings in the corpus of works attributed to Nichiren extensively employ the vocabulary and categories associated with medieval Tendai original enlightenment thought. However, of these, very few exist in Nichiren's holograph or as transcriptions made by his direct disciples, or appear in the earliest catalogues of his writings. Thus their authenticity has been questioned. Since these problems of authorship are unlikely to be resolved in the near future, if at all, it is hard to assess just how far Nichiren appropriated original enlightenment ideas.

Second, comparisons of Nichiren's doctrine and Tendai original enlightenment thought tend to overlook a key difference between the two that must be made clear from the outset. For all that they are both overtly concerned with the central Buddhist issue of liberation from the sufferings of birth and death, they are formulated vis-à-vis very different polemical targets. Medieval Tendai *kuden* texts assert the idea of innate enlightenment over and against conventional, "inferior" notions of enlightenment as achieved through a linear process of cultivating merit. The burden of their argument is to stress the importance of insight into being enlightened "originally"; how one achieves that insight is far less important. Nichiren's concern, however, was to declare the exclusive validity of the *Lotus Sūtra* in the Final Dharma age and to rebuke those who lacked faith in it. He himself created and inhabited a hermeneutical universe in which every significant event of his age was interpreted from this perspective. The rise of the *bushi* and the victory of the Minamoto clan over the Taira that resulted in the establishment of a warrior government in Kamakura; the retired emperor Gotoba's defeat in the Jōkyō Disturbance of 1221, when he attempted to challenge the power of the Kamakura *bakufu;* the earthquakes, famines, and epidemics that periodically decimated local populations; and the Mongol invasion fleets launched against Japan in 1274 and 1281 were all in his eyes connected to the failure of his contemporaries to recognize the unique validity of the *Lotus Sūtra*. Whether people are or are not enlightened inherently was not his central concern. This difference in polemical thrust is in turn related in part to social, institutional, and ideological differences in the respective positions of Nichiren and his community and the compilers of Tendai *kuden* texts. Simply enumerating continuities and breaks between Nichiren's thought and medieval Tendai *hongaku* doctrine does not take adequate account of this more fundamental difference in orientation.

Third, while examinations of such breaks and continuities have been useful in illuminating the sources of Nichiren's ideas and how they differed from contemporary Tendai thought, they have easily tended to degenerate into disputes about whether, or to what extent, Nichiren's thought is "original" or derivative of his parent tradition. This is a question of interest chiefly to those with partisan concerns and does not place the relationship between medieval Tendai and Nichiren in any broader perspective related to their historical and social context.

The argument advanced here is not that Nichiren did or did not embrace original enlightenment thought, but that Tendai original enlightenment thought and Nichiren's teaching both represent different appropriations and developments of a new, distinctively medieval paradigm of Buddhist liberation, embodied in different social and institutional contexts and given a different ideological thrust. The example of Nichiren and his later tradition will serve to illustrate that the doctrines of the new Kamakura Buddhism cannot be understood simply as emerging from the matrix of medieval Tendai original enlightenment thought, nor simply as reacting against it, nor as retaining its philosophical subtleties while eliminating its morally ambiguous areas. Rather, the various streams of both medieval Tendai and the new Kamakura Buddhism, in a complex web of mutual influences, now appropriating, now rejecting, together developed and were themselves expressions of a shared "nonlinear" reconception of the problem of salvation, which in each case was fleshed out in the specifics of a different religious vision and ideological orientation.

Two Soteric Modalities

Nichiren's teaching of exclusive commitment to the *Lotus Sūtra* in the Final Dharma age undergoes development from two perspectives. While it would be misleading to suggest that these exist as distinct categories in his thought, they may perhaps be thought of as two interconnected soteric modalities. The first is Nichiren's emphasis on the importance of readiness to give one's life for the *Lotus Sūtra*. Since, in Nichiren's thought, only the *Lotus* leads to salvation, its devotees, out of compassion, must confront nonbelievers in the sūtra and strictly point out their errors. By enduring the abuse such efforts are likely to call forth, one's past evil karma can be lessened or eradicated. To incur persecution for the *Lotus Sūtra*'s sake demonstrates the authenticity of one's faith; to give one's life for it is to guarantee one's future Buddhahood. Nichiren developed this soteriology through his own reading of the *Lotus* and other sūtras and commentaries over the course of two exiles, various attempts on his life, and other ordeals he and his followers confronted in the course of his turbulent career.

Second, Nichiren taught that in the Final Dharma age, by arousing the mind of faith in the sūtra and chanting its title or *daimoku* in the phrase "Namu-myōhō-renge-kyō," one can realize Buddhahood with this very body. In this act, the identity of the Buddha and the ordinary worldling is manifested, and the place of practice becomes the Buddha land. This modality has obvious continuities with the esoteric Tendai tradition from which Nichiren had emerged.

Of these two soteric modalities, the first—attaining Buddhahood by meeting persecution for the sūtra's sake—stands out more prominently in the body of Nichiren's writings. It is the "outward face," so to speak, of his religion and represents his response to immediate circumstances as he and his followers began to meet opposition from the *bakufu* and to wrestle with the doubts such persecution engendered. After Nichiren's death, the ethos of "not begrudging bodily life" for the practice and propagation of the *Lotus Sūtra* proved instrumental in enabling his fledgling community to emerge as an independent sect and to define and maintain its identity vis-à-vis older and more established institutions. It is in many ways definitive of his tradition, and no comprehensive account of his thought could ignore it. Informing it, however, is the second or "inner" soteric modality, that of realizing Buddhahood in the moment of chanting the *daimoku*. This is what ties Nichiren to the nonlinear model of salvation that characterizes much of medieval Japanese Buddhism. The chief task of this chapter will be to illuminate this "inner" soteric modality and its connection to that common model. The first part of the chapter will provide context with an outline of Nichiren's career. The second part will analyze the structure of his thought concerning the realization of Buddhahood in the moment of embracing the *Lotus Sūtra*.

An Outline of Nichiren's Career

In contrast to the compilers of medieval Tendai *kuden* texts, few of whom can positively be identified before the Muromachi period, a great deal is known about Nichiren, based on his own voluminous writings.[2] It is impossible in a brief space to do full justice even to the historical facts about Nichiren, let alone to the compelling mythic images and events elaborated by the hagiographies that have powerfully affected his later tradition. What follows here, then, must be understood simply as an outline.[3]

Nichiren was born in 1222 in the fishing village of Kominato in Tōjō in the Nagasa district of Awa Province (now Chiba Prefecture) at the tip of the Bōsō Peninsula.[4] Among all the leaders of the new Kamakura Buddhist movements, he alone was of common origins. In later life, he would describe himself as "the son of lowly people," "born of a *caṇḍāla* [outcaste] family," and "the child of a fisherman."[5] Attempts on the part of later hagiographers to furnish Nichiren with illustrious forebears are most likely unfounded.[6] Still, his family may not have been altogether as humble as he indicates. Recent scholarship suggests that his father may perhaps have been a manager *(shōshi)* or official *(shōkan)* of the local manor or *shōen,* perhaps in charge of administering the exercise of fishing rights held by the *shōen* proprietor.[7] In any event, Nichiren's marginal position as a person of low social position from a remote part of eastern Japan would profoundly influence both his career and his thought. His lack of status seems both to have hindered him in gaining patronage and imbued his teaching with a distinctly subversive edge. When challenging the monks of prominent temples, he would assert that religious authority stemmed not from birth or position, but from commitment to the *Lotus Sūtra.*

Early Studies

We have little information about Nichiren's early years. At the age of twelve, he entered the Kiyosumidera (or Seichōji), a local temple said to have been founded by a monk named Fushigi in 771 and to have been restored by Ennin, third *zasu* of the Enryakuji, during the Shōwa era (834–847). Most scholars hold that, in Nichiren's time, the Kiyosumidera was a Tendai temple, though it may have been a center for esoteric practice not specifically affiliated with either Tendai or Shingon.[8] Nichiren was ordained there at age sixteen by his teacher Dōzen-bō, taking the name Zeshō-bō Renchō. There exists today a transcription that Nichiren made at Dōzen-bō's cloister in 1238, of the first volume of the *Juketsu entaragishū tōketsu,* a medieval Tendai work attributed to Ennin, to which Hōchi-bō Shōshin had referred in his criticism of the original enlightenment doctrine.[9] From Dōzen-bō, Nichiren also learned to chant the *nenbutsu,* an act he would later come to regard as a grave sin.[10]

It is not certain why Nichiren decided to undergo ordination and pursue the study of Buddhism. His later writings say variously that he was motivated by an awareness of life's impermanence and a desire to escape the round of birth and death;[11] that he desired to know which, among the many sūtras and rival schools, represented the Buddha's true intention;[12] or that he wished to resolve doubts about why—when emperors are supposedly protected by the Buddhas and *kami*—Emperor Antoku had perished in the sea at the battle of Dan-no-ura where the Taira were defeated by the Minamoto, and Gotoba and two other retired emperors had been exiled to Oki and Sado following Gotoba's defeat by the forces of the Kamakura *bakufu.*[13] However, these are retrospective accounts, written decades after the fact, and may be more reflective of Nichiren's concerns at the time he wrote them than of autobiographical accuracy.[14] Whatever his reasons, however, it seems clear that, as an adolescent, he possessed an unusually strong desire for knowledge. Nichiren wrote that he prayed before an image of the bodhisattva Kokūzō (Skt. Ākāśagarbha), the Kiyosumidera's central *honzon* or object of worship, to become "the wisest man in Japan." This may indicate that he, like the young Kūkai, undertook the Kokūzō Bosatsu *gumonji hō,* an esoteric ritual for strengthening the powers of memory that centered on the repeated invocation of Kokūzō's name.[15] Nichiren's account, which was written later in life, says that "before my eyes, the bodhisattva Kokūzō became a dignified monk and presented me with a jewel of wisdom like a bright star," as a result of which he was able to understand the teachings of the various schools.[16]

Having exhausted the intellectual resources of his rural temple, Nichiren set out for the country's major Buddhist centers, first in Kamakura, and later in the region of the imperial capital. "For some twenty years, from the time I was twelve or sixteen until I was thirty-two, I traveled extensively, studying at Kamakura, the capital, Mt. Hiei, Onjōji, Kōya, Tennō-ji, and various temples throughout the many provinces."[17] But exactly what he studied, and under whom, is difficult to determine. In Kamakura he is thought to have studied the Pure Land teachings and Zen.[18] His earliest extant work, the *Kaitai sokushin jōbutsu gi* (The meaning of the precept essence and the realization of Buddhahood with this very body), written in 1242 evidently during a brief return to the Kiyosumidera, reflects the fruits of his study up until that point. Essentially it is a work of Taimitsu thought, asserting the original enlightenment of all beings and the immanence of the Pure Land in the present world. It also contains an attack on Hōnen's Pure Land doctrine, especially the notion of seeking a pure land apart from one's own body and mind. Nichiren condemned this idea as "deviating from the Hīnayāna sūtras and differing from the Mahāyāna. Its teacher is a devil and his disciples, the devil's people."[19] This is the earliest notice of his lifelong antipathy to Pure Land faith and practice, that of Hōnen in particular.[20]

After returning to the Kiyosumidera, Nichiren set out again for the vicinity of the capital, where he studied on Mt. Hiei and at other locations. Virtually nothing is known of his studies on Mt. Hiei. During his stay there, the master of instruction *(sōgakutō)* was Shunpan, a leading Tendai scholar and the current patriarch of the Sugiu line of the Eshin school. Traditional accounts maintain that Nichiren received from Shunpan the transmission of the Eshin lineage, which some modern scholars have upheld.[21] However, the few brief references to Shunpan in Nichiren's writings convey no sense of a personal relationship.[22] Takagi Yutaka argues that while Nichiren may have audited Shunpan's public lectures, his common birth would have precluded his entry into a master-disciple relationship with so eminent a prelate. Moreover, his Kantō accent would have instantly marked him as native of the eastern provinces, despised as culturally backward by people of the Kyoto region. Takagi further suggests that Nichiren's exclusion from the circles of initiates that formed around the leading masters on Mt. Hiei may have led to his habit of turning to written documents, rather than living teachers, for instruction and verification.[23] The first of the four reliances, "Rely on the

Dharma and not upon persons" *(ehō fuenin)*, would be his lifelong motto. Nonetheless, it is noteworthy that Shunpan was among those ranking Tendai prelates who vigorously opposed Hōnen's teaching. Even if Nichiren's only exposure to Shunpan were through public lectures, what he heard may have confirmed him in his objections to the exclusive *nenbutsu*.[24]

Traditional biographies, as well as Nichiren's own later writings, suggest that he formed his exclusive commitment to the *Lotus Sūtra* during this period of travel and study. While there is little concrete evidence by which to evaluate this claim, one can probably go so far as to say that, at this time, he laid the intellectual foundations upon which his distinctive reading of the *Lotus* would later be developed. The more than five hundred extant works attributed to him reflect a formidable knowledge, not only of the *Lotus* and T'ien-t'ai/Tendai thought but of a range of Buddhist sūtras, treatises and commentaries, Confucian classics, and other secular literature, a testament to the breadth of his early studies. He also seems to have gained a familiarity with certain Eshin and Danna transmissions, whether acquired from Shunpan or from others.[25] In the home provinces surrounding the capital, he would in addition have been exposed to a spectrum of Buddhist practices and institutions: not only the esoteric Taimitsu of Hiei and the Tōmitsu of Kōya, but the new Pure Land lineages of Hōnen's disciples, the beginnings of an independent Zen, the religious practices of a variety of *hijiri* (holy men), both itinerants and recluses, the popular preaching of the Agui school, and others.[26] One concrete piece of data that survives concerning Nichiren's studies during this period is his transcription, done in Kyoto in 1251, of the *Gorin kuji myō himitsu shaku* (Secret interpretation of the five-element stūpa and the nine-letter mantra) by the Shingon master Kakuban (1095–1143).[27] This work, which interprets Amida Buddha and the Pure Land from the standpoint of Tōmitsu, or Shingon Mikkyō, contains this passage:

> The Tripiṭaka master Śubhakarasiṃha said, "There is an adamantine mantra in just five chararacters, the heart of the *Vajraśekara*[*-sūtra*] and the essence of the *Mahāvairocana-sūtra*, the supreme field of blessings and the ultimate merit. If you embrace this [mantra], the merit that you shall obtain cannot be fathomed. You will always be free of disasters and hindrances, as well as all sickness and pain. Your heavy sins will be eradicated, all virtues will be gathered together, and, in [this present] body born of father and mother, you will quickly achieve the stage of great awakening.[28]

The reasoning behind the use of esoteric mantras in this and similar texts may well have influenced Nichiren's thinking concerning the *daimoku*.[29]

By 1253, at the age of thirty-two, Nichiren had returned to the Kiyosumidera. In later life, he would write that he "first began to speak of this teaching" at noon on 4/28/1253 "at the south side of the image hall" to a group of assembled fellow monks.[30] This first talk or sermon has long been regarded in the Nichiren tradition as Nichiren's declaration of the founding of a new sect, although it seems more likely that, at this early stage, his aim was simply to revive central emphasis on the *Lotus Sūtra* within the Tendai tradition. Presumably this first sermon included criticism of Pure Land practices, not only of Hōnen's exclusive *nenbutsu* but of the nonexclusive Tendai Pure Land practices being conducted at the Kiyosumidera. According to later hagiographies, on this day Nichiren rose before dawn, climbed the hill Takakamori behind the temple, and, facing the morning sun as it rose above the ocean, chanted "Namu-myōhō-renge-kyō" for the first time. On that same day he renamed himself "Nichiren."[31] At noon he preached his first sermon. His denunciation of the *nenbutsu* was reported to the local *bakufu*-appointed steward (*jitō*), Tōjō Kagenobu, an ardent Pure Land devotee. Kagenobu sent his warriors to the temple to arrest him, but Dōzen-bō, Nichiren's former teacher, had two senior monks help him escape.[32]

Actual events were probably more complex and unfolded over a longer time. Based on the evidence of Nichiren's writings, Takagi Yu-taka suggests that Nichiren's presence at the Kiyosumidera polarized its monks into two factions, those who embraced Pure Land along with *Lotus*-related practices, and those who, following Nichiren, stressed devotion chiefly to the *Lotus Sūtra*. Tensions between the two parties were aggravated by attempts on the part of the *jitō*, Kagenobu, to encroach on the rights of the local *ryōke* or *shōen* proprietor and assert control over temple lands. Tagaki suggests that the Pure Land faction at Kiyosumidera supported Kagenobu, while Nichiren intervened on behalf of the *shōen* proprietor, a widow to whom Nichiren's parents were in some way indebted and who appears in his writings as "the nun of the estate" (*ryōke no ama*).[33] Nichiren offered ritual prayers to free the temple from Kagenobu's influence and evidently helped to negotiate a successful lawsuit.[34] Though Nichiren's opponents were thus temporarily thwarted, the growing hostility of Kagenobu and the Pure Land faction at the Kiyosumidera eventually forced him to leave.[35] Whatever other dramatic license it may take, the hagiographical account does not exaggerate Kagenobu's animosity. When Nichiren returned briefly to Awa eleven years later to visit his mother and followers in the area, he was ambushed and nearly killed by a band of the *jitō*'s men.[36]

Driven from the Kiyosumidera, Nichiren went to Kamakura, where he lived at a place called Matsubagayatsu. There he began to attract followers, both monks and lay people. Most of the monks who joined him were Tendai monks, though later on, others would be ordained directly by Nichiren. The lay followers were chiefly middle- and lower-ranking samurai, who would form the core and economic support base of Nichiren's following. They included a number of direct vassals *(gokenin)* of the Hōjō who first met Nichiren while on tour of duty in Kamakura. They converted their own households and retainers and often built private chapels on their lands for Nichiren's disciples, who in turn provided them and their families with religious guidance and ritual services. This was the start of Nichiren communities in Kai, Suruga, Shimōsa, and elsewhere in the Kantō.[37]

At this time, Nichiren's thinking still remained largely within the framework of Tendai *Lotus* and Taimitsu teachings. He made drawings of two visions that had appeared to him, in the first month of 1254, of the "living forms" of the esoteric deities Aizen Myōō and Fudō Myōō, respectively. The "seed characters"—Sanskrit letters representing a particular deity—for these figures would later appear on a mandala that Nichiren devised, written there in Siddham, the medieval Sanskrit orthography. An inscription following the drawings says that he conferred on a "new Buddha" (i.e., a disciple initiate) a transmission he had received as twenty-third in a direct line from Mahāvairocana.[38] Nichiren's writings of this period also employ Tendai ideas of nonduality and original enlightenment to undermine the categories of Hōnen's thought, such as the distinction between "self-power" *(jiriki)* and "Other-power" *(tariki),* or between this impure world *(edo)* and the pure land. For example:

> The *Lotus Sūtra* establishes self-power but is not self-power. Since the "self" encompasses all beings of the ten realms, one's own person from the outset contains the Buddha realm of both oneself and of all beings. Thus one does not now become a Buddha for the first time. [The sūtra] also establishes Other-power but is not Other-power. Since the Buddha who is "other" is contained within us ordinary worldlings, this Buddha naturally manifests himself as identical to ourselves.[39]

> The originally enlightened Buddha of the perfect teaching abides in this world. If one abandons this land, toward what other land should one aspire? . . . The practitioner who believes in the *Lotus* and *Nirvāṇa* sūtras should not seek another place, for wherever one has faith in this sūtra is precisely the pure land. . . . For people of our day, who have not yet formed a bond with the *Lotus Sūtra,* to aspire to the Western Pure Land is to aspire to a land of rubble.[40]

Although Nichiren's thinking during this early period thus remained largely within the framework of Taimitsu, some of the beginnings of his distinctive teaching are nevertheless in evidence. Around this time, Nichiren began recommending to his disciples a practice that has since become almost uniquely associated with his tradition: chanting the *daimoku* or title of the *Lotus Sūtra*, in the formula "Namu-myōhō-renge-kyō." *Myōhō-renge-kyō* is the Sino-Japanese pronunciation for *Miao-fa-lien-hua ching*, the title of the Chinese translation of the *Saddharma-puṇḍarīka-sūtra* made by Kumārajīva in 406 and regarded as authoritative throughout East Asia. "Namu," a transliteration of the Sanskrit *namo-* (from *namas*), is an expression of devotion, veneration, praise, or the taking of refuge. Nichiren himself did not invent this practice. Use of the phrase "Namu-myōhō-renge-kyō" to express devotion to the Dharma is attested as early as the ninth century.[41] Throughout the late Heian period, single phrases expressing faith in the *Lotus* were chanted—though not nearly as widely—in the same manner as the *nenbutsu*. These expressions were not unified but included such variants as "Namu-myōhō-renge-kyō," "Namu-ichijō-myōden" (*Namu* to the wonderful scripture of the one vehicle), and so forth.[42] Nichiren, however, was the first to define the *daimoku* as an exclusive practice and to provide it with a doctrinal foundation. His emphasis on the *daimoku* as an exclusive practice no doubt reflects the influence of Hōnen's exclusive *nenbutsu* teaching, as others have pointed out.[43] But the doctrinal basis he provided for it has deep roots in Taimitsu and also reflects his own distinctive synthesis.

At this early stage, Nichiren's claims for the *daimoku* were still rather modest. He presents it as an alternative for "ignorant persons" unable to perform the introspective contemplation on the "three thousand realms in a single thought-moment," which those "who have the resolve" are encouraged to pursue.[44] As for the merits resulting from this practice, Nichiren says only that those who chant it, even without understanding its meaning, will not be pulled down by worldly evils into the lower realms of transmigration but will eventually reach the stage of non-retrogression.[45] Not until much later in life would he declare that "all persons, whether they have wisdom or not, should alike abandon other practices and chant Namu-myōhō-renge-kyō" and advocate the *daimoku* as the sole practice for the direct realization of Buddhahood in this very body.[46]

The beginnings of Nichiren's eventual thinking concerning the *daimoku* are, however, already present in his *Ichidai shōgyō taii* (The cardinal meaning of the sacred teachings of the Buddha's lifetime), written in 1258, which declares the *Lotus Sūtra* to be the Buddha's ultimate teaching and the purpose of his advent in this world. In this work, Nichiren identifies the five characters of the *daimoku*, the "Wonderful Dharma," with the "three thousand realms in one thought-moment" (*ichinen sanzen*), an identification that would be central to his later writings.[47] The *Ichidai shōgyō taii* also foreshadows the importance Nichiren would place on the concept of the "three thousand realms in one thought-moment" as the foundation of his mature thought. Unlike the majority of medieval Tendai *kuden* texts, Nichiren took as his doctrinal basis not the threefold contemplation in a single mind, but the three thousand realms in a single thought-moment. While both concepts express the idea of a perfectly interpenetrating universe in which all dharmas simultaneously encompass one another, the "three thousand realms in one thought-moment" explicitly includes two component principles that Nichiren would draw upon in developing his thought. One is the mutual inclusion of the ten dharma realms (*jikkai gogu*), which Nichiren used to focus more diffuse notions of nonduality on the mutual encompassing of the Buddha realm and the nine realms of unenlightened beings. The other is the concept of the land (*kokudo seken*), which is nondual with and inseparable from the beings who inhabit it. This concept would be important to Nichiren for two reasons. First, it underlies his claim that the land itself can manifest Buddhahood, that is, that the pure land can be realized in the present world. Second, its implication that insentient forms can manifest Buddhahood provided the doctrinal basis for his use of a mandala as a *honzon* or object of worship.[48]

The year 1254, when Nichiren arrived in Kamakura, saw the beginning of a grim wave of calamities: drought, storms, famine, epidemics, earthquakes, fires, and ominous astronomical portents.[49] The era name was changed four times between 1256 and 1260, in an attempt to stem disasters by renewing the cycle of time. Confronted by widespread death and misery, Nichiren consulted the sūtras in an effort to reach an understanding of their causes. In one among a group of essays written to express his conclusions, Nichiren wrote, "When prayers are offered for the peace of the land and still the three disasters occur within the country, then one should know that it is because an evil teaching has spread."[50] The "evil teaching" he saw as Hōnen's exclusive *nenbutsu*, which has "closed off the direct path of the *Lotus* and esoteric teachings" in favor of the hard and narrow route of the Pure Land teachings.[51] The most famous work to emerge from this period of study was Nichiren's memorial *Risshō ankoku ron* (Treatise on establishing the right [teaching] and bringing peace to the land), submitted on 7/16/1260 via an intermediary to Hōjō Tokiyori, the former regent to the shōgun.[52] Though officially retired, Tokiyori was then the most powerful figure in the *bakufu*. In this treatise, Nichiren argued that the protective *kami* had abandoned the nation because the people as a whole had "turned their backs upon the right"—the supreme teaching of the Buddha's lifetime, the *Lotus Sūtra*—and "given themselves to evil," which he identified, again, with Hōnen's exclusive *nenbutsu*.[53] Drawing on descriptions from the *Chin-kuang-ming ching* (*Suvarnaprabhāsa-sūtra*, Sūtra of the golden light), *Ta-chi ching* (*Mahāsaṃnipāta-sūtra*, Great collection of sūtras), *Jen-wang ching* (Sūtra of the benevolent kings), and *Yao-shih ching* (Sūtra of [the Buddha] Medicine Teacher *Baiṣajyaguru-vaidurya-prabhāsa-purva-praṇidhāna-viśesa-viṣtara*) of the miseries that will befall a country whose sovereign does not protect the True Dharma, Nichiren argued that Japan perfectly mirrored this situation. Already, just as the sūtras described, there had been violent and unseasonable storms, crop failure, famine, epidemics, and ominous portents in the heavens. If the situation were not rectified, he said, then, based on these scriptural predictions, two further disasters could be expected to occur—the "calamity of revolt within one's own domain" and "the calamity of invasion from foreign lands."[54]

Early references to this treatise in Western scholarship have often seen its chief argument as advocating an alliance of Buddhism and the state, as though these two had ever been separate.[55] In reality, Buddhist institutions had been intimately connected with the state from the time Buddhism first entered the country, a relationship described as "the mutual dependence of the imperial law and the Buddhist Law" (ōbō Buppō sōi ron), and which has been investigated in detail by Kuroda Toshio and other historians of the kenmitsu taisei.[56] In writing the treatise, Nichiren clearly saw himself as a successor to Myōe and other representatives of the Buddhist establishment who had written rebuttals to Hōnen's Senchakushū and appealed to the court to suppress the exclusive nenbutsu for the sake of the national welfare.[57] The fact that the Risshō ankoku ron stands within a larger, older discourse about Buddhism as a power for nation-protection (chingo kokka) has caused some Japanese scholars to see Nichiren as retaining elements of "old Buddhism" and thus not fully representative of the "New Buddhism."[58]

However, as Satō Hiroo has pointed out, Nichiren's idea of the relationship between Buddhism and worldly authority as reflected in the Risshō ankoku ron departs in important respects from traditional chingo kokka thought. Those representatives of the "old Buddhism" who had petitioned the court to suppress the exclusive nenbutsu had conflated the "country" (kokka) with the "imperial law" (ōbō); "nation protection" in their eyes was equated with protecting the system of aristocratic rule grounded in the authority of the emperor, the retired emperor, and the court. In Nichiren's eyes, however, the country and the rule of the court and aristocracy were entirely different matters, as indicated by his submission of the Risshō ankoku ron to the Kamakura bakufu. The "land" (koku) in his treatise is the kokudo seken, the external world, nondually related to sentient beings and capable of positive transformation through their faith in the "one vehicle." To ensure the spread of the one vehicle, the ruler's support is indispensable, but his role is relativized by his responsibility, in Nichiren's eyes, to discern the True Dharma from false teachings and protect the former while suppressing the latter. Nichiren points out that Hōnen's teaching first spread during the reign of Gotoba, "and the fate of that retired emperor is clear before our eyes."[59] In this way, he suggests that a ruler who fails to protect the True Dharma and suppress false teachings is likely to meet his downfall, as Gotoba did. This, Satō argues, invests Nichiren's early view of the relationship of Buddhism and worldly authority with a critical edge not seen in that of the older Buddhist establishment.[60]

The submission of the *Risshō ankoku ron* to Hōjō Tokiyori is regarded in the Nichiren tradition as Nichiren's first remonstration with the *bakufu.* However, it is important to note that, at this stage of his career, while he had come to identify the *Lotus Sūtra* as the Buddha's highest teaching, Nichiren was not yet making exclusive truth claims for it. In memorializing the *bakufu* with the *Risshō ankoku ron,* he was not seeking support for a new religion but instead identified himself with the "old Buddhism." He even implied that the ruler had a responsibility to protect the economic basis of *kenmitsu* temples, especially those of Tendai, against the encroachments of Hōnen's new Pure Land movement.[61]

By this time, nearly half a century had passed since Hōnen's death, and his disciples in the east had powerful patrons in Kamakura, including the shogunal regent's father, Hōjō Shigetoki. Nichiren was soon challenged to debate by the leading Jōdo prelates in Kamakura, Dō'a Dōkyō (a.k.a. Nenkū, d. 1287) of the Shinzenkōji, a second-generation disciple of Hōnen, and Nōan of the Chōanji. By Nichiren's account, his opponents were unable to respond after only a few exchanges. He writes that their lay followers then repeatedly attacked him and spread slanderous rumors about him to persons in authority.[62] A mob attacked his dwelling seeking to kill him, and he was forced to leave Kamakura temporarily.[63] The year after he submitted his memorial, the *bakufu* had him arrested and exiled to the Izu peninsula.[64]

Had Nichiren not publicly attacked Hōnen's teaching and come into conflict with the *bakufu,* his following might have remained simply another branch of medieval Tendai, and an independent Nichiren Hokke tradition might never have emerged. However, his failure to win an official hearing, followed by the sentence of exile, forced him into an adversarial position from which he would begin to define his religion over and against that of the ruling elites. Of low status from the outset and now under criminal sentence, Nichiren would increasingly articulate his message from the standpoint of someone on the margins in challenge to the center. More precisely, he would elaborate a world view and mythic vision in which center and periphery were reversed.

The Izu Period

Nichiren's writings during the Izu exile show the emergence of several new elements in his thought. One is a deepened sense of personal connection between himself and the *Lotus Sūtra*. The sūtra speaks of trials and difficulties that will attend its practice and propagation in the evil age after the Buddha's nirvāṇa. "Hatred and jealousy toward this sūtra abound even during the Buddha's lifetime; how much more so after his nirvāṇa!"[65] Such passages, cast in the form of predictions uttered by the Buddha or great bodhisattvas, probably served to give meaning to the opposition from established Buddhist schools encountered by the Mahāyāna community that had compiled the sūtra. In exile, Nichiren began to read them as speaking specifically to his own circumstances and expressed delight that he was able to live in his own person the persecutions predicted in the sūtra. "The devotees (*jikyōsha*) of the *Lotus Sūtra* in Japan have not yet experienced these scriptural passages. I alone have read them. This is the meaning [of the statement]: 'We do not value bodily life, but cherish only the unexcelled way.'"[66]

In his Izu writings, Nichiren began to refer to himself as the *gyōja*—practitioner or votary—of the *Lotus Sūtra*. In contrast to the more conventional term *jikyōsha*, one who "holds" the sūtra and recites it as his or her personal practice, *gyōja* for Nichiren meant one who lived the sūtra through one's actions, experiencing in one's own person the great trials that it predicts. His later writings would call this "reading with the body" (*shikidoku*). Having been exiled, as he saw it, for the sūtra's sake, Nichiren rejoiced that even when not specifically reciting it, he was in effect now practicing the sūtra continuously, walking, standing, sitting, and lying down, throughout all the hours of the day and night.[67]

Nichiren's Izu writings also reflect an increasingly exclusive emphasis on the *Lotus Sūtra*. During this period, he formulated his "five principles" (*gogi*), five interconnected perspectives from which the *Lotus Sūtra* is defined as the supreme teaching.[68] We will outline them here as a framework for introducing some of Nichiren's basic ideas, some of which he would not fully develop until later in life.

THE TEACHING (KYŌ) Following the traditional T'ien-t'ai classificatory schema of the five periods and eight teachings (*goji hakkyō*), Nichiren assigned the *Lotus Sūtra* to the last period of the Buddha's preaching life and asserted that all other, earlier sūtras are provisional (*gon*) while the *Lotus* alone is true (*jitsu*). For textual support, he often cited the passage from the *Wu-liang-i ching* (Sūtra of immeasurable meanings), the introductory scripture to the *Lotus*, which states: "In these forty years and more, I [Śākyamuni] have not yet revealed the truth," and another from the *Lotus* itself: "Among all those [sūtras] I [Śākyamuni] have preached, now preach, or will preach, this *Lotus Sūtra* is the hardest to believe, the hardest to understand."[69] Nichiren, like other T'ien-t'ai/Tendai scholars before him, saw the superiority of the *Lotus Sūtra* as lying in two teachings unique to this scripture and identified respectively with the trace and origin teachings—specifically, with the second chapter ("Skillful Means") and the sixteenth ("Fathoming the Lifespan of the Tathâgata").[70] The first is that persons of the two vehicles can attain Buddhahood *(nijō sabutsu).* Since those practicing the two vehicles of the *śrāvaka* and the *pratyekabuddha* are followers of the Hīnayāna path, a number of Mahāyāna sūtras deny their capacity for the Buddhahood. The *Lotus Sūtra*'s pronouncement that they can become Buddhas was taken as representing the potential for the Buddhahood of all beings. Second is the revelation of the Buddha's enlightenment in the remote past *(kuon ji-tsujō).* According to the sūtra, all other Buddhas are merely emanations or manifestations of Śākyamuni. Moreover, Śākyamuni is said to have displayed himself as entering final nirvāna as a "skillful means" to arouse people's longing for his teaching, but in reality, he is "always here in this Sahā world." As noted before, the Buddha's enlightenment in the far distant past was also widely understood in Nichiren's time to mean that the Buddha is eternal and constantly abides in this world. Like other Tendai thinkers of his day, Nichiren also associated these two teachings respectively with "principle" *(ri)* and "actuality" *(ji).*[71]

HUMAN CAPACITY (KI) This concept, often invoked in the context of *mappō* discourse, refers to innate receptivity or capacity for achieving salvation through a particular teaching. "Capacity" forms an element central to the exclusive *nenbutsu* teaching of Hōnen, who argued that the superiority of a teaching depends not on its depth of philosophical content but on whether or not people can actually practice it; hence he maintained that the *nenbutsu,* readily accessible even to those of limited capacity who predominate in this evil age, is superior. For Nichiren, as for Hōnen, "capacity" was to be understood in universal terms; being advocates of exclusive practices, neither man focused on individual differences in receptivity but maintained that all persons can be saved through a single teaching. However, Nichiren did not base his argument for the superiority of the *Lotus Sūtra* solely on ease of practice.[72] The *Lotus Sūtra* is the seed of Buddhahood; that is, encountering the *Lotus Sūtra* is the condition that enables salvation. Nichiren described the people of the Final Dharma age as "not yet having good [roots]" *(honmi uzen),* that is, without prior connection to the *Lotus Sūtra* that would ensure their enlightenment. Thus persons of this age should, he said, all be instructed in the *Lotus Sūtra;* whether they accept it or slander it, they will in either case receive the seed of Buddhahood and eventually become Buddhas.[73] Nichiren vehemently rejected the position of exclusive *nenbutsu* adherents, that the *Lotus* should be set aside as too profound for the benighted people of the Final Dharma age. He maintained, with Chan-jan, that "the more true the teaching, the lower the stage [of the practitioners it can bring to enlightenment]."[74] It was in part to stress the ability of the *Lotus* to save even the lowly and sinful that Nichiren would refer to himself, later in life, as "the son of lowly people" and born of a *caṇḍāla* family."[75]

THE TIME (JI) This category encompasses Nichiren's understanding of the Final Dharma age, which, like most Buddhist scholars of the time, he held to have begun in 1052. Here again, the comparison with Hōnen is instructive. For Hōnen, in the time of *mappō*, people are of limited capacity, and the easy practice of the *nenbutsu* is therefore appropriate. For Nichiren, the Buddha specifically intended the *daimoku* of the *Lotus Sūtra* for the Final Dharma age; thus this age is the very time when the *daimoku* is destined to spread. This element of historical inevitablity is a key aspect of Nichiren's thought and would later form the topic of one of his major treatises: *Senji shō* (The selection of the time).[76] By defining the beginning of the Final Dharma age as the precise historical moment when the Buddha's ultimate teaching, the *Lotus Sūtra,* shall spread, Nichiren was able to reverse the conventional gloomy connotations of the last age and celebrate it as the best possible time to be alive. He represented great teachers of the past, such as Chih-i, Chan-jan, and Saichō, as lamenting their inability to see the dawn of this age. "Rather than be great rulers during the two thousand years of the True and Semblance Dharma ages, those concerned for their salvation should be common people now in the Final Dharma age. . . . It is better to be a leper who chants Namu-myōhō-renge-kyō than be chief abbot *(zasu)* of the Tendai school."[77]

In this way, Nichiren was able to invert conventional hierarchies and define himself and his followers, rather than the nation's rulers or leading clerics, are the ones whose practice accorded with the time.

THE LAND OR COUNTRY (KOKU) "Country" here means a land inhabited by a specific people. From the viewpoint that the "self" at present is the concatenation of all past deeds, living beings represent primary karmic recompense *(shōhō)* and the land they inhabit, dependent recompense *(ehō)*. The two are understood as nondual *(eshō funi)*, like body and shadow. Thus in correspondence to the capacity of their inhabitants, lands or countries may be said to have an affinity to particular teachings. Following earlier Tendai thinkers such as Saichō, Annen, and Genshin, Nichiren argued that the country of Japan is related exclusively to the *Lotus Sūtra*.[78] However, such claims on the part of Annen and others were inevitably linked to the authority of their religious institution, the Enrya-kuji on Mt. Hiei, as a major cultic center for the rites of nation-protection. In Nichiren's hands, the same claim served to challenge the authority of Mt. Hiei and other leading cultic centers, as well as the rulers who supported them, by arguing that they did not preserve unadulterated the teaching of the *Lotus,* which alone could truly protect the country, but had contaminated it with Mikkyō, Pure Land, and other "inferior" teachings. Indeed, part of Nichiren's idea of Japan was that it had become "a country of slanderers of the Dharma"; hence one disaster was destined to follow upon another.

SEQUENCE OF DHARMA PROPAGATION (KYŌHŌ RUFU NO ZENGO) This is the principle that one should not attempt to spread in a particular country any teaching inferior to those that have already been propagated there. It was inappropriate, in Nichiren's view, to teach provisional Mahāyāna or Hīnayāna teachings in Japan, where the true Mahāyāna teaching (i.e, the *Lotus*) had already been established by Saichō. The efforts of men like Hōnen or Dainichi Nōnin and their followers to spread Pure Land or Zen teachings were thus like "discarding a jewel to take up [ordinary] rocks."[79]

In keeping with his increased emphasis on the *Lotus Sūtra* as the exclusive vehicle of salvation in the Final Dharma age, Nichiren's writings during the Izu period also show a growing concern with the evil of "slander of the Dharma" (*hōbō*), a sin elaborated in detail in a number of Mahāyāna sūtras but which Nichiren understood as willful disbelief in or rejection of the *Lotus Sūtra*.[80] Believers in the *Lotus Sūtra*, in his thought, ordinarily need not fear rebirth in the hells, whatever their misdeeds: "Apart from discarding faith in the *Lotus Sūtra* to follow an advocate of provisional teachings, all other worldly evil acts cannot equal [in weight] the merit of the *Lotus;* thus those who have faith in the *Lotus Sūtra* will not fall into the three evil paths."[81] Slander of the *Lotus Sūtra*, however, "exceeds a thousand times" the five perverse offenses (*gogyakuzai*) of killing one's mother, father, or an arhat; causing the body of the Buddha to bleed; or disrupting the harmony of the sangha; and is the cause for falling into the Avīci Hell.[82] Thus the practitioner of the *Lotus* has a duty to rebuke slander, whatever the personal consequences: "No matter what great good one may produce, even if one reads and transcribes the entire *Lotus Sūtra* a thousand or ten thousand times, or masters the way of contemplating the three thousand realms in one thought-moment, if one fails to rebuke enemies of the *Lotus Sūtra*, one cannot attain the Way."[83]

In later life, Nichiren's conviction that all the people of Japan in his day were slanderers of the *Lotus Sūtra* would underscore his advocacy of *shakubuku* (to "break and subdue"), the "stern method" of teaching the Dharma by assertively rebuking "wrong views."[84] To the rhetoric of rebuking slander he assimilated both the Buddhist ideal of bodhisattva conduct and the Confucian virtues of loyalty and filial piety. One rebukes another's slander to save that person from the hells and to provide the karmic connection to the *Lotus* that alone enables the realization of Buddhahood; thus Nichiren regarded *shakubuku* as an act of bodhisattva-like compassion and the highest form of service to that person. In addition, Nichiren argued that *not* to obey a sovereign or parent who opposed the *Lotus Sūtra* was the true form of loyalty and filial devotion, thus appropriating Confucian virtues in a way that could in some cases legitimize, or even mandate, defiance of worldly authority.[85]

Return to Kamakura

Nichiren was pardoned from his sentence of banishment on 2/22/1263.[86] For the next few years, he traveled in Awa, Suruga, and possibly also Kazusa and Shimōsa to preach and encourage followers.[87] By 1268 he was back in Kamakura. Early that year, envoys sent by Khubilai Khan had arrived with demands that Japan acknowledge the suzerainty of the Mongol empire or prepare to be subdued by force of arms. Subsequent envoys arrived with repeated demands in 1269. A sense of crisis mounted as the *bakufu* mobilized its defenses and the major temples and shrines offered prayers for the enemy's defeat. Around this time, Nichiren began holding commemorative lectures or Daishikō on the *Mo-ho chih-kuan* on the twenty-fourth of each month, the day of Chih-i (Tendai Daishi)'s death. These lectures were not merely for doctrinal instruction but were also conducted with the ritual purpose of praying, in the *Lotus Sūtra*'s words, for "peace and security in this life and birth in a good place in the next."[88] This may have been in part a response to general anxieties accompanying the Mongol threat.[89] At the same time, however, Nichiren and his community were emboldened by the fact that the prophecy made in the *Risshō ankoku ron* of "invasion from foreign lands" seemed about to be fulfilled. His following grew, and Nichiren took the opportunity to repeat his memorializing of top officials.[90] He also began to challenge actively the teachings represented by those monks of the major temples in Kamakura who enjoyed the patronage of the Hōjō.[91] Zen now joined the *nenbutsu* among his polemical targets, as did those who sought to promote observance of the precepts.[92] His criticism of *shingon*—by which term he frequently designated both Taimitsu and Tōmitsu—also begins around this same time or a bit later, evidently in conjunction with government sponsoring of esoteric rituals for protection from the Mongols.[93] Yet, while hopeful that his message might be heeded, having had one experience of exile, Nichiren knew that he was courting danger and wrote to a close follower that he had resolved to give his life for *Lotus Sūtra*.[94]

Nichiren's attacks on other forms of Buddhism did indeed make enemies. Chief among these, by Nichiren's account, was Ryōkan-bō Ninshō (1217–1303), a disciple of the *vinaya* restorer Eizon of Nara and inheritor of his Saidaiji precept lineage. A strict observer of the *vinaya* and an esoteric ritual specialist, Ninshō was widely revered among the nobility for his virtue and charitable activities. He had come to the Kantō in 1252. In 1271, when drought wasted the eastern provinces, the *bakufu* commissioned Ninshō to conduct prayer rituals for rain. According to Nichiren, events then transpired as follows. Nichiren sent Ninshō a challenge to produce rain within one month: if Ninshō succeeded, Nichiren would become his disciple; if he failed, Ninshō should embrace the *Lotus Sūtra*. When the rituals conducted by Ninshō and his hundreds of disciples failed to produce rain, Nichiren sent him another letter asking how Ninshō expected to achieve the difficult goal of Buddhahood, when he could not even accomplish the easy task of producing rain. Chagrined, the humiliated cleric then prompted *bakufu* authorities to move against Nichiren.[95] Unfortunately we have only Nichiren's word for it, and it seems unlikely that so prominent a cleric as Ninshō would have felt intimidated by an obscure monk without status like Nichiren.[96] Nevertheless, in criticizing Ninshō, Nichiren had spoken out against one of the most highly revered prelates in Kamakura. Ninshō's admirers and supporters in the *bakufu* might well have decided to have Nichiren silenced, whether Ninshō himself was personally involved or not.

Nichiren also wrote that Ninshō had joined forces against him with the Pure Land prelates Nen'a Ryōchū (1199–1287), of the Goshinji, a disciple of Hōnen's disciple Benchō, and Dō'a Dōkyō, whom Nichiren had earlier debated. Together they submitted a complaint to the *bakufu*, charging, among other things, that Nichiren had claimed all teachings other than the *Lotus Sūtra* were false; that his disciples had destroyed images of Amida and Kannon; that he was harboring "outlaws" *(kyōto)* and storing weapons. Nichiren denied only the iconoclasm of his disciples, demanding that a witness be produced. Citing the *Nirvāṇa Sūtra* and other sources, he declared that it was acceptable to bear arms in defense of the True Dharma.[97] It is possible that Nichiren's lay followers, many of whom were warriors, may have felt he needed protection.

On 9/12/1271, Nichiren was arrested by Hei (Taira) no Yoritsuna (Hei no Saemon-no-jō, d. 1294), deputy chief of the *samurai-dokoro*, the board of retainers for the Hōjō, and sentenced to exile on the remote island of Sado in the Japan Sea. He was remanded to the custody of Honma Shigetsura, deputy governor of the island. His arrest was probably part of a larger *bakufu* move to subdue unruly elements in mobilizing their defenses against the Mongols.[98] Nichiren himself wrote that, while he was formally sentenced to exile, Yoritsuna's real intent was to have him beheaded that night, and he was taken to the execution grounds at Tatsunokuchi, but for some reason his life was spared.[99] Later hagiographies, which elaborate on the drama of Nichiren's arrest and near-beheading, say he was saved when a dazzling object streaked across the night sky, terrifying his executioners.[100] Nichiren himself clearly felt that in some sense he had undergone a death and transformation: "On the twelfth night of the ninth month of last year, between the hours of the Rat and the Ox [11:00 p.m.–3:00 a.m.] the man called Nichiren was beheaded. This is his spirit *(konpaku)* that has come to the province of Sado and, in the second month of the following year, is writing this amid the snow."[101]

Second Exile and Reclusion

Under armed escort, Nichiren traveled to the northern port of Teradomari, where the party had to wait for storm winds to subside before making the crossing. On Sado, Nichiren was assigned as living quarters the Tsukahara Sanmaidō, a small abandoned and dilapidated temple, little more than a hut, in the midst of a graveyard. Especially during the first winter, he and the few disciples who accompanied him suffered terribly from cold and hunger and the hostility of local inhabitants. Nichiren was also anxious about his followers in Kamakura, who, along with himself, had been the target of *bakufu* suppression. Some were exiled or imprisoned; some among the laiety had their lands confiscated or were ousted from their clans; a majority simply abandoned their faith.[102] Those who remained questioned why they should meet such adversity when the *Lotus Sūtra* promises "peace and security in the present life," and similar doubts seem to have troubled Nichiren as well. Yet it was under these harsh circumstances that he developed his mature thought and produced some of his most important writings. Later he would write that his pre-Sado teachings were like the Buddha's provisional teachings preached before the *Lotus Sūtra*.[103]

Nichiren's letters of encouragement to his followers and other writings of this period show his efforts to discover, by reflecting on himself and on the sūtra, an explanation for his trials. On the one hand, he became convinced that his sufferings represented karmic retribution for his own sins in prior lifetimes—not such conventional sins as killing, theft, and so forth, but the most terrible sin of slander against the Wonderful Dharma. Meeting persecution for the *Lotus Sūtra*'s sake thus amounted in his eyes to an act of repentance that would enable him to purify himself of such past errors, and his hardships were therefore to be welcomed. In this context, he often identified his experience with that of Bodhisattva Never Despising (Sadāparibhūta, Jōfukyō), described in chapter 20 of the *Lotus Sūtra,* who was mocked and tormented when he preached the message of universal Buddhahood but in a future lifetime was able to become Śākyamuni Buddha. On the other hand, entwined with this emphasis on repentance, Nichiren also interpreted his sufferings as the inevitable concomitants of practicing the *Lotus Sūtra* in the evil, last age. Such trials were predicted in the sūtra itself and thus served as a validation of his teaching and mission.[104] From this perspective, he saw himself as the Buddha's messenger, sent to propagate the *Lotus Sūtra* in the Final Dharma age and to prove the truth of its words. In this connection, Nichiren began to identify his efforts with the work of Bodhisattva Superior Conduct (Viśiṣṭacāritra, Jōgyō), leader of a great multitude of bodhisattvas who spring forth from beneath the earth in chapter 15 of the *Lotus Sūtra,* and to whom, in chapter 21, Śākyamuni Buddha entrusts the sūtra for propagation in the age after his nirvāṇa.[105]

Nichiren's most eloquent statement of his victory over doubts appears in the *Kaimoku shō* (Opening of the eyes), completed during the first winter on Sado as a last testament to his followers in the event of his death.[106] Together with the *Kanjin honzon shō* (The contemplation of the mind and the object of worship), it is considered one of his two most important writings. In it he explores various reasons why he, as the *gyōja* or votary of the *Lotus Sūtra,* meets with evils: because of his own past slanders; because such obstacles must be met in order to prove the truth of the sūtra's words; because the protective *kami* have abandoned a country given over to slander of the True Dharma; and so forth. But the final point at which he arrives is a conviction that seeks no explanation for adversity and no guarantee of protection, a simple resolve to carry on with his mission, whatever may happen: "Let Heaven forsake me. Let ordeals confront me. I will not begrudge bodily life. . . . No matter what trials we may encounter, so long as we do not have a mind of doubt, I and my disciples will naturally achieve the Buddha realm."[107]

By the end of that first winter, Nichiren had won a small but committed following on the island. In the second month of 1272, Hōjō Tokisuke, the half brother of the shogunal regent, attempted to usurp the regency, and fighting broke out in Kyoto and Kamakura. This seemed to bear out the *Risshō ankoku ron*'s earlier prediction of "rebellion within one's own domain," and perhaps for that reason, Nichiren was transferred in the spring to slightly better quarters at the home of the landowner and *nyūdō* (lay monk) Ichinosawa.

During the Sado period, Nichiren articulated his own teaching, distinct from the Tendai of his day. In this regard, his increasing self-identification with the work of Bodhisattva Superior Conduct is significant for several reasons. According to the *Lotus Sūtra,* Superior Conduct and the other bodhisattvas who sprang up from the earth are the Buddha's "original disciples" *(honge);* that is, they are followers not of the historical Śākyamuni who attained enlightenment under the *bodhi* tree, but of the original Buddha, enlightened since the inconceivably remote past. In identifying his efforts with those of Bodhisattva Superior Conduct, Nichiren was claiming a direct connection to the original Buddha. In later years, he would state this explicitly: "Hidden in the fleshly heart within his breast, Nichiren maintains the secret Dharma of the sole great matter transferred from Śākyamuni, master of teachings, at Eagle Peak."[108] This claim was probably related to the idea that "the assembly on Sacred [Eagle] Peak is solemnly [present] and has not yet dispersed," which occurs repeatedly in medieval Tendai texts.[109] Nichiren elaborated three aspects of this "secret Dharma"—the *daimoku*, the object of worship, and the ordination platform—to be discussed below.

Being the teaching and transmission of the original Buddha, this "secret Dharma of the sole great matter" has its locus in the origin teaching *(honmon)* of the *Lotus Sūtra*. Up until this point, Nichiren had merely asserted the superiority of the *Lotus Sūtra* over all others; now he turned his attention to its latter fourteen chapters. "The teaching of three thousand realms in one thought-moment is found only in the origin teaching of the *Lotus Sūtra,* hidden in the depths of the text of the 'Fathoming the Lifespan' chapter,"[110] he wrote. Where Chih-i had derived the doctrine of three thousand realms in one thought-moment from the trace teaching, specifically from the "Skillful Means" chapter, Nichiren now identified it with the origin teaching: thus the "one thought-moment containing three thousand realms" becomes the thought-moment of the original Buddha. This was not entirely a novel move but was closely related to medieval Tendai associations of *kanjin* or "mind-contemplation" specifically with the origin teaching.[111] Nichiren's emphasis on the origin teaching was distinctive, however, in that he defined it as uniquely related to the Final Dharma age.[112] For him, the origin teaching mediated a "great secret Dharma," embodied as the five characters of the *daimoku,* that had been transferred by Śākyamuni Buddha to the bodhisattvas who had emerged from beneath the earth, especially for the *mappō* era:

> Now at the beginning of the Final Dharma age, Hīnayāna is used to attack Mahāyāna, the provisional is used to repudiate the true. East and west are confused, and heaven and earth are turned upside down. . . . The heavenly deities forsake the country and do not protect it. At this time, the bodhisattvas who sprang up from the earth will appear for the first time in the world to bestow upon the children the medicine of the five characters *myōhō-renge-kyō.*[113]

During the Sado exile, together with his reinterpretation of the five characters *myōhō-renge-kyō* as the teaching conferred by the original Buddha, a shift becomes evident in Nichiren's understanding of the *daimoku.* No longer would he speak of it as a practice accommodated to ignorant persons. Rather, in his writings of this period, it becomes the vehicle of direct access to the Buddha's enlightenment. It was also on Sado that Nichiren inscribed for the first time the calligraphic mandala or *daimandara* he devised, depicting the assembly of Eagle Peak, which served as an object of worship.[114]

On 2/14/1274 a pardon was issued;[115] on 3/26 Nichiren returned to Kamakura. Hei no Yoritsuna, who had had him arrested two and a half years before, sent for him on 4/8 and inquired when the Mongol attack might be expected. Nichiren replied (accurately, as it turned out) that they would strike within the year. He also admonished, as he had at the time of his arrest, that only reliance on the *Lotus Sūtra* could forestall the disaster; ritual prayers to subdue the enemy, especially those based on the *shingon* teachings, would simply bring worse calamities upon the country.[116] However, Yoritsuna was in no position to withdraw support from other schools as Nichiren desired. A biography written a few decades after Nichiren's death says that he was offered *bakufu* patronage if he would add his prayers to those offered by other temples and shrines, but he refused.[117]

The sudden release from Sado after his long years of danger and tribulation, especially the official summons from Yoritsuna on his return, must have raised Nichiren's hopes that his admonitions were at last to be heeded. His disappointment was acute. On 5/12, just one month after the interview and less than two months after his reunion with his followers, he left Kamakura for the last time. A letter to his longtime follower, Toki Jōnin, announces his intention to become a solitary wayfarer, drifting throughout Japan.[118] On 5/17 he stopped at Mt. Minobu in Kai Province, where the *jitō*, Hakii Sanenaga, was a follower. He intended only a brief stay. Soon, however, he learned that he had other followers in the nearby Fuji district of Suruga Province who had remained devoted to him. His first lodging at Minobu was of the most primitive sort, and his letters of this period tell of suffering from hunger and cold. But eventually a community of as many as sixty disciples formed around him. His temporary stay lasted nine years. During the years of reclusion on Minobu, Nichiren devoted himself to training disciples and to writing. More than half his extant writings are from this period. They include a number of moving letters to lay followers, expressing thanks for their support, encouraging them through personal trials, and explaining his teachings in terms relevant to their individual situations. Exhausted by years of privation, Nichiren fell ill in 1282 and in the tenth month was persuaded by his disciples to visit the hot springs in Hitachi. He died en route at Ikegami (now a suburb of Tokyo) on 10/13/1282. Though he had never won official recognition for his teaching, he seems to have died with the confidence it would one day happen. "If Nichiren's compassion is vast, Namu-myōhō-renge-kyō will flow for ten thousand years and beyond, into the future. . . . [The people] of the country of Japan will all [chant] Namu-myōhō-renge-kyō."[119]

"Nichiren is not the founder of any school," he wrote, "nor is he a leaf at the tip [i.e., of the branch of some existing school]."[120] The *Lotus Sūtra* as he understood it *was* Buddhism, the ocean in which the teachings and practices of the various schools would be absorbed. In later life, he dis-

tanced himself from the esoteric Tendai of his own day and denounced
earlier Tendai prelates such as Enchin, Ennin, and Annen for adulterat-
ing the *Lotus*-based Tendai teaching with esoteric teachings. On the one
hand, he clearly considered himself heir to the earlier tradition of Chih-i
and Saichō: "Nichiren of Awa Province has reverently received the transmission from the three teachers [Śākyamuni, Chih-i, and Saichō] and as-
sists the spread of the Hokke lineage in the Final Dharma age," he wrote.
"Together we are the four teachers in three countries."[121] Such passages
have led some to see Nichiren as attempting to revive a "pure" Tendai independent of esoteric accretions. There is no doubt that Nichiren saw
himself as standing within the Tendai tradition.[122] Nevertheless, in claiming possession of a Dharma teaching that (1) was received directly from
Śākyamuni; (2) was intended specifically for the Final Dharma age; and
(3) was to assume a concrete form—as the *daimoku,* the object of worship, and the ordination platform—that had never before been revealed
and transmitted, it appears that Nichiren was in effect establishing a new
religion. This distinctive doctrinal basis, along with Nichiren's fierce emphasis on devotion to the *Lotus* alone; the charisma of his image, which
survived his death, as prophet, martyr, and messenger of the Buddha to
the Final Dharma age; the establishment of ordination rites for his clerical followers independent of those of Mt. Hiei; and the formation among
his followers of lay patronage networks independent of older religious
institutions enabled the emergence and survival of a new sect.

Taira Masayuki has argued that, in their absolutizing of a single form
of practice that alone leads to salvation, Nichiren and the other founders
of the new Kamakura Buddhism in effect relativized the social hierarchy and established religious equality.[123] He sees Nichiren as declaring
an inner freedom from worldly authority, as exemplified in his famous
statement: "Having been born in the ruler's domain, I may have to follow him with my body but I don't have to follow him with my mind."[124]
It is true that, in establishing the *Lotus Sūtra* as the ultimate authority,
transcending that of the ruler, Nichiren provided his followers with a
transcendent religious and moral basis from which worldly structures of
power could be criticized and resisted.[125] However, in envisioning the order of things as they would be should his teaching win official acceptance,
he also wrote: "Of my disciples, the monks will be teachers to the emperor and retired emperors, while the laymen will be ranged among the
ministers of the left and right."[126] What Nichiren envisioned was not an
egalitarian restructuring of society—a modern idea—but a reversal of
the position that his teaching and community occupied within it. The
single-practice movements of the new Kamakura Buddhism were subversive of authority, not because single-practice discourse is inherently
antiauthoritarian, but because it was articulated by people on the mar-

gins, outside the "influential parties system" of rule, and was thus deployed as a critique of established religion.

The Structure of "Embracing" the *Lotus Sūtra*

As the above biographical outline suggests, it is the "outer" soteric modality of giving one's life for the *Lotus Sūtra* that frames the story of Nichiren's career. His refusal to compromise his exclusive devotion to the *Lotus,* his conviction in his unique mission, his intemperate attacks on influential clerics and deliberate provoking of authorities, and his fortitude in the face of danger and privation left for his followers a model of "not begrudging bodily life," and the persisting charisma of his image as prophet, martyr, and emissary of the Buddha formed the pivot around which the later Nichiren tradition would define its identity. However, behind Nichiren's mandate that one should be ready to give one's life for the *Lotus Sūtra* lies the question of what exactly about the *Lotus Sūtra* he thought worth dying for. This brings us to Nichiren's "inner" soteric modality, that of realizing Buddhahood in the moment of chanting the *daimoku* that lies at the heart of his mature teaching. This aspect of his thought is what ties Nichiren to the new paradigm or reconception of enlightenment described in the preceding chapter. In discussing Nichiren's particular use of this paradigm, this section will focus on the structure of the moment of "embracing" the *Lotus Sūtra,* that is, the moment of faith and chanting the *daimoku.*[127] It will draw chiefly on writings from the latter period of Nichiren's life, from the Sado exile and after.

The Basis of Buddhahood

"The doctrine of three thousand realms in one thought-moment *(ichinen sanzen)* first established by Great Master T'ien-t'ai [Chih-i] is the father and mother of the Buddhas,"[128] Nichiren wrote. Quoting Chan-jan, he praised it as "the ultimate truth of his [Chih'i's] teachings."[129] "It is clear that only the T'ien-t'ai [doctrine] of three thousand realms in one thought-moment is the path of attaining Buddhahood."[130] For Nichiren, the single thought-moment possessing three thousand realms was the heart of the *Lotus Sūtra* and the core of the Tendai teachings he had inherited. As Kanno Hiroshi has pointed out, it was by means of this doctrine that Nichiren sought to legitimize his own position within the T'ien-t'ai/Tendai Buddhist tradition originating with Chih-i, and at the same time, also expressed the innovative aspects of his own teaching.[131] It is Nichiren's own reading that will concern us here.

In a letter to a follower, Nichiren wrote:

There are two methods of contemplating the three thousand realms in one thought-moment. One is that of principle *(ri)*, and the other that of actuality *(ji)*. In the time of T'ien-t'ai [Chih-i] and Dengyō [Saichō], that of principle was appropriate. Now is the time for that of actuality. Because this [form of] contemplation is superior, the great ordeals [attending its propagation] are also more severe. One [i.e., that of principle] is *ichinen sanzen* of the trace teaching *(shakumon)*, while the other is *ichinen sanzen* of the origin teaching *(honmon)*. They differ, differ vastly, like heaven and earth.[132]

"Now" is of course the Final Dharma age: Nichiren's "three thousand realms in one thought-moment" represents teaching and practice expressly for the time of *mappō*. But what exactly is the "vast difference" he claims between his teaching of *ichinen sanzen* and that of the earlier T'ien-t'ai/Tendai masters?

First of all, the passage just cited alludes to a difference in textual locus. As indicated in chapter 4, Chih-i derived the concept of the three thousand realms in one thought-moment from the trace teaching or first fourteen chapters of the *Lotus Sūtra;* it represents his attempt to conceptualize the "true aspect of the dharmas" *(shohō jissō)* referred to in the "Skillful Means" chapter. For Nichiren, however, this doctrine "is found only in the origin teaching of the *Lotus Sūtra,* hidden in the depths of the text of the 'Fathoming the Lifespan' chapter."[133] This shift of textual grounding for the *ichinen sanzen* doctrine is related to the larger context of medieval Tendai thought, which, as discussed earlier, saw the latter part of the sūtra as superior to the former in its revelation of nonlinear, original enlightenment. Nichiren elaborates in the following passage:

When one arrives at the origin teaching, because [the view that the Buddha] first attained enlightenment [in this lifetime] is demolished, the fruits of the four teachings are demolished. The fruits of the four teachings being demolished, their causes are also demolished. The causes and effects of the ten realms of the pre–*Lotus Sūtra* and trace teachings being demolished, the cause and effect of the ten realms of the origin teaching are revealed. This is precisely the doctrine of original cause *(hon'in)* and original effect *(honga)*. The nine realms are inherent in the beginningless Buddha realm; the Buddha realm inheres in the beginningless nine realms. This represents the true mutual inclusion of the ten realms, the hundred realms and thousand suchnesses, and the three thousand realms in one thought-moment.[134]

To unpack the rather technical language of this passage, the "four teachings" here represent those other than the *Lotus Sūtra*.[135] Their "effects" refers to the attainment of Buddhahood, or to the Buddhas, represented in these teachings, and their "causes," to the practices for attaining Buddhahood, or to those still in the stages of practice. In terms of the ten dharma realms, "cause" represents the nine realms, and "effect," the Buddha realm. "Demolishing" the causes and effects of the pre–*Lotus Sūtra* teachings and the trace teaching of the *Lotus Sūtra* means to demolish linear views of practice and attainment, in which efforts are first made and then Buddhahood is realized as a later consequence. The origin teaching—specifically, the "Fathoming the Lifespan" chapter with its revelation of the Buddha's original enlightenment—is here seen as opening a perspective in which cause (nine realms) and effect (Buddhahood) are present simultaneously. It is passages such as this that led Tamura Yoshirō to assert that Nichiren maintained the notion of original enlightenment in the depths of his mature thought.[136]

It should be noted that, in the context of the *Kaimoku shō,* this "true *ichinen sanzen,*" the mutual encompassing of original cause and original effect that is "hidden in the depths" of the "Fathoming the Lifespan" chapter, comes as the culmination of a discussion of five successive levels of teaching, codified by later Nichiren scholars as the "fivefold comparison" *(gojū sōtai).* Though he did not state so explicitly, Nichiren was in effect here establishing his own doctrinal classification *(kyōhan).* In so doing, he drew on both traditional T'ien-t'ai categories and the medieval Tendai of his own day, assimilating them to his own insights. The five steps of the comparison are: (1) Buddhist teachings surpass those of non-Buddhist traditions, such as Confucianism and Brahmanism *(naige sōtai);* (2) within Buddhism, Mahāyāna surpasses Hīnayāna *(daishō sōtai);* (3) within the Mahāyāna, the *Lotus Sūtra,* being true, surpasses the other sūtras, which are provisional *(gonjitsu sōtai);* (4) within the *Lotus Sūtra,* the origin teaching surpasses the trace teaching *(honjaku sōtai);* and (5) within the origin teaching, "contemplative insight" *(kanjin)* surpasses the written text *(kyōsō).*[137] From the standpoint of the sūtra text, the "Fathoming the Lifespan" chapter reveals that Śākyamuni Buddha first achieved Buddhahood countless kalpas ago; yet, however inconceivably distant, that Buddhahood nonetheless had a beginning in time and represents the fruit of a linear process of cultivation. From the standpoint of *kanjin,* however, the same "Fathoming the Lifespan" chapter is seen to reveal the mutual encompassing of the beginningless nine realms and the beginningless Buddha realm, or the simultaneity of original cause and original effect. Unlike some of the later, more extreme medieval Tendai thinkers, Nichiren never regarded *kanjin* as a separate transmission independent of the *Lotus Sūtra;* the realm of "original cause and original effect" is always mediated by the sūtra text. Moreover, as will be discussed below, *kanjin* had for him a distinctive meaning: not insight into original enlightenment per se but exclusive faith in and commitment to the

Lotus Sūtra, manifested in chanting its title and declaring its unique validity to others, even at the risk of one's life. Nevertheless, for Nichiren as for his Tendai contemporaries, the ultimate teaching (which he identifies as "the three thousand realms in a single thought-moment in actuality") represents a shift in perspective, in which enlightenment is understood, not as the fruit of a process of cultivation having beginning, middle, and end, but as inherent from the outset.

It will also be noted in the above passage that Nichiren reads *ichinen sanzen* primarily in terms of the mutual encompassing of the ten realms (*jikkai gogu*). Elsewhere in the same text, he writes, "The three thousand worlds in one thought-moment begins with the mutual encompassing of the ten realms," that is, the nonduality and mutual inclusion of the nine realms of deluded beings and the enlightened realm of the Buddha.[138] Nichiren specifically identified the mutual encompassing of the ten realms as the ground of the *Lotus Sūtra*'s two great revelations on which claims for its superiority were based: that persons of the two vehicles have the capacity to attain Buddhahood, and that the Buddha originally realized enlightenment in the inconceivably remote past yet ever since has remained constantly in the world to preach the Dharma. Nichiren saw the promise of Buddhahood given to persons of the two vehicles in the trace teaching as indicating that the nine realms of unenlightened beings encompass the Buddha realm (*kukai soku bukkai*), and the eternity of the Buddha's presence set forth in the origin teaching as indicating that the Buddha realm encompasses the nine realms of deluded beings (*bukkai soku kukai*), both of these expressing the principle that a single thought-moment is the three thousand realms.[139] Thus in Nichiren's system, the "three thousand realms in one thought-moment"—represented by the mutual inclusion of the ten realms—becomes both the "deep structure" of the entire *Lotus Sūtra* and the ontological basis upon which the realization of Buddhahood can occur.

The Forms of Practice

To say that "the nine realms possess the Buddha realm" is a statement about ontology; it does not mean that deluded persons experience or perceive the world as Buddhas do, or that they act as Buddhas act. To transform consciousness, practice is necessary. The "three thousand realms in one thought-moment" represents not only the ontological basis for the actualization of Buddhahood, but also a "contemplation method" (*kanpō*). In this sense, as we have seen, Nichiren distinguishes his method of contemplating *ichinen sanzen* as that of "actuality" (*ji*), from the method of Chih-i and Saichō, which he terms that of "principle" (*ri*). The latter of course refers to the introspective method set forth in the *Mo-ho chih-kuan,* in which the practitioner's (deluded) thought of one moment is taken as the object of contemplation. But what did Nichiren mean in saying that his was the method of "actuality"? While the notion of "actuality" or *ji* in Nichiren's thought has undergone extensive interpretation,[140] there is one particular sense of *ji* to which Nichiren himself calls attention in this context. In the *Kanjin honzon shō*, he writes that while Hui-ssu and Chih-i had established the teaching of three thousand realms in one thought-moment, "[T]hey only discussed it as inherent in principle *(rigu)*" and did not reveal "the five characters of Namu-myōhō-renge-kyō, which represents concrete practice *(jigyō)*, or the object of worship of the teaching of origin."[141] Here, *ji* clearly carries the Mikkyō connotation of *jisō*, or "actual forms"—the mūdras, mantras, and mandalas employed in esoteric practice. In Nichiren's Buddhism, the three thousand realms in one thought-moment takes concrete, "actual" form as the *daimoku* and a specific object of worship *(honzon)*. These two, together with the ordination platform *(kaidan)*—or, more broadly, the place of practice—constitute what Nichiren called the "three great matters of the 'Fathoming the Lifespan' chapter of the origin teaching" *(honmon juryōhon no sandaiji)*[142] or, as the later tradition would call them, the "three great secret Dharmas" *(sandai hihō)*. In Nichiren's system, these three form the content of the transmission conferred by Sākyamuni Buddha upon Bodhisattva Superior Conduct at the assembly in the air above Eagle Peak and are destined expressly for the Final Dharma age. All three are entailed in the moment of "embracing" the *Lotus Sūtra*.

The Daimoku

From his earliest writings, Nichiren discusses "the *daimoku* in five or seven characters" as something far more potent than the mere title of a text.[143] The *Hokke daimoku shō* (On the title of the *Lotus*), written in 1266, one of his earliest extended discussions of the subject, defines it as "the heart of the eighty-thousand holy teachings and the eye of all the Buddhas."[144] This theme continues throughout his later writings as well. "People today think that *myōhō-renge-kyō* is just a name, but that is not so. . . . [I]t is neither the text nor the meaning but the heart of the entire sūtra."[145] Here Nichiren drew on the Chinese tradition of title exegesis, in which the entire meaning of a particular sūtra was held to be encompassed by its title. Chih-i, for example, had organized the major portion of the *Fahua hsüan-i*, his commentary on the *Lotus Sūtra*, as a discussion of the five characters that comprise the sūtra's title. While it is impossible in a short space to do full justice to Nichiren's concept of the *daimoku*, two aspects of it will be outlined here: the *daimoku* as perfectly inclusive, and the *daimoku* as the seed of Buddhahood.

The *daimoku*, which Nichiren equates with the one vehicle, is all-encompassing, a claim he develops from several interrelated perspectives, beginning with his early writings. For example, in the *Hokke daimoku shō,* the *daimoku* is said to contain all teachings:

> The teachings of the seven Buddhas and the thousand Buddhas of the past, and of all the Buddhas since long kalpas ago, as well as the sūtras preached by the Buddhas of the present throughout the ten directions, are all followers of the single character *kyō* [sūtra] of the *Lotus Sūtra.* . . . Within this single character *kyō* [of *myōhō-renge-kyō*] are contained all the sūtras in the dharma realms of the ten directions.[146]

In a yet more encompassing sense, the *daimoku* contains, or rather *is,* the entirety of the dharma realm. Another passage of the same text reads:

> The five characters *myōhō-renge-kyō* . . . contain all sentient beings of the nine realms and also the Buddha realm. And because they contain [all beings of] the ten realms, they also contain the lands of the ten realms, which are those beings' dependent recompense.[147]

Or in greater detail, from an earlier, 1260 writing:

> The doctrines of three thousand realms in one thought-moment and the Buddha's enlightenment in the distant past, the core of the "Skillful Means" and "Fathoming the Lifespan" chapters, are contained within the two characters *myōhō* [Wonderful Dharma]. . . . All Buddhas and bodhisattvas, the causes and effects of the ten [dharma] realms, the grasses and trees, rocks and tiles throughout the ten directions— there is nothing that is not included in these two characters. . . . Therefore, the merit of chanting the five characters *myōhō-renge-kyō* is vast.[148]

Here the *daimoku* is equated with three thousand realms in one thought-moment, the entirety of all that is. This identification can be found in some of Nichiren's earliest writings.[149]

A third aspect of the all-inclusiveness of the *daimoku* comes to the fore in Nichiren's writings after his banishment to Sado. This is the idea that the whole of the Buddha's enlightenment is contained within the *daimoku* and accessible to the practitioner in the act of chanting it. This theme is most clearly developed in a passage from the *Nyorai metsugo go gohyakusai shi kanjin honzon shō* (The contemplation of the mind and the object of worship first [revealed] in the fifth of the five-hundred-year periods following the nirvāṇa of the Tathâgata) or simply *Kanjin honzon shō,* regarded in the tradition as Nichiren's single most important writing.[150] In this work, written in question-and-answer style, a hypothetical interlocutor asks what is meant by the "contemplation of the mind" *(kanjin).* Nichiren responds that it is to "observe one's own mind and see [in it] the ten dharma realms"—specifically, to see that one's own mind contains the Buddha realm.[151] Several rounds of further questioning and explanation follow as the hypothetical interlocutor finds it "hard to believe that our inferior minds are endowed with the Buddha dharma realm."[152] This questioner may perhaps be thought to represent the people of the Final Dharma age, who are not capable of practicing introspective contemplation on the three thousand realms in a single thought-moment. Finally, in a passage considered by many within the Nichiren tradition to represent the very core of his teaching, Nichiren indicates that "contemplating the mind" in the Final Dharma age is not a matter of "seeing" the identity of the Buddha realm with one's own mind in introspective meditation, but of embracing the *daimoku*, which encompasses Buddhahood within it:

> The *Wu-liang-i ching* states, "Even if one is not able to practice the six *pāramitās*, the six *pāramitās* will naturally be present." The *Lotus Sūtra* states, "They wish to hear to the all-encompassing Way." . . . To impose my own interpretation may slight the original text, but the heart of these passages is that Śākyamuni's causal practices *(ingyō)* and their resulting merit *(katoku)* are inherent in the five characters *myōhō-renge-kyō*. When we embrace these five characters, he will naturally transfer to us the merit of his causes and effects."[153]

The practices carried out by the Buddha throughout his countless lifetimes (causes) and the resulting virtues of his enlightenment (effects) are contained within the *daimoku* and spontaneously accessed by the practitioner in the act of chanting.[154] We can see this idea developing in a personal letter that Nichiren wrote the year before the *Kanjin honzon shō:*

> This jewel of [the character] *myō* contains the merit of the Tathâgata Śākyamuni's *pāramitā* of giving *(danbaramitsu),* when in the past he fed his body to a starving tigress or [gave his life] to ransom a dove; the merit of his *pāramitā* of keeping precepts, when, as King Śruta-soma, he would not tell a lie; the merit gained as the ascetic Forbearance, when he entrusted his person to King Kāli; the merit gained when he was Prince Donor, the ascetic Shōjari, [etc.] He placed the merit of all his six perfections *(rokudo)* within the character *myō*. Thus, even though we persons of the evil, last age have not cultivated a single good, he confers upon us the merit of perfectly fulfilling the countless practices of the six perfections. This is the meaning [of the passage], "Now this threefold world / is all my domain. / The beings in it / are all my children." We ordinary worldlings, fettered [by defilements], at once have merit equal to that of Śākyamuni, master of teachings, for we receive the entirety of his merit. The sūtra states, "[At the start I made a vow / to make all living beings] / equal to me, without any difference." This passage means that those who take faith in the *Lotus Sūtra* are equal to Śākyamuni. . . .

> Commoners [i.e., the heirs chosen to succeed the emperors Yao and
> Shun] immediately achieved royal status. Just as commoners became
> kings in their present body, so ordinary worldlings can immediately
> become Buddhas. This is what is meant by the heart of [the doctrine
> of] three thousand realms in one thought-moment.[155]

Thus the "contemplation of the mind" in Nichiren's teaching is not the
introspective meditation on the moment-to-moment activity of one's (unenlightened) mind, but rather embracing the *daimoku,* which is said to
embody the enlightenment of the eternal Buddha of the origin teaching, that is, the three thousand realms in a single thought-moment in
actuality.

"Embracing" the *daimoku* has the aspects both of chanting and having the mind of faith *(shinjin);* for Nichiren, the two are inseparable.[156]
Faith is also all-inclusive: in the Final Dharma age, it substitutes for the
three disciplines of precepts, meditation, and wisdom. "That ordinary
worldlings born in the Final Dharma age can believe in the *Lotus Sūtra*
is because the Buddha realm is inherent in the human realm."[157] Thus
the "one thought-moment containing three thousand realms" is also the
"single moment of belief and understanding." In the moment of faith,
the three thousand realms of the original Buddha and those of the ordinary worldling are one. This moment of faith corresponds to the stage
of *myōji-soku.*[158] Like that of many medieval Tendai texts, Nichiren's
thought focuses on realizing Buddhahood at the stage of verbal identity, which he understood as the stage of embracing the *daimoku* of the
Lotus Sūtra and taking faith in it.

Nichiren accepted the received Mahāyāna view that "all sentient beings have the Buddha nature," as well as Tendai ideas about the Buddhahood of insentient beings, but did not himself develop a particular
theory of Buddha nature. Rather, as a number of postwar Nichirenshū
scholars have pointed out, he emphasized the *daimoku* as the "seed" of
Buddhahood.[159] While ideas about the "Buddha-seed" *(busshu)* have a
long and varied history, Nichiren's concept draws explicitly on Chih-i's
Fa-hua hsüan-i, which describes the Buddha as leading the beings to enlightenment by first sowing the seed of enlightenment by preaching them
the *Lotus Sūtra,* then bringing it to maturity, and finally reaping the harvest of liberation, a process transpiring over successive lifetimes.[160]
Nichiren makes explicit that it is always the *Lotus Sūtra* that sows the initial seed. While people in the True and Semblance Dharma ages might
have progressed spiritually and even reached the maturity of full enlightenment through other teachings, this was only because they had first
received the seed of Buddhahood by hearing the *Lotus Sūtra* in prior lifetimes. This idea also occurs in certain medieval Tendai texts attributed
to Saichō, and it is possible that Nichiren's emphasis on the seed of Bud-

dhahood reflects more general developments within the broader field of contemporary *Lotus Sūtra* interpretation.[161] However, Nichiren's reading is distinctive in that it identifies the seed of Buddhahood as the *daimoku* ("All Buddhas of the three time periods and ten directions invariably attain Buddhahood with the seed of the five characters *myōhō-renge-kyō*"[162]) or as the "three thousand realms in one thought-moment."[163] Nichiren also connects the notion of the seed of Buddhahood specifically to the Final Dharma age. People in this age, he claims, have never before received this seed in prior lifetimes; they are people "originally without good [roots]" *(honmi uzen):*

> At this time, Namu-myōhō-renge-kyō of the "Fathoming the Lifespan" chapter, the heart of the teaching of origin, should be planted as the seed [of Buddhahood in the minds] of the two kinds of persons who inhabit this defiled and evil age—those who commit the [five] perverse [offenses] and those who slander [the True Dharma].[164]

Although the very notion of a "seed" tends to suggest a gradual process of growth and maturation, in Nichiren's thought, because "original cause" and "original effect" are simultaneous, the "process" of sowing, maturing, and harvesting also occurs simultaneously. This is called, in the terminology of Nichirenshū doctrine, "the seed being simultaneously [the harvest of] liberation" *(shu soku datsu)*. Nichiren explains this idea in readily accessible terms to a lay follower:

> The *mahā-mandārava* flowers in heaven and the cherry blossoms of the human world are both splendid flowers, but the Buddha did not choose them to represent the *Lotus Sūtra*. There is a reason why, from among all flowers, he chose this [lotus] flower to represent the sūtra. Some flowers first bloom and then produce fruit, while others bear fruit before flowers. Some bear only one blossom but many fruit, others send forth many blossoms but only one fruit, while others produce fruit without flowering. In the case of the lotus, however, flowers and fruit appear at the same time. The merit of all [other] sūtras is uncertain, because they teach that one must first plant good roots and [only] afterward become a Buddha. But in the case of the *Lotus Sūtra,* when one takes it in one's hand, that hand at once becomes Buddha, and when one chants it with one's mouth, that mouth is precisely Buddha. It is like the moon being reflected in the water the moment it appears above the eastern mountains, or like a sound and its echo occurring simultaneously.[165]

As discussed thus far, the "three thousand realms in one thought-moment" both is the ontological basis on which the realization of Buddhahood can occur and is embodied in the *daimoku* as the "seed" that provides the condition of that realization.[166] These two meanings of *ichinen sanzen* can also be distinguished respectively as "principle" *(ri)* and "actuality" *(ji)*. The two perspectives are further brought out in the two aspects of human relation to the Buddha as described in the *Kanjin honzon shō*. On the one hand:

> Śākyamuni of subtle awakening [*myōkaku*] is our blood and flesh. Are not the merits of his causes [practice] and effects [enlightenment] our bones and marrow? . . . The Śākyamuni of our own mind is the ancient Buddha without beginning, who has manifested the three bodies since countless dust-particle kalpas ago *(gohyaku jindengō)*.[167]

Yet on the other hand,

> For those unable to discern the three thousand realms in one thought-moment, the Buddha, arousing great compassion, placed this jewel within the five characters and hung it from the necks of the immature beings of the last age.[168]

The true aspect of reality, the "three thousand realms in a single thought-moment," is both immanent and bestowed by a transcendent Buddha.[169] As the ontological basis of Buddhahood it is timeless and originally inherent. As the seed of Buddhahood embodied in the *daimoku* of the origin teaching, its revelation is dependent upon the particular historical moment that is the beginning of the Final Dharma age. In the moment that it is taught, upheld, or "embraced," the *daimoku*, as the "three thousand realms in a single thought-moment in actuality," embodies the intersection of the timeless realm of original enlightenment with temporal, concrete particulars.

The Object of Worship

Nichiren uses the term "object of worship" or *honzon* to mean not only a physical icon used for ritual, contemplative, or devotional purposes—the common meaning of the word in his time—but also the principle or reality which that object is said to embody. His various writings explain the object of worship in this latter sense from two perspectives. From one view, it is the original Buddha. For example:

> [The people of] Japan as well as all of Jambudvīpa should as one take Śākyamuni, master of teachings, of the origin teaching as their object of worship—that is to say, Śākyamuni and Many Jewels within the jeweled stūpa along with all the other Buddhas, flanked by Superior Conduct and the others of the four bodhisattvas.[170]

In other writings, the object of worship is said to be the *Lotus Sūtra*, or Myōhō-renge-kyō, itself:

Question: What should ordinary worldlings in the evil days of the last age take as their object of worship?

Answer: They should make the *daimoku* of the *Lotus Sūtra* their object of worship. . . .

Question: . . . Why do you not take Śākyamuni as the object of worship, but instead, the *daimoku* of the *Lotus Sūtra*?

Answer: . . . This is not my interpretation. Lord Śākyamuni and T'ien-t'ai [Chih-i] both established the *Lotus Sūtra* as the object of worship. . . . The reason is that the *Lotus Sūtra* is the father and mother of Śākyamuni and the eye of all Buddhas. Śākyamuni, Dainichi, and the Buddhas of the ten directions were all born of the *Lotus Sūtra*. Therefore I now take as object of worship that which gives birth [to the Buddhas.][171]

These two views at first seem contradictory. However, if "Śākyamuni" in the passage first cited is understood to be the eternal Buddha, the apparent contradiction dissolves. The eternal Śākyamuni and the Dharma (i.e., the *daimoku* of the *Lotus Sūtra*) are two aspects of an identity; the "three thousand worlds in one thought-moment as actuality" for Nichiren describes both the insight of the original Buddha and the truth by which that Buddha is awakened.

Whether imagined as Dharma or as Buddha, Nichiren's "object of worship of the origin teaching" is perfectly inclusive. As Dharma, its all-encompassing nature has already been discussed: *Myōhō-renge-kyō* contains all teachings, all phenomena, all merits. As Buddha, it is no less embracing:

Zentoku Buddha in the eastern quarter, Dainichi in the center, the [other] Buddhas of the ten directions, the seven Buddhas of the past, the Buddhas of the three time periods, Superior Conduct and the other bodhisattvas, Mañjuśrī and Śāriputra, the great heavenly King Brahmā, King Māra of the sixth heaven, King Indra, the sun god, the moon god, the gods of the stars, the seven stars of the Big Dipper, the twenty-eight constellations, the five stars, the seven stars, the eighty-four thousand countless stars, the asura kings, the *kami* of heaven, the *kami* of earth, the mountain *kami*, the *kami* of the seas, the *kami* of the clans, the *kami* of the villages, the persons who rule the various lands in all worlds—which of them is not the Lord Śākyamuni? Tenshō Daijin and Hachiman Daibosatsu also have Śākyamuni, master of teachings, as their original ground *(honji)*. Śākyamuni is like the single moon in the sky, while the various Buddhas and bodhisattvas are like its reflections in myriad bodies of water. One who makes an image of Śākyamuni [thereby] makes [images of] all Buddhas of the ten directions.[172]

This passage appears to draw on the *Lotus Sūtra*'s representation of all

Buddhas as emanations of Śākyamuni, as well as on Mikkyō concepts of an all-pervading Dharma-body Buddha. One notes not only that all Buddhas, bodhisattvas, and Buddhist tutelary deities emanate from Śākyamuni, but that the Japanese *kami* all have Śākyamuni as their original ground. This reflects Nichiren's distinctive, *Lotus*-centered *honji-suijaku* thought, in which all *kami* are seen as the local manifestations of Śākyamuni.[173]

In accordance with traditional T'ien-t'ai thought, as well as that of medieval Japanese Tendai, Nichiren understood the Śākyamuni of the origin teaching as eternal and possessing all three bodies. However, the "Tathāgata of original enlightenment" seen in medieval Tendai texts, while nominally triple-bodied, tends to be described chiefly as an all-pervasive Dharma body. The passage just cited presents a similar view. Nichiren's writings as a whole, however, present a spectrum of concepts of the Buddha, drawing on the implications, not only of the Dharma body, but of the recompense and manifested bodies as well. Nichiren's Buddha is at once both immanent and transcendent. He is "our blood and flesh"; his practices and resulting virtues are "our bones and marrow." Yet at the same time, he is "parent, teacher, and sovereign" to all beings of this, the Sahā world. In this connection, Nichiren also stressed that Śākyamuni was only the Buddha who, out of compassion for its beings, had actually appeared in this world—a frequent point in Nichiren's criticism of devotion to Amida.[174] Śākyamuni is lord of this threefold world; all lesser rulers hold their territories in fief from him. With this concept of the Buddha, Nichiren asserted the superior authority of the *Lotus Sūtra* over that of worldly rule.[175] Śākyamuni also presides over a pure land, the Pure Land of Eagle Peak *(ryōzen jōdo)*, discussed below, and Nichiren often assured his followers that their deceased relatives were with Śākyamuni there. In short, Nichiren's concept of the object of worship not only posits a Buddha who encompasses all things, but itself attempts to encompass all views of the Buddha.

In addition to its meaning as ultimate truth or principle, Nichiren also used the term *honzon* in its more conventional sense to mean a physical icon forming the focus of practice, in this case, *Lotus Sūtra* recitation and the chanting of the *daimoku*. His *honzon* in this sense had plural forms. During Nichiren's lifetime, the *honzon* most commonly used by his followers appears to have been a calligraphic mandala of his own devising, which he referred to variously as the "great mandala" *(daimandara)* or the "revered object of worship" *(gohonzon)*. On this mandala the *daimoku* is written vertically as a central inscription, flanked by the names of Śākyamuni, Many Jewels, and the other personages who were present at the assembly in open space above Eagle Peak where the core of the origin teaching of the *Lotus Sūtra* was expounded. Nichiren widely inscribed these mandalas for individual followers as personal *honzon*.[176] More than 120 of them still survive, and there are likely to have been many more.[177]

Some larger mandalas may have been enshrined in Hokkedō—lodging temples of disciples or other chapels maintained by lay followers—where congregations met.[178] Nichiren's writings also refer occasionally to the scrolls of the *Lotus Sūtra* being enshrined as an object of worship.[179] At the same time, at least three of his extant letters suggest that he or his disciples occasionally performed the eye-opening ritual *(kaigen kuyō)* for Buddha images made by his followers.[180] He is also known to have kept by him throughout much of his life a small personal image of Śākyamuni Buddha, which he enshrined wherever he happened to be living.[181] Yet another form of *honzon* possibly adopted during Nichiren's lifetime is known as the "one Buddha and four attendants" *(isson shishi)*. It probably derives from passages in Nichiren's writings such as the following, in a letter to his follower Toki Jōnin (1216–1299), dated 1279:

> You say in your letter: "I have heard before that an object of worship should be made of the Lord Śākyamuni of the origin teaching, who attained enlightenment in the remotest past, and that, as attendants, [images] should be made of the four leaders of the bodhisattvas emerged from the earth who are his original disciples. But when [is this object of worship to be established] as I have heard?"

> . . . Now in the Final Dharma age, in accordance with the Buddha's golden words, [an object of worship] should be made of the original Buddha and his original attendants.[182]

And in fact, Toki Jōnin's index of the writings, icons, and ritual implements preserved at the temple he established after Nichiren's death includes "a standing image of Śākyamuni and also the four bodhisattvas (in a small shrine)."[183] The presence of the four bodhisattvas signals that the central icon is the original or eternal, rather than the merely historical, Śākyamuni. The "one Buddha and four attendants" came into fairly widespread use among Nichiren's followers as a *honzon* almost immediately after his death.[184] There was also a more complex configuration consisting of the two Buddhas, Śākyamuni, and Many Jewels, seated together in the jeweled stūpa and flanked by the four bodhisattvas *(ittō ryōson shishi)*. The earliest attested grouping was made by Jōgyōin Nichiyū (1298–1374) of the Nakayama lineage in 1335.[185]

The variety of explanations in Nichiren's writings concerning the object of worship and the plurality of its iconic forms gave rise to considerable controversy after his death. Scholar-monks within the sect debated whether his true intent was represented by the "object of worship as Buddha" or as "person" *(butsu-honzon, nin-honzon)*, or by "the object of worship as Dharma" *(hō-honzon)*. Some argued that one represented Nichiren's true intention and the other a skillful means, while others tried in various ways to reconcile the two. These controversies have continued down to the present.[186] A related point of contention has concerned whether the physical object of worship employed in actual practice should be an image of Śākyamuni or Nichiren's calligraphic mandala. This represents one of the earliest fault lines along which rival factions among Nichiren's followers aligned themselves after his death. It is addressed primarily in writings of the Fuji school, originating with Byakuren Ajari Nikkō (1246–1333), whose differences with other leading disciples led to the first schism within the Nichiren community. Fuji documents cite as one reason for the schism Nikkō's opposition to the use of Buddha images and conviction that the mandala alone should be revered as the object of worship.[187]

From a contemporary perspective, it may seem puzzling that Nichiren himself did not clarify such matters more definitively. However, as the late Shioiri Ryōdō pointed out, the expectation that each sect of Buddhism should have a unified object of worship had not yet come into being in his time. Nichiren's treatment of the object of worship as a central issue of doctrine was, in Shioiri's view, of "epochal significance in the history of [Japanese] Buddhism."[188] Other research indicates that differentiation in *honzon* may have contributed to the formation of sectarian consciousness long before Nichiren's time.[189] Nonetheless, as Shioiri suggests, the debates that raged among Nichiren's successors over the meaning and form of the object of worship were instrumental in defining the power of a particular tradition's *honzon* to unify its faith and doctrine and to express its sense of unique identity.

Nichiren spoke of his object of worship as embodying "the three thousand realms in a single thought-moment as actuality," a statement that may be understood in two ways. First, as underscored by recent studies in Buddhist art history, icons and mandalas in premodern Japan were seen not as merely symbolic or representational but as participating in and actively embodying the sacred powers of the beings or principles they depicted. Nichiren explains this idea in terms of the concept of the Buddhahood of grasses and trees *(sōmoku jōbutsu),* or more broadly, of insentient beings, a principle encompassed by the doctrine of the three thousand realms in one thought-moment:

> Both inner and outer writings permit the use of wooden and painted images as objects of worship, but the reason for this has emerged [only] from the T'ien-t'ai school. If plants and trees did not possess cause and effect [i.e., the nine realms and the Buddha realm] in both physical and mental aspects, it would be useless to rely on wooden and painted images as objects of worship. . . . Were it not for the Buddha-seed which is the three thousand realms in one thought-moment, the realization of Buddhahood by sentient beings and [the efficacy of] wooden and

painted images as objects of worship would exist in name but not in reality.[190]

For this reason, Nichiren insisted that only the *Lotus Sūtra,* the textual source of the *ichinen sanzen* principle, was efficacious in the eye-opening ritual for consecrating Buddha images.[191]

Second, the object of worship not only is held physically to embody the three thousand realms in one thought-moment but also represents an attempt to depict this reality visually. In the case of configurations of statues, this enlightened reality of the eternal Buddha, described in the *Lotus Sūtra* as the assembly in open space above Eagle Peak, is only suggested by the presence of the Buddha's original disciples, the four bodhisattvas, or by the two Buddhas, Śākyamuni and Many Jewels (Prabhūtaratna, Tahō), seated side by side in the jeweled stūpa. Nichiren's mandala, however, is much more detailed. Namu-myōhō-renge-kyō is written vertically in large characters down the center. At the top, this central inscription is flanked by the two Buddhas, Śākyamuni and Many Jewels, who are in turn flanked by the four bodhisattvas. Below them, in the next row, are representatives of the bodhisattvas who are followers of the Buddha of the provisional and trace teachings, such as Fugen (Samantabhadra) and Monju (Mañjuśrī), and the great voice-hearers, Śāriputra and Maudgalyāyana, flanked by the Buddhist tutelary deities Brahmā and Indra, and King Māra of the *deva* realm. In lower rows still are representatives of the six realms: the *devas* of the sun, moon, and stars, King Ajātaśatru, the wheel-turning king, the asura king, the dragon king, the *rakṣasa* Kishimojin (Harītī) and her ten daughters, and the Buddha's cousin and traitorous disciple Devadatta. Also represented in the assembly are the sun goddess Tenshō Daijin and Hachiman Daibosatsu, who for Nichiren together represented the *kami* of Japan. Beside them, the patriarchs T'ien-t'ai Ta-shih (Chih-i) and Dengyō Daishi (Saichō) are also accorded a place. The four *deva* kings guard the four corners of the mandala, and to either side appear the Siddham "seed characters" for the esoteric deities Fudō Myōō and Aizen Myōō, representing, respectively, the doctrines of "saṃsāra is nirvāṇa" *(shōji soku nehan)* and "the defilements are bodhi" *(bonnō soku bodai).* Passages from the sūtra, expressing its blessings and protection, are inscribed to the right and left sides of the assembly; the choice of inscriptions sometimes varied according to the individual mandala.[192] At the bottom is Nichiren's signature and the words: "This is the great mandala never before revealed in Jambudvīpa during the more than 2,220 years since the Buddha's nirvāṇa."

As will be seen from the description above, Nichiren's mandala includes not only Buddhas, bodhisattvas, and deities but also representa-

tives of the evil realms, such as *rakṣasa* demons and the treacherous Devadatta. In including such figures, Nichiren followed not the text of *Lotus Sūtra* itself—in which all beings in the six realms of transmigration
are removed before the jeweled stūpa is opened—but the principle of
three thousand realms in one thought-moment, according to which even
the Buddha realm contains the nine unenlightened states. In short, the
mandala depicts the mutual inclusion of the ten realms. As noted above,
Nichiren saw this concept as central to the three thousand realms in a
single thought-moment, an emphasis visible in the mandala. A writing
attributed to Nichiren explains:

> The "Jeweled Stūpa" chapter states: "All in that great assembly were
> lifted and present in open space." All the Buddhas, bodhisattvas, and
> great saints, and in general all the beings of the two worlds [of desire
> and form] and the eight kinds of [nonhuman] beings who assembled
> in the introductory chapter, dwell in this *gohonzon*, without a single ex-
> ception. Illuminated by the light of the five characters of the Wonderful
> Dharma, they assume their originally inherent august attributes. This
> is called the object of worship.[193]

Nichiren's mandala draws on a number of earlier, sometimes overlapping iconographic traditions. Representations of the Buddhas and
their auditors found in the sūtras revered in particular schools, ranged
together in mandala-like "assemblies" with the patriarchs of those
schools, are attested in Japan as early as the eighth century and appear
to have played a role in the expression of sectarian doctrine and the formation of sectarian identity; Nichiren's mandala may well represent an
extension of these older forms.[194] It is certainly linked to the extremely
widespread and varied iconographic depictions of the two Buddhas
Śākyamuni and Many Jewels seated side by side within the jeweled stūpa.
Such representations appear in the Tendai tradition early on; for example, a jeweled stūpa of Tahō Nyorai together with images of Śākyamuni Buddha flanked by Mañjuśrī and Maitreya are said to have formed
the central images of the ordination platform erected on Mt. Hiei five
years after Saichō's death.[195] Jeweled stūpa representations are also associated with Taimitsu and with broader, nonsectarian currents of *Lotus*-
centered practice and devotion.[196] Nichiren's use of a mandala as an object of worship was also clearly influenced by the use of mandalas within
esoteric Buddhism, in which contemplation of mandalas or the deities
represented thereon was regarded, among the three mysteries of Mikkyō
practice, as the "mystery of the mind," by which the Buddha's mind and
the practitioner's mind were identified. In particular, Nichiren's mandala shows structural similarities to the Lotus mandala *(Hokke mandara)*,
employed in a Taimitsu ritual known as the "Lotus rite" *(Hokke hō)*. This
mandala, which depicts Śākyamuni and Many Jewels together on a lotus
in its central court, reflects a synthesis of *Lotus* and Mikkyō thought.[197]

Nichiren's mandala also shows connections with more contemporaneous Tendai developments in Buddhist ritual iconography. By the late thirteenth century, the practice hall of the cloister Ryōzen-in at Yokawa is said to have been adorned with a group of large paintings depicting the assembly of the *Lotus Sūtra*. Centering on a lifesize image of Śākyamuni Buddha, the configuration included to one side, a jeweled stūpa flanked right and left by paintings of the four leaders of the bodhisattvas of the earth and bodhisattvas of the provisional teachings, and to the other side, by paintings of other bodhisattvas and great śrāvaka disciples. The two adjoining walls were hung with silk paintings of further bodhisattvas, deities, King Ajātaśatru of the human world, the kings of the dragons and of other nonhuman beings, and other figures present in the assembly of the *Lotus Sūtra*. The effect would have been to make those entering the hall feel as though they were actually there in that assembly.[198] Or, to give another example, the *kuden* text *Shuzenji-ketsu,* discussed in the preceding chapter, contains the following passage:

> The transmission concerning the Master [Tao-sui]'s profound and secret practice states: "You should make pictures of images representing the ten realms [of beings] and enshrine them in in ten places. Facing each image, you should, one hundred times, bow [with your body], chant Namu-myōhō-renge-kyō with your mouth, and contemplate with your mind. When you face the image of hell, contemplate that its fierce flames are themselves precisely emptiness, precisely conventional existence, and precisely the middle, and so on for all the images. When you face the image of the Buddha, contemplate its essence being precisely the threefold truth.[199]

While Nichiren did not recommend the threefold contemplation, the use of iconographic representations of the ten realms as an aid to meditation as described in this passage is similar to his mandala. Since the chronology of such icons is not definite, it is impossible to say whether they came before or after Nichiren's mandala or whether one may have influenced the other; it is more useful to see Nichiren's *honzon* and these Tendai configurations as stemming from shared conceptions of *Lotus*-related thought and imagery of the early medieval period.

The most obvious difference between Nichiren's mandala and these Tendai iconographic groupings is that the former contains no pictures but is written entirely in characters. Each figure is indicated by the Chinese characters for its name, except for Fudō and Aizen, who are represented by their "seed characters" in Siddham, the Japanese Sanskrit orthography. Nichiren does not say why he decided on a calligraphic mandala, though it is probably related to the tradition of esoteric mandalas drawn consisting partly or entirely in Siddham characters, as well as his personal reverence for the characters of the *Lotus Sūtra,* which he regarded as not mere written words but the Buddha's mind.[200] However, as other scholars have pointed out, this mandala links Nichiren to other, near-contemporaneous instances of the use of calligraphic *honzon* in both "old" and "new" Buddhist traditions.[201] In his *Sanji raishaku* (Thrice-daily worship), written in 1215, Myōe (1173–1232) of the Kegon school describes a calligraphic mandala he devised consisting of a central vertical inscription of a phrase expressing devotion to the three treasures, flanked by four expressions for the *bodhicitta* or mind aspiring to enlightenment taken from the *Hua-yen ching*. Across the top, the three treasures were written horizontally in Siddham.[202] This mandala formed the focus of a simplified practice consisting in three times reciting the phrases inscribed upon it and performing three prostrations, three times each day. Shinran also made use of calligraphic scrolls with either the *nenbutsu* or a variant expression of devotion to Amida inscribed in the center.[203] It is not known whether or not Nichiren had knowledge of these earlier precedents, but clearly his mandala was one instance of a new form of *honzon* emerging in the Kamakura period. As Takagi Yutaka points out, these calligraphic objects of worship were not tied to the aesthetic concerns commonly associated with the production of Buddhist statues or paintings. Requiring for their production only paper, a brush, and ink, they could also be made available to persons lacking the means to commission a painter or sculptor or pay for expensive materials and thus represent a popularization of mandalas and Buddhist imagery previously available only to a few.[204]

Nichiren's writings say very little about the place of his mandala (or of Buddha images) in actual practice. There is one personal letter, the "Nichinyo gozen gohenji," cited above, which does touch on this issue, and though some modern scholars dispute its authenticity, it has historically been highly valued in the Nichiren tradition for its easily accessible description of the mandala and its relation to the practitioner's faith:

> Never seek this *gohonzon* elsewhere, [for] it abides only in the fleshly heart within the breast of persons like ourselves who embrace the *Lotus Sūtra* and chant Namu-myōhō-renge-kyō. This is called the capital city of suchness, the ninth consciousness that is the mind-ruler *(kushiki shinnō shinnyo no miyako)*. Being endowed with the ten realms means that [all] ten realms, not excepting a single one, are contained within a single realm, [that of Buddhahood]. That is the reason why this is called a mandala. "Mandala" is a word from India. Here [in Japan] it is called "perfect endowment" *(rinnen gusoku)* or "cluster of merits" *(kudokuju)*. This *gohonzon* is contained solely within the word "faith." That is the meaning of "gaining entrance by faith." By believing undividedly in [the *Lotus Sūtra,* in accordance with its words,] "honestly

Nichiren's calligraphic mandala representing the assembly of the *Lotus Sūtra*. This particular mandala, which Nichiren inscribed in 1280, is said to have been enshrined at his bedside during his last hours (*rinmetsu doji honzon*). Myōhonji; courtesy of Futabasha.

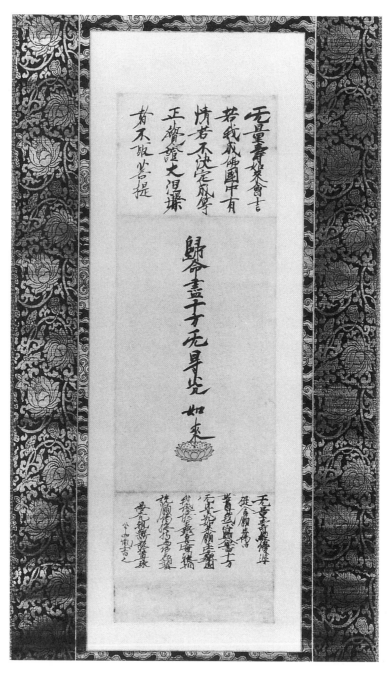

Calligraphic mandala inscribed by Shinran expressing devotion to Amida. The inscription reads "devotion to the Tathâgata whose light is unobstructed throughout the ten directions" (*kimyō jin jippō mugekō nyorai*). Senshūji; courtesy of Hōzōkan.

Calligraphic mandala inscribed by Myōe, expressing devotion to the three treasures of the Buddha, Dharma, and Sangha. Kōsanji; courtesy of George Tanabe.

The *Lotus Sūtra* mandala used in the esoteric *Hokke hō* ritual. Rather than Dainichi, the two Buddhas Śākyamuni and Many Jewels occupy the center of the lotus, reflecting the fusion of *Lotus* and Mikkyō elements. Hanging scroll; color on silk. Thirteenth to fourteenth century. Important cultural property. Taisanji; courtesy of Nara National Museum.

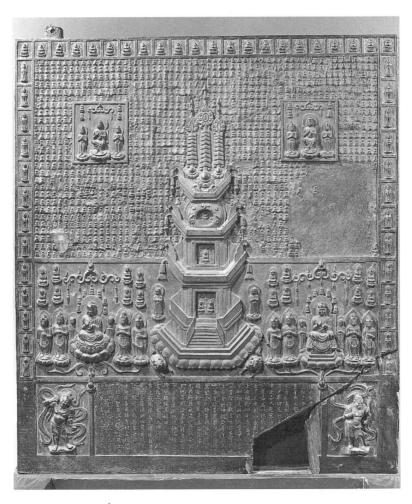

The two Buddhas Śākyamuni and Many Jewels seated together in the jeweled stūpa. Bronze; bas-relief and repoussé. Late seventh century. National treasure. Hasedera; courtesy of Nara National Museum.

Lotus Sūtra mandala, showing the two Buddhas seated in the jeweled stūpa. Unpainted wood; bas-relief. Eleventh century. Important cultural property. Yokokuraji; courtesy of Nara National Museum.

ection of a copy of the *Lotus Sūtra* inscribed so that each character is placed in a stūpa, as though were a Buddha (*ichiji hōtō Hokekyō*). Twelfth century. Important cultural property. Togakushi Jinja; ourtesy of Nara National Museum.

Lotus Sūtra jeweled-stūpa mandala, inscribed in gold and silver ink on deep blue paper. This is an example of a *moji-tō* or sūtra text inscribed in the form of a stūpa. Late twelfth to early thirteenth century. Ryū-honji; courtesy of Nara National Museum.

Detail from the scrolls of the Ryūhonji jeweled-stūpa mandala, showing the two Buddhas seated together in the stūpa. Courtesy of Nara National Museum.

discarding skillful means" and "not accept[ing] even a single verse from other sūtras," Nichiren's disciples and lay followers shall enter the jeweled stūpa of this *gohonzon*. How reassuring, how reassuring![205]

If one judges by this passage, it appears that the logic of Nichiren's mandala is quite similar to that of esoteric practice, wherein the practitioner visualizes the union of self and Buddha, known as "the Buddha entering the self and the self entering the Buddha" *(nyūga ganyū)*.[206] For Nichiren, however, the nonduality of the practitioner and the Buddha is realized neither by esoteric visualization techniques nor by introspective contemplation involving the application of mental categories, such as the threefold contemplation. Rather, it is by faith in the *Lotus Sūtra* that one enters the realm of the Buddha's enlightenment—the three thousand realms in a single thought-moment as actuality—and manifests its identity with oneself.

The Place of Practice

This actualizing of the identity of practitioner and object of worship in the act of "embracing" the *Lotus Sūtra* must occur in a specific place. The attention devoted to that "place" represents a distinctive feature of Nichiren's thought. This section will briefly consider his ideas on the place of practice in terms of (1) the ordination platform, (2) the Buddha land to be realized in this world, and (3) the Pure Land of Eagle Peak.

THE ORDINATION PLATFORM In its most specific sense, the place of practice is understood in terms of the "ordination platform of the origin teaching" *(honmon no kaidan)*, the third of the three great secret Dharmas entrusted by the original Śākyamuni to Bodhisattva Superior Conduct for the sake of persons in the Final Dharma age. However, as rules governing conduct, neither the *ssu-fen lü* precepts nor the bodhisattva precepts receive much attention in Nichiren's thought.[207] Although he maintained celibacy, refrained from meat-eating, and generally observed the standards of monastic conduct, he described himself as "a monk without precepts."[208] Like Hōnen, Nichiren saw the Final Dharma age as an age without precepts, when "there is neither keeping the precepts nor breaking them."[209] From a very early period, he held that "merely to believe in this [*Lotus*] sūtra is to uphold the precepts," a statement based on the sūtra's claim that one who can receive and keep the sūtra after the Buddha's nirvāṇa is "a keeper of the precepts."[210] A later writing explains this in terms of the all-inclusiveness of the *daimoku*:

> *Myōhō-renge-kyō*, the heart of the origin teaching of the *Lotus Sūtra*, assembles in five characters all the merit of the myriad practices and good

[acts] of the Buddhas of the three time periods. How could these five characters not contain the merit of [upholding] the myriad precepts? After the practitioner has once embraced this perfectly endowed, wonderful precept, it cannot be broken, even if one should try. No doubt this is why it has been called the *vajra* precept of the jeweled receptacle *(kongō hōki kai)*. By embracing this precept, the Buddhas of the three time periods realized the Dharma, recompense, and manifested bodies, becoming Buddhas without beginning or end. . . . Because so wonderful a precept has been revealed, the precepts based on the pre–*Lotus Sūtra* teachings and on the trace teaching are now without the slightest merit.[211]

In that embracing the *Lotus Sūtra* substitutes for the three disciplines of precepts, meditation, and wisdom, what did Nichiren intend by the expression "ordination platform"? No uncontested work in the collection of his writings gives any explanation beyond the words "ordination platform of the origin teaching." However, in that the ordination platforms of his day were state sponsored, one may assume that he intended the establishment of a similar, state-sponsored center for the dissemination of the *Lotus Sūtra,* which would in turn presume official recognition of his teaching.[212] Such an assumption is in fact born out by the *Sandai hihō honjō ji* (On the transmission of the three great secret Dharmas) or, more commonly, *Sandai hihō shō,* possibly the most hotly disputed of any writing in the Nichiren collection.[213] This work unambiguously describes the *kaidan* as an imperially sponsored ordination platform to supercede the "ordination platform of the trace teaching" *(shakumon no kaidan)* established by Saichō's efforts at Mt. Hiei:

When the Dharma of the ruler *(ōbō)* becomes one with the Dharma of the Buddha *(buppō),* the Buddha-Dharma accords with the Dharma of the ruler, when the ruler and his ministers all uphold the Three Great Secret Dharmas, and the past relationship between King Utoku and the monk Kakutoku[214] is again realized in the future in this impure and evil Final Dharma age, then surely an imperial edict and shogunal decree will be handed down, to seek out the most superlative site, resembling the Pure Land of Eagle Peak, and there to erect the ordination platform. You have only to await the time. This [ordination platform] will be the [establishment in] actuality *(ji)* of the Dharma of the precepts *(kaihō).* Not only will this be [the site of] the Dharma of the precepts by which the people of the three countries [India, China, and Japan] and all of Jambudvīpa will perform repentance *(sange)* and eradicate their offenses, but Brahmā and Indra will also descend and mount this ordination platform. Once this [actuality of] the Dharma of the precepts is established, the ordination

platform at the Enryakuji will become useless, as it pertains only to
the precepts in principle *(rikai)* of the trace teaching.[215]

This understanding of the *kaidan* as an actual institution that would
someday be established predominated throughout the medieval period.
During this time, following Nichiren's example in submitting the *Risshō ankoku ron* to Hōjō Tokiyori, leading Nichiren clerics repeatedly
memorialized the emperor or the shogun to uphold the *Lotus* exclusively in order to bring peace to the country. In this context, the establishment of an imperially sponsored ordination platform proved a
compelling ideal for leaders of the Hokkeshū, as Nichiren's following
had come to be called, and symbolized the eventual acceptance of their
teaching over all others. Rival lineages debated whether the *kaidan*
should be erected at Fuji or at Minobu. At the same time, perhaps because this "ordination platform in actuality" *(ji no kaidan)* could not immediately be realized, a corollary interpretation developed concerning
the "ordination platform in principle" *(ri no kaidan),* meaning wherever
one might chant the *daimoku.* This was also known as the *soku ze kaidan*
("[here] is itself the *kaidan*") based on a passage in the *Lotus* that says,
of any place where one keeps the sūtra: "You should know that this place
is itself the place of enlightenment."[216] Which interpretation predominated was to vary with political and social circumstances. Under Tokugawa rule, when religious proselytizing was restricted and the hope of
winning imperial sponsorship seemed increasingly remote, the translo-
cal understanding of the *kaidan,* as existing wherever one embraces the
Lotus Sūtra, became the dominant one. With the Meiji Restoration, however, the ideal of a state-sponsored ordination platform was revived and
reinterpreted, often in terms of militant Japanese imperialism, as a site
that would become the religious center of the world. Since World War
II, as part of a move to repudiate earlier concessions to wartime nationalism, many Nichirenshū sectarian scholars and others have interpreted the "ordination platform" only in the abstract and universal sense
of the place of practice and condemned the *Sandai hihō honjō ji* as apocryphal.[217] Whatever the provenance of the *Sandai hihō honjō ji,* it seems
altogether likely that Nichiren did envision the establishment of an imperially sponsored ordination platform.[218] However, the understanding
of the *kaidan* as being wherever one embraces the *Lotus Sūtra* is also
deeply connected to elements in Nichiren's thought concerning the
place of practice.

THE PRESENT WORLD AS THE BUDDHA LAND We have already seen that
Nichiren saw the Buddha's pure land as immanent in the present world,
based on the "Fathoming the Lifespan" chapter of the *Lotus Sūtra,* which

says, "I [Śākyamuni] am always in this Sahā world."[219] In the *Kanjin hon-zon shō,* Nichiren developed this idea specifically in terms of the origin teaching and the three thousand realms in a single thought-moment:

> Now *(ima)* the Sahā world of the original time *(honji)* [of the Buddha's enlightenment] is the constantly abiding pure land, freed from the three disasters and transcending [the cycle of] the four kalpas [for-mation, stability, decline, and extinction]. Its Buddha has not already entered nirvāṇa in the past, nor is he yet to be born in the future. And his disciples are of the same essence. This [world] is [implicit in] the three realms, which are inherent in the three thousand realms of one's mind.[220]

In a manner very similar to that of the *Sanjū shika no kotogaki* and other medieval Tendai writings, this passage conveys the sense of the moment of enlightenment as accessing a timeless, "constantly abiding" realm in which all change is suspended. "Original time" *(honji)* differs from lin-ear time. It has no distinction of past, present, and future, and no pro-ceeding from a deluded to an enlightened state; the Buddha and the or-dinary worldling—the Buddha realm and the nine realms—are always one. This "original time" is the "actuality" of the three thousand realms in one thought-moment of the original Buddha and is accessed in the "now" *(ima)* of embracing the *daimoku.* In the single thought-moment of faith, the three thousand realms of the practitioner are those of the original Buddha. And because the person and the land are nondual, in the moment of faith and practice, the Sahā world is the eternal Buddha land. In the words of Chan-jan, a passage Nichiren quotes in this con-text: "You should know that one's person and the land are [both] the single thought-moment comprising three thousand realms. Therefore, when one attains the Way, in accordance with this principle, one's body and mind in that moment pervade the dharma realm."[221]

The immanence of the pure land in the present world had long been asserted by both Tendai and Shingon schools and was by no means unique to Nichiren's teaching. Where Nichiren's position differed was that, for him, the identity of the Sahā world and the Buddha's land was not only to be realized subjectively in the moment of practice but man-ifested in actuality: as faith in the *Lotus Sūtra* spread from one person to another, there would occur an objective, visible transformation of the outer world. This vision is expressed in a letter written from Sado Island in 1273:

> When all people throughout the land enter the one Buddha vehicle and the Wonderful Dharma alone flourishes, because the people all chant Namu-myōhō-renge-kyō as one, the wind will not thrash the

branches nor the rain fall hard enough to break clods. The age will become like the reigns of [the Chinese sage kings] Yao and Shun. In the present life, inauspicious calamities will be banished, and the people will obtain the art of longevity. When the principle becomes manifest that both persons and dharmas "neither age nor die," then each of you, behold! There can be no doubt of the sūtra's promise of "peace and security in the present world."[222]

Thus the pure land is implicit in the ontological basis of the three thousand realms in one thought-moment but must be concretely realized through the practice and propagation of the *daimoku.* This aspect of Nichiren's thought draws on apotropaic notions that the proper Buddhist prayer rituals could rid the land of misfortune, grounding them in traditional Tendai teachings concerning the immanence of the pure land in the present world and in his own exclusive practice of the *Lotus.* Nichiren's idea that faith in the *Lotus* would materially transform the world inspired repeated memorializing of rulers throughout the medieval period and has underlain the political, activist, and millenarian aims of a number of Nichiren Buddhist movements in the modern era.

THE PURE LAND OF SACRED EAGLE PEAK Shortly before his exile to Sado, Nichiren began to refer in his letters and other writings to the "Pure Land of Sacred [Eagle] Peak" *(ryōzen jōdo).*[223] These references increase during the Sado period and especially during Nichiren's retirement on Mt. Minobu. "Sacred Eagle Peak" (or "Sacred Vulture Peak") translates Ryō-jusen (Chn. Ling-chiu-shan), the Chinese translation for Gṛdhrakūṭa (Vulture Peak), the name of the mountain in Rājāgṛha where the *Lotus Sūtra* is said to have been preached.[224] The notion of Eagle Peak as a pure land seems to arise from a conflation of this site with the sūtra's assertion that this Sahā world is the eternal dwelling place of the original Buddha:

> Throughout *asaṃkheya-kalpas*
> I am always on Sacred Eagle Peak
> as well as in other dwelling places.
> When the beings see the kalpa ending
> and [the world] being consumed in a great fire,
> this land of mine is safe and peaceful,
> always filled with gods and humans.
> In it are gardens, groves, halls, and towers . . .
> wherein the beings play and amuse themselves . . .
> My pure land is not destroyed,
> yet the multitude see it consumed in flames.
> Worried, they fear the torment of pains . . .
> Those who have cultivated merit,
> who are gentle and agreeable, straightforward and honest,

    all do, however, see my body
    dwelling here and preaching the Dharma.[225]

Kumārajīva (344–413), the sūtra's translator, is said to have interpreted the lines "My pure land is not destroyed / yet the multitude see it consumed in flames" to mean "the two qualities of purity and defilement dwelling in the same place."[226] Since his time, "Eagle Peak" was frequently understood as representing the ontological nonduality of delusion and enlightenment, or of the present, Sahā world and the Land of Ever-Tranquil Light.[227] This reading clearly informs Nichiren's understanding of the present world as potentially the Buddha land, discussed above. However, "Sacred Eagle Peak" was also known to be a specific place and, in the manner of many continental sacred sites, had manifested itself in Japan. Mt. Hiei, Ōmine, Kasagi, and other locations of mountain ascetic practice were all at times identified with "Eagle Peak."[228] Nichiren, too, occasionally equated Eagle Peak with Mt. Minobu, where he, the *gyōja* of the *Lotus Sūtra*, was living.[229]

    In Nichiren's appropriation, however, the notion of the Pure Land of Sacred Eagle Peak is used chiefly to indicate the destination of believers in the *Lotus Sūtra* after death, a place where those left behind can look forward to rejoining them in the next life. This interpretation was not altogether unique to Nichiren. As an early example, a poem of parting written by the scholar and courtier Sugawara no Michizane (845–903) expresses the hope of reunion after death on Eagle Peak.[230] Similar aspirations for birth after death in the Pure Land of Eagle Peak also occur in the Kamakura period, in collections of *setsuwa* or tales and in the writings of the scholar-monks Myōe (1173–1232) and Jōkei (1155–1213), both prominent figures within the Buddhist schools of Nara.[231] In the case of Myōe and Jōkei, aspiration to the Pure Land of Eagle Peak seems to have been linked to broader attempts to "return" to or recover the age of Śākyamuni Buddha, in response to a consciousness of living in an age of decline. While not as widespread as aspirations for Amida's Pure Land of Utmost Bliss, notions of the Pure Land of Eagle Peak as an ideal realm to be sought after death thus formed an aspect of the Kamakura period religious imagination held by representatives of both "old" and "new" Buddhism.

    In Nichiren's thought, aspiration for the Pure Land of Eagle Peak assumes a particular orientation, informed by his exclusive commitment to the *Lotus Sūtra*. Most *Lotus* practitioners of the Heian and Kamakura periods recited the sūtra in hopes of achieving Amida's western Pure Land.[232] Nichiren, however, had so thoroughly rejected any aspect of faith in Amida that he would not have been able to represent the next life in such terms.[233] The "Pure Land of Sacred Eagle Peak" provided him with a needed alternative image, consistent with his *Lotus* exclusivism, for conceptualizing what happens to believers after death. As others have suggested, Nichiren may also have begun to preach to his followers about this pure land in response to the sense of imminent danger accompanying the Mongol threat, and the concept was no doubt further stimulated by the suppressions experienced by Nichiren and his community. The "Pure Land of Eagle Peak" was thus posited in contrast to, and as recompense for enduring, the hardships occasioned by upholding exclusive faith in the *Lotus* in this present world.[234] Moreover, during his reclusion on Mt. Minobu, as Nichiren himself grew older, he was also faced increasingly with the need to console followers who had lost parents, spouses, and children; the promise of reunion in the Pure Land of Eagle Peak occurs frequently in his letters on such occasions.

It is important to note that Nichiren's aspiration for achieving the Pure Land of Eagle Peak after death never replaced his conviction that, by the spread of exclusive faith in the *Lotus* and in accordance with the principle of *risshō ankoku,* the pure land could be realized in the present world.[235] It also coexists in his thought with his teaching that enlightenment is manifested in the moment of faith and chanting. In other traditions as well, notions of directly accessible or even immanent Buddhahood did not rule out conceptions of an afterlife in a different realm but often existed alongside them: "Even though one knows Amida Buddha to be one's own mind, one forms a relationship with Amida of the west."[236] However, unlike some strands of Pure Land thought directed toward Amida, Nichiren's "Pure Land of Sacred Eagle Peak" lacks a sense of concreteness as an actual place postulated over and against the present world; it is never said to lie in a specific direction, nor does aspiring toward it involve repudiating the present world. In the few passages of Nichiren's writings where some sort of description is offered, it is usually along the lines of "[M]aster and disciples shall together visit the Pure Land of Sacred [Eagle] Peak and behold the faces of the three Buddhas [Śākyamuni, Many Jewels, and all the Buddhas who are Śākyamuni's emanations],"[237] or "If one enquires where the late Abutsu-bō is now, . . . he is within the jeweled stūpa of the Buddha Many Jewels on Sacred Eagle Peak."[238] In short, this pure land resembles the assembly in open space depicted on Nichiren's mandala and may be thought of as an extension of that realm to encompass the faithful dead.[239]

Such, in outline, is the structure of the moment of "embracing" the *Lotus Sūtra* as conceived in Nichiren's thought. It is a moment of intersection between the present time and the timeless realm of enlightenment, in which the Buddha, the practitioner, and the practitioner's outer world are all identified. It is described as the "three thousand realms in one thought-moment," which is implicit in the practitioner as the ontological basis of enlightenment, embodied in the *daimoku* and the object of worship, accessed in the act of faith and chanting, and manifested outwardly in the transformation of the world. This reality is both inherent in and mediated by the five characters *myōhō-renge-kyō* conferred by the original Śākyamuni Buddha upon the people of the Final Dharma age and is accessible in no other way. This understanding of the *Lotus Sūtra* as the sole vehicle of realizing Buddhahood underlies Nichiren's mandate to uphold it "without begrudging bodily life." It also enabled him and his followers to challenge the authority of established religious institutions and to define themselves as the unique possessors of truth.

Nichiren and the New Paradigm

Now let us consider how Nichiren's thought embodies the new paradigm of enlightenment identified in the preceding chapter.

NONLINEARITY In Nichiren's view, enlightenment is realized in the moment of practice. This enlightenment is a timeless state, in which original cause (the nine realms) and original effect (Buddhahood) exist simultaneously, and is ever accessible in the act of chanting the *daimoku*. The practitioner does not progressively expunge defilements or accumulate merit with a view to reaching eventual enlightenment, because all merit is inherent in the *daimoku* and "naturally transferred" to the person who embraces it. As in other Buddhist teachings of this time that assert direct and full accessibility of salvation or enlightenment in the present moment, Nichiren's doctrine nevertheless includes a discourse about the importance of continuing one's practice or further deepening one's faith. In the case of Tendai *kuden* texts, this element is, as we have seen, subordinated to an argument for enlightenment as originally inherent, while in Nichiren's writings the aspect of continued practice assumes much greater prominence. This was not because Nichiren was reasserting the primacy of practice vis-à-vis a decadent Tendai tradition that neglected it, but because he was in effect establishing a new religious order and needed to make clear its premises; because he had constantly to exhort his followers to maintain faith in the face of opposition and even suppression; and because exclusive commitment to the *Lotus* carried, in his view, a mandate to propagate it. "To accept *(ju)* [faith in the sūtra] is easy," he wrote to a follower, "to uphold it *(ji)* is difficult. But the realization of Buddhahood lies in upholding [faith]."[240] Even so, this "upholding" is not construed as progress toward the achievement of enlightenment as a future goal but is premised on the notion of an enlightenment continually accessed in the present.

SINGLE CONDITION As we have seen, in Nichiren's thought, enlightenment, or salvation, depends not on multiple factors but on one condition only—faith in the *Lotus Sūtra,* which is inseparable from the chanting of the *daimoku.* Anyone who chants the *daimoku,* man or woman, cleric or lay person, foolish or wise, realizes enlightenment. Correspondingly, there is but one single error or evil that can obstruct this enlightenment: "slander of the Dharma," or willful disbelief in the sūtra. To discard the *Lotus Sūtra,* Nichiren writes, "exceeds even the sin of killing one's parents a thousand or ten thousand times, or of shedding the blood of the Buddhas in the ten directions."[241] The modality of Nichiren's doctrine on this point appears at first absolutely either/or: "Disbelief is the cause of the *icchantika* and of slander of the Dharma, while faith is the cause of wisdom *(prajñā)* and corresponds to the stage of verbal identity."[242] So powerful is faith in the *Lotus* that no worldly evil can ever counteract it and pull the practitioner down into the evil paths. Conversely, slander of the *Lotus Sūtra* is so great an evil that no accumulation of worldly good deeds can ever offset it or save one who commits it from the Avīci Hell. On a deeper level, however, the dichotomy is dissolved, for even to slander the *Lotus Sūtra* is to form a connection with it. Thus in Nichiren's view, even if one's practice of *shakubuku* should arouse the enmity of others and cause them to slander the *Lotus Sūtra,* because it nonethless allows them to form a "reverse connection" with the sūtra, that is far preferable to their having no connection at all. Once the retribution of their slander is expiated, they will, by virtue of that connection, encounter the sūtra again and attain Buddhahood.[243]

ALL-INCLUSIVENESS As we have seen, the five characters of the *daimoku* are said to contain all teachings and to encompass all phenomena. They also contain the merit of all the good practices of the Buddhas, such as the six *pāramitās,* and the virtues of enlightenment in which they result. However, this is not the only sense in which the *daimoku* is claimed to be all-inclusive. By the logic of the single-practice position, being by definition the only practice a true devotee should uphold, the *daimoku* is also said to produce all possible benefits. Nichiren's teaching assimilates to the *daimoku* all the goods that religion in medieval Japan was thought to provide. In his various writings, faith in the *Lotus* is said to offer the realization of Buddhahood in this body, healing and other worldly benefits, protection of the nation, repentance or expiation of sin *(sange),* and birth after death in a pure land. Similarly, Nichiren's idea of the Buddha of the *Lotus Sūtra* encompasses all conceptions of the Buddha that were current in his day. Śākyamuni is "our blood and flesh," "our bones and marrow." But at the same time he is ruler of the world, compassionate parent, and wise teacher to all beings. Nichiren's use of *hongaku* ideas is also assimilated to this polemic of the all-inclusiveness of the *Lotus Sūtra.* The *Lotus* is presented as the only sūtra to reveal that the enlightened state of the Buddha and the nine realms of deluded beings are mutually encompassing and originally inherent; this is what makes the *Lotus* uniquely true and superior.

Nichiren has sometimes been criticized for adopting features of the very traditions he attacked. For example, it has been pointed out that Hōnen's exclusive *nenbutsu,* which Nichiren denounced, influenced his positing of the *daimoku* as an exclusive practice.[244] Or it has been noted that, while harshly criticizing Taimitsu, he nonetheless made use of mandalas.[245] While the single-practice orientation is itself open to criticism for the ease with which it can translate into dogmatic self-assertion, such observations miss the underlying logic of Nichiren's aim. This appears to have been not to eradicate the spectrum of religious interpretations current in his day, but to undercut their bases in other traditions and assimilate them to the *Lotus Sūtra.*[246] This is illustrated in the following passage:

> Once they enter the great ocean of the *Lotus Sūtra,* the teachings preached before the *Lotus* are no longer shunned as provisional. It is the mysterious virtue of the great ocean of the *Lotus Sūtra* that, once they are encompassed in the single flavor of *Namu-myōhō-renge-kyō,* there is no longer any reason to refer to the distinct names *"nenbutsu,"* "precepts," *"shingon,"* or "Zen." Thus the commentary states, "When the various rivers enter the sea, they assume the same unitary salty flavor. When the various kinds of wisdom [represented by the provisional teachings] enter the true teaching, they lose their original names.[247]

Nichiren's teaching is no less exclusivistic for its attempt to be all-encompassing, but it should be understood as one of a number of contemporaneous attempts at subsuming all teachings, virtues, and possibilities within a single formulation.

DEEMPHASIS ON MORAL CULTIVATION As in much of medieval Tendai thought and various schools of Kamakura Pure Land, Zen, and other traditions, no direct causal connection is drawn in Nichiren's thought between good deeds or the cultivation of virtue and the realization of enlightenment. As noted above, Nichiren did not stress observance of the precepts as necessary to liberation: the merit of keeping precepts is already contained within the *daimoku.* Moreover, he claimed that one who chants the *daimoku* cannot be drawn by evil acts into the lower realms of transmigration. Nichiren also participated in the discourse of the "realization of Buddhahood by evil persons" *(akunin jōbutsu),* usually in teachings to his warrior followers:

> Whether or not evil persons *(akunin)* of the last age attain Buddhahood does not depend on whether their sins are light or heavy but rests solely upon whether or not they have faith in this sūtra. You are a person of a warrior house, an evil man involved day and night in killing. Up until now you have not abandoned the household life [to become a monk], so by what means will you escape the three evil paths?

> You should consider this well. The heart of the *Lotus Sūtra* is that [all dharmas] in their present status are precisely the Wonderful [Dharma], without change of original status. Thus without abandoning sinful karma, one attains the Buddha Way.[248]

This does not mean that Nichiren's teaching legitimates evildoing, or that his community lacked for moral guidelines. His letters and other writings show that, in making personal decisions or advising his followers, Nichiren drew on a variety of ethical sources. Prominent among these is Confucian social morality, with its emphasis on the virtues of benevolence, righteousness, good faith, loyalty, and filial piety. Other ethical sources for Nichiren were generic Buddhist morality, including the virtues of almsgiving, forbearance, and equanimity; and the emerging warrior ethos, with its emphasis on courage and personal honor. However, such values are not central to Nichiren's formal doctrine, which does not explicitly articulate a set of ethical principles. Only faith in the *Lotus Sūtra* and the rebuking of "slander of the Dharma" are specifically enjoined as necessary to salvation. Like Shinran, Nichiren seems to have believed that a person of genuine faith would not do evil gratuitously ("one who chants [the *daimoku*] as the *Lotus Sūtra* teaches will not have a crooked mind"[249]). His denial of the necessity of keeping precepts—like the larger discourse about *mappō* as an age without precepts, of which it is part—was intended not to excuse wrongdoing but to bring salvation within reach of those unable to keep the precepts. Nichiren's followers, most of whom were *bushi*, definitely fell within this category. At the same time, however, the divorcing of Buddhahood or salvation from the observance of ethical norms tends to undercut any moral basis from which specific evils, such as killing in battle, might be resisted.[250]

In this way, Nichiren appropriated and developed the same, nonlinear paradigm of liberation that was variously elaborated in medieval Tendai *hongaku*-related texts and in the doctrines of a number of the new Kamakura Buddhist movements. The most distinctive characteristic of his appropriation was not a revival of Buddhist practice in the face of a corrupt Tendai tradition that supposedly denied its necessity, nor an emphasis on "relative duality" aimed at moderating the thoroughgoing immanentalism of Tendai *hongaku* ideas. Rather, it was his assimilation of the paradigm to an exclusive form, in which enlightenment is defined as accessible only through the *daimoku* of the *Lotus Sūtra* and all other forms of practice are condemned as slander of the Dharma. In Nichiren's case, the single-practice orientation was connected at least in part with the social composition of his following. He himself was a person of common origins, from a remote part of eastern Japan, without powerful backers, and whose followers were chiefly middle- and lower-ranking samurai— persons on the periphery, if not altogether outside, the "influential parties system" or *kenmon taisei*. At the same time, Nichiren's criticisms of leading religious figures and institutions, and of the rulers and officials who were their patrons, resulted in sanctions and suppressions that further marginalized him and his followers and prompted increasing self-definition in opposition to existing religious and political authority. In this process, Nichiren's assimilation of the new paradigm of enlightenment to an exclusive practice became, in effect, a challenge to the establishment. In his reading of the paradigm, direct access to enlightenment was possible only by the teaching of which he and his disciples were the bearers—a Dharma received directly from Śākyamuni Buddha for the Final Dharma age and alone capable of saving the country from disaster. Thus in his reading, the locus of authority and legitimacy was made to shift, and it was not the court, nor the *bakufu*, nor the clerics of the leading shrines and temples, but Nichiren and his disciples who held the center stage of their historical moment.

Chapter Seven

Hokke-Tendai Interactions and the Emergence of a Nichiren Hongaku Discourse

BY FAR, the majority of Japanese studies of the "new" Kamakura Buddhism have focused on the lives and teachings of the founders. This is due partly to Buddhist sectarian regard for the founder's thought as normative for a given tradition, and partly to Marxist-inspired secular historiography that has deemed the new movements worthy of attention chiefly at those moments when they could be seen as resisting the establishment, that is, at the moment of their founding or at times when they offered active opposition, as in the Hokke and Ikkō *ikki* or uprisings of the sixteenth century. Only recently have secular historians, both in Japan and elsewhere, begun to consider seriously the process by which the "new" schools institutionalized and accommodated their teachings in response to changing circumstances—in other words, the process by which they ceased to be "new" and instead became established religion.[1]

The very model of "old Buddhism" versus "new Buddhism" in the Kamakura period highlights the inception of new schools that broke away from established institutions. It does not, however, draw attention to the many new developments taking place within those established institutions, nor does it address the extent to which the new Buddhist movements appropriated the forms of older ones in the process of their own development and institutionalization. Investigation of such issues may be expected to raise questions about where exactly "new" and "old" begin and leave off, and thus, about the limitations of these categories for the study of religious institutions in the latter part of the medieval period.

In calling into question the usefulness of monolithic conceptions of "new" and "old," chapter 5 proposed an "interactive model" for understanding the relationship between the teachings of the new Kamakura Buddhist movements and those of medieval Tendai. The suggestion was made that, through a complex and ongoing process of borrowings, appropriations, and transformations, both the "old" Tendai establishment and the "new" Kamakura movements participated from their differing social and institutional standpoints in elaborating a shared "reimagining" of Buddhist liberation as nonlinear and accessible in the present moment. The various strands of Tendai original enlightenment thought, as well as the doctrines of the new movements, can be seen as specific readings of this new paradigm, which is characteristic of Japan's medieval period.

An interactive model is particularly useful in illuminating the development of original enlightenment thought beyond the Kamakura period. It was during the Muromachi era that the "new" Buddhist movements grew into powerful Buddhist orders *(kyōdan)*. From their inception, they had shared with the parent Tendaishū a particular paradigm of liberation; now, in formalizing their doctrine and solidifying their institutions, they began actively to appropriate many of the forms and conventions of the medieval Tendai tradition and develop them in new directions. "Original enlightenment thought" in particular ceased to be the monopoly of Tendai but was elaborated with particular colorations in several traditions. At the same time, aspects of Tendai Buddhism underwent change in response to these newer forms.

The present chapter will take such an interactive approach in exploring some aspects of how the Hokkeshū or "Lotus sect"—as the Nichiren tradition called itself up through the Muromachi period[2]—interacted with medieval Tendai institutions, and how some of the forms and ideas of medieval Tendai were adopted and transformed in the service of elaborating and promoting Nichiren's teaching. This discussion is by no means comprehensive, nor is it intended to suggest that Hokkeshū interactions with medieval Tendai were necessarily representative of interactions between "new" and "old" forms of Buddhism after the Kamakura period. Further research would be necessary before such a comparison could be made. Nonetheless, this discussion will serve to give some preliminary idea of the complexity of the appropriations that occurred and will suggest the future importance of studying the "new" movements, not in isolation, but in the context of their interaction with rival institutions.

The Hokkeshū after Nichiren's Death

While a detailed account of the medieval Hokkeshū would exceed the scope of this book, a brief sketch will be helpful as background. As described in the last chapter, Nichiren died on 10/13/1282, en route from Minobu to Hitachi. Realizing that his strength was failing and that death was near, he stopped on 9/18 at Ikegami in Musashi, where he had followers. On 10/8 he designated six disciples to whom he entrusted the leadership of his community after his death, specifying that no order of rank obtained among them.[3] All six were at this time active in proselytizing in various parts of the Kantō and had congregations of followers under their direct guidance. These early congregations were the origins of branch lineages within the Hokkeshū.

These six leading disciples and their lineages were as follows:

BEN AJARI NISSHŌ (1221–1323), the eldest of the six, was sixty-two at the time of Nichiren's death. He was based at the Hokkeji, a temple he had established at Hamado in Kamakura, and, together with Daikoku Ajari Nichirō, headed the community of Nichiren's followers in Kamakura. His lineage became known as the Nisshō or Hama *monryū*.

DAIKOKU AJARI NICHIRŌ (1245–1320) was based at the Myōhonji, which he had founded, in Hikigayatsu in Kamakura, and also headed the Honmonji in Ikegami. He is additionally regarded as the founder of the Hondoji at Hiraga in Shimōsa. His followers were known as the Hikigayatsu or Nichirō *monryū*. Among his many talented disciples, Higo Ajari Nichizō (1269–1342) was the first monk of the Hokkeshū to preach Nichiren's doctrine in Kyoto.

MINBU AJARI NIKŌ (1253–1314) was based in Mobara in Kazusa and later became the second chief abbot of Minobu (Nichiren is regarded as the first).

BYAKUREN AJARI NIKKŌ (1246–1333) was active in Suruga, Kai, and Izu. A disagreement between him and the aforementioned Nikō led in 1289 to the first schism among Nichiren's followers. Nikkō established himself at Omosu near Fuji, and his line is called the Fuji *monryū* or Nikkō *monryū*.

IYO AJARI NITCHŌ (1252–1317) was based at Mama and Wakamiya in Shimōsa, where he assisted the efforts of Nichijō (Toki Jōnin), originally a prominent lay supporter of Nichiren who had taken clerical vows after his death. Nitchō was Toki Jōnin's adopted son. However, for reasons that are not clear, there was a break between the two, and Nitchō left the area around 1292, retiring to Omosu, where he joined Nikkō. Nichijō's line came to be known as the Nakayama lineage, after Nakayama in Shimōsa where its main temple was located.

RENGE AJARI NICHIJI (1250–?) was based at Matsuno in Suruga. However, in 1295, he embarked on a journey, determined to spread Nichiren's teaching beyond the confines of Japan, and is said to have traveled north to Hokkaidō, crossing over into northern China and Manchuria. It has been argued that he did in fact reach Mongolia, but the evidence is inconclusive.[4]

ABBREVIATED LINEAGE CHART OF THE EARLY HOKKESHŪ

Nichiren

| Nichijō (Toki Jōnin, 1216-1299) (Nakayama *monryū*) | Nichiji (1250-?) | Nitchō (1252-1317) | Nikō (2) (1253-1314) (Minobu *monryū*) (Mobara *monryū*) | Nikkō (1246-1333) (Fuji *monryū*) (Taisekiji lineage) | Nichirō (1245-1320) (Hikigayatsu *monryū*) | Nisshō (1221-1323) (Hama *monryū*) |

Nichikō (1257-1314)

Nichiyū (1298-1374)

Nichizen (1294-1344)

Nisshū (1264-1334) (Mobara *monryū*)

Nisshin (3) (1271-1346?) (Minobu *monryū*)

Nichimoku (1260-1333)

Nichidō (1283-1341)

Nichizō (1269-1342) (Shijō *monryū*)

Nichiu (1409-1482)

Nichiei (7) (d. 1400)

Nichioku (8) (d. 1422)

Nichigaku (9) (d. 1459)

Nichien (10) (1430-1461)

Nisshutsu (1381-1459)

Nitchō (11) (1422-1500)

Nichii (12) (1444-1519)

Nichiden (13) (1482-1548)

Nichikyō (14) (1507-1559)

No. = *kanju* of Minobu

Based on *Nichirenshū jiten*, with reference to individuals mentioned in this chapter.

Congregations formed around each of these major disciples and their successors. As additional temples were founded or converted, and with the expansion of propagation efforts beyond the Kantō, new lineages and sublineages were formed. After the fall of the Kamakura *bakufu* and the subsequent shift of the center of political power back to Kyoto in 1333, virtually all the Hokke lineages established bases in Kyoto, where the process of expansion continued. New *monryū* also resulted from schisms.

Whatever their lineage, Hokke monks appear to have shared a sense of being Nichiren's disciples and of carrying out his mandate to spread exclusive devotion to the *Lotus Sūtra*. Conventions adopted by the sect worked to enhance this sense of shared identity. One obvious instance was the use, by virtually all Hokke monks and many nuns, of the *nichi-gō*, a clerical name beginning with the character *nichi* from Nichiren; in this way, the entire order became in a sense an extension of Nichiren, who was thus made to live on in his successors.[5] The *nichi-gō* represents a specific instance of more general naming conventions in Buddhist lineages, where the disciple typically would be given a name containing one character taken from that his master (e.g., Shinson, Songai, Kankai).

Activities of *shakubuku,* including debate with scholars of other sects and the memorializing of government officials, also instilled a sense of common purpose vis-à-vis other traditions, especially since such actions often provoked hostility. Rival Nichiren lineages were also able to join forces for mutual advantage or protection, as evidenced by the Kanshō-era accord (Kanshō *meiyaku*) signed in 1466 by the major Hokke temples in Kyoto in an effort to band together in the face of threats from Mt. Hiei.[6]

Nonetheless, the medieval Hokkeshū was in no way a monolithic tradition. Temples in different parts of the country had different social and economic bases. In the Kantō, local warrior patronage remained the rule, sons of the clan becoming incumbents of the local temple and offering ritual prayers for the family's fortunes. In the western cities of Kyoto and Sakai, however, the Hokkeshū drew its major support from the emerging urban mercantile class or *machishū* and was influential in the development of a distinctive *machishū* culture. Differences in doctrine and ritual observance developed among the various branches of the Hokkeshū and became the subject of dispute. The monk Kuonjō in Nisshin (1407–1488), who traveled extensively and compiled the first history of the Nichiren tradition, summed up these conflicts as follows: "Whether the origin and trace [teachings] represent a unity or a hierarchy; whether or not to mount the ordination platform of Mt. Hiei; whether or not to accept the alms of nonbelievers; whether or not to go pay respects at shrines and temples—such arguments are entangled like so many strands of hair."[7]

Of these points of tension enumerated by Nisshin, none was argued more vociferously throughout the Muromachi period than the first. A word is in order here about this controversy, as it will be relevant to subsequent discussion, and because its significance is far from obvious to one unfamiliar with the tradition. Nichiren, as outlined in the previous chapter, had grounded his concept of the single thought-moment comprising three thousand realms in actuality in the origin teaching or latter fourteen chapters of the *Lotus Sūtra.* Only the origin teaching, in his view, revealed the mutual inclusion of "original cause" (the nine realms) and "original effect" (the realm of Buddhahood). However, his later followers found it necessary to elaborate, on the basis he had established, the precise relationship that obtained between the dharmas of the origin teaching and of the trace teaching *(honjaku ron).* No debate over this issue appears in any authenticatable writing by the first generation of Nichiren's followers, who were chiefly concerned with establishing the superiority of the *Lotus Sūtra* itself over other teachings.[8] The controversy took shape in the Muromachi period and quickly became crucial to the self-definition of rival Hokke lineages. On this issue, the Hokkeshū divided broadly into two positions. Those who stressed the superiority of the origin teaching over the trace teaching were said to occupy the *shōretsu* ("superior versus inferior") position, while those who emphasized the essential unity of the two represented the *itchi* ("unified") position. Each comprised a number of variations.[9] Those who upheld the *shōretsu* position differed among themselves as to how the superiority of the origin teaching should be understood. Some said that its superiority lay in all fourteen chapters of the origin teaching; others held that it resided in the eight chapters that represent the assembly in open space presided over by Śākyamuni and Many Jewels seated side by side in the jeweled stūpa; or in the "Fathoming the Lifespan" chapter alone; or in the "Fathoming the Lifespan" chapter plus the latter part of the preceding "Emerging from the Earth" chapter and the first half of the subsequent "Discrimination of Merits" chapter ("one chapter and two halves"); or in the *daimoku* alone, and so forth. The *itchi* position was also variously argued. Some maintained that the origin and trace teachings were essentially one *(ittai)*, arguing, for example, that, while a distinction exists between origin and trace teachings with respect to the capacity of the people for whom they were expounded, they are one in the Buddha's intent; or that they are essentially one in being subsumed within the *daimoku*. Others held that the two teachings, while essentially different, were nonetheless inseparable *(itchi)*, for example, in representing the inherent nature of enlightenment and its realization in the act of practice; or that the two are unified when the trace teaching is read in light of understanding of the origin teaching. Since very few scholars upholding the *shōretsu* position went so far as to reject the trace teaching entirely, and since most *itchi* proponents acknowledged the doctrinal superiority of the origin teaching, the two positions tended to shade off into one another, rather than remaining in absolute confrontation. On the whole, however, those holding the *itchi* position tended also to be more accommodating in their dealings with other religious traditions, while those committed to the *shōretsu* position were frequently uncompromising in upholding the exclusive devotion to the *Lotus Sūtra* through *shakubuku* and the rebuking of "slander of the Dharma."

Unlike religious debates such as that between Saichō and the Hossō monk Tokuitsu, over whether or not all beings can attain Buddhahood, the Hokke controversy over the relationship between origin and trace teachings does not have immediately obvious soteriological implications. Nor—unlike the controversy among Hōnen's disciples over whether birth in the Pure Land requires many recitations of the *nenbutsu* or only one—is its relationship to actual practice immediately clear.[10] One imagines that the finer points of the debate lay beyond both the understanding and the concern of most Hokke lay followers. Nichiren scholars today differ on what significance this controversy has had in the history of their tradition. Some see it as an attempt, striking at the heart of Nichiren Buddhist thought, to grasp the relationship of the differentiated and the equal, the phenomenal and the real, the relative and the absolute, as represented by the two divisions of the sūtra.[11] Others have dismissed it as a dry, formulaic rehearsal of the terms of Nichiren's doctrine that misses its existential significance.[12] However, the *itchi/ shōretsu* controversy was never purely about doctrine, but about establishing the identity of the tradition, with respect to both the classical T'ien-t'ai that had preceded it (and which had emphasized the trace teaching) and the medieval Japanese Tendai that shared its historical moment (and which, although on different grounds, also emphasized the origin teaching). Even more importantly, it was about establishing legitimacy and authority vis-à-vis rival schools and lineages *within* the Hokkeshū. Command of the specialized vocabulary used in expressing the terms of the debate marked its participants as members of an elite within the tradition. Manipulating those terms in new ways and with ever more subtle distinctions served both to define one's own lineage within that elite and to contest the authority of others. In this respect, it was very similar to doctrinal debates in other clerical traditions.

Having outlined above some of the important developments within the early Hokke tradition, we can proceed to discuss its interactions with Tendai institutions in both eastern and western Japan. These, as shall become clear, were exceedingly complex and multivalent, changed over time, and resulted in transformations on both sides.

Early Rivalries in the Kantō

Among Nichiren's extant letters to his follower Toki Jōnin, an erudite samurai who had become a *nyūdō* or lay monk, is one congratulating Jōnin on having bested in debate the "vastly learned" Tendai monk Ryōshō-bō.[13] According to this letter, the debate turned in Jōnin's favor when Ryōshō-bō proved ignorant of the passage in Chan-jan's commentary on Chih-i's *Fa-hua wen-chü:* "To liberate oneself from the [threefold] world by means of the provisional [teachings] is called an ephemeral liberation."[14] Because of their distinctive claim that Buddhahood can be realized only through the *Lotus Sūtra,* Nichiren and his followers had probably familiarized themselves to a greater extent than had their Tendai contemporaries with those passages in the classical T'ien-t'ai literature that would serve to support this position.[15]

The monk Ryōshō-bō defeated in debate by Toki Jōnin was quite probably someone more commonly known as Kawataya Shinson of the Tendai Eshin school, whom traditional accounts identify as the first to introduce the Eshin doctrines to eastern Japan.[16] While modern scholarship has identified Tendai Eshin-school monks in the Kantō prior to Shinson, he was undeniably instrumental in establishing an Eshin presence there.[17] He is said to have founded a temple at Kawataya in Musashi called the Tōeizan [Eastern Mt.(Hi)ei] Senpukuji, about forty kilometers from Mama in Shimōsa where Toki Jōnin lived, and to have lectured there on the *Mo-ho chih-kuan* during the Kangen era (1243–1247). Shinson was also said to have been the compiler of the collection of oral transmissions known as the *Kawataya bōshō jūkutsū* (Nineteen main and subsidiary articles of Kawataya), a *kuden hōmon* collection influential in the development of Kantō Eshin thought. His disciple Songai (1253–1332) established the Senba *dangisho* at Kawagoe in Musashi, which, as mentioned in chapter 3, became a leading intellectual and institutional center of Eshin Tendai in eastern Japan.

If Ryōshō-bō was in fact Shinson, his debate with Toki Jōnin may have marked the beginning of confrontation that was to develop between Nichiren's followers and the emerging Kantō Tendai tradition, especially that branch of the Sugiu Eshin line based at the Senba *dangisho*. While the two fledgling traditions competed for influence and patronage, their rivalry was on both sides articulated in doctrinal terms, centering on the issue of the status of other Buddhist sūtras and teachings with respect to the *Lotus Sūtra*.

Scholars have called attention to the *Shoshin kangaku shō* (Encouraging beginners in study), a Muromachi period introductory text written and studied at the Senba *dangisho*. Under the heading "Oneness of the true and provisional teachings," it reads:

> Right at hand we have the transmissions passed down from virtuous teachers of the past, who have said, "The *Lotus Sūtra* itself has no essence. It takes as its essence the teachings expounded before it." Nonetheless, in the present age, the followers of Nichiren profoundly revere only the *Lotus* and deeply reject the teachings expounded before it. This is a grave error. While the *Lotus* is indeed to be revered, to slander other sūtras in fact destroys the intent of the *Lotus*. . . .

> Question: In their repudiation of the provisional teachings, we find that the Nichiren followers cite as their proof texts these passages from [the "Skillful Means" chapter] of the *Lotus:* "Honestly discarding skillful means, I will expound only the unexcelled Way" and "[There is the Dharma of only one vehicle, there are not two or three,] excepting the Buddha's preaching of skillful means." How do you respond?

> Answer: When one reads the character for "to discard" *(sha)* in "honestly discarding skillful means" as "to place" *(oku),* then it means that the skillful means of the provisional teachings, just as they are, are placed within the *Lotus*. This being the case, the fact that the "Skillful Means" chapter is placed among the [sūtra's] twenty-eight chapters expresses the meaning of skillful means being precisely true reality. As for "excepting the Buddha's preaching of skillful means," this is interpreted

to mean that attachment to these teachings is to be removed, not the dharma-teachings themselves. In other words, one is simply to remove emotional attachment to the [notion of] skillful means expounded before the *Lotus* as provisional teachings.[18]

The Kantō Tendai of Senba and Hokke positions on this issue can be seen as representing two poles in the interpretation of the notion of *kaie,* or the "opening and integration" of all other teachings into the one vehicle of the *Lotus Sūtra.* The Senba side, as represented in the above passage from the *Shoshin kangaku shō,* took this to mean that since all teachings are encompassed by the one vehicle, to practice other teachings is in effect to practice the *Lotus Sūtra.* This interpretation is sometimes termed "absolute integration" (or *zettai kaie*) and has enjoyed a prominent place in the history of Japanese Tendai thought. The Hokke side, on the other hand, maintained that *Lotus* is, quite simply, superior to all other teachings; when integrated into it, they lose their separate identity. This is the interpretation of "relative integration" *(sōtai kaie)* that Nichiren had emphasized.[19] The idea that all practices may be understood as aspects of the one vehicle and are thus the practice of the *Lotus Sūtra* had been well established in Tendai circles since Heian times. The invocation "Namu-Amida-butsu," for example, was often referred to as the "six-character *Lotus Sūtra.*" The fact that the scholars of Senba felt compelled to argue this already well established position in such detail suggests that they were being hard pressed by their Hokke counterparts.

Rivalry with the Nichiren Hokkeshū also provides an illuminating context for understanding the doctrine most distinctive of the Senba line of the Sugiu branch of Eshin-school Tendai: that *shikan,* or "calming and contemplation," surpasses the textual *Lotus Sūtra (shikan shō Hokke).* This doctrine is frequently represented in medieval Tendai *kuden* texts as originating with Songai and unique to the scholar-monks of Senba. It has a clear basis in the medieval Tendai doctrinal classification of the "fourfold rise and fall," discussed in chapter 4, and represents a particularly strong reading of its fourth and last stage—"When the great teaching of *kanjin* rises, the origin teaching is superceded." Here, however, *kanjin* (or *shikan*) is declared superior to the sūtra, not merely in the sense that contemplative insight resulting from practice is deemed superior to mere doctrinal understanding, but in representing a Dharma transmission independent of the sūtra text. Senba scholars distinguished between the "Hokke lineage" ("Hokkeshū")—here meaning not the Nichiren Hokkeshū, but the textual *Lotus Sūtra*—and the "Tendai lineage" (Tendaishū), transmitted directly from Śākyamuni Buddha in the jeweled stūpa. Where the "Hokkeshū" assumes a linear sequence of stages ranging from pre-*Lotus* to trace to origin teachings, the "Tendaishū" is prior to such distinctions and is grounded in original en-lightenment. The association of this doctrinal position with Senba is made clear, for example, in the *Nijō shō kenmon* of Sonshun (1451–1514):

> [Concerning the threefold interpretation of *isshin sangan* in terms of the trace teaching, the origin teaching, and the contemplation of the mind:] On the mountain side [i.e., Mt. Hiei], they do not postulate a Dharma of "contemplating the mind" *(kanjin)* that transcends the ori-gin and trace teachings. Hence they do not establish a difference be-tween the Tendai and Hokke [lineages]. Only on the *inaka* side [the Kantō] since the time of Songai, do they generally say that there ex-ists a Dharma transcending the origin and trace teachings, establish-ing the perspective of "the contemplation of the mind" *(kanjin)*. The trace and origin teachings pertain to the Hokkeshū; above these is pos-tulated the "contemplation of the mind," which pertains to the Ten-daishū. This [distinction] is not permitted on the mountain; it is taught only at Senba.[20]

In this way, Senba scholars arrogated to themselves the designation "Tendaishū," which they identified with their own characteristic doctri-nal position that there exists an ineffable Dharma known through med-itative insight—designated as *kanjin* or *shikan*—independent of and prior to the origin and trace teachings of the *Lotus Sūtra*. It appears that the Senba branch of Kantō Tendai in particular used this doctrine to chal-lenge the authority of, and assert its superiority to, the parent tradition of Mt. Hiei. The particularity of this doctrine to the Kanto, especially the Senba *dangisho,* is also indicated in a mid-Muromachi text by the Nichiren Hokke monk Shinnyo-in Nichijū (1406–1486) of the Hongakuji in Kyoto, who as a young man had studied on Hiei with the Tendai monk Jōgen of the Eastern Pagoda precinct. He writes:

> Within the Tendaishū, an interpretation is posited that *shikan* is su-perior and the *Lotus* inferior. Of the two schools, Eshin and Danna, the Danna school has taken no account of this [position], but in the Eshin school it is a valued doctrine. Within the Eshin school, it is the particular doctrine of the Sugiu line, but even within the Sugiu line, scholars of the main lineage on the mountain [Hiei] do not assert it. Because it is a doctrine of the Sugiu lineage, scholars such as Zōjō-bō Jōgen and others at the Kitadani of the Eastern Pagoda speak of it when it is natural to do so, but while speaking, they do not place faith in it. In general it is said to be asserted by [Tendai] scholars of the provinces. . . . It is a doctrine put forth by Songai Hōin (Dharma Seal) of Senba.[21]

This suggests that the doctrine of *"shikan* surpasses the *Lotus"* was known but not accepted among Eshin scholars on Mt. Hiei. Possibly it had been

introduced to Hiei from the Kantō, as a number of Eastern Tendai monks
traveled to Mt. Hiei and lived there for extended periods. As recorded
in a Nanbokuchō period text noted by Hayashi Senshō, "Throughout
Japan, those called the Senba disciples are everywhere. There are now
said to be forty of them on the mountain [Hiei]."²²

However, not all sources agree that the *"shikan* surpasses the *Lotus"*
doctrine began with Songai, or that it even originated in the Kantō. The
Tōkai kuden shō, a *kuden hōmon* collection compiled between 1343 and
1349, attributes a very similar idea to Shinga (fl. 1329), a monk of the
Gyōsen-bō Eshin line with whom Songai had studied on Mt. Hiei. Shinga
is quoted as saying: "*Shikan* was expounded by the wise man T'ien-t'ai
[Chih-i] and is the doctrine he practiced within his own mind. Because
this is the mysterious *shikan* of his inner enlightenment, it is not separately established on the basis of the *Lotus* [Sūtra]."²³ However, other
transmissions attributed to Shinga stress that the ultimate standpoint is
implicit in the origin teaching of the *Lotus Sūtra* text rather than distinct
from it. Thus, Shinga himself may not have gone so far as to assert that
"shikan surpasses the *Lotus,"* though this idea appears to be embryonic
in what has been transmitted of his thought.²⁴ A still different account,
dating from around the same time as the *Tōkai kuden shō,* is the *Hokke
mondō shōgishō* (Judgments on questions and answers concerning the
Lotus), written between 1332 and 1344 by Tōgakuin Nichizen (1294–
1344) of the Nakayama branch of the Nichiren Hokke sect. In this work,
Nichizen records that he had formerly studied on Mt. Hiei at the Nishidani of the Eastern Pagoda precinct, where the Ekō-bo lineage of the
Danna school had its base. There he was told that the doctrine of *"shikan*
surpasses the *Lotus"* had first been articulated by Seikai, a disciple of
Jōmyō and regarded as the founder of the Tsuchimikado-monzeki lineage of the Eshin school, during an examination held at the Senjudō.²⁵
According to Nichizen's account, Seikai, who was acting as judge
(shōgisha), declared: "Because *shikan* is the doctrine that the great teacher
[Chih-i] practiced within his mind, he realized it without reliance on sūtras and treatises." The examinee, a scholar of the Nishidani, expressed
doubt. "How can this be? The purpose of the Tathâgata Śākyamuni's advent in this world lies in the origin and trace teachings of the *Lotus.* . . .
Because *shikan* is the practice of the *Lotus Sūtra,* it is that which interprets *(nōshaku).* The *Lotus* is that which is interpreted *(shoshaku),* the fundamental Dharma." The next day, the scholar-monk Fuzen, also of the
Nishidani, sent Seikai a letter with questions: Why had his assertion never
appeared in the writings of Chih-i, Saichō, or any of their successors?
From whom had he received this transmission? Seikai replied that it was
not a master-disciple transmission; the insight had occurred to him during the debate, but careful reflection would show it to be correct. Fuzen
pressed the issue and, when Seikai eventually proved unable to answer,

wrote him admonishing: "From now on, the scholar-monks of the mountain should never uphold a perverse doctrine such as this which slanders the Dharma." In the east, however, Songai got word of this doctrine and inquired about it on Mt. Hiei from Seikai's disciple Ikkai. Ikkai advised him that it was not an established teaching and should not be communicated to others. Nevertheless, Songai regarded it as a most profound secret teaching and transmitted it to his disciples in the Kantō.[26]

Nichizen's account reflects the Hokkeshū's general hostility toward the *"shikan* surpasses the *Lotus"* position, a point addressed below. Nonetheless, his informant, Zenpu, was a disciple of Fuzen, the monk who had pressed Seikai on this issue, so it may have some credibility.[27] Ono Bunkō suggests that Nichizen's account can be read to mean that the doctrine of *"shikan* surpasses the *Lotus"* was probably known on Mt. Hiei around the time of Jōmyō (who was roughly contemporary with Nichiren) and his disciple Shinga, and was made public in debate for the first time by Jōmyō's disciple Seikai, who presented it as his personal insight. Under criticism, Sugiu Eshin scholars on the mountain ceased to uphold it outwardly, while Songai's successors in the Kantō maintained it as their distinctive position.[28] Hayashi Senshō, on the other hand, questions whether the *"shikan* surpasses the *Lotus"* doctrine can be traced back as far as Jōmyō; he suggests it developed from Shinga's time on, though he finds it to be still undeveloped in surviving transmissions attributed to Shinga.[29] Whatever the case, it is clear that by the first part of the fourteenth century, the doctrine was known in Buddhist scholarly circles in the Kantō and was associated specifically with Songai and the Senba *dangisho.*

As noted above, the claim that *"shikan* surpasses the *Lotus"* has obvious roots in the emphasis on the authority of *kanjin* or meditative insight that characterized much of medieval Tendai thought. However, interpretations were not uniform. For some scholar-monks, *kanjin* or *shikan* simply denoted the practice of the origin teaching of the *Lotus;* the two were not independent but were distinguished merely as contemplative insight and textual expression of the same truth. For others, however, *shikan* was a separate transmission, independent of and superior to the textual *Lotus Sūtra*—a move that in effect asserted the independence and superior authority of one's own lineage. This was an extreme position, and not all Tendai lineages endorsed it. Nichizen's account, for example, suggests that the doctrine of *shikan* surpassing the *Lotus* was repudiated by Danna scholars on Mt. Hiei.[30] Nor was it necessarily embraced by all scholars of the Eshin school, on Hiei or in the Kantō.[31] Why, then, did Senba scholars choose this particular doctrine with which to identify their new eastern Tendai tradition?

Although the idea of *"shikan* surpasses the *Lotus"* served rhetorically to define the emerging Senba tradition over and against Mt. Hiei, it also effectively countered the central claim of another competitor closer to home, namely, the Nichiren Hokkeshū. If insight into true reality is something independent of written teachings and is not based upon even the *Lotus Sūtra,* then it would become pointless to assert, as the Nichiren followers did, that the *Lotus Sūtra* is true and all other teachings are provisional. Their entire argument could be dismissed as one still pertaining to the inferior level of textual transmission, transcended by the Tendai transmission of *shikan.* One can easily imagine that the *"shikan* surpasses the *Lotus"* idea was asserted within the Senba lineage at least in part as a polemic against the position of the Nichiren Hokke followers, who maintained that the *Lotus Sūtra* alone represents the true vehicle of salvation and that all other teachings must be rejected.[32]

This suggestion gains some force when one considers the vehemence of Nichiren Hokke criticisms of this doctrine in the first several decades after Nichiren's death. Daien Ajari Nichiden (1277–1341), a Tendai monk converted by Nichiren's disciple Nichirō, was de facto founder of the Hondoji in Hiraga and also held the position of chief of instruction *(gakutō)* for the communities of monks at Hikigayatsu and Ikegami. His *Jūni innen shō* (On the twelvefold chain of dependent origination), written in 1322, roundly condemns the doctrinal classification of the fourfold rise and fall, from which *"shikan* surpasses the *Lotus"* derives: "There flourishes a perverted doctrine that makes contemplation of the mind the essence, abolishing the origin and trace teachings. . . . One should abide in Namu-myōhō-renge-kyō, in which origin and trace [teachings] are inconceivably one."[33]

Jōgyōin Nichiyū (1298–1374), third in the succession of the Nakayama lineage, was also critical: "To say that when the great teaching of *kanjin* rises the great teachings of the origin and trace teachings are superceded is an extremely distorted view."[34] Nichizen—author of the above-cited account of how Seikai allegedly invented the doctrine that *"shikan* surpasses the *Lotus"*—was Nichiyū's disciple. The *Hokke mondō shōgishō,* in which he relays this account, criticizes this doctrine as lacking textual support: "T'ien-t'ai [Chih-i] was an auditor on Sacred [Eagle] Peak. What he heard on Sacred [Eagle] Peak was the present *Sūtra of the Wonderful Dharma of the [Lotus] Blossom.* In [the preaching] of which chapter did he hear that there is a 'calming and contemplation' that surpassess the Wonderful Dharma?"[35] Nichizen added that he had written his criticism "to demolish this perverted doctrine and establish correct doctrine."[36]

Nichizen's teacher Nichiyū had studied for a time under Daishin Ajari Nisshin (1271–1346?), third abbot of the Kuonji at Minobu. Through his connection as Nichiyū's disciple, Nichizen had also studied with Nisshin. While we do not have an explicit statement from Nisshin himself with regard to the Senba doctrine of *"shikan* surpasses the *Lotus,"* he transcribed in 1325 the *Risshōkan jō* (On establishing correct contemplation).

This work is traditionally said to have been written by Nichiren in 1274 to Sairen-bō, a Tendai monk who had become his follower while both were in exile on Sado. It is virtually the only work in the Nichiren corpus to comment—negatively—on the doctrine of *"shikan* surpassing the *Lotus."*[37] To quote some excerpts:

> Among those who study Tendai doctrine in the world today, there appear to be many who revere the practice of contemplating the mind and discard the origin and trace teachings of the *Lotus.* . . . Those who abandon the *Lotus Sūtra* and regard only contemplation as primary are guilty of a grave slander of the Dharma, a great perverted view, an act of devils. . . . The Tendaishū today is so deplorable as to assert that because *shingon* [i.e., Taimitsu] sets forth both the principles and practices of the esoteric teachings, it surpasses the *Lotus Sūtra;* thus they find it completely reasonable that *shikan* [also] surpasses the *Lotus.* Next, with regard to the argument that when applying the interpretation of *kanjin,* the origin and trace teachings are to be abandoned: Based on what passage of the *Lotus Sūtra,* or of the commentaries from later teachers, are we to abandon the Buddha's teaching? Even if this were the interpretation of T'ien-t'ai [Chih-i], it violates the golden words of Śākyamuni and goes against the *Lotus Sūtra.* [This view] is absolutely never to be adopted. . . . If *shikan* is not grounded in the *Lotus Sūtra,* then the Tendai *shikan* becomes equivalent to the Daruma[shū]'s diabolical and false teaching of a separate transmission outside the scriptures.[38]

The *Risshōkan jō* does not survive in Nichiren's holograph, and its authenticity is a matter of considerable dispute. Since it represents the earliest reference outside the Tendai *kuden* literature to the doctrine of *"shikan* surpasses the *Lotus,"* inquiries into when this doctrine first appeared are often intertwined with arguments for or against Nichiren's authorship of the *Risshōkan jō.*[39] It is possible that, if this doctrine had been known on Mt. Hiei in Nichiren's latter years, he might have heard it from Sairen-bō, who had returned from exile and was living in Kyoto. The *Risshōkan jō* might then be exactly what it purports to be—Nichiren's response in the year 1274 to Sairen-bō's request for his opinion on this doctrine. It seems odd, however, that a doctrinal position so at odds with Nichiren's own would never again be addressed and criticized in his later writings, or for that matter, in the writings of his immediate disciples. Nisshin's transcription of the *Risshōkan jō* in 1325 coincides with a brief period of outcry on the part of Nichiren's second- and third-generation disciples in the first part of the fourteenth century against the *"shikan* surpasses the *Lotus"* doctrine as asserted by the monks of the increasingly influential Senba *dangisho.* Based on this coincidence of timing and his own research into the origins of the doctrine, Take Kakuchō has suggested that the superiority of *shikan* over the *Lotus* began to be asserted not long after Nichiren's death, and that Nisshin is in fact the *Risshōkan jō*'s author, voicing Hokke arguments against this doctrine in the persona of Nichiren.[40]

Not all Hokke scholars remained adamantly opposed to such ideas as the fourfold rise and fall and the superiority of *kanjin* over the sūtra text; many incorporated them into their interpretation of Nichiren doctrine, especially later in the medieval period.[41] However, at this early stage, it appears that at least some monks in the Kantō lineages of Hikigayatsu-Ikegami, Minobu, and Nakayama opposed the doctrine of *"shikan* surpasses the *Lotus."* Where the Senba scholars asserted *kanjin* as a truth transcending even the origin teaching, the Buddha's most profound textual statement, these Hokke monks took a position of the nonduality of text and contemplation *(kyōkan funi)*, meaning that truth accessed in contemplative practice (which in their case was equated with the *daimoku*) is not separable from the sūtra text. Given the status of Senba and the Kantō Nichiren Hokkeshū as competitors in the same geographic area and their clear opposition to one another's positions, it seems likely that these sharply contrasting doctrinal stances developed at least in part as statements of their rivalry and were reinforced as they defined their emerging traditions over and against one another.

The Appropriation of Shunpan

By the latter part of his career, Nichiren had in effect broken away from the Tendai Buddhism of Mt. Hiei, establishing a new movement. Yet his later followers still drew selectively upon that tradition for purposes of legitimization. One instance of this has already been noted, in Nichizen's invoking of the Danna scholars of the Eastern Pagoda precinct to condemn the *"shikan* surpasses the *Lotus"* doctrine of the Senba *dangisho*. Another example may be seen in the claim, evidently originating within the Fuji lineage of Byakuren Ajari Nikkō, to the effect that Nichiren had received the secret transmission of the Eshin school from Shunpan, who had been master of instruction *(sōgakutō)* on Mt. Hiei while Nichiren was studying there as a young man. As mentioned in the preceding chapter, Nichiren's extant writings contain only two brief, impersonal references to Shunpan; thus there is good reason to doubt that the two shared a close master-disciple relationship, although Nichiren may well have attended Shunpan's public lectures. However, within less than a hundred years after Nichiren's death, he was being represented within one branch of his own tradition as an inheritor of Shunpan's Eshin Sugiu line. The earliest known instance occurs in a writing by Hongaku Hōin Nichidai (1309–1369), a second-generation disciple of Nikkō active in Kyoto. Nichidai recorded two conversations he had on 12/23/1363 and

1/26/1364 with the Tendai monk Enjitsu-bō Hōin Jikken. Jikken, a leading Tendai scholar, held the rank of *gondaisōzu* and served as *tandai* on
Mt. Hiei.[42] Their conversation concerned the continuities and differences between their respective doctrines. According to Nichidai's account, Jikken informed him: "On this mountain [Hiei], there are no
[longer any] learned scholars. I am fourth in a line of transmission from
Shunpan. This lodging temple was formerly the site of Shunpan Hōin's
goma hall. The leadership of the Eshin school rests with me." To which
Nichidai replied: "'The great saint [*daishōnin*, i.e., Nichiren] inherited
the Tendai doctrine from Shunpan. I am fourth in the line of those who
propagate this sect. Is the Tendai transmission which the great saint received the same or different from the Tendai lineage that you uphold
in this lodging temple where I have encountered you?' We exchanged
opinions. What a mysterious karma."[43] Whatever Nichiren's relationship
to Shunpan may have been, we can glimpse here what appears to have
been an attempt on the part of Nichidai, a representative of a small sect,
still very new to the region of the capital, to place himself (and his lineage) on equal footing with the ranking Tendai prelate Jikken via a presumed common link to Shunpan.

In a later document of the Fuji school, a transmission on the subject
of Nichiren's mandala, Shunpan is shown as validating Nichiren's enlightenment concerning the object of worship:

> The master [Nichiren] said, "[In the past,] I prayed to [the bodhi-
> sattva] Kokūzō to know what should be established as the object of wor-
> ship for ordinary worldlings, the ignorant people of the last age. At
> that time, an old monk appeared to me and said, 'Make your own per-
> son the object of worship. Go look in Myōjō Pond [presumably located
> on or near the grounds of the Kiyosumidera].' At once I looked into
> the pond, and, strangely, my reflection appeared as what is now the
> great mandala *(daimandara)*." When he related this to Shunpan Hōin
> of Yokawa, Shunpan praised him, saying, "Well done, well done! You
> met the old monk Śākyamuni and, within the [jeweled] stūpa, he con-
> ferred [this upon you] directly. Admirable, admirable!"[44]

This passage draws on Nichiren's own account of the bodhisattva Kokūzō
appearing to him as an old monk and assimilates it to an origin story
for the great mandala. Shunpan of Mt. Hiei is made to play the role of
the teacher who validates the disciple's insight. In another document
of the Fuji school, Shunpan is cited as holding authoritative views on
the issue of the relation of the trace and origin teachings.[45] In this way,
Shunpan, the eminent scholar of Mt. Hiei, was appropriated by one
branch of the newly emerging Hokkeshū—the Fuji school—for purposes
of legitimation.

Curiously enough, on the Tendai side, Nichiren seems eventually to have been incorporated into narratives about Songai as the companion of his studies on Mt. Hiei. The earliest reliable reference appears in the writings of Ichinyo-in Nichijū (1549–1623), a leading scholar of Nichiren-shū: "Tendai scholars say that Master [Nichi]ren studied together with Songai, founder of Senba in Musashino. Both were of like mind and received from Shinga Hōin the threefold transmission [of the Eshin school]."[46] It is hard to know when, or why, this tradition began.[47] It may possibly have represented an attempt to counter Hokkeshū claims to uniqueness by subsuming Nichiren within the Eshin tradition, or have reflected intellectual exchange between Hokke and Tendai scholar-monks, which increased from the late fourteenth century on. Eventually it was appropriated by the Nichiren sect, as seen in this account by Tsūshin-in Nikkyō (1601–1659):

> Since the early times of our sect, oral transmissions have said that the Shōnin [Nichiren] studied together with Songai Hōin. They learned the same doctrines together on Mt. Hiei, and when they went together back down to the Kantō, the Shōnin announced his intention to spread the practice of chanting the title [of the *Lotus Sūtra*]. Songai Hōin replied that the time had not yet come. Later, hearing of the principles of the sect the Shōnin had established, Songai put forth the doctrine that *shikan* surpasses the *Lotus*. This doctrine is refuted in our founder's writings. The Shōnin's rebuke was directed toward Songai.[48]

Whatever the source of the tradition that Songai and Nichiren were fellow students on Mt. Hiei, it is a chronological impossibility. Songai was not born until 1253, by which time Nichiren had returned from Mt. Hiei to the Kiyosumidera.[49]

Mt. Minobu and the Senba Dangisho

As seen above, in the first part of the fourteenth century, leading Hokke scholar-monks in the Kantō region looked upon the Senba *dangisho* as a promulgator of heresy. By the latter part of the fourteenth century, however, intercourse developed between Hokke lineages and Kantō Tendai *dangisho*, encouraging the importation of features of medieval Tendai thought into interpretations of Nichiren doctrine.

Nichiren's teaching shares with Tendai a common textual and doctrinal basis in the *Lotus Sūtra* and the works of Chih-i, Chan-jan, and Saichō. For monks of the Hokkeshū, doctrinal training therefore involved a grounding in T'ien-t'ai/Tendai thought as well as in Nichiren's distinctive teaching. It was also necessary to understand the teachings of other Buddhist traditions, at least in outline, for purposes of *shakubuku* and debate. In Nichiren's own time, many of his monk-disciples were converts from Tendai and thus already possessed this background, but there remained the problem of providing such education for those who took the tonsure directly under Nichiren. Nichiren himself gave lectures to his disciples on the *Lotus Sūtra* and the *Mo-ho chih-kuan* and wrote texts for the instruction of those who did not live close to him. He also sent capable monks to Mt. Hiei for training, although—given that he regarded much about the Tendai Buddhism of his day to be corrupt and heterodox—he did so with considerable ambivalence.[50] After his death, his immediate disciples took over the task of pedagogy.[51] Eventually, *dangishō* were established and the position of head of instruction *(gakutō)* instituted at leading Hokke temples, such as Minobu, Omosu, Hiraga, Hikigayatsu, and Ikegami.[52] Usually, a *dangisho* would be established at the main temple *(honji)* of a given lineage and attended by monks of its branch temples *(matsuji)*. Some monks continued to go to Mt. Hiei for study. In the early decades of the tradition, these included Nisshin, who became third *kanju* or chief abbot of Minobu; Nichiyū, third chief abbot of the Nakayama Hokekyōji; and Sanmi Nichijun (1294–1354/1356), an important scholar of the Fuji lineage. Other Hokke monks went also to Mt. Kōya, the Nara temples, or other centers of Buddhist learning, probably to familiarize themselves with the doctrines of other schools for purposes of *shakubuku* and debate.

However, by the latter part of the fourteenth century, one finds the beginnings of intercourse with Tendai *dangisho,* especially in the Kantō, in the form of Tendai monks converting to the Hokkeshū and Hokke monks training at Tendai *dangisho* such as Senba and Kanasana. Here we will examine some aspects of this interaction by focusing on the Minobu lineage, in which it was especially marked.

An early connection between Minobu and medieval Tendai influences may have been established via Izumi-bō Nikkai (1336–1389), who became the fourth abbot of Mobaraji in Shimōsa. Said originally to have been a Tendai monk, Nikkai converted to the Hokkeshū and studied at Minobu under the sixth *kanju*, Jikkyō Ajari Nichiin. Eventually he was appointed head of instruction for Minobu. Nikkai's writings show strong influence of medieval Tendai thought.[53] Another such connection may have been through Jōgyōin Nichiei (d. 1400), who became seventh *kanju* of Minobu. Nichiei studied with Daiju Ajari Nissan (1338–1381), fourth abbot of both Hikigayatsu and Ikegami. Although the details of Nissan's early biography are not clear, he is said to have been an instructor at the Senba *dangisho* who had also received Tendai transmissions.[54] It has been suggested that Nichiei may have absorbed the influence of medieval Tendai through his connection with Nissan.[55]

Be that as it may, it is clear that after Nichiei's time, exchanges between Minobu and Kantō Tendai *dangisho* increased rapidly. A number of leading disciples of the ninth *kanju*, Jōjuin Nichigaku (d. 1459), had received transmissions in the Eshin and Danna Tendai lineages, including the man who became tenth abbot, Kangyōin Nichien (1430–1461). The increased intercourse with Tendai centers is reflected in the contents of the Minobu Bunko. The holdings of this archive in medieval Tendai *kuden* literature, including debate texts, outnumber those of any other premodern collection. Most numerous are *kuden* texts from Kantō branches of the Eshin school, especially those based at the Senba and the Kanasana *dangisho* in Musashi. Debate literature and texts dealing with the Eshin "seven-article transmission," received into the archive between the time of the seventh *kanju* Nichiei and the fourteenth, Zengakuin Nichikyō (1507–1559), comprise the largest categories of Minobu's holdings in medieval Tendai material.[56] When the ninth volume of *Tendaishū zensho* (Complete works of the Tendai school, published 1935), which contains the major Eshin *kuden hōmon* collections dealing with the "seven great matters," was being compiled, no copy of the *Ichijō shō,* the earliest collection of this kind, was to be found in any major Tendai temple archive. Four copies, however, were finally located at Minobu.[57]

The seven-article doctrines of the Eshin school—the "seven great matters" outlined in chapter 4—probably served as a pedagogical tool for conveniently summarizing and systematizing the great body of T'ient'ai/Tendai doctrine basic to both medieval Tendai and Hokke traditions. Asai Yōrin points out that a commentary on the seven articles of transmission by the Tendai monk Taigei (1444–1519) says, concerning the education of disciples: "First they should be given the *Lotus Sūtra,* then they should study and understand the three major works [of Chih-i], and after that, they should receive this transmission."[58] (Taigei, who converted to the Hokkeshū, became the twelfth chief abbot of Minobu, Engyōin Nichii.) The seven-article doctrines are mentioned in a number of medieval Hokke writings, not only of the Minobu lineage. Sometimes they were used to interpret Nichiren's teachings. For example, the three articles of the abbreviated transmission, which elaborate on the "deep meaning of the *Lotus Sūtra,*" were sometimes equated with Nichiren's three great secret Dharmas. That is, the "triple-bodied [Tathâgata] of the perfect teaching" *(engyō sanjin)* was equated with the object of worship; the causality of the *Lotus (renge inga)* with the *daimoku;* and the Land of Ever-Tranquil Light, with the ordination platform.[59]

The reasons for the sudden rise of interaction between Hokke scholars and those of the Kantō Tendai *dangisho,* and of Hokke scholarly interest in medieval Tendai doctrine, are not yet altogether clear. Though it will bear further investigation, one possible reason for the increased presence of Hokke monks at Kantō Tendai *dangisho* may have been growing antagonism between Mt. Hiei and the Hokke *monto* or temple-based confraternities in Kyoto. As the Kyoto Hokkeshū grew increasingly wealthy and powerful with the support of the *machishū,* friction with Mt. Hiei became more intense; thus one imagines that it may have become increasingly difficult for Hokke monks to study on the mountain, though some still continued to do so. It is also possible that the Kantō Tendai *dangisho* were simply more receptive. Songai is said to have abolished the tradition of transmission to a single person at Senba, creating an atmosphere in which monks desirous of studying Tendai doctrine were able to do so, whether or not they had Tendai affiliations.[60] The greatest role, however, seems to have been played by the forging of multiple lineage ties. This was a time when a number of prominent Tendai scholars converted to the Hokkeshū and then sent their (Hokke) disciples to Tendai *dangisho* where they had earlier connections. Thus the ranks of leading Hokke scholars came to include a growing number of persons who also had ties to one or more Tendai lineages and who had received Tendai transmissions.

To gain some sense of the complexity of interactions between the medieval Tendai and Hokke traditions during this period, it is useful to look briefly at the life and thought of a particular figure, Gyōgakuin Nitchō (1422–1500), eleventh *kanju* of Minobu and the leading scholar among the *itchi* faction of the Hokkeshū during the Muromachi period.[61] Nitchō was born at Usami in Izu. His father died when he was young, and at age eight he took the tonsure under Ichijō-bō Nisshutsu (1381–1459) of the Minobu lineage, who had founded a temple called the Hongakuji at Mishima in Izu Province. Nisshutsu, said to have formerly been a Tendai monk called Zeshō and an instructor at the Senba *dangisho,* had converted to the Hokkeshū and studied under the ninth *kanju* of Minobu, Nichigaku. As a young man, Nitchō also went to study at Senba, possibly at Nisshutsu's direction. Colophons of texts he transcribed while studying there place him at Senba from 1440 through 1445, that is, from the age of nineteen to twenty-four. However, this does not seem to have been a period of continuous residence. In 1441 he journeyed to Sado to visit the site of Nichiren's exile, and he seems also to have made a trip to Kyoto sometime during the Kakitsu era (1441–1443).

Several Hokke monks seem to have been studying at Senba at this time. The colophon to one Senba document records that the principals in a debate conducted in 1441 at the Butsuzō-bō, one of the major temples of the Senba complex, were both from the Kuonji in Kōshū (Kai Province), a clear reference to Mt. Minobu.[62] Of a number of fellow students mentioned in Nitchō's colophons, two have been conclusively identified: Izumi-kō of the Myōrenji in Kyoto, and Daiho-kō of the Shōgyōin of the Myōkakuji, also in Kyoto.[63] Their presence shows that—whether because of personal connections or because of friction between Mt. Hiei and Hokke temples in the capital—Hokke monks came to study at Senba from as far away as Kyoto, rather than going to Mt. Hiei. Among those whose signatures appear with that of Nitchō in colophons as transcribers, one Shūbō-kō has been tentatively identified as Myōkōin Nichii

(1421–1473), later seventh abbot of the Hondoji in Hiraga, a temple in Nichirō's line.[64]

While at Senba, Nitchō studied at the Butsuzō-bō and transcribed a number of debate texts; his colophons indicate that he copied these texts in preparation for the debates that constituted the core of the *dangisho*'s system of doctrinal training and which were held in conjunction with events of the temple's ritual calendar. Events at Senba accompanied by formal debates included the Satsurai-e, a ceremony held in the fourth month honor of the Sannō deity of the Hie shrine complex, a branch of which had been established at Senba as at most Kantō Tendai temples. The use of debate to celebrate the deity is thought to be a reenactment of the tradition that Jie Daishi Ryōgen, eighteenth *zasu* of Mt. Hiei, conducted a debate on the Hie shrine precincts and so brought about the prosperity of the Tendai debate tradition.[65] Others included the Ryōgon-e or Ryōgon-kō, formal lectures accompanied by debate, held to honor Genshin, who had lived at the Ryōgon-in at Yokawa, and which were used for the transmission of Eshin doctrine. Also there was the Kannon-kō, held in honor of the bodhisattva Kannon, who was enshrined as the central object of worship at the Muryōjuji, another of the main temples of the Senba complex.[66] One of Nitchō's colophons contains the triple invocation: "Namu-myōhō-renge-kyō, Namu-Sannō-nijū-issha [*Namu* to the twenty-one Sannō shrines], Namu-Jie-Daishi," hinting at the integration of his Nichiren faith with the conventions of the Tendai temple where he was studying.[67]

Nitchō is said to have inherited from his teacher Nisshutsu the abbacy of the Mishima Hongakuji in Izu and later that also of its branch temple, the Hongakuji in Kamakura. However, these must have been administered by representatives while Nitchō set off for further study.[68] He studied Confucian texts at the Ashikaga College in Shimotsuke and the various schools of Buddhism in Kyoto, Nara, and on Mt. Hiei. In Kyoto Nitchō is said to have studied Nichiren doctrine with Shinnyo-in Nichijū (1406–1486), a student of Daishōin Nichien, ninth abbot of the Myō-kakuji. As a young man, Nichijū also studied with Jōgen of the Sugiu line on Mt. Hiei, where he called himself Jōken, as well as with the Tendai scholars Keishun and Yūsai of the Kashiwabara and Kanasana Kantō lineages, respectively.[69] On Hiei Nitchō is said to have met the Tendai scholar Taigei, a student of Eigen of the Kanasana *dangisho,* and converted him to the Hokkeshū; Taigei, who took the name Engyōin Nichii, would eventually succeed Nitchō as twelfth *kanju* of Minobu.[70] Using the Mishima Hongakuji as his base, Nitchō is also said to have traveled to preach and practice *shakubuku* in Kai, Shinano, Suruga, Musashi, and Sagami. In 1454, at Koishiwa (or Kitaishiwa) in Kai, he is said to have been attacked during a sermon by followers of other sects, headed by one Yajirō, younger brother to the deputy of the *shugo* or provincial military governor. Being driven off with four of his disciples, Nitchō is said—in the best Hokke tradition—to have rejoiced at meeting persecution for the *Lotus Sūtra's* sake.[71]

Nitchō became the eleventh *kanju* or chief abbot of Minobu in 1462, a post he held until 1499. Since the beginning of the Muromachi period, the major strength of the Hokkeshū had shifted to Kyoto, the center of political power. Nitchō, however, was resolved to establish Minobu in Kai Province in the Kantō—where Nichiren had spent his last years and where his tomb was located—as a major Hokke institution and center of practice. He relocated the main temple structures at Minobu to a broader and more advantageous site and had built a number of halls, lodgings, and a pagoda to enshrine Nichiren's ashes. He established Minobu's calendar of ritual observances and instituted a system of debate training similar to that of the Tendai *dangisho.* The events marked by formal debates that Nitchō established included the Mitsugan-kō or Kōshi-e, held on the third of every month, the death date of Nikō, founder of the Minobu lineage; the Soshi-e, held monthly on the thirteenth, the date of Nichiren's death; and the Risshō-e, held yearly to commemorate the founding of the sect. He initiated in addition the Reikō Mondō, a debate that dealt with the doctrines of other sects; and also a Jie Daishi-kō and a Sannō-kō, presumably borrowings from the tradition of Senba.[72] Nitchō appears to have judged many of these debates himself, and voluminous records of them are contained in the Minobu archives. These accounts also record the presence of monks from a number of Hokke lineages, suggesting that they came from all branches of the sect to study with Nitchō.[73] Judging from the evidence of debate records as well as Nitchō's colophons and his inscriptions on mandalas conferred on disciples, he is thought to have had more than seventy disciples.[74] He also seems to have acquired a number of transmission texts, representing a variety of Tendai and Hokke lineages, and to have referred to these in developing his systematization of Nichiren doctrine.[75]

In addition to his administrative and pedagogical achievements, Nitchō made great efforts in the collecting, copying, and cataloguing of Nichiren's writings. Nitchō's own extant writings are voluminous, including five commentaries on the *Lotus Sūtra;* the *Ganso kedō ki,* a biography of Nichiren; the *Gosho kenmon,* a collection of commentaries in forty-four fascicles on several of Nichiren's major essays; several works on Nichiren doctrine; numerous essays on T'ien-t'ai/Tendai thought, spanning the entire tradition; and three writings on the doctrines of other schools. It would be impossible to outline the thought of so prolific a writer in a brief space; however, some of his representative ideas may be highlighted so as to indicate the influence of medieval Tendai thought on his interpretation of Nichiren's teachings.[76]

First of all, Nitchō appropriates the doctrinal classification of the "four-

fold rise and fall" to make clear the absolute and final status of the
daimoku. For example, he enumerates three meanings of realizing Buddhahood at the stage of verbal identity *(myōji-soku)*, that is, from the perspectives of the trace teaching, the origin teaching, and the "inconceivable sea of effects" of the origin teaching, "effects" here meaning what
the Buddha has realized:

> The trace teaching represents the realization of Buddhahood that is
> enlightenment acquired after practice *(shikaku)*. It is attaining the first
> *bhūmi*, the realization in this life of [the stage of] acquiescence to the
> unbornness of the dharmas. Hearing the [doctrine of] the true as-
> pect of the mind is called "realizing Buddhahood." With the origin
> teaching, one realizes the forms of the original realization of Bud-
> dhahood that is innately inherent and unproduced. As for the real-
> ization of Buddhahood in terms of Myōhō-renge-kyō, the inconceiv-
> able sea of effects of the origin teaching: Simply chanting Namu-
> myōhō-renge-kyō is the inner enlightenment of the Buddhas. . . . The
> realization of Buddhahood in terms of the *daimoku* is the final, ulti-
> mate inner enlightenment.[77]

Here, as in a number of medieval Tendai texts, the trace teaching is
associated with a linear process of enlightenment that proceeds from
practice to attainment, and with the mind; while the origin teaching is
associated with innate enlightenment and with the specific forms of phenomena, which are all said to be enlightened inherently. But transcending even the origin teaching is the *daimoku*, "Myōhō-renge-kyō, the
inconceivable sea of effects of the origin teaching."

The *daimoku* is concretely described in Nitchō's writings as the ultimate reality to which the Buddha is awakened, prior to the distinction
of the origin and trace teachings *(honjaku mibun)*. "The Dharma-essence
that encompasses provisional and true, trace and origin, in a single moment of thought is called the title. . . . The inner enlightenment in which
provisional and true, origin and trace, are not yet divided is called Myōhō-
renge-kyō."[78] The notion of the ultimate reality to which the Buddha is
awakened as prior to the conceptual and verbal distinctions of doctrinal
categories is, as we have seen, common to a number of medieval Tendai
transmissions. However, where these texts define this reality as *shikan* or
kanjin, Nitchō identifies it as "Myōhō-renge-kyō." Nichiren, as we have
seen, saw the *daimoku*, the three thousand realms in a single thought-
moment in actuality, as "hidden in the depths" of the "Fathoming the
Lifespan" chapter of the origin teaching; for Nichiren, however, it is not
"prior to" the trace-origin distinction but premised upon it. Gyōgakuin
Nitchō's idea of the *daimoku* as embodying an ultimate Dharma prior to
the distinction of origin and trace teachings shows influence of "strong

readings" of the fourfold rise and fall that understood *kanjin* or *shikan* as pointing to a reality independent of the sūtra text. This element in his interpretation may derive from the thinking of Shinnyo-in Nichijū, with whom Nitchō had studied in Kyoto.[79]

This ultimate Dharma, the *daimoku,* was for Nitchō none other than the innate enlightenment of all beings. Like his Tendai contemporaries, Nitchō interpreted the revelation of Śākyamuni Buddha's attainment of Buddhahood, described in the "Fathoming the Lifespan" chapter of the *Lotus Sūtra,* not as marking him off as a unique or transcendent figure, but as pointing to the inherently enlightened nature of all:

> This Buddha's realization of enlightenment is without beginning. In the final analysis, this is the Buddha without beginning or end. And such being the case, we, too, are without beginning or end. The ten realms all from the outset constantly abide and are without beginning or end; where one realizes this, the unproduced triple-bodied [Tathâgata] appears of itself. This is called the revelation of the realization [of Buddhahood] as a principle [originally inherent in all beings]. Therefore, [the Buddha's] actual realization [in the distant past] is [merely] an inducement. The point is the revelation of the constant abiding of the ten realms.[80]

The concrete instance of Śākyamuni's attainment of Buddhahood in the distant past *(jijō)* is merely to illustrate that all beings of the ten realms are, in principle, Buddhas inherently *(rijō).* Ultimately, the Buddha is not a person, whether transcendent or historical, but the all-pervasive triple-bodied Tathâgata that "constantly abides." Nitchō interprets the triple-bodied Tathâgata almost exclusively in terms of ordinary worldlings. For example, the Dharma body corresponds to principle; the recompense body to wisdom; and the manifested body to compassion, which are innate in all beings.[81] An alternative reading invokes the three categories of "nonenlightenment," "original enlightenment," and "acquired enlightenment" that derive from the *Awakening of Faith.* Prior to the arising of a single thought in the practitioner's mind (i.e., before conceptual or verbal distinctions) is the "triple-bodied Tathâgata in terms of innate principle, which is the original ground" *(honji honri sanjin)*—this corresponds to "nonenlightenment." The practitioner's wisdom capable of discerning the true nature of the thought-moment corresponds to "the unproduced triple-bodied Tathâgata of original enlightenment" *(musa hongaku sanjin),* and the actual moment of discernment, to the "triple-bodied Tathâgata of acquired enlightenment, which is produced" *(usa shikaku sanjin).*[82] Fundamental to Nitchō's various readings is the triple-bodied Tathâgata as the principle originally innate in all phenomena. The "real" Buddha is not the transcendent figure of Śākyamuni, but the Buddhahood inherent in all beings just as they are. In making such interpretations, Nitchō drew on medieval Tendai categories and terminology (such as "original enlightenment" and "unproduced triple-bodied Tathâgata") to interpret that aspect of Nichiren's thought which sees "Śākyamuni, the ancient Buddha without beginning" as "our mind" or "our blood and flesh," but took less account of Nichiren's Śākyamuni who is "sovereign, teacher, and parent" of the Sahā wold. This focus on the immanentalist side of Nichiren's teaching, and the use of medieval Tendai categories to elaborate it, was by no means limited to Nitchō but was quite widespread in Muromachi readings of Nichiren doctrine.

It should also be noted, however, that Nitchō's strong doctrinal emphasis on the original enlightenment of ordinary worldlings was modified by the presence of other elements in the context of practice. For example:

> [Question]: By upholding the truth and not abandoning it, one eventually arrives at the fruit of Buddhahood—if this is the case, then whether or not Buddhahood is realized depends solely on the mind. The power of the sūtra, it would appear, is not involved. How should this be understood?

> Answer: This is an essential matter. When it is said that one who maintains one's resolve without abandoning it will achieve great merit, in reliance upon what do we understand that great merit to be achieved? By relying for one's good roots upon the *Lotus Sūtra* and not losing one's resolve, any merit can be achieved. Thus even the slightest good roots can result in the fruit of Buddhahood. But should one not rely upon the *Lotus Sūtra,* no matter how vast one's good roots may be, one will not arrive at the fruit of Buddhahood.[83]

Or again:

> All persons, by receiving the Wonderful Dharma transmitted by Bodhisattva Superior Conduct and having faith in it, will eradicate within this lifetime the delusions of the three poisons of greed, hatred, and folly [accumulated] since beginningless vast kalpas and, when this life is ended, with their final breath, shall at once realize the cherished desire of going to [the Pure Land of] Eagle Peak.[84]

Side by side with his discussion of realizing enlightenment in the moment of chanting the *daimoku* are notions of realizing Buddhahood at the moment of death or going at death to the Pure Land of Eagle Peak.[85] Nitchō's case thus supports the suggestion, offered earlier in the context of medieval Tendai, that original enlightenment discourse was a rhetorical strategy rooted in commitment to a philosophical position of nonduality; in actual practice, it often existed side by side and was constrained by ideas that did not necessarily cohere with it logically, including the need to rely on superior powers (such as Buddhas or sūtras), the importance of cultivating lifelong faith, and birth after death in a pure land.

Gyōgakuin Nitchō affords a clear example of the close interaction between Tendai and Hokke traditions in the Muromachi period. An abbot of the leading Hokke temple in the Kantō and famed as the "restorer" of Minobu, he had studied both at a Tendai *dangisho* in the east and also on Mt. Hiei. He adopted medieval Tendai categories such as the fourfold rise and fall and notions of original enlightenment in his interpretation of Nichiren doctrine and instituted elements on Mt. Minobu of ritual and pedagogical practices borrowed from the Senba *dangisho*. He also converted leading Tendai scholars, such as his disciple and successor Nichii. Nichii's successor Hōju-in Nichiden (1482–1548)—formerly Jōkai—was also a convert from Tendai, a scholar of the Ekō-bō lineage of the Danna school.[86] Monks of Nitchō's lineage held the abbacy of Minobu up through the nineteenth *kanju*, Hōun-in Nichidō (1552–1601). Nitchō's doctrinal interpretations dominated the Minobu school of the Hokkeshū throughout the same period and were broadly representative of trends in medieval Hokke thought in general.

Not all Hokke scholars, it should be noted, were entirely sympathetic to the adoption of trends in medieval Tendai thought. One important exception was Keirin-bō Nichiryū (1385–1464), who, with Nitchō, is regarded as one of the two "pillars" of medieval Hokkeshū scholarship. Nichiryū, a leading figure of the *shōretsu* faction, was critical of the fourfold rise and fall and maintained emphasis on the transcendent person of Śākyamuni Buddha, rather than the Dharma innate in all persons.[87] On the whole, however, given the milieu of intellectual exchange and the receiving of transmissions from multiple lineages, medieval Hokke scholars drew freely on the medieval Tendai style of doctrinal expression in their readings of Nichiren's teachings.

By the middle of the sixteenth century, intercourse between the monks of Minobu and other Hokke lineages with Senba and other Kantō Tendai *dangisho* seems to have fallen off. War between the houses of Uesugi and Gohōjō in 1537 laid waste a number of temples in Musashi and Ueno provinces, including the Muryōjuji at Senba. Moreover, political changes spanning the latter half of the sixteenth century and the beginning of the seventeenth greatly affected the main body of the Hokkeshū in both western and eastern Japan, leading to new forms of sectarian organization and doctrinal interpretation and bringing about the end of what may be considered the "medieval period" in the history of the Hokkeshū.[88]

Almost all research to date on the intellectual history of the Hokkeshū during the medieval period has been done by the Nichirenshū scholars of Risshō University, often through painstaking work on unpublished primary documents. One finds in their evaluation, however, a tendency to see the incorporation of medieval Tendai thought into the Hokke doctrine of this time as a departure from the putative purity and originality of Nichiren's teaching and a compromise with the Taimitsu-influenced Tendai tradition that he had criticized. Asai Yōrin, who was among the very first to become aware of Muromachi period Hokke incorporations of medieval Tendai ideas, sounded the note that others have repeated:

> The unconditional importation of this naturalistic, original enlightenment-influenced esoteric Tendai thought casts doubt upon the particularity of our sect's doctrine. . . . Scholars of our sect in succession studied at [the Tendai *dangisho* at] Kashiwabara, or at Senba, or at Kanasana. Not only did they receive the transmission of the seven-article doctrine, the core of medieval Tendai, but they appear to have praised it and become infatuated with it.[89]

Shigyō Kaishū similarly remarks, of the Minobu Hokke scholars who studied at Tendai *dangisho:*

> At the outset, [the purpose of] their study of medieval Tendai doctrine was probably to acquire a basis for organizing their own sectarian doctrine. As to its result, however, one senses that, in their efforts to incorporate medieval Tendai doctrine, they instead became infatuated with that doctrine, and in the end turned into followers of it.[90]

Asai, Shigyō, and their successors were operating from a hermeneutical perspective which sought, through a rigorous sifting by modern critical methods of genuine from apocryphal texts, to recover the pure, authentic doctrine of the founder, Nichiren, as a standard for evaluating subsequent developments and establishing normative sectarian doctrine. However, this "return to the source" perspective was itself the product of a modern historical moment and would have been quite foreign to Muromachi period Nichiren Hokke scholar-monks, who, like many Japanese intellectuals of their time, valued not only original texts but the "dis-covering" of their deepest meanings in subsequent *kuden.* In view of their need to ensure the instruction of their disciples in Tendai doctrine and their close involvement with medieval Tendai institutions such as the Kantō *dangisho,* it is not surprising in the least that they adopted much of the language and form of the Tendai of their day and incorporated it into their readings of Nichiren's teaching. In so doing, they often chose to emphasize the immanentalist aspects of Nichiren's thought, clearly regarding these as more important than other elements. However, to see this as an "infatuation" with medieval Tendai thought that compromised the originality of Nichiren's doctrine is to impose on the past a particular (and problematic) modern sectarian reading of

Nichiren, one that defines his uniqueness as a rejection of Tendai original enlightenment thought. The emphasis on *hongaku* perspectives in the doctrinal writings of Muromachi period Hokke scholars should rather be seen as reflecting the circumstances surrounding that juncture in their sect's history. Having successfully established a new religious institution *(kyōdan)*, monks of the Hokkeshū now had the leisure to explore how their founder's thought might be developed in terms of the intellectual paradigm that reigned in the Buddhist circles of their day—namely, that of original enlightenment.

Doctrine is, moreover, only one of many ways in which religious traditions have historically defined their "particularity," and the Nichiren Hokkeshū was no exception. If the doctrine of medieval Hokke scholars came in many respects to resemble closely that of their Tendai contemporaries, they were at the same time engaged in behavior that very much set them apart as followers of Nichiren. First, the use of the *nichi-gō* in their clerical names immediately identified them with the Hokkeshū. Second, they embraced a distinctive form of Buddhist practice. Regardless of doctrinal interpretation—which varied among lineages— the status of the *daimoku* as the central form of Nichiren Buddhist practice was consistently upheld, although meditation, copying the sūtra, and so forth, were sometimes endorsed as subsidiary good acts. Third, and perhaps most definitively, Hokke monks engaged in *shakubuku,* or rebuking the "wrong views" of other sects, which took the form of assertive proselytizing, doctrinal debate, and the memorializing of government officials. This last activity, known as "admonishing the state" *(kokka kangyō)*, was modeled on Nichiren's memorializing of Hōjō Tokiyori via the *Risshō ankoku ron* and usually entailed submitting a letter of admonition *(mōshijō)* to the ruler—the emperor, or more often the *shogun*— or to his local representatives, warning that all other teachings should be discarded and the *Lotus Sūtra* alone embraced, to ensure the peace of the country. Going up to Kyoto to "admonish the state" is said to have been almost de rigeur for the heads of the various Kantō Hokke lineages.[91] Such confrontational activities carried a certain risk, and Hokkeshū chronicles and hagiographies celebrate those monks who endured official sanctions, even imprisonment and torture, for defying prohibitions against repeated memorializing. The various forms of *shakubuku,* including debate, preaching, and the memorializing of local and high officials, as well the legends that grew up around those who excelled in these endeavors, comprised a distinctive Hokkeshū culture, and the Hokke monks spoken of in the preceding paragraphs were very much a part of it. In 1436, Nitchō's teacher Nisshutsu challenged and defeated in debate the influential Tendai monk Shingai of the Kongōhōkaiji, braving the wrath of Shingai's powerful patron, the *kanrei* or shogunal representative, Ashikaga Mochiuji.[92] Nitchō himself, as noted above, prac-

ticed *shakubuku* in the Kantō prior to his appointment as *kanju* of Minobu. Nichiden, a close disciple of Nitchō and the thirteenth abbot of
Minobu, went up to Kyoto repeatedly to memorialize the shogun. Such
men were hardly dependent on doctrine alone to define their sectarian
orthodoxy; their practice of *shakubuku*, emerging as it did from the stance
of *Lotus* exclusivism peculiar to the Hokkeshū, would have set them apart
as followers of Nichiren far more effectively than doctrinal originality.

Even so, it would still be inappropriate to regard medieval Hokke doctrine as a mere offshoot of medieval Tendai. In appropriating elements
of medieval Tendai to interpret Nichiren's teachings, Hokke scholars
thoroughly assimilated and developed their own readings of these appropriations and used them to begin producing what may be regarded
as a new, distinctively Nichirenist mode of *hongaku* discourse. Some aspects of this discourse are discussed below.

Transmissions Concerning the Mandala

In the Muromachi period, different lineages within the Hokkeshū began to produce and transmit what purport to be records of secret oral
transmissions containing their distinctive interpretation of Nichiren's
teachings. This adoption of *kuden* forms on one hand reflected trends
in the broader culture; by this time, secret master-disciple transmission
had become the normative mode of passing on knowledge in religion,
literature, and the arts. More specifically, however, it was undoubtedly
a product of Hokke-Tendai interactions. Hokke monks studying at
Tendai *dangisho* or on Mt. Hiei would have been exposed to Tendai *kuden* literature, while Tendai scholar-monks converting to the Hokkeshū
would also have been familiar with these forms. It is also possible that
increasing rivalry among Hokke lineages may have encouraged adoption of medieval Tendai forms of *kuden* and secret transmissions as a way
of asserting the superior authority of one's own school.[93]

The greatest number of Hokke *kuden* are devoted to secret teachings
concerning the calligraphic mandala that Nichiren had devised. This
mandala, variously termed the *daimandara* or *gohonzon*, continued to occupy a vital place in Hokkeshū practice and ritual after Nichiren's death,
as it had during his lifetime. Mandalas were enshrined as the object of
worship in Hokke temples, either by themselves or behind a Buddha
image.[94] Abbots produced them for the parishioners of their temples as
personal *honzon*, and teachers sometimes inscribed them for disciples
as proof of the transmission of lineage.[95] However, Nichiren's own writing contains very little in the way of detailed explanation of the mandala. Probably in response to the need for explanations of this ritually
central object, interpretations of the mandala were elaborated after his
death in the various Hokke lineages. Written down, these take the form

of master-to-disciple *kirikami* transmissions or collections of such transmissions, and some, like medieval Tendai *kuden* texts, assume the convention of secret transmission. For example, in this text of the Fuji lineage
of Nikkō:

> This [transmission] represents the great matter of our sect, the inner
> meaning of its secret repository. Do not transmit it to anyone who lacks
> the proper capacity, not even for a thousand in gold. I ask that you
> choose a[n appropriate] Dharma-vessel from among the disciples and
> confer this secretly in a personal interview.[96]

Or this one, from the Hama lineage of Nisshō:

> The above doctrines represent the oral transmissions of successive gen-
> erations of our school, first set down on paper during the abbacy of
> Nichiden. [The choice of] the person to whom it is transferred should
> be restricted to those who have: first, faith; second, wisdom; and third,
> lack of arrogance. . . . Beyond that, it should be transferred only to a
> single person.[97]

It is hard to determine exactly when these transmission texts were compiled. While some are attributed—probably retrospectively—to immediate disciples of Nichiren, or to their close followers, a greater number
identify themselves as collections made by Muromachi period Hokke
scholar-monks of oral and *kirikami* transmissions passed down through
their respective lineages. Most appear to have been compiled roughly
around the latter half of the fifteenth century. How long the transmissions may have been in existence before being written down is, of course,
all but impossible to judge.[98] Though many of them purport to represent the secret transmissions of particular schools and lineages within
the Hokkeshū, overlapping content suggests that considerable communication and sharing of transmissions occurred among the various
schools.[99] This too parallels the Tendai case, where, despite a rhetoric of
absolute secrecy and transmission to a single disciple, ample evidence
exists of individuals receiving more than one transmission and of considerable exchange among lineages.

   The formation and compilation of these transmissions appears to have
roughly coincided with the peak of intellectual exchange between Hokke
scholar-monks and their counterparts at Tendai *dangisho*. Not surpris-
ingly, they appropriate much of the vocabulary and interpretive style of
medieval Tendai *kuden* literature to discuss Nichiren's mandala. Though
there are individual differences of interpretation to be found among transmissions of different lineages, their commonalities are far more striking.
Generally, the articles included in individual collections can be grouped
into four categories, namely, transmissions concerning (1) the significance of the mandala as a whole; (2) the significance of the individual

figures whose names appear on the mandala and of their relationship
to the central inscription of the *daimoku;* (3) the significance of established conventions concerning the inscription of the mandala; and (4)
the relationship of the *kami* appearing on the mandala to the *Lotus Sūtra*
and to Nichiren. Here we will touch briefly on each of these.

First, the mandala is interpreted from an immanentalist view. It is seen
not as representing the enlightenment of an individual transcendent
Buddha, but as a ritual object that enables the practitioner to discern
and actualize a realm of enlightenment already innate within oneself.
Since the ten realms are depicted by the names of their representatives
on the mandala, this innate realm of enlightenment is usually discussed
in terms of the mutual inclusion of the ten realms:

> The ultimate teaching of the *Lotus Sūtra* is the original inherence of
> the ten realms. When you face this object of worship, the realm of one-
> self, the realm of the Buddha, and the realm of living beings are all
> the essence of the Wonderful Dharma, the suchness which is original
> enlightenment. . . .
>
> Now [in our school, we] do not establish contemplation [as the
> method of realizing the three thousand realms in one thought-moment].
> We display it on a sheet of paper, so that one can directly see, in a sin-
> gle thought-moment, three thousand realms.[100]

> What is the true mutual inclusion of the ten realms? The teacher
> [Nichiren] said: "The seven characters that are chanted are the Bud-
> dha realm. We who chant them are the nine realms. When the cause
> and effect of the four teachings are demolished, the true cause and
> effect of the ten realms is revealed." At that time, we are the unpro-
> duced triple-bodied [Tathâgata], the true Buddha *(jitsubutsu),* who
> dwells in the Land of Tranquil Light. The Buddha who appeared in
> this world was a manifested trace *(suijaku),* a provisional Buddha who
> benefits the beings through provisional teachings. Keep this secret!
> Keep this secret![101]

Such readings are on the one hand rooted in Nichiren's treatise *Kanjin honzon shō,* which discusses the object of worship as embodying the
mutual inclusion of the ten dharma realms and the importance of believing that one's own deluded thought-moment contains the Buddha
realm. However, there is also strong evidence of medieval Tendai
thought, in the privileging of the ordinary worldling over the Buddha
who appeared in this world—something rarely found in Nichiren's authenticated writings. As noted earlier, it was often the immanentalist side
of Nichiren's doctrine that most engaged his Muromachi period successors, who also drew on medieval Tendai conventions in interpreting
it. The second quotation immediately above, for example, represents an

instance of the reversals common in Tendai *kanjin*-style readings informed by notions of original enlightenment: The Buddha depicted in the sūtra is dismissed as a mere provisional Buddha, while the ordinary worldling is identified as the true Buddha.

The individual figures whose names are written on the mandala are also interpreted as representing not themselves as historical or legendary personages, but the originally inherent reality of the practitioner. For example, the *Honzon sando sōden,* a transmission of the Fuji school, discusses the two Buddhas, Śākyamuni and Many Jewels, who appear in the *Lotus Sūtra* and whose names flank the central inscription of the *daimoku* on Nichiren's mandala. In Chih-i's interpretation of the *Lotus,* these two Buddhas seated side by side in the jeweled stūpa are said to represent the nonduality, realized in meditative practice, of truth as object of contemplation (*kyō,* represented by Many Jewels) and the wisdom by which it is cognized (*chi,* represented by Śākyamuni).[102] The *Honzon sando sōden* appropriates this reading as follows:

> What is this nonduality of object and wisdom? It is precisely the [round of] birth and death that we living beings have undergone since the beginningless past until the present. . . . Many Jewels having already entered nirvāṇa represents death. Śākyamuni having not yet entered nirvāṇa represents birth. . . . Many Jewels represents the aspect of death in our repeated deaths, and Śākyamuni represents the aspect of birth in our successive births. The two Buddhas seated in the stūpa represent precisely birth and death and also death and birth. This oneness of birth and death is the great nirvāṇa that is unborn and unperishing.[103]

Other figures on the mandala are similarly interpreted in Hokke transmissions to represent the innate enlightenment of ordinary worldlings. For example, the two esoteric deities Fudō and Aizen, whose Sanskrit seed characters appear on the mandala, are discussed as follows: "As for Fudō, his black color represents the evil deeds performed [in the round of] transmigration in the [threefold] world. And Aizen's red color represents the intensity of sexual desire. In the Dharma-position of the Wonderful Dharma (*myōhō*), they represent the worldly passions being precisely *bodhi* and birth and death being precisely nirvāṇa."[104] This is a standard Mikkyō explanation of the two deities, here assimilated to Nichiren's mandala, which occurs in a number of Hokke transmissions. Another frequent interpretation regarding figures on the mandala takes the four leaders of the bodhisattvas who emerge from the earth—Superior Conduct, Boundless Conduct, Firm Conduct, and Pure Conduct—as representing the four universal elements of fire, wind, earth, and water, which form all things. Thus the entire dharma realm is seen as the four bodhisattvas:

The four bodhisattvas who are the leaders of the Buddha's original disciples manifest themselves as the four great elements. . . . Because [one constantly] receives and makes use of the four elements of earth, water, fire, and wind that comprise the dharma realm, they might evoke no particular feeling of respect, but when one inquires into their essence, then the benefits they confer are unexpectedly vast. Day and night, the land and its inhabitants *(eshō)*, and the myriad things all display the benefits conferred by the four bodhisattvas.[105]

This equation of the four leaders of the bodhisattvas who emerged out of the earth with the four universal elements appears in medieval Tendai commentaries on the *Lotus Sūtra* and also in some writings attributed to Nichiren.[106] This identification is developed through the *kanjin*-style hermeneutical technique of association by isomorphic resemblance discovered between the behavior of the four elements and the names of the four bodhisattvas. Earth is stable and is associated with "Firm Conduct." Water cleanses and is consequently identified with "Pure Conduct." Fire rises and is therefore assimilated to "Superior Conduct." Wind is unrestrained and is thus equated with "Boundless Conduct." In the following transmission on the mandala, attributed to Nichizō, a disciple of Nichirō of the Hikigayatsu lineage, the identification of the four bodhisattvas with the four elements is invoked to suggest that the Wonderful Dharma shall, in the *Lotus Sūtra's* words, be "widely declared and spread" *(kōsen-rufu)*:

The placement of Superior Conduct [together with Boundless Conduct] and Pure Conduct [together with Firm Conduct] opposite one other [on either side of the central inscription of the mandala] expresses the meaning that the fire of wisdom represented by Superior Conduct, in dependence on the wind represented by Boundless Conduct, shall be widely declared *(kōsen)*, and that the water of wisdom represented by Pure Conduct, in conformity with the earth represented by Firm [Conduct], shall spread *(rufu)*.[107]

A number of conventions surround the style of brushstrokes and the writing of particular characters on the mandala, and the Hokke *kuden* texts contain transmissions explaining these conventions. For example, calligraphic style is assimilated via the hermeneutical technique of association by resemblance to the exclusive doctrine of the Hokkeshū and its ethos of assertive proselytizing: "As to the way of writing the characters: According to secular transmissions, there are various styles, such as the suspended needle, fish scales, tiger claws, and sword shapes. . . . In the Dharma of this sect, *shakubuku* is regarded as our pride, so the brush method of sword shapes and tiger claws should naturally be used."[108]

Similarly, the extremely long, bold, diagonal strokes employed in writ-

ing the central inscription of the *daimoku,* often extending into the surrounding characters, are described as representing "the mind profoundly compassionate, assiduous in propagation, that seeks to spread
the Wonderful Dharma throughout Jambudvīpa [i.e., the world]. They
mean that, like the flow of water that never ceases, Nichiren's compassion is vast and great."[109]

We have already mentioned that some sections of these transmission
texts deal with individual figures whose names are inscribed on the mandala. Among these figures are the *kami* Hachiman and Tenshō Daijin,
who represented for Nichiren the deities of Japan. The specific transmissions dealing with these two figures represent one aspect of the
specifically Nichiren Buddhist appropriations of *kami* that would come
to be called "Hokke Shintō." While not nearly as developed as those of
Ryōbu Shintō or Sannō Shintō, these transmissions attempt, using the
kanjin-style hermeneutical techniques of word play and association by
resemblance, to identify *kami* with the sacred sites and persons of the
Hokkeshū. For example:

> Śākyamuni appeared in the Western realm [India] and, in accordance
> with the original intent of all Buddhas, preached the *Sūtra of the Won-
> derful Dharma of the Lotus Blossom* and declared, "Now this threefold
> world is all my domain." In our country, he appeared as Tenshō Dai-
> jin [the Sun Goddess], and, through the ruler, protects honest peo-
> ple. This means that Śākyamuni and the Sun Goddess are one entity.
> In the Final Dharma age, he appeared as Nichiren, who made mani-
> fest the essential Dharma [of the *daimoku*], which is the true intent of
> the Buddhas. Thus Śākyamuni, [Bodhisattva] Superior Conduct, the
> sun *kami*, and Nichiren are simply one entity. One should reflect on
> these [names]: Sun Seed [an epithet of Śākyamuni], Sun Deity *(nis-
> shin),* and Sun Lotus [Nichiren].[110]

Equations of specific Buddhist and Shinto deities often involve claims
about the legitimacy and authority of particular institutions. Here the
authority of the Sun Goddess and the throne are assimilated to the
Hokkeshū via the person of Nichiren, carrying an implicit challenge to
the authority of other religious traditions, such as the Sannō Shintō of
Mt. Hiei, which also identifies Śākyamuni with the Sun Goddess enshrined at Ise, or the esoteric traditions of both Tendai and Shingon that
equated Dainichi with the Sun Goddess. The identification of Nichiren
with the Sun Goddess is especially pronounced in transmissions of the
Fuji school, which exalt the status of Nichiren to that of the original Buddha. Consider, for example, this passage from the *Ubuya sōjō no koto,* a
Fuji transmission that deals not with the mandala specifically, but with
Nichiren's parentage and the significance of his name. It presents itself
as Byakuren Ajari Nikkō's transcription of Nichiren's words:

"Nichiren" is the natural name of Mt. Fuji. Fuji is [simply] the name
of the district. [The mountain's] real name is Dainichi-renge-zan
[Great Sun Lotus Blossom Mountain]. Because of my practice of the
Middle Way, the country is thus called Nihon [Sun Origin], and its
kami is the Sun Deity. The Buddha's childhood name was Crown Prince
Sun Seed, and my childhood name was Zennichi [Good Sun]. My temporary [monastic] name was Zeshō [written "person born under the
sun"], and my true name is Nichiren.[111]

Here again, Śākyamuni, the Sun Goddess, and Nichiren are identified
by the shared element of "sun" in their respective names. By one of the
temporal reversals common in *kanjin*-style interpretations, the word
"sun" in the name of both the country and its major deity are made to
derive from the name of Nichiren. Mt. Fuji, location of the first temple
in Nikkō's lineage, is also drawn into the equation. Medieval documents
of the Fuji school employ such interpretations in arguing that the *kaidan*
of the origin teaching should eventually be erected at Mt. Fuji.[112]

In this way, virtually all Hokke lineages drew on the *kuden* genre, conventions of secret transmission, notions of original enlightenment, *kanjin*-style interpretation, and other forms associated with medieval Tendai
in explicating Nichiren's mandala that served as their focus of practice.
Now let us consider how these forms were uniquely appropriated in the
distinctive doctrine of one particular lineage of the Hokkeshū.

The Particular Doctrines of the Fuji School

As rivalries developed among the various lineages of the Hokkeshū, different branches within the sect began to formulate distinct interpretations of Nichiren's teaching by which they each asserted their own legitimacy. However, no Hokke lineage has been more sharply divided from
the rest of the tradition, or developed so distinct a doctrinal position, as
the Nikkō or Fuji school, which derives from Byakuren Ajari Nikkō
(1246–1333). The Fuji school is best known today through one of its descendants, Nichiren Shōshū, with whom the Sōka Gakkai—largest of
Japan's contemporary "new religions"—was affiliated from the time of
its founding until 1991.[113] From about the sixteenth century on, Fuji doctrine divided into two streams, that of the Taisekiji, located near Mt. Fuji,
and that of the Yōhōji in Kyoto. Since Taisekiji doctrine became dominant within the Nikkō school during the Edo period, Fuji doctrine is often referred to—not entirely accurately—as synonymous with that of the
Taisekiji.[114] The interpretations discussed here precede the split but
would become particularly characteristic of Taisekiji doctrine. While the
Fuji school has long claimed to represent the only legitimate form of
Nichiren Buddhism, other branches of the Hokkeshū have denounced

it as heretical.[115] Like the scholar-monks of other Hokke lineages, those of the Fuji school drew on medieval Tendai thought in systematizing their doctrine. However, they did so in a particular way that supported their distinctive reading of Nichiren's teaching.

The Fuji school was the product of the first schism within the Hokkeshū, which is said to have occurred in the following manner.[116] After Nichiren's death, in accordance with his wishes, the six senior disciples established a rotating custodianship of his grave on Mt. Minobu. Each of the six was to watch over the grave for two months out of the year. However, each had his own local following to attend to, and those in Kamakura had to contend with suppression from *bakufu* officials, which had been renewed following Nichiren's death. The watch was soon reduced from two months to one, and additional monks were added to the rotation. For logistical reasons, these additional monks came largely from among Nikkō's followers, who were based chiefly in Kai and Suruga provinces. Even with these modifications, however, the watch proved difficult to maintain. Within two years, the custodianship system seems to have broken down entirely. When Nikkō arrived at Minobu in 1284 for the founder's third annual memorial service (that is, two years after Nichiren's death), he found the gravesite desolate and neglected and resolved to reside permanently on the mountain in order to protect it.[117] Not long after, Minbu Ajari Nikō, another of the six leading disciples, was able to return to Minobu and took up residence there. While Nikkō held overall responsibility for Kuonji, the temple that had been established on Minobu, Nikō became its doctrinal instructor (*gakutō*). Before long, friction developed between the two. According to Fuji sectarian histories, their disagreement concerned the behavior of Hakii Nanbu Rokurō Sanenaga, the *jitō* or steward of Minobu and lay patron of Nichiren while the latter had lived on the mountain. Sanenaga is said to have committed the following acts, which in Nikkō's mind violated the pure exclusivism of Nichiren's teaching: (1) He enshrined an image of Śākyamuni and refused to heed Nikkō's admonition that such an image was not that of the original Buddha of the "Fathoming the Lifespan" chapter, unless flanked by additional images of the four bodhisattvas; (2) he visited and worshiped at a shrine in Mishima, which Nikkō saw as a violation of Nichiren's teaching, expressed in the *Risshō ankoku ron,* that the *kami* have abandoned the country;[118] and (3) he made offerings for the construction of a Pure Land stūpa in Fuji.[119] Though it was Nikkō who had originally converted Sanenaga, the *jitō* now refused to accept his remonstrances and eventually transferred his allegiance to Nikō, whose more tolerant, accommodating attitude contrasted with Nikko's strict purism. This, it is said, led to a rupture between the two and to Nikkō's departure.

However, this traditional account may be subject to qualification. It is possible that Nikkō felt compelled to leave Minobu not on account of Sanenaga's "slanderous acts," but because, despite Nikkō's own close connections to the mountain, Minbu Ajari Nikō had been chosen over him by the other leading disciples to be Minobu's chief abbot.[120] Whatever the reason, Nikkō felt he could no longer reasonably remain on Minobu, and he left early in 1289.[121] A letter written from him to a follower laments the necessity of his departure.[122] Returning to his home in Suruga Province, he established two temples: the Taisekji in the Fuji district, and the Honmonji in the neighboring district of Omosu. Most of his life was spent at Omosu, where he established a seminary and trained a number of talented followers.

It is by no means certain that Nikkō himself actually intended to break decisively with Nichiren's other leading disciples and establish his own school.[123] Among his disciples, however, the tradition quickly emerged that only he, of the six senior monks, had correctly maintained the purity of Nichiren's teaching. From there, it was but a short step to the claim that Nichiren had in fact transferred his teaching to Nikkō alone. The "Minobu sōjō" (Minobu transmission), an apocryphal transfer document, probably written at least a hundred years after Nichiren's death, says, "Nichiren transfers the Dharma that he spread throughout his lifetime to Byakuren Ajari Nikkō, who is to be the great leader of the propagation of the origin teaching." A second such document, the "Ikegami sōjō" (Ikegami transmission), transfers to Nikkō, in Nichiren's name, the fifty years of Śākyamuni's Dharma preaching and entrusts to him the charge of Minobusan Kuonji.[124] Transmission texts were also produced that purport to be Nikkō's record of oral teachings conferred by Nichiren on him alone, or that were written down by Nikkō for Nichiren. During the Edo period, the doctrines expressed in these transmission texts would be systematized by the Fuji Taisekiji scholar Kenju-in Nichikan (1665–1726) as the framework for interpreting Nichiren's writings. The transmission texts themselves, however, were produced in the Muromachi period and draw heavily on the structures of medieval Tendai thought to formulate and legitimate the unique doctrinal interpretations emerging among Nikkō's later followers.

Two of these transmission texts most important in the history of the Fuji lineage are the *Hon'in-myō shō* (On the original cause) and the *Hyaku rokka sōjō* (106-article transmission), together known as the "two transmission texts" *(ryō kechimyaku sho)*. They were probably compiled roughly at least a hundred years after Nichiren's death.[125] The *Hon'in-myō shō* presents itself as Nichiren's explanation, from the standpoint of the origin teaching, of a secret transmission concerning Chih-i's three major works that Tao-sui purportedly conferred upon Saichō during the latter's journey to China. It follows the structure of the *Sandai shōsho shichimen sōjō kuketsu* (Verbal decisions on the seven-article transmission of [Chih-i's] three major writings), a medieval Tendai text attributed to Saichō, which purports to record this transmission.[126] The *Hyaku rokka sōjō,* which has similarities of content with the *Hon'in-myō shō,* consists of 106 articles concerning the superiority of the origin over the trace teaching. The Fuji school adopted a very strong *shōretsu* position, although, as discussed below, its scholars defined what constitutes the "origin teaching" in a distinctive fashion. A detailed discussion of these two texts is not possible here, but a few of their major ideas can be summarized, showing how they appropriate structures from medieval Tendai thought to assert the legitimacy of the Fuji doctrinal position.

The *Hon'in-myō shō* develops a fourfold interpretation, in increasing levels of profundity, of "name and essence"—two of the five aspects of the *Lotus Sūtra* set forth in Chih-i's *Fa-hua hsüan-i*—name, essence, gist, function, and teaching:

> First, name and essence both have the meaning of impermanence; this corresponds to the sūtras preached before the *Lotus Sūtra* and to the schools based upon them. Second, the essence is real but the name is temporary; this corresponds to the trace teaching and to acquired enlightenment, which is impermanent *(shikaku mujō)*. Third, name and essence are both real; this corresponds to the origin teaching and to original enlightenment, which constantly abides *(hongaku jōjū)*. Fourth, name and essence are [both] inconceivable; this corresponds to the direct realization of the contemplation of the mind *(kanjin jikidatsu)*, which is Namu-myōhō-renge-kyō.[127]

This amounts to a comparative classification of teachings and is structurally comparable to the Eshin school's "fourfold rise and fall." The fourth and highest category, ranking as even more profound than the text of the origin teaching of the *Lotus Sūtra* itself, is here equated with the *daimoku,* the core of Nichiren Buddhist practice, and the direct realization of Buddhahood. This understanding is very similar to the interpretation of Gyōgakuin Nitchō of the Minobu lineage, cited above, and the readings of other Muromachi period Hokke scholars.

As discussed in the previous chapter, Nichiren had spoken of the *daimoku* as "hidden in the depths of the text of the 'Fathoming the Lifespan' chapter" of the origin teaching.[128] His claim here bears some resemblance, and is perhaps partially indebted, to medieval Tendai notions of an ultimate truth or insight—*kanjin*—that is not explicitly stated in the sūtra itself. However, since he held the *daimoku* to be "hidden in the depths" of the origin teaching, it would appear that he did not see it as independent of the sūtra, in the way that some medieval Tendai lineages would come to define "the contemplation of the mind" as a Dharma prior to, and transmitted separately from, the scriptural text. Later scholars within the Nichiren tradition would discuss the origin teaching of the

Lotus Sūtra and the *daimoku* as being inseparably related, respectively, as "doctrinal teaching" *(kyōsō)* and the "contemplation of the mind" *(kanjin),* or as "the surface of the text" *(monjō)* and "the depths of the text" *(montei).* In the early fourteenth century, as mentioned above, a number of Hokke scholars asserted that the sūtra and the *daimoku*—or doctrine and contemplative practice—are nondual *(kyōkan funi),* probably in part to counter the claims of the Eshin Tendai lineage based at Senba that *shikan* is altogether independent of the written *Lotus Sūtra.* (This "nondual" position is also held today by the mainstream Nichiren denomination, Nichirenshū.[129]) Later, however, under the influence of such medieval Tendai ideas as the "fourfold rise and fall" and "*shikan* surpasses the *Lotus,*"the *daimoku* was often said to be superior to the origin teaching. The uniqueness of Fuji doctrine lies in the extreme to which this position was carried, assigning to the *daimoku* the status of a Dharma virtually independent of the *Lotus Sūtra* text.

In the two transmission texts, this argument is developed in the following manner. The origin teaching, the last fourteen chapters of the *Lotus Sūtra,* is said to express the "subtlety of original effect" *(honga-myō),* that is, the state of Buddhahood that Śākyamuni achieved as a result of practice in the distant past, as discussed in the "Fathoming the Lifespan" chapter of the *Lotus.*[130] It does not, however, explicitly reveal the "subtlety of original cause" *(hon'in-myō)*—here, the "seed" or practice by which he achieved that Buddhahood. Thus it served to lead to enlightenment only those people who had lived in the Buddha's lifetime or in the True and Semblance Dharma ages, who had already received and nurtured the seed of Buddhahood in prior lifetimes; therefore it is called the "origin teaching of the harvest" *(datchaku no honmon).* In the Final Dharma age, when no one has received the seed of Buddhahood in prior lifetimes, this origin teaching is useless. The only valid teaching in this age is held to be that of "the original cause," Nichiren's *daimoku,* which represents the seed of Buddhahood. This claim is based on Nichiren's assertion in the *Kanjin honzon shō:*

> The origin teaching of the Buddha's lifetime and [that of] the beginning of the Final Dharma age are both alike the pure perfect *(jun'en)* [teaching]. However, the former corresponds to [the harvest of] emancipation and the latter, to the seed. The former is one chapter and two halves [i.e., the "Fathoming the Lifespan" chapter and the adjacent, framing sections of the preceding and following chapters], and the latter, solely the five characters of the *daimoku.*[131]

For many Hokke scholars, the above passage referred to two aspects of the origin teaching: in the past, in the form of the "one chapter and two halves," the origin teaching had served to bring about the harvest of emancipation; in the present age of *mappō,* as the five characters of the *daimoku,* it served to sow the seed. The same Dharma, in other words, could function as either the harvest or the seed, depending upon whether those who received it had formerly planted good roots by receiving the seed of Buddhahood *(hon'i uzen)* or not *(honmi uzen).*[132] For Fuji scholars, however, this passage referred to two separate teachings: Śākyamuni's origin teaching and Nichiren's *daimoku.*[133] The superiority of the *daimoku* over the origin teaching of the *Lotus Sūtra* is expressed in the *Hon'in-myō shō* as follows: "In the *Lotus* [*Sūtra*] of the harvest, the origin and trace [teachings] are both the trace [teaching]. . . . The *Lotus* [*Sūtra*] that sows the seed [of Buddhahood] is the one and only origin teaching."[134] By this definition, all twenty-eight chapters of the *Lotus Sūtra* are relegated to the status of "trace teaching," and the "real" origin teaching is the seed of Buddhahood—the *daimoku*—alone.[135]

Defining the "seed" and the "harvest" of liberation in this way as two distinct teachings could also imply two different teachers, and this is precisely the direction in which Fuji doctrine moves. Chapter 16 of the *Lotus Sūtra* states, "Once I [Śākyamuni] practiced the bodhisattva way," a passage read by Chih-i as pointing to the original cause of Śākyamuni's enlightenment.[136] Based on this passage, the Fuji transmission texts postulate a teacher prior to Śākyamuni's attainment of enlightenment in the remote past, who first conferred upon Śākyamuni the seed of Buddhahood and enabled him to realize the stage of verbal identity. In contrast to Śākyamuni, the "teacher of the subtlety of original effect" *(hongamyō no kyōshu),* this prior Buddha is characterized as the "teacher of the subtlety of original cause" *(hon'in-myō no kyōshu).* He resembles the "unproduced triple-bodied Tathâgata" of medieval Tendai thought in being prior even to the distant enlightenment of Śākyamuni as described in the sūtra text. This teacher's sowing of the seed of Buddhahood in the beginningless past enabled Śākyamuni to achieve the stage of verbal identity, thus beginning the process of cultivation that would culminate in his enlightenment in the remote past, as described in the "Fathoming the Lifespan" chapter. It is said to be recapitulated in the Final Dharma age with Nichiren's propagation of the *daimoku:*

Today, the origin and trace teachings of maturing and harvesting are both "trace," and the origin teaching that corresponds to [the stage of] verbal identity [achieved by Śākyamuni] in the distant past is "origin." . . . The Buddha is master of the teachings of maturing and harvesting, while I [Nichiren] am master of the Dharma of sowing . . . What Śākyamuni practiced in the remotest past when he realized the stage of verbal identity has now at this time, in the Final Dharma age, been transposed to the person of Nichiren, who also represents the stage of verbal identity.[137]

The Final Dharma age is the moment when present time and the time-less realm of the original Buddha (the "teacher of original cause") are united in the act of practice. The dispensation of the historical Śākya-muni from his lifetime through the True and Semblance Dharma ages—a period when people attained enlightenment through the teaching of the "harvest" and a linear process of cultivation—is short-circuited, and, via the *daimoku,* the seed of Buddhahood, timeless original enlighten-ment is realized in the present moment.

Mappō as the historical moment of intersection with the enlighten-ment of the original Buddha is a notion present in Nichiren's writings. However, in his thought, the Śākyamuni Buddha who attained enlight-enment in the remote past as described in the sūtra text and the origi-nally enlightened Buddha without beginning or end appear to be mu-tually identified and inseparable, the one corresponding to the doctrinal teaching *(kyō)* and the other, to that which is realized through faith and practice *(kan).*[138] In Fuji doctrine, however, these two tended to become distinguished as the "teacher of original effect" and the "teacher of orig-inal cause," the latter being increasingly identified with the person of Bodhisattva Superior Conduct and with Nichiren. From the perspective of the sūtra text, Śākyamuni Buddha is the teacher of Bodhisattva Su-perior Conduct. In Fuji doctrine, this is dismissed as a provisional view, the reality being that Superior Conduct is the teacher of Śākyamuni. The *Hon'in-myō shō* simply identifies Nichiren as "the practitioner of the sub-tlety of original cause" *(hon'in-myō no gyōja).*[139] However, the *Hyaku rokka sōjō* is more explicit: "The subtlety of original effect corresponds to Śākya-muni Buddha, and the subtlety of original cause, to Bodhisattva Supe-rior Conduct."[140] It also says:

> What Nichiren now practices does not differ from the conduct of [the Buddha] in the most distant past when he achieved the stage of ver-bal identity, not by so much as a single mustard seed. . . . The "Fath-oming the Lifespan" chapter of my [Nichiren's] inner enlightenment is the subtlety of original cause hidden in the depths of the "Fath-oming the Lifespan" [chapter] of the harvest, and its teacher is my-self . . . From the standpoint of beginningless time *(kuon ganjō),* "In heaven and earth, I alone am worthy of respect" refers to Nichiren. . . . Nichiren, constantly abiding throughout the three time periods [of past, present, and future], [confers] the benefits of [the stage of] ver-bal [identity]. . . . The Buddha of sowing is [like] the moon in the sky, while the Buddha of the harvest is [like] the moon reflected in a pond. [141]

By the latter part of the Muromachi period, such ideas would be sys-tematized in the Fuji school's idiosyncratic doctrinal position, elabo-rated particularly within the Taisekiji line, that equates Nichiren with the original Buddha *(Nichiren honbutsu ron).*[142] A few passages from the Muromachi period writings of this school will suggest some of the various ways in which this doctrine was developed. For example, Nichiu (1409–1482), ninth abbot of the Taisekiji, argues that for people of the Final Dharma age who are at the beginning stage of practice, Nichiren as the teacher of the original cause is a more appropriate focus of devotion than Śākyamuni:

> In our school, we do not enshrine as the object of worship the Śākyamuni who, during his lifetime, taught people able to extirpate delusion and thus reach the ultimate principle. . . . Because this Śākyamuni, who taught for the sake of those at advanced stages of practice, is beyond the deluded perception of [beings like ourselves], who are at the stage of verbal identity and have but newly produced the aspiration for enlightenment, we take as our object of worship that which Śākyamuni practiced as the cause for his enlightenment. This is why we rely on the eminent founder, Nichiren Shōnin.[143]

Nichiyō, a contemporary of Nichiu and of the same Fuji lineage, interprets Nichiren as manifesting in his behavior a reality that Śākyamuni only theoretically expressed: "[Nichiren] Daishōnin is the essence of the *Lotus Sūtra*. Śākyamuni's *Lotus Sūtra* is the *Lotus Sūtra* in words alone. . . . When [Nichiren] practiced the *Lotus Sūtra* in actuality, then it became the true *Lotus Sūtra*."[144] Similarly, Sakyō Ajari Nikkyō (b. 1428), a disciple of Nichiu, developed the argument for Nichiren as the original Buddha in his *Musaka shō*. He argues that Bodhisattva Superior Conduct, who represents the stage of practice, is the teacher of all Buddhas and surpasses Śākyamuni, who represents only the stage of attainment. Thus Nichiren, who is the embodiment of Superior Conduct in the time of *mappō*, is all-inclusive: "Simply believing in Nichiren Shōnin encompasses the virtues of faith in Śākyamuni, Many Jewels, Superior Conduct, and all Buddhas."[145]

The equation of Nichiren with the original Buddha represents a bold if convoluted attempt to free Nichiren from the context of the preceding historical tradition of Śākyamuni's Buddhism and to relocate Śākyamuni within the context of Nichiren's teaching. Structurally, it resembles medieval Tendai claims that Chih-i's inner enlightenment is prior to and surpasses the text of the *Lotus Sūtra* preached by Śākyamuni. It also suggests the nonlinearity and reversals of time and hierarchy characteristic of medieval Tendai *kanjin*-style interpretations: The seed surpasses the harvest; the stage of practice surpasses that of attainment; Superior Conduct, a bodhisattva, is superior to Śākyamuni, a Buddha; and Nichiren, who lived after Śākyamuni in historical time, becomes his teacher in beginningless time. In the reading of the three jewels of Buddhism adopted by most schools within the Nichiren tradition, the

Buddha is defined as the original Śākyamuni of the "Fathoming the Lifespan" chapter of the *Lotus Sūtra,* the Dharma is Namu-myōhō-renge-kyō, and the Sangha is represented by Nichiren. In the Fuji school, however, the Buddha is Nichiren, the Dharma is Namu-myōhō-renge-kyō, and the Sangha is represented by Nikkō. Founder worship is hardly uncommon in Japanese Buddhism, but nowhere has it been provided with a more elaborate doctrinal rationale than in the Fuji lineage of the Nichiren tradition.

Fuji interactions with Tendai institutions are less easy to document than in the case of Minobu, but they nevertheless occurred. Sanmi Nichijun (1294–1354/1356), a noted scholar of the lineage, studied both Eshin and Danna teachings on Mt. Hiei. The sixth abbot of the Taiseki-ji, Nichiji (d. 1406), is said to have studied Tendai doctrine at the Senba *dangisho.*[146] Nichiu, the ninth abbot, mentioned above, appears as a young man to have received the transmission of the Tendai *kuden* text *Nijō shō.*[147] Whatever the nature and extent of such contacts, there appear to be several points of structural similarity between Fuji doctrine and medieval Tendai thought. First, the supreme Dharma, in this case the *daimoku,* is held to be prior to and virtually independent of the text of the *Lotus Sūtra,* as is "mind contemplation" or *kanjin* in the transmissions of some medieval Tendai lineages. Second, the supreme Dharma is associated with a Buddha who is postulated prior even to the Śākyamuni who attained enlightenment in the remote past as described in the sūtra text: the "unproduced triple-bodied Tathâgata" in the case of Tendai documents and the "teacher of original cause" in the case of the Fuji school. And third, a reversal of conventional hierarchies occurs in which the ordinary worldling is accorded status higher than the Buddha who attained enlightenment in the sūtra. In the case of the Fuji school, the "ordinary worldling" refers very specifically to Nichiren, and more generally to his followers who chant the *daimoku.*

The equation of Nichiren with the original Buddha is not easily reconciled with Nichiren's own clear expressions of reverence for Śākyamuni as "parent, teacher, and sovereign" of all living beings, and this particular strand of Nichiren Buddhist thought has been much criticized by other Nichiren schools. In recent decades, it has come under attack for lack of basis in Nichiren's writings by those sectarian scholars of Nichirenshū intent on purifying the Nichiren corpus of apocryphal works as a basis for establishing a normative doctrine, a project in which the present-day inheritors of the Fuji lineage—Nichiren Shōshū—have evinced little interest. But authenticated writings of a founder are not the only basis upon which religious traditions have, historically, chosen to argue their authority. Scholars of the medieval Fuji school, like the Tendai lineages of their day, based their interpretations of doctrine and their claims to legitimacy less on original texts than on secret transmissions, a hermeneutical approach that its modern descendents have in large measure inherited.

Reinventing the Lotus: The Production of Sūtra Commentaries

The medieval period, especially the Muromachi era, saw the production of a number of commentaries on the *Lotus Sūtra* in both Tendai and Nichiren traditions, drawing on what was becoming a shared tradition of transmissions concerning notions of original enlightenment. These commentaries were often compiled from series of lectures given on the sūtra, representing either the lecturer's own revision of his notes or a compilation made by disciples. On the Tendai side, such works ranged from highly technical discussions based upon or taking the form of commentaries on Chih-i's own commentary on the *Lotus Sūtra,* the *Fa-hua wen-chü* (Words and phrases of the *Lotus Sūtra*), to a more accessible style of *Lotus* commentary known as *Hokke jikidan-mono,* recording lectures on the *Lotus* that were often conducted for audiences of laiety as well as clergy, and which frequently included *waka* poetry and didactic tales *(setsuwa).*[148] On the Nichiren side as well, one finds a variety of *Lotus Sūtra* commentaries from this period, aimed not merely at elucidating the sūtra text but also at clarifying and promoting Nichiren doctrine.[149] Medieval *Lotus Sūtra* commentaries of both traditions offer a rich and scarcely tapped field for studying transsectarian developments in *Lotus*-related Japanese Buddhist thought, and justice cannot be done to them in a brief space. The following discussion will touch only briefly on three medieval *Lotus* commentaries—one Tendai and two Hokke—to suggest how the *Lotus* was being interpreted as a teaching of original enlightenment, and how this shared understanding was appropriated by both traditions.

First we will consider the *Mongu ryaku taikō shikenmon* (Private record of lectures on an abbreviated outline of the *Wen-chü*) by the Tendai monk Sonshun (1451–1514) in the Kantō Eshin lineage of Songai. Like a number of medieval *Lotus* commentaries, this work adopts a *kanjin*-style interpretive approach in which the text is passed through the hermeneutical filter of original enlightenment perspectives. The *Lotus Sūtra* in itself contains only a few passages that could perhaps be considered suggestive of original enlightenment, such as "the dharmas from the outset always of themselves bear the marks of quiet extinction" or "the dharmas dwell in a Dharma-position, and the worldly aspect constantly abides"; the latter in particular, as we have seen, is in fact widely quoted in medieval Tendai *kuden* literature.[150] However, the sūtra had for centuries been read through the lens of T'ien-t'ai commentaries, which interpreted it as teaching the mutual encompassing and identification of the

344   NICHIREN AND HIS SUCCESSORS

mind and all dharmas. T'ien-t'ai readings of the *Lotus* in terms of such
holistic doctrines as the threefold truth and the three thousand realms
in a single thought-moment helped lay the foundation for understanding the sūtra from a *hongaku* perspective. This foundation was further
strengthened by the fusion of *Lotus*-based teachings and Mikkyō in the
Taimitsu thought developed by such early Japanese Tendai figures as Ennin, Enchin, and Annen. Yet, even so, read at face value, the text of the
Lotus hardly suggests itself as a prime source of original enlightenment
doctrine. If anything, it upholds traditional notions of Buddhahood as
realized through a long and gradual process of cultivation: "Śāriputra,
you, in an age to come, beyond incalculable, limitless, inconceivable
kalpas, . . . having upheld the True Dharma and having acquired to per-
fection the path trodden by bodhisattvas, shall be able to become a Buddha."[151] Nonetheless, a number of the medieval Japanese commentaries
on the sūtra in effect "reinvent" the *Lotus* as a teaching of original enlightenment. Sonshun's *Mongu ryaku taikō shikenmon* serves to illustrate
the hermeneutical strategies by which this was accomplished. Since it
not only presents Sonshun's own interpretations but also cites *kuden* from
earlier centuries, it offers considerable insight into how *hongaku* readings of specific passages developed over time.

In his commentary on the "Introductory" chapter of the sūtra, Sonshun asserts that the *Lotus* represents the direct path of the realization
of Buddhahood for all living beings; wherever it may be preached is the
pure land of Sacred Eagle Peak.[152] Moreover, the Buddha revealed in
the *Lotus Sūtra* is different from the Buddha of any other teaching. Sonshun discusses three textually based views of the Buddha: in terms of the
pre–*Lotus Sūtra* teachings, the trace teaching, and the origin teaching.
The pre–*Lotus Sūtra* teachings pertain to "the teacher Śākyamuni of the
present world, who renounced the household life at nineteen, attained
the Way at thirty, and manifested himself as the one solely worthy of respect in the threefold world." According to the trace teaching, "Buddha"
is to be understood as "the principle of suchness *(shinnyo)* or the true aspect *(jissō)*, apart from the delusion and impurity of the dharmas." But
the origin teaching reveals that "the myriad dharmas that are the three
thousand realms" are to be understood as "the unproduced triple body,
the Buddha-essence of original enlightenment." Then, based on the origin teaching, Sonshun asserts the importance of the "Buddha in terms
of *kanjin*," which is the realization that "our mind-nature is from the outset endowed with the dharmas of the three thousand realms, and at the
same time, permeates them."

The various schools all reject as delusion the false objects of our
moment-to-moment thoughts and understand by "Buddha" the origin
where a single thought has not [yet] arisen, where neither good nor

evil is hindered. But the Tendai interpretation is that the arising of the thought-moment is precisely practice, and the false [objects] are precisely the dharma realm. Thus our moment-to-moment thoughts, precisely as they are, are the workings of the Tathâgata of original enlightenment who receives [the Buddha body] for his own use. This is called the doctrine that surpasses [those of] other schools. It should be kept secret.[153]

In the twenty-first section of his commentary on the sūtra's "Introductory" chapter, a section titled "The teacher of the *Lotus* is the unproduced triple body," Sonshun further elaborates:

First, what is this unproduced Buddha? It is the ordinary worldling, who is actually deluded. This is not a Buddha who first aroused the thought of enlightenment, launched his practice, and, on attaining awakening, transformed delusion, but simply the original Buddha, who from the outset constantly abides while we living beings undergo the beginningless round of transmigration. This is called "the true Buddha prior to awakening" *(kakuzen no jitsubutsu).* Because we do not know that we are Buddha, we perform evil deeds, and with respect to good and evil objects, we produce one-sided thoughts of hatred and desire. But when we realize that we are Buddha originally, then naturally we refrain from evil and promote good. Toward objects that differ [from our wishes] we do not [arouse] hate, and toward those that accord [with our wishes] we do not [arouse] desire. With a mind equal and without discrimination, we naturally dwell in unconditioned compassion. Thus all our actions—walking, sitting, standing, and lying down— are the Buddha's conduct. This is called the direct path of realizing Buddhahood in this very body. The above doctrine is truly the most profoundly secret of secret transmissions. It is a secret Dharma to be transmitted only to one person. It should never be spoken of to those who lack faith.[154]

That the sūtra's true intent is to reveal that all beings are Buddha inherently is a theme running throughout Sonshun's commentary. His discussion of the "Fathoming the Lifespan" chapter, for example, like a number of earlier *kuden* texts, interprets the revelation of the Buddha's enlightenment in the distant past in two senses: *ji kenpon,* the revelation that Śākyamuni, as an individual, attained Buddhahood inconceivable dust particle-kalpas ago; and *ri kenpon,* the revelation that "our beginningless physical and mental [dharmas], undergoing transmigration through birth and death, are the subtle wisdom and its subtle object that are unproduced original enlightenment." For Sonshun, as for most medieval Tendai thinkers, the latter interpretation is fundamental. The purpose of Śākyamuni's revelation about his own enlightenment in the remote past was to make clear, through his own example, that "living beings of the nine realms are the constantly abiding Buddha fruit." The first-person pronoun "I" in the statements in this chapter, "Since I in actuality attained Buddhahood" and "Since I attained Buddhahood," is explained as having both a provisional and a true meaning. The provisional "I" is the individual Śākyamuni; the true "I" is all living beings of the ten realms.[155]

Upon this fundamental claim that the *Lotus* reveals a constantly abiding original Buddha innate in all beings, the *Ryaku taikō shikenmon*, like other medieval *Lotus* commentaries, ingeniously reconstructs those passages in the sūtra that do not support the *hongaku* perspective. One obvious instance, occurring in the early chapters, is the prophecies of future Buddhahood conferred by Śākyamuni on his great *śrāvaka* disciples. The *Ryaku taikō shikenmon* raises the question: "This sūtra is the subtle exposition of sudden realization. Why then does [the Buddha] confer prophecies [to be fulfilled] countless kalpas in the future?" and responds that the Buddha here addresses himself to the level of his disciples' understanding, which is still constrained by the conceptual framework of the pre–*Lotus Sūtra* teachings. Thus they mistakenly "think that 'Buddha' means to possess the thirty-two major and eighty minor excellent marks like Śākyamuni, and desire to become such a Buddha." However, from the standpoint of the origin teaching, which represents the teaching of original enlightenment, the notion of Buddhahood set forth in the trace teaching, in which the prophecies occur, is informed by the deluded perspective that enlightenment is acquired at a particular time *(shikaku)*. Thus when Kāśyapa, for example, is given a prophecy that he will eventually become a Buddha named "Light Bright," the name signifies the state of having "dispelled the darkness of [the view of] acquired enlightenment set forth in the trace teaching and perfected the awakening of original enlightenment that is unproduced, as revealed in the origin teaching."[156]

Another passage in the sūtra at variance with the perspective of original enlightenment is the episode of the dragon king's daughter, who, in the "Devadatta" chapter, demonstrates her capacity for enlightened wisdom by first transforming herself into a male and then becoming a Buddha. Sonshun observes: "'Transforming [the female] and becoming a male' *(henjō nanshi)* is not the attainment of Buddhahood in this very body. [This doctrine] injures the *Lotus,* which teaches that the ordinary worldling is precisely the ultimate. In fact, interpretation in light of the esoteric teachings establishes that, having a female body, she must have attained Buddhahood in that very body."[157] After discussing several interpretations of this point, Sonshun takes up the question of whether or not there are female Buddhas:

According to the transmissions of scholars, from the standpoint of acquired enlightenment, there are not. But from the standpoint of original enlightenment, their oral transmissions maintain that there are. The reason is that, from the perspective of acquired enlightenment, delusion is cut off and awakening realized; because [this entails] transformation into male form, there are no female Buddhas. However, from the perspective of original enlightenment, delusion and enlightenment are originally inherent; thus a man as a man [on realizing original enlightenment] pervades and illuminates the dharma realm, and a woman as a woman, just as she is, [likewise] pervades the dharma realm. Because [these transmissions] teach that one's present status is precisely the wonderful [Dharma], they teach that there are female Buddhas.[158]

It need hardly be said that the soteriological potential of actual women is not the issue here, nor are traditional assumptions of male superiority fundamentally challenged. Rather, the Buddhahood of women becomes a locus for arguing the superiority of the *hongaku* perspective.

A similar difficulty occurs in the chapter on "Bodhisattva Medicine King," in the passage that reads: "If there is a woman who, on hearing this sūtra text, practices as it preaches, then at the end of this life she shall go at once to the world of Peace and Bliss, to the dwelling place of the Buddha Amida where he is surrounded by a multitude of great bodhisattvas, and be born there on a jeweled pedestal within a lotus blossom."[159]

This statement presents a triple challenge to notions of original enlightenment: first, in singling out women as a particular case; second, in implying that salvation is to be achieved after death; and third, in locating that salvation in a place other than this world. Sonshun acknowledges: "[The phrase] 'at the end of this life' *(kono myōju ni oite)* suggests that a woman does not go directly [to the land of Peace and Bliss] as a woman [but implies that she must first discard her female body]." However, he says, this is only the superficial meaning. As to the real meaning, the text should be repunctuated to read "ending within this life" *(kono myō ni oite owaru),* meaning that one achieves the pure land in this very body, not upon casting away the body at death. Sonshun cites an older Eshin-school interpretation to the effect that "at the end of this life" means that the "life" of evil acts is brought to an end, and that to "go directly to the world of Peace and Bliss" means to abide in peaceful practices. To "practice as it teaches" means that "once we encounter the Wonderful Dharma [of the *Lotus Sūtra*], then day and night, the four modes of conduct [walking, standing, sitting and lying down] are all the practice of the Wonderful Dharma." To "be born on a lotus pedestal" means that the eight-petaled lotus of the mind opens and the original Buddha who is the mind-king manifests. Amida Buddha is similarly reinterpreted in light of the threefold truth: "*a*" signifies emptiness; "*mi,*" conventional existence; and "*da,*" the middle, while "Buddha" is the achievement of the threefold contemplation in a single mind, a reading that dates back to the latter Heian period.[160] As for the specific reference to women, Sonshun concludes that all beings of the last age are universally referred to in this passage as "women" because of their "foolishness and ignorance."[161]

The foregoing examples will give some idea of the ingenious and even playful qualities found in medieval commentaries on the *Lotus*. The entire arsenal of *kanjin*-style hermeneutical devices is marshalled to "reinvent" the sūtra as a teaching of original enlightenment. However, as suggested by the example of Sonshun's passages dealing with women, the reversals and inversions of meaning performed on the sūtra text were intended solely to establish the *hongaku* perspective and were not extended in such a way as to challenge or rearrange social hierarchies.

We turn now to two *Lotus* commentaries from the Nichiren Hokkeshū. Both purport to be records of lectures on the sūtra given by Nichiren at Mt. Minobu in the last years of his life. One is the *Ongi kuden* (Oral transmission of the sacred meanings), whose colophon describes it as a lecture given by Nichiren for his six senior disciples and transcribed by Byakuren Ajari Nikkō, who obtained Nichiren's endorsement on 1/1/1278. The other is the *Onkō kikigaki* (Lectures heard and recorded), which presents itself as a record of a series of lectures on the *Lotus Sūtra* given by Nichiren from 3/19/1278 to 5/28/1280 and recorded by Minbu Ajari Nikō. Until recent decades, both documents were regarded as direct records of Nichiren's teaching on the innermost meaning of the *Lotus Sūtra*. However, the earliest notices of these texts do not occur until the beginning of the sixteenth century, and the balance of scholarly opinion now holds them to be Muromachi period productions.[162] It is not clear what significance, if any, may attach to the fact that the two commentaries are attributed respectively to the founders of the Fuji and the Minobu lineages, whose differences are said to have led to the first schism within the Nichiren community.

Both these texts, like Sonshun's *Mongu ryaku taikō shikenmon,* take as their premise that the true intent of the *Lotus Sūtra* is to teach the doctrine of original enlightenment: Śākyamuni of the text is considered an ephemeral Buddha, while the true Buddha is held to be the beings of the ten realms just as they are. The dramatic events of the sūtra—the apparition of the jeweled stūpa, the emergence of the bodhisattvas from beneath the earth, and the revelation of the Buddha's enlightenment in the remote past—are taken as pointing not to a transcendent state of Buddhahood, but to the enlightenment innate in ordinary worldlings. The *Ongi kuden* in particular includes some of the same material as the *Ryaku taikō shikenmon.* For example, both Sonshun's text and the *Ongi kuden* interpret the stūpa of the Tathâgata Many Jewels as the body of the ordinary worldling, who is the only true Buddha. Sonshun observes:

> In terms of its concrete representation *(ji)* [in the sūtra text], the jeweled stūpa was a stūpa built by Many Jewels in the land called Jewel Pure, wielding an axe with his own hand. . . . But in terms of universal principle *(ri)*, the stūpa was made in the land of the formless repository. This land indicates the mother's womb. The five *skandhas* that constitute the dharma realm lodge in the womb and form the five-foot frame [of a person]. In this case, the stūpa that is the beginningless and originally inherent five elements of all living beings and their mind that is originally endowed with the virtue of the [Buddha] nature is represented in concrete form as the jeweled stūpa five hundred *yojanas* in height.[163]

Similarly, the *Ongi kuden* reads:

> The realm called "Jewel Pure" is our mother's womb. "In it was a Buddha" indicates the Buddha who is all dharmas manifesting the true aspect; that is why he is called the Buddha Many Jewels. [Again,] the womb indicates the defilements, but amid the mire and muck of the defilements is the Buddha who is suchness. This refers to us, living beings. Now, when Nichiren and his followers chant Namu-myōhō-renge-kyō, we are the Buddha who is the Lotus as the Dharma itself.[164]

The texts have other similarities as well. For example, both the *Ryaku taikō shikenmon* and the *Ongi kuden* interpret the four leaders of the great bodhisattvas who emerge from the earth—Superior Conduct, Boundless Conduct, Pure Conduct, and Firm Conduct—as representing the four elements of fire, wind, water, and earth that constitute all things, and the "remote past" *(kuon)* when Śākyamuni first attained enlightenment, not as a literal past but as an originally enlightened state that is described as "unadorned" *(tsukurowazu)* and "being as it is originally" *(moto no mama).*[165] Such duplications of content do not necessarily mean that the compiler of one text had reference to the other, but more likely, that Tendai and Hokke exegetes were drawing on a by-now-common fund of traditions and transmissions concerning the interpretation of the *Lotus Sūtra.*

As suggested by the passage above interpreting the jeweled stūpa, the compilers of the Hokke commentaries not only read the *Lotus Sūtra* as a teaching of original enlightenment—as did their Tendai counterparts—but assimilated that enlightenment to the distinctive practice of their sect, the chanting of the *daimoku.* The *daimoku* is defined in these texts as the sole vehicle for realizing that one is Buddha inherently. For example, in the parable of the good physician in the "Fathoming the

Lifespan" chapter, the physician addresses his children, saying, "This excellent good medicine I now leave here. You should take and drink it, and not fear that you will not be cured."[166] The *Ongi kuden* comments:

> "This excellent good medicine" can refer either to [the Buddha's] scriptural teachings or to his *śarīra*. In the Final Dharma age, it indicates Namu-myōhō-renge-kyō. "Excellent" means that what all Buddhas of the three time periods prefer is the five characters of the *daimoku*.[167] "Now leave" indicates the Final Dharma age. "Here" indicates, within all of Jambudvīpa, the country of Japan. "You" is all beings of the Final Dharma age. "Take" refers to the ritual in which one embraces the *Lotus Sūtra*.[168] "Drink" is to chant [the *daimoku*]. From the time that one "drinks," one is the unproduced triple-bodied Buddha. This cures one of the sickness and pain [of the notion] that the Buddha first attained enlightenment in this lifetime. Now, Nichiren and his followers who chant Namu-myōhō-renge-kyō are the ones to whom this passage refers.[169]

Here the *daimoku* is said to cure one of the "sickness and pain" of thinking that enlightenment must be attained, and not realizing that one has always been enlightened inherently. The *Onkō kikigaki* similarly assimilates to the *daimoku* the medieval Tendai tradition that the transmission of the "threefold contemplation in a single phrase" was received directly from Śākyamuni:

> According to the Great Sage [Śākyamuni]'s verses of transmission [conferred] in the [jeweled] stūpa, the true intent of his one lineage resides in a single phrase. This "single phrase" is interpreted as the single phrase "nonduality of quiescence and illumination" (*jakushō funi*) or as the single phrase "ultimately equal from beginning to end" (*honmatsu kukyō-tō*). [However,] its true meaning is Namu-myōhō-renge-kyō. "Beginning" indicates the ordinary worldling. "End" indicates the Buddha. "Ultimate" is living beings and the Buddha being a single suchness. The essence of living beings and the Buddha being a single suchness is Namu-myōhō-renge-kyō.[170]

Other passages in both the two Hokkeshū commentaries employ the techniques of *kanjin*-style interpretation by resemblance and reversal to read the specifics of the sūtra as referring to Nichiren's followers and their distinctive practices: not only chanting the *daimoku*, but the practice of *shakubuku* as well. The *Lotus* represents the Buddha as preaching the sūtra "of his own accord, without being asked" by an interlocutor (*mumon jisetsu*); the *Ongi kuden* interprets this as referring, in the present time, to Nichiren's disciples, who "of their own accord, without being asked" uphold the *Lotus* by rebuking other sects.[171] Similarly, in chapter 7, the guide dissolving the magically conjured city is read as indicating the destruction of the temples of those who slander the Dharma.[172] In the *Onkō kikigaki,* the sūtra's promise of "peace and security in this life" is interpreted as meeting great persecution for the sūtra's sake, for encountering such difficulties assures the practitioner of achieving Buddhahood.[173] The sūtra describes the bodhisattvas who emerge from beneath the earth in chapter 15 as "untainted by worldly dharmas,/like a lotus blossom in the water"; "untainted by worldly dharmas" is interpreted as "not accepting alms from those who slander the Dharma."[174] Such texts clearly illustrate how Hokke scholar-monks appropriated and modified the doctrines and interpretive techniques of medieval Tendai to illuminate, and support their own claims for the supremacy of, Nichiren's teaching.

Conclusion

Hokke-Tendai interactions in the medieval period point up the limitations of the categories "old Buddhism" and "new Buddhism" once one looks beyond the moment of their institutional divergence in the Kamakura period. Such interactions were exceedingly complex. In the early fourteenth century, the emerging Hokkeshū defined itself over and against Tendai yet at the same time occasionally invoked the authority of Mt. Hiei for purposes of self-legitimization, for example, to enhance their founder's status by incorporating the Tendai master Shunpan into accounts of Nichiren's life, or to counter the doctrinal claims of a major competitor in the Kantō, the Tendai *dangisho* at Senba. By the end of the fourteenth century, however, Hokke monks were widely studying at Kantō Tendai institutions and drawing on Tendai intellectual resources to develop and systematize the doctrines of their sect and of its various subbranches. These were not simple borrowings but refigurations that employed Tendai ideas, conceptual structures, and interpretive styles to argue the superiority of Hokke teachings. So thoroughly integrated were these appropriations and transformations that one might legitimately speak of a medieval Nichiren *hongaku* discourse; by this time, Tendai clearly no longer held a monopoly on the ideas and interpretative techniques associated with this doctrine, if indeed it ever had.

Was there Hokke influence on medieval Tendai as well? We have seen above that the controversial doctrine of *"shikan surpassing the Lotus,"* associated with Senba, the leading Tendai *dangisho* in eastern Japan, may have been formulated at least in part as a defense against Hokke claims for the exclusive validity of the *Lotus Sūtra.* In addition, judging from the number of Tendai scholars who converted to the Hokkeshū during the Muromachi period, the influence resulting from contact between the two traditions was by no means one-sided. The practice of Nichiren Buddhist monks may also have influenced their Tendai counterparts in some degree. Iwata Kyōen, editor of the volume of the *Tendaishū zensho* (Complete works of the Tendai school) containing the major Eshin *kuden hōmon,* draws attention to the following passage in the *Zōda shō,* compiled by Songai's disciple Gōkai (fl. 1347):

> Question: What is the abbreviated method of practice of the threefold *Lotus Sūtra* [advocated by] the Great Teacher [Saichō]?
> According to transmission, [this method consists of three lines. One:] *"Namu* to the *Sūtra of the Lotus Blossom of the Wonderful Dharma,* which opens the three [vehicles] to reveal the one [vehicle] and opens the recent [attainment of the Buddha in this world] to reveal the distant [i.e., his original enlightenment in the remote past], the single vehicle in which the mind, the Buddha and all living beings [are without distinction]" *(Namu-kaisan-kennichi-kaigon-kennon-shin-butsu-shujō-ichijō-myōhō-renge-kyō).* (This represents the fundamental *Lotus Sūtra.*) [Two:] *"Namu* Buddha." (This represents the hidden and secret *Lotus Sūtra.*) [Three:] "Namu-myōhō-renge-kyō." (This represents the *Lotus Sūtra* that was preached explicitly.) According to transmission, one should recite these three lines morning and evening, without neglect.[175]

As touched upon in earlier chapters, the chanting of single phrases designed to encompass the essence of the *Lotus Sūtra* definitely predated Nichiren, and references to such practices occur occasionally in medieval Tendai literature. However, it is also possible that passages such as the one above represent the direct influence of Nichiren Hokke practice upon the medieval Tendai tradition, and that the *daimoku,* while subject to differing interpretations, was to some extent chanted within Tendai circles.

A feature of great interest in medieval Hokke-Tendai interactions is the way that strong sectarian consciousness, especially on the side of the Hokkeshū, existed together with intellectual exchange and the production of a shared fund of traditions, transmissions, and interpretations related to the *Lotus Sūtra.* One notices in particular how distinctive interpretations within both traditions were constructed on the basis of strikingly similar doctrinal classifications. Peter N. Gregory's analysis of the project of doctrinal classification in China, cited in the first chapter of this study, notes that it encompassed hermeneutical, sectarian, and soteriological dimensions.[176] The same observation holds true for Tendai and Hokke doctrinal classification in the late Kamakura and Muromachi periods. Scholar-monks engaged in interpreting the *Lotus Sūtra* and commentarial traditions based upon it shared, across institutional and sectarian boundaries, what were generally the same four categories. These four categories, which correspond on the whole to the stages of the Eshin school's classification of the "fourfold rise and fall," were endlessly interpreted, argued, and deployed in a great variety of ways to locate specific traditions within the overall sweep of Buddhism, to establish distinct sectarian and lineage identities, and to clarify issues of practice and liberation.

The first of the four shared categories was that of the pre–*Lotus Sūtra* teachings, widely held to be incomplete, in that they denied the possibility of Buddhahood to certain groups: followers of the two "Hīnayāna" vehicles of the voice-hearer *(śrāvaka)* and the condition-perceiver *(pratyeka-buddha),* women, and evil men. Their relationship to the *Lotus Sūtra,* however, was an issue of profound disagreement, most particularly between the Tendai and Nichiren Buddhist traditions. Many Tendai scholars maintained that, read in the light of the *Lotus,* all these earlier teachings could be integrated within the one vehicle as expressions of its various aspects *(zettai kaie);* from this hermeneutical perspective, the practices associated with them, such as the *nenbutsu,* could all be regarded as the practice of the *Lotus Sūtra.* For Nichiren and his later followers, however, all earlier teachings were to be rejected in favor of the *Lotus Sūtra,* which was to be embraced and practiced exclusively *(sōtai kaie).* From the standpoint of thought and practice, this represents the greatest point of cleavage between the two traditions.

The second and third shared categories were, respectively, the trace and origin teachings, the two divisions within the *Lotus* itself. These, too, were generally understood in a common, transsectarian fashion. The trace teaching allowed the possibility of Buddhahood for all, but—in that it concerned only the historical Śākyamuni who attained Buddhahood in this world—was held to represent a linear view of liberation as the culmination of a process of cultivation, that is, the perspective of acquired enlightenment. The origin teaching, on the other hand, which contains the revelation of Śākyamuni's original enlightenment in the inconceivably remote past, was read as representing the perspective of original enlightenment. Though details of interpretation differed, wide consensus held the doctrinal perspective of the origin teaching to be superior. As mentioned in chapter 3 of this study, both Eshin and Danna lineages arrogated the "origin teaching" to themselves and identified the "trace teaching" with their rivals. However, even acknowledging the doctrinal superiority of the origin teaching, it was still possible to "go back" and consider how the dharmas of the two teachings were actually related, and whether they represented a unity or a hierarchy. This line of hermeneutical inquiry—the *itchi-shōretsu* debate—and the disputes surrounding it were peculiar to the Nichiren Hokkeshū. Where one stood on this particular issue was a marker of lineage identification within the Hokke tradition and was used to define individual schools and lineages over and against one another.

There was also a consensus in outline, though by no means in the details, about a fourth category—something not explicitly stated in the

Lotus Sūtra text, that was variously denoted as "mind contemplation" *(kanjin)*, "calming and contemplation" *(shikan)*, "the depths of the text" *(montei)*, "the single thought-moment being three thousand realms in actuality" *(ji no ichinen sanzen)*, the "three great secret Dharmas" *(sandai hihō)*, or "Namu-myōhō-renge-kyō." This fourth category referred to the ultimate standpoint and also provided the hermeneutical basis for rereading texts to yield an a priori meaning. But exactly what it was— a perspective or insight, an actual Dharma transmission, or a specific form of practice—and how it was related to the preceding categories, those of the *Lotus Sūtra* text, were issues of profound divergence, both between Tendai and Hokke traditions and internally among their respective lineages.

At one end of the hermeneutical spectrum, the "origin teaching" and *kanjin* were seen as inseparable and nonhierarchical, being related simply as scriptural text or doctrinal teaching *(kyō)* and its internalization through faith or contemplative insight *(kan)*. At the other end of the spectrum, the fourth category was seen as a separate transmission independent of the sūtra or as a reality prior to, and not mediated by, verbal distinctions and doctrinal categories such as those of the trace and origin teachings *(honjaku mibun)*. This "strong reading" is most characteristically expressed by the formulation that *"shikan surpasses the Lotus,"* or the distinction between a scriptural transmission ("Hokkeshū") and a mind-to-mind transmission ("Tendaishū"), both associated with the Senba *dangisho*.

The "weak reading"—that the origin teaching and *kanjin* are inseparable, representing respectively the doctrinal statement and intuitive cognition of the same reality—was also found in a number of Tendai lineages and is expressed in the account of the debate at Nishidani of the Eastern Pagoda precinct, outlined above, where the candidate for examination protested the claim that *"shikan surpasses the Lotus,"* saying: "How can this be? The purpose of the Tathâgata Śākyamuni's advent in this world lies in the origin and trace teachings of the *Lotus*. . . . Because *shikan* is the practice of the *Lotus Sūtra*, it is that which interprets. The *Lotus* is that which is interpreted, the fundamental Dharma."[177] It is also possible to read Nichiren in this way. His "true *ichinen sanzen*" is "hidden in the depths of," not prior to, the origin teaching, and he refers to his three great secret Dharmas as the *daimoku*, object of worship, and ordination platform "of the origin teaching" *(honmon no daimoku, honmon no honzon, honmon no kaidan)*. In the *Kanjin honzon shō*, he uses the term "origin teaching" to refer both to the second half of the *Lotus Sūtra* text and to the ultimate perspective.[178] A number of his later followers thus interpreted him as teaching that the ultimate perspective, the three thousand realms in a single thought-moment as actuality, is inseparable from and mediated by the sūtra text *(kyōkan funi)*. This is the doctrinal position of Nichirenshū today. However, Nichiren also spoke of being the bearer of a new Buddha-Dharma, received directly from Śākyamuni on Eagle Peak. In emphasizing the *daimoku* as an exclusive practice, he even wrote, "Now in the Final Dharma age, neither the *Lotus Sūtra* nor the other sūtras are of use. Namu-myōhō-renge-kyō alone is valid."[179] Thus it is not surprising that, in some medieval Hokke lineages, the *daimoku* was understood as somehow independent of, or prior to, the sūtra text. This position reaches its extreme in the doctrine of the Fuji school, in which the three great secret Dharmas represent a transmission not only separate from the textual *Lotus Sūtra* but originating with a different teacher— the original Buddha, who is identified with Nichiren. This is the doctrinal position of today's Nichiren Shoshū. In both Tendai and Hokke traditions, "strong readings" of the fourth category served as markers by which particular schools distinguished themselves both from other lineages of their own tradition and from other forms of Buddhism, and laid claim to a superior standpoint. For scholars of Senba, the doctrine that *"shikan* surpasses the *Lotus"* served both to distinguish their lineage from that of their counterparts on Mt. Hiei, and to counter the assertions of the early Nichiren Hokkeshū, while the Fuji school's identification of the founder Nichiren as the original Buddha, prior even to Śākyamuni of the origin teaching, became grounds for arguing their diffference from, and superiority to, other Hokke lineages and, indeed, the whole of Buddhism.

The widespread use and elaboration by both Tendai and Nichiren lineages of the categories of "trace teaching," "origin teaching," and *"kanjin"* form a useful lens through which to examine both intellectual exchange and strategies of sectarian differentiation. Interactions between the medieval Hokke and Tendai traditions may represent a special case, in that they shared so much in terms of doctrine and foundational texts; thus, how far one can generalize from their example to other medieval Japanese Buddhist traditions remains open to question. Nonetheless, their exchange and mutual influence underscore the importance of considering the new schools, subsequent to their founding, in connection with their interaction with older institutions—a process instrumental in shaping both.

Conclusion

THIS BOOK HAS SOUGHT to introduce the subject of medieval Japanese "original enlightenment thought" and the major issues involved in its study. By now the reader will have a sense both of its multivalence as a scholarly category and of the complexity of its embeddedness in medieval Japanese religious institutions, as well as culture and society more generally.

Even when viewed purely as doctrine, "original enlightenment thought" does not have a simple or unified meaning. It denotes, first of all, an influential strand of continental Buddhist thought, deriving from the *Awakening of Faith* and the Hua-yen and Ch'an traditions of "original enlightenment" as the potential for enlightenment in ordinary worldlings, grounded in suchness or the *tathâgata-garbha*. In its Japanese incarnation, "original enlightenment thought" developed chiefly within the Tendai tradition; to a far greater extent than had its Chinese antecedents, it incorporated the Madhyamaka-derived T'ien-t'ai thought, according to which all phenomena manifest the true aspect of reality: empty, yet at the same time existing provisionally in dependence upon conditions. Japanese *hongaku* thought was also profoundly influenced by esoteric Buddhism, specifically, the Mikkyō-*Lotus* synthesis that developed within the Tendai school and became known as Taimitsu. Scholars such as Shimaji Daitō and Tamura Yoshirō have therefore broadly distinguished medieval Japanese Tendai *hongaku* thought from the *hongaku* thought of the continent: Here, "original enlightenment" is no longer simply a potential innate in deluded beings to be realized through cultivation and the eradication of defilements but the true status of all phenomena just as they are.

Nonetheless, the existence of a distinct Japanese form of *hongaku* thought does not necessarily imply doctrinal consistency. Some texts, such as the *Shinnyo kan*, hold that the deluded realms of experience and

356

the whole samsaric process originate from failure to discern or believe in one's identity with "suchness that is original enlightenment," while others maintain that birth and death are themselves the natural expressions of original enlightenment. And as we have seen, outright controversy occurred within medieval Tendai over the issue of whether the ultimate insight, the innate and self-luminous "mind-contemplation," is dependent on the *Lotus Sūtra* text or transmitted independently of it. Even narrowly construed as doctrine, original enlightenment thought was not univalent but encompassed a range of positions.

Original enlightenment thought, however, was more than doctrine. It represented a hermeneutical perspective from which scholar-monks attempted to rethink the entire T'ien-t'ai/Tendai doctrinal system, as seen, for example, in the Eshin school's "threefold seven great matters." Applied to practice, it undercut purely instrumental understandings of religious disciplines as a means to reach the goal of enlightenment, recasting them as the paradigmatic expressions of enlightenment itself. It also served polemical ends. *Hongaku* thought is grounded in a philosophical commitment to the nonduality of the Buddha and the ordinary worldling, of ultimate reality and the world of visible forms. The nondual position was assumed, in and of itself, to be superior; hence, to lay claim to the "nondual" *hongaku* position was to arrogate to oneself the doctrinal high ground. More broadly, original enlightenment entailed a metaphysical premise about concrete phenomena instantiating ultimate reality, which exists nowhere apart from them. This premise not only shaped Tendai doctrine and ritual practice but also influenced the development of the medieval arts, Buddhist vocal music, mountain asceticism, Shintō doctrine, and the *kanjin*-style interpretations found in a variety of *kuden* transmissions. In this larger sense, original enlightenment thought involved a particular way of seeing and understanding the world and was linked to a transsectarian "reimagining of liberation" in nonlinear terms as accessible in the present moment and in one's immediate circumstances. It is in these expanded senses that original enlightenment is referred to as "discourse," as well as "thought" or "doctrine."

What original enlightenment thought was not, however was a unified, totalizing system. As we have seen, it coexisted with a number of other discourses, practices, and ideas that did not necessarily mesh with it in a logical fashion, including thaumaturgical rituals to manipulate and transform the present reality, moral and ethical traditions governing behavior, aspirations for the western Pure Land after death, and prayers invoking the superior powers of Buddhas, bodhisattvas, and *kami*. One imagines that the "*hongaku* mode" was situational, adopted in contexts of transmission, interpretation, debate, or other circumstances where appropriate, but also supplemented by other approaches. In short, the im-

plications of nondual original enlightenment were not systematically
worked out to logical conclusions, nor was it deemed necessary to implement them on all occasions.

Having said this much, we can begin to assess and refine two of the
major claims made about medieval Tendai original enlightenment
thought that have been reiterated in modern scholarship. One, asserted
by Shimaji Daitō and Tamura Yoshirō, is that *hongaku* thought represents
a position of "absolute affirmation" of reality. The second, proposed by
Kuroda Toshio, is that it was "archetypical" of *kenmitsu* ideology.

Hongaku thought has been called a doctrine of "absolute affirmation"
in that all phenomena, including one's most ordinary acts and deluded
thoughts, just as they are, are seen as the expressions of original enlightenment. However, this statement requires some qualification. Being committed to a nondual position, *hongaku* rhetoric strives to collapse
any tension, separation, or disjuncture between the visible phenomena
of this world and ultimate reality, or between the Buddha's enlightenment and the state of ordinary worldlings. But on investigation, its "absolute affirmation" proves to be not quite absolute. It is, after all, Buddhist thought, and thus also committed to a distinction between suffering
and liberation from suffering. Thus while asserting nonduality as a fundamental premise, it also acknowledges a profound experiential divide
between knowing that "all dharmas are the Buddha-Dharma" and not
knowing it. A close reading of texts suggests that such statements as "the
defilements are none other than enlightened insight" are articulated
from the standpoint of having realized nonduality, not that of having yet
to realize it. Great as the attempt has been to minimize or even elude it,
inevitably, something remains here of the notion of "acquired enlightenment." We have seen how Nichirenshū scholars in the early decades
of the century distinguished between Tendai original enlightenment
thought as a statement of naturally inherent enlightenment (*jinen hongaku*), and Nichiren's teaching as the actualizing of inherent enlightenment through practice (*shikaku soku hongaku*). The distinction, however,
is overdrawn. Even the nondual Tendai original enlightenment stance
remains, ultimately, one of *shikaku soku hongaku,* for the insight into original enlightenment and the transformation such insight is said to bring
about are mediated by the knowledge (or faith) that "all dharmas are
the Buddha-Dharma," achieved at the stage of verbal identity. It is only
from the standpoint of this nondual insight that the *hongaku* doctrine
may be accurately characterized as "absolute affirmation."

Failure to grasp this qualification has led to the questionable assumption that original enlightenment thought, in its "absolute affirmation" of the enlightenment of ordinary worldlings just as they are, in effect denies the need for practice. This charge should now be laid to rest.
Tendai *kuden* transmissions make clear that statements about "nothing

to practice and nothing to achieve" were to convey some sense of what an enlightened person is supposed to see, or to repudiate purely functional understandings of practice as a means to an end—not to deny its necessity. Because original enlightenment is seen as the true status of all phenomena, practice cannot be the "cause" of enlightenment. Thus its role becomes ambiguous. It must undergo redefinition, whether as predisposing one to the insight that "all dharmas are the Buddha-Dharma," or as solidifying and deepening such insight, or as the exemplary form of the nonduality of the Buddha and the beings. But just as some version of "acquired enlightenment" cannot ultimately be dispensed with, neither can practice, as becomes clear from a close reading of texts. And from the perspective of history, medieval Tendai monks participating in *hongaku* discourse can be shown to have engaged in diverse forms of religious practice.

Nor was the "absolute affirmation" of *hongaku* thought a unifying political ideology. In that it provided the basis for the *kanjin*-style interpretations that formed the content of secret transmissions, original enlightenment discourse supported the elite culture of closed, aristocratic lineages. But it was not used explicitly to endorse the structure of social hierarchy, the system of rule, or the value of accepting one's lot. It flourished in a society in which world renunciation, in the form of reclusion, was a viable possibility. In this respect, medieval original enlightenment thought was quite different from the immanentalist world view and metaphysics that supported what has been called "Tokugawa ideology." Early modern Japan saw the rise of a religiously grounded, totalizing, and highly ethicized legitimation of social hierarchy, in which to strive diligently and cheerfully in one's given circumstances—whether as samurai, peasant, merchant, or artisan—was to complete the Way of Heaven.[1] As the "critical Buddhists" have warned, the danger of sacralizing the status quo, and thus of undermining efforts to reform it, is potentially inherent in immanentalist systems of thought; this danger is well illustrated by much of Tokugawa orthodoxy. In the medieval period, however, immanentalist Tendai original enlightenment thought was not assimilated to a particular ideology of rule as was, say, the discourse of the mutual dependence of the Buddhist law and the imperial law *(ōbō buppō sōi ron)*. Nor was it translated into a theory of social obligations. Rather, it was fluid and open to appropriation by a range of ideological positions.

Lastly, the "world affirming" tendencies of *hongaku* thought did not mean that it endorsed wrongdoing. Though the degree of decline in clerical behavior during Japan's medieval period has often been exaggerated— then and now—for polemical purposes, violation of the monastic precepts was an issue of contemporary concern. Sometimes it was rationalized by rhetoric about the degenerate last age. At other times, it was the subject of internal critique, whether explicitly, by the leaders of *vinaya* revival movements, or implicitly, by *hijiri* who left the monastic establishment to practice in reclusion. *Hongaku* thought is not a moral discourse and there was little about it that would have worked actively in such circumstances to counter clerical misbehavior and promote good conduct. However, it is extremely difficult to establish causal links between doctrines and social behavior. That ranking monks not infrequently had sexual relations, accumulated wealth, bore arms, or engaged in political intrigues is probably due less to the world-affirming tendencies of original enlightenment thought than to the circumstances of the *kenmon taisei,* in which leading temple-shrine complexes had emerged as one of the major rival governing parties and had to protect their own interests. Over time, other factors had also contributed to a less than strict observance of the monastic code. These included the Tendai adoption of bodhisattva precept ordinations; notions of "formless precepts" as conveying an underlying Mahāyāna spirit, rather than a set of rules for behavior; the discourse of *mappō,* with its rhetoric of the impossibility of upholding the precepts in a degenerate age; and the swelling of the higher clerical ranks with the sons of the nobility, who adapted monastic life to their aristocratic preferences. Original enlightenment thought may have been, at most, only one of several "passive enablements" leading to a relaxed interpretation of the monastic rules.[2]

The criticism that nondual original enlightenment thought undermines proper distinctions between good and evil is not something peculiar to this doctrine but has recurred throughout the history of the Mahāyāna. The Mahāyāna denial of duality aims at liberation from attachment by undercutting notions of self-existing entities to which one might cling; in repudiating the idea that there can be "self" independent of "other," it also serves to foster responsibility and compassion. Its denial of "good" and "evil" as independent ontological entities is not a denial of morality; from the perspective of conventional truth, good and evil must be distinguished. But the Mahāyāna rhetoric of nonduality, such as "saṃsāra is nirvāṇa" and "the defilements are enlightened insight," has at times been taken as a license to commit evil and exposed the tradition to criticism. The same holds true with the recondite language of those tantric texts that equate sexual activity or even killing with the practice of the Way.[3] Thus Kūkai warned that such statements are metaphors whose true meaning can be grasped only through esoteric meditation, which must be taught directly by master to disciple.[4]

Andō Toshio, a leading scholar of T'ien-t'ai Buddhism, has suggested that in China before Chih-i's time, sūtras such as the *Shou-lou-yen ching* (*Śūraṃgama-samādhi-sūtra*) and the *Wei-mo ching* (*Vimalakīrti-nirdeśa*)— which explicitly teach the ontological identity of opposing categories such as the worldly passions and enlightenment—had been facilely misread and misappropriated as endorsements of immoral conduct, eventually opening the sangha to attack. Chih-i himself saw this as a key factor that had precipitated anti-Buddhist persecution (574–577) during the Northern Chou dynasty.[5] Chih-i's own thought stresses that delusion and enlightenment, the nine realms and Buddha realm, are inherent in any phenomenon; thus those who live in evil circumstances and have no opportunity to contemplate the perfections are not excluded from the Way but can make that evil the subject of liberative contemplation. Nevertheless, he was extremely careful to clarify that the ontological nonduality of good and evil did not obviate the need to make firm conventional distinctions between them; he also inveighed against monks who interpreted the teaching of nonduality as legitimizing antinomian behavior or who taught it irresponsibly without regard for their listeners' ability to understand.[6] Medieval Japanese Tendai thought might conceivably be deemed potentially more "dangerous" than its continental antecedent in that its nondual message was not tempered by an emphasis on successive stages of cultivation but was wedded to a position of "realizing Buddhahood with this very body." Nonetheless, the moral questions raised by its *hongaku* doctrine are far from unique. But if it shared with the larger tradition of nondual Mahāyāna thought a susceptibility to antinomian readings, it also shared its appeal found in the collapse of any ultimate distinction between the Buddha and the ordinary worldling, or the pure land and the present world. As Tamura Yoshirō has noted, "When interpreted with a mind ready to understand its meaning, we can state that the thesis that 'the common worldling is the essential Buddha' has uncovered a deep value in the condition of being a common worldling, who in pain and sorrow struggles to live through factual reality."[7]

The qualifications suggested above to the characterization of original enlightenment thought as "absolute affirmation" both allow for a more accurate understanding of this medieval Tendai discourse in its own right and also make possible a reassessment of its relationship to the doctrines of the new Kamakura Buddhist movements. Since Tendai *hongaku* thought does not deny the necessity of Buddhist practice, the new Kamakura schools cannot accurately be characterized as a countermovement to revive it: This notion, too, should be allowed to lapse permanently. As Shigyō Kaishū pointed out long ago, unlike Hōchi-bō Shōshin, none of the founders of the new schools advocated an "acquired enlightenment" model of gradual cultivation culminating in enlightenment.[8] In that their teachings hold enlightenment or salvation to be accessed in the present moment and inseparable from the act of faith or practice, all adopted an "original enlightenment" orientation. In medieval Tendai thought, the nonduality of the ordinary worldling and the Buddha forms the focus of argument; the particular form of practice one adopts is less important.

In the new movements, this "nondual" standpoint is assimilated to claims for the sole validity of a particular form of faith or practice, which itself becomes the polemical touchstone, as the exclusive validity of the *Lotus Sūtra* does in the case of Nichiren. But this shift in focus is neither a rejection nor a fundamental transformation of the *hongaku* stance: Acceptance or denial of original enlightenment thought was not the fault line along which the "old"/"new" divide occurred. Far more important to the emergence of the new movements were such factors as their success in forming new institutions or *kyōdan* (including, as Matsuo Kenji has noted, the adoption of ordination procedures independent of the state-sponsored *kaidan*); their grounding in social and economic bases different from those of the Tendai temple-shrine complexes of the capital; and the particular ideological orientation inherent in their commitment to single practice, which served to define them over and against other Buddhists. That successors of Nichiren, Dōgen, or Shinran actively appropriated elements of the *hongaku* discourse and developed them in terms of their founder's teaching does not mean that they broke faith with a founder who had rejected, criticized, or retreated from original enlightenment thought. Rather it is an indication that their institutions and distinctive forms of practice were by then sufficiently well established that they could devote themselves to working out the philosophical implications of their founder's message with respect to the interpretive model—that of original enlightenment—then reigning in leading Buddhist circles.

The present study has approached *hongaku* thought as representative of a new paradigm or "reimagining" of liberation that emerged and became influential in the early medieval period. This paradigm was characterized by nonlinearity, that is, by the conviction that enlightenment is directly accessible in the present moment, and that practice represents the expression of enlightenment, not merely the means to achieve it. This way of thinking about Buddhist liberation also stressed dependence upon a single factor, whether faith, insight, or a specific practice; accessibility, at least in theory, to all persons, even (or especially) those of limited capacity; and a deemphasis on moral cultivation as a causal factor necessary to salvation. This paradigm was shared by both Tendai and the new Kamakura schools. Given the difficulties of chronology, and the fact that the doctrines of medieval Tendai and of the new schools continued to undergo elaboration throughout the Kamakura and Muromachi periods, it is difficult to say that this paradigm simply and unproblematically "emerged" from Tendai. It developed within both Tendai and the new schools and was influenced by their interaction. By the latter medieval period, it had become an orthodoxy. The present study has considered only Tendai Buddhism and the new movements that emerged from it—particularly the Nichiren Hokkeshū. Whether or not, and if so, to what extent, its findings apply to developments in other parts of the medieval Buddhist world, such as Shingon and the Nara schools, remains to be determined.

Seeing *hongaku* thought as representative of a "reimagining" of liberation characteristic of the medieval period and shared by both "new" and "old" Buddhisms allows us better to evaluate a second, oft-invoked characterization: in Kuroda Toshio's words, that *"kenmitsu* ideology in its most archetypal form is found in the Tendai doctrine known as *hongaku shisō."*[9] "We could go so far," Kuroda suggests, "as to describe *hongaku* thought as esoteric Buddhism, in both essential concept and actual practice, operating under the title of Tendai."[10] As Sueki Fumihiko has pointed out, Kuroda's concept of *kenmitsu* Buddhism is complex, in that it encompasses both the intellectual and ideological aspects of the fusion of exoteric and esoteric doctrine *(kenmitsu-shugi)* and also a religious system involving the organizational structure and ritual activities of temple-shrine complexes and their relationship to political authority and medieval society more generally (i.e., the *kenmitsu taisei*).[11] Concerning the first aspect, the incorporation of Mikkyō by the various Buddhist schools, Kuroda writes:

> Within this [Heian period] trend toward esotericization, where did the individuality of the respective schools lie? What, for instance, characterized the Tendai school *as* Tendai? . . . It was not that there was a pure and immutable body of Tendai *Lotus* thought onto which the esoteric teachings were grafted and later flourished. Rather, a unique form of the esoteric teaching endowed with the features of Tendai *Lotus* thought—specifically, found in its doctrinal dimensions at the time Annen lived—emerged and reached full maturity. The Tendai school's individuality lies here.[12]

This perfectly describes the Taimitsu thought that developed within Heian period Tendai Buddhism through the efforts of Enchin, Ennin, Annen, and others. But is medieval Tendai *hongaku* thought merely a "maturing" of Taimitsu? As doctrine or "thought," original enlightenment definitely drew on a Taimitsu sensibility. Its emphasis on the all-pervasiveness of an originally enlightened Tathâgata who is identified with all concrete phenomena, its insistence on the direct accessibility of enlightenment, and its "mandalization" of time and space, all reflect Mikkyō influence and can be seen as a continuation of the effort, begun in early Heian period Taimitsu thought, to understand traditional T'ien-t'ai/Tendai texts, doctrines, and categories in an esoteric mode. The milieu in which it was developed, including conventions of initiation rituals and secret master-disciple transmission, was heavily influenced by Taimitsu ritual culture and that of Mikkyō more generally. However, one notes, broadly speaking, a difference in focus: Where Taimitsu thought aims at synthesizing traditional *Lotus*-based studies with Mikkyō scriptures and categories, medieval Tendai *hongaku* doctrine assumes this synthesis and directs itself instead to the reinterpretation and reassertion of traditional T'ien-t'ai/Tendai categories and emphasis on the uniqueness of the *Lotus Sūtra* from the standpoint of original enlightenment. It must also be noted that the scholar-monks engaged in the kuden transmissions of the Eshin and Danna schools and their sublineages termed these "exoteric" lineages, distinct from those of Taimitsu ritual. It is this in particular that leads Sueki Fumihiko to assert that, "although influenced by esoteric Buddhism, *hongaku* thought is not essentially esoteric in nature."[13] This of course raises the question of whether the "essential" feature of *hongaku* thought is its esoteric structure or its distinctively T'ien-t'ai/Tendai exoteric doctrinal content, a point that one imagines could be debated endlessly to little purpose. However, in the Tendai case, the category of *kenmitsu* doctrine would seem to require a further distinction: There was Taimitsu thought proper, the distinctively Tendai mode of esoteric Buddhism thought developed by such Heian period thinkers as Ennin, Enchin, and Annen, and the *hongaku* teachings of the medieval *kuden hōmon*, which, while esoteric in structure and sensibility, gave greater attention to traditional Tendai doctrinal categories and were classed by their transmitters as "exoteric." Whether or not one calls *hongaku* thought "esoteric" then comes down to how broadly "esoteric" should be defined.[14]

When one considers the institutional aspects of *kenmitsu* Buddhism, the *kenmitsu taisei*, the place of *hongaku* thought becomes yet more elusive. Seen in the context of Mt. Hiei, Onjōji and other major Tendai temple-shrine complexes of the region of the imperial capital, original enlightenment thought unquestionably developed within the *kenmitsu taisei* and helped legitimize the culture of secret transmission that supported it. However, as this study has shown, there were other important loci where original enlightenment thought developed. These included the Tendai seminaries or *dangisho* of the Kantō region, not all of which performed Taimitsu rituals. Another such locus was the Nichiren Hokke temples of the Muromachi period, which developed a distinctively Nichiren Buddhist mode of original enlightenment thought but were not necessarily incorporated into the *kenmitsu taisei*. The same may be true for distinctive appropriations and developments of *hongaku* thought by other schools of "new" Buddhism. Original enlightenment thought, it would appear, transcended any one particular institutional system.

The same may be said of exoteric-esoteric syntheses more generally. Within the *kenmitsu taisei*, as Kuroda has pointed out, the new Buddhist movements represented heterodox elements: they were not part of the system of ruling elites and their single-practice orientation was potentially subversive, in that it implicitly challenged the religious authority of the major temple-shrine complexes. Nor did they define themselves as *kenmitsu* Buddhism. Nevertheless, their teachings, like those of medieval Tendai *hongaku* thought, suggest esoteric influence. This is particularly striking in the case of Nichiren, whose practice reflects Mikkyō ritual use of mantra and mandala, and whose later tradition conducted apotropaic prayer rituals.[15] The "nonlinear" paradigm of liberation itself, which was characteristic of the medieval period and shared by both "old" and "new" Buddhism, may itself be seen as an expression of *"kenmitsu"* thought. Its emphasis on the direct accessibility of enlightenment in the moment of faith and practice strongly suggests the Mikkyō concept of realizing union with the cosmic Buddha in the act of esoteric practice. To this basic, non-linear structure were assimilated the specifics of a variety of "exoteric" traditions: Tendai, Pure Land, Nichiren, and Zen. As illustrated by the examples of both original enlightenment thought and the "nonlinear" paradigm of liberation of which it was one expression, the fusion of es-oteric and exoteric teachings, to which Kuroda has drawn attention, in fact transcends the *kenmitsu* system itself.

Original enlightenment thought, and the "nonlinear" paradigm more generally, cross and blur the traditional categories that have used to ana-lyze Kamakura Buddhism: "old" and "new," *kenmitsu* orthodoxy and het-erodox *itan*. It thus has much to reveal, synchronically, about the com-plexity of Buddhist thought and practice during this period. Viewed diachronically, it also raises important questions about the history of Japanese Buddhism. As Hazama Jikō pointed out, the *hongaku* discourse flourished for some six hundred years, from the latter Heian through the mid-Tokugawa periods. A deeper investigation of its beginning and end points—what preceded it and what followed—might be expected to shed light on aspects of Japanese Buddhism that are as yet but little understood. At its source, of course, lie the complex developments of Heian religion. All the significant features of *hongaku* discourse—the direct accessibility of Buddhahood, the concern for people of limited capacity, the "shortening of the path," the equation of wordly phe-nomena with Buddhist truth, the weakening of the causal links between moral conduct and liberation—can be traced to the Heian period. Com-pared to that of the Kamakura period, Heian Buddhism has been little studied, and yet its formative influence was profound. Sueki Fumihiko writes:

> In my view, the basis of Japanese Buddhist thought was formed in the early Heian period. For example, one can point to the establishment of Saichō's ideas concerning the Buddha nature and the Mahāyāna precepts, or Kūkai's thought on the realization of Buddhahood with this very body. The fundamental theoretical issues were for the most part already present in this period. We can probably say that the so-called

Kamakura Buddhism developed on this basis, as an extension of new, multifaceted issues related to practice.[16]

The key intellectual developments that Sueki notes; the religious, political, and cultural importance of esoteric ritual pointed out by Kuroda Toshio and others; and the emergence of the new model of conceiving liberation addressed in this study all underscore the need to understand better the religious life and thought of the Heian period, not merely as the precursors to Kamakura Buddhism but in their own right. Here, one hopes not merely for the history of particular schools, ideas, and institutions, important as they are, but for interdisciplinary and "interactive" approaches that will illuminate the mutual influences of Mikkyō and other Buddhist schools; of Buddhism and other religious traditions; and of religion and art, literature, politics, and society.[17]

Almost more intriguing than the question of how original enlightenment discourse began is that of how it ended. In one sense, it is still with us, for the doctrinal orthodoxy of many Japanese Buddhist traditions today retains a *"hongaku"* orientation in holding that liberation is accessed in the act of practice. However, only vestiges remain of the medieval sensibility in which that discourse was embedded, including the culture of secret transmission and *kanjin*-style interpretation. Here our attention is drawn to the eighteenth century. The rise to influence on Mt. Hiei of the monks of the Anraku school—their advocacy of the *ssu-fen lü* precepts, their call for suppression of the *genshi kimyōdan kanjō*, and their espousal of the Sung T'ien-t'ai thought of Chih-li as a new orthodoxy, replacing that of the medieval Tendai *kuden*—were representative of profound but little-understood epistemological shifts. New modes of learning stressed a return to original source documents as normative sources of authority. Crossing traditions, this emphasis on "classicism and fundamentalism" was to be found in eighteenth-century schools of Neo-Confucianism, in Nativism *(kokugaku)* and in Buddhism.[18] This was the era when Buddhist scholars "rediscovered" their respective founders as definitive of their traditions, collated and edited their writings, and wrote extensive commentaries. Aided by improved printing and circulation, the study of publicly available documents began to compete with *kuden* as a major source of knowledge. Long dismissed by scholars as "corrupt," Tokugawa Buddhism is at the time of this writing at last coming into its own as a rich field of study. Understanding the shifts that occurred during this period in Buddhist sources of legitimation, modes of transmission of knowledge, and hermeneutical strategies will be important to understanding the complex transitions that took place in religious and intellectual life in early modern Japan.

Besides illuminating, by the manner of its rise and fall, important shifts in Japanese religious thought and practice, *hongaku* discourse during its own historical moment exerted an immense impact on medieval thought and culture. Its valorizing of the phenomenal world as equivalent to the ultimate reality that exists nowhere apart from it was profoundly inter-twined with developments in Buddhist thought and ritual, theories about the *kami,* modes of interpretation and transmission, and medieval aesthetic ideals and artistic forms. Scholars have only begun to study the historical significance of this discourse. This study is an introduction; much more waits to be done.

Notes

Chapter One: What Is "Original Enlightenment Thought"?

1. There is no scholarly consensus as to the best English translation of the term *hongaku*. "Original enlightenment," "innate enlightenment," and "inherent enlightenment," have all been used. In his editor's introduction to the June–September 1987 issue of the *Japanese Journal of Religious Studies* 14/2–3, Paul Swanson notes: "None of these is entirely satisfactory: 'original enlightenment' has too strong a temporal implication, while the terms 'innate' and 'inherent' smack of a substantialist heresy" (p. 74). More recently, Ruben L. F. Habito, taking account of these difficulties, has decided to use "originary enlightenment" (see his *Originary Enlightenment*, pp. 79–80, n. 1). "Originary," however, seems problematic in that it carries the connotation of "producing" or "causing to exist." For this study, I have decided to use "original enlightenment." Not only has this precedent been set by Yoshito Hakeda in his translation of the *Awakening of Faith* and by Robert Buswell in his translation of the *Chin-kang san-mei ching (Vajrasamādhi-sūtra)*, but "original enlightenment" seems particularly appropriate in the medieval Tendai context, precisely because of the temporal implications of the word "original." Texts of this tradition often play on the ambivalence of *hon* as meaning both "the beginning" and "inherent." For example, the Buddha's "original" (i.e., "first") realization of enlightenment in the distant past, as described in chapter 16 of the *Lotus Sūtra*, is consistently reinterpreted as a metaphor for the "original" (i.e., "innate") enlightenment of all beings.

2. "Hongakumon no shinkō," a lecture given by Shimaji in 1906 and published in 1928, deals with "original enlightenment thought" in the broad sense. *Hongaku* as an interpretive category in medieval Japanese Tendai is discussed in several of Shimaji's books and essays. These include "Chūko Tendai no gakugo toshite mitaru hongaku no gainen" (1916); *Nihon Bukkyō hongaku shisō no gaisetsu* (1931), the published edition of Shimaji's first lectures at the University of Tokyo following his appointment there as lecturer in 1919; *Nihon Bukkyō kyōgakushi* (1933), the published edition of lectures Shimaji gave at the University of Tokyo in 1924 and 1925; and "Nihon ko Tendai kenkyū no hitsuyō o ronzu" (1926).

3. "Nihon ko Tendai kenkyū no hitsuyō o ronzu."

4. For extremely useful bibliographies on Tendai original enlightenment thought, see Sueki Fumihiko, "Tendai hongaku shisō kenkyū no shomondai," pp. 299–311, and Asai Endō, ed., *Hongaku shisō no genryū to tenkai*, pp. 461–74.

5. A good example of this way of understanding original enlightenment thought can be found in Nakamura Hajime, "Kichō kōen: Shizen ni ikiru," p. 7. See also Nakamura's *Ways of Thinking of Eastern Peoples*, pp. 350–51. Echoes of the same argument can be found in some essays by Tamura Yoshirō; for example, "Japanese Culture and the Tendai Concept of Original Enlightenment," pp. 207–209.

6. See, for example, Matsumoto Shirō, "Bukkyō to shingi: Han-Nihonshugiteki kōsatsu," and Hakamaya Noriaki, "'Wa' no han-Bukkyōsei to Bukkyō no hansensei" and "Tennōsei hihan."

7. For early studies of the genealogy of original enlightenment thought, see Shimaji Daitō, *Nihon Bukkyō hongaku shisō no gaisetsu*, esp. pp. 21–38, and Mochizuki Kankō, "Hongaku hōmon ni tsuite." A more recent account is Tamura Yoshirō, "Tendai hongaku shisō gaisetsu," pp. 483–521.

8. The *Awakening of Faith* was probably compiled after the *Jen-wang ching* but before the *Chin-kang san-mei ching*. On the dating of the *Jen-wang ching* and the *Awakening of Faith*, see Mochizuki Shinkō, *Bukkyō kyōten seiritsushi ron*, pp. 425–41, 532–641. The *Jen-wang ching* is also discussed in Paul Swanson, *Foundations of T'ien-t'ai Philosophy*, pp. 45–50. The *Chin-kang san-mei ching* is discussed and translated in Robert E. Buswell, Jr., *The Formation of Ch'an Ideology in China and Korea*. Buswell suggests that this sūtra was composed in Korea in the late seventh century (see esp. pp. 170–77).

9. English translations of the *Ta-sheng ch'i-hsin lun* include D. T. Suzuki's *Aśvaghosha's Discourse on the Awakening of Faith in the Mahayana* (1900), Rev. Timothy Richard's *The Awakening of Faith in the Mahayana Doctrine* (1907), Bikshu Wai-tao and Dwight Goddard's "Awakening of Faith" (1952), and Yoshito S. Hakeda's *The Awakening of Faith* (1967). Goddard (*Buddhist Bible*, p. 668) also refers to an English translation of a Sanskrit version of the text reconstructed from the Chinese and published in the magazine *Shrine of Wisdom* in 1929–30 (one assumes that this project was undertaken before the Chinese origins of the *Awakening of Faith* were generally recognized). There exists a formidable body of secondary literature on the question of the treatise's authorship. See the list of references in Kashiwagi Hiroo, *Daijō kishinron no kenkyū*, pp. 498–501. For two recent considerations of this issue in English, see Whalen W. Lai, "A Clue to the Authorship of the *Awakening of Faith*: 'Śikṣānanda's' Redaction of the Word 'Nien'," and William H. Grosnick, "The Categories of *T'i, Hsiang* and *Yung*."

10. For a detailed discussion of this problem in early Chinese Buddhism, see Robert Gimello, "Chih-yen (602–668) and the Foundations of Hua-yen Buddhism," pp. 212–337. For its treatment in the specific context of the *Ta-sheng ch'i-hsin lun*, see Peter N. Gregory, "The Problem of Theodicy in the *Awakening of Faith*," and Buswell, *Ch'an Ideology*, pp. 78–92.

11. According to Yūki Reimon, this emerged as one of the major issues in the distinctively Chinese forms of Buddhism that arose during the Sui and T'ang dynasties. See, for example, his "Shotō Bukkyō no shisōshiteki mujun to kokka kenryoku

to no kōsaku," pp. 5–7. Yūki's theory has been developed with respect to Hua-yen Buddhism in Gimello, "Chih-yen (602–668)" (e.g. pp. 96ff), and Peter N. Gregory, *Tsung-mi and the Sinification of Buddhism.*

12. *T* 32:576b12.

13. *T* 32:576b15–16; Hakeda, *The Awakening of Faith,* p. 38.

14. Tamura Yoshirō, "Tendai hongaku shisō gaisetsu," pp. 486–90. See also Itō Zuiei, "Chūgoku Kegonshū ni okeru hongakuteki shisō."

15. "Chih-yen," p. 411.

16. Hua-yen concepts of origination as developed by Chih-yen are discussed in Gimello, "Chih-yen," pp. 421–45; by Fa-tsang, in Gregory, *Tsung-mi,* pp. 157–58; and by Tsung-mi, in Gregory, *Tsung-mi,* pp. 187–92, 232–33, and 242–43. My discussion here of Hua-yen concepts of origination is indebted to these sources.

17. *Ta-sheng ch'i-hsin lin i-chi, T* 44:255c20–21; *Hua-yen yu-hsin fa-chieh chi, T* 45:644a1–3.

18. *T* 32: 576c11–13, 578a7–10. See also Hakeda, *The Awakening of Faith,* pp. 41, 55, and the discussion in Gregory, *Tsung-mi,* pp. 160–61.

19. *T* 46:54a9–10, 15–16. Translation follows Wm. Theodore de Bary et al., eds, *Sources of Chinese Tradition,* vol. 1, p. 328, slightly modified.

20. For a synopsis of the threefold truth and threefold contemplation, see Neal Donner and Daniel Stevenson, *The Great Calming and Contemplation,* pp. 9–13. The threefold truth as an expansion of Madhyamaka doctrine and the underlying structure of Chih-i's thought is discussed in Swanson, *T'ien-t'ai Philosophy,* esp. pp. 6–8, 115–56. (I have also followed Swanson in using "conventional existence" to translate *chia;* "provisional existence" is also frequently used.) See in addition Yu-kwan Ng, *T'ien-t'ai Buddhism and Early Mādhyamika,* who argues, against Swanson and others, that the "Middle Way-Buddha Nature," rather than the threefold truth, represents the key to Chih-i's thought. He also stresses the disjuncture, rather than the continuity, between Chih-i and Nāgārjuna. Swanson's response appears in his "Understanding Chih-i: Through a Glass, Darkly?," pp. 349–56. See also Susan Mattis, "Chih-i's Appropriation of Madhyamaka."

21. *Mo-ho chih-kuan* 1, *T* 46:1c24–25. This oft-quoted passage is actually from the preface by Chih-i's disciple Kuan-ting. On the status of "conventional existence" in Chih-i's thought, see Satō Tetsue, "Santai sangan shisō no kigen oyobi hattatsu," and Tamura Yoshirō, *Kamakura shin Bukkyo shisō no kenkyū,* pp. 73–75.

22. The locus classicus for this doctrine is the *Kuan-yin hsüan-i* 1, *T* 34:882c8–883a11. See also Andō Toshio, *Tendaigaku,* pp. 165–72, and Heng-ching Shih, "T'ien-t'ai Chih-i's Theory of Buddha Nature," both of whom treat the *Kuan-yin hsüan-i* as Chih-i's work. Satō Tetsue, however, argues that it is in fact the work of Chih-i's disciple Kuan-ting (561–632), to whom the doctrine of innate evil should be attributed (*"Kannon gengi* narabi ni *Gisho* no seiritsu ni kansuru kenkyū").

23. Tamura Yoshirō, "Tendai hongaku shisō gaisetsu," p. 495.

24. *Chin-kang pei, T* 46:782c4–5, as translated in Linda Penkower, "T'ien-t'ai during the T'ang Dynasty," pp. 454–55. On Chan-jan's appropriation of Hua-yen concepts, see Lang Eun Ra, "The T'ien-t'ai Philosophy of Non-duality," esp. pp. 175–77,

186–94; and Chi-wah Chan, "Chih-li (960–1028) and the Formation of Orthodoxy in the Sung T'ien-t'ai Tradition of Buddhism," pp. 52–74. Against claims that Chan-jan compromised T'ien-t'ai orthodoxy by borrowing Hua-yen ideas of origination from suchness, Ra argues that Chan-jan was faithful to the T'ien-t'ai position of mutual inclusivity of the mind and all dharmas. This argument is also upheld by Chan and Penkower, who additionally stress that Chan-jan deliberately adopted such terminology because his intention was to criticize the arguments of *tathâgata-garbha* and Hua-yen thinkers in their own language, which was popular in the Buddhist circles of his day. See Chan, pp. 42–47, and Penkower, pp. 366–68, as well as *passim* in Penkower's commentarial notes on her translation of the *Chin-kang pei* included in this study, esp. n. 108 (pp. 455–56), n. 119 (pp. 463–64), n. 122 (p. 465), and n. 128 (pp. 467–81).

25. *Chin-kang pei, T* 46:782c19–26. See also the translations of this passage in Chan ("Chih-li," pp. 53–54) and Penkower ("T'ien-tai," pp. 463–65). Chan-jan's argument obviously rests on the equation of the Buddha nature with suchness, a position that Hua-yen teachers such as Fa-tsang and Ch'eng-kuan did not necessarily accept. For a summary of Sui and T'ang understandings of the Buddha nature, see Penkower, "T'ien-t'ai," pp. 467–81, n. 128.

26. For an analysis of the complex issues involved in this controversy, see Ra, "The T'ien-t'ai Philosophy of Non-Duality," esp. chap. 3; Chan, "Chih-li (960–1028)"; and Donner and Stevenson, *The Great Calming and Contemplation,* pp. 84–96. Where Ra focuses on doctrinal issues, Chan also analyzes the social context of the schism, and Donner and Stevenson discuss the relation of the doctrinal controversy to different emphases in the forms of T'ien-t'ai practice.

27. See Tamura Yoshirō, *Kamakura shin Bukkyō shisō no kenkyū,* pp. 73–82, and "Tendai hongaku shisō gaisetsu," p. 485.

28. See Robert Gimello, "Apophatic and Kataphatic Discourse in Mahāyāna." Gimello argues that the paired terms *li* and *shih* parallel but are not identical to the Indic terms "emptiness" (*śūnyatā, k'ung*) and "form" (*rūpa, se*), whose implications they serve to clarify and expand. *Li,* he says, may be understood as the principle *that* particular forms are empty of metaphysical substance, thus subsuming within itself the relationship of the two. This move serves to emphasize the *modal* status of the notion of emptiness, avoiding its reification either as a "thing" or as "nothingness." (However, as noted by Gregory in *Tsung-mi and the Sinification of Buddhism,* p. 7, n. 8, "principle" in the Hua-yen tradition came increasingly to be understood as the "one mind" from around Fa-tsang's time.) *Shih* for its part includes both dharmas as the basic constituents of existence and the things and events constituted by dharmas; since both are empty, the use of this term implies the emptiness of both dharmas and common-sense phenomena. It therefore enables insight into the nonsubstantial nature of the world in broad terms, freed from the need to focus on the emptiness of the specific dharma categories imported into the early Mahāyāna by way of Abhidharma studies. This new language, in Gimello's view, enabled each particular to be seen, not only as empty, but also as *full,* in the sense of encompassing in itself the nonduality of principle and phenomena. This in turn enabled a positive revalorizing of the phenomenal world.

For an introduction to the influence and reception of the categories of *li* and *shih* in Japanese Tendai, see Tamura Yoshirō, "Ri kenpon to ji jōjū."

29. See Gimello, "Chih-yen, esp. pp. 449–51, and "Apophatic and Kataphatic Discourse in Mahāyāna." Many of the observations Gimello makes here with regard to Hua-yen apply also to T'ien-t'ai.

30. As others have noted, there is no single English word that will adequately handle all connotations of the Japanese *shū* (Ch. *tsung*), which can mean "doctrine" or "teaching" as well as the lineage of followers of that teaching. Both "school" and "sect" have been used to translate *shū* in the latter sense. Following James H. Foard, I have generally used "school" in the case of premodern Tendai and Shingon, and "sect" for the independent Pure Land, True Pure Land, and Nichiren Buddhist institutions that emerged during the Kamakura period (see "In Search of a Lost Reformation," pp. 272–74). I have also used "sect" in referring to contemporary Japanese Buddhist denominations. Through its use in the context of the church-sect theory of Ernst Troelsch, H. Richard Niebhur, and others in the study of Christian institutions, "sect" has often come to imply a closed, schismatic group that has broken away from a larger, established church. See, however, William M. Bodiford, who draws on recent sociological theory for a definition of the term "sect" freed from Christian overtones and more applicable to the Japanese case (*Sōtō Zen in Medieval Japan*, pp. 4–5).

31. On the ninth stage of mind, represented by the Kegon teachings, see Kūkai's *Himitsu mandara jūjūshin ron* 9, *KDZ* 1:369–96, trans. in Yoshito S. Hakeda, *Kūkai*, pp. 211–17, and *Hizō hōyaku* 3, *KDZ* 1:459–65. The mutual influence of Hua-yen and Chen-yen in China and Korea is noted by Shimaji Daitō, *Nihon Bukkyō hongaku shisō no gaisetsu*, pp. 26–27. The *Shih Mo-ho-yen lun*, a Hua-yen-influenced treatise mentioned below that greatly influenced Kūkai, also shows signs of Chen-yen influence (see Morita Ryūsen, "Shaku Makaen ron," *BKD* 5:25a).

32. Nāgārjuna's authorship was already suspect by Kūkai's time (see, for example, Saichō's dismissal of this text as apocryphal in *Shugo kokkai shō* 1b, *DDZ* 2:278). Mochizuki Shinkō concludes that it was produced in Korea between 720 and 779 (*Bukkyō kyōten seiritsushi ron*, pp. 651–70).

33. On this subject, see Shimaji Daitō, *Nihon Bukkyō hongaku shisō no gaisetsu*, pp. 25–26, 60–64, and Kashiwagi Hiroo, "*Shaku makaen ron* ni okeru hongaku shisō."

34. *Shih Mo-ho-yen lun* 5, *T* 32:637b29–c1, c7–8.

35. For example: "If living beings also possess the Dharma body of original enlightenment and are equal to the Buddha" (*Shōji jissō gi*, *KDZ* 1:533) and "Great Vairocana is the Dharma body that is one's own nature, that is, the body in principle *(rishin)* of innate, original enlightenment." (*Dainichi-kyō kaidai*, *KDZ* 1:640). On Kūkai's reading of the *Shih Mo-ho-yen lun*, see Shimaji Daitō, *Nihon Bukkyō hongaku shisō no gaisetsu*, pp. 27–30, 64–68; Tamura Yoshirō, "Mikkyō to hongaku shisō," pp. 383–87; Katsumata Shunkyō, "Kōbō Daishi ni okeru hongaku shisō to sono haikei"; and Matsuzaki Keisui, "Kūkai oyobi sono monka no hongaku yōgorei oyobi sono igi," pp. 121–32.

36. On Kūkai's ideas of original enlightenment and the identification of the practitioner with the cosmic Buddha Mahāvairocana, see Fukuda Ryōsei, "Kōbō Daishi no hongakuteki shutaikan."

37. *Shugo kokkai shō* 1b reads: "The *Yūmon* states, '. . . The essence of wisdom, the

pure suchness of original enlightenment *(hongaku)* that is within oneself is expressed [in the *Lotus Sūtra*] as "the Buddha's knowledge." . . . When hindrances have not yet been fully removed, that is called dwelling in delusion. Original enlightenment is still obscured. When hindrances are fully removed, that is called emerging from delusion. When original enlightened has [thus] appeared, that is called the Dharma body'" *(DDZ* 2:230–31).

The *Yūmon* (properly *Joshō Hokke yūmonshū*) is a no longer extant work attributed to a monk named Hinbō or Hinpō, whose biographical details are unclear. On Saichō's understanding of original enlightenment, see Asai Endō, *Jōko Nihon Tendai honmon shisō shi,* pp. 137–40.

38. *MFLHC, p'in* 2, *T* 9:8a17–18; Hurvitz, p. 34.

39. For how the relation of the three vehicles to the one vehicle has been understood historically, see Fujita Kōtatsu, "One Vehicle or Three?" On the concept of skillful means in the *Lotus Sūtra,* see Michael Pye, *Skilful Means,* pp. 18–83. Pye takes an inclusive reading of the sūtra, interpreting the "one vehicle" as a formless truth that can have no expression apart from the "skillful means" that are the differentiated vehicles or teachings. For a historical treatment emphasizing exclusive appropriations of the one-vehicle doctrine to particular traditions, especially as this occurred in Japan, see Carl Bielefeldt, "The One Vehicle and the Three Jewels."

40. Tokuitsu's communications with Saichō do not survive, and the content of their debate is known only through Saichō's writings. However, these give an account detailed enough to be able to reconstruct Tokuitsu's position. For convenient summaries of key issues in the debate, see Asai Endō, *Jōko Nihon Tendai honmon shisōshi,* pp. 140–50, and Paul Groner, *Saichō,* pp. 91–106.

41. This assertion seems to derive from the *Yüan-chüeh ching* (Sūtra of perfect enlightenment), an apocryphal Sinitic sūtra. Following the *Awakening of Faith* and other sources, it asserts the inherent potential for Buddhahood in all beings and, especially as interpreted by Tsung-mi, helped shape the continental original enlightenment tradition. Saichō cites its assertion that the principle of suchness in living beings has the nature of knowing. See the discussion in Asai Endō, *Jōko Nihon Tendai honmon shisōshi,* p. 146.

42. See Tamura Yoshirō, *Kamakura shin Bukkyō shisō no kenkyū,* p. 171, n. 26, for examples of scholary studies noting the Kegon influences on Saichō's thought.

43. *Shugo kokkai shō* 1b and 3b, *DDZ* 2:237, 567–68.

44. See Take Kakuchō, *Tendai kyōgaku no kenkyū,* pp. 10–13.

45. On the background and development of Chinese *p'an-chiao,* see Gregory, *Tsung-mi,* pp. 93–114.

46. Ibid., p. 115.

47. The "five periods" organizes the body of Buddhist teachings according to an assumed sequence of preaching. The five periods are: (1) the Flower Ornament period, the first three weeks following the Buddha's enlightenment, during which he is said to have preached the Flower Ornament Sūtra (Skt. *Avataṃsaka-sūtra,* Chn. *Hua-yen ching*); (2) the Āgama period, or the next twelve years, during which he is said to have preached the āgamas or the Hīnayāna teachings; also called the period

of the Deer Park; (3) the Extended (Skt. *vaipulya*) period, or next eight years, when he is said to have expounded various introductory Mahāyāna sutras; (4) the Prajñā period, or next twenty-two years, during which the Buddha is said to have expounded the *prajñā-pāramitā* sūtras; and the Lotus-Nirvāṇa period, comprising the final eight years of his life, during which he is said to have preached the *Lotus Sūtra*, and the last day of his life, when he is said to have preached the *Nirvāṇa Sūtra*. See *T'ien-t'ai ssu-chiao i*, T 46:774c20–776a5; Hurvitz, *Chih-i*, pp. 230–44; and David Chappell, ed., *T'ien-t'ai Buddhism*, pp. 55–82.

The "eight teachings" consist of the "four methods of conversion" and the "four teachings of conversion." The four methods of conversion *(hua-i ssu-chiao, kegi no shikyō)* is a classification of the body of teachings according to the method the Buddha is said to have used in expounding them. They are: (1) the sudden teaching *(tun-chiao, tonkyō)*, which the Buddha preaches directly without preparatory teachings, as in the case of the *Flower Ornament Sūtra;* (2) the gradual teaching *(chien-chiao, zengyō)*, through which the Buddha gradually cultivates the beings' capacity, as he did with the *āgamas* and early Mahāyāna teachings; (3) the secret teaching *(pi-mi-chiao, himitsukyō)*, through which the Buddha enables the beings to benefit differently from the same preaching according to their capacities without their being aware of this; and (4) the indeterminate teaching *(pu-ting-chiao, fujōkyō)*, by which the beings knowingly receive different benefits from the same preaching. See *T'ien-t'ai ssu-chiao i*, T 46:774c21–775b 11; Hurvitz, *Chih-i*, pp. 244–48; and Chappell, *T'ien-t'ai Buddhism*, pp. 55–61.

The four teachings of conversion *(hua-fa ssu-chiao, kehō no shikyō)* represents a T'ien-t'ai classification of the Buddhist teachings according to their content. They are: (1) the Tripiṭaka teaching *(tsang-chiao, zōgyō)*, named for the three canonical divisions of *sūtra, vinaya* and *abhidharma;* (2) the shared teaching *(t'ung-chiao, tsūgyō)*, which stresses the doctrine of emptiness and is shared by the first teaching and the third and fourth teachings; (3) the separate or distinct teaching *(pieh-chiao, bekkyō)*, taught exclusively for bodhisattvas, which is distinct from the other three teachings; here the truth of the middle is cognized as separate from the truths of emptiness and conventional existence; and (4) the perfect teaching *(yüan-chiao, engyō)*, encompassing all three truths in their perfect interfusion. See *T'ien-t'ai ssu-chiao i*, T 46:776a5–780a21; also Hurvitz, *Chih-i*, pp. 248–71; Chappell, *T'ien-t'ai Buddhism*, pp. 83–173; and Donner and Stevenson, *The Great Calming and Contemplation*, pp. 13–17.

While it was long thought that the classification system of the five periods and eight teachings had originated with Chih-i (an assumption reflected in Hurvitz's study), the recent scholarship of Sekiguchi Shindai suggests that it developed later, through the efforts of Chan-jan and especially the Korean monk Chegwan (d. 971), author of the influential *T'ien-t'ai ssu-chiao i*, which sets forth this system. For example, instead of the "five periods," Chih-i had emphasized the level of the practitioner's cultivation with the analogy of the "five flavors" *(wu-wei, gomi)* corresponding to the successive steps in the manufacture of ghee or clarified butter: fresh milk, cream, curds, butter, and ghee. The "five flavors" distinguishes differences in the level of human spiritual development, rather than establishing a fixed hierarchy among sūtras. The "five periods," however, ranks the sūtras according to their content and thus has a more strongly polemical thrust. The system of the five periods and eight teachings is thought to have developed in response to growing sectarian consciousness and the need to defend the T'ien-t'ai school against its rivals. For a summary of Sekiguchi's findings, see Chappell, *T'ien-t'ai Buddhism,* pp. 36–40; and Penkower, "T'ien-t'ai," pp. 225–80, which lists the relevant Japanese scholarship. See also Minoru Kiyota, "The Structure and Meaning of Tendai Thought."

48. The two approaches take as their textual basis Chih-i's general interpretation of *miao* (Jpn. *myō*) or "subtle"—the first character of the *Lotus Sūtra*'s title— from the standpoint of the absolute *(zettai myō)* and the relative *(sōtai myō).* The subtlety of the Dharma in an absolute sense is beyond conceptualizing; its "absoluteness" is not established with respect to anything else, for there is nothing apart from it to which it might be compared. In a relative sense, however, "subtlety" is established by comparison with the "crude" or coarse (*Hsüan-i T* 33:696b9–697b21; translated in Swanson, *Foundations of T'ien-t'ai Philosophy,* pp. 199–206). See also the discussion in Tamura Yoshirō, *Kamakura shin Bukkyō shisō no kenkyū,* pp. 3–12, 95–117, as well as his "Nihon Tendai ni okeru ichijō kaie no shisō."

49. For example, *Hokke shūku* 1a and 3, *DDZ* 3:38, 241, 244, and 277. See also the discussion in Asai Endō, *Jōko Nihon Tendai honmon shisōshi,* pp. 86–97. The terms derive from *Shih-ti-ching lun* 2, *T* 26:134a1ff and are developed especially in Hua-yen/Kegon doctrine. See also the entry "Inbun kabun" in *BD* 1:192b–193a.

50. *Shugo kokkai shō* 1c, *DDZ* 2:348–49. See also the discussion in Groner, *Saichō,* pp. 183–90.

51. Asai Endō, *Jōko Nihon Tendai honmon shishōshi,* p. 184. Saichō's views on the length of time required to attain enlightenment are discussed on pp. 179–91.

52. *Hokke shūku* 3, *DDZ* 3:266. Saichō based his concept of "realizing Buddhahood within three lifetimes" *(sanshō jōbutsu)* on the passage from the *Fo-shuo kuan P'u-hsien P'u-sa ching,* the capping sūtra to the *Lotus,* which reads, "After devoting their minds to practice and being mindful with each thought of the Great Vehicle, after one day to three weeks, they will be able to see [Bodhisattva] Samantabhadra. . . . Those with heavy obstructions will be able to see him within this lifetime, or in a second lifetime, or in a third" (*T* 9:389c22–26).

53. Asai Endō, *Jōko Nihon Tendai honmon shisōshi,* pp. 99–106; Groner, *Saichō,* pp. 181–83.

54. *MFLHC, p'in* 2, *T* 9:7b26–27, c9.

55. *Shugo kokkai shō* 1a, *DDZ* 2:171. As Tamura Yoshirō points out, Saichō draws here on the doctrinal classification schemes of Chi-tsang (549–623), regarded as the patriarch of the Chinese San-lun school (*Kamakura shin Bukkyō shisō no kenkyū,* pp. 143–44).

56. The tradition that Saichō received the transmission of four schools *(shishū sōjō,* often enumerated as *en mitsu zen kai)* is based on the *Naishō Buppō kechimyaku fu,* Saichō's record of the lineages that he inherited. There he gives five lineages: the Ch'an lineage of Bodhidharma, Tendai *Lotus* teachings, bodhisattva precepts of the Tendai perfect teaching, Matrix and Diamond realm esoteric traditions, and mis-

cellaneous esoteric mandala traditions (*DDZ* 1:199). Some questions remain about the details of these transmissions. See Groner, *Saichō,* pp. 251–60.

57. Groner, *Saichō,* pp. 249–50.

58. Ibid., pp. 255–63.

59. This sūtra has been translated into French by J. J. M. DeGroot, in his *Le Code du Mahayana en Chine,* pp. 14–88.

60. Groner, *Saichō,* p. 8.

61. Ibid., pp. 190–91, 202–203.

62. For the relationship of the *Fan-wang ching* and the *Lotus Sūtra* in Saichō's understanding of the bodhisattva precepts, see *ibid.,* pp. 206–12.

63. *Kenkairon* 3, *DDZ* 1:197. See also Groner, *Saichō,* pp. 190–94.

64. "Inherent Enlightenment *(hongaku shisō)* and Saichō's Acceptance of the Bodhisattva Precepts." Of the four sources Shirato draws upon, one, the *Denjutsu isshin kaimon,* is by Saichō's disciple Kōjō, while another, the *Ju bosatsukai gi* quoted below, may also be a disciple's work. Thus they may not exactly represent Saichō's own thinking. Nevertheless, the immanentalist interpretation of the precepts that they offer did emerge very early in Japanese Tendai.

65. *T* 24:1003c22–24, 28; translation from Shirato Waka, p. 115.

66. *Ju bosatsukai gi, DDZ* 1:304; translation from Shirato Waka, "Inherent Enlightenment," p. 120, slightly modified. Saichō also speaks of the bodhisattva precepts as "unmoving like empty space within the body of the Buddha" in *Chū Muryogikyō* 1, *DDZ* 3:583.

67. Groner, *Saichō,* pp. 187–90.

68. Recorded in *Eizan Daishi den, DDZ* 5 *(furoku):* 40–41. See also Groner, *Saichō,* pp. 159–62.

69. For Saichō's understanding of this "provisional Hīnayāna ordination" *(keju shōkai)* and why it was not successfully implemented, see Groner, *Saichō,* pp. 195–205.

70. Ibid., pp. 286–303.

71. See Asai Endō, *Jōko Nihon Tendai honmon shisōshi,* pp. 780–812, and Paul Groner, "Annen, Tankei, Henjō, and Monastic Discipline in the Tendai School" and "The *Fang-wang ching* and Monastic Discipline in Japanese Tendai."

72. Groner, *Saichō,* pp. 206–207; "The *Fang-wang ching,*" p. 279.

73. Asai Endō suggests that, despite Saichō's intentions, his adoption of bodhisattva precept ordinations served as a remote cause for the clerical misconduct of later times, as well as for a more widespread devaluating of the precepts that became characteristic of Japanese Buddhism (*Jōko Nihon Tendai honmon shisōshi,* p. 210). Taga Munehaya (*Eisai,* pp. 237–38) and Takagi Yutaka (*Kamakura Bukkyōshi kenkyū,* p. 55) also suggest that the reading by Annen (b. 841) of the precepts was interpreted by later generations of monks as a rationale for breaking the precepts.

74. A key text in this development was the apocryphal *Mappō tōmyō ki,* attributed to Saichō. See the translation by Robert F. Rhodes, "Saichō's *Mappō Tōmyōki:* A Candle for the Latter Dharma."

75. Shingonshū (Shingon school) is the name given to the tradition founded by Kūkai. However, it was also used in premodern sources to indicate esoteric Buddhism

in general, and some Tendai monks referred to their own esoteric tradition in this way. Where the term does not refer specifically to Kūkai's Shingon tradition, I have translated it as "*shingon* school" or "*shingon* lineage," italicized and in lower case.

76. For an introduction to Shingon esoteric practice in English, see Taikō Yamasaki, *Shingon*, pp. 106–22.

77. Charles D. Orzech has eloquently argued this point with respect to esoteric Buddhism in its Chinese context, in his "Seeing Chen-yen Buddhism."

78. The *ryōbu* tradition is now generally thought to have emerged around the time of Amoghavajra (705–774), teacher to Kūkai's Chinese master Hui-k'o (746–805). Matsunaga Yūkei has suggested that the two lineages may not have been fully unified until Hui-k'o's time (*Mikkyō no rekishi*, pp. 146–47).

79. For the details of Saichō's esoteric initiations in China and the scholarly questions surrounding them, see Groner, *Saichō*, pp. 52–63.

80. Ryūichi Abé, "Saichō and Kūkai: A Conflict of Interpretations."

81. On Saichō's view of the esoteric teachings, see Asai Endō, *Jōko Nihon Tendai honmon shisōshi*, pp. 79–82, and Katsumata Shunkyō, *Mikkyō no Nihonteki tenkai*, pp. 250–72.

82. From the time of Saichō's disciple Ennin (794–866), it became possible for Tendai ordinands following the "esoteric course" to specialize in the *Chin-kang-ting ching* and *Su-hsi-ti ching* as well, completing the threefold division of Tendai esoteric Buddhism (Groner, *Saichō*, p. 70).

83. Ōya Tokujō proposed a third branch of esoteric Buddhism that he termed Nanmitsu ("southern esoteric Buddhism"), which developed within the temples of Nara ("Heian-chō ni okeru sandai seiryōku no kōsō to chōwa," p. 387).

84. The few occurrences of the word *hongaku* in the authenticated works of Saichō, Ennin, and Enchin are all given in Asai Endō, "Jōko Nihon Tendai ni okeru hongaku hōmon tenkaijō no genkai." Asai suggests three reasons why they did not use this term, despite both their familiarity with the Hua-yen texts in which it occurs and the mutual influence that obtained between Tendai and the Shingon school of Kūkai, who had employed the concept in arguing the superiority of the esoteric teachings. (1) The *Shih Mo-ho-yen lun*, from which Kūkai had derived the concept of "original enlightenment," had been rejected by Saichō as apocryphal; (2) "original enlightenment" was understood in early Tendai as synonymous with other terms indicating the universal potential for enlightenment, such as the "nature of realization and knowledge inherent in suchness" (*shinnyo no kakuchishō*) or "active Buddha nature" (*gyō-busshō*). In other words, it did not yet represent a distinct concept that could only be expressed through this phrase; and (3) in his argument with Tokuitsu, Saichō's concern was to establish that universal suchness is not merely a quiescent principle but also has the active nature of realizing and knowing. The notion that all beings are originally enlightened could not precede such an argument but had to follow from it.

Annen, who was of a later generation, did make use of the *Shih Mo-ho-yen lun*. For his use of the term *hongaku*, see Asai Endō, *Jōko Nihon Tendai honmon shisōshi*, pp. 741–46.

85. For discussion of Kūkai's ten stages, see, for example, Katsumata Shunkyō, *Mikkyō no Nihonteki tenkai*, pp. 179–226; Hakeda, *Kūkai*, pp. 67–75; and Minoru Kiyota, *Shingon Buddhism*, pp. 37–56.

86. *Kongochō-daikyōō-kyō shō* 1, *T* 61:16b1–8. Ennin attributes the idea of the "one great perfect teaching" to the esoteric master Yüan-cheng ("the *ācārya* of the Ta-hsing-shan-ssu"), under whom he had studied in China. As its scriptural source, he cites the *Ta-jih ching:* "All the bodily acts, all the verbal acts, and all the mental acts of Vairocana are, at all places and all times, expounding for sentient beings the phrases and teachings of the path of *shingon*" (*T* 18:848a29–b2). However, in the same work he writes that when the *Lotus Sūtra* states, "Within the Buddha lands of the ten directions, there is the Dharma of only One Vehicle" (*T* 9:8a17), that one vehicle includes the *Chin-kang ching* (*T* 61:13a21–27). As Asai Endō notes, this sūtra passage closely resembles the one on which Saichō based his concept of the "three kinds of Lotus Sūtra," and Ennin's "one great perfect teaching" may have roots in Saichō's earlier concept (*Jōko Nihon Tendai honmon shisōshi*, p. 286).

87. On Ennin's distinctions between esoteric and exoteric, see Shimaji Daitō, *Tendai kyōgaku shi*, pp. 361–67; Asai Endō, *Jōko Nihon Tendai honmon shisōshi*, pp. 284–94; and Katsumata Shunkyō, *Mikkyō no Nihonteki tenkai*, pp. 276–80.

88. *Soshitsuji-kyō sho* 1, *T* 61:393b16–26.

89. See Asai Endō, *Jōko Nihon Tendai honmon shisōshi*, pp. 422–36, and Katsumata Shunkyō, *Mikkyō no Nihonteki tenkai*, pp. 280–84.

90. These arguments are elaborated in the body of Enchin's *Dainichi-kyō shiki*. For a convenient summary, see Katsumata Shunkyō, *Mikkyō no Nihonteki tenkai*, pp. 281–82. The views of Kuang-hsiu and Wei-chüan are expressed in the *Tōketsu* (T'ang decisions), collections of answers from Chinese T'ien-t'ai monks to doctrinal questions posed by their Japanese counterparts (see *Nihon daizōkyō*, 46:365a, 394a).

91. *T* 75:374a19–20, 26–29. Translation from Sueki Fumihiko, "Annen: The Philosopher Who Japanized Buddhism," pp. 79–80, slightly modified. See also Asai Endō's discussion of the "four ones" in *Jōko Nihon Tendai no honmon shisōshi*, pp. 639–46.

92. For detailed discussions of Annen's comparative classification schemes, see Asai Endō, *Jōko Nihon Tendai honmon shisōshi*, pp. 646–55, and Katsumata Shūnkyō, *Mikkyō no Nihonteki tenkai*, pp. 284–91.

93. *Taizō kongō bodaishin gi ryaku mondō shō* 5, *T* 75:554b2–c2.

94. *MHFLC*, *T* 9:32c–33b; Hurvitz, pp. 185–87.

95. See Take Kakuchō, "Tendai Daishi Chigi no honjaku ron."

96. *T* 9:42b9–16, 23–25, c20–23; Hurvitz, pp. 237–38, 239. In the vocabulary of T'ien-t'ai/Tendai *Lotus* exegesis, the vast span of time that has passed since this original realization is referred to as *gohyaku jindengō: gohyaku* ("five hundred") for the five hundred thousand myriads of millions of nayutas of asaṃkheyas of thousand millionfold worlds that are first reduced to atoms, and *jindengō* meaning "an atom represents a kalpa."

97. The history of Tendai *honmon* thought forms the focus of Asai Endō's *Jōko Nihon Tendai honmon shisōshi*. Asai's stated concern in this volume is to establish the

antecedents of *honmon* thought in the teachings of Nichiren (1222–1282), who based his understanding of the *Lotus Sūtra* on a distinctive reading of the origin teaching. However, Asai's is also among the most detailed studies available of Heian period Tendai thought in its own right.

98. *Ta-fang-kuang fo hua-yen ching* 4 lists "Śākyamuni" and "Vairocana" as two of the many names of the Buddha of this world (*T* 9:419a11–13). *Chüan* 57 of the same sūtra additionally names Śākyamuni's mother, Lady Māyā, as "the mother of the Buddha Vairocana" (763c12).

99. *T* 9:392c15–17; English translation from Katō Bunnō et al., trans, *The Three-fold Lotus Sutra,* p. 362, slightly modified.

100. *T* 24:1003b-c. See also Ōyama Kōjun, *Mikkyōshi gaisetsu to kyōri,* p. 490.

101. Ōyama Kōjun, *Mikkyōshi gaisetsu to kyōri,* pp. 488–92.

102. *Wen-chü* 9b, *T* 34: 128a16–19. See also Chih-i's identification of P'i-lu-che-na with the subtlety of objects; Lu-che-na, with the subtlety of wisdom; and Śākyamuni, with the subtlety of practice. Here again, the three Buddhas are said to be "neither identical nor differentiated, nor vertical nor horizontal" (*Hsüan-i* 6a, *T* 33:746c13–15).

103. Before Chih-i, most Chinese Buddhist exegetes at first interpreted the Buddha of the "Fathoming the Lifespan" chapter as representing the Dharma body, while later scholars such as Fa-yün (467–529) interpreted this Buddha as the manifested body. See Andō Toshio, *Tendaigaku ronshū,* pp. 314–15. Chih-i identifies the Buddha of the "Fathoming the Lifespan" chapter with the recompense body specifically at *Wen-chü* 9b, *T* 34:129a19–25. The denial of sequence or hierarchy among the three bodies is mentioned at 128b6–9. On Chih-i's view of the three bodies, see also Andō Toshio, *Tendaigaku,* pp. 157–60, and *Tendaigaku ronshū,* pp. 314–36.

104. I-hsing suggests the identity of the two Buddhas in the *Ta-p'i-lu-che-na ch'eng-fo ching shu* 7 and 12, *T* 39:658a13–18 and 709b7. Ennin reports that Yüan-cheng ("the *ācārya* of the Ta-hsing-shan-ssu of the Great T'ang") similarly identified them (*Kongōchō daikyōō-kyō sho* 3, *T* 61:39b14–16).

105. See Shioiri Ryōchū, "Dengyō Daishi no hongaku shisō," and Asai Endō, *Jōko Nihon Tendai honmon shisōshi,* pp. 125–28.

106. Groner, *Saichō,* pp. 255–63.

107. Asai Endō discusses the positions of individual Taimitsu thinkers on this issue in his *Jōko Nihon Tendai honmon shisōshi,* as follows: Gishin, Tokuen, Kōjō, and Enchō, pp. 227–32; Ennin, pp. 310–14; Enchin, pp. 443–56; and Annen, pp. 707–18.

108. The sūtra text appears in *HTC* 15:409–13. The verse itself is at p. 409a *recto.* The *Renge sanmai-kyō* is also referred to in some Heian period texts as the *Mushōge-kyō.* According to Annen, it was introduced from China to Japan by Kūkai (*Taizō kongō bodaishin gi ryaku mondō shō* 5, *T* 75:541b3–7), while the monk Unshō (1614–1693) wrote that it had been brought over by Enchin, who had excerpted it from a longer work (*Jakushōdō kokkyō shū* 10, *DNBZ* 149:172b). The opening verse and the subsequent prose section were composed separately. Citations of the *Renge sanmai-kyō* in Heian period texts seem to refer only to the opening verse; the prose section was probably not composed until the Nanbokuchō or Muromachi period. The verse came eventually to be known as the *Hongaku san* and appears under this title in *THR,* p.

98. The *Renge sanmai-kyō* is first cited in the *Kōen Hokke gi* attributed to Enchin, but some scholars have questioned Enchin's authorship. Annen quotes it in several of his works; Mizukami Bungi has suggested that it may have been composed by Annen himself or by someone close to him ("Genkōbon *Renge sanmai-kyō* no seiritsu ni tsuite," "*Renge sanmai-kyō* no seiritsu o megutte," and "*Renge sanmai-kyō* [*Hongaku san*] o meguru ichi, ni no mondai"). For the role of the *Renge sanmai-kyō* in Annen's thought, see Misaki Ryōshū, "Godaiin Annen to *Hongaku san*."

109. These are Dainichi and the attendant Buddhas and bodhisattvas who compose the central court of the Diamond-Realm mandala.

110. The *Chū hongaku san* (*THR*, pp. 99–100) is attributed to Ryōgen (912–985), and the *Hongaku san shaku* (pp. 101–18), to Genshin (942–1017).

111. I am indebted to William Bodiford for initially pointing out to me the importance of this understanding of *ri* and *ji* in the context of Japanese Buddhism.

112. Shioda Gisen notes this shift from *ri* to *ji* with respect to practices associated with Tendai and the *Lotus Sūtra* but does not connect it to Mikkyō influence ("Asa daimoku to yū nenbutsu," pp. 66–67). Asai Endō similarly notes a general trend from "formless contemplation" to "ritual having form" as part of the "Japanization" of Buddhism but also does not link it to Mikkyō influence ("Nichiren no ibun to hongaku shisō," pp. 293–94).

113. The phrase "the real is identical with phenomena" is taken from Chih-i's *Hsüan-i* 2a and 6b, *T* 33:696c27, 760c25. (The first of these two passages is translated in Swanson, *Foundations of T'ien-t'ai Philosophy,* p. 202.) The "constant abiding of the worldly truth" probably represents a variant of *MFLHC, p'in* 2, *T* 9:9b10. See n. 115 below.

114. The association of the origin teaching with *ji* was first made by Chan-jan. According to Chan-jan, the opening of the three provisional vehicles to reveal the one true vehicle, set forth in the trace teaching, represents the perfect teaching in terms of principle *(li-yüan, rien),* while the revelation of the Buddha's enlightenment in the remote past, set forth in the origin teaching, represents the perfect teaching in terms of concrete actuality *(shih-yüan, jien)* (*Shih-ch'ien* 1, *T* 33:817b29–c1). In medieval Tendai texts, however, the "concrete actuality" associated with origin teaching is the phenomenal world understood as identical to ultimate reality.

115. *MFLHC, p'in* 2, *T* 9:9b10. This passage has a long history of varying interpretations. If one goes by the grammar of the Sanskrit version *("dharma-sthitiṃ dharma-niyāmatāṃ ca nitya-sthitāṃ loki imām akampyām"),* it should be construed as "This is the abode of the dharmas, the position of the dharmas, and the [impermanent] aspect of the world is also constant"—where the initial "this," referring back to the preceding lines of verse, indicates the nonsubstantiality of the dharmas that arise through dependent origination. In other words, arising and perishing in dependence upon conditions is the constant mode of the dharmas (Sakamoto Yukio and Iwamoto Yutaka, trans., *Hokekyō* 1:120, 352). If one follows Chih-i's interpretation, however, the passage would be read, "These dharmas abide in a Dharma-position. . . ." In Chih-i's reading, both the "Dharma-position" and the "aspect of the world" denote principle or suchness, which is the same in Buddhas and unenlightened beings (*Wen-*

chü 4b, *T* 34:58a9–17). Of the readily available English translations, those by H. Kern (*The Saddharma-puṇḍarīka*, p. 53) and Leon Hurvitz (*Scripture of the Lotus Blossom of the Fine Dharma*, pp. 41, 352 [n. 12]) follow or refer to the Sanskrit, while those by Katō Bunnō, Tamura Yoshirō, and Miyasaka Kōjirō (*The Threefold Lotus Sutra*, p. 70) and by Burton Watson (*The Lotus Sutra*, p. 41) are based on Chih-i's reading.

In Japanese Tendai, this same passage was interpreted as indicating the constant abiding of the worldly truth *(zokutai jōjū)*. Ennin in particular found in this passage the rationale for asserting that the *Lotus Sūtra* is "equal in principle" to the esoteric teachings (*THR*, p. 419b; Asai Endō, *Jōko Nihon Tendai honmon shisōshi*, pp. 306, 354). The translation above follows the interpretation commonly found in medieval Tendai texts.

116. On this topic see Sakamoto Yukio, "Sōmoku jōbutsu ni tsuite"; Miyamoto Shōson, "'Sōmoku kokudo shikkai jōbutsu' no busshōronteki igi to sono sakusha"; Hanano Michiaki, "*Sanjū shika no kotogaki* no senja to shisō ni tsuite" (2), (3), and (4); and Sueki Fumihiko, *Heian shoki Bukkyō shisō no kenkyū*, pp. 363–421.

117. On Tao-sheng's argument for the Buddha nature of the *icchantika*, see Penkower, "T'ien-t'ai," pp. 393–96, n. 15, which also references the relevant studies in Japanese and English. Chi-tsang's argument appears in his *Ta-sheng hsüan-lun* 3, *T* 45:40a21–41b8; he is the first to refer to plants and trees possessing the Buddha nature and realizing Buddhahood (40b19–20, 23). See also the discussion of Chi-tsang's position in Sueki Fumihiko, *Heian shoki Bukkyō shisō no kenkyū*, pp. 365–68, and Penkower, pp. 459–62, n. 114.

118. For Chan-jan's interpretation, see *Hung-chüeh* 1b, *T* 46:151c27–152a23, as well as the translation and discussion by Penkower, "T'ien-t'ai," pp. 420–23, n. 54.

119. *Hizō ki, KDZ* 2:37.

120. Asai Endō, *Jōko Nihon Tendai honmon shisōshi*, pp. 155–59.

121. See his *Shinjō sōmoku jōbutsu shiki*, published with annotations in Sueki Fumihiko, *Heian shoki Bukkyō shisō no kenkyū*, pp. 705–85, as well as Sueki's discussion, pp. 377–416.

122. William R. LaFleur, "Saigyō and the Buddhist Value of Nature," and Donald H. Shively, "Buddhahood for the Nonsentient."

123. *Sōmoku hosshin shugyō jōbutsu ki, DNBZ* 24:345a, attributed to Ryōgen (912–985), the eighteenth *zasu* or chief abbot of the Enryakuji. Early essays on the subject of *sōmoku jōbutsu*, such as those of Sakamoto Yukio and Miyamoto Shōson cited in n. 116 above, treat this text as Ryōgen's work. However, later textual scholarship has made clear that it was not composed until much later and belongs to the medieval Tendai original enlightenment tradition. See Sueki Fumihiko, *Heian shoki Bukkyō shisō no kenkyū*, pp. 416–17.

124. LaFleur, "Saigyō" (1), pp. 111–12.

125. Tamura Yoshirō, "Tendai hongaku shisō gaisetsu," pp. 482–515 *passim*.

126. For a summary of the scholarship on this issue, see Paul Groner, "The *Lotus Sutra* and Saichō's Interpretation of the Realization of Buddhahood with This Very Body." My use of "realizing Buddhahood with this very body" as a translation for *sokushin jōbutsu* also follows Groner.

127. *T* 32:572c13.

128. Translated by Hakeda in *Kūkai,* pp. 225–34. For a discussion of Kūkai's views on *sokushin jōbutsu* and a comparison with Saichō's, see Katsumata Shunkyō, *Mikkyō no Nihonteki tenkai,* pp. 131–78.

129. *MFLHC, p'in* 12, *T* 9:35b15–c26; Hurvitz, pp. 198–201. Saichō derived the term *sokushin jōbutsu* from Chan-jan, who interprets the dragon girl's attainment as the "realization of Buddhahood with this very body" in his commentary on Chih-i's lecture on the *Lotus Sūtra* (*Chi, T* 34:314b23–24).

On Saichō's views of *sokushin jōbutsu,* see Asai Endō, *Jōko Nihon Tendai honmon shisōshi,* pp. 179–201, and Groner, "The *Lotus Sutra.*"

130. *Hokke shūku, DDZ* 3:261.

131. Groner, "The *Lotus Sutra,*" pp. 61–68. Both the six stages of identity and the fifty-seven stages of bodhisattva practice in the perfect teaching were models of the path employed in T'ien-t'ai Buddhism. The six stages of identity are discussed in chapter 5. See also Neal Donner, "Sudden and Gradual Intimately Conjoined," pp. 204–205; Chappell, *T'ien-t'ai Buddhism,* pp. 160–61; and Donner and Stevenson, *The Great Calming and Contemplation,* pp. 207–18. The fifty-seven stages consist of five preliminary stages for disciples (*gohon deshi-i*), based on chapter 17 of the *Lotus Sūtra,* plus a fifty-two-stage schema of the bodhisattva path based on the *P'u-sa ying-lo pen-yeh ching.* These are discussed in Hurvitz, "Chih-i," pp. 264–71, 363–68. For the correlation between the two models, see Chappell, *T'ien-t'ai Buddhism,* pp. 32–34.

132. Sueki Fumihiko, "Nihon Bukkyō: Sokushin jōbutsu o chūshin ni."

133. Asai Endō discusses the views of Saichō's followers concerning *sokushin jōbutsu* in his *Jōko Nihon Tendai honmon shisōshi* as follows: Gishin, Enchō, Tokuen, Kōjō, and Anne, pp. 240–54; Ennin, pp. 358–68; Enchin, pp. 579–99; and Annen, pp. 765–79. See also Paul Groner, "Shortening the Path," and Sueki Fumihiko, *Heian shoki Bukkyō shisō no kenkyū,* pp. 278–361.

134. The most detailed study on this subject is Satō Tetsuei's *Eizan Jōdokyō no kenkyū.*

135. This system is described in detail in Daniel B. Stevenson, "The Four Kinds of Samādhi in Early T'ien-t'ai Buddhism."

136. On Ennin's introduction of the Wu-t'ai *nenbutsu* and its development on Mt. Hiei as the *fudan nenbutsu,* see Sonoda Kōyō, "Yama no nenbutsu," which is probably the most detailed treatment to date. As Sonoda points out (p. 169), the *fudan nenbutsu,* which aims at eradicating sin and achieving birth in Amida's Pure Land, differs in purpose from the T'ien-t'ai "constantly walking samādhi," in which the contemplation of Amida serves as a vehicle for achieving nondual insight.

137. A portion of this treatise is translated in A. K. Reischauer, trans., "Genshin's *Ōjō Yōshū.*" See also the study by Allan A. Andrews, *The Teachings Essential for Rebirth.*

138. Hori Ichirō, *Folk Religion in Japan,* pp. 117–27.

139. The three stages are the age of the True Dharma (*shōbō*), the age of the Semblance Dharma (*zōhō*), and the age of the Final Dharma. According to K'uei-chi (632–682), founder of the Chinese Fa-hsiang school, in the age of the True Dharma, the Buddha's teaching flourishes, people practice it correctly, and receive the "proof" of enlightenment. In the Semblance Dharma age, teaching and practice remain, but

people no longer gain their proof. And in the Final Dharma age, the teaching alone survives; there is neither practice nor proof (*Ta-sheng fa-yüan i-lin chang, T* 45:334b3–5). Most Japanese scholars held to the theory that the True and Semblance Dharma ages each lasted for a thousand years, and the Final Dharma age, for ten thousand. Based on the East Asian tradition that placed the Buddha's *pari-nirvāṇa* in 949 B.C.E., they calculated that the Final Dharma age had begun in 1052. For a summary of the textual bases of *mappō* thought in Japan, see my "Seeking Enlightenment in the Last Age" (1), pp. 29–33. (However, the larger argument of this article—that the new Buddhist movements of the Kamakura period represented the only successful responses to the perceived crisis of the last age—now requires critical reassessment.) For the development of the three-stage theory of decline in East Asia, see Jan Nattier, *Once Upon a Future Time*, pp. 65–118.

140. See Sueki Fumihiko, "Amida santai-setsu o megutte." On Tendai Pure Land Buddhism and original enlightenment thought more generally, see Tamura Yoshirō, *Kamakura shin Bukkyō shisō no kenkyū*, pp. 475–506, and Ishida Mizumaro, *Jōdokyō no tenkai*, pp. 227–52.

141. For some problems in the definition of *chūsei* in Japanese historiography, see John Whitney Hall, "Terms and Concepts in Japanese Medieval History," pp. 4–9.

142. "Nihon ko Tendai kenkyū no hitsuyō o ronzu," pp. 174–76. *"Ko"* in the title of this essay is an abbreviation of *"chūko."*

143. Hazama Jikō, *Chūko Nihon Tendai no kenkyū*, p. 1.

144. Ibid., p. 2.

145. On Myōryū, Reikū, and the Anraku school, see Shimaji Daitō, *Tendai kyōgaku shi*, pp. 471–72, and Uesugi Bunshū, *Nihon Tendai shi*, vol. 1, pp. 715–48.

146. "Tendai hongaku shisō gaisetsu," pp. 479, 521.

147. In the study of medieval Tendai, the term *kuden hōmon* is employed in a specific sense to indicate the teachings contained in these doctrinal systematizations. More broadly, it is used to indicate any teaching taking the form of a recorded oral transmission.

148. Tamura Yoshirō, "Tendai hongaku shisō gaisetsu," p. 538.

149. "Chūko Tendai no gakugo toshite mitaru hongaku no gainen," pp. 109–15.

150. The following discussion draws on a number of Tamura's works. See, for example, *Kamakura shin Bukkyō no kenkyū*, pp. 107–8; "Hongaku shisō to honmon shisō"; "Ri kenpon to ji jōjū," especially pp. 312–13; and "Tendai hongaku shisō gaisetsu," pp. 482, 514–15.

151. *THR*, p. 176. In some of his discussions, Tamura cites a later version of the *Sanjū shika no kotogaki* called *Makura sōshi*. For the corresponding passage in *Makura sōshi*, see *DNBZ* 32:115b.

152. Shōshin's critique of "original enlightenment" appears in his *Hokke gengi shiki* 7, *DNBZ* 21:285a–88b. For discussions, see Tamura Yoshirō, "Hongaku shisō ni taisuru hihan ron" (a version of which has been translated into English by Jan Van Bragt as "Critiques of Original Awakening Thought in Shōshin and Dōgen"); Yamanouchi Shinnyū, *Dōgen Zen to Tendai hongaku hōmon*, pp. 724–30; and Ōtani Gyōkō, "Hōchi-bō Shōshin no hongaku shisō hihan." In his *Shikan shiki* 1 (*DNBZ* 22:248a–

252b), Shōshin also attacked the view that grasses and trees can of themselves arouse the *bodhicitta,* cultivate practice, and achieve awakening. See also Miyamoto Shōson, "'Sōmoku kokudo shikkai jōbutsu' no busshōron teki igi to sono sakusha," p. 681–83.

153. *Shasekishū* 10 *(matsu):* 2, p. 444; English translation from Robert Morrell, *Sand and Pebbles,* p. 260 (slightly modified).

154. *Sōkonshū,* nos. 2526 and 9495, in *Shikashū taisei* 5:612, 818.

155. I am indebted to William Bodiford for first pointing out to me the importance of Buddhist monks as disseminators of shrine-related traditions and practices.

156. Kuroda Toshio, "Shinto in the History of Japanese Religion." Kuroda's study, which argues that notions of the *kami* were formed largely under Buddhist influence, is part of a recent, revisionist move challenging earlier assumptions of an unchanging entity called "Shintō" that can be traced back to Japan's earliest times. See also Allan G. Grapard, "Institution, Ritual and Ideology," and Neil McMullin, "Historical and Historiographical Issues in the Study of Pre-Modern Japanese Religions," pp. 4–8. Although not in agreement on all points, these three scholars suggest from different perspectives that Buddhist institutions and "Shintō" shrines of the medieval period, as well as the discourses emanating from them, were inextricably connected and cannot be properly understood apart from one another.

157. This was first pointed out by Shimaji Daitō ("Nihon ko Tendai kenkyū no hitsuyō o ronzu," pp. 184–85) and has been explored to some extent by Tamura Yoshirō ("Hongaku shisō to Shintō riron").

158. *Nakatomi no harae kunge, KDZ* 5:179.

159. Tamura Yoshirō, "Hongaku shisō to Shintō riron," pp. 444–47. For the influence of original enlightenment thought on Ise Shintō, see also Kuroda Toshio, *Nihon chūsei no shakai to shūkyō,* pp. 51–56, and "The Discourse on the 'Land of Kami' *(Shinkoku)* in Medieval Japan," pp. 361–66.

160. *Hsüan-i* 7a, *T* 33:766b18–19.

161. See Grapard, "Institution, Ritual and Ideology," pp. 264–65. For Grapard's discussion of the principles of association between *kami* and Buddhas or bodhisattvas at specific temple-shrine complexes, see his "Linguistic Cubism," pp. 215–220 (the Hiei-Sannō complex), and *The Protocol of the Gods,* pp. 74–97 (the Kōfukuji-Kasuga complex).

162. *Mongu ryaku taikō shikenmon* 6, *DNBZ* 18:189b.

163. "Nihon ko Tendai kenkyū no hitsuyō o ronzu," pp. 184–85.

164. Tamura Yoshirō draws attention to the influence on Yuiitsu Shintō of the Tendai monks Jihen and Ryōhen ("Hongaku shisō to Shintō riron," pp. 448–49). Jihen, the brother of Yoshida Kenkō, author of *Tsurezure-gusa,* trained on Mt. Hiei and later became interested in the transmissions of Ise, where he went to study. Ryōhen similarly trained on Mt. Hiei and then developed an interest in theories of the *kami.* On Jihen, see Kubota Osamu, *Chūsei Shintōshi no kenkyū,* pp. 139–59; Sugawara Shinkai, *Sannō Shintō no kenkyū,* pp. 165–196; and Allan G. Grapard, "The Shinto of Yoshida Kanetomo, pp. 34–36. On Ryōhen, see Kubota, pp. 277–300.

165. *Jindai no maki shikenmon,* Kōyasan University Library Archives, cited in Tamura Yoshirō, "Nihon chūsei shichō to Tendai hongaku shisō," p. 463.

166. For an outline of this subject, see Tamura Yoshirō, "Karon to hongaku shisō," and Misaki Gisen, "Mono no aware o utau michi to hongaku shisō to no kanren."

167. On the perceived tensions involved in Buddhists composing poetry, see Herbert E. Plutschow, "Is Poetry a Sin?," and William R. LaFleur, *The Karma of Words,* pp. 1–9. "Floating phrases and fictive utterances" (Chn. *k'uang-yen i-yu,* Jpn. *kyōgen kigo*) is LaFleur's translation of the poet Po Chü-i (772–846)'s deprecatory reference to his own verses, when he presented them to a Buddhist library in offering to the Dharma. The phrase was often invoked in medieval Japanese poetic circles in the context of attempts to reconcile poetry and Buddhism.

168. *MFLHC, p'in* 19, *T* 9:50a23–24; translation from Hurvitz, *Scripture of the Lotus Blossom of the Fine Dharma,* p. 276, slightly modified.

169. *Fo-shuo kuan P'u-hsien P'u-sa hsing-fa ching, T* 9:392c26–27. This is the capping sūtra to the *Lotus.*

170. *Korai fūtei shō* 1, *Nihon shisō taikei* 23, p. 263. This passage was translated with reference to the more elegant rendition in LaFleur, *The Karma of Words,* pp. 90–91. My intent here was to be very literal.

171. Konishi Jin'ichi, "Shunzei no yūgenfū to shikan."

172. LaFleur, *The Karma of Words,* p. 93.

173. *Shinkokinshū* 258; translation from Jacqueline Stone, "An Introduction to the Poetry of Jien," p. 215.

174. LaFleur, *The Karma of Words,* chap. 4: "Symbol and Yūgen: Shunzei's Use of Tendai Buddhism," pp. 80–106. (The same piece also appears as the first chapter of James H. Sanford, William R. LaFleur, and Masatoshi Nagatomi, eds., *Flowing Traces,* pp. 16–46.) Also relevant here is LaFleur's "Saigyō and the Buddhist Value of Nature" (1), especially pp. 121–26, which explores the nonduality of symbol and symbolized in the work of Shunzei's contemporary Saigyō (1118–1190). LaFleur connects this nonduality with the concept of *samaya* ("symbol") in Kūkai's thought, in which a concrete physical symbol simultaneously stands for the body of Dainichi and is integral to it. This understanding of symbol was also found in Taimitsu thought and, by the time of Shunzei and Saichō, had become part of a general Buddhist milieu. On Shunzei and the Tendai identification of the phenomenal with the true, see also Manaka Fujiko, *Kokubungaku ni sesshū sareta Bukkyō,* pp. 221–24.

175. See Sanford, LaFleur, and Nagatomi, eds., *Flowing Traces,* "Introduction," pp. 5–7.

176. *Shūgyokushū,* cited in Misaki Gisen, "Chūsei biishiki no chūjiku toshite no 'shikanteki bigaku'", p. 46.

177. *Hōmon hyakushū, GR* 24:698b–99a. Mujū Ichien similarly invokes the "every form and fragrance" passage from the *Mo-ho chih-kuan* in defense of the Buddhist value of poetry (*Shasekishū* 5A12, *Nihon koten bungaku taikei* 85, p. 224; Morrell, trans., *Sand and Pebbles,* p. 165).

178. *GR* 27:502a, b.

179. *Azuma mondō, Nihon koten bungaku taikei* 66, p. 233. Shūgi refers to the passage of the *Lotus Sūtra* which reads, "The dharmas that he preaches shall accord with those [unfathomable, boundless] meanings, and in every case there will be no con-

tradiction to the true aspect" (*MFLHC*, *p'in* 19, *T* 9:50a22–23). This sūtra passage immediately precedes that cited in n. 168 above.

180. Early studies include Shimaji Daitō's "Nihon Tendai no kuden hōmon" (1910) and Oka Kyōzui's "Nihon Tendai kuden hōmon no yurai oyobi sono hattatsu" (1911–1912).

181. Kojima Michimasa, Kodera Bun'ei, and Take Kakuchō, "Tendai kuden hō-mon no kyōdō kenkyū" (1), p. 372.

182. *TZ*, vol. 9, contains records of oral commentaries on the doctrines of the E-shin school, compiled in the late Kamakura and Muromachi periods. Vol. 2 of Uesugi Bunshū's *Nihon Tendaishi* contains examples of both Eshin and Danna texts, as well as some *kuden* relating to precept initiation. A number of *kuden* retrospectively attributed to Saichō appear in *DDZ*, vol. 5. Several of the *hongaku*-related essays written from a Pure Land perspective and attributed to Genshin are in *ESZ*. Some *kuden* are also included in *DNBZ* and other collections. The multi-volume *Zoku Tendaishū zensho*, now being compiled, edited, and published by the Tendai Shūten Hensanjo (Tendai Research Foundation), will make available many hitherto unpublished documents.

183. Tada Kōryū, Ōkubo Ryōjun, Tamura Yoshirō, and Asai Endō, eds., *Nihon shisō taikei*, vol. 9, published by Iwanami Shoten. This collection is subsequently referred to as *THR*. Unfortunately, the editors do not clarify their selection principle in choosing the texts for this volume. One notes, however, that several of those included had already drawn the attention of earlier researchers such as Shimaji Daitō and Hazama Jikō.

184. Tamura Yoshirō, "Tendai hongaku shisō gaisetsu," p. 521.

185. *Hokke sho shiki* 8, *DNBZ* 22:109a. The years 1165 and 1207 are the dates traditionally given for the beginning and completion of Shōshin's commentary, but Ishii Ryōkun suggests that 1190–1198 may be more probable (*BKD* 10:76a-b).

186. See Tamura Yoshirō, *Kamakura shin Bukkyō shisō no kenkyū*, pp. 403–51, and "Tendai hongaku shisō gaisetsu," pp. 523–41. Major texts as dated by Tamura include:

1. 1100–1150: *Honri taikōshū, Entaragishū.*

2. 1150–1200: *Tendai Hokkeshū gozu hōmon yōsan, Gobu kechimyaku, Chū hongaku san, Hongaku san shaku.*

3. 1200–1250: *Shinnyo kan, Sanjū shika no kotogaki (Makura sōshi).*

4. 1250–1300: *Shuzenji-ketsu, Sandai shōsho shichimen sōjō kuketsu, Kankō ruijū, Hokke ryakugi kenmon.*

5. 1300–1350: *Hokke kan'yō ryakuchū shūku shū, Kōyō shō, Kawataya bōshō jūkutsū, Ichijō shō, Nijō shō, Hachijō shō.*

6. 1350–1400: *Zōda shō, Tōkai kuden shō, Hachijo shō kenmon, Nijō shō kenmon, Hokke jurin shūyō shō.*

187. "Tendai hongaku shisō gaisetsu," pp. 523, 550–53.

188. Ibid., p. 520.

189. "Ri kenpon to ji jōjū," p. 314. See also "Tendai hongaku shisō gaisetsu," pp. 528–31, 567.

190. Hanano Michiaki, following Shimaji Daitō and Hazama Jikō, maintains that the *Kotogaki* may actually be Kōkaku's work ("*Sanjū shika no kotogaki no sensha to*

shisō ni tsuite" (1), pp. 154–63). Sueki Fumihiko, while unwilling to accept Kōkaku as the actual compiler, places it not long after Kōkaku's time and agrees with Hanano that Tamura's dating is too late ("Tendai hongaku shisō kenkyū no shomondai," pp. 155–57). For details, see chap. 5, n. 33. Sueki's argument is in my opinion the most convincing.

191. In *Kamakura shin Bukkyō shisō no kenkyū*, published in 1965, Tamura expresses general agreement with Hazama's claim that *hongaku* thought matured in the late Heian period (pp. 370–71); his position appears to shift, however, in later articles such as "Tendai hongaku shisō gaisetsu," where he places the full flowering of Tendai *hongaku* thought around the mid-thirteenth century. This rather late date was anticipated by Tamamuro Taijō, *Nihon Bukkyōshi gaisetsu*, pp. 239–44, and Shigyō Kaishū, "Nichiren Shōnin no shisōshiteki kenkyū no ichi kōsatsu," pp. 46–49. However, neither scholar developed a detailed chronological scheme as Tamura did.

192. Several of these are discussed in Sueki Fumihiko, "Tendai hongaku shisō kenkyū no shomondai," pp. 289–96.

193. "Nichiren Shōnin kyōgaku no shisōshi teki kenkyū joron," pp. 139–40. Hanano's chronology is as follows (compare with Tamura's given in n. 18b above):

1. Before 1100 (emergence of *kanjin*-style interpretation): *Honri taikōshū, Entaragishū*.

2. Before 1150 (compilation of *kuden hōmon* and *kirikami* transmissions): *Gobu kechimyaku, Gozu hōmon yōsan, Sanjū shika no kotogaki*.

3. Before 1200 (establishment of the "fourfold rise and fall" classification system): *Shuzenji-ketsu, Danshō ketsujōshū, Sandai shōsho shichimen sōjō kuketsu, Jigyō nenbutsu mondō*.

4. Before 1250 (establishment of the Eshin school's doctrinal system of the seven great matters): *Ichijō shō, Kankō ruijū, Hokke ryakugi kenmon*.

5. Before 1300 (general systematizing of *kuden hōmon*): *Nijō shō, Kawata jūkutsū, Kōyō shō, Hachijō shō*.

6. After 1300 (systematizing of commentaries on the *kuden hōmon*): *Hokke kan'yō ryakuchū shūku shū, Zōda shō, Tōkai kuden shō*.

194. These texts include the *Kanjin ryaku yōshū, Jigyō nenbutsu mondō, Myōgyōshin yōshū, Shinnyo kan*, and others.

195. See, for example, Hanano Michiaki, "Chūko Tendai bunken to nenbutsu shisō," especially pp. 335–36; Satō Tetsue, "Eizan Jōdokyō kobunken no chōsa to kenkyū"; and Ishida Mizumaro, *Jōdokyō no tenkai*, pp. 227–52.

Among the better studied texts in this category is the *Kanjin ryaku yōshū*, possibly the earliest example of such literature. Attributed to Genshin, it follows the format of Genshin's *Ōjō yōshū* and interprets the *nenbutsu* from the standpoint of *kanjin*, or introspective contemplation. A number of scholars maintain that the *Kanjin ryaku yōshū* actually is Genshin's work (see, for example, Taira Ryōshō, "Eshin Sōzu no *Kanjin ryaku yōshū* ni tsuite"; Ishida Mizumaro, *Jōdokyō no tenkai*, pp. 112–15; and Hanano Michiaki, "Chūko Tendai bunken to nenbutsu shisō"). However, though he himself treated the *Kanjin ryaku yōshū* as genuine, Satō Tetsue noted that some had doubts

(*Eizan Jōdokyō no kenkyū*, p. 158). Tamura Yoshirō pointed out that it represents a leap beyond the *Ōjō yōshū* in interpreting the *nenbutsu* in terms of original enlightenment thought and placed it between 1150 and 1200 (*Kamakura shin Bukkyō shisō no kenkyū*, pp. 481–83). Nara Hiromoto also questioned its authenticity ("Genshin no chosaku ni tsuite"). Sueki Fumihiko at first upheld Tamura's dating ("*Kanjin ryaku yōshū* no senja ni tsuite") but later revised his opinion. He argues convincingly on grounds of both style and content that the *Kanjin ryaku yōshū* cannot be Genshin's work but concludes that it was probably compiled not long after Genshin's death ("*Kanjin ryaku yōshū* no kenkyū," especially pp. 253–55; "*Myōgyōshin yōshū* no shomondai," pp. 286–87; and "Tendai hongaku shisō kenkyū no shomondai," p. 291). Nishimura Keishō has suggested that the *Kanjin ryaku yōshū* was compiled in 1077 by the teacher of a monk named Eikai, whom he presumes to be the author of a related work, the *Myōgyōshin yōshū*, which is based on the *Kanjin ryaku yōshū* ("*Kanjin ryaku yōshū* seiritsu kō"). The above is representative of the kind of scholarly disagreement that arises in attempts to date medieval Tendai literature.

196. See, for example, "Nihon shisōshi ni okeru hongaku shisō," pp. 123–26.

197. "Japanese Culture and the Tendai Concept of Original Enlightenment," p. 205.

198. Nakamura Hajime et al., eds. *Iwanami Bukkyō jiten*, pp. 745–46. Tamura was among the dictionary's editors and, according to its preface, played a central role in its planning, compiling, and editing.

199. This problem was first pointed out to me by Paul Groner.

200. Paul Groner, "A Medieval Japanese Reading of the *Mo-ho chih-kuan*," pp. 55–58.

201. In the interests of resisting reification, this study uses alternatively such terms as original enlightenment thought, original enlightenment ideas, original enlightenment discourse, and original enlightenment notions. However, none of these alternatives individually solves the problem.

202. "Nihon ko Tendai kenkyū no hitsuyō o ronzu," pp. 189–91. On the contemporary debate over whether "philosophy" was purely a Western import or had previously existed in Japan, see John C. Maraldo, "Tradition, Textuality, and the Translation of Philosophy."

203. "Japanese Culture and the Tendai Concept of Original Enlightenment," pp. 205, 207–208. Similar statements appear in a number of Tamura's articles.

204. Tamura's claim is related to Nakamura Hajime's identification of "the phenomenal world [seen] as absolute" and "this-worldliness" as characteristics of Japanese mentality (*Ways of Thinking of Eastern Peoples*, pp. 350–72). For another argument that original enlightenment thought should be considered "Japanese" rather than "Buddhist," see Nitta Masaaki, "Hongaku hōmon no keisei no shisōshiteki imi," pp. 707–12.

205. For a recent example, see Kurita Isamu, *Saichō to Tendai hongaku shisō* (1994), which is directed toward the general reader.

206. *Chung-hua ch'uan-hsin-ti ch'an-men shih-tzu ch'eng-hsi t'u*, HTC 110:435 *verso* b; English translation from Gregory, *Tsung-mi*, p. 237.

Chapter Two: Tendai *Hongaku* Thought
and the New Kamakura Buddhism: Rival Theories

1. Jeffrey P. Mass, "The Kamakura Bakufu," pp. 2–14.
2. These have been noted independently by James C. Dobbins, "Envisioning Kamakura Buddhism," pp. 26–28, and Matsuo Kenji, *Kamakura shin Bukkyō no seiritsu,* pp. 2–9. Matsuo refers to these two approaches as "theory A" and "theory B."
3. This analogy was suggested to me by Sueki Fumihiko.
4. Joseph M. Kitagawa, "Japanese Religion: An Overview," *Encyclopedia of Religion,* 7:529. I have also been guilty of perpetuating the assumption of "old Buddhist" decadence, in "Seeking Enlightenment in the Last Age."
5. The comparison was first made in Hara's "Tōsai no shūkyō kaikaku." Its subsequent adoption and criticism by later Japanese scholars is outlined in Sasaki Kaoru, *Chūsei kokka no shūkyō kōzō,* pp. 3–12, and in Funaoka Makoto, *Nihon Zenshū no seiritsu,* pp. 105–15, which also includes an overview of the historiography of Kamakura Buddhism. The history of the "Reformation theory" in English-language scholarship is summarized and evaluated in James H. Foard, "In Search of a Lost Reformation."
6. "In Search of a Lost Reformation," p. 262.
7. See, for example, Umehara Takeshi's introduction to *Shinran, Dōgen, Nichiren,* p. 13.
8. *Foundations of Japanese Buddhism,* vol. 2: *The Mass Movement,* p. 7.
9. James L. Ford points this out in his "A Life Ignored: Jōkei (1155–1213) and 'Old' Kamakura Buddhism Reexamined," (Ph.D. dissertation, cited by permission of the author).
10. Kuroda's major works on this subject include *Jisha seiryōku, Nihon chūsei no kokka to shūkyō,* and "Chūsei jisha seiryoku ron." In English, see Mikael S. Adolphson, "Monks, Courtiers and Warriors in Premodern Japan," pp. 7–17, and James C. Dobbins, guest editor, *The Legacy of Kuroda Toshio,* which contains several translations and discussions of Kuroda's work. Of the articles it includes, Kuroda's "The Development of the *Kenmitsu* System as Japan's Medieval Orthodoxy" serves as a particularly useful introduction to his thought.
11. This is less evident in Kuroda's own work than in that of others influenced by him, such as Taira Masayuki. Sueki Fumihiko comments on this point in his "Kamakura Bukkyō kenkyū o megutte," p. 276, and "A Reexamination of the *Kenmitsu Taisei* Theory," p. 463.
12. "Kamakura Bukkyō kenkyū o megutte," p. 276.
13. Examples by Western scholars include Robert E. Morrell, *Early Kamakura Buddhism;* Frédéric Girard, *Un Moine de la Secte Kegon a l' Époque de Kamakura, Myōe (1173–1232)* et le "Journal de ses Rêves"; George J. Tanabe, Jr., *Myōe the Dreamkeeper;* and Richard K. Payne, ed., *Re-visioning "Kamakura" Buddhism.*
14. Scholars of the *kenmitsu taisei* have participated in this redefinition in that they tend to regard the Jishū—usually categorized with the "new Buddhism"—as incorporated within the *kenmitsu* system, rather than as part of the marginal *itan-ha.*
15. "In Search of a Lost Reformation."
16. *Kamakura shin Bukkyō no seiritsu,* pp. 180–81, 292.
17. *Chūsei kokka no shūkyō kōzō.* See, for example, pp. 49–52.
18. "Nihon ko Tendai kenkyū no hitsuyō o ronzu," p. 191.

19. Shimaji Daitō, *Nihon Bukkyō hongaku shisō no gaisetsu,* pp. 5–6.

20. *Nihon Bukkyō kyōgakushi,* p. 473. Shimaji, like a number of later scholars, also saw the *kuden* tradition as exerting a corrupting influence on Tendai scholarship. See his *Tendai kyōgaku shi,* p. 470.

21. This connection between immanentalist forms of Buddhist thought and the absorption of indigenous elements anticipates by several decades similar criticisms of original enlightenment thought leveled by "critical Buddhism," discussed below. Hakamaya Noriaki in particular sees *hongaku* thought as an expression in Buddhist terms of indigenous thinking that relies on the fundamentally non-Buddhist idea of "topos," or unchanging substantial ground (see n. 83 below).

22. *Nihon Bukkyō hongaku shisō no gaisetsu,* pp. 4–6.

23. *Tendai kyōgaku shi,* p. 469. Later scholarship has opened grounds for disputing Shimaji's claim that *hongaku* thought was purely concerned with the individual. Examples include the suggestions of Taira Masayuki, who, following Kuroda Toshio, regards it as an ideology of the ruling elite, and Alan Grapard, who has pointed to a connection between *hongaku* thought and development of cultic sites ("Linguistic Cubism," pp. 223–27).

24. *Nihon Tendai shi,* vol. 1, p. 597. Uesugi, like Shimaji, seems to have assumed that oral transmissions attributed to late Heian period figures such as Renjitsu-bō Shōhan (996–1077) and Chūjin (1065–1138) really were the work of these men; these writings are now thought to be the product of the mid-Kamakura period or later. Thus Uesugi, too, assumed that Tendai *hongaku* thought was fully developed before the new Kamakura schools appeared.

25. Ibid., p. 470. This argument finds its visual analogue in the Great Lecture Hall (Daikōdō) in the East Pagoda precinct on Mt. Hiei, where the portraits of the new Kamakura Buddhist founders are enshrined together with those of the great Tendai masters, thus in effect subsuming them within the domain of Tendai Buddhism. Needless to say, this is a modern interpretative move; influential clerics on Mt. Hiei in the Kamakura period saw such individuals as Eisai and Hōnen as heterodox and took action against them.

26. "Shin Kamakura Bukkyō kōki no in'yu," p. 2.

27. I use "Nichirenshū" in the strict sense to mean that denomination within the larger tradition of Nichiren Buddhism whose head temple is Kuonji on Mt. Minobu. Risshō University, which is affiliated with Nichirenshū, and particularly its Nichiren Kyōgaku Kenkyūjo (Center for Nichiren Doctrinal Studies), represents the leading institutional base for the scholarly study of Nichiren Buddhism.

28. For the Tendai antecedents of Hōnen and his immediate disciples, as well as possible influences of original enlightenment thought on their doctrine, see Hirokawa Gyōbin, ed., *Kamakura shin Bukkyō to chūko Tendai to no kōshō ni kansuru kenkyū.* Kumoto Noboru's "Hōnen Shōnin ni okeru hongaku shisō" contains some intriguing suggestions concerning continuities and discontinuities between Hōnen's doctrine and original enlightenment thought. The appropriation and transformation of original enlightenment thought by Shinran and some of his later disciples are discussed in Fugen Daien, "Shinshū kyōgaku to hongaku shisō" and "Shinshū nyorai ron no tokushoku." In contrast, Ishihara Toshio argues that Shinran's doctrinal standpoint differs fundamentally from original enlightenment thought ("Hongaku shisō to Shinran").

29. Among Nichirenshū sectarian scholars, Shimizu Ryūzan located Nichiren in the Eshin line (*Nichiren Shōnin no gakusetsu no yurai ni tsuite,* p. 206); Oka Kyōzui saw him as emanating from the Danna school ("Danna-ryū ni ranshō seru tōke no shūgi"); and Shima Chiryō believed that he had studied the teachings of both schools ("Taitō kōshō shikō" [1], p. 37), as did Yamakawa Chiō ("Eizan ni okeru Nichiren Shōnin no shiyū no kenkyū," p. 147). Outside Nichirenshū, Shimaji Daitō believed that Nichiren had "transmitted the doctrinal studies of the Eshin school" (*Tendai kyōgaku shi,* p. 469), while Uesugi Bunshū speculated that Nichiren's *daimoku* had originated in certain Danna transmissions (*Nihon Tendaishi* vol. 1, p. 712).

30. *Kanjin honzon shō, STN* 1:719; "Toki Nyūdō-dono gohenji," *STN* 2:1522.

31. See Asai Endō, "Ji no hōmon," pp. 2–3, and Lucia D. Dolce, "Esoteric Patterns in Nichiren's Thought," pp. 15–16. The above remarks by no means exhaust Nichiren's use of the term *ji* or its importance as a category in subsequent Nichiren Buddhist doctrinal scholarship. In addition to Asai's article, see also Mochizuki Kankō, *Nichiren kyōgaku no kenkyū,* pp. 118–22.

32. Nichiki elaborates on the *ri/ji* distinction between T'ien-t'ai/Tendai and Nichiren thought in section 5 of his major work *Ichinen sanzen ron, Jūgoen zenshū* 3, pp. 43–103. For a discussion of the importance of these categories in his thought, see Ono Bunkō, "Udana-in Nichiki," pp. 32–39.

33. For examples of this kind of argument, see Mochizuki Kankō, "Juryō shoken hongaku sanjin ron" (3), especially pp. 25–28, and Takada Enin, "Hongaku shisō Taitō kōshō shiron" (3). See also Shioda Gisen, *Honmon jikan shi* (1940), which interprets Nichiren sectarian scholarship since the latter Edo period as an attempt to retrieve Nichiren's normative meaning of *ji.*

34. "Tendaishū kōyō," *Maeda Eun zenshū,* vol. 2, p. 22. Maeda was writing before critical methods of scholarship made clear that the *hongaku*-related texts attributed to Saichō are apocryphal.

35. *Tendai kyōgaku shi,* p. 469. In the same vein, see also his *Nihon Bukkyō kyōgaku shi,* p. 11.

36. *Nihon Tendai shi,* vol. 1, p. 505.

37. Takahashi Ken'yū, "Shimizu Ryūzan," p. 254.

38. Included in *Shimizu Ryūzan chosakushū,* vol. 1, p. 368. This text, a collection of essays, was first published in 1919.

39. Asai's most important work is the posthumously published *Nichiren Shōnin kyōgaku no kenkyū.* Chapter 6 in particular calls into question the authenticity of Nichiren-attributed texts showing medieval Tendai influence and develops the thesis that Nichiren's doctrine differs essentially from that of Tendai *hongaku* thought. The specific response to Shimaji and others appears on pp. 194–95.

40. Ibid., p. 221.

41. Ibid., p. 80. On *chigo* and monastic homosexual practices, see Margaret Childs, "*Chigo Monogatari:* Love Stories or Buddhist Sermons?" and Paul Gordon Schalow, "Kūkai and the Tradition of Male Love in Japanese Buddhism."

42. For example, Kawazoe Shōji criticized Asai's methodology as "ahistorical" for its failure to take Nichiren's medieval Tendai background into consideration ("Nichiren no shūkyō keisei ni okeru nenbutsu haigeki no igi [2]," pp. 52–3); Suguro Shinjō expressed concern about the consequences of excluding all but absolutely unimpeachable texts from the interpretation of Nichiren's thought ("Shūgaku kenkyūjō no nisan no mondaiten," pp. 365–66); and Hanano Michiaki questioned

the feasibility of establishing a fixed, singular, and normative Nichiren doctrine ("Junsui Nichiren gi kakuritsu no shomondai"). See also my "Some Disputed Writings in the Nichiren Corpus," especially chapter 1.

43. "Nichiren Shōnin kyōgaku no shisōshiteki kenkyū no ichi kōsatsu."

44. Ibid., pp. 46–49.

45. Ibid., p. 45.

46. Ibid., pp. 45–46.

47. If original enlightenment thought developed primarily as a counter to the rising influence of the new Buddhism, it is not altogether obvious how Hōnen and Shinran could have been reacting against it. This point remains unclear in Shigyō's argument.

48. Ibid., pp. 49–54. Shigyō did note in passing (pp. 53–54) that none of the Kamakura founders returned to the position of *shikaku*—i.e., that enlightenment is acquired as the result or conclusion of a linear process of cultivation. This is a crucial observation, meriting a more detailed treatment than he gave it.

49. *Jōko Nihon Tendai honmon shisō shi*, p. 17.

50. Asai Endō, "Shūso ni okeru kannenron daha no shisō," p. 146.

51. Ibid., p. 145.

52. There are three main versions of this story: (1) the account given identically in Dōgen's earliest biographies, *Eiheiji sanso gyōgoki* (*SZ* 16:1b) and *Sandaison gyōjōki* (16:11b–12a). According to Azuma Ryūshin, these two may have derived from the same text and diverged in the process of transmission. The *Sandaison gyōjōki*, he suggests, remains closer to the original version, which may have been composed by the Sōtō patriarch Keizan (1264–1325) ("Gyōgōki to Gyōjōki" and *Keizan Zenji no kenkyū*, pp. 122–27); (2) the *Eihei kaisan gogyōjō ki*, the so-called Zuichō ms. of Dōgen's biography *Kenzei ki*, compiled by Kenzei (1415–1474), fourteenth abbot of the the Eiheiji, between 1468–73 and recopied by Zuichō in 1589 from a 1552 transcription (Kawamura Kōdō, *Shohon taikō Eihei kaisan Dōgen Zenji gyōjō Kenzei ki*, p. 10b); and (3) *Teiho Kenzei ki*, dated 1754 and edited by Menzan (1683–1769) (*SZ* 17:16a; also in Kawamura, pp. 7–8f). The quotation above is translated from this version.

53. Seiryū Sōji suggests this as a possible reason for Dōgen's departure from Mt. Hiei, based on *Zuimonki* 4:8 (*DZZ* 7: 109–11, "Dōgen Zenji no shoki sangaku ni okeru gidan no shinsō ni tsuite," pp. 136–37).

54. This has been suggested by Ōkubo Dōshū, *Shūtei zōho Dōgen Zenji den no kenkyū*, pp. 80–81.

55. This has in fact been suggested by Seiryū Sōji, "Dōgen Zenji no shoki sangaku ni okeru gidan no shinsō ni tsuite," pp. 135–37. For a passage very similar in its concern to the "great doubt," see, for example, the opening sentences of Dōgen's *Fukan zazengi*, which also raise the question of the relationship between inherent enlightenment and practice (*DZZ* 5:4; Carl Bielefeldt, *Dōgen's Manuals of Zen Meditation*, p. 175). I am indebted to Steven Heine for pointing this out to me.

56. Dōgen's "great doubt" was to the best of my knowledge first interpreted as Dōgen's youthful questioning of Tendai *hongaku* thought by Hazama Jikō in his 1942 essay, "Kamakura jidai ni okeru shinjō sōmetsu ron ni kansuru kenkyū," p. 317. This reading has been followed by Kagamishima Genryū, "Honshō myōshū no shisōshiteki haikei," pp. 97–98; Tamura Yoshirō, *Kamakura shin Bukkyō shisō no kenkyū*, p. 552; Ōkubo Dōshū—who varies the theme by suggesting that the "great doubt" represents Dōgen's response to an overly ceremonialized atmosphere where Taimitsu rit-

ual was emphasized over traditional T'ien-t'ai/Tendai studies (*Shūtei zōho Dōgen Zenji den no kenkyū*, pp. 78–80); Tamamuro Taijō, *Dōgen*, pp. 26–28; Shinno Kōryō, "Dōgen Zenji no gidan ni tsuite no ichi kōsatsu"; Ōno Tatsunosuke, "Dōgen no hongaku shisō" pp. 1–2; Imaeda Aishin, *Dōgen*, pp. 30–31 and "Dōgen no shōgai," pp. 44–46; Hee-Jin Kim, *Dōgen Kigen*, pp. 25–27; and Masao Abe, "The Oneness of Practice and Attainment," pp. 99–100. This is not an exhaustive list.

57. This has been suggested by Kagamishima Genryū, "Eisai, Dōgen sōken mondai ni tsuite," based on a comparison of Menzan's *Teiho Kenzei ki* (1754) with two earlier manuscripts of the *Kenzei ki*, dated 1589 and 1694, that were only recently discovered. According to the *Teiho* version, Dōgen studied on Mt. Hiei for a mere three years, from 1212 to 1214, when, at age fifteen, he left and sought out Kōin, who directed him to Eisai. However, the older versions say that Dōgen had studied on Hiei from 1212 until 1217, when he was eighteen, and then went to Kōin. In this they concur with Dōgen's earliest biographies, the *Eihei sandai gyōgōki* and *Sandaison gyōjōki*. Since Kōin died in 1216, this would not have been possible, but it is not altogether clear why Menzan placed Dōgen's departure from Hiei as early as 1214. As Seiryū Sōji notes, if Dōgen left Hiei in connection with his teacher Kōen's resignation as *zasu*, the earlier date gains plausibility because Kōen resigned toward the end of 1213 ("Dōgen Zenji no shoki sangaku ni okeru gidan no shinsō ni tsuite," p. 134). However, as both Seiryū (p. 133) and Kagamishima (p. 47) point out, the *Honchō kōsōden* says that Dōgen met Kōin in 1216 (*DNBZ* 102:211a), the year of Kōin's death. If this is the case, then Dōgen might have spent as many as five years on Mt. Hiei, rather than two, as Menzan suggests. In any event, it appears that Menzan deliberately minimizes the role of the Tendai master Kōin in the course of Dōgen's studies. Where the earlier *Kenzei ki* manuscripts say that Kōin directed Dōgen to go study in China, the *Teiho* version has him direct Dōgen to Eisai.

58. *Hōkyō ki, DZZ* 7:6.

59. *Kamakura shin Bukkyō shisō no kenkyū*, pp. 552–53.

60. "Honshō myōshū no shisōteki haikei." The quotations are at pp. 98–99, 104.

61. A useful summary of this large volume appears in Ikeda Rosan's review, "Yamanouchi Shun'yū cho *Dōgen Zen to Tendai hongaku hōmon*."

62. *Dōgen Zen to Tendai hongaku hōmon*, p. 671.

63. Ibid., pp. 94–95.

64. This translation of *honshō myōshū* is taken from Norman Waddell and Masao Abe, "Dōgen's *Bendōwa*," p. 144.

65. *Dōgen Zen to Tendai hongaku hōmon*, p. 547.

66. Ibid., p. 551.

67. Ibid., p. 727. Here Yamanouchi's argument contrasts with that of Tamura. While Tamura agreed that both Shōshin and Dōgen were critical of *hongaku* thought, he saw Shōshin as advocating the traditional idea of a linear process of cultivation culminating in Buddhahood, but Dōgen as inverting the relationship of practice and enlightenment, regarding the two as simultaneous. See his "Critique of Original Awakening Thought in Shōshin and Dōgen," p. 265.

68. *Dōgen Zen to Tendai hongaku hōmon*, pp. 730–31.

69. See Kagamishima Genryū, *Dōgen Zenji to sono shūhen*, pp. 111–16, and Yamanouchi Shun'yū, "*Shōbō genzō shō* to Tendai hongaku hōmon." See also Bodiford, *Sōtō Zen in Medieval Japan*, p. 48.

70. Yamanouchi Shun'yū, "*Shōbō genzō shō*," pp. 104–5.

71. "Tendai kyōgaku to Dōgen," p. 21.

72. An early example (1960) is Kagamishima Genryū's "Dōgen Zenji to Tendai hongaku hōmon," which notes that, of the passages from the *Lotus Sūtra* cited in the *Shōbō genzō,* the majority are from the first fourteen chapters or "trace teaching" *(shakumon)* section of the sūtra, rather than from the latter fourteen chapters or "origin teaching" *(honmon),* to which medieval Tendai thought gives priority. Morever, from the commentarial literature, Dōgen cites not medieval Japanese Tendai sources but the work of Chinese T'ien-t'ai teachers such as Chih-i, and especially the *Hung-chüeh,* the sixth patriarch Chan-jan's commentary on Chih-i's *Mo-ho chih-kuan.* Kagamishima concluded that "the connection between Tendai original enlightenment doctrine and the Zenji is a slight one" (p. 57).

In response, Tamura Yoshirō pointed out that, despite their privileging of the "origin teaching" of the *Lotus Sūtra,* medieval Tendai transmission texts also quote widely from the "trace teaching" and from Chan-jan's *Hung-chüeh;* the fact that Dōgen does not cite medieval Tendai texts does not preclude the possibility of a connection between his ideas and original enlightenment thought (*Kamakura shin Bukkyō shisō no kenkyū,* pp. 552, 569–71 [n. 39]). However, Kagamishima's argument is defended by Yamanouchi Shun'yū, who sees Kagamishima's research as helping to establish important connections between Dōgen and earlier, classical T'ien-t'ai/Tendai thought, an issue that Tamura does not address (see *Dōgen to Tendai hongaku hōmon,* part III, chap. 2, especially pp. 623–40). More recently, in his analysis of the "Hokke ten Hokke" fascicle of the *Shōbō genzō,* Ikeda Rosan has also suggested that Dōgen's understanding of the *Lotus Sūtra* is more consistent with traditional T'ien-t'ai than with its medieval Japanese incarnation ("Dōgen to chūko Tendai hongaku shisō.").

73. "Kamakura jidai ni okeru shinjō sōmetsu ron ni kansuru kenkyū."

74. *Bendōwa, DZZ* 2:549.

75. For example, "Sokushin ze butsu" condemns as equivalent to the Śrenika heresy the position that the discriminating intellect of beings, prior to arousing of the *bodhicitta,* is itself Buddha (DZZ 1:53–54). "Daishugyō," in discussing the *kōan* about Pai-chang's fox, condemns as the "heresy of an original self" the view that the enlightened person at death "returns to the ocean of the [true] nature of original enlightenment" (2:189). See also the similar passage in "Jinshin inga," 2:393.

76. See *Ta-pan nieh-p'an ching* 39, *T* 12:594a14–596b10.

77. See Hazama Jikō, "Kamakura jidai ni okeru shinjō sōmetsu ron ni kansuru kenkyū," pp. 305–14, for a discussion of the origins of this idea and the texts in which it appears.

78. *Gobu kechimyaku, DDZ* 5:360, cited in Hazama, ibid., p. 303.

79. See for example Yamanouchi Shun'yū, *Dōgen Zen to Tendai hongaku hōmon,* pp. 642–73, and Hakamaya Noriaki, *Hongaku shisō hihan,* p. 141.

80. Hui-chung's comments appear in *Ching-te ch'uan-teng lu* 28, *T* 51:437c17–439b19. The passages referred to above occur at 437c–438a.

81. Tamura Yoshirō sees Dōgen's criticism as directed primarily at certain strands of Southern Sung "sudden enlightenment" Ch'an, especially the doctrines of the Lin-chi master Ta-hui Tsung-kao (1089–1163), which were upheld by followers of Nōnin's Darumashū (*Kamakura shin Bukkyō shisō no kenkyū,* pp. 556–64). Bernard Faure argues convincingly that Dōgen's criticisms were aimed at the Darumashū ("The Daruma-shū, Dōgen and Sōtō Zen," pp. 41–44). As both scholars point out, some

connection may also have existed between Darumashū doctrine and Tendai *hongaku* discourse.

82. The most important sources for an understanding of "critical Buddhism" are Hakamaya Noriaki, *Hongaku shisō hihan,* and *Hihan Bukkyō,* as well as Matsumoto Shirō, *Engi to kū.* For a discussion of these three works and other articles by Hakamaya, and of responses to the critical Buddhism movement, see Paul L. Swanson, "Zen is Not Buddhism." For a response to Hakamaya by an American scholar, see Peter N. Gregory, "Tsung-mi and the Problem of *Hongaku shisō.*" Implications for a rereading of Dōgen's thought in light of "critical Buddhism" are suggested in Ishii Shūdō, "Recent Trends in Dōgen Studies." *Pruning the Bodhi Tree,* a volume of essays on critical Buddhism edited by Jamie Hubbard and Paul L. Swanson, appeared after this book had been submitted for copy editing and promises to generate interest outside Japan in issues raised by critical Buddhism. I regret that I was unable to refer to it for this study.

83. See, for example, Hakamaya Noriaki, *Hongaku shisō hihan,* p. 9, and Matsumoto Shirō, *Engi to kū,* pp. 79–81 (n. 11).

84. These are introduced in the introductory chapter of *Hongaku shisō hihan,* pp. 9–10, and developed in subsequent chapters.

85. *Hongaku shisō hihan,* pp. 152–54.

86. See, for example, Hakamaya Noriaki, "Sabetsu jishō o umidashita shisōteki haikei ni kansuru shiken." This particular essay was written in the context of Sōtō attempts to revise discriminatory practices against the *burakumin,* on which see also William M. Bodiford, "Zen and the Art of Religious Prejudice." "Critical Buddhists" further argue that "topical" Buddhism has been used to bolster nationalism and ethnocentrism. See chapter 1, n. 6.

87. *Hongaku shisō hihan,* pp. 294–95.

88. Ibid. pp. 322–23.

89. Ibid., p. 396.

90. Ibid., pp. 327–37.

91. For more on Hakamaya's controversial privileging of the twelve-fascicle version of *Shōbō genzō* over the earlier sixty- and seventy-five-fascicle versions, see chapters 14 and 19, *Hongaku shisō hihan,* as well as Hakamaya's *Dōgen to Bukkyō: Jūni kanbon Shōbō genzō no Dōgen.* His arguments are summarized along with the responses of other Sōtō scholars in Steven Heine, "'Critical Buddhism' *(Hihan Bukkyō)* and the Debate Concerning the 75–fascicle and 12–fascicle *Shōbōgenzō* Texts."

92. See the summary of these responses in Habito, *Originary Enlightenment,* p. 73.

93. Ibid., chap. 4, "The Logic of Nonduality and Absolute Affirmation."

94. *Tendai Hokkeshū gozu hōmon yōsan, THR.* p. 38; translation by Habito, *Originary Enlightenment,* p. 48–49.

95. *Ta-pan-nieh-p'an ching* 25, *T* 12:510b29.

96. *Nihon chūsei no kokka to shūkyō,* p. 443 (see also pp. 443–45, 487–88). Translation from Kuroda Toshio, "The Development of the *Kenmitsu* System as Japan's Medieval Orthodoxy," trans. James C. Dobbins, p. 262.

97. *Nihon chūsei no kokka to Bukkyō,* p. 57.

98. "Kamakura Bukkyō ron," pp. 270–71. See also Taira Masayuki, *Nihon chūsei no shakai to Bukkyō,* pp. 473–75. Taira's assertions about the connection between *hongaku* thought and the activities of warrior monks are based on Akamatsu Toshihide's "'Akusō' no shinjō to Kamakura Bukkyō," discussed in chapter 5.

99. Kuroda Toshio actually saw the new Kamakura Buddhist movements (the *itan-ha*) as engaged with issues that overlapped original enlightenment thought and not in direct or complete opposition to it (*Nihon chūsei no kokka to shūkyō*, p. 488). In contrast, Taira Masayuki sees all the *itan* thinkers (except Dainichi Nōnin) as "grounded in a stance opposed to *hongaku* discourse" ("Kamakura Bukkyō ron," p. 289).

100. See Tamura Yoshirō, "Tendai hongaku shisō gaisetsu," pp. 477–521.

101. Tamura's theory of the relation between the new Kamakura Buddhism and Tendai *hongaku* thought is discussed in several of his books and articles. Its most thorough elaboration is to be found in his *Kamakura shin Bukkyō shisō no kenkyū*. A shorter version is his "Kamakura shin Bukkyō no haikei toshite no Tendai hongaku shisō." A convenient summary of his argument, complete with diagrams, appears in the final chapter of his *Nichiren: Junkyō no nyoraishi*, pp. 202–209. For further discussion of Tamura's theory in English, see Habito, *Originary Enlightenment*, pp. 17–22.

A slight disjuncture appears to exist between this aspect of Tamura's work and his dating of medieval Tendai texts: his chronology, as discussed in the last chapter, locates the full flowering of Tendai *hongaku* thought in the mid-thirteenth century, yet all the new Kamakura founders except Nichiren were active well before this point. Presumably Tamura saw them as responding to *hongaku* thought at an earlier stage in its development, though he does not make this clear.

102. *Kamakura shin Bukkyō shisō no kenkyū*, pp. 467–68, 469.

103. Ibid., pp. 511, 517–518, 535.

104. *Tanni shō, SCZ*, p. 678.

105. Tamura follows Shimaji in regarding Shinran as one of several among Hōnen's disciples who sought to impart a greater philosophical sophistication to their teacher's message by supplementing it with original enlightenment thought. See Shimaji Daitō, "Nihon ko Tendai kenkyū no hitsuyō o ronzu," pp. 181–82; Tamura Yoshirō, *Kamakura shin Bukkyō shisō no kenkyū*, pp. 511, 534.

106. See *Ichinen tanen mon'i, SCZ*, pp. 527–28, and *Yuishin shō mon'i, SCZ*, pp. 550–51.

107. For example, *Mattō shō, SCZ*, pp. 585, 586.

108. *Kamakura shin Bukkyō shisō no kenkyū*, pp. 539–40.

109. Nakanishi Chikai, "Shinran Shōnin ni okeru hongaku to jitsuzon no mondai."

110. *Bendōwa, DZZ* 2:470.

111. Section 28, *DNBZ* 32:121b. The same transmission also appears in *Sanjū shika no kotogaki, THR*, p. 180.

112. "Shōji," *Shōbō genzō, DZZ* 2:528. See also *Bendōwa*, 2:473.

113. *Tendai Hokkeshū gozu hōmon yōsan, THR*, p. 35.

114. The expression "dwelling in a Dharma-position" comes from the *Lotus Sūtra*: "The dharmas dwell in a Dharma-position, and the worldly aspect constantly abides" (*MFLHC, p'in* 2, T 9:9b10). See chap. 1, n. 115, for the interpretation of this passage. For Dōgen's understanding of "dwelling in a Dharma-position," see Hee-Jin Kim, *Dōgen Kigen*, pp. 200–203.

115. "Genjō kōan," *Shōbō genzō, DZZ* 1:2.

116. *Makura sōshi*, section 32, *DNBZ* 32:123b.

117. Tamura's illustrations of points of resemblance between Dōgen and Tendai *hongaku* thought are given in *Kamakura shin Bukkyō shisō no kenkyū*, pp. 548–52.

118. "Gyōbutsu igi," *Shōbō genzō, DZZ* 1:66.

119. *Bendōwa, DZZ* 2:460.

120. "Busshō," *Shōbō genzō, DZZ,* 1:22.

121. *DZZ* 2:470. Translation from Waddell and Abe, "Dōgen's *Bendōwa,*" p. 144, slightly modified.

122. Tamura was one of the first scholars to move substantially beyond the traditional sectarian periodicization of Nichiren's teachings into before and after his exile to Sado (1271–1274) and to clarify in more nuanced terms the process of his intellectual development *(Nichiren: Junkyō no nyoraishi).* Dōgen's thinking on the subject of original enlightenment may also have undergone change and development, but Tamura does not explore this. The issue has been taken up by Hakamaya Noriaki, who, as we have seen, regards Dōgen as becoming increasingly critical of *hongaku* ideas toward the end of his life.

123. *Kaitai sokushin jōbutsu gi, STN* 1:14.

124. *Kaimoku shō, STN* 1:576.

125. *Kanjin honzon shō, STN* 1:711.

126. *Kamakura shin Bukkyō shisō no kenkyū,* p. 625.

127. Ibid., p. 626.

128. See, for example, "Junsui Nichirengi kakuritsu no mondaiten," p. 9ff. While he establishes grounds for criticizing Asai Yōrin and Tamura Yoshirō's extreme position in ruling out of consideration any Nichiren-attributed writing dealing with original enlightenment thought, Hanano on his part does not always take adequate note of textual difficulties. See my "Some Disputed Writings in the Nichiren Corpus," pp. 228–29.

129. "Nichiren no shōdai shisō to Danna-ryū no kanjō genshi kuden," p. 149.

Chapter Three: The Culture of Secret Transmission

1. For the history of Mt. Hiei, see Murayama Shūichi, "Hieizan no kankyō to soshiki" and *Hieizan shi,* and Adolphson, "Monks, Courtiers and Warriors," pp. 18–69. For specific aspects of the culture and practices of Mt. Hiei, see, for example, Kageyama Haruki, *Hieizan;* Kageyama Haruki et al., *Hieizan I;* Murayama Shūichi, ed., *Hieizan to Tendai Bukkyō no kenkyū;* Setouchi Jakuchō et al., *Hieizan II;* Watanabe Shujun et al., *Hieizan;* and Arai Eizō et al., *Eizan no bunka.*

2. See Neil McMullin, "The Sanmon-Jimon Schism in the Tendai School of Buddhism."

3. On the physical layout and administrative structure of Mt. Hiei, see Kageyama Haruki, "Santō, kuin, jūrokudani" and *Hieizan,* pp. 68–79, as well as Adolphson, "Monks, Courtiers and Warriors," pp. 42–45, 242–43.

4. *Nichūreki,* cited in Kageyama Haruki, *Hieizan,* p. 142. See also Adolphson, "Monks, Courtiers and Warriors," pp. 45–46, n. 92.

5. Kuroda Toshio includes *hijiri* or *shōnin* as a third category of monks in "Chūsei jisha seiryoku ron," pp. 254–55. See also his *Jisha seiryoku,* pp. 78–88, and "The Development of the *Kenmitsu* System," pp. 259–61.

6. On the shrine system of Mt. Hiei, see Sugawara Shinkai, *Sannō Shintō no kenkyū;* Kageyama Haruki, *Hieizan,* pp. 169–75; and Grapard, "Linguistic Cubism," pp. 212–16.

7. On the role of *kami* in Enryakuji's "forceful appeals" *(gōso)* in the capital, see Adolphson, "Monks, Courtiers and Warriors," pp. 198–233.

8. Ibid., p. 6. For a partial list of these estates, their location, the sources in which they are mentioned, and the purpose for which their income was designated, see Kageyama Haruki, *Hieizan,* pp. 211–18.

9. See Kageyama Haruki, "Santō, kuin, jūrokudani," pp. 59–62, and *Hieizan,* pp. 176–82; Adolphson, "Monks, Courtiers and Warriors," pp. 66–67, 83.

10. For summarized accounts of these conflicts, see Tsuji Zennosuke, *Nihon Bukkyōshi,* vol. 2: *Chūsei* 1, pp. 40–106; Akamatsu Toshihide, ed., *Nihon Bukkyōshi (Chūsei-hen),* pp. 335–39; Inoue Mitsusada, *Nihon Jōdokyō seiritsu shi no kenkyū,* pp. 173–77, 180–81, 270–71, 272–75; and Murayama Shūichi, "Hieizan no kankyō to sōshiki." For a detailed study in English of the warrior monks of Mt. Hiei, see Adolphson, "Monks, Courtiers and Warriors."

11. Adolphson, "Monks, Courtiers and Warriors," p. 66.

12. Inoue Mitsusada, for example, cites growing "secularization," increased participation of monastic warriors in internal disputes, and decline in scholarship as the salient characteristics of the Tendai institution during the Insei period (*Nihon Jōdokyō seiritsu no tenkai,* pp. 173–85).

13. For a discussion of the ideological aspects of *mappō* thought, see Taira Masayuki, "Mappō matsudaikan no rekishiteki igi." Taira's article is especially valuable in calling attention to the way in which temple-shrine complexes of the "old Buddhism" used *mappō* discourse to further their interests.

14. For examples, see Tsuji Zennosuke, *Nihon Bukkyōshi,* vol. 2: *Chūsei* 1, pp. 133–41.

15. McMullin, "History and Historiographical Issues," pp. 32–33.

16. *Re-visioning "Kamakura" Buddhism,* "introduction."

17. Kuroda Toshio, "Chūsei jisha seiryoku ron," p. 247.

18. *Jisha seiryoku,* p. 34.

19. "Influential parties" is Neil McMullin's translation of the term *kenmon* (*Buddhism and the State in Sixteenth-Century Japan,* p. 8). James C. Dobbins uses "ruling elites" ("Editor's Introduction," p. 219).

20. "Chūsei jisha seiryoku ron," p. 248.

21. For discussion of Jimon Tendai during this period, see Hazama Jikō, *Chūko Nihon Tendai no kenkyū,* pp. 207–40.

22. Among the earliest references, if authentic, are Nichiren's "Shijō Kingo-dono gohenji" (*STN* 1:635) and "Risshōkan jō sōjō" (1:870), dated 1272 and 1275, respectively. While Nichiren's authorship of both texts has been questioned, the "Risshō kanjō sōjō" exists in a 1325 transcription and so had definitely been written by that time. Other notices occur in the *Tangi hōshin shō* by Saien, written in 1275 (cited in Hazama Jikō, *Chūko Nihon Tendai no kenkyū,* p. 23, and in Ōkubo Ryōjun, "Edan ryōryū kengaku [zōden] no yōsō," p. 308); and in the works of Gyōnen (1240–1321), such as the *Sangoku Buppō dentsū engi* 3 (*DNBZ* 101:128b), *Gokyōshō tsūryakki* 12 (9:175a), and *Naiten jinro shō* (3:58a). The *Kitadani hiten,* which bears a colophon dated 1304, also refers to the two schools (cited in Ōkubo Ryōjun, p. 311).

23. *Chūko Nihon Tendai no kenkyū,* pp. 24, 43.

24. That is, around the time of the monks Shinga and Shinson (both fl. 1329). See Ōkubo Ryōjun, "Edan ryōryū ni kansuru shiron," p. 9.

25. The *Kankō ruijū* is said to have been compiled by Chūjin (1065–1138), but this is a retrospective attribution. The precise dating of this text, and hence, of the origin myth of the two schools, is difficult to determine. Hazama Jikō places the *Kankō ruijū* in the late Heian or early Kamakura period (*Chūko Nihon Tendai no kenkyū,* pp. 14–17). Tamura Yoshirō places it later, assigning it to the fourth period, 1250–1300, in his organization of the original enlightenment literature ("Tendai hongaku shisō

gaisetsu," p. 532). Ōkubo Ryōjun suggests that it was probably compiled around the time of Jōmyō (d. 1286), regarded as the founder of the Gyōsen-bō branch of the Eshin school, and may possibly even be his work (*"Kankō ruijū," THR*, pp. 576–77). However, Hayashi Senshō argues that it is not Jōmyō's work but dates from around the time of Jōmyō's disciple Shinga or later ("Shikan shō Hokke shisō to Senba kyō-gaku," p. 258).

26. The symbolism of the two Buddhas seated side by side in the jeweled stūpa played a vital role in the medieval Tendai tradition and in *Lotus*-related practices more generally. The emergence of the stūpa from beneath the earth is described in chapter 11 of the *Lotus Sūtra*. See *MFLHC, p'in* 11, *T* 9:32b–33c; Hurvitz, pp. 183–88.

27. *Kankō ruijū* 1 and 4, *THR*, pp. 188–89, 284–85.

28. *Sui T'ien-t'ai Chih-che Ta-shih pieh-chuan*, *T* 50:191c22. See also *Hsü kao-seng chuan*, *T* 50: 564b15–6.

29. Taira Ryōshō, "Ryōzen dōchō ni tsuite."

30. *Naishō Buppō sōjō kechimyakufu*, *DDZ* 1:225. For a discussion of this work and the scholarship concerning it, see Groner, *Saichō*, pp. 251–60. The story of Hui-ssu and Chih-i being present in the assembly on Eagle Peak evidently impressed Saichō, as he mentions it in a number of his writings (*Shugo kokkai shō* 1a and 1b, *DDZ* 2:183, 236; *Hokke shūku* 3, *DDZ* 3:279; *Ehyō Tendaishū*, *DDZ* 3:363; and *Fuhō engi*, *DDZ* 5:33). It also appears in works by Saichō's immediate disciples, such as Kōjō (779–858)'s *Denjutsu isshin kaimon* (*DDZ* 1:594, 626) and Ninchū's *Eizan Daishi den* (*DDZ* 5 [*furoku*]:10, 33). However, Shioiri Ryōchū sees the *Kechimyakufu* as especially important because it connects the idea of Hui-ssu and Chih-i's presence on Eagle Peak with the construction of a Tendai lineage ("Dengyō Daishi no hongaku shisō," pp. 22, 24).

31. *DDZ* 1:225. The sutra quote is at *Fo-shuo kan P'u-hsien P'u-sa hsing-fa ching, T* 9:392c15–16. The identification of Śākyamuni with Vairocana is discussed in chap. 1.

32. This phrase, whose symbolism was central to the initiation rituals of a number of medieval Tendai *kuden* lineages, has roots in the important but understudied area of interactions between Tendai and Zen traditions. It first occurs in recorded teachings of the Ch'an master Ta-hui (1098–1163), such as the *Ta-hui P'u-chiao Ch'an-shih yü-lun* 23, where it is used to express Chih-i's enlightenment (*T* 47:907a23–24). Its first appearance in a Japanese text is Eisai's *Kōzen gokoku ron* 2, where it also refers to Chih-i's awakening (*T* 80:9a25–26). The phrase recurs throughout the Tendai *kuden* literature. For example, the *Nijō shō kenmon* says that Ta-hui, fifth in line of succession from Bodhidharma, had originally been a T'ien-t'ai monk and established a temple on Mt. Chin-feng to the northwest of Mt. T'ien-t'ai. There he erected a stone stele incribed with praise of Chih-i, which included this statement (*TZ* 9:206a). See also Hiroumi Kōken, "Kuden hōmon to Daie Zenji."

33. *DDZ* 5:10. For discussion of the dating and significance of this work, see Ōkubo Ryōjun, *"Tendai Hokkeshū denbō ge ni tsuite."*

34. According to Saichō, the lineage of the bodhisattva precepts originates with Vairocana, the central Buddha of the *Fan-wang ching*, in which the bodhisattva precepts are expounded, and is then transmitted to Śākyamuni on Eagle Peak (*Naishō Buppō sōjō kechimyakufu, DDZ* 1:230). Hui-ssu and Chih-i are also incorporated into the lineage as "auditors on Sacred [Eagle] Peak" (232). Saichō was probably the first to incorporate the idea of a transmission originating with Śākyamuni on Eagle Peak into the lineages of both the T'ien-t'ai/Tendai school and the bodhisattva precepts

(Taira Ryōshō, "Ryōzen dōchō ni tsuite, p. 10; Groner, *Saichō*, p. 259). A biography of Saichō traditionally attributed to his disciple Ninchū (fl. 824) also cites Saichō as saying that Hui-ssu and Chih-i received the transmission of the threefold bodhisattva precepts when the *Lotus Sūtra* was preached on Eagle Peak (*Eizan Daishi den, DDZ* [*furoku*] 5:33). For examples of the direct transmission of the perfect precepts from Śākyamuni to Hui-ssu and Chih-i on Eagle Peak in medieval Tendai precept lineages, see *Isshin myōkai shō, ZTZ, Enkai* 1:299–300, and *Tendai Hokkeshū gakushōshiki mondō, DDZ* 1:369–75. On the dating of the latter text, see Groner, *Saichō*, pp. 206–7 (n. 3).

35. See Taikō Yamasaki, *Shingon Buddhism*, pp. 8, 86–89.

36. *Kankō ruijū* 4, *THR*, pp. 279–80.

37. Shimaji Daitō, *Nihon Bukkyōshi kenkyū*, pp. 481–85; Hazama Jikō, *Chūko Nihon Tendai no kenkyū*, pp. 13–14, 190. See also Uesugi Bunshū, *Nihon Tendai shi*, vol. 1, pp. 417–34.

38. "Shijō Kingo-dono gohenji," *STN* 1:635. Nichiren's authorship of this letter has been questioned by both Asai Yōrin (*Nichiren Shōnin kyōgaku no kenkyū*, pp. 182–85) and Tamura Yoshirō (*Kamakura shin Bukkyō shisō no kenkyū*, pp. 596, 615–16).

39. *Shūyōshū shikenmon*, cited in Hazama Jikō, *Chūko Nihon Tendai no kenkyū*, p. 44.

40. Hazama Jikō, *Chūko Nihon Tendai no kenkyū*, pp. 190–91.

41. For example, the *Nihon daishi sentoku myōshō ki*, written by Jōchin in 1580, says that the Eshin school maintains the transmission of meditative disciplines handed down from Tao-sui through Genshin, while the Danna schools maintains the transmission of doctrinal studies taught by Hsing-man and passed down through Kakuun (*DNBZ* 111:270).

42. Hazama Jikō, *Chūko Nihon Tendai no kenkyū*, pp. 21–22, 51–52.

43. *Kenkai roni 1, DDZ* 1:35.

44. Sasaki Kentoku, *Tendai kyōgaku*, p. 39–41. Sasaki notes that the Sung T'ien-t'ai master Chih-li criticized Tao-sui for unorthodox readings (see *Shih pu-erh men chih-yao ch'ao* 1, *T* 46:710c12–14).

45. See Groner, *Saichō*, pp. 45–46.

46. Hazama Jikō, *Chūko Nihon Tendai no kenkyū*, pp. 17–18; Sueki Fumihiko, "Chūsei Tendai to hongaku shisō," p. 321.

47. Hazama Jikō, *Chūko Nihon Tendai no kenkyū*, pp. 45–47.

48. See, for example, *Maka shikan kenmon tenchū* 1a, *DNBZ* 29:18a.

49. For a partial list and discussion of lineages not included in the traditional "eight schools," see Hazama Jikō, *Chūko Nihon Tendai no kenkyū*, pp. 61–68.

Like the Eshin and Danna schools, these subsidiary lineages are referred to in primary sources as *ryū*. However, since they represent divisions within Eshin and Danna, I have for clarity's sake translated Eshin-ryū and Danna-ryū as "Eshin school" and "Danna school," while referring to the subsidiary *ryū* as "sublineages."

50. Ibid., p. 68.

51. Hazama Jikō cites Gyōnen's *Sangoku Buppō dentsū engi* and *Gokyōshō tsūryakki*, which mention, in addition to the Eshin and Danna, the Sugiu and Hōchi-bō lines; Saien's *Tangi hōshin shō*, which mentions the Ishiizumi-bō, Tōyō-bō, Ekō-bō and Inokuma lines; and the "Risshōkan jō sōjō" attributed to Nichiren, which states, "Within the single Tendai school, although there are various divisions of lineage, they do not go beyond the two schools, Eshin and Danna," thus suggesting the existence of numerous subdivisions. All these sources are given in n. 22 above as early notices of the existence of the Eshin and Danna schools.

52. Of the four Danna lineages, the Ekō-bō lineage, considered the main Danna line, traces itself from Chōgō (1049–1133); the Chikurin-bō and Bishamondō lines, from Chōgō's disciples Chōyō and Chikai, respectively; and the Inokuma line, from Chōyō's disciple Shōyū—all persons of approximately the Insei period. Of the four Eshin lines, the main, Sugiu line traces itself from Kōkaku, a disciple of Chūjin (1065–1138), and the Hōchi-bō line traces itself from Hōchi-bō Shōshin—again, both persons of the Insei period. In contrast, the persons regarded as founders of the Gyōsen-bō and Tsuchimikado-monzeki lines—respectively, Jōmyō (d. 1286) and his disciple Seikai—were people of the mid-Kamakura period. Sueki suggests the possibility of a connection between the datings of these two clusters of founders and important developments in the *kuden* literature. For example, for reasons that are not altogether clear, a number of important medieval Tendai works are attributed to Insei figures, such as Kōkaku and Chūjin. Works attributed to Chūjin—such as the *Kankō ruijū*—often quote Jōmyō, and so were probably written around his time or slightly later. See Sueki Fumihiko, "Chūsei Tendai to hongaku shisō," pp. 322, 324–25. Hanano Michiaki similarly suggests that the works attributed to Chūjin were produced by a group of monks centered around Jōmyō (Nichiren Shōnin kyōgaku no shisōshiteki kenkyū joron," p. 139).

53. Shōshin was at various times assimilated to both Eshin and Danna traditions. See Ōkubo Ryōjun, "Edan ryōryū kengaku (zōden) no yōsō," pp. 309–310.

54. Hayami Tasuku, *Heian kizoku shakai to Bukkyō,* pp. 33–35. Hayami's represents one of very few studies of *shuhō* and their social roles.

55. Ibid., pp. 104–22. See also his *Nihon Bukkyōshi,* pp. 248–49.

56. Shimaji Daitō, *Tendai kyōgaku shi,* pp. 412–19, and Uesugi Bunshū, *Nihon Tendai shi,* vol. 1, pp. 444–48. These figures for the number of Taimitsu and Tōmitsu lineages appear to have been retrospectively projected from a later period; exactly how many lineages had formed by the Insei period is not certain (Hayami Tasuku, *Heian kizoku shakai to Bukkyō,* p. 122). The Taimitsu lineages are said to have originated from three major lineages: two originating from the Mikkyō transmissions received in China by Saichō and Ennin respectively and transmitted on Mt. Hiei (the Konpon Daishi-ryū and Jikaku Daishi-ryū), and a third, the Chishō Daishi-ryū, originating with Enchin and transmitted by the Jimon branch of Tendai at the Onjōji. However, this too appears in some respects to be a retrospectively created tradition, and details are unclear.

57. On Taimitsu ritual, see Shimaji Daitō, "Taimitsu no jisōteki kitō ni tsuite" and *Tendai kyōgaku shi,* pp. 420–29.

58. Hayami Tasuku, *Heian kizoku shakai to Bukkyō,* p. 125.

59. A parallel with secret transmission in schools of poetry was noted by Hazama Jikō (*Chūko Nihon Tendai no kenkyū,* p. 25).

60. On the beginnings of *waka no ie,* see Jin'ichi Konishi, *A History of Japanese Literature,* vol. 3, pp. 31–34. On the rise of the ideal of *michi,* see his *Michi* and also "Michi and Medieval Writing," especially pp. 181–96.

61. On Kōkei, see Uesugi Bunshū, *Nihon Tendai shi,* vol. 1, p. 448; *BD* 2:1038a–b; Inoue Mitsusada, *Nihon Jōdokyō seiritsu no tenkai,* pp. 185–86; and Hayami Tasuku, *Heian kizoku shakai to Bukkyō,* pp. 123–25, and *Nihon Bukkyōshi,* pp. 250–51.

62. This appears in a colophon to fascicle seventeen of the so-called *Chōen-bon,* a version copied by Chōen's disciple Raishō (see Tajima Tokuon, "*Shijūjō-ketsu,*" *BKD* 4:191b–c). This colophon does not appear in the version of *Shijūjō-ketsu* included in the Taishō canon.

63. Hazama Jikō, *Chūko Nihon Tendai no kenkyū*, pp. 70–71.

64. Tamura Yoshirō, "Tendai hongaku shisō gaisetsu," p. 520.

65. Nakanishi Zuikō has drawn attention to aristocratic factions as the "social basis" *(shakai kiban)* of the Eshin and Danna *kuden* lineages (see particularly his "Kuden hōmon keiseiki no kōsatsu," which expands upon material presented in two earlier articles: "Kuden hōmon seiritsu no shakai kiban" and "Kuden hōmon tenkai no igi").

66. *Heian jidai no kenkyū*, pp. 17–20. See also his *Sōhei to bushi*, pp. 90–98.

67. Hirata Toshiharu, *Sōhei to bushi*, pp. 105–108.

68. For Ryōgen's relationship with Morosuke and his descendants and its consequences for Mt. Hiei, see Neil McMullin, "The *Lotus Sutra* and Politics in the Mid-Heian Period."

69. Nakanishi Zuikō, "Kuden hōmon keiseiki no kōsatsu," p. 76–77, 79–84.

70. Inoue Mitsusada, *Nihon Jōdokyō seiritsushi no kenkyū*, pp. 178–79. See also Murayama Shūichi, *Hieizan shi*, p. 156.

71. Adachi Naoya, "Hōshinnō no seijiteki igi," pp. 179–80, 192; Taira Masayuki, *Nihon chūsei no shakai to Bukkyō*, p. 471; Adolphson, "Monks, Courtiers and Warriors," p. 59.

72. *Tendai zasu ki*, p. 17.

73. Adachi Naoya, "Hōshinnō no seijiteki igi," p. 192.

74. On Enryakuji *monzeki*, see Kageyama Haruki, *Hieizan*, pp. 163–68, and "Santō, kuin, jūrokudani," pp. 56–58; Fukuyama Toshio, "Monzeki jiin tanjō"; Watanabe Shujun, Amano Denchū and Mizukami Fumiyoshi, "Tendai no monzeki"; and Adolphson, "Monks, Courtiers and Warriors," pp. 60–61.

75. Inoue Mitsusada, *Nihon Jōdokyō seiritsushi no kenkyū*, p. 275; Kuroda Toshio, "Jisha seiryoku ron," p. 264.

76. Kuroda Toshio, "Jisha seiryoku ron," pp. 263–64.

77. Kageyama Haruki, *Hieizan*, p. 164.

78. Adachi Naoya, "Hōshinnō no seijiteki igi," p. 190.

79. Kageyama Haruki, *Hieizan*, p. 164.

80. *Ama no mokuzu*, a work dealing with ceremony and etiquette written in 1420, says, "The arts of the various *monzeki* include assemblies for [Chinese and Japanese] poetry, tea and incense-smelling" (*GR* 28:92a).

81. Watanabe Shujun, Amano Denchū and Mizukami Fumiyoshi, "Tendai no monzeki," pp. 264–66.

82. Takeuchi Rizō, "Kuden to kyōmei," cited in Nakanishi Zuikō, "Kuden hōmon seiritsu no shakai kiban" and "Kuden hōmon keiseiki no kōsatsu," p. 77.

83. Takeuchi Rizō, "Kuden to kyōmei" (1). On the "diary houses," especially the Kujō, see also Matsuzono Hitoshi, "Nikki no ie."

84. For the history of debate in the Tendai tradition, see Ozaki Kōjin, *Nihon Tendai rongishi no kenkyū*.

85. The Yuima-e, a lecture on the *Wei-mo ching* (Skt. *Vimālakīrti-nirdeśa;* Jpn. Yuima-gyō), is said to have been initiated in 657 by Fujiwara no Kamatari. It was conducted from the 10th through 16th day of the tenth month at the Kōfukuji. The Misai-e, featuring a lecture on the *Chin-kuang-ming tsui-sheng-wang ching* (*Konkōmyō saishōō-kyō)*, one of the "nation protecting sutras," was established in 766 or 768 and held annually at the court from the 8th through 14th of the first month. The Saishō-e, which included a lecture on the same sūtra, was established in 829 or 830 and held annually at the Yakushiji from the 7th through 13th of the third month. Paralleling

these "three assemblies of the Southern capital" *(nankyō sandai-e)*, which were dominated by monks of the Nara schools, three further annual assemblies were established by the Tendai school in the eleventh century: the Hokke-e, begun in 1072 and held at the Enshūji; the Saishō-e, begun in the same year and also held at the Enshūji; and the Daijō-e, established in 1078 and held at the Hosshōji. These Tendai assemblies also featured debate.

86. Willa Jane Tanabe, "The Lotus Lectures," especially pp. 397–99.

87. McMullin, "The *Lotus Sutra*," pp. 129–33.

88. On the political and ideological aspects of such debates, see Neil McMullin, "The Sutra Lecture and Doctrinal Debate Traditions in Early and Medieval Japan."

89. Tendai *ryūgi* are sometimes said to have begun during the time of Saichō and his successor Gishin, but the sources are not altogether reliable. See Groner, "The Significance of Ryōgen's (912–984) Revival of the Tendai Examination System," pp. 123–27 (cited by permission of the author).

90. Ibid., pp. 132–37.

91. For the education system on Mt. Hiei in the Heian and Kamakura periods, see Ikeyama Saien, "Eizan no kyōiku."

92. Ibid., p. 94.

93. Ibid,. p. 96.

94. Different texts give variant accounts of the lecture schedule. See Ogami Kanchū, "Yokawa no shūgaku seido," p. 59, and Groner, "The Significance of Ryōgen's (912–984) Revival," pp. 131–32, n. 14.

95. Ogami Kanchū, "Yokawa no shūgaku seido," pp. 58, 61.

96. Ikeyama Saien, "Eizan no kyōiku," pp. 101–102.

97. Ibid., p. 102.

98. Ogami Kanchū, "Yokawa no shūgaku seido," p. 60.

99. Ozaki Kōjin, *Nihon Tendai rongishi no kenkyū*" pp. 141–43.

100. On these two texts, see Ozaki Kōjin, *Nihon Tendai rongishi no kenkyū*, pp. 178–80; Ogami Kanchū, "*Shūman shū oyobi Shūen shū ni tsuite*"; and Ōkubo Ryōjun, "Tendai kuden hōmon no seiritsu to bunkenka," pp. 193–205.

101. *DNBZ* 16:13a–b. This debate is also recounted in Henku's biography in *Honchō kōsōden* 10, *DNBZ* 102:174a–b.

102. See Ozaki Kōjin, *Nihon Tendai rongishi no kenkyū*, pp. 143–48.

103. Taira Masayuki, *Nihon chūsei no shakai to Bukkyō*, p. 358.

104. Oka Kyōzui suggests a distinction to be made between "mystical oral transmissions" and "oral transmissions concerning debate topics" ("*Shūen shū, Shūman shū* no kenkyū," cited in Ōkubo Ryōjun, "Tendai kuden hōmon no seiritsu to bunkenka," p. 196). Ōkubo suggests a similar distinction on pp. 192–93.

105. Ozaki Kōjin, *Nihon Tendai rongishi no kenkyū*, p. 184.

106. Ogami Kanchū, "Kantō ni okeru chūko Tendai" (2), p. 2; Hazama Jikō, *Chūko Nihon Tendai no kenkyū*, pp. 88–89.

107. See, for example, *T* 46:50c16 and 112c12.

108. *Hung-chüeh 1a, T.* 1912.46:147b19–29; translated in Donner and Stevenson, *The Great Calming and Contemplation*, pp. 104–105, n. 39.

109. *DDZ* 1:35.

110. *DDZ* 2:266.

111. Hazama Jikō, *Chūko Nihon Tendai no kenkyū*, p. 53. See also Osabe Kazuo, "Kuden hōmon ni okeru hiden no kigen to Tōketsu to no kankei." Osabe agrees that

there was no established tradition of secret transmission in Sui and T'ang Buddhism but points out that there was in Taoism; this tradition, he suggests, may have filtered into Buddhist circles and entered Japan via *Tōketsu* ("T'ang decisions"), or verbal explanations of doctrine on which Japanese monks traveling in China made notes. There may be a remote connection, Osabe says, between these *Tōketsu* and medieval Tendai transmissions.

112. *TZ* 9:107a–b.

113. "Edan ryōryū hōmonchū no Dengyō Daishi," p. 89. See the entirety of this article for a discussion of the treatment of the two phrases in Eshin and Danna oral transmission texts.

114. *Dōsui Oshō fuhōmon, DDZ (furoku)* 5:115.

115. Ōkubō Ryōjun, "Edan ryōryū hōmonchū no Dengyō Daishi," pp. 74–75.

116. *THR*, pp. 42–43.

117. *THR*, pp. 49–50.

118. *THR*, pp. 50–52.

119. *TZ* 9:31a.

120. *TZ* 9:190b–92b.

121. *Heike monogatari* 2, *Nihon koten bungaku taikei*, vol. 32, p. 144; English translation from Helen Craig McCullough, *The Tale of the Heike*, p. 59, slightly modified.

122. *Chih-kuan* 1b, *T* 46:9a2–3, translated in Donner and Stevenson, *The Great Calming and Contemplation*, p. 195. See also the discussion in *THR*, pp. 426–27.

123. *THR*, pp. 25–29; *DNBZ* 24:350–51. On transmissions concerning "the mirror and its images" in medieval Tendai *kuden* texts, see also Shimaji Daitō, "Nihon Tendai kuden hōmon," pp. 63–65; Uesugi Bunshū, *Nihon Tendai shi*, vol. 1, pp. 613–23; and Sueki Fumihiko, "Tendai hongaku shisō kenkyū no shomondai," p. 291.

124. For example, *Ichijō shō, TZ* 9:30b–31a; *Nijō shō kenmon*, p. 193a–b.

125. *THR*, pp. 44–45.

126. *Koshinjū ki, DNBZ* 24:351b. A virtually identical passage occurs in *Ichijō shō, TZ* 9:31a, and *Kawataya bōshō jūkutsū, TZ* 9:108a.

127. *Genshi kanjō shiki*, cited in Ōkubo Ryōjun, "Edan ryōryū hōmonchū no Dengyō Daishi," p. 87.

128. See Ōkubo Ryōjun, "Jūju kai kanjō no kōki," p. 6, and also Nomoto Kakujō, "Genshi kanjō yori kai kanjō e," pp. 718–19.

129. See Alex Wayman, "The Mirror as a Pan-Buddhist Metaphor-Simile."

130. The relationship of *hongaku* thought to the transmissions of the chroniclers and the *shōmyō* chanters was first pointed out by Hazama Jikō, *Chūko Nihon Tendai no kenkyū*, pp. 245–74.

131. I have borrowed "chroniclers," as a translation for *kike*, from Kuroda Toshio, "Historical Consciousness and *Hon-jaku* Philosophy in the Medieval Period on Mt. Hiei," trans. Allan G. Grapard (see p. 156, n. 7). "Documents" as English for *kiroku* also comes from Grapard's translation. Kuroda's essay and Hazama Jikō's *Chūko Nihon Tendai no kenkyū*, pp. 245–66, are the two major studies of *kike* to date.

132. *T* 76:503b19–20.

133. *GR* 24:563a; translation from Kuroda Toshio, "Historical Consciousness and *Hon-jaku* Philosophy," trans. Grapard, p. 149.

134. Hazama Jikō, *Chūko Nihon Tendai no kenkyū*, pp. 254–55.

135. *Kuin bukkaku shō, GR* 24:563b–64a; *Keiran shūyō shū, T* 76:504a12–18.

136. *Chūko Nihon Tendai no kenkyū*, pp. 252–53. Kuroda also distinguishes between

kike texts that are "written in the style of basic documents and have very little mystical or philosophical content" and those that "do have a religious coloration" and whose "contents are even surreal" ("Historical Consciousness and the *Hon-jaku* Philosophy," p. 153).

137. *Keiran shūyō shō* 107, *T* 76:861a21–24.

138. See Misaki Gisen, "Hieizan no kaihyōgyō to sono rironteki konkyo." On the *kaihōgyō* walking pilgrimage generally, see Robert Rhodes, "The *Kaihōgyō* Practice of Mt. Hiei," and, for a popular treatment, John Stevens, *The Marathon Monks of Mt. Hiei.*

139. Hazama Jikō, *Chūko Nihon Tendai no kenkyū,* pp. 263–65. On Sannō Shintō, see n. 6 above.

140. For interpretations of Sannō in Tendai *kuden* texts, see Kojima Michimasa, "Sannō isshin sangan kuden dokugo" and "Tendai kuden hōmon to shingi," as well as Grapard, "Linguistic Cubism."

141. Kubota Tesshō, "Kaike to kike no kōshō," pp. 240–41.

142. For example, *Keiran shūyō shō, T* 76:504a4; *Kuin bukkaku shō, GR* 24:563b.

143. Arguments on this point have centered around the dating and attribution of the *Sange yōryakki,* of which several versions survive, and which bears interpolations by Gigen (c. 1289–1351). Hazama Jikō suggested that, even acknowledging the later additions, the possibility of Kenshin's authorship should not hastily be dismissed, and that *kike* transmissions probably existed from his time (*Chūko Nihon Tendai no kenkyū,* pp. 257–61). In contrast, Kubota Osamu argued that the *Yōryakki* is Gigen's compilation, retrospectively attributed to Kenshin, and that the *kike* transmissions date from the late Kamakura period (*Chūsei Shintō no kenkyū,* pp. 270–72). More recently, Kubota Tesshō has established that *kike* transmissions are cited in works by Ejin (d. 1289?), which would mean that they existed by the mid-Kamakura period ("Kaike to kike no kōshō"). Nomoto Kakujō suggests that the *Sange yōryakki* may have been the product not of one individual but of multiple *kike* lineages, a process that preceded Gigen ("*Sange yōryakki* no seikaku").

144. Hazama Jikō, *Chūko Nihon Tendai no kenkyū,* p. 261–62.

145. On the Kurodani precept lineage, see Ishida Mizumaro, *Kairitsu no kenkyū,* vol. 2, pp. 398–406 (an earlier version of the same essay appears in his *Nihon Bukkyō ni okeru kairitsu no kenkyū,* pp. 469–78); Shikii Shūjō, ed., *Tendai Shinseishū shūgaku hanron,* pp. 185–99, and his *Kaikanjō no nyūmonteki kenkyū,* pp. 1–16; and Kubota Tesshō, "Chūko Tendai ni okeru kai shō shikan no hōmon." A number of *kaike* texts are included in the recently published *Enkai* 1 volume of *ZTZ.* The "Kaidai" or notes on these texts, by Shikii Shūjō, Nomoto Kakujō, and Ōkubo Ryōjun, provide useful biographical information on *kaike* figures.

146. See Groner, "The *Fan-wang ching,*" p. 279.

147. See the lineage charts in his *Isshin myōkai shō, ZTZ, Enkai* 1, pp. 300, 301.

148. Because of the connection to Hōnen, the Kurodani precept lineage has sometimes been treated as a Pure Land lineage, for example, by Etani Ryūkai in his "Eizan kaihō fukkō undō no shomondai." However, Ishida Mizumaro demonstrates that this was in fact a Tendai lineage (*Kairitsu no kenkyū,* vol. 2, pp. 399–401). Matsuo Kenji suggests that, especially from the time of Echin, a third-generation disciple of Ejin, these revivers of the precepts should be seen as representing a new Buddhist *vinaya* movement, different in character from traditional Tendai, in that they constituted a new order and ordained followers independently of the state-sponsored ordination platform on Mt. Hiei (*Kanjin to hakai no chūseishi,* p. 168ff; also personal conversation, March 13, 1997).

149. *Sokenki, DNBZ* 74:302a. According to this text, black robes had been standard on Mt. Hiei before Ryōgen's time, but Ryōgen deemed the color black inappropriate to a temple devoted to prayers for the imperial welfare and decreed that a white robe be worn instead. See also Matsuo Kenji's discussion in *Kanjin to hakai no chūseishi*, pp. 172–73.

150. A printed edition of this biography appears in *Sange gakuhō* 21 (April 1925).

151. *Denshin Kashō den*, p. 17. A "period" here would be the equivalent of two hours.

152. Ibid., p. 11.

153. Kubota Tesshō, "Kaike to kike no kōshō," p. 232.

154. Matsuo Kenji, *Hakai to kanjin no chūseishi*, pp. 167–94.

155. *ZTZ, Enkai* 1, p. 258b.

156. Cited in Kubota Tesshō, "Chūko Tendai ni okeru kai shō shikan no hōmon," p. 47.

157. Kōen's biography represents him as stating explicitly that the inherent nature of the perfect precepts in principle can be realized only by the actual observance of the ten major and forty-eight minor precepts (*Denshin Kashō den*, pp. 2–3).

158. Mibu Taishun and Miyasaka Yūshō, *Nihon no Bukkyō: Tendai-Shingon*, p. 102.

159. Watanabe Shujun et al., *Hieizan*, p. 272.

160. *Shōmyō* lineages are given in *Genkō shakusho* 29 (*DNBZ* 101:487b) and the *Shōmyō genryū ki* (*T* 84:864c–65b), both by Gyōnen (1240–1321). See also Hazama Jikō, *Chūko Nihon Tendai no kenkyū*, pp. 267–71; Kuroda Toshio, *Nihon chūsei no shakai to shūkyō*, p. 268; and Mibu Taishun and Miyasaka Yūshō, *Nihon no Bukkyō: Tendai-Shingon*, pp. 103–105.

161. *Shōritsu hiyō shō*, cited in Hazama Jikō, *Chūko Nihon Tendai no kenkyū*, pp. 271–72. The five Buddhas are Dainichi Nyorai and the four other Buddhas who surround him on esoteric mandalas. Together they symbolize the "five wisdoms" *(gochi)* or aspects of Dainichi's enlightenment (see Taikō Yamasaki, *Shingon Buddhism*, pp. 94–95).

162. *Chūko Nihon Tendai no kenkyū*, pp. 267–74.

163. Nomoto Kakujō, "Genshi kankō yori kai kanjō e," p. 703.

164. Ibid., p. 706.

165. The earliest modern study of the *genshi* and *kimyōdan kanjō* rituals is Oka Kyōzui's 1911 essay, "Genshi kimyōdan no enkaku oyobi kyōri jisō no ippan." The most detailed study to date is Hazama Jikō, *Chūko Nihon Tendai no kenkyū*, pp. 135–181. Also helpful are Ōkubo Ryōjun, "Genshi kimyōdan kanjō" and "Tendai genshi kimyōdan kanjō ni tsuite," and Nomoto Kakujō, "Genshi kanjō kara kai kanjō e." A study in English by James Sanford is forthcoming. Some of the ritual texts related to the *genshi kimyōdan kanjō* have been published in Uesugi Bunshū, *Nihon Tendai shi*, vol. 2, pp. 830–96, and in *Shinkō sōsho*, pp. 18–122. Different texts give variant accounts of the rituals; the brief sketch given here is based chiefly on Hazama Jikō's study.

166. See Shimaji Daitō, *Nihon Bukkyō kyōgakushi*, pp. 474–78; Hazama Jikō, *Chūko Nihon Tendai no kenkyū*, pp. 165–69; Ōkubo Ryōjun, "Genshi kimyōdan kanjō," pp. 40–41, and "Tendai genshi kimyōdan kanjō ni tsuite," p. 317–18; and Nomoto Kakujō, "Genshi kanjō kara kai kanjō e," pp. 708–709.

167. For the text of this transmission, see, for example, *Genshidan hishō, Shinkō sōsho*, p. 18. It is also reproduced in Hazama Jikō, *Chūko Nihon Tendai no kenkyū*, pp. 165–66. For a discussion of the text and some of its problems, see Hanano Michiaki, "Nichiren no shōdai shisō to Danna-ryū no kanjō genshi kuden," pp. 127–33.

168. *Genshidan hishō, Shinkō sōsho*, pp. 34b–35a, 51a–b.

169. *Naishō Buppō sōjō kechimyaku fu, DDZ* 1:215.

170. Yuiken's (1289–1387) compilation of transmissions received from Ejin and Echin says that Ejin had received "five transmissions concerning the threefold contemplation in a single mind, of Kyōyū's lineage of the Ekōin" (*Santsū kuketsu, ZTZ, Enkai* 1, p. 370b). Another, external source is the *Risshōkan jō*, said to have been written by Nichiren in 1274, which makes reference to the *kanjō genshi* and to the tradition of the stone stūpa (*STN* 1:849). Although some question exists as to the authenticity of the *Risshōkan jō*, it appears that the *genshi kanjō* transmission was in existence during Nichiren's time. See Ōkubo Ryōjun, "Tendai genshi kimyōdan kanjō ni tsuite," pp. 311–14, and Nomoto Kakujō, "Genshi kanjō kara kai kanjō e," pp. 712–13.

171. When this happened is not entirely clear. However, according to the *Danna monryū sōjō shi* (1380) by the monk Jūkaku, Genshun, a second-generation disciple of Kyōyū, criticized his fellow disciple Gen'un for incorporating the *honzon* of the constantly-walking samādhi [Matarajin] into the *genshi kanjō* (cited in Ōkubo Ryōjun, "Tendai genshi kimyōdan kanjō ni tsuite," p. 316); thus the introduction of Matarajin may date from Gen'un's time. See also Nomoto Kakujō, "Genshi kanjō kara kai kanjō e," pp. 713–15.

172. According to the *Keiran shūyō shō*, while Ennin was aboard ship returning to Japan with the transmission of the *inzei nenbutsu*, this deity spoke to him in empty space, saying, "Those who do not reverence me cannot achieve the aspiration of birth in the Pure Land"; thereafter he was installed as a protector of the *jōgyōdō* (*T* 76:632c24–28). A slightly earlier source, the *Sange yōryakki*, identifies Matarajin with the *kami* of the Shoshinji, now the Usa-no-miya, one of the seven upper shrines of the Hie shrine complex (cited in Nomoto Kakujō, "Genshi kanjō kara kai kanjō e," p. 715). The deity of this shrine was further said to be the *suijaku* of Amida. See also Kageyama Haruki, "Matarajin shinkō to sono ihō."

173. Hazama Jikō, *Chūko Nihon tendai no kenkyū*, pp. 143–45, 152. Kageyama Haruki points out that both ginger and bamboo grass grow in profusion in the area of the Kitadani of the Eastern Pagoda precinct, then a major stronghold of the Danna school. He suggests these plants were at first used simply as offerings but were later incorporated into the symbolism of Danna ritual ("Matarajin shinkō to sono ihō," p. 324).

174. It is not clear when the *kimyōdan kanjō* originated, nor when it was combined with the *genshi kanjō*. Nomoto Kakujō suggests that it must have developed after the beginning of the sixteenth century ("Genshi kanjō kara kai kanjō e," pp. 707–11).

175. *Genshi jū daiji*, cited in Hazama Jikō, *Chūko Nihon Tendai no kenkyū*, p. 146.

176. *Kimyōdan denju no koto*, cited in Hazama Jikō, *Chūko Nihon Tendai no kenkyū*, p. 174.

177. On Amida as the breath of life, see Hazama Jikō, *Chūko Nihon Tendai no kenkyū*, pp. 275–97, and James H. Sanford, "Breath of Life."

178. *Kimyōdan denjū no koto*, cited in Hazama Jikō, *Chūko Nihon Tendai no kenkyū*, p. 146.

179. For Taoist influences on invocations of the seven stars in Buddhist ritual, see Herbert Franke, "The Taoist Elements in the *Great Bear Sūtra (Pei-tou ching)*."

180. Hazama Jikō, *Chūko Nihon Tendai no kenkyū*, pp. 149–50.

181. The tantric elements of the ritual will be discussed in James Sanford's forthcoming study.

182. *Chūko Nihon Tendai no kenkyū,* pp. 176–80.

183. On the origins of *kai kanjō,* see Shikii Shūjō, ed., *Tendai Shinseishū shūgaku hanron,* pp. 188–93; Ishida Mizumaro, *Nihon Bukkyō ni okeru kairitsu no kenkyū,* pp. 479–89, or *Kairitsu no kenkyū,* vol. 2, pp. 406–14; and Ōkubo Ryōjun, "Jūjukai kanjō no kōki." Ishida suggests that *kai kanjō* may have been initiated by Tankū, Ejin's teacher. Ōkubo, however, notes that the *kai kanjō* developed in connection with the *genshi kanjō* and suggests that its origins may not be so simple to identify.

184. *Denshin Kashō den,* p. 6. According to this work (p. 3), Egi performed this *kanjō* for Kōen when the deceased Ejin appeared to him in a dream and reproached him for not having done so sooner.

185. *ZTZ, Enkai* 1, pp. 76–115. Other texts related to *kai kanjō* are included in this volume and in Uesugi Bunshū, *Nihon Tendai shi,* vol. 2, pp. 897–912.

186. For descriptions of contemporary *kai kanjō,* see Shikii Shūjō, "Jūjukai kanjō" and *Kai kanjō no nyūmonteki kenkyū.*

187. See, for example, *Enkai jūroku chō, ZTZ Enkai* 1, p. 79a, and *Tonchō himitsu kōyō,* p. 330a. Both these texts cite *kike* records for their authority, suggesting that the *kaike* appropriated to their transmissions a more general story about Saichō's transmission of the Dharma. The "eight-pronged key" relates these precept texts to another Saichō myth that exists in several variations. Its essential elements are as follows. When ground was being broken for the Shikan-in on Mt. Hiei, an eight-pronged key was unearthed, which Saichō later took with him to China. On Mt. T'ien-t'ai was a sūtra repository that no one had been able to open since Chih-i's time. Saichō was able to unlock it with the key found on Mt. Hiei, which established his identity as Chih-i reborn. See, for example, *Sanmon hiden kenmon* and *Sanmon konryū hiketsu,* cited in Hanano Michiaki, "Nichiren no shōdai shisō to Danna-ryū no kanjō genshi kuden," pp. 124–25, and the *Maka shikan kenmon tenchū* 1c, *DNBZ* 29:119a–b. The story of the eight-pronged key may have been inspired by the somewhat similar legend that Kūkai hurled a vajra into the air from China that was later discovered on Mt. Kōya.

188. *ZTZ, Enkai* 1, pp. 88b–89a.

189. Ibid., p. 90b.

190. Ibid, p. 88b.

191. Ibid., p. 76.

192. Ibid., pp. 103a–105a. The "three kinds of *Lotus Sūtra*" are discussed in chap. 1.

193. See Shikii Shūjō, "Kai kanjō to gasshō."

194. *ZTZ, Enkai* 1, p. 97b.

195. "Jūjukai kanjō," especially p. 306.

196. This ritual is mentioned in the *Keiran shūyō shū, T* 76:503b23. See also Ōkubo Ryōjun, "Wakō dōjin kanjō ni tsuite."

197. See Ōkubo Ryōjun, "'Namu myōhō isshin kanbutsu' ni tsuite" and "Tendai Hokkeshū no dentō," pp. 4–5.

198. See, for example, *Dainijū shichika daiji kuden,* in Uesugi Bunshū, *Nihon Tendai shi,* vol. 2, pp. 820a–21a.

199. Hazama Jikō, *Chūko Nihon Tendai no kenkyū,* pp. 78–80.

200. *TZ* 9:165a–b.

201. It is not clear how Shinga's document was thought to differ from the transfer document that, according to the same text, was given by Jōmyō to Isen for his son Jōhan.

202. Ōkubo Ryōjun, "Edan ryōryū ni kansuru shiron," p. 6.

203. On *jisshi sōzoku*, see Takeshima Hiroshi, "Jiin no shishi sōzoku to kettō sō-zoku"; Hazama Jikō, *Chūsei Nihon Tendai no kenkyū*, pp. 78–83; and Nishiguchi Junko, *Onna no chikara*, pp. 186–201.

204. *Shasekishū, Nihon koten bungaku taikei*, vol. 85, p. 480b. See also Tuji Zenno-suke, *Nihon Bukkyōshi, Chūsei* 1, pp. 392–95, and Ishida Mizumaro, "Nyohan: Sono furerarenai jittai ni tsuite."

205. *Ryō no gige, Kokushi taikei* 24b, p. 99.

206. Nishiguchi Junko, *Onna no chikara*, p. 199.

207. Ibid., pp. 201–209.

208. "Chūsei jisha seiryoku ron," p. 267.

209. *Onna no chikara*, pp. 200–201.

210. *Ushidan sho kikigaki, FSY* 2:155–56. This version of the account follows a claim that Sanmi Ajari Nichijun (1294–1354/1356), a prominent scholar of the early Fuji lineage, had received an oral transmission from Jōmyō.

211. This is a transmission text appended to the *Naishō Buppō kechimyaku tō shiken-mon* held by the Kanazawa Bunko and recently published in Komazawa University's *Bukkyō gakubu kenkyū kiyō* 54 (March 1996). The episode discussed above is on p. 261. See also the discussion by Ōkubo Ryōjun in "Edan ryōryū ni kansuru shiron," pp. 6–9. Ōkubo reads the name of the false successor in this account as Jitsugen, while Takahashi Shūei, who edited the *Isshin sangan kanjin sūken* for publication, reads it as Jisshin. I have seen the original ms. but cannot determine which is correct.

212. Ōkubo Ryōjun, ibid., pp. 7–9. Ōkubō uses these two accounts to argue that, in the time of the events they refer to, the Eshin and Danna schools had not yet as-sumed clear rival identities and that considerable communication and exchange oc-curred among lineages.

213. *DNBZ* 28:1192b.

214. *THR*, p. 184.

215. Hazama Jikō, *Chūko Nihon Tendai no kenkyū*, pp. 74–75.

216. "Endon-bō Songai kishōmon o tatemōsu koto," appended to the *Kawataya bōshō jūkutsū*, transmissions said to have been compiled and conferred upon Songai by his teacher Shinson (*TZ* 9:116b).

217. "Ekō-bō-[ryū] hōmon sōjō keiyaku jōjō," reproduced in Uesugi Bunshū, *Ni-hon Tendaishi*, vol. 2, p. 860.

218. *SSH*, p. 350.

219. "Kanjin honzon shō soejō," *STN* 1:721.

220. *TZ* 9:160b–61a. This statement occurs in the course of explaining a variant of this practice observed in the tradition of the Tendai *dangisho* or seminary at Senba in Musashi Province, in which two persons, rather than one, were permitted to hear the teachings at a time.

221. "Chūsei jiin no kōzō to kokka," pp. 30–31, 37.

222. "Edan ryōryū kengaku (zōden) no yōsō," p. 322.

223. Hazama Jikō, *Chūko Nihon Tendai no kenkyū*, pp. 85–86.

224. *Keiran shūyō shū* 9, *T* 76:540c8–17. There appears to be a transcription error in the text; "to be purchased according to one's ability" *(chikara ni makasete kau nari)* is Hazama's reconstruction (*Chūko Nihon Tendai no kenkyū*, p. 84).

225. *STN* 1:850. This work does not survive in Nichiren's holograph, and several scholars have deemed it a forgery. However, based on the existence of an early (1325) transcription by Nisshin (1271–1334), third abbot of the Minobu lineage, as well as

on content shared with another, authenticated work of Nichiren, Asai Endō maintains that it should be regarded as genuine (*NSIJ*, p. 1181a; *NJ*, p. 419b). Take Kakuchō, on the other hand, suggests that it is Nisshin's work ("Eizan, Mii to Nichiren monka to no kōryū," p. 418). See also chap. 7, n. 39.

226. Ogami Kanchū, "Kantō ni okeru chūko Tendai" (1), pp. 1–2.

227. *Shūyō byakkō, TZ,* 18:28a. This text, dated 1321, records the teachings of Echin (1281–1356), mentioned earlier in connection with the *kaike.* The event in question is represented as having occurred during the time of Yōben, a disciple of Chōgō (1049–1133), founder of the Ekō-bō line of the Danna school.

228. There are divergent accounts of Shinson's biography. He may have been from the Kantō region originally and established the Kawataya *dangisho* after a period of study on Mt. Hiei. See Takahashi Ken'yū, "Tendai gakusō Shinson ni tsuite."

229. *Eshin-ryū kyōjū sōjō shishō,* reproduced in Uesugi Bunshū, *Nihon Tendai shi,* vol. 2, p. 813.

230. Ibid., p. 814. This description calls to mind those parties of the court where recently promoted officials were compelled to drink as much sake as possible (Ivan Morris, *The World of the Shining Prince,* p. 161). Asai Yōrin's reading of this passage, that monastic standards on Mt. Hiei had degenerated to a point where transmission was actually made dependent on such things as the ability to drink quantities of sake, seems overly literal (*Nichiren Shōnin kyōgaku no kenkyū,* p. 82, n. 6).

231. *Nijō shō kenmon* 1, *TZ* 9:160a–b. There are variant accounts of these events. See, for example, *Eshin-ryū kyōjū sōjō shishō,* included in Uesugi Bunshū, *Nihon Tendaishi,* vol. 2, pp. 814, 815. On Songai, see also *Honchō kōsōden* 16 (*DNBZ* 102:248a–249a); *Nihon daishi sentoku myōshōki* (*DNBZ* 111:278–79); Shima Chiryō (a.k.a. "Enrei Gakunin"), "Endon Hōin Songai" (which draws on documents from the Minobu Bunko); and *BD* 4, pp. 3165–66.

232. Cited in Shima Chiryō, "Endon Hōin Songai" (1), p. 56.

233. *Senji shō, STN* 2:1046.

234. See Hazama Jikō, *Chūko Nihon Tendai no kenkyū,* pp. 91–94, and Ōgami Kanchū, "Kantō chiiki ni denpan shita Danna-ryū no keitō."

235. Hazama Jikō, *Chūko Nihon Tendai no kenkyū,* p. 92. The *Azuma kagami* reference is at *Kokushi taikei* 32:677.

236. *Azuma kagami, Kokushi taikei* 33:58–59. See also Ogami Kanchū, "Kantō ni okeru chūko Tendai" (1), pp. 2–3.

237. Ogami Kanchū, "Kantō ni okeru chūko Tendai" (1), pp. 3–4.

238. The foundational scholarship on Kantō Tendai *dangisho* has been done by Ogami Kanchū, who laboriously pieced together a picture of these institutions by studying and collating the information contained in the colophons of writings in archival collections, chiefly debate texts, that were produced and copied at these centers. See, for example, his "Chūko Tendai ni okeru dangisho," "Shinano no Tendaishū dangisho," "Dangisho to Tendai kyōgaku no ryūden," "Kantō no Tendai dangisho," "Kashiwabara dangisho no hatten," and others. Also useful is Murata Eiden, "Kantō no Tendai dangisho."

239. Ogami Kanchū, "Kantō no Tendaishū dangisho" (2), p. 10.

240. There were, however, some Taimitsu temples in the Kantō. See Ogami Kanchū, "Dangisho to Tendai kyōgaku no ryūden," p. 18.

241. Ogami Kanchū, "Chūko Tendai ni okeru dangisho," p. 257.

242. Ibid., p. 258.

243. *Jikidan* form the subject of a recent study by Hirota Tetsumichi, *Chūsei Hokekyō chūshakusho no kenkyū.*

244. There is evidence of some sort of early head-temple/branch-temple arrangements between the Butsuji-in (by then called the Chū-in) and other Kantō Tendai temples by the year 1571. The Butsuji-in may have gained this degree of influence by virtue of having been able to establish ties with the *monzeki* cloister Shōren-in on Mt. Hiei. See Udaka Ryōtetsu, "Chūsei no Kawagoe Senba dangisho ni tsuite," pp. 66–67.

245. Ogami Kanchō, "Shinano no Tendaishū dangisho," p. 614; "Dangisho to Tendai kyōgaku no ryūden," p. 24.

246. Ogami Kanchū, "Dangisho to Tendai kyōgaku no ryūden," p. 19.

247. Ogami Kanchū, "Kantō no Tendaishū dangisho" (1), p. 3.

248. This point has been raised by Brian Ruppert in "Buddha Relics and Power in Early Medieval Japan," p. 307, n. 5.

Chapter Four: Hermeneutics, Doctrine, and "Mind-Contemplation"

1. "Buddhism in the Kamakura Period," p. 572.

2. *Nihon Jōdokyō seiritsu shi no kenkyū,* pp. 184–85.

3. See, for example, Shimaji Daitō, *Tendai kyōgaku shi,* p. 470; Asai Yōrin, *Nichiren Shōnin kyōgaku no kenkyū,* p. 221; Uesugi Bunshū, *Nihon Tendai shi,* vol. 1, p. 597; and Inoue Mitsusada, *Nihon Jōdokyō seiritsu shi no kenkyū,* p. 290.

4. *THR,* p. 70. The same text also mentions a transmission Saichō received on the first day of the third month, Chen-yüan 24 (p. 42).

5. *THR,* p. 191.

6. Some examples are discussed in Takahashi Ken'yū, "Nichiren Shōnin to *Shuzenji-ketsu.*" See pp. 82–90.

7. See, for example, Hazama Jikō, *Chūko Nihon Tendai no kenkyū,* p. 41.

8. Ōtani Daigaku library, cited in Nakanishi Zuikō, "Kuden hōmon keisei ki no kōsatsu," p. 73.

9. Eizan library, Shinnyo archive, cited in ibid., p. 74.

10. "Nichiren no shōdai shisō to Danna-ryū no kanjō genshi kuden," p. 133.

11. Paul Williams, *Mahāyāna Buddhism,* p. 30.

12. See Groner, "The Significance of Ryōgen's Revival," pp. 155–56.

13. On the work of these three scholars, see Hazama Jikō, *Chūko Nihon Tendai no kenkyū,* pp. 26–33. Hazama characterizes their mode scholarship as displaying *kyōsō-shugi,* or an emphasis on textual fidelity, in contrast to the more personal, subjective *kanjin-shugi* interpretive mode of the *kuden*—a distinction that has been widely cited.

14. "A Medieval Japanese Reading of the *Mo-ho chih-kuan,*" p. 56.

15. Winston Davis, *Dōjō,* p. 95.

16. *T* 9:465c29.

17. *Hsüan-i* 2a, *T* 33:696a14–17. This passage is translated in Swanson, *Foundations of T'ien-t'ai Philosophy,* p. 197. Chih-i discusses the three dharmas of sentient beings, the Buddha, and the mind in detail in the section of this text interpreting the character "dharma" (*fa, hō*) of the *Lotus Sūtra*'s title (pp. 693a4–696b8; Swanson, pp. 177–99). See also *Chih-kuan* 1b, where Chih-i uses the inseparability of the three dharmas as a basis on which to assert that the Buddha-Dharma is fully contained within one's own mind (*T* 46:9a5–10; Donner and Stevenson, *The Great Calming and Contemplation,* p. 195).

18. The "four teachings of conversion" *(hua-fa ssu-chiao, kehō no shikyō)* represents one aspect of Chih-i's doctrinal classification of the Buddhist teachings. See chap. 1, n. 47.

19. The "four modes of interpretation" are enumerated at *Wen-chü* 1a, *T* 34:2a22–b10, and employed throughout the text. See also Sekiguchi Shindai, *Tendai shikan no kenkyū,* pp. 39–41.

20. *Wen-chü* 1a, *T* 34:4a28–b1.

21. *Wen-chü* 1a, *T* 34:4c3–5.

22. *Wen-chü* 8b, *T* 34:113c14–15 and 114b3–4. This mode of interpretation, in which the sūtra text is understood as expressive of meditative discernment, is also called *t'o-shih kuan (takuji-kan),* the contemplation of particulars, in which concrete phenomena are seen as embodiments of truth. This is one of three contemplations mentioned in Chan-jan's *Chih-kuan yi-li,* the other two being *yüeh fa-hsiang kuan (yaku hossō-kan)* or *fu-fa kuan (fuhō-kan),* contemplation according with doctrine, in which doctrines are internalized as the objects of meditation; and *ts'ung-hsing kuan (jugyō-kan),* or formal meditative practice (*T* 46:458a10–16). Later T'ien-t'ai scholarship identifies these three respectively with the *Wen-chü, Hsüan-i,* and *Chih-kuan.* See Andō Toshio, *Tendai gaku,* p. 32; Sekiguchi Shindai, *Shikan no kenkyū,* p. 231; and Ōkubo Ryōjun, "Kanjin ni tsuite," pp. 10–12.

23. For this reason, I have used such expressions as "*kanjin*-style interpretation" or "*kanjin* mode of interpretation" to translate *kanjin-shugi,* reserving "*kanjin* interpretations" *(kanjin-shaku)* specifically for the readings given in Chih-i's *Wen-chü.*

24. "A Medieval Japanese Reading of the *Mo-ho chih-kuan,*" pp. 58–62.

25. It is reproduced in *THR,* pp. 411–13.

26. Groner, "A Medieval Japanese Reading of the *Mo-ho chih-kuan,*" pp. 62–64.

27. "Busshō," *Shōbō genzō, DZZ* 1:14. See also the discussion in Hee-Jin Kim, *Dōgen Kigen,* pp. 160–67. Dōgen's alteration of passages from sūtras and other continental sources to accord with his own views of time, practice, and Buddha nature is discussed in Kagamishima Genryū, *Dōgen Zenji no in'yō kyōten-goroku no kenkyū,* pp. 63–83.

28. *Kyōgyōshinshō, SCZ,* p. 115; Alfred Bloom, *Shinran's Gospel of Pure Grace,* pp. 48–49.

29. *Jinden ainō shō* 16, which relates another clever repunctuation attributed to Chūzan at the time of the Ōwa debate, is often cited in error as the source of this tradition. It actually appears in *Hokekyō jikidan shō* 3b (vol. 1, p. 510). Both were compiled several centuries after the debate and do not represent firsthand accounts.

30. Such a transmission is referred to, for example, in the *Sōmoku jōbutsu kuketsu,* attributed to Nichiren (*STN* 1:533). See also *Jinden ainō shō* 16, *DNBZ* 150:399a.

31. *Mongu ryaku taikō shikenmon* 5, *DNBZ* 18:159b.

32. See Yoshino Hiroko, *Kamigami no tanjō,* p. 273, for a chart of the major associations of fives, and also Joseph Needham, *Science and Civilisation in China,* vol. 2, pp. 261–65.

33. *The Medieval Vision,* pp. 218, 219.

34. *Theories of Macrocosms and Microcosms,* p. 134.

35. *The Order of Things,* p. 17. The relevance of Foucault's discussion of the premodern European episteme to that of medieval Japan has been proposed by Allan G. Grapard, "The Textualized Mountain—Enmountained Text," pp. 182–84, and

by George Tanabe, *Myōe the Dreamkeeper,* p. 139. For further analysis of the Japanese esoteric Buddhist episteme, see Fabio Rambelli, "True Words, Silence, and the Adamantine Dance."

36. The equation of Amida with the threefold truth recurs in Tendai literature of the Heian and medieval periods, for example, in the *Kanjin ryaku yōshū* attributed to Genshin (*DNBZ* 31:157a) or the *Sandai shōsho shichimen kuketsu* attributed to Saichō (*DDZ* 5:151). See also Sueki Fumihiko, "Amida santai-setsu o megutte."

37. "Linguistic Cubism," p. 226.

38. *Mongu ryaku taikō shikenmon* 1, *DNBZ* 18:26a.

39. By Kawai Tadaakira, "Hongaku gainen no koperunikusu-teki tenkai."

40. Mt. Gṛdhrakūṭa means "vulture peak." However, the Chinese Ling-chiu-shan (Jpn. Ryōjusen) admits of being read either as "sacred vulture peak" or "sacred eagle peak." The Japanese *washi no yama,* found in classical *waka* poetry, also clearly means "eagle peak" and suggests that the image of the sacred mountain had been reconceptualized in this more poetic fashion. Translators of the *Lotus Sūtra* from Chinese into English such as Leon Hurvitz and Burton Watson have used "eagle" rather than "vulture," and I have followed suit in this study. However, for some passages, such as the one that follows, "Vulture Peak" is clearly more appropriate.

41. *Mongu ryaku taikō shikenmon* 1, *DNBZ* 18:26b–27a.

42. Buddhaghosa includes, among forty subjects of meditation, the "ten impurities," all involving contemplation of the decomposition of corpses (*Visuddhi-magga,* chap. 3).

43. "Virtual enlightenment" and "wondrous enlightenment" are, respectively, the penultimate and final stages in a traditional fifty-two-stage T'ien-t'ai *mārga* scheme. To move from virtual enlightenment to wondrous enlightenment thus denotes the completion of the path according to the linear model of acquired enlightenment. "Identity in principle," mentioned subsequently, the first of the six stages of identity, denotes the potential for Buddhahood inherent in deluded beings prior to practice (see chap. 1, n. 131). Here, "moving from virtual enlightenment to identity in principle" indicates a return to original enlightenment.

44. This may also refer to offerings of tea, often made in a Buddhist context. See "Chatō: le thé et l'eau chaude," *Hōbōgirin,* vol. 3, pp. 281–283. I am indebted to James Benn for the reference.

45. The section of this passage detailing the second reason is translated in chap. 1, p. 42 [n. 162].

46. *Mongu ryaku taikō shikenmon* 6, *DNBZ* 18:189a–190a.

47. Sueki Fumihiko, in examining medieval debate literature, finds that while "there are a number of [examination] topics shared with the orally transmitted doctrines," generally speaking, "the discussion in debate literature rarely exhibits extreme *hongaku* thought to the extent of the orally transmitted doctrines. Perhaps this is a distinction between debate, which was conducted publicly, and oral transmissions" ("Chūsei Tendai to hongaku shisō," p. 325). Similarly, Kuroda Toshio, in his study of the chroniclers *(kike),* found that they produced two kinds of documents, one that he characterizes as symbolic, secret, and mandalic, and the other, as historical and discursive ("Historical Consciousness and *Hon-jaku* philosophy," pp. 153–54).

48. *Hsüan-i* 2a, *T* 33:697b11–21; translated in Swanson, *Foundations of T'ien-t'ai Philosophy,* pp. 205–206. The four category names also correspond to the "four modes of interpretation," discussed above, that occurs at *Wen-chü* 1a, *T* 34:2a22–b10.

49. Tamura Yoshirō places the compilation of both texts between 1250 and 1300, slightly after Jōmyō's time (*Kamakura shin Bukkyō shisō no kenkyū,* p. 428). On differences of opinion concerning the dating of the *Kankō ruijū* and Jōmyō's possible authorship, see chap. 3, n. 25. Jōmyō is often referred to in these texts by the name "Awataguchi," the area of the capital where he maintained his residence. See also Tamura's "Tendai hongaku shisō ni okeru shō no mondai," pp. 185–87.

50. *DNBZ* 16:9a.

51. I have drawn here on Shimaji Daitō, *Nihon Bukkyō kyōgaku shi,* pp. 486–503.

52. See chap. 1, n. 48.

53. The "perfect" or "round teaching" *(engyō)* is one of the "four teachings of conversion" *(kehō no shikyō)* in Chih-i's comparative classification of teachings (see chap. 1, n. 47).

54. Both the concept and term, *chōhachi* (Ch. *ch'ao-pa*), appear to have originated with Chan-jan (see *Shih-ch'ien* 2 and 5, *T* 33:825c20–21 and 962c25, and *Chi* 1b, *T* 34:159c12–16). On *chōhachi* thought and its influence on medieval Japanese Buddhism, see Hazama Jikō, *Nihon Tendai to Kamakura Bukkyō,* pp. 193–219, and Tamura Yoshirō, *Kamakura shin Bukkyō shisō no kenkyū,* pp. 129–39.

55. *Chu Wei-mo-ch'i ching* 1, *T* 38:327a–b. The two terms were also applied to the *Lotus Sūtra* by two others of Kumārajīva's disciples, Seng-jui and Hui-kuan, although not in the same way that Chih-i did. See Take Kakuchō, "Tendai Daishi Chigi no honjaku ron," pp. 138–39, and *BD* 5:4691c–4692a.

56. *Hsüan-i* 7a, *T* 33:764b18–765a11. See also Take Kakuchō, "Tendai Daishi Chigi no honjaku ron."

57. On the history of *honmon* thought, see Asai Endō, *Jōko Nihon Tendai honmon shisōshi.*

58. Traditionally, it was believed that the only the Eshin school asserted the superiority of *honmon* over *shakumon,* and that the Danna school acknowledged them to represent a single principle. Shimaji Daitō appears to have accepted this view (*Nihon Bukkyō kyōgakushi,* pp. 481–82). However, Hazama Jikō suggests that this distinction between the position of the two schools derives chiefly from Eshin texts, which make this assertion to stress the uniqueness of their own position, and that Danna transmissions also uphold the superiority of *honmon*. In addition, considerable variation exists from one text to another in how far the trace/origin distinction is developed (*Chūko Nihon Tendai no kenkyū,* pp. 197–99).

59. See Shimaji Daitō, *Nihon Bukkyō kyōgakushi,* pp. 497–500, and *Tendai kyōgaku shi,* pp. 460–622; Hazama Jikō, *Chūko Nihon Tendai no kenkyū,* pp. 199–201.

60. Chih-i distinguishes the trace and origin teachings in terms of *li* and *shih* at *Hsüan-i* 7a, *T* 33:764b19–24. Chan-jan also states, "The revelation of the Buddha's original attainment [in the origin teaching] is the perfect teaching in actuality *(shih-yüan, jien);* the opening of the [three] provisional [vehicles to reveal the one vehicle as taught in the trace teaching] is the perfect teaching in principle *(li-yüan, rien)*" (*Shih-ch'ien* 1, *T* 33:817b29–c1). The application of the *li/shih* distinction to the perfect teaching is further developed by Chih-li (Shimaji Daitō, *Tendai kyōgaku shi,* p. 457).

61. *T* 46:1a12. See also Chan-jan's commentary (*Hung-chüeh* 1a, *T* 46:143c26–28) and the supplementary note for *"Tenjin dokurō no shikan," THR,* pp. 445b–446a.

62. Chih-i gave as his textual ground for both concepts the passage: "Only a Buddha and a Buddha together can fathom the true aspect of the dharmas, that is to say, the suchness of their characteristics, the suchness of their nature, the suchness

of their essence, the suchness of their power, the suchness of their activity, the suchness of their causes, the suchness of their conditions, the suchness of their effects,
the suchness of their recompenses and the suchness of their ultimate equality from
beginning to end" (*MFLHC, p'in* 2, *T* 9:5c11–13). Chih-i read this passage as expressing the three truths (*Hsüan-i* 2a, *T* 33:693b13–25. See also the translation of this section of the *Hsüan-i* in de Bary et al., eds., *Sources of Chinese Tradition,* vol. 1, pp. 319–20,
as well as the explanation of the three ways of reading the sūtra text in Leon Hurvitz,
Chih-i, pp. 290–92). Briefly, in the Chinese text of the sūtra, each of the ten suchnesses is expressed in three characters. The word "suchness" is *nyoze,* meaning literally "like this" or "like such." Thus, if one punctuates the text to read, "These their
characteristics are such" (*ze sō nyo*), that indicates the truth of emptiness (or suchness). If one reads it as "their such-like characteristics" (*nyo ze sō*), that emphasizes
the truth of conventional existence. And if one reads it as "their characteristics are
like this" (*sō nyo ze*), that emphasizes the truth of the middle. Thus this passage can
be made to yield the meaning of the threefold truth and the threefold contemplation. The "three thousand realms in a single thought-moment" represents Chih-i's
attempt to clarify the content of the "true aspect of the dharmas" (*shohō jissō*) in the
same passage.

63. These terms present particular translation problems in the medieval Tendai
context. As Neal Donner and Daniel B. Stevenson have noted, Chih-i's term *chih-
kuan* (*shikan*) can be glossed in three ways. From the causal standpoint, as practice,
it can be understood as "calming and contemplation"; in terms of the effect of practice, as "tranquility and insight" or "stillness and clarity"; and, as a description of
the nature of ultimate reality, as "quiescence and illumination" (Donner and
Stevenson, *The Great Calming and Contemplation,* p. 8). The term *kanjin,* too, can be
understood from these three standpoints. In the *kuden* literature, it is not always
clear which perspective is intended; sometimes all three are invoked simultaneously.
Therefore, rather than make a choice in each case, I have translated *shikan* throughout as "calming and contemplation," and *kanjin,* as "the contemplation of the mind."
However, it should be borne in mind that these terms are often referring to original enlightenment as a priori ground, rather than to contemplative practice or its
effects.

64. Take Kakuchō notes evidence of the linking of the origin teaching with *kanjin* in the *Jigyō nenbutsu mondō, Makura sōshi (Sanjū shika no kotogaki),* and *Entaragishū.*
See his "Eizan, Mii to Nichiren monka to no kōryū," p. 409.

65. A "single moment's faith and understanding" (*ichinen shinge*) is the first of four
stages of faith set forth in *Wen-chü* 10a on the basis of the "Discrimination of Merits" chapter of the *Lotus Sūtra* (*T* 34:137b17ff). On the "contemplation of actuality,"
see Shimaji Daitō, *Nihon Bukkyō kyōgakushi,* pp. 502–503, and Hazama Jikō, *Chūko Nihon Tendai no kenkyū,* pp. 203–204.

66. *Chūko Nihon Tendai no kenkyū,* pp. 203, 204.

67. See, for example, *Ichijō shō, TZ* 9:40b.

68. Tamura Yoshirō, "Nihon Tendai hongaku shisō no keisei katei," pp. 347–51.
The possibility of Zen influence on medieval Tendai concepts of *kanjin* and *shikan*
had been suggested earlier by Shimaji Daitō (*Nihon Bukkyō kyōgakushi,* pp. 500–501),
and by Yamakawa Chiō, who noted the connection between Enni and Jōmyō ("*Risshōkan jō* ni taisuru gigi ni tsuite," pp. 39–40).

69. *Genkō shakusho* 7, *DNBZ* 101:218b–19a. The relevant passage is translated in
Groner, "A Medieval Japanese Reading of the *Mo-ho chih-kuan,*" p. 54.

70. *Dainichikyō kenmon* 1, *Nihon Daizōkyō* 14:69a.
71. See, for example, Sonshun's *Maka shikan kenmon tenchū* 1, *DNBZ* 29:122b.
72. *STN* 1:849. For references to arguments for and against Nichiren's authorship, see chap. 7, n. 39.
73. *THR,* pp. 207–208.
74. *TZ* 9:75b.
75. *DNBZ* 31:201a. The "first kind of Amida" here follows the account given in the *Pei-hua ching,* according to which King Lacking Contentious Thoughts (Musōnen, Aranemin) encountered the Buddha Jewel Store, renounced the world, took bodhisattva vows, and received a prediction that he would become the Buddha Immeasurable Life, presiding over the western pure land of Peace and Bliss. This differs from the better-known account of Amida Buddha's prior bodhisattva practice as the monk Dharmakāra (Hōzō) under the Buddha Lokeśvarāja (Sejizaiō), given in the *Wu-liang-shou ching.*
76. The possibility of such a connection was first pointed out by Ishida Mizumaro. Ishida argues that the "four kinds of Amida" discussed in the *Jigyō nenbutsu mondō* influenced Hōnen's disciple Kōsai (1163–1247), famous for his advocacy of the *ichinen gi* or "single calling" doctrine, in establishing his schema of the "four stages of rejecting and practicing" *(shijū shagyō):* (1) rejecting contemplative good disciplines and practicing noncontemplative good disciplines; (2) rejecting manifold disciplines and practicing the calling on the Buddha's name; (3) rejecting many callings and practicing one calling; (3) and rejecting the many Buddhas and practicing with respect to Amida alone *(Gengibun shō).* Ishida finds the logical structure of Kōsai's four stages to be similar to that of the "fourfold rise and fall" and suggests that the compilation of the *Jigyō nenbutsu mondō* and the formation of the *shijū kōhai* both precede Kōsai's text ("Kuden hōmon ni okeru shijū kōhai no seiritsu," pp. 774–75, and *Jōdokyō no tenkai,* pp. 245–47). Ishida's argument is upheld by Hanano Michiaki, who also dates the formation of the fourfold rise and fall from the Insei period ("Shijū kōhai no seiritsujiki ni kansuru ichi kōsatsu," pp. 44–45). However, Sueki Fumihiko counters that the structure of Kōsai's "four stages of rejecting and practicing" much more closely resembles that of Hōnen's *Senchaku hongan nenbutsu shū* than it does the *shijū kōhai,* and cannot be used to help date either the *Jigyō nenbutsu mondō* or the formation of the fourfold rise and fall ("Tendai hongaku shisō kenkyū no shomondai," pp. 295–96). As Tamura Yoshirō asserts, the fourfold rise and fall, as a comparative classification of teachings, would seem to date from around the time of Jōmyō or slightly later (*Kamakura shin Bukkyō shisō no kenkyū,* pp. 422–28), though the category names clearly existed much earlier.

For further discussion of the dating of the *Jigyō nenbutsu mondō,* see Satō Tetsue, who attributes it to, or places it around the time of, Shingen (1064–1136) (*Eizan Jōdokyō no kenkyū,* pp. 282–84, 337). Satō argues against Tamura Yoshirō, who alone dates it later than the Insei period, placing it between 1250 and 1300. Tamura sees the "four kinds of Amida" as representing the influence of, rather than a precursor to, the classification of the fourfold rise and fall seen in medieval Tendai *kuden* texts (*Kamakura shin Bukkyō shisō no kenkyū,* pp. 488–90).
77. *Nihon Tendai rongishi no kenkyū,* pp. 187–89.
78. "Chūko Tendai to Hokke shisō no kanren," pp. 606–607.
79. "Chūsei Tendai to hongaku shisō," p. 342.
80. Shimaji Daitō, *Nihon Bukkyō kyōgaku shi,* pp. 467–78; Hazama Jikō, *Chūko Nihon Tendai no kenkyū,* pp. 132–34.

81. On the formation of the threefold seven great matters, see Hazama Jikō, *Chūko Nihon Tendai no kenkyū*, pp. 115–19, and Tamura Kansei, "Eshin-ryū sanjū shichika kuden hōmon no keisei ni kansuru shiron." Also useful in the study of this doctrinal system is Uesugi Bunshu, *Nihon Tendai shi*, vol. 1, pp. 599–712, which collates interpretations from a number of Eshin texts in explaining the individual categories.

82. Ōkubo Ryōjun, "*Tendai Hokkeshū denbōge* ni tsuite," p. 128. The relevant passage in the *Tendai Hokkeshū denbōge* is at *DDZ* 5:28.

83. *TZ* 9:47a. A series of colophons is at pains to invest this text with the imperial aura. Shinsō's colophon says that he, like Shunpan, presented the *Ichijō shō* to the throne in response to a subsequent imperial command. His colophon is followed by the text of an edict dated Karyaku 4 (1329), purportedly from the retired emperor Hagiwara (Hanazono), acknowledging that the text had been submitted to him by Shinsō and identifying it as "the most profound and secret transmission of the unique lineage of Eshin." Another colophon, by Shinsō's disciple Shin'ei, reports that the document was returned to the lineage following Hagiwara's death (47b). The theme is continued in later *kuden hōmon* texts: Sonshun's *Nijō shō kenmon* says that when Shunpan submitted the "seven great matters" to Gosaga, they were found to accord exactly with "seven great matters" submitted some generations earlier by Tōyō-bō Chūjin to the retired emperor Shirakawa, thus establishing that the "unique lineage" of the Sugiu line of the Eshin school represented the legitimate stream of Tendai (*TZ* 9:164b–165a).

84. On Gosaga's interactions with Tendai monks, see Shibuya Ryōtai, "Gosaga Jōkō to chūko Tendai no bokkō," and Adolphson, "Monks, Courtiers and Warriors in Premodern Japan," pp. 161–97 *passim*.

85. In addition to the above-mentioned *Ichijō shō* of Shinsō, these commentaries, together with their traditional attributions, are as follows: the *Zōda shō* compiled by Songai (1253–1332)'s disciple Gōkai, said to record transmissions he had received verbally from Shinsō in 1347, elaborating on those in the *Ichijō shō*; the *Ichiryū sōden hōmon kenmon*, better known as the *Nijō shō*, a collection of transmissions said to have been conferred verbally by Shinga to Songai and to have been transcribed by Shinga's disciple Ikkai; the *Nijō shō kenmon*, also formally titled *Ichiryū sōden hōmon kenmon*, a collection of transmissions elaborating on the *Nijō shō* compiled in 1501 by Sonshun (1451–1514) of Hitachi in Songai's line; the *Hachijō sho*, said to be Ikkai's record of transmissions received verbally from his teacher Shinga, supplementing the *Nijō shō*; the *Hachijō shō kenmon*, compiled in 1367 by Jikkai, a disciple of Ikkai's disciple Jikken; and the *Tōkai kuden shō*, the largest of these *kuden hōmon* collections, compiled by Tōkai, a disciple of Ikkai's disciple Shōkai, between 1343 and 1349. All these commentaries are included in *TZ* 9, and their attribution to specific compilers or transcribers on the whole is probably reliable (Tamura Yoshirō, "Tendai hongaku shisō gaisetsu," p. 539). See also Iwata Kyōen, "Eshin-ryū shichika kuden hōmon ni tsuite."

86. *Chūko Nihon Tendai no kenkyū*, p. 119. Hazama's argument is questioned by Hanano Michiaki, who is inclined to uphold Shunpan's authorship of the *Ichijō shō* ("Nichiren Shōnin kyōgaku no shisōshiteki kenkyū joron," pp. 117–20).

87. On the significance of the three truths in Chih-i's thought, see Swanson, *Foundations of T'ien-t'ai Philosophy*.

88. *T* 46:24a–25c. See also Swanson, *Foundations of T'ien-t'ai Philosophy*, pp. 116–23, and Donner and Stevenson, *The Great Calming and Contemplation*, pp. 9–13.

89. These are the first two of the "four teachings of conversion" *(kehō no shikyō)*,

into which T'ien-t'ai doctrine divides the Buddha's teachings. The separate and perfect teachings, mentioned subsequently, are the other two. See chap. 1, n. 47.

90. *TZ* 9:32a.

91. Although the concept is set forth in the *Chih-kuan,* the precise expression *i-nien san-ch'ien* or *ichinen sanzen* was evidently first used by Chan-jan in his commentary (*Hung-chüeh* 5–3, *T* 46:296a5–6). Satō Tetsue has suggested that the concept itself may in fact represent Kuan-ting's interpolation into the *Chih-kuan* (*Tendai Daishi no kenkyū,* p. 674, and *"Maka shikan* no ichinen sanzen-setsu ni taisuru gigi").

92. See Donner and Stevenson, *The Great Calming and Contemplation,* pp. 20–21.

93. The most detailed explanation in English to date is Hurvitz, "Chih-i," pp. 271–318. See also Swanson, *Foundations of T'ien-t'ai Philosophy,* pp. 11–13. In Japanese, Kanno Hiroshi's *Ichinen sanzen to wa nani ka* is particularly accessible.

94. *Chih-kuan* 5a, *T* 46:54a5–9; English translation quoted from de Bary et. al., eds., *Sources of Chinese Tradition,* vol. 1, p. 328, slightly modified.

95. *T* 46:54a9–10, a13–18; de Bary et. al., eds., *Sources of Chinese Tradition,* vol. 1, p. 328, slightly modified.

96. Chih-i's scriptural source(s) for the ten dharma realms is not entirely certain. Kanno Hiroshi (*Ichinen sanzen to wa nani ka,* pp. 40–41, n. 1) suggests these possibilities: *Hua-yen ching* 27, *T* 9:572a2–8; *Ta-chi tu lun* 27, *T* 25:257c27–258b6; and *MFLHC, p'in* 19, *T* 9:47c25–48a4.

97. See chap. 1, n. 22.

98. *MFLHC p'in* 2, *T* 9:5c11–13.

99. *Hsüan-i* 2a, *T* 33:694a11–15; English translation from Swanson, *Foundations of T'ien-t'ai Philosophy,* p. 184, slightly modified.

100. Chih-i discusses in detail how the ten suchnesses are manifested in each of the ten dharma realms in the *Hsüan-i* 2a, *T* 33:694a19–696a4; translated in Swanson, *Foundations of T'ien-t'ai Philosophy,* pp. 184–96.

101. The three realms are enumerated in the *Ta-chi-tu lun, T* 25:402a 22–24, 546b29–c2.

102. *Foundations of T'ien-t'ai Philosophy,* p. 12.

103. *Ichinen sanzen to wa nani ka,* pp. 44–45.

104. *TZ* 9:35a.

105. As discussed above, this claim for a direct, nonverbal transmission may reflect Zen influence. The *Ichijō shō* reads: "The inner enlightenment of the Buddhas is a secret matter and is referred to as *shikan.* Throughout his life the Lord Śākyamuni did not expound it. But when his preaching was done, he extended his feet from within his golden coffin. This is called *shikan,* and Kāśyapa understood it" (*TZ* 9:40b). This appears to represent a conflation of the tradition that Kāśyapa (Pāli Kassapa) reverenced the Buddha's feet on the funeral pyre (*Dīgha-nikāya,* no. 16, *Mahā-parinibbāna-sutta,* 6.22) with Ch'an/Zen claims for the origin of the mind-to-mind transmission in a nonverbal insight conveyed from the Buddha to Kāśyapa.

106. The English versions of these chapter titles are taken from Donner and Stevenson, *The Great Calming and Contemplation,* p. 18.

107. *TZ* 9:36a.

108. *TZ* 9:39b.

109. These English names for the five principles follow Swanson, *Foundations of T'ien-t'ai Philosophy,* p. 159.

110. Use of the name of the *Lotus Sūtra* to indicate the Dharma, or ultimate truth,

predates the medieval Tendai tradition. Beginning as early as the ninth century, invocations to the three treasures of the Buddha, Dharma, and Sangha include, among invocations to the Dharma, such phrases as "Namu-myōhō-renge-kyō" (*Namu* to the Sūtra of the Lotus Blossom of the Wonderful Dharma), "Namu-ichijō-myōhō-renge-kyō" (*Namu* to the one vehicle, the Sūtra of the Lotus Blossom of the Wonderful Dharma), etc. Among invocations of the three treasures to be uttered on one's deathbed, Genshin gives "Namu-byōdō-daie-myōhō-renge-kyō" (*Namu* to the Great Impartial Wisdom, the Sūtra of the Lotus Blossom of the Wonderful Dharma) as one of several invocations of the Dharma (*Ōjō yōshū, Genshin*, p. 210). For further examples, see Takaki Yutaka, *Heian jidai Hokke Bukkyō shisō no kenkyū*, pp. 430–47, and my "Chanting the August Title of the *Lotus*"). Such uses of the title of the *Lotus Sūtra* represent important antecedents to Nichiren's *daimoku* practice but can also be found in traditions not based specifically on the *Lotus*. For example, the *Eihei shingi*, a Sōtō Zen text on monastic observances, gives the title of the *Lotus Sūtra* as one of a list of names of Buddhas and bodhisattvas to be recited at meals (*T* 82:327a29). I am indebted to William Bodiford for this reference.

111. *TZ* 9:42b.

112. Uesugi Bunshū, *Nihon Tendai shi*, vol. 1, p. 674.

113. *Chūko Nihon Tendai no kenkyū*, p. 128.

114. *Eshin-ryū kyōjū sōjō shishō*, reproduced in Uesugi Bunshū, *Nihon Tendai shi*, vol. 2, p. 815b.

115. For a general introduction to this subject, see Nagao Gadjin, "On the Theory of the Buddha-body *(Buddha-kāya)*," and Paul Williams, *Mahāyāna Buddhism*, pp. 167–84.

116. See chap. 1, n. 102.

117. Swanson, *Foundations of T'ien-t'ai Philosophy*, p. 10. The term *musa* (Ch. *wu-tso*) is taken from the fourth of four ways of interpreting the four noble truths: as arising and perishing, as neither arising nor perishing, as immeasurable, and as unproduced. *Chih-kuan* 1a correlates these four, respectively, with the realm of change, emptiness, conventional existence, and the middle (*T* 46:5b13–6a7, translated in Donner and Stevenson, *The Great Calming and Contemplation*, pp. 157–63); while *Hsüan-i* 2b correlates them with Chih-i's classication of the four teachings: Tripiṭaka, shared, separate, and perfect (*T* 33:700c15–702a12, translated in Swanson, pp. 226–34). See also Swanson's discussion, pp. 8–10.

118. Shimaji Daitō, *Nihon Bukkyō kyōgakushi*, p. 471.

119. In response to the Hossō monk Tokuitsu, who maintained that the recompense body, being produced through practice, is not eternal by nature, Saichō upheld the T'ien-t'ai position that the recompense body, like the manifested body, is inseparably related to the Dharma body as function and essence, respectively. Being one with the Dharma body, as potential, it constantly abides. In this context, he wrote, "The conditioned recompense body is a provisional result [achieved] in a dream; the unproduced triple body is the real Buddha [appearing] before [one who has] awakened" *(musa sanjin kakuzen jitsubutsu)* (*Shugo kokkai shō* 3b, *DDZ* 2:567). This is the sole occurence of the term "unproduced triple body" *(musa sanjin)* in Saichō's authenticated writings. For the medieval Tendai *kuden* tradition, however, "kakuzen jitsubutsu" is prior to the distinction between delusion and enlightenment and refers to the ordinary worldling, who is enlightened inherently. Asai Endō argues that, in the context of the *Shugo kokkai shō*, Saichō was addressing the issue of whether the triple-

bodied, recompense-body-centric Buddha of traditional T'ien-t'ai *Lotus* exegesis was impermanent or constantly abiding, and not whether or not ordinary worldlings were inherently enlightened. *Kakuzen jitsubutsu,* he says, should not be construed as the Buddha "prior to awakening" *(satoru mae),* as medieval *kuden* texts would have it, but as the Buddha "subsequent to" or "from the perspective of awakening" *(satotte kara saki)* ("Musa sanjin kō," pp. 104–105; *Nihon Jōko Tendai honmon shisō shi,* pp. 112–14; *Tendai hongaku ron,* p. 436a–b). Hanano Michiaki, however, while agreeing that Saichō's use of the term "unproduced triple body" refers to the constant abiding of the recompense body and not to the innate Buddhahood of ordinary worldlings, disputes Asai's reading of *kakuzen jitsubutsu* as "the real Buddha subsequent to awakening." Hanano argues that Saichō's concept of *musa sanjin* was not the traditional T'ien-t'ai concept of the recompense body realized and manifested through the cultivation of practice but was influenced by esoteric notions of the Dharma body ("Nihon chūko Tendai bunken no kōsatsu (1)," p. 342 [endnote]). The influence of esoteric concepts of the Dharma-body Buddha Vairocana on Saichō's *musa sanjin* idea has also been suggested by Shioiri Ryōchū, "Dengyō Daishi no hongaku shisō," pp. 25–26.

120. *TZ* 9:43b, 44a.

121. *TZ* 9:44a–b.

122. *Wei-mo ching lüeh-shu* 1, *T* 38:564a28ff.

123. *TZ* 9:45a–b.

124. *TZ* 9:46a.

125. This tradition is found in a number of Tendai transmission texts and appears to derive from Taimitsu literature. See the note for "Fundarike" (*THR,* p. 453b), and Kuroda Toshio, "The Discourse on the 'Land of Kami' *(Shinkoku)* in Medieval Japan," trans. Fabio Rambelli, p. 366.

126. Hazama Jikō, *Chūko Nihon Tendai no kenkyū,* p. 120–21.

127. The three are outlined in Hazama Jikō, *Chūko Tendai no kenkyū,* pp. 126. When this threefold division was formulated is not easy to determine. The *Shuzenji-ketsu,* dating probably no later than the mid-Kamakura period, discusses the four broad categories in terms of teaching, practice, and realization, but does not apply this threefold division to the three abbreviated transmissions. Nor is the threefold division set forth in Shinsō's *Ichijō shō,* the earliest extant presentation of the seven great matters in fully developed form. For its subsequent development, see Tamura Kansei, "Eshin-ryū sanjū shichika kuden hōmon no keisei ni kansuru shiron."

128. Sonshun's *Nijō shō kenmon* describes a ritual in which all three "folds" are transmitted on the same occasion (*TZ* 9:161a–162a). However, the *Eshin-ryū kyōjū sōjō shishō* indicates that the three were transmitted at separate stages in a disciple's development (Uesugi Bunshū, *Nihon Tendai shi,* vol. 2, p. 815a). See also Tada Kōryū's notes on the *Sōden hōmon kenmon (Nijō shō)* in *THR,* pp. 586–87. There was probably considerable variation in the way transmissions were conducted.

129. Shimaji Daitō, *Nihon Bukkyō kyōgakushi,* pp. 462–63; Tamura Kansei, "Eshin-ryū sanjū shichika kuden hōmon no keisei ni kansuru shiron," p. 367.

130. Tamura Kansei, "Eshin-ryū sanjū shichika kuden hōmon no keisei ni kansuru shiron," pp. 363, 366.

131. *Hsüan-i* 5b, *T* 33:740c25–26.

132. See, for example, K'uei-chi (632–682)'s *Ta-sheng fa-yüan i-lin chang, T* 45:344b3–5.

133. Shimaji Daitō, *Nihon Bukkyō kyōgakushi*, p. 464. Shinran may also have been influenced by their much more longstanding use in connection with *mappō* thought.

Chapter Five: Tendai *Hongaku* Thought and the New Kamakura Buddhism: A Reappraisal

1. *Kankō ruijū, THR*, p. 193.

2. *Ichijō shō, TZ* 9:35a.

3. *THR*, pp. 120–49. This edition, as well as those reproduced in *DNBZ* 33 and *ESZ* 1, is based on a Genroku 5 (1692) printed text. There is also a partial transcription dated Meiō 2 (1493) held at the library of Ryūkoku University. Recently, a transcription of the *Shinnyo kan* dated Karyaku 2 (1327) was discovered at the Shinpukuji in Nagoya (Satō Tetsuei, *Eizan Jōdokyō no kenkyū*, p. 297).

4. The opening passage of the *Shinnyo kan* refers to a work called the *Bodai yōshū* (Essentials of *bodhi*). A work that appears to be the *Bodai yōshū* in question, also attributed to Genshin, was discovered in 1933 at the Kanazawa Bunko. According to its colophon, it was transcribed in the year Chōji 2 (1105). If this date is accurate, the *Bodai yōshū* must have been written before then, while the *Shinnyo kan* would have to be later. For the relationship between the two texts, see Sato Tetsuei, *Eizan Jōdokyō no kenkyū*, pp. 292–96. See also Tamura Yoshirō, "Tendai hongaku shisō gaisetsu," p. 565. The *Shinnyo kan* is also mentioned by name in the *Hōbutsu shū* (*DNBZ* 147:426b), a *setsuwa* collection attributed to Taira no Yasuyori (fl. 1190–1200), and in Hōnen's *Hyaku shijūgokajō mondō* (*SSH*, p. 648), which questions Genshin's authorship of the *Shinnyo kan* and dismisses its teachings as ineffective for attaining the Pure Land. Since both the *Hōbutsu shū* and the *Hyaku shijūgokajō mondō* were written around the end of the twelfth or the beginning of the thirteenth century, that would place the composition of the *Shinnyo kan* before these works but after the *Bodai yōshū*, or in other words, sometime during the twelfth century. Tamura has suggested "around 1200" ("Tendai hongaku shisō gaisetsu," p. 566). Tajima Tokuon suggested that this work dates from the Muromachi period (*BKD* 6:230b); however, this hypothesis has been rejected in the light of subsequent research.

5. However, Tajima Tokuon cites the suggestion of some unidentified person that there may have been a *kanbun* original that was later rendered into Japanese (*BKD* 6:230a).

6. *THR*, p. 120.

7. *THR*, pp. 120–21.

8. *DNBZ* 31:212b.

9. *THR*, p. 125.

10. *Originary Enlightenment*, p. 25.

11. *THR*, p. 121. The passage from the *Lotus* is at *p'in* 3, *T* 9:15b28–c1.

12. *THR*, p. 123.

13. *THR*, p. 125.

14. *THR*, pp. 140–41. See also pp. 128–9, 130–31.

15. *THR*, pp. 133–34.

16. *DNBZ* 147:426b. Sueki takes note of this passage in "*Hōbutsu shū* to *Shinnyo kan*," p. 2.

17. *THR*, p. 124.

18. *THR*, p. 128.

19. *THR*, p. 145.

20. *T* 46:10b7–11a14; Donner and Stevenson, *The Great Calming and Contemplation*, pp. 207–18. See also Donner, "Sudden and Gradual Intimately Conjoined," pp. 204–205.

21. *THR*, p. 146.

22. See Groner, "Shortening the Path."

23. As Paul Groner has noted, the suggestion that the realization of Buddhahood in this body could occur at the stage of verbal identity is found as early as the writings of Ennin (794–864)'s disciple Rinshō in his *Tendai Hokkeshū sokushin jōbutsu gi*, question and answer #50 (reproduced in Sueki Fumihiko, *Heian shoki Bukkyō shisō no kenkyū*, p. 664; translated in Groner, "Shortening the Path," p. 447).

24. *THR*, p. 144.

25. *THR*, p. 143.

26. *THR*, p. 142.

27. *THR*, p. 148.

28. *THR*, pp. 152–85 (annotated text in Japanese), pp. 357–69 *(kanbun)*. The *Sanjū shika no kotogakai* is also included in Shigematsu Akihisa, *Nihon Jōdokyō seiritsu katei no kenkyū*, pp. 346–64. These printed editions are based on a transcribed manuscript found at the Kanazawa Bunko. A cover sheet gives the name of Tan'ei (1271–1346), who was third abbot of the Shōmyōji, suggesting that this copy of the *Kotogaki* was his possession. However, the handwriting of the text differs from that of the cover sheet, indicating that the actual transcription was done by someone else. See Tamura Yoshirō, "Tendai hongaku shisō gaisetsu," p. 568.

29. "Ri kenpon to ji jōjū," p. 314; "Tendai hongaku shisō gaisetsu," p. 531.

30. *THR*, p. 184.

31. For references to Kōkaku in contemporary documents, see Taga Munehaya, "Kōkaku oyobi *Makura sōshi* ni tsuite," pp. 6–7.

32. The order of the thirty-four sections of the *Kotogaki* and of the *Makura sōshi* is not the same, and two of the sections in each text are completely different. In addition, some individual sections of the *Kotogaki* still retain the *gedai* or "outer titles" originally written on the sheet of paper in which individual *kirikami* were enclosed, while these are entirely missing from the *Makura sōshi*. Where the colophon to the *Kotogaki* gives the lineage of transmission of the Eshin school from Genshin to Jōmyō (fl. 1250), the *Makura sōshi* lists six additional names in the lineage beyond Jōmyō. The *Makura sōshi* also has appended at its very end a discussion of "the single thought-moment being three thousand realms" not found in the *Kotogaki*. For these reasons, the *Makura sōshi* is generally regarded as a later version of the *Kotogaki*. For differences between the two texts, see Hanano Michiaki, "Nihon chūko Tendai bunken no kōsatsu (5)," and Tamura Yoshiro, "Tendai hongaku shisō gaisetsu," pp. 566–68. The *Makura sōshi* survives in a number of printed editions, most dating from the sixteenth century (for a discussion of the various editions of the *Makura sōshi*, see Hanano Michiaki, "Nihon chūko Tendai bunken no kōsatsu [4].)" The *Makura sōshi* is included in *DNBZ* 32:105–29 and *ESZ* 3:469–520.

33. Earlier researchers, including Hazama Jikō and Satō Tetsue, had generally concurred that the *Kotogaki* might very well be Kōkaku's work (see Shigematsu Akihisa, *Nihon Jōdokyō seiritsu katei no kenkyū*, pp. 364–66). Tamura Yoshirō, however, argued that the *Kotogaki* contains all the essential elements of Tendai *hongaku* thought; subsequent developments are merely those of systematization. Based on his premise that *hongaku* thought had not reached the height of its development until the mid-

Kamakura period, Tamura suggested that the *Kotogaki* could not have been compiled as early as Kōkaku's time but was probably written between 1200 and 1250—perhaps closer to 1250 (*Kamakura shin Bukkyō shisō no kenkyū*, pp. 413–14; "Tendai hongaku shisō gaisetsu," p. 531).

Recent counterarguments, however, date the *Kotogaki* from the late Heian. Hanano Michiaki has reasserted the argument for Kōkaku's authorship. He points out that Hōchi-bō Shōshin, in his criticism of the original enlightenment doctrine, criticizes the concepts of the "unproduced triple-bodied Tathâgata" (*musa sanjin*) and the "four phrases of attaining the Way" (*shiku jōdo*) (*Hokke gengi shiki* 7, *DNBZ* 21:288b–89a, 289b–290a). However, the *Kotogaki* is at present the earliest known medieval Tendai text to develop these concepts. Hanano therefore argues that the ideas presented in the *Kotogaki* must have existed by Shōshin's time; hence there is no objection to the premise that Kōkaku compiled the text ("*Sanjū shika no kotogaki* no senja to shisō ni tsuite [1]").

Sueki Fumihiko, while somewhat critical of Hanano's argument, suggests that the *Kotogaki* probably dates from not too long after Kōkaku's time. Sueki points out that the interpretations of the "unproduced triple-bodied Tathâgata" and the "four phrases of attaining the Way" criticized by Shōshin are presented as merely "the conventional reading" in the *Kotogaki*, which further develops them from a more radically *hongaku* position. Thus Sueki argues that Shōshin's criticism must have been based on texts predating the *Kotogaki*. However, like Hanano, Sueki is unwilling to accept a date for this text as late as Tamura's. He notes Taga Munehaya's finding that a Taimitsu ritual text in the hand of the *zasu* Jien (1155–1225) kept in the Nankeizō collection on Mt. Hiei contains a passage on "fundamental darkness" (*ganpon no mumyō*) very similar to a discussion of this concept in the *Kotogaki*. Taga suggests a probable connection between Jien and Kōkaku's disciple Hangen, noting that Jien and Hangen's disciple Shunpan were well acquainted ("Kōkaku oyobi *Makura sōshi* ni tsuite," pp. 7–8). These are good grounds, Sueki suggests, for arguing that the *Kotogaki* might reasonably date from around Kōkaku's or Hangen's time. On the other hand, he also cites Shigematsu's argument that the notion of "realizing Buddhahood in a single moment" set forth in the *Kotogaki* may be related to the *ichinen gi* doctrine of Hōnen's disciple Kōsai (1163–1247). If so, this would argue against a very early date, although not quite as late as Tamura proposes ("Tendai hongaku shisō kenkyū no shomondai," pp. 292–94). As Sueki also points out, the fact that all thirty-four transmissions were compiled in a single text does not necessarily mean that they all date from the same time; some may express later stages in development of medieval Tendai thought than others.

34. *THR*, p. 155.
35. *Hsüan-i* 7a, *T* 33:766b18–19, 767a7–8. See also *THR*, p. 456b.
36. *THR*, p. 153. See also p. 165.
37. *THR*, p. 177.
38. *THR*, p. 156.
39. *MFLHC, p'in* 2, *T* 9:9b10. See also chap. 1, n. 115.
40. See chap. 2, n. 114.
41. *THR*, p. 157.
42. See Kouda Ryōsen, ed., *Wayaku Tendaishū rongi hyakudai jizaibō*, pp. 103–109. On the development of the *sōmoku jōbutsu* doctrine in medieval Tendai *kuden* literature, see chap. 1, n. 116.

43. *THR*, p. 167.

44. *Shōbō genzō, DZZ* 1:2; English translation from Norman Waddell and Abe Masao, "Shōbō genzō Genjō kōan," p. 133. I am indebted to William Bodiford for pointing out to me the similarity here with "Genjō kōan" and with Dōgen's concept of the "total exertion of a single thing" mentioned below. Such similarities have also been noted by Tamura Yoshirō, for example, in *Kamakura shin Bukkyō shisō no kenkyū,* pp. 549–51, and "Critique of Original Awakening Thought in Shōshin and Dōgen," pp. 260–61.

45. "Chūsei Tendai to hongaku shisō," p. 328ff; "Two Seemingly Contradictory Aspects of the Teaching of Innate Enlightenment *(Hongaku)* in Medieval Japan," pp.7–8.

46. See Hee-Jin Kim, *Dōgen Kigen,* pp. 82–83, 159–60, 200–201.

47. *THR*, p. 176.

48. *THR*, p. 169.

49. *THR*, p. 172.

50. *THR*, p. 158. "Wondrous awakening" *(myōkaku)* is the final stage in the fifty-two stage *mārga* scheme elaborated in classical T'ien-t-'ai. See chap. 1, n. 131.

51. The phrase *gend_ hongaku* first appears in Fa-tsang's commentary on the *Awakening of Faith* (*Ta-sheng ch'i-hsin lun i-chi, T* 44:c22–23). Its first occurrence in a Japanese Tendai text is Annen's *Taizō kongō bodaishin gi ryaku mondō shū* (*T* 74:373b26). For its use in medieval Tendai texts, see Hiroumi Kōken, "Tendai kuden hōmon ni okeru gendō usō ni tsuite."

52. *THR*, p. 180.

53. Ibid.

54. *THR*, p. 154–55.

55. "Chūsei Tendai to hongaku shisō," pp. 337–38. See also Sueki's "Two Seemingly Contradictory Aspects of the Teaching of Innate Enlightenment *(Hongaku)* in Medieval Japan," pp. 10–14.

56. See chap. 1, n. 96.

57. *THR*, pp. 163–64.

58. *DNBZ* 32:112b–113a. This passage appears in a transmission preceding the one just quoted.

59. On this point, see Tamura Yoshirō. "Ri kenpon to ji jōjū."

60. *THR*, pp. 180–81.

61. See chap. 1, n. 18.

62. I am indebted to William Bodiford for this suggestion about the "mandalic" quality of the world view set forth in this text.

63. *THR*, pp. 41–96. This edition is based on manuscripts belonging to Gyōgakuin Nitchō (1422–1500) and Engyōin Nichii (1444–1519), respectively, the eleventh and twelfth chief abbots of Minobu-san Kuonji, head temple of the Minobu line of the Nichiren Hokkeshū. The *Shuzenji-ketsu* also appears in *DDZ* 5:69–138, which is based on a transcription from the Keichō era (1596–1614). *Shuzenji-ketsu* is actually an inclusive title for two smaller, closely related works: the *Shuzenji sōden shiki* (Personal annotations on the transmissions of Hsiu-ch'an-ssu), called *Shuzenji sōden shichū* in the *DDZ* version, and the *Shuzenji sōden nikki* (Diary of the transmissions of Hsiu-ch'an-ssu).

64. For summaries of the major arguments on this issue, see Hanano Michiaki, "Nichiren kyōgaku to *Shuzenji-ketsu,*" and Jacqueline Stone, "Chanting the August Title of the *Lotus Sūtra.*"

65. See Takagi Yutaka, *Heian jidai Hokke Bukkyōshi kenkyū*, pp. 430–47, and my "Chanting the August Title of the *Lotus Sūtra*," which summarizes Takagi's findings. See also chap. 4, n. 110.

66. The theory of a latter Heian date for the *Shuzenji-ketsu* is maintained by Takagi Yutaka (*Heian jidai Bukkyōshi kenkyū*, pp. 447–65) and by Hanano Michiaki ("Nichiren kyōgaku to *Shuzenji-ketsu*" pp. 149–53). Tamura Yoshirō, on the other hand, places it between 1250 and 1300 (*Kamakura shin Bukkyō shisō no kenkyū*, pp. 414–17; "Tendai hongaku shisō gaisetsu," pp. 532–34). Ōkubo Ryōjun has suggested that it may postdate Nichiren ("*Shuzenji-ketsu* o chūshin to suru ni-san no mondai," p. 7).

67. *THR*, p. 44.

68. This was first pointed out by Shimaji Daitō in "Shōdai shisō ni tsuite," p. 500. Chapter 6 of the *Ōjō yōshū* discusses *nenbutsu* practice for "special times," which are divided into special *nenbutsu* sessions and practice for the moment of death. See also the discussion in Andrews, *The Teachings Essential for Rebirth*, pp. 75–86.

69. I am indebted to William Bodiford for suggesting this to me.

70. *THR*, p. 45.

71. Ibid.

72. *THR*, p. 46.

73. See Stevenson, "The Four Kinds of Samādhi," pp. 75–84.

74. *THR*, p. 46.

75. *THR*, pp. 48–49.

76. *THR*, p. 50.

77. *THR*, pp. 63–65.

78. *THR*, p. 65.

79. *THR*, p. 75. The name of Hsing-man's temple was actually Fo-lung-ssu.

80. *THR*, p. 76.

81. *THR*, pp. 51, 96.

82. *Nihon Bukkyō kyōgakushi*, p. 502.

83. Paul Groner makes this point with respect to the *Kankō ruijū* in "A Medieval Japanese Reading of the *Mo-ho chih-kuan*," p. 75.

84. *THR*, p. 65. The text gives this as an illustration of "the doctrine of penetrating and arriving at [truth] from one's original position" *(honjo tsūdatsu mon)*, which it attributes to the *Mo-ho chih-kuan*. The *Chih-kuan* does not in fact contain this exact phrase, which probably derives from Taimitsu (see the note at *THR*, pp. 444b–445a). However, Chih-i does assert that, because the ten realms interpenetrate, good and evil are mutually inclusive; thus those who live in evil circumstances are not thereby barred from the Way but may achieve insight by using that very evil as the object of meditation (*Chih-kuan* 2b, *T* 46:17b16–c29). See also the discussion in Donner, "Chih-i's Meditation on Evil," especially p. 54.

85. *THR*, p. 179.

86. *THR*, p. 196.

87. "A Medieval Japanese Reading of the *Mo-ho chih-kuan*, p. 72. See also Donner, "Chih-i's Meditation on Evil."

88. *DNBZ* 17:40b–41a.

89. Perhaps the most famous articulation of this idea appears in the *Tanni shō*, sections 13 and 14, though it occurs elsewhere in Shinran's writings. See also Dobbins, *Jōdo Shinshū*, pp. 53–56.

90. Several examples of "evil persons" achieving the Pure Land occur in late Heian-

period *ōjōden* or "accounts of those born in the Pure Land." See Ishida Mizumaro, *Ōjō no shisō,* pp. 285–92.

91. *Shasekishū, Nihon koten bungaku taikei* 85, p. 497. This passage occurs in a supplementary section of the text and is not included in Robert Morrell's translation, *Sand and Pebbles.*

92. See James Sanford, "The Abominable Tachikawa Skull Ritual."

93. These events have been historically verified. See *Tendai zasu ki,* p. 99, and Adolphson, "Monks, Courtiers and Warriors in Premodern Japan," pp. 128–29.

94. *Shōzōmatsu wasan, SCZ,* p. 459.

95. Akamatsu Toshide, "'Akusō' no shinjō to Kamakura Bukkyō." Akamatsu's understanding of Shinran's reception of original enlightenment thought draws heavily on Tamura Yoshirō's work. The incident of the verse being recited while the Kiyomizudera burned occurs in the *Enkyō, Nagato, Genpei jōsuiki* and *Shibu gassenjō* versions of the *Heike* and does not appear in available English translations.

96. See, for example, Adolphson, "Monks, Courtiers and Warriors in Premodern Japan," pp. 234–35.

97. Nishi Giyū, "Kamakura shin Bukkyō kōki no in'yu," p. 12.

98. On the shift of residence of aristocratic scholar-monks from Mt. Hiei to the capital, see Ishida Mizumaro, *Nihon Jōdokyō seiritsushi no kenkyū,* pp. 283–84.

99. *Honchō kōsōden* 13, *DNBZ* 102:209a. The thrust of this account is of course to praise Shōshin's unworldliness and devotion to learning. It is a modern reading that would condemn such ignorance as a callous indifference to events.

100. *Hongaku sanshaku, THR,* p. 103. The wording of "has no beginning, nor does it perish" *(funen fumetsu)* is drawn from *Wei-mo-chieh so-shuo ching* 1, *T* 14:540b5–6, 541a20–21. The Sanskrit reads "what does not burn is not extinguished," indicating the emptiness of both saṃsāra and nirvāṇa. However, the Chinese character for "burn" *(jan, nen)* can also be read as "so" or "in that way"; thus, in Chinese, the sūtra passages could also be read to mean that the dharmas are not "so" in the sense of having a beginning; that is, they are unproduced. This is the reading adopted in the note given in *THR.*

101. *Tendai Hokkeshū gozu hōmon yōsan, THR,* p. 38.

102. *Nihon Bukkyōshi: Kodai,* p. 253.

103. *Nihon chūsei no shakai to Bukkyō,* pp. 473–74; "Kamakura Bukkyō ron," pp. 270–71.

104. On the *akunin shōki* doctrine, see, for example, Ienaga Saburō, *Chūsei Bukkyō shishōshi kenkyū,* pp. 204–208; Tamura Enchō, "Akunin shōki-setsu no seiritsu"; Shigematsu Akihisa, *Nihon Jōdokyō seiritsu katei no kenkyū,* pp. 502–39; and Sueki Fumihiko, "Akunin shōki-setsu o megutte." Sueki's article contains a note listing other important studies of this subject (p. 438).

105. See Dobbins, *Jōdo Shinshū,* pp. 47–62.

106. *Shichikajō kishōmon,* article 4, *SSH,* p. 788; English translation from Dobbins, *Jōdo Shinshū,* p. 17.

107. *Shinran Shōnin goshōshoku shū, SCZ,* p. 626; English translation from Dobbins, *Jōdo Shinshū,* p. 55. In the same vein, see also *Mattō shō,* letters 16, 19, and 20, *SCZ,* pp. 605–606, 610, 614–15.

108. See LaFleur, *The Karma of Words,* pp. 48–59.

109. *Kamakura shin Bukkyō shisō no kenkyū,* pp. 539–40.

110. On Shinran's embeddedness in Confucian social ethics, see James Dobbins,

"Buddhist Modernism, Shinran's Teachings and Shin Buddhism in Medieval Japan" (cited by permission of the author). For a discussion of Nichiren's advice to individual followers on matters involving social ethics, see Takagi Yutaka, *Nichiren to sono montei*, pp. 222–53.

111. I use the term "paradigm" here simply to mean a model, and not, in the sense often derived from Thomas Kuhn's *Structure of Scientific Revolutions*, to indicate an overarching explanatory framework. Nor am I arguing that there occurred a "paradigm shift."

112. *Tendai Hokkeshū gozu hōmon yōsan, THR*, p. 39.

113. See Shigematsu Akihisa, *Nihon Jōdokyō seiritsu katei no kenkyū*, pp. 367–85.

114. *Jimyō Hokke mondō shō, STN* 1:283; translation from *Major Writings* 5:34. Traditionally it has been said that Nichiren's disciple Nichiji wrote this essay in Nichiren's name, obtaining Nichiren's endorsement (*NSIJ*, p. 476d).

115. *Bendōwa, DDZ* 2:470.

116. *THR*, p. 180.

117. I am indebted to Carl Bielefeldt for first pointing out this structure to me as something shared by the teachings of the new Kamakura Buddhist movements.

118. *Tendai Hokkeshū gozu hōmon yōsan, THR*, p. 35.

119. *THR*, p. 123.

120. See, for example, Kuroda Toshio, *Shōensei shakai*, p. 203; and Taira Masayuki, *Nihon chūsei no shakai to Bukkyō*, pp. 240–55, and "Kamakura Bukkyō ron," pp. 292–97.

121. Hazama Jikō, *Chūko Nihon Tendai no kenkyū*, pp. 241–44.

122. Ienaga Saburō, *Chūsei Bukkyō shisōshi kenkyū*, pp. 93–94.

123. This has been suggested by Funaoka Makoto, *Nihon Zenshū no seiritsu*, pp. 59–63, 127–28. See also the summary of Funaoka's argument in Bodiford, *Sōtō Zen in Medieval Japan*, pp. 7–8.

124. *Nihon Tendai to Kamakura Bukkyō*, pp. 149–58.

125. *Shishin gohon shō, STN* 2:1294–1300; *Kanjin honzon shō, STN* 1:702–21.

126. See, for example, *Mattō shō* 3, *SCZ*, pp. 585, 586.

127. *Senchakushū*, chap. 3, *SSH*, p. 319.

128. *Kanjin honzon shō, STN* 1:711.

129. *Shugo kokka ron, STN* 1:127–28; *Shō Hokke daimoku shō*, 1:184; *Hokke daimoku shō*, 1:391, 393.

130. *DNBZ* 17:40b.

131. *Mattō shō* 20, *SCZ*, p. 615; translation from Dobbins, *Jōdo Shinshū*, pp. 55–56.

132. "Myōmitsu Shōnin goshōsoku," *STN* 2:1166.

133. See, for example, Willa Tanabe's discussion of what she terms the "merit of surfeit," in her *Paintings of the Lotus Sūtra*, pp. 24–28.

134. *MFLHC, p'in* 25, *T* 9:56c21.

Chapter Six: Nichiren and the New Paradigm

1. The present study grew out of an attempt to answer questions that arose in investigating, for an earlier project, the scholarly dispute surrounding the authenticity of those *hongaku*-influenced writings attributed to Nichiren that Asai had questioned. See my "Some Disputed Texts in the Nichiren Corpus," especially chapter 1.

2. The standard edition of Nichiren's collected works, the 1989 revised version of the four-volume *Shōwa teihon Nichiren Shōnin ibun* (hereafter *STN*), contains a total of 498 writings, including doctrinal essays and letters to his followers; 66 charts

and outlines; and records of two oral teachings attributed to him. It also contains 391 holographic fragments of additional writings. These have come down to us in three forms: Nichiren's autographs, transcriptions (either of individual writings or collections of writings), and xylographs published during the Edo period. Of Nichiren's letters and essays, 115 complete autographs survive, and another 25 autographs, lost in a fire at the Nichirenshū head temple at Minobu in 1875, are known to have existed. In addition, there are 54 transcriptions of individual works made by Nichiren's immediate or second-generation disciples. However, there are no authenticated external contemporary references to him. See also Miyazaki Eishū, "Ibun," in *Nichiren jiten*, pp. 19b–21a.

3. Recent scholarly biographies of Nichiren tend to rely primarily on his own writings, focusing on those whose authenticity has been established, and to pass over the legendary or miraculous elements found in traditional hagiographies. Among the best of these are Takagi Yutaka's *Nichiren to sono montei* and *Nichiren: Sono kōdō to shisō*. Also useful is Tamura Yoshirō, *Nichiren: Junkyō no nyoraishi*. Among prewar biographical studies, Yamakawa Chiō's *Nichiren Shōnin den jikkō* is the most detailed and authoritative. Though now somewhat dated in many respects, it still serves as a valuable reference. To understand how the image of Nichiren was elaborated by, and affected, his later tradition, the study of traditional hagiographies is also important. Several of the most important from the Muromachi and Edo periods are found in *Nichiren Shōnin denki shū*. Another useful research tool is the *Nichiren Daishōnin denki shiryō sakuin*, an index to Nichiren biographical literature produced from 1314 through 1981.

4. The year 1222 is determined by calculating backward from various references in Nichiren's writings. His earliest biography, the *Goden dodai* by Nichidō (1283–1341), gives the date as "the sixteenth day of the the second month of the first year of the Jōō era" (*NSZ* 2:236). However, the era name did not change until 4/13, so 2/16 would have been Jōkyū 4, rather than Jōō 1. While such mistakes were probably common in a time when era names changed frequently, the fact that 2/16 happens to be the day after the date traditionally assigned to the Buddha's *parinirvāṇa* suggests that it may represent a later hagiographic addition.

5. "Zenmui Sanzō shō," *STN* 1:465; *Sado gosho*, 1:614; *Honzon mondō shō*, 2:1580.

6. For example, the Muromachi period biographical accounts *Ganso kedōki* and *Nichiren Daishōnin chūgasan* say that Nichiren's father was one Nukina Shigetada of the Mikuni family, son of a samurai from Tōtōmi Province who had been exiled to Awa following the defeat of the Taira. According to several traditional hagiographies, the Mikuni were descended from Emperor Shōmu. Other accounts, such as the Edo period *Honge betsuzu busso tōki*, trace Nichiren's ancestry to the aristocrat Fujiwara no Fuyutsugu. While these most likely represent attempts by later hagiographers to compensate for Nichiren's obscure origins, Tamura Yoshirō points out that the *Hokke honmonshū yōshō*, an apocryphal autobiographical account produced about fifty years after Nichiren's death, refers to him as "the son of the fisherman *gon no kami* at the bay of Kominato in Tōjō" (*STN* 3:2158). Since the title *gon no kami* was used to designate exiled nobles and members of powerful families and their descendants, Tamura suggests it is not impossible that Nichiren came from a family of some note (*Nichiren: Junkyō no nyoraishi*, p. 16).

7. Takagi Yutaka, *Nichiren: Sono kōdō to shisō*, pp. 14–15.

8. Kubota Tesshō, "Awa Seichōzan gumonjihō gyōja no keifu." See also *NJ*, p.

480b–d. Not long after Nichiren's death, the Kiyosumidera established formal ties with Shingon, which were retained until 1949, when it became a temple of Nichirenshū.

9. Nichiren's colophon appears in *STN* 4:2875; here he uses the name "Zeshō-bō." The transcription itself is held by the Kanazawa Bunko (*Kanazawa bunko komonjo, shikigo hen* 164).

10. See, for example, *Sado gosho, STN* 1:615. Nichiren never fully persuaded Dōzen-bō to adopt his views on exclusive devotion to the *Lotus,* but he retained a lifelong gratitude to his old teacher. One of his major essays, the *Hōon shō* (*STN* 2:1192–1250; Watson and Yampolsky, pp. 250–318), was written to commemorate Dōzen-bō's death in 1276.

11. "Myōhō-ama gozen gohenji," *STN* 2:1535, and "Myōhō-bikuni gohenji," 2:1553.

12. *Hōon shō, STN* 2:1194; "Myōhō-bikuni gohenji," 2:1553.

13. *Shinkokuō gosho, STN* 1:882–85.

14. Tamura Yoshirō, *Nichiren: Junkyō no nyoraishi,* pp. 18–21, 24–27. Tamura points out, for example, that Nichiren's statements about his desire to solve the problem of birth and death occur in letters to a woman recently bereaved; and his doubts about the fate of Gotoba and other emperors appear in the context of an argument about the futility of relying for thaumaturgical support on prayer rituals *(kitō)* based not on the *Lotus Sūtra* but on Mikkyō—something the Taira had done in their struggle with the Minamoto, and Gotoba, in challenging the *bakufu.*

15. Takagi Yutaka, "Kiyosumi no Nichiren," p. 1. For a discussion in English of the *gumonji hō* and a description of its practice today, see Taikō Yamasaki, *Shingon,* pp. 182–90.

16. "Zenmui Sanzō shō," *STN* 1:473; "Seichōji daishu chū," 2:1133.

17. "Myōhō-bikuni gohenji," *STN* 2:1553.

18. "Teachings such as those left by Shan-tao and Hōnen have been known to me from the age of seventeen or eighteen" ("Nanjō Hyōe Shichirō-dono gosho," *STN* 1:326); "First, I listened to [the teachings of] Jōdo and Zen" ("Ha Ryōkan-tō gosho," 2:1283). Nichiren would already have been exposed to Tendai Pure Land thought and practice—not necessarily that of Hōnen—at the Kiyosumidera.

19. *STN* 1:11.

20. The medieval biographical account *Nichiren Daishōnin Chūgasan* by Enmyōin Nitchō suggests that Nichiren began to doubt the Pure Land teachings when he learned that the Pure Land master Dai Amida-butsu had died shrieking in agony (p. 35). While the connection with Dai Amida-butsu, one of Hōnen's disciples, is probably a later invention, Takagi Yutaka points out that a good death was taken very seriously as a sign of the deceased person's salvation, and suggests that, while still very young, Nichiren may indeed have conceived an aversion to the Pure Land teachings as a result of seeing some Pure Land devotee close to him die unpleasantly (*Nichiren: Sono kōdō to shisō,* pp. 22–23).

21. See, for example, Yamakawa Chiō, "Eizan ni okeru Nichiren Shōnin no shiyū no kenkyū," pp. 114–17. Yamakawa bases this on the *Nichidai Jikken taitō mondō ki, NSZ* 2:427, which is discussed in the next chapter.

22. Shunpan is mentioned in Nichiren's *Nenbutsusha tsuihō senjō ji* (*STN* 3:2261) and *Jōdo kuhon no koto* (*STN* 3:2310), in both cases, in connection with his opposition to Hōnen's exclusive *nenbutsu.* Recently, drawing on newly published transmis-

sions attributed to Shunpan, Kubota Tesshō has explored possible connections between Nichiren's thought and that of the Tendai master ("Shunpan kyōgaku no ichi kōsatsu"). However, though he establishes that Nichiren was influenced by some elements of medieval Tendai thought generally the question of a specific relationship with Shunpan remains inconclusive.

23. *Nichiren: Sono kōdō to shisō,* pp. 30–33.

24. Nichiren's corpus includes the *Nenbutsusha tsuihō senjō ji* (*STN* 3:2258–72), a collection of extracts from petitions to suppress the exclusive *nenbutsu* and edicts issued against it by both court and *bakufu.* The *Kinkōshū,* a work by Nichiren's disciple Minbu Ajari Nikō, also includes a section containing documents relating to the suppression of Hōnen's *nenbutsu* (*NSZ* 13:158–221). Taira Masayuki suggests that Nichiren may possibly have received these documents through Shunpan (*Nihon chūsei no shakai to Bukkyō,* p. 358).

25. See, for example, Hanano Mitsuaki, "Nichiren no shōdai shisō to Danna-ryū no kanjō genshi kuden."

26. Takagi Yutaka discusses the forms of Buddhism Nichiren is likely to have encountered during this period of study in *Nichiren: Sono kōdō to shisō,* pp. 25–29.

27. Nichiren's colophon appears in *STN* 4:2875. The transcription itself, the earliest one extant, is kept in the archives of the Nakayama Hokekyōji in Chiba. The translation of the title was suggested to me by Ryūichi Abé.

28. *T* 79:12c2–6.

29. Sakai Kyōjun, "Nichiren Shōnin ni miru taimitsu no eikyō," p. 62. The *Rishōin kechimyaku,* a Shingon lineage of the Daigoji, also gives the name "Nichiren" as twenty-fifth in a line of esoteric transmission beginning with Dainichi (*Kanazawa Bunko komonjo, butsuji hen* 6622). However, Takagi Yutaka has argued that this Nichiren was a different person ("'Futari no Nichiren' kaikō").

30. "Shōnin gonanji," *STN* 2:1672. "Seichōji daishū chū," 2:1134.

31. The name "Nichiren" is written with the characters for "sun" and "lotus." Judging from Nichiren's own account ("Shijō Kingo nyobō gosho" *STN* 1:484; "Jakunichi-bō gosho," 2:1669–70), the name derives from two passages in the *Lotus Sūtra:* "Just as the light of the sun and moon illuminate all obscurity, this person [who upholds the *Lotus*] will practice in the world and dispel the darkness of all beings" (*T* 9:52b26–27), and a reference to the bodhisattvas who emerge from beneath the earth in chapter 15 as "untainted by worldly dharmas,/like a lotus in the water" (42a5–6).

32. These elements appear very early in the hagiographical literature. Nichiren's chanting of the *daimoku* while facing the rising sun and an attack by Tōjō Kagenobu are mentioned in the *Hokke honmonshū yōshō* (*STN* 3:2159), an apocryphal work attributed to Nichiren, probably dating from about forty to fifty years after his death.

33. "Seichōji daishu chū," *STN* 2:1135. Takagi Yutaka argues that "indebted" here means "in the service of," one reason for supposing that Nichiren's father may have been a *shōen* official (*Nichiren to sono montei,* p. 4). This woman may also have helped finance Nichiren's early travels for study (*NJ,* p. 563c).

34. "Seichōji daishū chū," *STN* 2:1135; "Myōhō-bikuni gohenji," 2:1562.

35. *Nichiren: Sono kōdō to shisō,* pp. 49–54. See also Takagi's "Kiyosumi no Nichiren," pp. 2–6, where he suggests that Nichiren may have remained at the Kiyosumidera until late in the year 1254.

36. This incident, known in the Nichiren tradition as the Komatsubara Persecution (Komatsubara *hōnan*), is described in the "Nanjō Hyōe Shichirō-dono gosho," *STN* 1:326–27; *Major Writings* 6:32.

37. For the social composition of Nichiren's following, see Takagi Yutaka, *Nichiren to sono montei*, pp. 51–81.

38. "Fudō Aizen kankenki," *STN* 1:16. The content of the transmission is not indicated.

39. *Ichidai shōgyō taii, STN* 1:73.

40. *Shugo kokka ron, STN* 1:129, 130.

41. The earliest authenticated use of this phrase in a Japanese context occurs in a written prayer or *ganmon* offered by Sugawara no Michizane on the occasion of a memorial service for his deceased parents in 881, which contains the invocation "Namu-Kanzeon-Bosatsu, Namu-myōhō-renge-kyō" ("Kichijō-in Hokke-e ganmon," *Kanke bunsō* 11, no. 650, *Nihon koten bungaku taikei* 72:599).

42. See chap. 4, n. 110.

43. See, for example, Shimaji Daitō, "Shōdai no shisō," p. 502; Ienaga Saburō, *Chūsei Bukkyō shisōshi kenkyū*, pp. 71–81; and Kawazoe Shōji, "Nichiren no shūkyō keisei ni okeru nenbutsu haigeki no igi" (1), p. 63.

44. *Shō Hokke daimoku shō, STN* 1:202.

45. In this vein, see *Shugo kokka ron, STN* 1:127–28; *Shō Hokke daimoku shō,* 1:184; and *Hokke daimoku shō,* 1:391–93, *Major Writings* 3:3,6.

46. *Hōon shō, STN* 2:1248. The *Isshō jōbutsu shō,* traditionally assigned the date 1255, along with the *Ichinen sanzen hōmon* and *Jūnyoze no koto,* both traditionally dated 1258, associate the *daimoku* with realizing Buddhahood in this very body. However, the authenticity of all three works has been questioned (see my "Some Disputed Writings in the Nichiren Corpus," pp. 135–76).

47. *STN* 1:71. This identification may have roots in earlier medieval Tendai transmissions. See Hanano Michiaki, "Nichiren no shōdai shisō to Danna-ryū no kanjō genshi kuden." The *daimoku* is identified with *ichinen sanzen* in the *kaike* text *Isshin myōkai shō* 2, *ZTZ* (*Enkai* 1):293b–294a.

48. The notion of potential Buddhahood inherent in the outer world is already implicit in Chih-i's *Mo-ho chih-kuan,* for example, where he states, in explaining the *ichinen sanzen* principle: "The realm of the land *(kokudo seken)* also possesses the ten kinds of dharmas. That is to say, an evil land has [its own] characteristics, nature, essence, etc." (*T* 46:54a3–4). Chan-jan also comments: "You should know that one's person and the land are [both] the single thought-moment comprising three thousand realms. Therefore, when one attains the Way, in accordance with this principle, one's body and mind in that moment pervade the dharma realm" (*Hung-chüeh* 5–3, *T* 46:295c23–24). This passage from Chan-jan is often quoted in Nichiren's writings.

49. Nichiren mentions in particular an unprecedented earthquake on 8/23/1257, a storm on 8/1/1258, a major famine in 1259 and an epidemic in the same year continuing throughout 1260, by which time "more than half the people had already died" ("*Ankoku ron* gokan yurai," *STN* 1:421). A more complete list of disasters and portents has been extracted from the *bakufu* record *Azuma kagami* and translated in Laurel Rasplica Rodd, *Selected Writings of Nichiren,* pp. 24–25, n. 46.

50. *Shugo kokka ron, STN* 1:116.

51. Ibid., p. 89.

52. Translations of the *Risshō ankoku ron* include, in English, Watson and Yampolsky, pp. 11–41, and Laurel Rasplica Rodd, *Nichiren: Selected Writings*, pp. 59–81.

53. *Risshō ankoku ron, STN* 1:209.

54. Ibid., p. 225. Translation from Watson and Yampolsky, p. 38.

55. For example, Charles Elliot, *Japanese Buddhism*, p. 277; G. B. Sansom, *Japan: A Short Cultural History*, p. 334.

56. The relationship between the "imperial law" and the "Buddhist Law" was closely explored by the late Kuroda Toshio. See, for example, his "Ōbō to buppō," and, in translation, "The Imperial Law and the Buddhist Law."

57. Nichiren names specifically Kōin's *Jōdo ketsugi shō*, Jōshō's, *Dan Senchaku*, and Myōe's *Zaijarin* (*Shugo kokka ron, STN* 1:90). Nichiren's criticism of Hōnen has particular resonance with Myōe's, as Takagi Yutaka has noted (*Kamakura Bukkyōshi kenkyū*, pp. 243–44). Myōe's criticism of Hōnen is discussed in Tanabe, Jr., *Myōe the Dreamkeeper*, pp. 96–110. For an earlier example of criticism of Hōnen on the part of the Buddhist establishment, see the *Kōfukuji sōjō* (Kōfukuji petition) of the monk Jōkei (1155–1213), translated in Morrell, *Early Kamakura Buddhism*, pp. 75–88.

58. For example, Ienaga Saburō, *Chūsei Bukkyō shisōshi kenkyū*, pp. 66–71.

59. *Risshō ankoku ron, STN* 1:219. The reference is to Gotoba's defeat in the Jōkyū Disturbance of 1221, when he issued a military challenge to the *bakufu*, and his subsequent exile to the island of Oki.

60. "Shoki Nichiren no kokkakan."

61. Kawazoe Shōji, "Nichiren no shūkyō keisei ni okeru nembutsu haigeki no igi" (1), pp. 66–68; Ikegami Songi, "Nichiren to kokka," p. 75. See also Satō Hiroo, "Shoki Nichiren no kokkakan," pp. 19–20, 26 (n. 8).

62. "Rondan tekitai gosho," *STN* 1:274.

63. This incident, known as the Matsubagayatsu Persecution (Matsubagayatsu *hōnan*), is mentioned in *Shimoyama goshōsoku, STN* 2:1330.

64. The legal basis for Nichiren's exile may have been article 12 of the Jōei Shikimoku, the *bakufu*'s legal code, which prohibited slander (Yamakawa Chiō, *Nichiren Shōnin den jikkō*, pp. 252–53). Takagi Yutaka further points out that there may have been physical violence between Nichiren's followers and those of the Pure Land contingent, which was prohibited under article 13. He also suggests there may have been some influence from ideas expressed in the regulations for clergy under the old Ritsuryō code, which forbade monks and nuns from reading astronomical portents and prognosticating concerning matters of state (*Nichiren: Sono kōdō to shisō*, pp. 76–78). Hōjō Shigetoki is also thought to have numbered among his vassals Nichiren's enemy Tōjō Kagenobu; Nichiren wrote that Kagenobu had earlier conspired with Shigetoki (Gokurakuji-dono) and others in his attempt to seize control of the *shōen* on which the Kiyosumidera was located ("Myōhō-bikuni gohenji," *STN* 2:1562). It is possible that Nichiren's opposition to Kagenobu at that time was a factor in the decision to have him exiled (*NJ*, p. 563c).

65. *MFLHC, p'in* 10, *T* 9:31b20–21.

66. "Nanjō Hyōe Shichirō-dono gosho," *STN* 1:327. The quoted statement is at *MFLHC, p'in* 13, *T* 9:36c18.

67. "Shion shō," *STN* 1:236.

68. The "five principles" are sometimes called the "five ropes" (*gokō*) in the later Nichiren tradition. Nichiren first outlines them in his *Kyō ki ji koku shō* (1262), *STN* 1:241–46; *Major Writings* 4:7–21, and also in "Nanjō Hyōe Shichirō-dono gosho"

(1264), *STN* 1:319–28; *Major writings* 6:19–33. For the background of the five principles, see Asai Endō, "Gogihan no keisei katei no kōsatsu."

69. *Wu-liang-i ching,* *T* 9:386b1–2; *MFLHC, p'in* 10, *T* 9:31b17–18.

70. The identification of these two chapters as the core of the trace and origin teachings can be traced to Chan-jan (*Shih-chien* 1, *T* 33:820c8–821a9, *passim*).

71. *Shingon kenmon, STN* 1:657.

72. In the *Shugo kokka ron,* an early writing, Nichiren does say that faith in the *Lotus Sūtra* represents an "easy practice" (*STN* 1:111). Later, however, he would more commonly speak of the practice of the sūtra as "difficult," because of the hardships to be encountered by those who uphold it in the Final Dharma age.

73. For an early example of this argument, see *Shō Hokke daimoku shō* (1260), *STN* 1:204–205.

74. *Hung-chüeh* 6–4, *T* 46:353b5–6. This is also a recurring theme in medieval Tendai literature. See Shigyō Kaishū, "Chūko Tendai to Hokke shisō no renkan," pp. 611–13.

75. See Tokoro Shigemoto, "Tami no ko no jikaku no keisei to tenkai," pp. 489–90.

76. *STN* 2:1003–1061. Translations include Kenneth Dollarhide, *Nichiren's Senjishō,* and Watson and Yampolsky, pp. 181–249. For discussions of time in Nichiren's thought, see also Kenneth Dollarhide, "History and Time in Nichiren's *Senji-shō,*" and Lucia Dolce, "Awareness of *Mappō.*"

77. *Senji shō, STN* 2:1009.

78. Saichō had argued that the faculties of the Japanese as a group were mature and therefore suited to the *Lotus Sūtra* (*Ehyō Tendaishū, DDZ* 3:343. See also Groner, *Saichō,* pp. 181–82). Annen cites the *Yü-ch'ieh lun,* attributed to Maitreya or Asaṅga, as saying that there is a small country to the east whose people's faculties are related solely to the Mahāyāna; however, no such statement appears in extant versions of the *Yü-ch'ieh lun* (*Futsū jubosatsukai kōshaku* 1, *T* 74:757c24). Genshin says that the faculties of the Japanese are pure and unified, suited to the perfect teaching (*Ichijō yōketsu* 2, *T* 74:351a3).

79. *Kyō ki ji koku shō, STN* 1:245.

80. For a discussion of the concept of "slander of the Dharma" in Nichiren's thought, see Watanabe Hōyō, "Nichiren Shōnin no shūkyō ni okeru 'hōbō' no igi."

81. *Shugo kokka ron, STN* 1:128.

82. *Ken hōbō shō, STN* 1:255.

83. "Nanjō Hyōe Shichirō-dono gosho," *STN* 1:321.

84. *Shakubuku* stands in contrast to *shōju* ("to embrace and accept"), the mild method of leading others gradually without criticizing their position. The two terms occur in the *Sheng-man shih-tzu-hou i-ch'eng ta-fang-pien fan-kuang ching,* where they are described as "enabling the Dharma to long endure" (*T* 12:217c13). Nichiren drew on the work of Chih-i, who associated *shakubuku* with the *Lotus Sūtra* (*Hsüan-i* 9a, *T* 33:792b17. See also *Wen-chü* 8b, 34:118c20–24; and *Chih-kuan* 10b, 46:137c25–29.) For examples of Nichiren's discussions of *shakubuku,* see the *Kaimoku shō, STN* 1:605–607, translated in Watson and Yampolsky, pp. 142–45; *Sado gosho, STN* 1:611–12, translated in *Major Writings* 1:34; and *Nyosetsu shugyō shō, STN* 1:735–36, *Major Writings* 1:104–105.

85. One sees this in Nichiren's advice given later in life to his lay followers, such as the Ikegami brothers Munenaka and Munenaga, whose father opposed their faith,

or Shijō Yorimoto, whose lord commanded him to abandon his allegiance to Nichiren. See Takagi Yutaka, *Nichiren to sono montei,* pp. 221–53.

86. Nichiren would later credit Hōjō Tokiyori ("Saimyōji-dono") with his pardon ("Ha Ryōkan-tō gosho," *STN* 2:1286). It has been suggested that Hōjō Shigetoki's death, which transpired shortly after Nichiren's exile, prompted Tokiyori to have him released.

87. Nichiren returned to his home province of Awa in 1263 or 1264, possibly to see his mother, who was quite ill. He is also thought to have engaged in preaching and to have renewed connections with those monks from the Kiyosumidera who were favorably disposed to him. On 10/14/1264 he met again with his old teacher, Dōzen-bō, and admonished him to renounce faith in Amida ("Zenmui sanzō shō," *STN* 1:474). In the course of this visit, on 11/11/1264, he and his party were ambushed on the road by Tōjō Kagenobu's men. One died defending Nichiren, who was himself wounded. After returning to Kamakura, in 1265, Nichiren went briefly to Ueno in the Fuji district of Suruga Province, to perform a funeral for his lay follower, Nanjō Hyōe Shichirō, whose bereaved family would number among his most devoted supporters in his later years. The same year, or possibly 1266, he again visited Awa. See Takagi Yutaka, *Nichiren: Sono kōdō to shisō,* pp. 79–83, 87–89; Tamura Yoshirō, *Nichiren: Junkyō no nyoraishi,* pp. 63–70.

88. *MFLHC, p'in* 5, *T* 9:19b19–20.

89. Takagi Yutaka, *Nichiren to sono montei,* p. 185; *Nichiren: Sono kōdō to shisō,* pp. 96–97.

90. These memorializing efforts include the *"Ankoku ron* gokan yurai," written on 4/5/1268 to one Hōkan-bō, presumably a monk with connections to the Hōjō, restating the message of the *Risshō ankoku ron* and giving Nichiren's reasons for writing it (*STN* 1:421–24; translated in Watson and Yampolsky, pp. 42–47), and two letters to Yadoya Nyūdō, an official in service to the Hōjō, the first pointing out that the prophecy of the *Risshō ankoku ron* was being fulfilled and asking him to report this to the Regent ("Yadoya Nyūdō gari gojō," *STN* 1:424–25), and the second inquiring why no response had been forthcoming ("Yadoya Nyūdō sai gojō," *STN* 1:425). In a letter to one of his lay followers thought to have been written in 1270, Nichiren notes that letters he had sent to various persons the year before had gone unanswered, but that letters of admonition sent in the present year had garnered some response, and that he hoped people were becoming more receptive ("Kingo-dono gohenji," *STN* 1:458). See also Takagi Yutaka, *Nichiren to sono montei,* p. 174. There are in addition the so-called eleven letters (*jū ittsū no jō, STN* 1:427–36), dated 10/11/1268, from Nichiren to *bakufu* officials and prominent clerics. However, their authenticity is in dispute. See Asai Yōrin, who questions it in *Nichiren Shōnin kyōgaku no kenkyū,* pp. 354–73, and Miyazaki Eishū, who upholds it in "Jū ittsū no jō," *NSIJ,* pp. 491d–92b.

91. See Takagi Yutaka, *Nichiren to sono montei,* pp. 154–61, for those schools and lineages that constituted a significant presence in Kamakura at this time.

92. Nichiren criticized Zen as early as 1255 in the "Renjō shō" and *Shoshū mondō shō,* and again in the *Kyō ki ji koku shō* (1262), but on purely doctrinal grounds. Only after the arrival of the Mongol envoy in 1268 did he begin to attack it as a contributing cause to the nation's disasters (Takagi Yutaka, *Nichiren to sono montei,* pp. 168–69). On the other hand, Tamura Yoshirō questions the authenticity of the 1255

writings and holds that Nichiren's critique of Zen did not start until this time (*Kamakura shin Bukkyō no kenkyū*, pp. 591, 598). The Zen figures who feature in Nichiren's polemics are Dainichi Nōnin and Enni (Shōichi Kokushi) in the area of the capital and Lan-ch'i Tao-lung in Kamakura. On the doctrinal bases of Nichiren's critique of Zen, see Kawazoe Shōji, "Nichiren no Zenshū ha ni tsuite."

93. On Nichiren's criticism of *shingon*, see Kawazoe Shōji, "Nichiren no shikan to shingon haigeki."

94. "Kingo-dono gohenji," *STN* 1:458.

95. *Shuju onfurumai gosho, STN* 2:964–65, Watson and Yampolsky, pp. 324–25; *Yorimoto chinjō*, 2:1353–55, *Major Writings* 5:219–22; and *Shimoyama goshōsoku, STN* 2:1322–23.

96. Nichiren's accounts of this event were all written retrospectively, several years after the events described. Satō Hiroo suggests that they may have been prompted by the fact that Ninshō and his teacher Eizon had been asked by the *bakufu* to perform prayer rituals to repel the Mongols, an undertaking that, in Nichiren's view, could only be conducted successfully by one devoted to the *Lotus Sūtra* ("Nichiren no kōki no shisō," pp. 56, 60 (n. 9).

97. "Gyōbin sojō goetsū," *STN* 1:497–500.

98. Takagi points out that two extant *bakufu* directives dated the day after Nichiren's arrest, issued to retainers with landholdings in Kyushu, order them to go south to establish defenses and to put down troublesome elements *(akutō)* within their territory (*Nichiren to sono montei*, p. 189; *Kamakura ibun, Komonjo hen* 14:300–301, document nos. 10873, 10874).

99. *Shimoyama goshōsoku, STN* 2:1332. It has long been thought that Nichiren may have been spared execution because the wife of the shogunal regent *(shikken)*, Hōjō Tokimune, was pregnant, executions often being commuted when an heir was about to be born (Tsuji Zennosuke, *Nihon Bukkyōshi, Chūsei* 2, p. 33). Takagi Yutaka suggests that Nichiren's life may have been saved through the efforts of his follower Daigaku Saburō, a close associate of Adachi Yasumori, who was the child's maternal grandfather (*Nichiren: Sono kōdō to shisō*, pp. 107–108).

100. This incident, known as the Tatsunokuchi or Ryūkō persecution (Ryūkō *hōnan*), is also related in three of Nichiren's writings: "Shijō Kingō-dono goshōsoku" (*STN* 1:504–505); *Shuju onfurumai gosho* (2:967, translated in Watson and Yampolsky, pp. 326); and "Myōho-bikuni gohenji" (*STN* 2:1562). The "Shijō Kingō-dono goshōsoku" says, "The god of the moon manifested as a luminous object and saved my head at Tatsunokuchi" (1:505). However, some scholars have questioned the authenticity of this section of the text, and the historicity of the "luminous object" is disputed. See Tamura Yoshirō, *Nichiren: Junkyō no nyoraishi*, pp. 89–90.

101. *Kaimoku shō, STN* 1:590.

102. See Takagi Yutaka, *Nichiren to sono montei*, pp. 181–85, for the impact of the 1271 persecution on Nichiren's followers.

103. "Misawa shō," *STN* 2:1446–47. The distinction between pre- and post-Sado in Nichiren's teaching has been accorded great importance in traditional Nichiren Buddhist doctrinal studies.

104. Nichiren was so convinced of the legitimizing function of his ordeal that he rebuked as disloyal those of his followers who were negotiating with the *bakufu* for his pardon ("Shingon shoshū imoku," *STN* 1:638).

105. While Nichiren's later followers would explicitly equate him with Bodhisattva

Superior Conduct, he spoke of himself in humbler terms, for example, as a "forerunner" of the bodhisattva.

106. *STN* 1:535–609; Watson and Yampolsky, pp. 50–147.

107. *STN* 1:601, 604.

108. "Nanjō Hyōe Shichirō-dono gohenji," *STN* 2:1884. The phrase "sole great matter" *(ichidaiji)* is a reference to chapter 2 of the *Lotus:* "The Buddhas, the World-Honored Ones, by reason of the sole great matter appear in the world" (*MFLHC, T* 9:7a21–22). The term occurs frequently in medieval Tendai transmissions and also in Zen writings.

109. See chap. 3, n. 32.

110. *Kaimoku shō, STN* 1:539.

111. See chap. 4, n. 64.

112. Take Kakuchō, "Nihon Tendai to Nichiren," pp. 57–58.

113. *Kanjin honzon shō, STN* 1:719. "Bestow upon the children the medicine," etc., is a reference to the parable of the good physician in chapter 16 of the *Lotus Sūtra.*

114. The earliest of Nichiren's extant mandalas was inscribed while he was in custody on 10/9/1271, the day before he left under guard for the coast of the Japan Sea where he would make the crossing to Sado. It is said to have been written with a twig or piece of bark broken off from a tree branch. However, its form appears embryonic. See Yamanaka Kihachi, ed., *Gohonzon shū,* plate 1, and *Gohonzon shū mokuroku,* pp. 3–4, as well as *NJ,* p. 412d. A mandala inscribed by Nichiren on Sado on 7/8/1273 was the first to bear all the figures typically appearing on Nichiren's mandalas, and carried an inscription that read in part "Nichiren inscribes this for the first time." This mandala was lost in a fire on Mt. Minobu, headquarters of Nichiren-shū, in 1875, but a copy of it appears in the *Shūso gohonzon shū* made by the thirty-third abbot of Minobu, Nichikō (1646–1721) (*NJ,* p. 117b).

115. The reasons for his release are not entirely clear. Nichiren himself wrote that because he was innocent, and because his predictions had proved accurate, the Regent Tokimune decided over the objections of other influential members of the Hōjō clan to pardon him ("Nakaoki Nyūdō goshōsoku," *STN* 2:1716). It is also possible, that despite Nichiren's disapproval, his followers continued their efforts to negotiate a pardon for him with the *bakufu*. Tsuji Zennosuke suggests that one of Nichiren's followers who appears in his writings as "Yagenta-dono" was in fact Hōjō Yagenta Tokimori, great-uncle of Tokimune, and that Nichiren's pardon may have been obtained through his mediation (*Nihon Bukkyōshi, Chusei* 2, p. 39). However, Takagi Yutaka suggests that key figure in obtaining the pardon may have been Daigaku Saburō, prevailing upon his connections with Adachi Yasumori (see n. 99 above). (*Nichiren: Sono kōdō to shisō,* pp. 183–84.)

116. See, for example, *Senji shō, STN* 2:1053–54; Watson and Yampolsky, p. 241.

117. *Goden dodai, NSZ* 2:250.

118. "Toki-dono gosho," *STN* 1:809. Later, after settling at Minobu, Nichiren began to write of his reclusion there as something he had decided upon from the outset, following the Chinese precedent that one who admonishes the ruler three times and is not heeded should retire into the mountains. See Takagi Yutaka, *Nichiren: Sono kōdō to shisō,* pp. 192–200.

119. *Hōon shō, STN* 2:1248, 1249.

120. "Myōmitsu Shōnin goshōsoku," *STN* 2:1165.

121. *Kenbutsu mirai ki, STN* 125.1:743.

122. During the Sado period and after, Nichiren continued to speak of the Tendai school as representing the orthodox stream of Buddhism and himself as the representative of orthodox Tendai. "All schools except the Tendai school have gone astray as to the object of worship" (*Kaimoku shō, STN* 1:578); "The Tendai-Hokke lineage is called the Buddha-founded lineage *(butsuryū shū)*, because it was established by the Buddha himself" ("Shōmitsu-bō gosho," 1:825–26); "Those [monks] in this country of Japan who are not disciples of the Great Teacher Dengyō [Saichō] are followers of heterodox paths and evil persons" (*Senji shū*, 2:1016); "The ceremony for opening the eyes of painted or wooden Buddha images should be conducted only on the basis of the *Lotus Sūtra* and the Tendai school" ("Shijō Kingo Shakabutsu kuyō ji," 2:1183), and so forth. Such passages stand in contrast to those in which Nichiren speaks of being the bearer of a Dharma never before revealed. His later tradition has sought to resolve this ambiguity by speaking of Nichiren as having received both an "outer transmission" *(ge sōjō)*, which is historical and intellectual, placing him within the historical flow from Śākyamuni through Chih-i and Saichō, and an inner transmission *(nai sōjō)*, religious and intuitive, inherited directly from Śākyamuni Buddha (*NJ*, pp. 243d–44b). This "inner transmission" parallels Tendai claims for Chih-i's receipt of a direct transmission from Śākyamuni on Eagle Peak (Sekiguchi Shindai, "Ryōzen jikiju to nenge mishō," pp. 584–85).

123. "Kamakura Bukkyō ron," pp. 296–97.

124. *Senji shō, STN* 2:1053.

125. On this point, see my "Rebuking the Enemies of the *Lotus Sūtra*."

126. "Shonin gohenji," *STN* 2:1479.

127. "Embracing" is the translation of *juji*, literally, "to receive and keep," the first of five forms of practice of the *Lotus Sūtra* enumerated in the "Dharma Preacher" (10th) chapter: to receive and keep, read, recite, explain, and transcribe the sūtra. Nichiren wrote that "embracing the *Lotus Sūtra* and chanting Namu-myōhō-renge-kyō in itself contains all five kinds of practice" ("Nichinyo gozen gohenji," *STN* 2:1377). In some contexts, it is convenient to translate *juji* in a way that preserves the distinction of the two characters, for example, in the *Ta chi tu lun:* "One accepts *(ju)* by the power of faith; one upholds *(ji)* by the power of contemplation" (*T* 25:461a9). In Nichiren's writings, *juji* is often used to indicate a single (though continued) act; thus it seems preferable in most cases here to use one word. "Embrace" is the translation used in both Watson and Yampolsky and *Major Writings*. I am indebted to the work of Ōtani Gyōkō, which points out the centrality to Nichiren's thought of the concept of "embracing" the *Lotus Sūtra*. See, for example, his *Nichiren Shōnin kyōgaku kenkyū* or his entry on "juji" in *NJ*, pp. 189b–191d.

128. "Shōmitsu-bō gosho," *STN* 1:822.

129. *Hung-chüeh* 5–3, *T* 46:296a9–10, cited by Nichiren in *Kanjin honzon shō, STN* 1:702–703. Andō Toshio has argued that the "three thousand realms in one thought-moment" was for Chih-i simply one form of meditation and not the foundation of his system ("Ichinen sanzen-setsu no keisei"). This argument, however, is extraneous to Nichiren's reception of the doctrine.

130. *Kaimoku shō, STN* 1:604.

131. *Ichinen sanzen to wa nani ka*, pp. 61–63.

132. "Toki Nyūdō-dono gohenji," *STN* 2:1522.

133. *Kaimoku shō, STN* 1:539. See also *Jisshō shō:* "The three thousand realms in

one thought-moment has its textual source in the [passage of the trace teaching concerning] the ten suchnesses and the true aspect . . . but its meaning is confined to the teaching of origin" (*STN* 1:489).

134. *Kaimoku shō, STN* 1:552.

135. The Tripiṭaka, shared, separate and perfect teachings. These are the four teachings of conversion *(kehō no shikyō)*, a T'ien-t'ai classification of the Buddhist teachings according to content. See chap. 1, n. 47. In T'ien-t'ai doctrine, a distinction was drawn between the "pure perfect teaching," or the *Lotus Sūtra*, which is not mixed with provisional teachings, and the perfect teaching as a doctrinal strand found in sūtras other than the *Lotus.* Ch'an-jan, however, asserted that the *Lotus Sūtra* transcends the eight categories, a position developed in Japan by Enchin and upheld by Nichiren. See Hazama Jikō, *Nihon Tendai to Kamakura Bukkyō,* pp. 193–219.

136. *Kamakura shin Bukkyō shisō no kenkyū,* p. 623. Other works in the Nichiren collection explicitly state this understanding of *ichinen sanzen,* or the mutual inclusion of the ten realms, in terms of original enlightenment. For example, an early work, the *Jippōkai ji,* written in 1259, reads, "The trace teaching merely expounds the mutual inclusion of the ten worlds in terms of acquired enlightenment *(shikaku).* It does not yet reveal the inherent mutual inclusion of the ten realms with respect to original enlightenment *(hongaku)*" (*STN* 1:142). The *Kyōgyōshō gosho,* assigned the date of 1278 in *STN,* interprets the Buddha's enlightenment in the remote past, described in the "Fathoming the Lifespan" chapter of the *Lotus,* to mean that "the realm of living beings, or ordinary worldlings like ourselves, submerged since the beginningless past in the sufferings of the round of birth and death, who never even dreamed of reaching the other shore of the Buddha Way, is defined as the triple body of [the Tathâgata of] unproduced original enlightenment. Truly it teaches the ultimate principle of three thousand realms in one thought-moment" (*STN* 2:1485). The earliest notice of this text is a fifteenth-century transcription. Asai Yōrin (*Nichiren Shōnin kyōgaku no kenkyū,* pp. 294, 304–305) and Tamura (*Kamakura shin Bukkyō shisō no kenkyū,* pp. 619, 623) have questioned it because of its use of original enlightenment ideas, while Yamakawa Chiō regarded it as authentic (*Nichiren Shōnin den jikkō,* p. 634), as, apparently, does Miyazaki Eishū (*NSIJ,* p. 246a–d). It does not in my opinion contain anything at odds with Nichiren's authenticated writings.

137. A useful discussion of the fivefold comparison is Komatsu Kuniaki, "Gojū sōtai," *NJ,* pp. 96c–97c. Nichiren does not use the terms *kyōsō* and *kanjin* in the *Kaimoku shō;* the term *kanjin* in the last stage of the fivefold comparison derives from his other major essay, *Kanjin honzon shō,* discussed below.

138. *Kaimoku shō,* p. 539. For Nichiren's emphasis on the mutual encompassing of the ten realms as central to the *ichinen sanzen* concept, see Mochizuki Kankō, *Nichiren kyōgaku no kenkyū,* p. 116, and Kanno Hiroshi, *Ichinen sanzen to wa nani ka,* pp. 68–69. While the possibility of influence on Nichiren remains to be investigated, it is worth noting that this concept plays an important role in the Taimitsu thought of Annen, who used it to argue the essential unity of the *Lotus* and the esoteric teachings (Asai Endō, *Jōko Nihon Tendai honmon shisōshi,* pp. 763–64).

139. See, for example, *Senji shō,* 2:1003–1004; Watson and Yampolsky, pp. 183–84. The identification of the *Lotus Sūtra*'s promise of universal Buddhahood with the mutual possession of the ten realms occurs in Nichiren's first extant essay, the *Kaitai*

sokushin jōbutsu gi, STN 1:10–11, and is explored in later writings as his thinking developed. See also *Ichidai shōgyō taii, STN* 1:70, 73 and *Kanjin honzon shō* 1:704–707; Watson and Yampolsky, pp. 153–57.

140. See chap. 2, n. 31.

141. *STN* 1:719.

142. "Shijō Kingo-dono gohenji," *STN* 1:635.

143. Strictly speaking, *Myōhō-renge-kyō*, the title of the *Lotus Sūtra*, is written with five Chinese characters, while the chanted invocation, Namu-myōhō-renge-kyō, is written with seven. However, Nichiren often uses them interchangeably.

144. *STN* 1:392.

145. "Sōya Nyōdō-dono gohenji," *STN* 267.2:1410.

146. *STN* 1:396.

147. STN 1:395.

148. *Shō Hokke daimoku shō, STN* 1:202, 203.

149. See, for example, *Ichidai shōgyō taii, STN* 1:71.

150. The "fifth of the five hundred year periods" is a reference to five stages of decline following the nirvāṇa of the Buddha described in the *Ta-chi ching* and refers to the beginning of the Final Dharma age (*T* 13:363a29–b5). Interpretation of the phrase *kanjin honzon* has been an issue of longstanding controversy within the Nichiren tradition; variant readings include "contemplating the object of worship, which is the mind" *(kokoro no honzon o kanzu);* "the object of worship for contemplating the mind" *(kanjin no honzon);* and "the contemplation of the mind and the object of worship" *(kanjin to honzon)* (*NSIJ*, p. 888a). I have opted for the last of these, as it allows for the most interpretive flexibility. English translations include Murano Senchū, trans., *Nyorai metsugo go gohyakusai shi kanjin honzon shō, or The True Object of Worship,* and Watson and Yampolsky, pp. 148–180.

151. *STN* 1:704.

152. *STN* 1:706.

153. *STN* 1:711. The sūtra quotes are at *T* 9:388b12–13 and 6c6.

154. The idea that this enlightenment is transferred "naturally" *(jinen ni)* in the act of embracing the *daimoku* has parallels in notions about the natural working of Amida's vow *(jinen hōni)* and the naturalness *(jinen)* of original enlightenment. See, for example, Takagi Yutaka, *Heian jidai Hokke Bukkyōshi kenkyū,* pp. 474–82.

155. "Nichimyō Shōnin gosho," *STN* 1:644–45. The quotations from the *Lotus* are at *T* 9:14c26–27 and 8b4–5, respectively.

156. No major controversy seems to have occurred within the premodern Nichiren tradition over the importance of faith versus the verbal act of chanting, or over the importance of the number of *daimoku* recited, as happened among Hōnen's disciples with respect to the *nenbutsu.* Nor does Nichiren's idea of faith lend itself to more modern debates about interiority versus outward ritual or praxis, etc. The mind of faith and the chanting of the *daimoku* are always coordinated in his thought.

157. *Kanjin honzon shō, STN* 1:706.

158. *Shishin gohon shō, STN* 2:1296.

159. See, for example, Watanabe Hōyō, "Nichiren Shōnin no busshu ron," and Ōtani Gyōkō, "Nichiren Shōnin no san'yaku ron."

160. *Hsüan-i* 1a, *T* 33:684a9–14; *Wen-chü* 1a, *T* 34:2c1–9. See also Hibi Senshun, "Tendai kyōgaku ni okeru busshu no geshu to busshō," and Asai Endō, "San'yaku," *NJ*, pp. 138b–139a. I have borrowed the translation of these terms as "sowing" *(shu),*

"maturing" *(juku)* and the "harvest [of liberation]" *(datsu)* from Watson and Yampolsky, p. 106.

161. For examples, see Asai Endō, *Jōko Nihon Tendai honmon shisōshi,* p. 151.

162. "Akimoto gosho," *STN* 2:1731.

163. *Kaimoku shō, STN* 1:579, Watson and Yampolsky, p. 106; *Kanjin honzon shō,* p. 711, Watson and Yampolsky, p. 164.

164. *Kyōgyōshō gosho, STN* 2:1480. Nichiren's major discussions of the *daimoku* as the seed of Buddhahood in the Final Dharma age occur here, pp. 1479–80, and in the *Kanjin honzon shō, STN* 1:714–15, Watson and Yampolsky, pp. 168–71.

165. "Ueno-ama gozen gohenji," *STN* 2:1890. This passage seems related to medieval Tendai transmissions which assert that the lotus flower derives its name from the *Lotus* as Dharma, rather than the other way around.

166. As Asai Endō points out, Nichiren's idea that all beings, while endowed with the Buddha nature, must have received the seed of Buddhahood to realize it has a precedent in Saichō, who speaks of the bodhisattva precepts as conferring the "seed of the Buddha nature" ("Nihon Tendai no busshō ron," pp. 358–59).

167. *Kanjin honzon shō, STN* 1:711, 712. See chap. 1, n. 96.

168. Ibid., p. 720.

169. Scholars who stress the cleavage between Nichiren's thought and that of medieval Tendai often cite as evidence for their position his emphasis on the need to receive the seed of Buddhahood, which does in fact differ in emphasis from the idea of a purely immanent original enlightenment. However, it should be noted in passing that there are writings in the Nichiren collection—albeit deemed problematic by some scholars—that discuss the *daimoku* in more immanentalist terms. For example, this passage in the *Hokke shōshin jōbutsu shō:*

[T]he Buddha nature of us, sentient beings; the Buddha nature of Brahma and Indra; the Buddha nature of Śāriputra and Maudgalyāyana; the Buddha nature of Mañjuśrī and Maitreya; and the Wonderful Dharma that represents the awakening of all Buddhas of the three time periods are one and nondual: This principle is called Myōhō-renge-kyō. When once we chant [Namu-]myōhō-renge-kyō, with just that single sound we summon forth and manifest [the Buddha nature of] all Buddhas, all dharmas, all bodhisattvas, all śrāvakas, all Brahmās, Indras, Dharma King Yamas, the sun and moon, the stars, the gods of heaven and earth, down to all hell dwellers, hungry ghosts, beasts, asuras, humans and devas, and the Buddha nature within the minds of all sentient beings. This merit is unfathomable and boundless. When we venerate Myōhō-renge-kyō that is our own mind as the object of worship, the Buddha nature within our own mind is summoned by our chanting of Namu-myhō-renge-kyō and appears; this is called Buddha. (*STN* 2:1432–33).

A very similar passage appears in the *Shōgu mondō shō* (*STN* 1:387). The authenticity of both works has been questioned (*NSIJ*, pp. 1039b, 534b).

170. *Hōon shō, STN* 2:1248.

171. *Honzon mondō shō, STN* 2:1573, 1574–75.

172. "Nichigennyo Shakabutsu kuyō ji," *STN* 2:1623.

173. On Nichiren's view of the *kami,* see Ueda Honshō, "Nichiren Shōnin no shingikan"; Fujii Manabu, "Nichiren to shingi"; and Takagi Yutaka, "Nichiren no shisō no keishō to hen'yō," pp. 582–89.

174. That the Buddha possesses the "three virtues" *(santoku)* of parent, teacher, and sovereign is a frequent theme in Nichiren's writings and derives from the verse

in the "Parable" (third) chapter of the *Lotus:* "Now this threefold world/is all my domain./The beings in it/are all my children. /Yet this world has many cares and troubles/from which I alone can save and protect them" (*T* 9:14c26–28). For an early example of this aspect of Nichiren's thought, see "Nanjō Hyōe Shichirō-dono gosho," *STN* 1:320–21; *Major Writings* 6:22.

175. On this concept of the Buddha in Nichiren's thought, see Satō Hiroo, "Nichiren no kōki no shisō," pp. 51–55, and, for its development among his later followers, Takagi Yutaka, "Nichiren no shisō no keishō to hen'yō," pp. 589–95.

176. Takagi Yutaka, *Nichiren to sono montei,* p. 68.

177. The revised edition of the *Gohonzon shū mokuroku,* Yamanaka Kihachi, ed., contains photographic plates and descriptions of 123 mandalas in Nichiren's hand. Watanabe Hōyō and Kitagawa Zenchō identify five additional holographic mandalas that are not included in this collection (*Nichiren no iitakatta koto,* p. 179). As noted by Mochizuki Kankō (*Nichiren kyōgaku no kenkyū,* p. 170), also missing from this count are those holographic mandalas belonging to the Taisekiji, head temple of Nichiren Shōshū, or to its branch temples. This sect of Nichiren Buddhism accords the mandala *(gohonzon)* an absolute sacrality and does not permit those in its possession to be photographed.

178. Takagi Yutaka, *Nichiren to sono montei,* p. 56; Watanabe Hōyō, "Daimandara to Hokkedō," pp. 90–95.

179. For an early example, see *Shō Hokke daimoku shō, STN* 1:202. Mochizuki Kankō also suggests, based on the evidence of several of Nichiren's letters, that he had enshrined the scrolls of the sūtra, placing them before an image of Śākyamuni, in his small temple on Mt. Minobu (*Nichiren kyōgaku no kenkyū,* pp. 162–63).

180. See, for example, "Mama Shakabutsu gokuyō oijō," *STN* 1:457; "Shijō Kingo Shakabutsu kuyō ji," *STN* 2:1182–83, *Major Writings* 6:159–63; and "Nichigennyo Shakabutsu kuyō ji," *STN* 2:1623–25. The merit of making statues or paintings of Śākyamuni is also praised in "Zenmui Sanzō shō," *STN* 1:469, *Major Writings* 4:69.

181. This was a *zuishinbutsu,* or personal image small enough to carry. According to tradition, during his exile to Izu, Nichiren received this image from the *jitō* or steward of Ito, in gratitude for Nichiren's prayers for his recovery from illness. The Buddha image, it is said, had been drawn up from the sea in a catch of fish ("Funamori Yasaburō moto gosho," *STN* 1:230; *Major Writings* 2:54). However, the authenticity of the writing in which these events appear is in dispute, so their historicity is difficult to assess (Stone, "Some Disputed Texts in the Nichiren Corpus," pp. 201–203). Nichiren mentions his personal image of Śākyamuni in several personal letters. It was given after his death to his disciple Daikoku Ajari Nichirō (*Goyuimotsu haibun no koto, NSZ* 1:55).

182. "Shibosatsu zōryū shō," *STN* 2:1647, 1648.

183. "Jōshūin honzon shōgyō no koto," *STN* 3:2729.

184. Mochizuki Kankō, *Nichiren kyōgaku no kenkyū,* pp. 175–76.

185. "Ikki shoshū zenkon kiroku," *NSZ* 1:445.

186. In the late 1920s and early 1930s, a number of heated exchanges on this issue took place, the chief participants being Tanabe Zenchi, Honda Nisshō, Shimizu Ryūzan, and Yamakawa Chiō. Their arguments are outlined in Takahashi Ken'yū, "Shimizu Ryūzan," pp. 265–69. Among postwar contributors to the debate, Mochizuki Kankō (1881–1967) argued that Nichiren intended the eternal Buddha to have primacy as object of worship (*Nichiren kyōgaku no kenkyū,* pp. 141–83); Tokoro Shige-

moto (1911–1977) asserted that the Dharma as object of worship represents orthodoxy (*Nichiren kyōgaku no shisōshi kenkyū*, pp. 409–62); and Motai Kyōkō (b. 1904),
maintained that the object of worship unites the aspects of both "Buddha" and
"Dharma" ("Honzon no genri to keisei").

187. See, for example, *Fuji isseki monto zonchi no koto, NSZ* 2:124. This position
cannot be confirmed as Nikkō's own view and probably represents a retrospective
construction on the part of his later followers (Mochizuki Kankō, *Nichiren kyōgaku
no kenkyū*, pp. 291–92; Shigyō Kaishū, *Kōmon kyōgaku no kenkyū*, p. 112). This difference in *honzon* as a marker of sectarian identity can still be observed among modern Nichiren denominations. Nichiren Shōshū, a modern descendant of the Fuji
school, insists on the exclusive orthodoxy of the mandala, while Nichirenshū, which
represents the Minobu line, frequently employs images of Śākyamuni flanked by the
four bodhisattvas.

188. "'Honzon' zakkō." The reference to Nichiren appears on p. 20.

189. See, for example, Sonoda Kōyū, "Sentokuzō to honzon."

190. *Kanjin honzon shō, STN* 1:703, 711.

191. See, for example, *Mokue nizō kaigen no koto, STN* 1:791–94, translated in *Major Writings* 4:28–35; and "Shijō Kingo Shakabutsu kuyō ji," *STN* 2:1183; *Major Writings,* 6:161–62.

192. See Watanabe Hōyō, "Daimandara to Hokkedō," pp. 95–110.

193. "Nichinyo gozen gohenji," *STN* 2:1375.

194. This has been suggested by Sonoda Kōyū, "Sentokuzō to honzon." Sonoda's
discussion focuses on the "assemblies" depicted on six shrines *(zushi)* used for holding texts, one for each of the six Buddhist schools, that were installed in the Tōdaiji
near the time that the great Buddha image was completed (752). He has also found
(p. 223) that Nichiren's mandala almost exactly replicates the configuration of a
painting of the preaching of the *Lotus Sūtra (Hokke sessō zu),* dated 686, that is preserved at the Hasedera in Nara.

195. Asai Endō, *Jōko Nihon Tendai honmon shisōshi,* p. 108; Tsumori Kiichi, "Ryōzen
jōdo shinkō no keifu," p. 32.

196. For Tendai *honzon* incorporating jeweled stūpa imagery, see Kawakatsu Kenryō, "Tendai Tahōtō no honzon." On jeweled stūpa mandalas, see Tanabe, *The Paintings of the Lotus Sūtra,* pp. 102–108. Several essays on the concept and iconography
of the jeweled stūpa in Japanese Buddhism are collected in Kawakatsu's *Tahōtō to
Hokekyō shisō.*

197. Sakai Kyōjun, "Nichiren Shōnin ni miru taimitsu no eikyō," pp. 58–60. See
also Komatsu Kuniaki, "Nichiren Shōnin to shingon mikkyō," in which he argues,
against Sakai, that Nichiren's mandala cannot be seen as a simple extension of Taimitsu antecedents but reflects his doctrinal grounding in the origin chapter of the
Lotus Sūtra. On the origins of the *Hokke mandara* and its development within Taimitsu, see Asai Endō, *Jōko Nihon Tendai honmon shisōshi,* pp. 456–527, and "Honzon ron
no tenkai."

198. *Yokawa Ryōzen-in zōryū anmon* (1296), reproduced in Kageyama Haruki,
Hieizanji, pp. 124–27. Since this document includes a request for necessary repairs,
the iconographic configuration itself would be older than this. See also Haruki's discussion, pp. 128–29. The paintings are also mentioned in *Keiran shūyō shū* 92, *T*
76:800b8–11. My thanks to Kevin Carr for explaining to me iconographic terms in
the Yokawa document.

199. *THR*, pp. 71–72.

200. See, for example, "Shijō Kingo-dono gohenji," *STN* 1:666, *Major Writings* 5:147; *Mokue nizō kaigen no koto, STN* 1:792, *Major Writings* 4:32.

201. This has been noted by Takagi Yutaka, *Nichiren: Sono kōdō to shisō*, pp. 169–70, and by Watanabe Hōyō and Kitagawa Zenchō, *Nichiren no iitakatta koto*, pp. 173–77.

202. *Sanji raishaku, DNBZ* 13:131a–44b; Tanabe, *Myōe the Dreamkeeper*, pp. 112–14.

203. These are discussed in his *Songō shinzō meimon*, translated as *Notes on the Inscription on Sacred Scrolls*, ed. Yoshifumi Ueda.

204. *Nichiren: Sono kōdō to shisō*, pp. 167–71. On the other hand, when Nichiren's later disciples began to proselytize in Kyoto and won converts among the aristocracy, they sometimes felt the need to modify the mandala in response to the aesthetic demands of their patrons, for example, by painting part or all of it in visual images rather than characters (*NJ*, p. 378b).

205. *STN* 2:1376. "Gaining entrance by faith" is a reference to *MFLHC, p'in* 2, *T* 9:15b18; "honestly discarding skillful means," to 10a19; and "not accepting even a single verse from other sūtras," to 16a28–29.

Asai Yōrin (*Nichiren Shōnin kyōgaku kenkyū*, pp. 272–73, 278–80) and Tamura Yoshirō (*Kamakura shin Bukkyō shisō no kenkyū*, p. 619) have questioned the authenticity of the "Nichinyo gozen gohenji" on account of its use of *hongaku* ideas. Miyazaki Eishū, however, finds such criticisms to be subjective and lacking in concrete demonstration (*NSIJ*, p. 863a–b).

206. See, for example, Taikō Yamasaki, *Shingon*, pp. 156–63 *passim*.

207. For Nichiren's understanding of the precepts, see Kageyama Gyōō, "Nichiren Shōnin no kai shisō ni tsuite."

208. "Onkoromo narabi ni hitoe gosho," *STN* 2:1111; "Myōmitsu Shōnin goshō-soku," 2:1165. A longstanding tradition holds that Nichiren's sole personal violation of the precepts was the drinking of sake. This is probably based on the fact that his letters thanking lay followers for offerings of food, clothing, and other necessities sometimes list sake among the items received. One such letter written the winter before Nichiren's death specifically states that he drank the offered sake for medicinal purposes ("Ueno-dono haha ama gozen gohenji," 2:1896–97).

209. See, for example, "Nanjō Hyōe Shichirō-dono gosho," *STN* 1:322.

210. *Jippōkai myōinga shō, STN* 1:183. See also *Ichidai shōgyō taii*, 1:70, and *Shugo kokka ron*, 1:95. The sūtra quote is at *MFLHC, p'in* 11, *T* 9:34b17.

211. *Kyōgyōshō gosho, STN* 2:1488. This passage assimilates to the chanting of the *daimoku* Saichō's concept of precept ordination as guaranteeing one's realization of Buddhahood. See note 136 above for varying opinions on the authenticity of this text.

212. Watanabe Hōyō suggests that, since such a center could be established only after victory in debate and confrontation with other sects, Nichiren deliberately refrained from writing or speaking about it in detail for reasons of discretion (*Nichiren-shū shingyōron no kenkyū*, pp. 71–72).

213. The earliest notice of this text appears in the *Hon'in-myō kuketsu* of Sanmi Nichijun (1294–1354/56) of the Fuji school (*FSY* 2:72). Throughout the premodern period, with some exceptions, it was generally accepted as authentic. In modern times, its authenticity was challenged by Tanabe Zenchi, Shioda Gisen, and others but upheld by Yamakawa Chiō. The arguments to date on both sides are summarized by Suzuki Ichijō, who suggests the text may be a transcription made by one of Nichiren's leading disciples of his oral teachings (*Nichiren Shōnin goibun kōgi* 7:352–56),

and in the entry "Sandai hihō honjō ji" (*NSIJ*, pp. 420c–22a) by Miyazaki Eishū, who assesses doubts about the text's authenticity as "for the most part subjective arguments that stop at mere assertion." Computer analyses, conducted in 1980 and 1992 under the auspices of the Ministry of Education, suggest that it is probably authentic. See Itō Zuiei and Murakami Masakatsu, "*Sandai hihō honjō ji* no keiryō bunkengaku-teki shin kenkyū." However, these findings have already found at least one challenger (Kanmuri Ken'ichi, "Monbusho tōkei sūri kenkyūjo no *Sandai hihō honjō ji* shinsaku-setsu ni taisuru gigi"), who identifies serious problems with the data base that might possibly affect the analysis. Thus the matter remains inconclusive. The text does indeed present some questionable points; for example, it explicitly identifies Nichiren as the leader of the bodhisattvas who emerged from the earth (*STN* 2:1865), whereas Nichiren's authenticated writings tend to be more indirect in speaking of his connection with Superior Conduct. However, this could also be the result of later interpolation and does not necessarily prove the entire text apocryphal.

214. When the True Dharma of the Buddha Joy Increasing was reaching its end, the monk Awakened Virtue (Jpn. Kakutoku) was attacked by evil monks who violated the precepts, and King Possessing Virtue (Utoku) came to his defense. In a later lifetime, the king was reborn as Śākyamuni Buddha (*Ta-pan-nieh-p'an ching* 3, *T* 12:383c20–384a18). Nichiren used this story to illustrate both the ruler's obligation to defend the Dharma and the blessings that accrue from so doing. See, for example, the *Risshō ankoku ron*, *STN* 1:222; Watson and Yampolsky, pp. 33–34.

215. *STN* 2:1864–65.

216. *MFLHC*, p'in 21, *T* 9:52a25–26.

217. See, for example, Tokoro Shigemoto, *Nichiren no shisō to Kamakura Bukkyō*, pp. 152–67. In the introduction to his translation of the *Sandai hihō shō*, Pier P. Del Campana rightly assesses this move as "stem[ming] from the desire of many of Nichiren's followers and sympathizers to bring his doctrine in line with the modern idea of separation between Church and State" ("'*Sandai hihō-shō*: An Essay on the Three Great Mysteries' by Nichiren," p. 209). It should be noted, however, that some Nichiren denominations still maintain the ideal of a establishing a formal *kaidan*, though not necessarily an imperially sponsored one. These include Nichiren Shōshū and the Kokuchūkai.

218. This has been argued by Suzuki Ichijō (*Nichiren Shōnin goibun kōgi*, 7:355) and by Watanabe Hōyō (*Nichirenshū shingyōron no kenkyū*, pp. 71–76).

219. *MFLHC*, *T* 9:42b26–27.

220. *STN* 1:712. The phrase "original time" derives from Chih-i, who uses it to denote the the time of the Buddha's original enlightenment (*Hsüan-i* 7a, *T* 33:767a13–15). There has been considerable controversy within the Nichiren tradition over whether the "three thousand realms of one's mind" (*koshin sanzen*) in this passage refers to the thought-moment of the original Buddha or the thought-moment of ordinary worldlings. See, for example, Mochizuki Kankō, *Nichiren kyōgaku no kenkyū*, p. 115; Tokoro Shigemoto and Takagi Yutaka, eds., *Nichiren*, p. 431a–b.

221. *Hung-chüeh* 5–3, *T* 46:295c23–24. See also n. 48 above.

222. *Nyosetsu shugyō shō*, *STN* 1:733.

223. For discussion of the "Pure Land of Sacred Eagle Peak" in Nichiren's thought, see, for example, Mochizuki Kankō, *Nichiren kyōgaku no kenkyū*, pp. 225–52, and Komatsu Yasutaka, "Nichiren no ryōzen ōkei shisō."

224. See chap. 4, n. 40.

225. *MFLHC, p'in* 16, *T* 9:43c4–17; Hurvitz, pp. 243–44, modified.

226. Cited in Chi-tsang (549–623)'s *Fa-hua hsüan-lun* 9, *T* 34:441c4–5.

227. Tsumori Kiichi, "Ryōzen jōdo shinkō no keifu," pp. 24–25. The actual term *ryōzen jōdo* may have first been used by Saichō, who employs it to refer to the pure land of Śākyamuni Buddha in his original ground, and as equivalent to the "truth that is the highest meaning" (*Naishō Buppō kechimyaku fu, DDZ* 1:215).

228. For these and other examples, see Tsumori Kiichi, "Ryōzen jōdo shinkō no keifu," pp. 30–31.

229. "Shijō Kingo-dono gohenji," *STN* 2:1801; "Nanjō Hyōe Shichirō-dono gohenji," 2:1884.

230. *Kanke bunsō* 4, no. 250, *Nihon koten bungaku taikei* 72:301.

231. Tsumori Kiichi, "Ryōzen Jōdo shinkō no keifu," pp. 33–44. In particular, Tsumori offers a detailed discussion of a liturgy *(kōshiki)* composed by Jōkei expressing aspiration for the Pure Land of Sacred Eagle Peak.

232. See Takagi Yutaka, *Heian jidai Hokke Bukkyōshi kenkyū,* pp. 456–63.

233. In the *Hokke daimoku shō* (1266), Nichiren says that women who have faith in the *Lotus Sūtra* can achieve birth in the Pure Land of Utmost Bliss (*STN* 1:404; *Major Writings* 3:26). This is probably in reference to a passage of the sūtra itself, which says that a woman who practices the sūtra will go after death to the Tranquil and Happy Land, the Pure Land of Amitāyus (*MFLHC, p'in* 23, *T* 9:54b29–c2). Later, Nichiren wrote that the Buddha referred to in this chapter is not the Amida of the Western Pure Land but an emanation of Śākyamuni (*Hokke shoshin jōbutsu shō, STN* 2:1429; *Major Writings* 6:202).

234. Komatsu Yasutaka, "Nichiren no ryōzen ōkei shisō," pp. 110–11; Satō Hiroo, "Nichiren no kōki no shisō," pp. 57–58.

235. This has been convincingly argued by Satō Hiroo, "Nichiren no kōki no shisō," pp. 55–59.

236. *Jigyō nenbutsu mondō, DNBZ* 31:212b.

237. "Kanjin honzon shō sōejō," *STN* 1:721.

238. "Sennichi-ama gohenji," *STN* 2:1761.

239. Komatsu Yasutaka, "Nichiren no ryōzen ōkei shisō," pp. 103–105.

240. "Shijō kingo-dono gohenji," *STN* 1:894.

241. "Kyōdai shō," *STN* 1:921.

242. *Shishin gohon shō, STN* 2:1296.

243. A structural similarity exists here between Nichiren's idea of salvation through "reverse connection" and Saichō's concept of the embracing the bodhisattva precepts. In his *Isshin denjitsu kaimon,* Saichō quotes the *P'u-sa ying-lo pen-yeh ching* to the effect that it is better to embrace the precepts and break them than never to receive them at all, because by receiving them, one enters the company of the bodhisattvas, while one who never receives them remains a nonbeliever (*T* 24:1021b15–16, cited in *DDZ* 1:555–56 and translated by Groner, *Saichō,* p. 151).

244. See, for example, Tokoro Shigemoto, *Nichiren no shisō to Kamakura Bukkyō,* p. 476.

245. Sakai Kyōjun, "Nichiren Shōnin ni miru taimitsu no eikyō."

246. I am partially indebted for this insight to the essays of Suguro Shinjō. See, for example, his "Nichiren ni okeru kaie no shisō to kyōdan no mondai."

247. *Shoshō mondō shō, STN* 1:25. The "commentary" here referred to appears to be Hsüan-i 3b, T 33:713a27–28, but the wording has been somewhat altered.

248. "Hakii Saburō-dono gohenji," *STN* 1:749. See also "Kōnichi-bō gosho," in

which Nichiren assures a follower that her faith in the *Lotus Sūtra* will expiate the sins committed by her son, a warrior, who killed others and was killed himself in battle (*STN* 2:1158–61; *Major Writings* 4:164–67).

249. "Myōmitsu Shōnin goshōsoku," *STN* 2:1166.

250. A critique of Nichiren's teaching in this regard appears in Tokoro Shigemoto, *Nichiren no shisō to Kamakura Bukkyō*, pp. 504–22.

Chapter Seven: Hokke-Tendai Interactions and the Emergence of a Nichiren *Hongaku* Discourse

1. Two significant examples in English are Dobbins' *Jōdo Shinshū* and Bodiford's *Sōtō Zen in Medieval Japan*.

2. During the Muromachi period, the term "Nichirenshū" was occasionally used by persons outside the Hokkeshū, usually with pejorative connotations. By the end of the medieval period, however, the designation "Nichirenshū" had come to be employed both inside and outside the tradition (*Zenshi*, p. 80).

3. *Shūso gosenge kiroku*, *NSZ* 2:101–102.

4. See *NJ*, p. 604c–d, for references to the scholarship on this issue.

5. The *nichi-gō* was employed almost universally among monks of the Nichiren tradition up until the Meiji period. It is still used by some ranking clerics and has occasionally been assumed by lay leaders (such as Niwano Nikkyō, founder of the new religious movement Risshō Kōsei Kai). Nichiren himself instituted this practice, giving names beginning with character *nichi* to his monk disciples and to some of his female followers, both lay women and those who had taken religious vows. (These are the women who appear in his writings as Nichimyō Shōnin, Nichinyo, Nichigennyo, Nichigon-ama, etc.) While use of the *nichi-gō* in premodern and early modern times no doubt served to instill a sense of identity with the founder, Nichiren, the proliferation over time of names beginning with *nichi-* can be confusing when reading or writing about the history of the tradition. To minimize such confusion, whenever a particular figure is introduced, I have given, in addition to the *nichi-gō*, either that person's *ācārya* title *(ajari-gō)* or the name of the cloister or hall *(in-gō, bō-gō)* at his temple of residence by which he was also known.

6. *Zenshi*, pp. 300–306.

7. *Dentō shō*, *NSZ* 18:30.

8. Watanabe Hōyō, "Honjaku ron no tenkai," pp. 279–81.

9. These are discussed in detail in Mochizuki Kankō, *Nichiren kyōgaku no kenkyū*, pp. 253–362. See also Asai Yōrin, *Nichiren Shōnin kyōgaku no kenkyū*, pp. 611–32, and Watanabe Hōyo, "Honjaku ron," *NJ*, pp. 372a–373d.

10. A sole, early exception was a debate within Nikkō's lineage, which belonged to the *shōretsu* faction, over whether or not the "Skillful Means" chapter of the trace teaching should be recited (*Zenshi*, pp. 178–80; Watanabe Hōyō, "Honjakuron no tenkai," pp. 284–92).

11. Mochizuki Kankō, *Nichiren kyōgaku no kenkyū*, pp. 271–72.

12. Motai Kyōkō, "Chūsei ni okeru Nichiren kyōgaku no tenkai," especially pp. 574, 577.

13. "Toki Nyūdō-dono gohenji," *STN* 2:1588–91; *Major Writings* 7:129–34. *STN* assigns this letter to the year 1278. Alternative suggestions include 1277, 1279, or sometime during the Bun'ei era (1264–1275). See Takahashi Ken'yū, "Tendai gakusō Shinson ni tsuite," n. 2, pp. 63–64.

14. *Chi* 9c, *T* 34:337a25.

15. Ono Bunkō, "Senba to Nichiren monka to no kōryū," p. 429.

16. The identification of Ryōshō-bō with Shinson appears in the *Tōke shūshi myōmoku* by Honjōin Nichijitsu (n. d.) of the Nakayama school (*Nichiren Shōnin denki shū*, p. 553a). The date of this work is uncertain: the colophon gives 1461, which is upheld by Mochizuki Kankō in *Nichirenshū shūgakushi* (p. 260). However, Shigyō Kaishū points out that the text contains a reference to the year Ōnin 1 (1467) and so would have to be later than that (*Nichirenshū kyōgakushi*, p. 69). The *Nihon daishi sentoku myōshō ki* also says that Shinson was called Ryōshō-bō (*DNBZ* 111:273). Although these notices are late, the evidence for the identity of Shinson and Ryōshō-bō is strong and has been upheld by Shima Chiryō ("Taitō kōshō shikō" 1, p. 41) and Oka Kyōzui ("Nihon Tendai kuden hōmon no yurai oyobi sono hattatsu" 3, pp. 40–41). For discussion in postwar scholarship, see Takahashi Ken'yū, "Tendai gakusō Shinson ni tsuite," pp. 53–54, and Ono Bunkō, "Senba to Nichiren monka to no kōryū," pp. 427–30. Ono additionally points out that Ryōshō-bō's arguments in the debate with Jōnin as represented in Nichiren's letter are consistent with what is known of Shinson's thought. On the *kuden* collection, mentioned below, that is traditionally attributed to Shinson, see Tajima Tokuon, "*Kawata Jūkutsū* ni tsuite."

17. Hazama Jikō, *Chūko Nihon Tendai no kenkyū*, pp. 91–92.

18. Taishō University Library ms. no. 130.38.1, vol. 1, p. 15. I am indebted to Stephen G. Covell and Zeng Ying for their assistance in obtaining a copy of this text. The two sūtra passages are at *MFLHC, p'in* 2, *T* 9:10a19 and 8a17–18. The importance of this text for understanding early relations between Kantō Tendai and the Hokkeshū has been noted by Shima Chiryō, "Endon Hōin Songai" (2), p. 26, and Ono Bunkō, "Senba to Nichiren monka to no kōryū," p. 444.

19. See also chap. 1, n. 48, and chap. 6, n. 246.

20. *TZ* 9:207a.

21. *Gosho shō* 2, p. 1580.

22. *Hōzenji monjo,* cited in Hayashi Senshō, "Shikan shō Hokke shisō to Senba kyōgaku," p. 236.

23. *TZ* 9:381b. Oka Kyōzui has also called attention to ideas related to notions of *"shikan* surpasses the *Lotus"* that appear in transmissions attributed to Shinga in the *Tōkai kuden shō* ("Nihon Tendai kuden hōmon no yurai oyobi sono hattatsu" [3], pp. 38–39).

24. Hayashi Senshō, "Shikan shō Hokke shisō to Senba kyōgaku," pp. 253–54, 261.

25. Ono Bunkō, "Senba to Nichiren monka to no kōryū," p. 442. According to Ono, this debate began on 1/3/1273, the anniversary of Ryōgen's death.

26. Risshō Library ms., fascicle 22, pp. 2–4. This ms. is a copy made by Saitō Yōrin in 1932 from a Meiō-era (1492–1501) transcription held by the archives of the Nakayama Hokkekyōji and destroyed in a fire in 1944. The section referred to above is reproduced in Hayashi Senshō, "Shikan shō Hokke shisō to Senba kyōgaku," pp. 242–43. See also the discussion in Ono Bunkō, "Senba to Nichiren monka to no kōryō," pp. 437–44, which draws in part on Hayashi's essay.

27. Ono Bunkō, "Senba to Nichiren monto to no kōryū," p. 443.

28. Ibid., p. 449, n. 45.

29. "Shikan shō Hokke shisō to Senba kyōgaku." In this article, Hayashi argues against Yamakawa Chiō, who had earlier proposed that the doctrine of *"shikan* sur-

passes the *Lotus*" originated with Jōmyō (*"Risshōkan jō* ni taisuru gigi ni tsuite," pp. 39–42).

30. The "Risshōkan jō sōjō," attributed to Nichiren, also represents the Danna school as rejecting the position that *"shikan* surpasses the *Lotus"* (*STN* 1:870–72). The *Tendai myōshō kuketsu shō* similarly suggests a division between Danna and Eshin schools on this point (*DNBZ* 18:268b–269b). Ono Bunkō suggests that the term "Danna" in these texts may not necessarily refer to actual Danna lineages but rather indicates those Tendai scholars who favored a more textually based approach over an extreme emphasis on *kanjin* ("Senba to Nichiren monka to no kōryū," p. 445).

31. See, for example, Hayashi Senshō, "Shikan shō Hokke shisō to Senba kyō-gaku," p. 260.

32. This has been suggested by Ono Bunkō, "Senba to Nichiren monka to no kōryū," p. 430. See also Take Kakuchō, "Eizan, Mii to Nichiren monka to no kōryū," p. 418.

33. *Jūni innen shō, NSZ* 1:302–303.

34. *Kanjin honzon shō shikenmon,* cited in Ono Bunkō, "Senba to Nichiren monka to no kōryū," p. 435.

35. Quoted in Asai Yōrin, *Nichiren Shōnin kyōgaku no kenkyū,* p. 261.

36. "On the relative superiority of the *Lotus* and Tendai *shikan,*" in *Hokke mondō shōgishō,* vol. 22, cited in Hayashi Senshō, "Shikan shō Hokke shisō to Senba kyō-gaku," p. 242.

37. The *Jippōkai ji,* a work assigned in *STN* to the year 1259, mentions the four-fold rise and fall uncritically (*STN* 1:140) but does not deal with *"shikan* surpassing the *Lotus.*" The "Risshōkan jō sōjō," which appears to be a summary of the *Risshōkan jō,* also criticizes the doctrine of *"shikan* surpasses the *Lotus* (1:870–72).

38. *STN* 1:844, 846, 849.

39. Nichiren's authorship of the *Risshōkan jō* has been questioned by Asai Yōrin, who holds that the *"shikan* surpasses the *Lotus"* doctrine was first asserted by Songai, who belonged to the generation after Nichiren (*Nichiren Shōnin kyōgaku no kenkyū,* pp. 197–202). The text's authenticity has been upheld by Yamakawa Chiō, who claims that this doctrine originated with Jōmyō (*"Risshōkan jō* ni taisuru gigi ni tsuite"), and by Hanano Michiaki, in "Nihon chūko Tendai bunken no kōsatsu" (2). A criticism of Yamakawa's position can be found in Hayashi Senshō, "Shikan shō Hokke shisō to Senba kyōgaku." While the authenticity of the *Risshōkan jō* is not Hayashi's chief concern, his thesis—that *"shikan* surpasses the *Lotus"* has roots in Shinga's thought but was only explicitly put forth by later Senba scholars—implicitly calls Nichiren's authorship into question, as, by his chronology, this doctrine would not have been known in Nichiren's lifetime.

40. "Hiei, Mii to Nichiren monka to no kōryū," pp. 416–18. Take points out that the first Tendai text to set forth the fourfold rise and fall that can be dated with certainty is the *Ichijō shō,* compiled by Shinsō in 1329. Since Shinsō and Songai were both Shinga's disciples, Take suggests that the classification of the fourfold rise and fall appeared around their time; thus the doctrine of *"shikan* surpasses the *Lotus"* would not have come into being during Nichiren's lifetime. However, if Nisshin is to be proposed as the author of the *Risshōkan jō,* one must then address the problem posed by the writing *Honjaku no koto,* which affirms the fourfold rise and fall as a teaching established by Hui-ssu and Chih-i. The *Honjaku no koto* exists in a tran-

scription made in 1614 by Jakushōin Nichiken (1560–1635), the twenty-first chief abbot of Minobu, who suggests in a colophon that it may be Nisshin's work (Asai Yōrin, *Nichiren Shōnin kyōgaku no kenkyū*, p. 266, n. 36; Nakajō Gyōshū, "Muromachi jidai no Nichiren kyōgaku to hongaku shisō," pp. 349–50).

41. See, for example, the *Gojū enki* (*NSZ* 2:90) attributed to Nikkō and the *Nichiman shō* (*NSZ* 2:405–406) of Sado Ajari Nichiman (d. 1360). Gyōgakuin Nitchō (1422–1500) also adopts the fourfold rise and fall in his *Kanjin honzon shō shiki* (*NSZ* 16:116, 203, 205, 246) and *Kanjin honzon shō kenmon* (16:324–25, 361). Shinshōin Nichion (1572–1642) also used it to argue the superiority of the *daimoku* over all other objects of worship (*Konke honzongi rakukyo, Honzon ron shiryō* 2, 530–33).

42. Takagi Yutaka, "Shunpan no hongaku shisō," pp. 174–75.

43. *Nichidai Jikken Taitō mondō ki, NSZ* 2:427.

44. *Gohonzon shichika sōjō, FSY* 1:32–33.

45. *Hyaku rokka sōjō, NSZ* 2:19.

46. *Kenmon guan ki* 3, cited in Yamakawa Chiō, "Eizan ni okeru Nichiren Shōnin no shiyū no kenkyū," p. 110.

47. An earlier (1504) work, the anti-Nichirenist polemic *Ha Nichiren gi* by the Tendai monk Enshin of Mt. Hiei, has a different and hostile version: "Nichiren was a servant of Songai Hōin of the Mudōji. A stubborn and arrogant man, he read texts of middle antiquity, aroused false views and founded a sect. He did not receive a proper transmission in Tendai studies from anyone" (cited in Yamakawa Chiō, "Eizan ni okeru Nichiren Shōnin no shiyū no kenkyū," p. 108). However, it is not certain if the "Songai Hōin of Mudōji" referred to here is the same Songai as the founder of the Senba *dangisho.* Moreover, since this statement is not addressed in the *Nisshutsu Taiin ki,* a rebuttal to the *Ha Nichiren gi* by Enmyōin Nitchō, written the same year, Yamakawa suggests that it may be a later interpolation (p. 109).

48. *Endonkai kechimyaku no koto,* cited in Asai Yōrin, *Nichiren Shōnin kyōgaku no kenkyū,* pp. 204–205.

49. This was first pointed out by Shima Chiryō in his "Taitō kōshō shikō" (1), pp. 36–37. Uesugi Bunshū erroneously accepts the tradition in *Nihon Tendai shi,* vol. 1, pp. 476–77.

50. "In general, when Nichiren's disciples go up to the capital, at first they do not seem to forget [their purpose], but later, devils possess them and they become deluded" (*Hōmon mōsarubekiyō no koto, STN* 1:448). This letter carries Nichiren's admonitions to his disciple Sanmi-bō, then studying on Mt. Hiei, as does the *Jisshō shō,* which urges Sanmi-bō to return home as soon as his studies are completed (*STN* 1:492).

51. The *Kinkō shū* of Minbu Ajari Nikō (*NSZ* 13 and 14), based on instruction he had received from Nichiren, contains a rebuttal of the doctrines of other sects, as does the *Hokke mondō shōgi shō* of Nichizen, mentioned above. These appear to have been handed down in their respective lineages as secret texts and were probably used for training in debate. See Kageyama Gyōō, *Nichiren kyōdan shi gaisetsu,* p. 37; *Zenshi,* p. 294.

52. *Zenshi,* p. 129; Kitagawa Zenchō, *Nichiren kyōgaku kenkyū,* pp. 380–81.

53. Shigyō Kaishū, *Nichirenshū kyōgaku shi,* pp. 60–62.

54. Ono Bunkō, "Senba to Nichiren monka to no kōryū," p. 437. Nissan's Danna lineage is given in the *Ichiji gogi kuden, Honzon ron shiryō* 2, pp. 290–91.

55. Shigyō Kaishū, *Nichirenshū kyōgaku shi,* p. 83.

56. For details on medieval Tendai texts in the Minobu collection, see Tamura Kansei, "Minobu bunko shozō no chūko Tendai kuden bunken ni tsuite," and Kitagawa Zenchō, *Nichiren kyōgaku kenkyū*, pp. 432–33.

57. Iwata Kyōen, "Eshin-ryū shichika kuden hōmon ni tsuite," p. 32.

58. *Ichiryū sōden hōmon shikenmon* (Minobu Bunko), cited in Asai Yōrin, "Nichiren kyōgakuchū ni kōsaku seru chūko Tendai no shisō oyobi yōsō," p. 81. Gyōgakuin Nitchō's (1422–1500) lecture on Sonshun's *Nijō shō kenmon* mentions a variety of pedagogical approaches, including cases in which disciples were first given the seven-article transmission and then instructed in the details of classic texts (cited in Shima Chiryō, "Endon Hōin Songai" [2], p. 20).

59. This appears, for example, in the *Nichiman shō* of Sado Ajari Nichiman, *NSZ* 2:404; the *Hokkeshū honmon gukyō shō* of Keirin-bō Nichiryū (1385–1464), *Nichiryū Shōnin zenshū* 11:5–6; and the *Shinryū shōden shō*, a compilation by Shōseiin Nisshū (1532–1594) of transmissions passed down from Jōfukyōin Nisshin (d. 1528), *NSZ* 10:232–33. All three are cited in Asai Yōrin, "Nichiren kyōgakuchū ni kōsaku seru chūko Tendai no shisō oyobi yōsō," pp. 69–71.

60. Tamura Kansei, "Minobu Bunko shozō no chūko Tendai kuden bunken ni tsuite," p. 647. For Songai's repudiation of his earlier vow that he would pass on the transmission he had received only to one person, see Shima Chiryō, "Endon Hōin Songai" (1), p. 56.

61. For Nitchō's biography, see in particular Murozumi Ichimyō, *Gyōgakuin Nitchō Shōnin*, and Kitagawa Zenchō, "Gyōgakuin Nitchō no kenkyū" and *Nichiren kyōgaku kenkyū*, pp. 373–86.

62. *Gengi daiichi taikō kenmon* 3, Minobu Bunko, cited in Ogami Kanchō, "Kantō no Tendaishū dangisho" (2), p. 15.

63. Kitagawa Zenchō, "Gyōgakuin Nitchō no kenkyū," p. 762.

64. The *Hiraga Hondoji keizu shidai* says that Nichii as a young man was a fellow student with Nitchō at Senba, where he was known as Shūbō-kō (*NSZ* 18:79). See Kitagawa Zenchū, "Gyōgakuin Nitchō no kenkyū," p. 762.

65. Ogami Kanchō, "Chūko Tendai ni okeru dangishō," p. 258.

66. Ibid.; "Kantō no Tendaishū dangisho" (2), p. 14–15.

67. Colophon to *Sanjin gi*, cited in Kitagawa Zenchū," "Gyōgakuin Nitchō no kenkyū," p. 763.

68. Kitagawa Zenchū, *Nichiren kyōgaku kenkyū*, p. 378.

69. Shigyō Kaishū, *Nichirenshū kyōgaku shi*, p. 79. On Shinnyo-in Nichijū and his possible influence on Nitchō's thought, see Kitagawa Zenchō, *Nichiren kyōgaku kenkyū*, pp. 387–92.

70. Tamura Kansei, "Minobu Bunko shozō no chūko Tendai kuden bunken ni tsuite," p. 650. Another, Edo period account says that Taigei, hearing of Nitchō's fame as a scholar, came to visit him on Minobu, and became his disciple after being bested in a debate that lasted three days and three nights (*Honge betsuzu Buttō ki*, p. 301).

71. *Nishidani myōmoku shi kikigaki* (Minobu Bunko), cited in Murozumi Ichimyō, *Gyōgakuin Nitchō Shōnin*, p. 41; Nakajō Gyōshū, "Muromachi jidai no Nichiren kyōgaku to hongaku shisō," p. 363, n. 7; and *Zenshi*, pp. 306–307. This record was written by Nitchō's disciple Nittō.

72. Kitagawa Zenchū, "Gyōgakuin Nitchō no kenkyū," p. 764, and *Nichiren kyōgaku kenkyū*, pp. 382–83; *Zenshi*, p. 308.

73. *Zenshi*, p. 308.

74. Kitagawa Zenchū, *Nichiren kyōgaku kenkyū*, p. 384.

75. Shigyō Kaishū, *Nichirenshū kyōgaku shi*, p. 84; *Zenshi*, pp. 308–309.

76. For discussion of Nitchō's thought, see Shigyō Kaishū, *Nichirenshū kyōgaku shi*, pp. 85–88; Mochizuki Kankō, *Nichirenshū gakusetsu shi*, pp. 116–38; Kitagawa Zenchō, *Nichiren kyōgaku kenkyu*, pp. 404–38; Serizawa Kazuo, "Gyōgakuin Nitchō to chūko Tendai shisō to no kanren ni tsuite"; and Nakajō Gyōshū, "Muromachi jidai no Nichiren kyōgaku to hongaku shisō." Kitagawa's study is particularly detailed in tracing textual evidence for Nitchō's appropriations from medieval Tendai thought (pp. 420–31).

77. *Hokke sōan shō*, cited in Mochizuki Kankō, *Nichirenshū gakusetsu shi*, p. 136.

78. *Honjaku nimon no koto*, cited in Mochizuki Kankō, *Nichirenshū gakusetsu shi*, p. 118.

79. Shigyō Kaishū, *Nichirenshū kyōgaku shi*, p. 85.

80. *Hokke sōan shō* 8:17, cited in Mochizuki Kankō, *Nichirenshū gakusetsu shi*, p. 121.

81. Kitagawa Zenchō, *Nichiren kyōgaku kenkyū*, p. 409.

82. Ibid, pp. 411–12.

83. *Hokke sōan shō* 1:46, cited in Mochizuki Kankō, *Nichirenshū gakusetsu shi*, p. 132.

84. *Hokke sōan shō* 1:9, cited in Mochizuki Kankō, *Nichirenshū gakusetsu shi*, p. 135.

85. See Mochizuki Kankō, *Nichirenshū gakusetsu shi*, pp. 135–37; Shigyō Kaishū, *Nichirenshū kyōgaku shi*, p. 88.

86. Tamura Kansei, "Minobu Bunko shozō no chūko Tendai kuden bunken ni tsuite," p. 650. Thus far I have not been able to determine Tamura's source for this information on Nichiden.

87. A leading scholar of Nichiryū's thought is Ōhira Kōryū. For Nichiryū's criticism of medieval Tendai thought—whose influence he did altogether escape—see Ōhira's "Nichiryū Shōnin no chūko Tendai gi hihan ni tsuite"; "Nichiryū kyōgaku ni okeru chūko Tendai gi"; "Muromachi jidai no Nichiren kyōgaku to hongaku shisō," etc. Also useful are Mochizuki Kankō, *Nichiren kyōgaku no kenkyū*, pp. 386–405; Kitagawa Zenchō, *Nichiren kyōgaku kenkyū*, pp. 494–621; and Serizawa Kazuo, "Kyōhanron no ichi kōsatsu."

88. In their efforts to unify Japan under their rule, the "three hegemons"—Oda Nobunaga, Toyotomi Hideyoshi, and Tokugawa Ieyasu—strove to break the autonomous power of the Buddhist institutions, including the Hokkeshū. Under Ashikaga rule, Hokke temples had usually been able to win exemptions from participating in *bakufu*-sponsored religious ceremonies, in accordance with the sect's principle that those who believe in the *Lotus* should neither receive offerings from non-believers nor give them (i.e., in the form of ritual services). However, the power of the sect had been significantly weakened by suppression under Nobunaga, and when Hideyoshi demanded in 1595 that monks representing all sects participate in a series of monthly memorial services for his deceased relatives, most of the leading Hokkeshū clerics in Kyoto felt they had no choice but to obey. Only a few dissenting voices urged that, in order to uphold the Hokke teachings, Hideyoshi should be defied, even if persecution were to result. In time, the dissenters gained considerable lay support, giving rise to the *fuju fuse* ("neither receiving [offerings] nor giving them") movement. The Hokkeshū was thus split between proponents of *fuju fuse* and *ju fuse* ("receiving but not giving"), a conciliatory position that deemed it ac-

ceptable to receive offerings from a ruler who did not yet embrace the *Lotus Sūtra*. With the establishment of the new capital in Edo, the conflict moved from western to eastern Japan. Ieyasu perceived the danger of the *fuju fuse* movement as a potential source of resistance to *bakufu* authority and moved to suppress it. In the name of protecting the sect, the *ju fuse* faction actively collaborated with the *bakufu* in this suppression. Prominent *fuju fuse* supporters were exiled or ousted from the leadership and administration of the sect's temples and seminaries, virtually all of which came under the control of the *ju fuse* faction. All *itchi* schools within the Hokkeshū were reorganized at this time with Minobu as their main head temple *(sōhonzan)*, and the doctrine of the lineage of Ichinyo-in Nichijū (1549–1623), a leading *ju fuse* figure, was adopted as the new orthodoxy. Nichijū himself became twentieth *kanju* of Minobu. Nichijū's interpretation of doctrine stressed accommodation, rather than the confrontational approach of *shakubuku* and—in part as a reaction against the medieval Tendai influence on earlier Hokke scholarship—focused heavily on the study of Chinese T'ien-t'ai. This included both the early T'ien-t'ai of Chih-i and and also Sung T'ien-t'ai, especially of the Shan-wai school. On the *fuju fuse* movement, see Miyazaki Eishū, *Fuju fuse-ha no genryū to tenkai,* and Jeffrey Hunter, "The *Fuju Fuse* Controversy in Nichiren Buddhism." On shifts in Hokke doctrinal interpretation between medieval and early modern periods, see Mochizuki Kankō, *Nichirenshū gakusetsu shi,* part 3, and Shigyō Kaishū, *Nichirenshū kyōgaku shi,* part 3. See also Ono Bunkō, "Kinsei Nichirenshū kyōgaku ni okeru kanjin shisō no tenkai" (1), pp. 92–94.

89. "Nichiren kyōgakuchū ni kōsaku seru chūko Tendai no shisō oyobi yōsō," pp. 70, 81.

90. *Nichirenshū kyōgaku shi,* p. 83.

91. On the practice of *shakubuku* and *kokka kangyō* in the medieval period, see *Zenshi,* pp. 254–77, and my "Rebuking the Enemies of the *Lotus,*" pp. 237–40.

92. According to the contemporary chronicle *Dentō shō* of Kuonjō-in Nisshin (1407–1488), as a consequence of the debate, Mochiuji ordered all believers in the Hokkeshū to be assembled, having resolved to confiscate the city's sixteen Hokkeshū temples, exile the monks, seize the fiefs of those lay followers who were samurai and behead those who were commoners. The Hokkeshū followers as a body defied his officials to do their worst, and Mochiuji was ultimately dissuaded from carrying out his threats when he received a supernatural sign *(NSZ* 18:37–38). This event is known in Nichiren Buddhist history as the Eikyō-era persecution (Eikyō *hōnan*). See *Zenshi,* pp. 256–57, 259–62.

93. Asai Yōrin, "Nichiren kyōgakuchū ni kōsaku seru chūko Tendai no shisō oyobi yōsō," p. 81.

94. *Zenshi,* pp. 125–27.

95. Shigyō Kaishū, *Kōmon kyōgaku no kenkyū,* p. 288.

96. *Honzon sando sōden, FSY* 1:41.

97. *Gohonzon sōden shō, Honzon ron shiryō* (2), p. 245.

98. On the dating of these texts, see Shigyō Kaishū, "Honzon kuden sōjōsho no kenkyū," pp. 288–93. This is to my knowledge the only work of secondary scholarship on these documents.

99. See, for example, Shigyō Kaishū's discussion of the complex textual filiation of *kuden* belonging to the Hikigayatsu, Mobara and Fuji lines *(Kōmon kyōgaku no kenkyū,* p. 58, and "Honzon kuden sōjōsho no kenkyū," pp. 293–97).

100. *Mandara sōden, NSZ* 1:221–22.

101. *Gohonzon shichika sōjō, FSY* 1:31. The quotation from Nichiren is a restatement of a passage from his *Kaimoku shō, STN* 1:552, cited in p. 264.

102. *Wen-chü* 8b, *T* 34:113b27–29.

103. *FSY* 1:36.

104. *Mandara sōden, NSZ* 1:225.

105. *Gohonzon sōden shō, Honzon ron shiryō* (2), pp. 312–13.

106. See for example *Shōji ichidaiji kechimyaku shō, STN* 1:524; *Major Writings* 1:24.

107. *Mandara sōden, NSZ* 1:226.

108. *Mandara sōden, NSZ* 1:228.

109. *Gohonzon shichika sōjō, FSY* 1:31. This quotation alludes to a passage from Nichiren's *Hōon shō:* "If Nichiren's compassion is vast and great, Namu-myōhō-renge-kyō will spread into the future for ten thousand years and more" (*STN* 2:1248).

110. *Gohonzon jikkaishū no koto, Honzon ron shiryō* (2), pp. 378–79. A very similar passage appears in the *Honzon no kikigaki, Honzon ron shiryō* (2), pp. 324–25. "Sun seed" is given as one of five personal names of the Buddha in the *Shih-chia-shih p'u, T* 50:85a12–13. According to Nichiren, the Buddha was called "Sun Seed" as a child because his mother, Lady Māyā, dreamt that she had conceived the sun (*Senji shō, STN* 2:1045; Watson and Yampolsky, p. 232). His source may have been the *Fo-pen-hsing chi ching, T* 3:674b28.

111. *FSY* 1:28.

112. See, for example, *Hon'in-myō kuketsu, FSY* 2:78.

113. The Sōka Gakkai dates its founding from 11/18/1930, publication date of the first volume of *Sōka kyōiku-gaku taikei* (System of value-creating education), written by its founder Makiguchi Tsunesaburō (1871–1944). However, the organization—then known as the Sōka Kyōiku Gakkai—was not formally inaugurated until 1937. It was reorganized after the war as Sōka Gakkai. Friction between its leaders and those of Nichiren Shōshū led to a break in 1991. On this schism, see Trevor Astley, "A Matter of Principles"; Daniel A. Métraux, *The Soka Gakkai Revolution,* pp. 71–97; and Brian Wilson and Karel Dobbelaere, *A Time to Chant,* pp. 232–45.

114. Shigyō Kaishū, *Kōmon kyōgaku no kenkyū,* p. 6.

115. See, for example, the criticisms of Eishōin Nichikan (1806–1869) in his *Kongō kin'yō ben, NSZ* 6:347–418. Criticisms of Taisekiji doctrine have also appeared since the postwar period. These appear to stem from (1) reactions of other Nichiren denominations to the remarkable postwar growth of the Sōka Gakkai, which disseminated Taisekiji (Nichiren Shōshū) doctrine on a broad scale; and (2) tension between the incommensurable heremeneutical approaches of certain Nichirenshū scholars based at Risshō University, who have inherited Asai Yōrin's project of formulating a normative doctrine based on the authenticated writings of Nichiren, and scholars within Nichiren Shōshū, who base their understanding of Nichiren on medieval transmission texts said to derive from the founder of their lineage, Nikkō.

116. A more detailed account of the events described appears in Shigyō Kaishū, *Kōmon kyōgaku no kenkyū,* pp. 81–85, and *Zenshi,* pp. 52–53, 67–79. For modern studies by scholars within Nikkō's lineage, see Hori Nichiko, *Fuji Nikkō Shōnin shōden,* vol. 1, pp. 215–93, and Fuji Gakurin Kenkyūka, *Nikkō Shōnin Minobu rizan shi.*

117. "Misa-bō gohenji," *NSZ* 2:145.

118. Nichiren's extant remarks on the place of *kami* worship in his religion are not entirely consistent (see the references given in chap. 6, n. 173). Historically, this

issue has been variously interpreted in different Nichiren lineages. The Taisekiji line of the Fuji school has traditionally adopted an extreme purist position that disallows *kami* worship altogether. Other Nichiren lineages, however, have developed distinctive cults devoted to specific deities, such as Kishimojin (Hārītī) or the thirty protector deities *(sanjūbanjin)*. The latter cult was originally appropriated from Mt. Hiei and became particularly associated with Nichiren Buddhism. From the late medieval period, influences from Yoshida Shintō were also incorporated. See Ueda Honshō, "Nichirenshū to shingi," and "Hokke Shintō," *Shintō jiten*, p. 443.

119. These incidents are mentioned in Nikkō's letters, "Yo Hakii Sanenaga sho" *(NSZ* 2:169) and "Hara-dono gohenji" (2:173). Sanenaga wrote to Nikkō protesting his innocence in the matter of the *nenbutsu* stūpa *(Fuji shiryō ruijū* 1, *FSY* 8:13), but Nikkō seems not to have been convinced.

120. This has been suggested by Mochizuki Kankō, *Nichiren kyōgaku no kenkyū*, pp. 283–86. Mochizuki points to evidence that Nikkō had vowed to remain perpetually at Minobu, the site of Nichiren's grave, and had in fact defended the *jitō*'s behavior to other disciples. Sanenaga's acts of "Dharma-slander," he argues, would not in themselves have been sufficient to drive Nikkō from Minobu.

121. Nikkō is said to have left Minobu in the twelfth month of the year Shōō 1 (1288). However, since the twelfth month of the year Shōō 1 began on 12/24 of the Western calendar, his departure probably corresponds to the beginning of 1289. See Fuji Gakurin Kenkyūka, *Nikkō Shōnin Minobu rizan shi*, pp. 133–48.

122. "Hara-dono gohenji," *NSZ* 2:173–74.

123. Mochizuki Kankō, *Nichiren kyōgaku no kenkyū*, pp. 281–86.

124. Both transfer documents appear in *NSZ* 2:33. For a discussion of textual problems and issues of dating, see Shigyō Kaishū, *Kōmon kyogaku no kenkyū*, pp. 91–96, and *NJ*, pp. 294c–95a.

125. The earliest notice of the *Hon'in-myō shō* is a citation in the *Hon'in-myō kuketsu*, attributed to Sanmi-bō Nichijun (1294–1354/1356), a direct disciple of Nikkō. However, there is room to suspect that the *Hon'in-myō kuketsu* itself may have been a later work attributed retrospectively to Nichijun. The earliest transcription of the *Hon'in-myō shō* is of uncertain date but was made by the sixth abbot of the Taisekiji, Nichiji (1348–1406). The first reliable references to both the *Hon'in-myō shō* and the *Hyaku rokka sōjō* appear in *Hyaku gojūkajō* of Honze-in Nikkyō (1428–1489). For questions raised historically within the Nichiren tradition over the authenticity of these transmissions, see Asai Yōrin, *Nichiren Shōnin kyōgaku no kenkyū*, pp. 623–32, and for a discussion of probable dating, see Shigyō Kaishū, *Kōmon kyōgaku no kenkyū*, pp. 18–24.

126. *DDZ* 5:139–57. For a comparison of the *Hon'in-myō shō* with this and with another medieval Tendai oral transmission text, the *Tōkai kuden shō*, see Shigyō Kaishū, *Kōmon kyōgaku no kenkyū*, pp. 35–39, and Takahashi Ken'yū, "*Hon'in-myō shō* ni miru Kōmon kyōgaku no shisō haikei ni tsuite."

127. *FSY* 1:1; *NSZ* 2:2. In the *NSZ* version, this text appears under its alternative name *Hokke honmonshū kechimyaku sōjō no koto*.

128. *Kaimoku shō, STN* 1:539.

129. See, for example, Ōtani Gyōkō, "Nichiren Shōnin kyōgaku ni okeru honmon to kanjin."

130. The "subtlety of original cause" and the "subtlety of original effect" are the first two of ten "subtleties" *(miao, myō)* of the origin teaching, set forth by Chih-i (*Hsüan-i*, *T* 33:765a–771c). See also Swanson, *The Foundations of T'ien-t'ai Philosophy*, p. 136.

131. *STN* 1:715

132. This too represents the standard reading of Nichirenshū today. See for example Ōtani Gyōkō, "Nichiren Shōnin no san'yaku ron." In the Muromachi period, the relationship of original cause (seed) and original effect (harvest), formed another focus of complex doctrinal controversy within the Hokkeshū. See Mochizuki Kankō, *Nichiren kyōgaku no kenkyū*, pp. 363–85.

133. The English translation of the *Kanjin honzon shō* in *Major Writings* and its revision in Watson and Yampolsky contain some of the very few instances where these collections exhibit a distinctively sectarian reading, inherited via Sōka Gakkai from its former affiliate Nichiren Shōshū. For example, the passage from the *Kanjin honzon shō* given immediately above has been translated to read: "The essential teaching of Shakyamuni's lifetime and that revealed at the beginning of the Latter Day are both pure and perfect [in that both lead directly to Buddhahood]. However, Shakyamuni's is the Buddhism of the harvest, and this is the Buddhism of sowing. The core of his teachings is one chapter and two halves, and for me it is Myōhō-renge-kyō alone" (Watson and Yampolsky, p. 171, slightly modified from *Major Writings* 1:71–72.) Another instance occurs earlier in the text, in a passage which asserts that the difference between *ichinen sanzen* of the trace teaching and of the essential teaching is as vast as heaven and earth. A subsequent statement, posed by way of comparison, is translated as: "However, even the difference between *ichinen sanzen* of the theoretical [*shakumon*] and essential [*honmon*] teachings pales into insignificance before the ultimate principle hidden within the Lotus Sutra" (*Major Writings* 1:70; Watson and Yampolsky, p. 169. For the original see *STN* 1:714). The Watson and Yampolsky version notes that this sentence has been transposed in translation from its original location in the passage "for clarity's sake" (p. 406, n. 105). In its original location, however, it could also be read to mean that "[However,] *ichinen sanzen* [in actuality] differs hardly at all [from the teaching of the mutual inclusion of the ten realms and the realm of the land expounded in the origin teaching]." (Compare also the contrasting explanations of the passage in question under the entry *"chikumaku"* ["bamboo and its membranous lining," i.e., a metaphor for "extremely close"] in the Nichirenshū dictionary *NSJJ*, p. 737a, and *"chikumaku o hedatsu"* in the Sōka Gakkai's *Nichiren Daishōnin gosho jiten*, p. 738.) The translations of such passages in *Major Writings* and Watson and Yampolsky follow traditional interpretations long established within the Taisekiji branch of the Fuji school and serve to emphasize its distinctive interpretation, that Nichiren's *daimoku* represents a teaching independent of, and superior to, Śākyamuni's *Lotus Sūtra*.

134. *FSY* 1:3; *NSZ* 2:3–4.

135. The *Hon'in-myō shō* speaks of the *daimoku*, the seed of Buddhahood, as the "real origin teaching" *(shinjitsu no honmon)* or the "one and only origin teaching" *(dokuitsu honmon)* (*FSY* 1:2,3; *NSZ* 2:2,4).

136. *Hsüan-i* 7a, *T* 33:765b1–3. The sūtra quote is at *MFLHC, T* 9:42c22.

137. *FSY* 1:3, 8; *NSZ* 2:4, 9.

138. For a detailed analysis of Nichiren's understanding of the Buddha's revelation of his original enlightenment in the "Fathoming the Lifespan" chapter, see Kitagawa Zenchō, "Nichiren ni okeru 'Juryōhon no hotoke' ni tsuite."

139. *FSY* 1:1; *NSZ* 2:1.

140. *NSZ* 2:20.

141. *FSY* 1:16, 18; *NSZ* 2:21, 24. "In heaven and earth, I alone am worthy of respect" are said to have been the first words spoken by Śākyamuni at the time of his birth. See *Chang a-han ching* 1, *T* 1:4c1–2.

142. For a detailed though rather unsympathetic account of the development of this doctrine, see Shigyō Kaishū, "Kōmon kyōgaku no shisōteki tenkai no ichi kōsatsu" and *Kōmon kyōgaku no kenkyū*. For one of the more accessible in-house explanations of this doctrinal position, see Yasuji Kirimura, ed., *Outline of Buddhism*, pp. 81–90.

143. *Ushi kegi shō, FSY* 1:78.

144. *Tōtaigi shō kenmon*, cited in Shigyō Kaishū, "Kōmon kyōgaku no shisōteki tenkai no ichi kōsatsu," p. 87.

145. *FSY* 2:254, 284.

146. *Fuji monkachū kenmon, FSY* 5:251.

147. *Ushidan sho kikigaki, FSY* 2:155.

148. Suguro Shinjō, "Hokke chūshaku no dōkō," discusses in some detail four medieval Tendai commentaries that are available in printed editions: the *Hokke mongu yōgi kikigaki*, attributed to Chūjin (1065–1137); the *Hokke kirin yūfū dan*, attributed to Ryōjo (1268–1350); and the *Hokke ryaku taikō shikenmon* and *Hokekyō jurin shūyō shō* of Sonshun. The first two texts may date from as early as the mid- to late Kamakura period. *Jikidan-mono* on the *Lotus Sūtra* flourished from roughly 1450 through 1550 and form the subject of Hirota Tetsumichi's study, *Chūsei Hokekyō chūshakusho no kenkyū*.

149. See Watanabe Hōyō, *Nichirenshū shingyōron no kenkyū*, pp. 79–119. This essay includes a discussion of three medieval Nichiren *Lotus* commentaries: the *Hokkeshū honmon gukyō shō* of Keirin-bō Nichiryū (1385–1464), the *Hokke sōan shō* of Gyōgakuin Nitchō (1422–1500), and the *Hokke Keiun shō* of Enmyōin Nitchō (1441–1510).

150. *MFLHC, p'in* 2, *T* 9:8b25, 9b10. See also chap. 1, n. 115.

151. *MFLHC, p'in* 3, *T* 9:11b16–18; Hurvitz, trans., *Scripture of the Lotus Blossom of the Fine Dharma*, p. 53.

152. *DNBZ* 18:24b, 26b.

153. *DNBZ* 18:24a.

154. *DNBZ* 18:27a.

155. *DNBZ* 18:157a–b.

156. *DNBZ* 18:85a–86a.

157. *DNBZ* 18:130a–b.

158. *DNBZ* 18:131a.

159. *MFLHC, p'in* 23, *T* 9:54b29–c3.

160. See pp. 34, 162.

161. *DNBZ* 18:201a–202a.

162. Mention of the *Ongi kuden* first occurs in the *Hokke Keiun shō* of Enmyōin Nitchō, completed in Bunki 3 (1503). As for the *Onkō kikigaki*, the colophon to the earliest printed edition (Genroku 16, or 1704) says that it follows a manuscript dated Meiō 9 (1500). It is possible that some portions of these texts, especially the *Onkō kikigaki*, may come from Nichiren (see my "Some Disputed Writings in the Nichiren Corpus," pp. 293–95). On the dating of these texts, see in particular Shigyō Kaishū, "Ongi kuden no kenkyū" and "Nichiren kyōgakujō ni okeru *Ongi kuden* no chii"; and Asai Endō, "*Onkō kikigaki* kō." Arguments offered for and against their authenticity of these texts are summarized in "Some Disputed Writings in the Nichiren Corpus," pp. 262–96.

163. *DNBZ* 18:111b.

164. *STN* 3:2646–47. "The lotus as the Dharma itself" *(tōtai renge)* contrasts with the lotus as metaphor *(hiyu renge),* or the the lotus plant that is used to illustrate the Dharma (*Hsüan-i* 7b, *T* 33:771c18–772a7).

165. *STN* 3:2660 and *DNBZ* 18:150a; *STN* 3:2671 and *DNBZ* 18:159b.

166. *MFLHC, p'in* 16, *T* 9:43a26–27.

167. A play on the character *kō,* meaning both "good" or "excellent" *(yoi)* and "to like or prefer" *(konomu).*

168. Probably a reference to the ceremony for conferring the precepts as observed in the Hokkeshū, in which receiving the precepts is interpreted as embracing faith in the *Lotus.*

169. *STN* 3:2666–67.

170. *STN* 3:2553.

171. *STN* 3:2611.

172. *STN* 3:2638.

173. *STN* 3:2567.

174. *STN* 3:2578. The sūtra passage is at *T* 9:42a5–6.

175. *TZ* 9:81a–b. The above-quoted section is followed by an interpretation of the practice of the three phrases in terms of the three mysteries of body, mouth and mind. Iwata notes this passage in "Eshin-ryū shichika kuden hōmon ni tsuite," p. 32.

176. *Tsung-mi and the Sinification of Buddhism,* p. 115.

177. *Hokke mondō shōgishō,* cited in Hayashi Senshō, "Shikan shō Hokke shisō to Senba kyōgaku," p. 242–43.

178. *STN* 1:714, lines 4, 6; Watson and Yampolsky, pp. 169, 406, n. 106.

179. "Ueno-dono gohenji," *STN* 2:1492.

Conclusion

1. For the totalizing ideological dimensions of religion in early modern Japan, see Robert N. Bellah, *Tokugawa Religion,* and Herman Ooms, *Tokugawa Ideology.*

2. In a different context, Winston Davis distinguishes between direct causal agents and "passive enablements"—factors that contribute to particular historical developments by simply not getting in the way ("The Weber Thesis and the Economic Development of Japan").

3. See Matsunaga Yūkei, *Mikkyō kyōten seiritsushi ron,* pp. 64–81.

4. See Ryūichi Abe, "Saichō and Kūkai," p. 125.

5. Ando Toshio, *Tendaigaku ronshū,* pp. 276–77.

6. See Neal Donner, "Chih-i's Meditation on Evil," pp. 58–63.

7. "Critique of Original Awakening Thought in Shōshin and Dōgen," p. 246.

8. "Nichiren Shōnin kyōgaku no shisōshiteki kenkyū no ichi kōsatsu," pp. 53–54.

9. *Nihon chūsei no kokka to shūkyō,* p. 443; "The Development of the *Kenmitsu* System as Japan's Medieval Orthodoxy," trans. Dobbins, p. 262.

10. *Nihon chūsei no kokka to shūkyō,* p. 445; "The Development of the *Kenmitsu* System," trans. Dobbins, pp. 264–65.

11. "A Reexamination of the *Kenmitsu Taisei* Theory," p. 456.

12. "The Development of the *Kenmitsu* System," trans. Dobbins, pp. 250, 251.

13. "A Reexamination of the *Kenmitsu Taisei* Theory," p. 459.

14. Kuroda himself notes the difficulty of defining "esoteric Buddhism" and anticipates objections to characterizing *hongaku* thought in these terms. *Nihon chūsei*

no kokka to shūkyō, p. 447, n. 5; "The Development of the *Kenmitsu* System," trans. Dobbins, p. 265, n. 19.

15. On this subject, see Miyazaki Eishū, *Nichirenshū no kitōhō.*

16. "Kamakura Bukkyō kenkyū o megutte," pp. 282–83.

17. Since writing this conclusion, I have had the opportunity to read the manuscript of Ryūichi Abé's *The Weaving of Mantra: Kūkai and the Construction of Esoteric Buddhist Discourse,* forthcoming from Columbia University Press, which in fact addresses a number of these issues.

18. Peter Nosco, "Introduction: Neo-Confucianism and Tokugawa Discourse," pp. 18–19.

Character Glossary

Adachi Yasumori 安達泰盛
Agui school 安居院流
Aizen Myōō 愛染明王
ajari 阿闍梨
ajari-gō 阿闍梨号
aji no ichigon 阿字の一言
akunin 悪人
akunin jōbutsu 悪人成仏
akunin ōjō 悪人往生
akunin shōki 悪人正機
akusō 悪僧
akutō 悪党
Amida 阿弥陀
Amida santai-setsu 阿弥陀三諦説
A-mi-t'o ching (Amida-kyō) 阿弥陀経
ango 安居
Anne 安慧
Annen 安然
Anraku school 安楽派
Antoku 安徳
Ashikaga College 足利学校
Ashikaga Mochiuji 足利持氏
Awa 安房
Awataguchi school 栗田口流
bakufu 幕府
Benchō 弁長
bessho 別所
betsuin 別院
betsuji no isshin sangan 別時の一心三観
bettō 別当
Birushana 毘盧遮那

Bishamondō lineage 毘沙門堂流
Bishamon-kō 毘沙門講
biwa 琵琶
Biwa, Lake 琵琶湖
Bizen 備前
bodai 菩提
bodaishin 菩提心
Bodai yōshū 菩提要集
bō-gō 房号
bonbu 凡夫
bonnō soku bodai 煩悩即菩提
bukkai soku kukai 仏界即九界
Bukkyō University 仏教大学
bundan shōji 分段生死
bunshin-soku 分真即
buppō 仏法
buppon shinjaku 仏本神迹
bushi 武士
busshu 仏種
butsu-honzon 仏本尊
Butsuji-bō (Butsuji-in, Butchi-in) 仏地房、仏地院
butsuryū-shū 仏立宗
Butsuzō-bō 仏蔵房
Buzan branch 豊山派
Ch'an (Zen) 禅
Chang-an (Kuan-ting) 章安（潅頂）
Chan-jan 湛然
Chegwan 諦観
Ch'eng-kuan 澄観
Chen-yen (Shingon) 真言
Chen-yüan (era) 貞元

461

chi 智

chia 假

chiao-hsiang (kyōsō) 教相

chiao-p'an (kyōhan) 教判

chien-chiao (zengyō) 漸教

Chien-chen (Ganjin) 鑑真

chien-ssu-huo (kenji-waku) 見思惑

chigo 稚児

Chih-i (T'ien-t'ai Ta-shih, Tendai
    Daishi) 智顗（天台大師）

chih-kuan (shikan) 止観

Chih-yen 智儼

Chih-li 智礼

Chikai 智海

chikumaku 竹膜

chikumaku o hedatsu 竹膜を隔つ

Chikurin-bō lineage 竹林房流

Chin-feng, Mount 金峯山

chingo kokka 鎮護国家

Chin-kang-ting ching (Kongochō-kyō)
    金剛頂経

Chin-kuang-ming ching (Konkōmyō-kyō)
    金光明経

Chin-kuang-ming tsui-sheng-wang ching
    (Konkōmyō saishōō-kyō) 金光明
    最勝王経

chi no isshin sangan 智の一心三観

Chinzei 鎮西

Chishō Daishi-ryū 智証大師流

Chi-tsang 吉蔵

Chizan branch 智山派

Chōanji 長安寺

Chōen 長宴

Chōen-bon 長宴本

Chōgen 重源

Chōgō 長豪

chōhachi (ch'ao-pa) 超八

Chōken 澄憲

chō-taisei Bukkyō 超体制仏教

Chōyō 長耀

Chūin 中院

Chūjin (Tōyō-bō) 忠尋（東陽房）

chūko Tendai 中古天台

chung 中

chūsei 中世

chū shinri 中真理

chūtai 中諦

Chūzan 仲算

Dai Amida-butsu 大阿弥陀仏

Daigaku Saburō 大学三郎

Daigoji 醍醐寺

Daiho-kō 大輔公

daiichi gi 第一義

daiji 大事

daijikidō 大直道

Daijō-e 大乗会

Daikōdō 大講堂

Daikōfushōji 大光普照寺

daimandara 大曼荼羅

daimoku 題目

Dainichi 大日

Dainichi Nōnin 大日能忍

Dainichi Nyorai 大日如来

Dainichi-renge-zan 大日蓮華山

Daishikō 大師講

daishōnin 大聖人

daishō sōtai 大小相対

daishu 大衆

Daitōmon lineage 大塔門流

danbaramitsu 檀波羅蜜

dangisho 談義所

Danna-in 檀那院

Danna monryū sōjō shi 檀那門流相
    承資

Danna school 檀那流

Danna Sōzu 檀那僧都

Dan-no-ura 壇ノ浦

danrin 檀林

Dan senchaku 弾撰択

Darumashū 達磨宗

datchaku no honmon 脱益の本門

datsu 脱

denbō yōge no shika 伝法要偈の四箇

Dengyō Daishi (Saichō) 傳教大師
    （最澄）

Dengyō Daishi-kō 傳教大師講

denju dan 伝授壇

denke 伝家

Dō'a Dōkyō (Nenkū) 道阿道教
    （念空）

Dōgen 道元

dōjō 道場

dokuitsu honmon 独一本門

dōri 道理

dōshū 堂衆

Dōsui (Shōkaku-bō) 道邃（聖
    覚房）

Dōzen-bō 道善房

Echin (Enkan) 恵鎮（円観）
edo 穢土
Egi 恵顗
ehō 依報
ehō fuenin 依法不依人
Eigen 栄源
Eihei kaisan gogyōjō 永平開山御
　　業状
Eikai 恵快
Eikū 叡空
Eikyō hōnan 永亨法難
Eisai (or Yōsai) 栄西
Eizon (or Eison) 叡尊
Ejin 恵尋
Ekō-bō lineage 恵光房流
Ekōin 恵光院
en 円
Enchin 円珍
Enchō 円澄
endonkai 円頓戒
Endonkai hiketsu yōshū 円頓戒秘決
　　要集
Endonkai kechimyaku no koto 円頓戒
　　血脈事
engi ron 縁起論
engyō 円教
engyō sanjin 円教三身
enkai 円戒
enke 円家
Enkyō ms. 延慶本
enmitsu itchi 円密一致
en mitsu zen kai 円密禅戒
Enni (Bennen, Shōichi Kokushi)
　　円爾（弁円, 聖一国師）
Ennin 円仁
enri edo gongu jōdo 厭離穢土欣求
　　浄土
Enryakuji 延暦寺
Enshin 円信
Enshūji 円宗寺
Eshin-in 恵心院
Eshin school 恵心流
Eshin Sōzū (Genshin) 恵心僧都
　　（源信）
eshō 依正
eshō funi 依正不二
fa (hō) 法
fa-chieh yüan-ch'i 法界縁起
Fa-hsiang (Hossō) school 法相宗

Fa-tsang 法蔵
Fa-yün 法雲
fei-hsing fei-tso san-mei (higyō hiza
　　sanmai) 非行非座三昧
Fo-chao Te-kuang 仏照徳光
Fo-li-ssu 仏立寺
Fo-lung-ssu 仏龍寺
fudan nenbutsu 不断念仏
Fudō Myōō 不動明王
fu-fa kuan (fuhō-kan) 附法観
Fugen 普賢
fuhen shinnyo 不変真如
fuhen shinnyo no ri 不変真如
　　の理
Fuji 富士
Fuji *monryū* 富士門流
Fujishima-shō 藤島庄
Fujiwara no Akisue 藤原顕季
Fujiwara no Fuyutsugu 藤原冬嗣
Fujiwara no Kamatari 藤原鎌足
Fujiwara no Morosuke 藤原師輔
Fujiwara no Mototoshi 藤原基俊
Fujiwara no Mototsune 藤原基経
Fujiwara no Saneyori 藤原実頼
Fujiwara no Shunzei 藤原俊成
Fujiwara no Sukeyoshi 藤原資能
Fujiwara no Tadahira 藤原忠平
Fujiwara no Teika 藤原定家
fujōshō 不定性
fuju fuse 不受不施
fukaku 不覚
fundarike 分陀利華
funen fumetsu 不然不滅
furigana 振り仮名
Fushigi 不思議
fushigi ichi 不思議一
fushikyō no isshin sangan 不至竟の
　　一心三観
Fushimi 伏見
Fuzen 扶全
gakuryō 学侶
gakushō 学生
gakutō 学頭
Ganjin (Chien-chen) 鑑真
ganjō 元初
ganjō no ichinen 元初の一念
ganmon 願文
Gannōji 元応寺
ganpon mo mumyō 元品の無明

Gansan Gohakkō (Gansan-e) 元三御八講 (元三会)

gasshō 合掌

gedai 外題

gedō-setsu 外道説

gendō hongaku 還同本覚

Gengibunshō 玄義分抄

Gengi daiichi taikō kenmon 元義第一大綱見聞

Genpei jōsuiki 源平盛衰記

Genpei War 源平の争乱

genjō 現成

Genroku (era) 元禄

genshi 玄旨

Genshi jū daiji 玄旨重大事

genshi kanjō 玄旨潅頂

Genshi kanjō shiki 玄旨潅頂私記

genshi kimyōdan kanjō 玄旨帰命壇潅頂

Genshin (Eshin Sōzu) 源信 (恵心僧都)

genshō 現証

genshō soku jissō 現象即実相

ge sōjō 外相承

Genshun 玄俊

Gen'un 玄吽

Gigen 義源

gika 義科

Gishin 義真

gochi 五智

gogi 五義

gogyakuzai 五逆罪

Gohōjō 後北条

gohon deshi-i 五品弟子位

gohonzon 御本尊

gohyaku jindengō 五百塵点劫

goji 五時

goji hakkyō 五時八教

Goji-kō 五時講

gojū gengi 五重玄義

gojū sōtai 五重相対

Gōkai 豪海

goka sōden 五箇相伝

gokenin 御家人

Gokikigaki shō 御聞書抄

gokō 五綱

goma 護摩

gon 権

gondaisōzu 権大僧都

gongen 権現

Gonijō 後二条

gonjitsu sōtai 権実相対

gon no kami 権頭

goryō 御霊

Gosaga 後嵯峨

Goshinji 悟真寺

goshintai 御神体

Goshirakawa 後白河

Goshō 御抄

goshō kakubetsu 五性各別

Gosho kenmon 御書見聞

gōso 強訴

gō soku gedatsu 業即解脱

Gotoba 後鳥羽

Gukanshō 愚管抄

gyō 行

gyō-busshō 行仏性

Gyōgen 行玄

Gyōhyō 行表

gyōja 行者

Gyōnen 凝然

Gyōsen-bō lineage 行泉房流

Hachiman Daibosatsu 八幡大菩薩

Hagiwara (Hanazono) 萩原 (花園)

hakarai はからい

Hakii Nanbu Rokurō Sanenaga 波木井南部六郎実長

Hama *monryū* 浜門流

Hanazono 花園

Hanazono University 花園大学

Hangen 範源

han honji-suijaku 反本地垂迹

Ha Nichiren gi 破日蓮義

han-taisei Bukkyō 反体制仏教

Hasedera 長谷寺

Heikija hen (Byakuja hen) 闢邪編

Hei (Taira) no Yoritsuna (Hei no Saemon-no-jō) 平頼綱 (平佐衛門尉)

Henku 偏救

hennyaku shōji 変易生死

henjō nanshi 変成男子

hen shinri 偏真理

Hie Taisha 日吉大社

Hiei, Mount 比叡山

Hieizanji 比叡山寺
hihan Bukkyō 批判仏教
hihō 秘法
hijiri 聖
Hikigayatsu 比企谷
Hikigayatsu *monryū* 比企谷門流
himitsu shuhō 秘密修法
Hinbō (or Hinpō) 賓法
Hiraga 平賀
Hitachi 常陸
hiyu renge 比喩蓮華
hōben 方便
hōbō 謗法
Hōchi-bō lineage 宝地房流
hōe 法会
hōgu 法具
hō-honzon 法本尊
hōi 法位
hōjin 報身
Hōjō 北条
Hōjō Shigetoki (Gokurakuji-dono) 北条重時 (極楽寺殿)
Hōjō Tokimune 北条時宗
Hōjō Tokisuke 北条時輔
Hōjō Tokiyori (Saimyōji-dono) 北条時頼 (最明寺殿)
Hōjō Yagenta Tokimori 北条弥源太時盛
Hōkan-bō 法鑒房
hokkai 法界
Hokekyō no gyōja 法華経の行者
Hokke chōhachi 法華超八
Hokke-e 法華会
Hokke Hakkō 法華八講
Hokke hō 法華法
Hokke Hōtō-in 法華宝塔院
Hokke ichijōkai 法華一乗戒
Hokke *ikki* 法華一揆
Hokke inga 法華因果
Hokkeji 法華寺
Hokke jikidan-mono 法華直談物
Hokke jingi 法華深義
Hokke Keiun shō 法華啓運抄
Hokke kirin yūfū dan 法華輝臨遊風談
Hokke mandara 法華曼荼羅
Hokke mondō shōgishō 法華問答正義抄

Hokke mongu yōgi kikigaki 法華文句要義聞書
Hokke no en 法華の円
Hokke senpō 法華懺法
Hokke sessō zu 法華説相図
Hokke Shintō 法華神道
Hokkeshū 法華宗
Hokkeshū honmon gukyō shō 法華宗本門弘経抄
Hokke sōan shō 法華草案抄
"Hokke ten Hokke" 法華転法華
Hokke Zanmai-dō 法華三昧堂
hon 本
honbutsu 本仏
Honda Nisshō 本多日生
Hondoji 本土寺
Hōnen 法然
honga 本果
hongaku (pen-chüeh, pon'gak) 本覚
hongaku hōmon 本覚法門
Hongakuji 本覚寺
hongaku jōjū 本覚常住
hongakumon 本覚門
hongaku shinnyo 本覚真如
hongaku shisō 本覚思想
honga-myō 本果妙
honga-myō no kyōshu 本果妙の教主
honge 本化
honge no isshin sangan 本解の一心三観
hon'in 本因
hon'in-myō 本因妙
hon'in-myō no gyōja 本因妙の行者
hon'in-myō no kyōshu 本因妙の教主
hon'i uzen 本已有善
honjaku mibun 本迹未分
Honjaku nimon no koto 本迹二門の事
Honjaku no koto 本迹の事
honjaku ron 本迹論
honjaku sōtai 本迹相対
honji (original ground) 本地
honji (main temple) 本寺
honji (original time) 本時
honji-butsu 本地仏
honji honri sanjin 本地本理三身
honji-suijaku 本地垂迹
honjo tsūdatsu mon 本所通達門

Honma Shigetsura　本間重連
honmatsu kukyō-tō　本末究竟等
honmatsu kukyō-tō no ichigon　本末究
　竟等の一言
honmi uzen　本未有善
honmon　本門
Honmonji　本門寺
honmon juryōhon no sandaiji　本門寿
　量品の三大事
honmon no daimoku　本門の題目
honmon no honzon　本門の本尊
honmon no kaidan　本門の戒壇
hon mushōji　本無生死
honrai jikaku-butsu　本来自覚仏
honshō myōshu　本証妙修
hontai　本体
honzon　本尊
Horikawa　堀河
hōshinnō　法親王
Hoshino-san Muryōjuji　星野山無量
　寿寺
hosshin　法身
hosshin seppō　法身説法
hosshō　法性
Hosshōji　法勝寺
Hossō school　法相宗
hōtō gyōhōshiki　宝塔行法式
Hōzenji monjo　逢善寺文書
Hōzō (Ratnagarbha)　宝蔵
Hōzō (Dharmakāra)　法蔵
hsiang　相
hsing　性
hsing-ch'i　性起
hsing-chü　性具
hsing-chü-shuo (shōgu-setsu)　性具説
Hsing-man　行満
hsin-hsing (shinshō)　心性
hsing-o (shōaku)　性悪
Hsin-yao (Shin'yō)　心要
Hsiu-ch'an-ssu　修禅寺
Hsüan-tsang　玄奘
hua-fa ssu-chiao (kehō no shikyō)　化法
　四教
hua-i ssu-chiao (kegi no shikyō)　化儀
　四教
Hua-yen　華厳
hu-chü　互具
Hui-k'o　慧可

Hui-kuan　慧観
Hui-neng　慧能
Hui-ssu (Nan-yüeh Ta-shih)　慧思
　(南岳大師)
Hui-wen　慧文
Hung-chou lineage　洪州宗
Hyaku gojūkajō　百五十箇条
ichidai engyō　一大円教
ichidaiji　一大事
ichijō kaie　一乗開会
Ichijō Shikan-in　一乗止観院
ichinen　一念
ichinen gi　一念義
ichinen hokkai　一念法界
ichinen jōbutsu　一念成仏
ichinen sanzen　一念三千
ichinen shinge　一念信解
Ichinosawa Nyūdō　一谷入道
Ichiryū sōden hōmon shikenmon　一流相
　伝法門私見聞
I-hsing　一行
Iimurodani　飯室谷
Ikegami　池上
Ikegami Ajari (Kōkei)　池上阿闍梨
　(皇慶)
Ikegami Munenaga　池上宗長
Ikegami Munenaka　池上宗仲
Iken　惟賢
Ikkai　一海
Ikkō *ikki*　一向一揆
ikō　已講
ima　今
in　院
inaka Tendai　田舎天台
inbun　因分
inga senjin　因果浅深
inge　院家
in-gō　院号
ingyō　因行
i-nien san-ch'ien (ichinen sanzen)　一念
　三千
injin　印信
inmyō　因明
innenshō no isshin sangan　因縁生の
　一心三観
Inokuma lineage　猪熊流
Insei　院政
inzei nenbutsu　引声念仏

Ippen 一遍
ippō gūjin 一法究尽
Ise Shintō 伊勢神道
Ise Shrine 伊勢神宮
Isen 惟暹 (or 維仙)
Ishii Ryōkun 石井亮勲
Ishiizumi-bō lineage 石泉房流
ishin denshin 以心伝心
isshin fushō no ichigon 一心不生の
    一言
isshin sangan 一心三観
isshin sangan den 一心三観伝
isshin sangan dennō ichigon 一心三観
    伝於一言
isshin sangan ki 一心三観記
isshō jōbutsu 一生成仏
isson shishi 一尊四士
itan-ha 異端派
itchi 一致
itchi/shōretsu 一致勝劣
ittai 一体
ittō ryōson shishi 一塔両尊四士
Izu 伊豆
Izumi-kō 和泉公
jakushō funi 寂照不二
jakushō funi no isshin sangan 寂照不
    二の一心三観
jakushō no ichigon 寂照の一言
Jakuzen 寂然
ji (actualities) 事
ji (time) 時
Jichin Kashō-kō 慈鎮和尚講
Jie Daishi (Ryōgen) 慈慧大師
    (良源)
Jie Daishi-kō 慈慧大師講
jien 事円
Jien 慈円
jigyō 事行
Jihen 慈遍
jihi no ichigon 慈悲の一言
ji jissō 事実相
jijō 事成
Jikaku Daishi-ryū 慈覚大師流
jikan 事観
ji kenpon 事顕本
jikidan 直談
jikidō 直道
jikkai 十界

Jikkai 直海
jikkai gogu 十界互具
Jikken (Enjitsu-bō Hōin) 直兼 (円
    実房法院)
jiko dōitsusei 自己同一性
jikyōsha 持経者
jimitsu 事密
Jimon 寺門
Jindai no maki shikenmon 神代巻私
    見聞
jinen 自然
jinen hongaku 自然本覚
jinen hōni 自然法爾
jinen ni 自然に
jinnin 神人
ji no kaidan 事の戒壇
Jinzen 尋禅
jiri gumitsu 事理倶密
jiriki 自力
jisha 寺社
Jishū 時衆
jisō 事相
jisshi sōzoku 実子相続
jissō 実相
jissō no in 実相の印
jissō ron 実相論
jitō 地頭
jitsu 実
jitsubutsu 実仏
Jitsugen (Jisshin) 実源 (実深)
Jizō-bō 地蔵房
Jōchin 定珍
jōdo 浄土
Jōdo ketsugi shō 浄土決疑抄
Jōdo Shinshū 浄土真宗
Jōdoshū 浄土宗
Jōei Shikimoku 貞永式目
Jōfukyō 常不軽
Jōgen (Zōjō-bō) 定源 (蔵乗房)
Jōgyō 上行
jōgyōdō 常行堂
jōgyō zanmai 常行三昧
Jōhan 静範
Jōhen 浄遍
jō jakkōdo daiichigi tai 常寂光土第
    一義諦
jō jakkōdo gi 常寂光土義
jōjū 常住

Jōkai 乗海
Jōkei 貞慶
Jōken 常憲
Jōkyū no ran 承久の乱
Jōmyō (Awataguchi) 静明 (栗
　田口)
Jōraku-in 常楽院
Jōren 浄蓮
Jōsan 浄算
Jōsen 定仙
Jōshō 定照
Joshō Hokke yūmon shū 助照法華融
　文集
jōyō no isshin sangan 常用の一心
　三観
Ju-ching 如浄
jūhōi 住法位
jūin shika 従因至果
jū ittsū no jō 十一通の状
ju fuse 受不施
juji 受持
jūjukai kanjō 重授戒潅頂
jūka kōin 従果向因
Jūkaku 什覚
juku 熟
ju-lai-tsang yüan-ch'i 如来蔵縁起
jun'en 純円
jūnyoze 十如是
jūrokuin 十六院
kabun 果分
kadō soku butsudō 歌道即仏道
kai 戒
Kai 甲斐
kaidan 戒壇
kaie 開会
kaigen kuyō 開眼供養
kaihō 戒法
kaihōgyō 回峰行
kai kanjō 戒潅頂
kaike 戒家
kaitai 戒体
Kajii *monzeki* 梶井門跡
Kakitsu (era) 嘉吉
Kakuban 覚鑁
kakuchi shō 覚知性
Kakuchō 覚超
Kakugyō 覚行
Kakutoku 覚徳

Kakuun 覚運
kakuzen jitsubutsu 覚前実仏
kami 神
kan (contemplation) 観
kan (monetary unit) 貫
Kanasana *dangisho* 金讃談義所
Kanazawa bunko komonjo, butsuji hen
　金沢文庫古文書、仏事篇
Kanazawa bunko komonjo, shikigo hen
　金沢文庫古文書、識語篇
kanbun 漢文
Kangakkō 勧学講
kangyō-soku 観行即
kanjin 観心
kanjin honzon 観心本尊
Kanjin honzon shō shikenmon 観心本
　尊抄私見聞
kanjin jikidatsu 観心直達
kanjin no ichigon 観心の一言
kanjin-shaku (kuan-hsin-shih) 観心釈
kanjin-shugi 観心主義
kanjō 潅頂
kanju 貫首 (or 貫主)
Kankai 寛海
Kanmu 桓武
Kannon 観音
Kannon-kō 観音講
kanpaku 関白
kanpō 観法
kanrei 管領
Kanryū 観隆
Kanshō *meiyaku* 寛正盟約
Kasagi 笠置
Kashiwabara 柏原
Kasuga Shrine 春日神社
katoku 果徳
Kawa school 川流
Kawataya 河田谷
Kazusa 上総
ke 仮
kechimyaku 血脈
kechimyaku sōjō 血脈相承
Kegon 華厳
kehō no shikyō 化法四教
Keishun 慶舜
Keiun 景雲
Keizan 瑩山
keju shōkai 仮受小戒

kekkai 結界

ken 顕

kengyō 顕教

kengyō kanjō 顕教灌頂

kenmitsu 顕密

kenmitsu-shugi 顕密主義

kenmitsu taisei 顕密体制

kenmon 権門

Kenmon guan ki 見聞愚案記

kenmon taisei 顕密体制

kensetsu Hokke 顕説法華

Kenshin 顕真

Kenzei 建撕

kesetsu 仮説

ketai 仮諦

ki 機

kike 記家

Kimyōdan denju no koto 帰命壇伝授
　　之事

kimyōdan kanjō 帰命壇灌頂

kirikami (or *kirigami*) 切紙

kiroku 記録

Kishimojin 鬼子母神

Kitadani 北谷

Kitadani hiten 北谷秘典

Kita-in 喜多院

kitō 祈祷

kitō sō 祈祷僧

Kiyomizudera 清水寺

Kiyosumidera (or Seichōji) 清澄寺

kō 講

kōan 公安

kōden shika 広伝四箇

Kōen 興円

Kōen Hokke gi 講演法華儀

Kōfukuji 興福寺

Kōfukuji sōjō 興福寺奏状

kōgaku ryūgi 広学竪義

Kōin Sōjō 公胤僧正

Koishiwa (Kitaishiwa) 小石和 (北
　　石和)

kōji 講師

Kojiki 古事記

Kōjō 光定

Kōkai 広海 (or 光海)

Kōkaku 皇覚

Kōkei (or Kōgyō) 皇慶

kokka 国家

kokka kangyō 国家諫暁

kokoro ikan 意如何 (north valley)
　　心何 (west valley)

koku 国

Kokuchūkai 国柱会

kokudo seken 国土世間

kokugaku 国学

Kokūzō 虚空蔵

Kokūzō Bosatsu *gumonji hō* 虚空蔵
　　菩薩求聞持法

Komatsubara *hōnan* 小松原法難

Komazawa University 駒沢大学

Kominato 小湊

Kongōhōkaiji 金剛宝戒寺

kongō hōki kai 金剛宝器戒

Kongōkai 金剛界

konpaku 魂魄

Konpon Chūdō 根本中堂

Konpon Daishi-ryū 根本大師流

konpon Hokke 根本法華

Kōsai 幸西

kōsen-rufu 広宣流布

Kōshi-e 向師会

kōshiki 講式

koshin sanzen 己心三千

Kōsō (or Kōshū) 光宗

kotodama-gaku 言霊学

k'ou-chüeh (*kuketsu*) 口決

Kōya (or Kūya) 空也

Kōya, Mount 高野山

Kōyō shō 紅葉抄

kū 空

kuan-hsin (*kanjin*) 観心

kuan-hsin-shih (*kanjin-shaku*) 観心釈

Kuang-hsiu 廣修

kuan pu-k'o-ssu-i ching (*kan fukashigi kyō*)
　　観不可思議境

Kuan-ting 灌頂

kuden 口伝

kuden hōmon 口伝法門

kudokuju 功徳聚

K'uei-chi 窺基

Kujō 九条

Kujō Kanezane 九条兼実

Kūkai 空海

kukai soku bukkai 九界即仏界

kūkan 空観

kukyō-soku 究竟即

Kumano shrine　熊野神社
k'ung　空
Kuo-ch'ing-ssu　國清寺
kuon　久遠
kuon ganjō　久遠元初
kuon jitsujō　久遠実成
Kurita-shō　栗太庄
Kurodani lineage　黒谷流
kushiki shinnō shinnyo no miyako　九識
　　心王真如の都
kusō　供僧
kūtai　空諦
kyō (object of contemplation)　境
kyō (teaching)　教
kyō (sūtra)　経
kyōchi funi no isshin sangan　境智不二
　　の一心三観
kyōchi myōgō　境智冥合
kyōchi no ichigon　境智の一言
kyōdan　教団
kyōgen kigo (*k'uang-yen i-yu*)　狂言
　　綺語
Kyōgō　経豪
kyōhan　教判
Kyōhō (era)　亨保
kyōhō rufu no zengo　教法流布の前後
Kyōkai　経海
kyōkan funi　教観不二
kyōmei　教命
kyō no isshin santai　境の一心三諦
kyōsō　教相
kyōsō hanjaku　教相判釈
kyōsō-shugi　教相主義
kyōto　凶徒
Kyōyū　経祐
kyōzō en'yū　鏡像円融
kyōzō en'yū kuketsu　鏡像円融口決
kyū Bukkyō　旧仏教
Lan-ch'i Tao-lung　蘭渓道隆
li　理
Lin-chi (Rinzai)　臨済
Ling-chiu-shan (Ryōjusen)　霊鷲山
liu-chi (*rokusoku*)　六即
li-yüan (*rien*)　理円
Lu-che-na (Rushana)　盧舎那
machishū　町衆
Makiguchi Tsunesaburō　牧口常
　　三郎

mappō　末法
mappō mukai　末法無戒
Mappō tōmyō ki　末法燈明記
Matarajin　摩多羅神
Matsubagayatsu *hōnan*　松葉谷法難
matsuji　末寺
Matsuno　松野
Ma-tsu Tao-i　馬素道一
Meiun　明雲
Memyō　馬鳴
Menzan Zuihō　面山瑞方
miao (*myō*)　妙
michi　道
Miidera　三井寺
Mikkyō　密教
Mikohidari school　御子左派
Mikuni　三国
Minamidani　南谷
Minamoto　源
Minamoto no Yoritomo　源頼朝
Minazuki-e Hokke Dai-e　六月会法
　　華大会
Minobu, Mount　身延山
Minobu Bunko　身延文庫
Minobu-san Kuonji　身延山久遠寺
Misai-e (or Gosai-e)　御斎会
Mishima　三島
mitsu　密
Mitsugan-kō　三日講
miyako Tendai　都天台
Mobara　藻原
Mobaraji　藻原寺
monja　問者
monjō　文上
Monju　文殊
Monjushiri　文殊師利
monryū　門流
monshō　文証
montei　文底
monto　門徒
mon'yō　問要
Mon'yōki　門葉記
monzeki　門跡
monzeki jiin　門跡寺院
monzen-machi　門前町
Morita Ryūsen　森田龍僊
mōshijō　申状
Mudōji　無動寺

Mudōji-dani　無動寺谷

muga no ichigon　無我の一言

mu ichi fu jōbutsu　無一不成仏

Mujū Ichien (Dōgyō)　無住一円（道暁）

mumon jisetsu　無問自説

mumyō-waku　無明惑

Muryōjuji　無量寿寺

musa (wu-tso)　無作

musa hongaku sanjin　無作本覚三身

musa kongō hōkai　無作金剛宝戒

musa sanjin　無作三身

musa sanjin kakuzen jitsubutsu　無作三身覚前実仏

Musashi　武蔵

Mushōge-kyō　無障礙経

Musōnen　無諍念

myō　妙

Myōe　明恵

Myōgyōshin yōshū　妙行心要集

myōhō　妙法

Myōhonji　妙本寺

myōhō no ichigon　妙法の一言

Myōhō-renge-kyō　妙法蓮華経

myōji-soku　名字即

Myōjō Pond　明星池

Myōkai　明快

myōkaku　妙覚

Myōkakuji　妙覚寺

Myōkōin　妙香院

Myōrenji　妙蓮寺

Myōryū　妙立

myōtai no isshin sangan　妙体の一心三観

Myōzen　明全

Naganuma　長沼

Naganuma Gorō Munemitsu　長沼五郎宗光

Nagasa　長狭

Nagato ms.　長門本

naige sōtai　内外相対

Naishō denbō-ketsu　内証伝法決

nai sōjō　内相承

Nakayama Hokekyōji　中山法華経寺

Nakayama lineage　中山門流

Namu-Amida-butsu　南無阿弥陀仏

Namu-byōdō-daie-myōhō-renge-kyo
南無平等大慧妙法蓮華経

Namu-ichijō-myōden　南無一乗妙典

Namu-ichijō-myōhō-renge-kyo　南無一乗妙法蓮華経

Namu-Jie-Daishi　南無慈慧大師

Namu-kaisan-kennichi-kaigon-kennon-shin-butsu-shujō-ichijō-myōhō-renge-kyo　南無開三顕一開近顕遠心仏衆生一乗妙法蓮華経

Namu-Kanzeon-Bosatsu　南無観世音菩薩

Namu-myōhō-renge-kyo　南無妙法蓮華経

Namu-Sannō-nijū-issha　南無山王二十一社

Nanjō Hyōe Shichirō　南条兵衛七郎

Nankeizō　南渓蔵

nankyō sandai-e　南京三大会

Nanmitsu　南密

nanto hokurei　南都北嶺

Nan-yang Hui-chung　南陽慧忠

Nashimoto *monzeki*　梨下門跡

Nen'a Ryōchū　然阿良忠

nenbutsu　念仏

nenju　念誦

Nichidai (Hongaku Hōin)　日大（本覚法印）

Nichiden (Hōju-in)　日伝（宝聚院）

Nichiden (Daien Ajari)　日伝（大円阿闍梨）

Nichidō　日道

Nichidō (Hōun-in)　日道（法雲院）

Nichiei (Jōgyōin)　日叡（上行院）

Nichien (Daishōin)　日延（大聖院）

Nichien (Kangyōin)　日延（観行院）

Nichigaku (Jōju-in)　日学（成就院）

Nichigennyo　日眼女

nichi-gō　日号

Nichigon-ama　日厳尼

Nichii (Engyōin)　日意（円教院）

Nichii (Myōkōin)　日意（妙光院）

Nichiin (Jikkyō Ajari)　日院 (実教
　阿闍梨)

Nichiji (sixth abbot of Taiseki ji)
　日時

Nichiji (Renge Ajari)　日持 (蓮華阿
　闍梨)

Nichijitsu (Honjōin)　日実 (本
　成院)

Nichijō (Toki Jōnin)　日常 (富木常
　忍)

Nichijū (Ichinyo-in)　日重 (一
　如院)

Nichijū (Shinnyo-in)　日住 (真
　如院)

Nichijun (Sanmi Ajari)　日順 (三位
　阿闍梨)

Nichikan (Eishōin)　日鑑 (永昌
　院)

Nichikan (Kenju-in)　日寛 (堅樹
　院)

Nichiken (Jakushōin)　日乾 (寂
　照院)

Nichiki (Udana-in)　日輝 (優陀
　那院)

Nichikō　日亨

Nichikyō (Zengakuin)　日鏡 (善
　学院)

Nichiman (Sado Ajari)　日満 (佐渡
　阿闍梨)

Nichimyō Shōnin　日妙聖人

Nichinyo　日女

Nichion (Shinshōin)　日遠 (心
　性院)

Nichiren　日蓮

Nichiren Hokkeshū　日蓮法華宗

Nichiren *honbutsu ron*　日蓮本仏論

Nichiren Shōshū　日蓮正宗

Nichirenshū　日蓮宗

Nichirō (Daikoku Ajari)　日朗 (大国
　阿闍梨)

Nichirō *monryū*　日朗門流

Nichiryū (Keirin-bō)　日隆 (慶
　林坊)

Nichiu　日有

Nichiyō　日要

Nichiyū (Jōgyōin)　日祐 (浄行
　院)

Nichizen (Tōgakuin)　日全 (等
　覚院)

Nichizō (Higo Ajari)　日像 (肥後阿
　闍梨)

Nichūreki　日中歴

Nihon shoki　日本書記

Nijō　二条

nijō sabutsu　二乗作仏

Nijū Hakkō　二十八講

Nikkai (Izumi-bō)　日海 (和泉房)

nikki no ie　日記の家

Nikkō　日光

Nikkō (Byakuren Ajari)　日興 (白蓮
　阿闍梨)

Nikkō *monryū*　日興門流

Nikkyō (Honze-in)　日教 (本是院)

Nikkyō (Sakyō Ajari)　日教 (左京阿
　闍梨)

Nikkyō (Tsūshin-in)　日境 (通心
　院)

Nikō (Minbu Ajari)　日向 (民部阿
　闍梨)

nikon　而今

Ninchū　仁忠

nin-honzon　人本尊

Ninkai　仁快

Ninshō (Ryōkan-bō)　忍性 (良
　観房)

nin'un　任運

Ninzen　仁全

Nishidani　西谷

Nishidani myōmoku shi kikigaki　西谷
　名目私聞書

Nishi Honganji　西本願寺

Nissan (Daiju Ajari)　日山 (大鷲阿
　闍梨)

nisshin　日神

Nisshin (Daishin Ajari)　日進 (大進
　阿闍梨)

Nisshin (Jōfukyōin)　日真 (常不
　軽院)

Nisshin (Kuonjōin)　日親 (久遠
　成院)

Nisshō (Ben Ajari)　日昭 (弁阿
　闍梨)

Nisshō *monryū*　日昭門流

Nisshū (Shōseiin)　日修 (證誠院)

Nisshutsu (Ichij-bō)　日出 (一
　　乗房)
Nisshutsu Taiinki　日出台隠記
Nitchō (Enmyōin)　日澄 (円明院)
Nitchō (Gyōgakuin)　日朝 (行
　　学院)
Nitchō (Iyo Ajari)　日頂 (伊予阿
　　闍梨)
Nittō　日藤
Niwano Nikkyō　庭野日敬
nizen　爾前
nizen no en　爾前の円
Nō　能
Nōan　能安
nōshaku　能釈
Nukina Shigetada　貫名重忠
nyorai　如来
Nyorai juryōhon　如来寿量品
nyo ze sō　如是相
nyūdō　入道
nyūga ganyū　入我我入
ōbō　王法
ōbō buppō sōi ron　王法仏法相依論
Oda Nobunaga　織田信長
Ōhara　大原
Ōhara *bessho*　大原別所
Ōhara lineage　大原流
Ōhara Shōrin-in　大原勝林院
ōjin　応身
ōjō　往生
ōjōden　往生伝
Okada Kōtama　岡田光玉
Ōmi　近江
omikoshi　御神輿
Ōmine　大峰
Omosu　重須
Ōnamuchi-no-mikoto　大已貴命
Onjōji　園城寺
onmitsu Hokke　隠密法華
Onmyōdō　陰陽道
Ono-no-miya　小野宮
Ōtani University　大谷大学
Ōtsu　大津
Ōwa debate　応和の宗論
Ōyamagui-no-mikoto　大山咋命
Pai-chang　百丈
p'an-chiao　判教

Pei-hua ching　悲華経
pen-chi (honjaku)　本迹
pieh-chiao (bekkyō)　別教
P'i-lu-che-na (Birushana)　毘盧舎那
pi-mi-chiao (himitsukyō)　秘密教
Po Chü-i　白居易
pu-chüeh　不覚
pu-erh mo-ho-yen (funi makaen)　不二
　　摩訶衍
Pu-k'ung　不空
pu-pien　不変
pu-ting-chiao (fujōkyō)　不定教
raigō　来迎
Raigō-in　来迎院
Raishō　頼昭
reichi　霊知
Reikō Mondō　例講問答
Reikū　霊空
renge　蓮華
renge inga　蓮華因果
ri　理
ri-busshō　理仏性
rien　理円
rigu　理具
rijō　理成
rikai　理戒
rikan　理観
ri kenpon　理顕本
rimitsu　理密
rinjū　臨終
rinjū no isshin sangan　臨終の一心
　　三観
rinmetsu doji honzon　臨滅度時
　　本尊
rinnen gusoku　輪円具足
ri no kaidan　理の戒壇
Rinshō　燐昭
Rinzaishū　臨済宗
Rinzai Zen　臨済禅
rishin　理身
Rishōin kechimyaku　理性院血脈
ri-soku　理即
rissha (ryūgisha)　竪者 (or 立者), 竪
　　義者
risshō ankoku　立正安国
Risshō-e　立正会
Risshō Kōsei Kai　立正佼成会

Risshō University　立正大学
Risshū　律宗
ritsu-e　律衣
Ritsuryō　律令
rokudo　六度
Rokujō school　六条派
rongi　論義
ryakuden sanka no daiji　略伝三箇の
　　　大事
ryō　両
ryōbu　両部
Ryōbu Shintō　両部神道
Ryōgen (Jie Daishi)　良源（慈慧
　　　大師）
Ryōgon-e　楞厳会
Ryōgon-kō　楞厳講
Ryōgon-in　楞厳院
Ryōhen　良遍
Ryōjo　良助
Ryōjusen (Ling-chiu-shan)　霊鷲山
ryōke　領家
ryō kechimyaku sho　両血脈書
ryōke no ama　領家の尼
Ryōnin　良忍
Ryōshō-bō　了性房
ryōshu　領主
ryōzen ichie gennen misan　霊山一会
　　　儼然未散
Ryōzen-in　霊山院
ryōzen jōdo　霊山浄土
ryōzen jōdo kuon jitsujō　霊山浄土久
　　　遠実成
ryū　流
ryūgi　竪義（or 立義）
Ryūju　龍樹
Ryūkō *hōnan* (or Tatsunokuchi *no*
　　　hōnan)　竜口法難
Ryūkoku University　竜谷大学
Sado　佐渡
Saga　嵯峨
Saichō　最澄
Saidaiji　西大寺
Saien　宰円
Saigyō　西行
Saikyōji　西教寺
Sairen-bō　最蓮房
Saishō-e　最勝会
Saitō　西塔

Saitō Yōrin　斉藤要輪
Saiun　最雲
Sakamoto　坂本
samurai-dokoro　侍所
sandai　算大
sandai-e　三大会
sandai hihō　三大秘法
san'e　三会
sangaku　三学
sange　懺悔
Sange Daishi　山家大師
Sange yōryakki　山家要略記
sanjin　三身
Sanjin gi　三身義
sanjin-setsu　三身説
Sanjō-Shirakawa　三条白河
sanjū　三重
sanjūbanjin　三十番神
sanju jōkai　三聚浄戒
Sanjū-kō　三十講
sanjū shichika no daiji　三十七箇の
　　　大事
sanku kuketsu　三句口決
San-lun　三論
sanmaijo　三昧処
Sanmai lineage　三昧流
sanmaya　三昧耶
Sanmi-bō　三位房
sanmitsu　三密
Sanmon　山門
Sanmon hiden kenmon　山門秘伝
　　　見聞
Sanmon konryū hiketsu　山門建立
　　　秘決
Sannō　山王
Sannō Gongen-kō　山王権現講
Sannō-kō　山王講
Sannō Shintō　三王神道
san seken　三世間
sanshō jōbutsu　三生成仏
sanshu Hokke　三種法華
santoku　三徳
Sanzen-in *monzeki*　三千院門跡
sato-bō　里坊
Satsurai-e　察礼会
se　色
Seii Taishōgun　征夷大将軍
Seikai (disciple of Jōmyō)　政海

Seikai (disciple of Songai) 盛海
Seikaku (or Shōkaku) 聖覚
Seishi 勢至
seitō-ha 正統派
Sejizaiō 世自在王
sekkanke 摂関家
Senba 仙波
senchaku 選択
Seng-chao 僧肇
Seng-jui 僧叡
senju 専修
Senjudō 千手堂
Senne 詮慧
senni gedō 先尼外道
sesshō 摂政
setsuwa 説話
shakai kiban 社会基盤
shakubuku 折伏
shakumon 迹門
shakumon no kaidan 迹門の戒壇
shanagō 遮那業
shan-chia 山家
Shan-tao 善導
shan-wai 山外
She-lun school 摂論宗
Shibu gassenjō ms. 四部合戦状本
shidai sangan 次第三観
shih 事
shih-chüeh (shikaku) 始覚
shih-hsiang 実相
shih-hsiang lun (jissō ron) 実相論
shih-yüan (jien) 事円
Shijō Yorimoto 四条頼基
Shijūjō-ketsu 四十帖決
shijū kōhai 四重興廃
shijū shagyō 四重捨行
shikaku 始覚
shikaku mujō 始覚無常
shikaku soku hongaku 始覚即本覚
shikan 止観
shikangō 止観業
Shikan-in 止観院
shikan no ichigon 止観の一言
Shikan shin'yō 止観心要
shikan shō Hokke 止観勝法華
shikan taishi 止観大旨
shiki 私記
shikidoku 色読

Shiki-kō 四季講
shikken 執権
shiku jōdō 四句成道
shikyō no isshin sangan 至境の一心
　　三観
Shimōsa 下総
Shimotsuke 下野
Shimozuki-e Hokke Dai-e 霜月会法
　　華大会
shin Bukkyō 新仏教
shin deshi 真弟子
Shin'ei 心栄
Shinga 心賀
Shingai 心海
Shingen 真源
Shingon, *shingon* 真言
Shingonshū 真言宗
shinjin 信心
shinjitsu no honmon 真実の本門
shinjō 信条
Shinkokinshū 新古今集
shinkoku 神国
Shinkū 信空
Shinkurodani 新黒谷
shinkyōgi 心境義
shinnyo 真如
shinnyo fuhen 真如不変
shinnyo no ichigon 真如の一言
shinnyo no kakuchishō 真如の覚
　　知性
shinnyo zuien 真如随縁
shinpon busshaku 神本仏迹
Shinpukuji 真福寺
Shinran 親鸞
Shinsei 真盛
shinshō jōjū 心性常住
Shinsō 心聡
Shinson (Kawataya) 信尊（河
　　田谷）
shintai 真諦
shintei 真弟
Shintō 神道
shin'yō no ichigon 心要の一言
Shin'yū 心瑜
Shinzenkōji 新善光寺
Shinzōji 神蔵寺
shinzoku ichinyo 真俗一如
Shirakawa 白河

shishin ekō 　至心廻向

shishū sōjō 　四宗相承

shō (sage) 　聖

shō (realization) 　證

Shōbō genzō gokikigaki 　正法眼蔵御
　　聞書

Shōbō genzō shō 　正法眼蔵抄

shōdō 　唱導

shōen 　荘園

shōgisha 　精義者

shōgu-setsu 　性具説

Shōgyōin 　正行院

Shōhan (Renjitsu-bō) 　勝範（蓮
　　実房）

shōhō 　正報

shohō jissō 　諸法実相

Shōichi Kokushi (Enni) 　聖一国師
　　（円爾）

Shōjari 　尚闍梨

shōji kakuyō no isshin sangan 　生死覚
　　用の一心三観

shōji no ichigon 　生死の一言

shōji soku jissō 　声字即実相

shōji soku nehan 　生死即涅槃

shōji wa moto raku nari 　生死は本楽
　　なり

shōjōju 　正定聚

shōju 　摂受

Shōkai 　承海

shōkaku dan 　正覚壇

shōkan 　荘官

Shōkō 　聖光

Shokoku ikken hijiri monogatari 　諸国一
　　見聖物語

Shōkū 　証空

shomin 　庶民

Shōmu 　聖武

shōmyō 　声明

Shōmyōji 　称名寺

shōmyō jōbutsu 　声明成仏

shōnin 　上人

Shōren-in 　青蓮院

Shōren-in (Awataguchi) school 　青蓮
　　院（粟田口）流

shōretsu 　勝劣

Shōrin-bō 　勝林坊

Shōrin-in 　勝林院

Shōritsu hiyō shō 　声律秘要抄

shoshaku 　所釈

shōshi 　荘司

Shōshin (Hōchi-bō or Hōji-bō) 　証真
　　（宝地房）

Shōtatsu 　聖達

Shōtetsu 　正徹

Shou-leng-yen ching 　首楞厳経

Shōyū 　聖融

Shōwa (era) 　承和

shu 　種

shū (tsung) 　宗

Shūbō-kō 　周防公

Shūen shū 　宗円集

shūgaku 　宗学

Shugendō 　修験道

Shūgi 　宗祇

shugo 　守護

Shūgyokushū 　拾玉集

shuhō 　修法

shukke 　出家

Shūkōji 　宗光寺

shūkyō 　宗教

Shūman shū 　宗満集

Shun 　農

Shunjō 　俊芿

Shunpan 　俊範

Shunzei 　俊成

Shuryōgon-in 　首楞厳院

shūshi (or *shūji*) 　宗旨

shushō ittō 　修証一等

Shūso gohonzon shū 　宗祖御本尊集

shu soku datsu 　種即脱

shussongyō 　出尊形

shuto 　衆徒

shūyō 　宗要

Shūyōshū shikenmon 　宗要集私見聞

Sōan shō 　草案抄

sōgakutō 　総学頭

Sōgō 　僧綱

sōhonzan 　総本山

sōji-soku 　相似即

sōjō 　相承

Sōka Gakkai 　創価学会

Sōka Kyōiku Gakkai 　創価教育学会

Sōka Kyōiku-gaku taikei 　創価教育学
　　体系

soku 　即

sokuchū no ichigon 即中の一言
sokuji nishin 即事而真
sokushin jōbutsu 即身成仏
sokushin jōbutsu gyōhōshiki 即身成仏
    行法式
soku ze kaidan 即是戒壇
sōmoku jōbutsu 草木成仏
Son'en 尊円
Songai (Endon-bō) 尊海（円頓房）
Sonshun 尊舜
sō nyo ze 相如是
Sōō 相応
Sōō Kashō-kō 相応和尚講
Soshi-e 祖師会
sōtai kaie 相対開会
sōtai myō 相対妙
Sōtōshū 曹洞宗
Sōtō Zen 曹洞禅
sōzu 僧都
ssu fen lü 四分律
Ssu-ming Chih-li 四明智礼
ssu-shih (shishaku) 四釈
Sugawara no Michizane 菅原道真
Sugiu lineage 椙生流
Su-hsi-ti ching (Soshitsuji-kyō) 蘇悉
    地経
suijaku 垂迹
suijaku-butsu 垂迹仏
sui-tzu-i (zuijii) 随自意
sui-yüan 随縁
Sūkyō Mahikari 崇教真光
Suruga 駿河
Tachikawa school 立川流
Tahō 多宝
Tahō Nyorai 多宝如来
tahō tatchū Ōmuni seson 多宝塔中大
    牟尼世尊
Ta-hsing-shan-ssu 大興善寺
Ta-hui Tsung-kao 大慧宗杲
Taigei 泰芸
Taiheiki 大平記
Taimitsu 台密
Taira 平
Taira no Yasuyori 平康頼
taisei Bukkyō 体制仏教
Taisekiji 大石寺
Taishō University 大正大学
Taizōkai 胎蔵界

Ta-jih ching (Dainichi-kyō) 大日経
Takakamori 嵩かもり
takuji-kan 託事観
Tanabe Zenchi 田辺善知
Tanaka Chigaku 田中智学
Tanba 丹波
tandai 探題
Tan'ei 湛睿
Tangi hōshin shō 彈偽褒真鈔
Tani Ajari (Kōkei) 谷阿闍梨
    （皇慶）
Tani school 谷流
Tankū 湛空
Tao-sheng 道生
Tao-sui 道邃
tariki 他力
Ta-su, Mount 大蘇山
tatchū hōmon 塔中法門
"Ta-i" 大意
Tendai 天台
Tendai Eshin-ryū gojū sōden kanjō 天台
    恵心流五重相伝潅頂
Tendai kanjō genshi 天台潅頂玄旨
Tendaishū 天台宗
tenjin dokurō 天真独朗
tenjin dokurō naru honri no ichinen
    sanzen 天真独朗本理一念
    三千
tenjin dokurō no ichigon 天真独朗の
    一言
tenjin dokurō no shikan 天真独朗の
    止観
Tenkai 天海
Tennōji 天王寺
Tenshō Daijin (Amaterasu Ōmikami)
    天照大神
Teradomari 寺泊
t'i 体
T'ien-t'ai 天台
T'ien-t'ai Ta-shih (Chih-i) 天台大師
    （智顗）
Ti-lun school 地論宗
Toba 鳥羽
Tōdaiji 東大寺
Tōeizan Senpukuji 東叡山泉福寺
Tōfukuji 東福寺
tōgaku 等覚
Tōji 東寺

Tōjō　東条

Tōjō Kagenobu　東条景信

Tōkai　等海

Tōketsu　唐決

Toki Jōnin　富木常忍

Tokuen　徳円

Tokugawa Ieyasu　徳川家康

Tokuitsu　徳一

Tōmitsu　東密

t'o-shih kuan (takuji-kan)　託事観

Tōtaigi shō kenmon　当体義抄見聞

tōtai renge　当体蓮華

tōtai soku myōkaku　当体即妙覚

Tōtō　東塔

Tōtomi　遠江

Tōyō-bō lineage　東陽房流

Toyotomi Hideyoshi　豊臣秀吉

tsang-chiao (zōgyō)　蔵教

Tsuchimikado-monzeki lineage　土御
　　門門跡流

tsūgyō　通教

Tsukahara Sanmaidō　塚原三昧堂

ts'ung-hsing kuan (jugyō-kan)　従行観

Tsung-mi　宗密

Tsurezure gusa　徒然草

Tsurugaoka Hachiman Shrine　鶴岡
　　八幡宮

tun-chiao (tonkyō)　頓教

t'ung-chiao (tsūgyō)　通教

tz'u-ti san-kuan (shidai sangan)　次第
　　三観

u　有

Ueno　上野

Uesugi　上杉

Unshō　運敞

usa shikaku sanjin　有作始覚三身

Utoku, King　有徳王

waka　和歌

waka no ie　和歌の家

wakō dōjin　和光同塵

wakō dōjin kanjō　和光同塵潅頂

wasan　和譜

washi no yama　鷲の山

Wei-chüan　維蠲

wo (ga)　我

wu-shih pa-chiao (goji hakkyō)　五時八教

Wu-t'ai, Mount　五台山

wu-wei (gomi)　五味

Yadoya Nyūdō　宿屋入道

Yagenta-dono　弥源太殿

Yajirō　弥次郎

Yakushi Nyorai　薬師如来

Yakushiji　薬師寺

Yamashita Hiroaki　山下宏明

Yamasue-no-ōnushi　山末の大主

yang　陽

Yang (Emperor)　煬

Yao　羲

Yao-shih ching (Yakushi-kyō)　薬師経

yin　陰

yin-yüan (innen)　因縁

Yōben　永辨

yōfu　遥附

Yōhōji　要法寺

Yokawa　横川

Yokawa Ryōzen-in zōryū anmon　横川霊
　　山院造立案文

yomikudashi　読み下し

Yoshida Kanetomo　吉田兼倶

Yoshida Kenkō　吉田兼好

Yoshida Shintō　吉田神道

Yüan-cheng　元政

yüan-chiao (engyō)　円教

yüan-ch'i　縁起

yüan-ch'i lun (engi ron)　縁起論

yüan-tun chih-kuan (endon shikan)
　　円頓止観

Yü-ch'ieh lun　瑜伽論

yüeh-chiao (yakkyō)　約教

yüeh fa-hsiang kuan (yaku hossō kan)
　　約法相観

yūgen　幽玄

Yuiitsu Shintō　唯一神道

yuiju ichinin　唯授一人

Yuiken　惟堅

Yuima-e　維摩会

yukan　遊観

yung　用

Yung-chen (era)　永貞

Yūsai　祐済

yūzū nenbutsu　融通念仏

Zaijarin　摧邪輪

zaike　在家

zasu　座主

zazen 座禅

ze ho jū hōi/seken sō jōjū 是法住法位・世間相常住

Zen 禅

Zenkai 全海

Zennichi 然日

Zenpu 禅芙

Zentoku 善徳

Zen'yū 禅瑜

Zeshō (Nisshutsu) 是生

Zeshō-bō Renchō (Nichiren) 是生房蓮長

ze sō nyo 是相如

zettai funi 絶対不二

zettai ichigen ron 絶対一元論

zettai kaie 絶対開会

zettai myō 絶対妙

zōaku muge 造悪無碍

Zōga 増賀

zōgyō 蔵教

zōhō 像法

zokutai 俗諦

zokutai jōjū 俗諦常住

Zuichō ms. 瑞長本

zuien shinnyo 随縁真如

zuien shinnyo no chi 随縁真如の智

zuijii 随自意

zuishinbutsu 随身仏

zuitai 随他意

zuryō 受領

zushi 厨子

Bibliography

Collections and Reference Works

Bukkyōgo daijiten 佛教語大辞典. Nakamura Hajime 中村元, ed. 1975. 3 vols. Reduced-size ed. (*shukusatsuban* 縮刷版). 1 vol. Tokyo: Tōkyō Shoseki, 1981.

Bukkyō daijiten 佛教大辭典. Mochizuki Shinkō 望月信亨. 1909. Expanded and revised by Tsukamoto Zenryū 塚本善隆 and Sekai Seiten Kankō Kyōkai 世界聖典刊行協会. 10 vols. Kyoto: Sekai Seiten Kankō Kyōkai, 1954–1971.

Bussho kaisetsu daijiten 佛書解説大辭典. Ono Genmyō 小野玄妙, ed. 14 vols. Tokyo: Daitō Shuppansha, 1933–1936. Revised 1964–1967. Supplementary vols. 12 and 13, ed. by Maruyama Takao 丸山孝雄. Reprint 1974–1978.

Dai Nihon Bukkyō zensho 大日本佛教全書. Busshō Kankōkai 佛書刊行会, ed. 150 vols. Tokyo: 1912–1922.

Dengyō Daishi zenshū 傳教大師全集. Hieizan Senshūin 比叡山專修院, ed. 5 vols. Tokyo: Sekai Seiten Kank戯 Kyōkai, 1989.

Dōgen Zenji zenshū 道元禅師全集. Kawamura Kōdō 河村孝道 et al., eds. 7 vols. Tokyo: Shunjūsha, 1988–1993.

Eshin Sōzu zenshū 惠心僧都全集. Hieizan Senshūin 比叡山專修院, ed. 5 vols. Kyoto: Shibunkaku, 1971.

Fuji shūgaku yōshu 富士宗学要集. Hori Nichikō 堀日亨, ed. 10 vols. Tokyo: Sōka Gakkai, 1974–1979.

Gunsho ruijū 群書類從. Hanawa Hokiichi 塙保巳一 (1746–1821), ed. Revised, Ōta Tōshirō 太田藤四郎, ed. 29 vols. Tokyo: Zoku Gunsho Ruijū Kansei-kai, 1939–1943.

Hōbō girin: Dictionnaire encyclopédique du bouddhisme d'après les sources chinoises et japonaises. Under the direction of Sylvain Lévi and Takakusu Junjirō. Paul Demiéville, ed. in chief. Tokyo: Maison franco-japonaise, 1929–.

Honzon ron shiryō 本尊論資料. Sozan Gakuin Shuppanbu 祖山學院出版部, ed. Tokyo: by the editor, 1909.

Hsü tsang ching 續藏經. Reprint of *Dai Nihon zoku zōkyō* 大日本續藏經. 150 portfolios. Shanghai, 1923.

Iwanami Bukkyō jiten 岩波仏教辞典. Nakamura Hajime 中村元 et al., eds. Tokyo: Iwanami Shoten, 1989.

481

Jūgōen zenshū 充洽園全集. Jūgōen Zenshū Kankōkai 充洽園全集刊行会, ed. 5 vols. Tokyo: Daitō Shuppan, 1975.

Kamakura ibun 鎌倉遺文. Komonjo hen 古文書編. Takeuchi Rizō 竹内理三, ed. 42 vols. Tokyo: Tōkyōdō Shuppan, 1971–1991.

Kamakura kyū Bukkyō 鎌倉舊仏教. Kamata Shigeo 鎌田茂雄 and Tanaka Hisao 田中久雄, eds. *Nihon shisō taikei* 日本思想大系, vol. 15. Tokyo: Iwanami Shoten, 1971.

Kanke bunsō kanke kōshū 管家文草・管家後集. Kawaguchi Hisao 川口久雄, ed. *Nihon koten bungaku taikei* 日本古典文學体系, vol. 72. Tokyo: Iwanami Shoten, 1966.

Kōbō Daishi zenshū 弘法大師全集. Mikkyō Bunka Kenkyūjo 密教文化研究所, ed. 8 vols. Revised, Ito-gun, Wakamiya Prefecture: by the editor, 1965–1968.

Kokushi taikei 國史大系. Kuroita Katsumi 黒板勝美 and Kokushi Taikei Henshūkai 國史大系編修會, eds. 60 vols. 1926. Revised and expanded (*shintei zōho* 新訂増補), 66 vols. Tokyo: Yoshikawa Kōbunkan, 1929–1966.

Kōtei zōho Tendai zasu ki 校訂増補天台座主記. Shibuya Jigai 渋谷慈鎧, ed. Tokyo: Daiichi Shobō, 1973.

The Major Writings of Nichiren Daishōnin. The Gosho Translation Committee, ed. and trans. 7 vols. Tokyo: Nichiren Shōshū International Center, 1979–1994.

Nichiren 日蓮. Tokoro Shigemoto 戸頃重基 and Takagi Yutaka 高木豊, eds. *Nihon shisō taikei* 日本思想大系, vol. 14. Tokyo: Iwanami Shoten, 1970.

Nichiren Daishōnin denki shiryō sakuin 日蓮大聖人伝記資料索引. Fujinomiya, Shizuoka Prefecture: Taisekiji, 1982.

Nichiren Daishōnin gosho jiten 日蓮大聖人御書辞典. Sōka Gakkai Kyōgakubu 創価学会教学部 ed., with editorial supervision of Ikeda Daisaku 池田大作. Tokyo: Seikyō Shinbunsha, 1976.

Nichiren jiten 日蓮辞典. Miyazaki Eishū 宮崎英修, ed. Tokyo: Tōyōdō Shuppan, 1987. Revised 1997.

Nichiren Shōnin denki shū 日蓮上人傳記集. Kyoto: Honmanji, 1974.

Nichiren Shōnin goibun kōgi 日蓮聖人御遺文講義. 19 vols. Nichiren Shōnin Roppyaku Gojū Onki Hōon Kinenkai 日蓮聖人六百五十遠忌報恩記念會, ed. Tokyo: Ryūginsha, 1932–1933. Reprint ed. Nihon Bussho Kankōkai, 1957–1964.

Nichiren Shōnin ibun jiten 日蓮聖人遺文辞典. Risshō Daigaku Nichiren Kyōgaku Kenkyūjo 立正大学日蓮教学研究所, ed. Minobu-chō. Yamanashi Prefecture: Minobusan Kuonji, 1985.

Nichirenshū jiten 日蓮宗事典. Nichirenshū Jiten Kankō Iinkai 日蓮宗事典刊行委員会, ed. Tokyo: Nichirenshū Shūmuin, 1981.

Nichirenshū shūgaku zensho 日蓮宗宗學全書. Risshō Daigaku Nichiren Kyōgaku Kenkyūjo 立正大學日蓮教學研究所, ed. 23 vols. Tokyo: Sankibō Busshorin, 1968–1978.

Nihon Daizōkyō 日本大藏經. Nihon Daizōkyō Hensankai 日本大藏經編纂會, ed. 50 vols. By the editor, 1914–1922.

Selected Writings of Nichiren. Philip B. Yampolsky, ed., with Burton Watson, trans. New York: Columbia University Press, 1990.

Shinkō sōsho 信仰叢書. Hayakawa Junsaburō 早川純三郎, ed. Tokyo: Kokusho Kankōkai, 1915.

Shinran chosaku zenshū 親鸞著作全集. Kaneko Daie 金子大栄, ed. Kyoto: Hōzōkan, 1964.

Shintō jiten 神道事典. Kokugakuin Daigaku Nihon Bunka Kenkyūjo 國學院大學日本文化研究所, ed. Tokyo: Kōbundō, 1994.

Shōwa genson Tendai shoseki sōgō mokuroku 昭和現存天台書籍総合目録. Shibuya Ryōtai 渋谷亮泰, ed. 3 vols. Kyoto: Hōzōkan, 1978.

Shōwa shinshū Hōnen Shōnin zenshū 昭和新修法然上人全集. Ishii Kyōdō 石井教道, ed. Kyoto: Heirakuji Shoten, 1955. Reprint 1974.

Shōwa teihon Nichiren Shōnin ibun 昭和定本日蓮聖人遺文. Risshō Daigaku Nichiren Kyōgaku Kenkyūjo 立正大學日蓮教學研究所, ed. 4 vols. Minobuchō, Yamanashi Prefecture: Minobusan Kuonji, 1952–1959. Revised 1988.

Sōtōshū zensho 曹洞宗全書, 1929–35. Sōtōshū Zensho Kankōkai 曹洞宗全書刊行会, ed. Revised and expanded. 18 vols. Tokyo: Sōtōshō Shūmuchō, 1970–1973.

Taishō shinshū daizōkyō 大正新修大藏經. Takakusu Junjirō 高楠順次郎, Watanabe Kaigyoku 渡邊海旭 et al., eds. 85 vols. Tokyo: Taishō Issaikyō Kankōkai, 1924–1934.

Tendai hongaku ron 天台本覚論. *Nihon shisō taikei* 日本思想大系, vol. 9. Tada Kōryū 多田厚隆 et al., eds. Tokyo: Iwanami Shoten, 1973.

Tendaishū zensho 天台宗全書. Tendaishūten Kankōkai 天台宗典刊行會, ed. 25 vols. 1935–1937. Reprint ed. Tokyo: Daiichi Shobō, 1973–1974.

Zoku gunsho ruijū 續群書類從. Hanawa Hokiichi 塙保己一, ed. Revised, Ōta Tōshirō 太田藤四郎, ed. 33 vols. Tokyo: Zoku Gunsho Ruijū Kanseikai, 1923–1928.

Zoku Tendaishū zensho 續天台宗全書. Tendai Shūten Hensanjo 天台宗典編纂所, ed. 15+ vols. Tokyo: Shunjūsha, 1987–.

Canonical Works

Ch'ang a-han ching (Dīrgha-āgama) 長阿含經. *T* 1.1:1–149.

Chih-kuan fu-hsing ch'uan-hung chüeh 止觀輔行傳弘決. *T* 1912.46:141–446.

Chih-kuan yi-li 止觀義例. *T* 1913.46:447–59.

Chin-kang pei 金剛錍. *T* 1932.46:781–86.

Chin-kang san-mei ching (Kŭmgang sanmae-kyŏng, Vajrasamādhi-sūtra) 金剛三昧經. *T* 273.9:365–73.

Chin-kang-ting yü-ch'ieh-chung fa o-nou-to-lo san-miao san-p'u-t'i-shin lun 金剛頂瑜伽中發阿耨多羅三藐三菩提心論. *T* 1665.32:572–74.

Ching-te ch'uan-teng lu 景德傳燈録. *T* 2076.51:196–467.

Chung-hua ch'uan-hsin-ti ch'an-men shih-tzu ch'eng-hsi t'u 中華傳心地禪門師資承襲圖. *HTC* 110:433–38.

Chu Wei-mo-ch'i ching 注維摩詰經. *T* 1775.38:327–420.

Fa-hua hsüan-i shih ch'ien 法華玄義釋籤. *T* 1717.33:815–963.

Fa-hua hsüan-lun 法華玄論. *T* 1720.34:361–450.

Fa-hua wen-chü chi 法華文句記. *T* 1719.34:151–360.

Fan-wang ching 梵網經. *T* 1484.24:997–1010.

Fo-pen-hsing chi ching 佛本行集經. *T* 190.3:655–932.

Fo-shuo kuan P'u-hsien P'u-sa hsing-fa ching 佛説觀普賢菩薩行法經. *T* 277.9:389–93.

Fo-shuo wu-liang-shou ching (Sukhāvatī-vyūha) 佛説無量壽經. *T* 360.12:265–79.

Hsü kao-seng chuan 續高僧傳. *T* 2060.50:425–707.

Hua-yen ching 華嚴經. See *Ta-fang-kuang fo hua-yen ching.*

Hua-yen yu-hsin fa-chieh chi 華嚴遊心法界記. *T* 1877.45:641–50.

Jen-wang ching 仁王經:

    Jen-wang hu-kuo po-jo po-lo-mi ching 仁王護國般若波羅蜜經. *T* 245.8: 825–34.

    Jen-wang po-jo po-lo-mi ching 仁王般若波羅蜜經. *T* 246.8:834–45.

Kuan-yin hsüan-i 觀音玄義. *T* 1726.34:877–92.

Miao-fa lien-hua ching (Saddharma-puṇḍarīka-sūtra) 妙法蓮華經. *T* 262.9:1–62.

Miao-fa lien-hua ching hsüan-i 妙法蓮華經玄義. *T* 1716.33:681–814.

Miao-fa lien-hua ching wen-chü 妙法蓮華經文句. *T* 1718.34:1–149.

Mo-ho chih-kuan 摩訶止觀. *T* 1911.46:1–140.

Myōhō-renge sanmai himitsu sanmaya kyō 妙法蓮華三昧秘密三摩耶經. See *Renge sanmai-kyō.*

P'u-sa ying-lo pen-yeh ching 菩薩瓔珞本業經. *T* 1485.24:1010–23.

P'u-t'i-hsin lun 菩提心論. See *Chin-kang-ting yü-ch'ieh-chung fa o-nou-to-lo san-miao san-p'u-t'i-shin lun.*

Renge sanmai-kyō (or *Renge zanmai-kyō*) 蓮華三昧經. *HTC* 15:409–13.

Sheng-man shih-tzu-hou i-sheng ta-fang-pien fang-kuang ching (Śrīmālā-devi siṃhanāda-sūtra) 勝鬘師子吼一乘大方便方廣經. *T* 353.12:217–23.

Shih-chia-shih p'u 釋迦氏譜. *T* 2041.50:84–99.

Shih Mo-ho-yen lun (Sŏk Mahayon-ron) 釋摩訶衍論. *T* 1668.32:591–668.

Shih pu-erh men chih-yao ch'ao 十不二門旨要鈔. *T* 1928.46:705–20.

Shih-ti-ching lun 十地經論. *T* 1522.26:123–203.

Sui T'ien-t'ai Chih-che Ta-shih pieh-chuan 隋天台智者大師別傳. *T* 2050.50:191–98.

Ta-chi ching 大集經. See *Ta-fang-teng ta-chi ching.*

Ta-chih tu lun 大智度論. *T* 1509.25:57–756.

Ta-fang-kuang fo hua-yen ching 大方廣佛華嚴經 (*Buddhāvataṃsaka-nāma-mahā-vaipulya-sūtra*). *T* 278.9:395–788; 279.10:1–444.

Ta-fang-kuang yüan-chüeh hsiu-to-lo liao-i ching 大方廣圓覺修多羅了義經. *T* 842.17:913–22.

Ta-fang-teng ta-chi ching 大方等大集經. *T* 397.13:1–407.

Ta-hui P'u-chüeh Ch'an-shih yü-lu 大慧普覺禪師語録. *T* 1998.47:811–957.

Ta-pan nieh-p'an ching (Mahā-parinirvāṇa-sūtra) 大般涅槃經. *T* 374.12:365–603.

Ta-p'i-lu-che-na ch'eng-fo ching (Ta-p'i-lu-che-na ch'eng-fo shen-pien chia-ch'ih ching) 大毘盧遮那成佛神變加持經. *T* 848.18:1–55.

Ta-p'i-lu-che-na ch'eng-fo ching shu 大毘盧遮那成佛經疏. *T* 1796.39:579–789.

Ta-sheng ch'i-hsin lun 大乘起信論. *T* 1666.32:575–83.

Ta-sheng ch'i-hsin lun i-chi 大乘起信論義記. *T* 1846.44:240–87.

Ta-sheng fa-yüan i-lin chang 大乘法苑義林章. *T* 1861.45:245–374.

Ta-sheng hsüan lun 大乘玄論. *T* 1853.45:15–77.

T'ien-t'ai ssu-chiao i (Chŏnt'ae sa kyoŭi) 天台四教儀. *T* 1931.46:773–80.

Wei-mo chieh so-shuo ching (Vimalakīrti-nirdeśa-sūtra) 維摩詰所説經. *T* 474.14:537–57.

Wei-mo ching lüeh-shu 維摩經略疏. *T* 1778.38:562–710.

Wu-liang-i ching 無量義經. *T* 276.9:383–89.

Wu-liang-shou ching 無量壽經. See *Fo-shuo wu-liang-shou ching.*

Yüan-chüeh ching 圓覺經. See *Ta-fang-kuang yüan-chüeh hsiu-to-lo liao-i ching.*

Japanese Tendai Works

Byakuja hen (Hekija hen) 闢邪編. Taishō University Library ms. no. 139.19.1.

Chū Hongaku san 註本覚讃. *THR*, pp. 99–100.

Chū Muryōgikyō 註無量義經. *DDZ* 3:555-675.

Dainichi-kyō shiki (Dai Birushana-kyō shiki) 大日經指歸（大毘盧遮那經指歸）. *T* 2212.58:12–23.

Dainijū shichika daiji kuden 第二重七ヶ大事口傳. In Uesugi Bunshū, *Nihon Tendai shi,* 2:818–21.

Danshō ketsujō shū 斷證決定集. *DDZ* 5:221–64.

Denjutsu isshin kaimon 傳述一心戒文. *DDZ* 1:523–648.

Denshin Kashō den 傳信和尚傳. *Sange gakuhō* 山家學報 21 (April 1925):1–24.

Dōsui Oshō fuhōmon [or *Dōzui Kashō fuhōmon*] 道邃和尚付法文. *DDZ* 5 (*furoku* 附録): 115–16.

Ehyō Tendaishū 依憑天台集. *DDZ* 3:343-66.

Eizan Daishi den 叡山大師傳. *DDZ* (*furoku* 附録) 5:1–48.

"*Ekō-bō* [*ryū*] *hōmon sōjō keiyaku jōjō*" 惠光坊「流」法門相承契約條條. Uesugi Bunshū, *Nihon Tendai shi,* 2:860.

"*Endon-bō Songai kishōmon o tatemōsu koto*" 立申圓頓房尊海起請文事. *TZ* 9:116b.

Enkai jūroku chō 円戒十六帖. *ZTZ, Enkai* 圓戒 1:76–115.

Entaragishū 圓多羅義集. *DNBZ* 28:1139–93.

Eshin-ryū kyōjū sōjō shishō 惠心流教重相承私鈔. Uesugi Bunshū, *Nihon Tendai shi,* 2:813–17.

Eshin-ryū naishō sōjō hōmon shū 惠心流内證相承法門集. See *Ichijō shō.*

Fuhō engi 付法縁起. See *Tendai Hokkeshū fuhō engi.*

Futsū jubosatsukai kōshaku 普通授菩薩戒廣釋. *T* 2381.74:757–79.

Genshidan hishō 玄旨壇秘鈔. *Shinkō sōsho*, pp. 18–122.

Gobu kechimyaku 五部血脈. *DDZ* 5:357–66.

Hachijō shō 八帖抄. *TZ* 9:299–318.

Hachijō shō kenmon 八帖抄見聞. *TZ* 9:319–42.

Hokekyō jikidan shō 法華経鈔直談隙. 3 vols. Ikeyama Saien 池山一切圓, ed. Kyoto: Nozomigawa Shoten, 1979. Reprint 1989.

Hokekyō jurin shūyō shō 法華經鷲林拾葉鈔. *DNBZ* 30:1–724.

Hokke gengi shiki 法華玄義私記. *DNBZ* 21:1–382.

Hokke kan'yō ryakuchū shūku shū 法華肝要略注秀句集. *DDZ* 5:279–326.

Hokke ryakugi kenmon 法華略義見聞. *DNBZ* 16:1–88.

Hokke shūku 法華秀句. *DDZ* 3:1–280

Hokke sho shiki 法華疏私記. *DNBZ* 21:383–550; 22:1–237.

Hongaku san 本覚讃. *THR*, p. 98.

Hongaku san shaku 本覚讃釈. *THR*, pp. 101–18.

Honri taikōshū 本理大綱集. *THR*, pp. 7–22.

Ichijō shō (Eshin-ryū naishō sōjō hōmon shū) 一帖抄（惠心流内證相承法門集）. *TZ* 9:27–48.

Ichijō yōketsu 一乗要決. *T* 2370.74:327–72.

Ichiryū sōden hōmon kenmon 一流相傳法門見聞. See *Nijō shō.*

Isshin myōkai shō 一心妙戒鈔. *ZTZ, Enkai* 圓戒 1:254–316.

Isshin sangan kanjin sūken 一心三観観心枢検. Takahashi Shūei 高橋秀栄, ed., *Komazawa Daigaku Bukkyōgakubu kenkyū kiyō* 駒澤大學佛教學部研究紀要 54 (March 1996): 260–62.

Jigyō nenbutsu mondō 自行念佛問答. *DNBZ* 31:197–213.

Ju bosatsukai gi 授菩薩戒儀. *DDZ* 1:303–34.

Juketsu entaragishū tōketsu 授決圓多羅義集唐決. See *Entaragishū*.

Kanjin ryaku yōshū 観心略要集. *DNBZ* 31:155–83.

Kankō ruijū 漢光類聚. *DNBZ* 17:1–114; *THR*, pp. 187–286 (*maki* 1, 4).

Kawataya bōshō jūkutsū 河田谷傍正十九通. *TZ* 9:91–118.

Keiran shūyō shū 渓嵐拾葉集. *T* 2410.76:503–888.

Kenkai ron 顯戒論. *DDZ* 1:25–198.

Kongōchō daikyōō-kyō sho 金剛頂大教王經疏. *T* 2223.61: 7–114.

Koshinjū ki 己心中記. *DNBZ* 24:350–51.

Kuin bukkaku shō 九院佛閣抄. *GR* no. 439, 24:563–89.

Maka shikan kenmon tenchū 摩訶止觀見聞添註. *DNBZ* 29:1–500.

Makura sōshi 枕雙紙. *DNBZ* 32:105–29; *ESZ* 3:469–520.

Mongu ryaku taikō shikenmon 門句略大綱私見聞. *DNBZ* 18:1–237.

Naishō Buppō kechimyaku tō shikenmon 内証仏法血脈等私見聞. Takahashi Shūei 高橋秀栄, ed., *Komazawa Daigaku Bukkyōgakubu kenkyū kiyō* 駒澤大學佛教學部研究紀要 54 (March 1996): 219–62.

Naishō Buppō sōjō kechimyaku fu 内證佛法相承血脈譜. *DDZ* 1:199–248.

Nijō shō (Ichiryū sōden hōmon kenmon) 二帖抄 (一流相傳法門見聞). *TZ* 9:119–55.

Nijō shō kenmon 二帖抄見聞. *TZ* 9:157–298.

Nihon daishi sentoku myōshō ki (or *Nihon daishi sentoku meishō ki*) 日本大師先徳明匠記. *DNBZ* 111:265–89.

Ōjō yōshū 往生要集. Genshin 源信. Ishida Mizumaro 石田瑞麿, ed. *Nihon shisō taikei* 日本思想体系, vol. 6. Tokyo: Iwanami Shoten, 1970.

Sandai shōsho shichimen sōjō kuketsu 三大章疏七面相承口決. *DDZ* 5:139–57.

Sanjū shika no kotogaki 三十四箇事書. *THR*, pp. 151–85.

Santsū kuketsu 三通口決. *ZTZ, Enkai* 圓戒 1:370–75.

Shikan shiki 止觀私記. *DNBZ* 22:237–591.

Shingonshū kyōji gi 眞言宗教時義. *T* 2396.75:374–450.

Shinjō sōmoku jōbutsu shiki 甚定草木成仏私記. Sueki Fumihiko, *Heian shoki Bukkyō shisō no kenkyū*, pp. 705–85.

Shinnyo kan 真如観. *THR*, pp. 119–49.

Shoshin kangaku shō 初心勸學鈔. Taishō University Library ms. no. 130.38.1.

Shugo kokkai shō 守護國界章. *DDZ* 2:151–682.

Shūyō byakkō 宗要白光. *TZ* 18.

Shuzenji-ketsu 修禪寺決. *THR*, pp. 41–96; *DDZ* 5:69–138.
> *Shūzenji sōden nikki* 修禪寺相傳日記. *THR*, pp. 54–96; *DDZ* 5:91–138.
> *Shuzenji sōden shiki* 修禪寺相伝私記. *THR*, pp. 42–53 (*Shuzenji sōden shichū* 修禪寺相傳私注. *DDZ* 5:69–90.)

Sokenki 素絹記. *DNBZ* 74:283–302.

Sōmoku hosshin shugyō jōbutsu ki 草木發心修行成佛記. *DNBZ* 24:345–46.

Soshitsuji-kyō sho (Soshitsuji kara-kyō ryakusho) 蘇悉地羯羅經略疏. *T* 2227.61:389–484.

Taizō kongō bodaishin gi ryaku mondō shō 胎藏金剛菩提心義略問答抄. *T* 2397.75:451–559.

Tendai Hokkeshū denbōge 天台法華宗傳法偈. *DDZ* 5:1–30.

Tendai Hokkeshū fuhō engi 天台法華宗付法縁起. *DDZ* 5:31–38.

Tendai Hokkeshū gakushōshiki mondō 天台法華宗學生式問答. *DDZ* 1:335–414.

Tendai Hokkeshū gozu hōmon yōsan 天台法華宗牛頭法門要纂. *THR*, pp. 23–40.

Tendai Hokkeshū sokushin jōbutsu gi 天台法華宗即身成仏義. Sueki Fumihiko, *Heian shoki Bukkyō shisō no kenkyū*, pp. 655–89.

Tendai mon'yō jizai-bō 天台問要自在房. See *Wayaku Tendaishū rongi hyakudai jizai-bō.*

Tendai myōshō kuketsu shō (or *Tendai meishō kuketsu shō*) 天台名匠口決抄. *DNBZ* 18:239–388.

Tokai kuden shō 等海口傳抄. *TZ* 9:343–571.

Tōketsu 唐決. *Nihon daizōkyō* 40:363–83, 391–405.

Tonchō himitsu kōyō 頓超秘密綱要. *ZTZ, Enkai* 圓戒 1:317–33.

Wayaku Tendaishū rongi hyakudai jizai-bō 和訳天台宗論義百題自在房. Revised. Kouda Ryōsen 古宇田亮宣, ed. Tokyo: Ryūbunkan, 1977.

Zōda shō 藏田抄. *TZ* 9:49–90.

Works by or Attributed to Nichiren

"Akimoto gosho" 秋元御書. *STN* 360.2:1729–40.

"*Ankoku ron* gokan yurai" 安国論御勧由来. *STN* 48.1:421–24.

"Fudō Aizen kankenki" 不動愛染感見記. *STN* 3.1:16.

"Funamori Yasaburō moto gosho" 船守弥三郎許御書. *STN* 26.1:229–31.

"Gyōbin sojō goetsū" 行敏訴状御會通. *STN* 84.1:497–501.

"Hakii Saburō-dono gohenji" 波木井三郎殿御返事. *STN* 127.1:745–49.

"Ha Ryōkan-tō gosho" 破良観等御書. *STN* 236.2:1278–86.

Hokke daimoku shō 法華題目鈔. *STN* 44.1:391–405.

Hokke honmonshū yōshō 法華本門宗要鈔. *STN* (*zokuhen* 續篇) 44.3:2150–68.

Hokke shōshin jōbutsu shō 法華初心成佛鈔. *STN* 270.2:1413–33.

Hōmon mōsarubekiyō no koto 法門可被申様之事. *STN* 70.1:443–56.

Honzon mondō shō 本尊問答抄. *STN* 307.2:1573–86.

Hōon shō 報恩抄. *STN* 223.2:1192–1250.

Ichidai shōgyō taii 一代聖教大意. *STN* 10.1:57–75.

Ichinen sanzen hōmon 一念三千法門. *STN* (*zokuhen* 續篇) 14.3:2033–40.

Isshō jōbutsu shō 一生成佛鈔. *STN* 7.1:42–45.

"Jakunichi-bō gosho" 寂日房御書. *STN* 341.2:1669–71.

Jimyō Hokke mondō shō 持妙法華問答鈔. *STN* 33.1:274–85.

Jippōkai ji 十法界事. *STN* 16.1:137–44.

Jippōkai myō inga shō 十法界明因果鈔. *STN* 22.1:171–83.

Jisshō shō 十章鈔. *STN* 81.1:488–93.

Jōdo kuhon no koto 浄土九品之事. *STN* (*zuroku* 圖録) 15.3:2306–11.

Jūnyoze no koto 十如是事. *STN* (*zokuhen* 續篇) 13.3:2030–33.

Kaimoku shō 開目鈔. *STN* 98.1:535–609.

Kaitai sokushin jōbutsu gi 戒體即身成佛義. *STN* 1.1:1–15.

Kanjin honzon shō 觀心本尊抄. *STN* 118.1:702–21.

"Kanjin honzon shō sōejō" 觀心本尊鈔副状. *STN* 119.1:721.

Kenbutsu mirai ki 顕佛未来記. *STN* 125.1:738–43.

Ken hōbō shō　顯謗法鈔. *STN* 31.1:247–73.

"Kingo-dono gohenji"　金吾殿御返事. *STN* 73.1:458–59.

"Kōnichi-bō gosho"　光日房御書. *STN* 213.2:1152–61.

"Kyōdai shō"　兄弟鈔. *STN* 174.1:918–34.

Kyōgyōshō gosho　教行證御書. *STN* 281.2:1479–89.

Kyō ki ji koku shō　教機時國鈔. *STN* 29.2:241-46.

"Mama Shakabutsu gokuyō oijō"　眞間釋迦佛御供養逐状. *STN* 72.1:457.

"Misawa shō"　三澤鈔. *STN* 275.2:1443–50.

Mokue nizō kaigen no koto　木繪二像開眼供養之事. *STN* 138.1:791–94.

"Myōhō-ama gozen gohenji"　妙法尼御前御返事. *STN* 301.2:1535–37.

"Myōhō-bikuni gohenji"　妙法比丘尼御返事. *STN* 305.2:1551–71.

"Myōmitsu Shōnin goshōsoku"　妙密上人御消息. *STN* 214.2:1162–70.

"Nakaoki Nyūdō goshōsoku"　中興入道御消息. *STN* 354.2:1712–19.

"Nanjō Hyōe Shichirō-dono gohenji"南條兵衛七郎殿御返事. *STN* 411.2:1883–85.

"Nanjō Hyōe Shichirō-dono gosho"　南條兵衛七郎殿御書. *STN* 38.1:319–28.

Nenbutsusha tsuihō senjō ji　念仏者追放宣状事. *STN* (*zuroku*　圖録) 7.3:2258–72.

"Nichigennyo Shakabutsu kuyō ji"　日眼女釋迦佛供養事. *STN* 327.2:1623–25.

"Nichimyō Shōnin gosho"　日妙聖人御書. *STN* 107.1:641–48.

"Nichinyo gozen gohenji"　日女御前御返事. *STN* 256.2:1374–77.

Nyorai metsugo go gohyakusai shi kanjin honzon shō　如来滅後五五百歳始觀心本尊抄. See *Kanjin honzon shō*.

Nyosetsu shugyō shō　如説修行鈔. *STN* 124.1:731–38.

Ongi kuden　御義口傳. *STN* (*kōki*　講記) 3:2606–728.

Onkō kikigaki　御講聞書. *STN* (*kōki*　講記) 3:2544–96.

"Onkoromo narabi ni hitoe gosho"　御衣竝單衣御書. *STN* 195.2:1111–12.

"Renjō shō"　蓮盛鈔. *STN* 4.1:17–22.

Risshō ankoku ron　立正安國論. *STN* 24.1:209–26.

Risshōkan jō　立正觀抄. *STN* 158.1:844–51.

"Risshōkan jō sōjō"立正觀抄送状. *STN* 165.1:870–72.

"Rondan tekitai gosho"　論談敵對御書. *STN* 32.1.274.

Sado gosho　佐渡御書. *STN* 100.1:610–19.

Sandai hihō honjō ji (Sandai hihō shō)　三大秘法禀承事（三大秘法鈔）. *STN* 403.2:1862–66.

"Seichōji daishu chū"　清澄寺大衆中. *STN* 205.2:1132–36.

Senji shō　撰時抄. *STN* 181.2:1003–61.

"Sennichi-ama gohenji"　千日尼御返事. *STN* 371.2:1759–66.

"Shibosatsu zōryū shō"四菩薩造立鈔. *STN* 335.2:1647–50.

"Shijō Kingo-dono gohenji"　四條金吾殿御返事. *STN* 105.1:634–37.

"Shijō Kingo-dono gohenji"　四條金吾殿御返事. *STN* 112.1:660–67.

"Shijō Kingo-dono gohenji"　四條金吾殿御返事. *STN* 169.1:894–95.

"Shijō Kingo-dono gohenji"　四條金吾殿御返事. *STN* 384.2:1799–1801.

"Shijō Kingō-dono goshōsoku"　四條金吾殿御消息. *STN* 87.1:504–5.

"Shijō Kingo nyobō gosho"　四條金吾女房御書. *STN* 78.1:484–85.

"Shijō Kingo Shakabutsu kuyō ji"四條金吾釋迦佛供養事. *STN* 220.2:1182–89.

Shimoyama goshōsoku　下山御消息. *STN* 247.2:1312–45.

Shingon kenmon　眞言見聞. *STN* 110.1:649–60.

"Shingon shoshū imoku"　眞言諸宗違目. *STN* 106.1:638–41.

Shinkokuō gosho　神國王御書. *STN* 168.1:877–93.

"Shion shō" 四恩鈔. *STN* 28.1:233–41.

Shishin gohon shō 四信五品鈔. *STN* 242.2:1294–1300.

Shōgu mondō shō 聖愚問答鈔. *STN* 43.1:350–91.

Shō Hokke daimoku shō 唱法華題目鈔. *STN* 23.1:184–208.

Shōji ichidaiji kechimyaku shō 生死一大事血脈鈔. *STN* 95.1:522–24.

"Shōmitsu-bō gosho" 聖密房御書. *STN* 148.1:820–27.

"Shonin gohenji" 諸人御返事. *STN* 280.2:1479.

"Shōnin gonanji" 聖人御難事. *STN* 343.2:1672–75.

Shoshū mondō shō 諸宗問答鈔. *STN* 5.1:22–33.

Shugo kokka ron 守護國家論. *STN* 15.1:89–136.

Shuju onfurumai gosho 種種御振舞御書. *STN* 176.2:959–86.

Sōmoku jōbutsu kuketsu 草木成佛口決. *STN* 97.1:532–34.

"Sōya Nyūdō-dono gohenji" 曾谷入道殿御返事. *STN* 267.2:1407–10.

"Toki-dono gosho" 富木殿御書. *STN* 144.1:809.

"Toki Nyūdō-dono gohenji" 富木入道殿御返事. *STN* 294.2:1517–22.

"Toki Nyūdō-dono gohenji" 富木入道殿御返事. *STN* 310.2:1588–91.

"Ueno-ama gozen gohenji" 上野尼御前御返事. *STN* 415.2:1890–94.

"Ueno-dono gohenji" 上野殿御返事. *STN* 282.2:1490–92.

"Ueno-dono haha ama gozen gohenji" 上野殿母尼御前御返事. *STN* 418.2:1896–98.

"Yadoya Nyūdō gari gojō" 宿屋入道許御状. *STN* 50.1:424–25.

"Yadoya Nyūdō sai gojō" 宿屋入道再御状. *STN* 51.1:425.

Yorimoto chinjō 頼基陳状. *STN* 249.2:1346–61.

"Zenmui Sanzō shō" 善無畏三藏鈔. *STN* 76.1:461–76.

Other Works in Premodern or Early Modern Nichiren Collections

Daishōnin gosōsō nikki 大聖人御葬送日記. *NSZ* 1:53–57.

Dentō shō 傳燈鈔. *NSZ* 18:1–60.

Fuji isseki monto zonchi no koto 富士一跡門徒存知事. *NSZ* 2:118–28; *FSY* 1:51–59.

Fuji monkachū kenmon 富士門家中見聞. *FSY* 5:147–266.

Fuji shiryō ruijū 富士史料類聚. *FSY* 8.

Ganso kedōki 元祖化導記. *Nichiren Shōnin denki shū*, pp. 7–55.

Goden dodai 御傳土代. *NSZ* 2:236–47.

Gohonzon jikkaishū no koto 御本尊十界習事. *Honzon ron shiryō* (2), pp. 378–80.

Gohonzon shichika sōjō 御本尊七箇相承. *FSY* 1:31–33.

Gohonzon sōden shō 御本尊相傳鈔. *Honzon ron shiryō* (2), pp. 237–46.

Gohonzon sōden shō 御本尊相傳鈔. *Honzon ron shiryō* (2), pp. 300–17.

Gojū enki 五重圓記. *NSZ* 2:88–92.

Gosho shō 御書鈔. 2 vols. Kyoto: Honmonji, 1976.

Goyuimotsu haibun no koto 御遺物配分事. *NSZ* 2:107–10.

"Hara-dono gohenji" 原殿御返事. *NSZ* 2:170–76.

Hiraga Hondoji keizu shidai 平賀本土寺繼圖次第. *NSZ* 18:73–80.

Honge betsuzu busso tōki 本化別頭佛祖統記. Kyoto: Honmanji, 1973. Reprint 1980.

Hon'in-myō kuketsu 本因妙口決. *FSY* 2:69–84.

Hon'in-myō shō (Hokke honmonshū kechimyaku sōjō no koto) 本因妙抄（法華本門宗血脈相承事）. *NSZ* 2:1–10; *FSY* 1:1–8.

Honzon no kikigaki 本尊ノ聞書. *Honzon ron shiryō* (2), pp. 324–27.

Honzon sando sōden 本尊三度相伝. *FSY* 1:35–42.

Hyaku rokka sōjō 百六箇相承. *NSZ* 2:11–32; *FSY* 1:9–25.

Ichiji gogi kuden 一字五義口傳. *Honzon ron shiryō* (2), pp. 289–91.

Ichinen sanzen ron 一念三千論. *Jūgōen zenshū* 3:19–232.

"Ikegami sōjō" 池上相承. *NSZ* 2:33.

Ikki shoshū zenkon kiroku 一期所修善根記録. *NSZ* 1:441–50.

Jōshūin honzon shōgyō no koto 常修院本尊聖教事. *STN* (*mokuroku* 目録) 3:2729–32.

Jūni innen shō 十二因縁抄. *NSZ* 1:283–318.

Kanjin honzon shō kenmon 觀心本尊鈔見聞. *NSZ* 16:269–378.

Kanjin honzon shō shiki 觀心本尊鈔私記. *NSZ* 16:103–378.

Kinkō shū 金綱集. *NSZ* 13, 14.

Kongō kin'yō ben 金剛龜羊辨. *NSZ* 6:347–418.

Konke honzon rongi rakukyo 今家本尊論義落居. *Honzon ron shiryō* (2), pp. 530–33.

Mandara sōden 漫荼羅相傳. *NSZ* 1:221–30.

"Minobu sōjō" 身延相承. *NSZ* 2:33.

"Misa-bō gohenji" 美作房御返事. *NSZ* 2:145–47.

Musaka shō 槾作抄. *FSY* 2:247–88.

Nichidai Jikken Taitō mondō ki 日大直兼台當問答記. *NSZ* 2:422–32.

Nichiman shō 日満抄. *NSZ* 2:397–407.

Nichiren Daishōnin chūgasan 日蓮大聖人註畫讃. *Nichiren Shōnin denki shū*, pp. 69–112.

Shinryū shōden shō 眞流正傳鈔. *NSZ* 10, 11:1–235.

Shūso gosenge kiroku 宗祖御遷化記録. *NSZ* 2:101–5.

Tōke shūshi myōmoku 當家宗旨名目. *Nichiren Shonin denki shū*, pp. 518–74.

Ubuya sōjō no koto 産湯相承事. *FSY* 1:27–29.

Ushidan sho kikigaki 有師談書聞書. *FSY* 2:139–62.

Ushi kegi shō 有師化儀抄. *FSY* 1:61–80.

"Yo Hakii Sanenaga sho" 與波木井實長書. *NSZ* 2:169–70.

Other Primary Sources

Ama no mokuzu 海人藻芥. *GR* no. 492, 28:85–111.

Azuma kagami 吾妻鏡. *Kokushi taikei* 32, 33.

Azuma mondō 吾妻問答. *Renga ronshū hai ronshū* 連歌論集俳論集. Kidō Saizō 木藤才藏 and Imoto Nōichi 井本農一, eds., pp. 205–37. *Nihon koten bungaku taikei* 日本古典文學大系, vol. 66. Tokyo: Iwanami Shoten, 1961. Reprint 1974.

Bendōwa 辨道話. *DZZ* 2:460–81.

"Busshō" 仏性. *Shōbō genzō*. *DZZ* 1:14–44.

Dainichi-kyō kaidai 大日經開題. *KDZ* 1:633–89.

Dainichi-kyō kenmon 大日經見聞. *Nihon daizōkyō* 14.

"Daishugyō" 大修行. *Shōbō genzō*. *DZZ* 2:185–95.

Eiheiji sanso gyōgō ki 永平寺三祖行業記. *SZ* 16:1–10.

Eihei shingi (Eihei genzenji shingi) 永平元禪師清規. *T* 2584.82:319–42.

Fukan zazengi 普勧坐禅儀. *DZZ* 5:4–12.

"Genjō kōan" 現成公安. *Shōbō genzō*. *DZZ* 1:2–7.

Genkō shakusho 元亨釋書. *DNBZ* 101:223–512.

Gorin kuji myō himitsu shaku 五輪九字明秘密釋. *T* 2514.79:11–22.

Gokyōshō tsūryakki 五教章通略記. *DNBZ* 9:1–331.

"Gyōbutsu igi" 行仏威儀. *Shōbō genzō*. *DZZ* 1:59–75.

Heike monogatari 平家物語. Takagi Ichinosuke 高木市之助 et al., eds. *Nihon koten bungaku taikei* 日本古典文學体系, vols. 32 and 33. Tokyo: Iwanami Shoten, 1959. Reprint 1974.

Himitsu mandara jūjūshin ron 秘密漫茶羅十住心論. *KDZ* 1:125–415.

Hizō hōyaku 秘藏寶鑰. *KDZ* 1:417–73.

Hizōki 秘藏記. *KDZ* 2:1–73.

Hōbutsu shū 寶物集. *DNBZ* 147:303–460.

Hōkyō ki 宝慶記. *DDZ* 7:2–51.

Hōmon hyakushū 法門百首. *GR* no. 445, 24:697–717.

Honchō kōsōden 本朝高僧傳. *DNBZ* 102, 103.

Hyaku shijū gokajō mondō (Ippyaku shijūgokajō mondō) 百四十五箇條問答. *SSH*, pp. 647–69.

Ichinen tanen mon'i 一念多念文意. *SCZ*, pp. 510–32.

Jakushōdō kokkyō shū 寂照堂谷響集. *DNBZ* 149:1–188.

Jinden ainō shō 塵添壒囊鈔. *DNBZ* 150:1–529.

"Jinshin inga" 深信因果. *Shōbō genzō*. *DZZ* 2:387–94.

Jūjūshin ron 十住心論. See *Himitsu mandara jūjūshin ron*.

Kenzei ki 建撕記. See *Teiho Kenzei ki*.

"Kichijō-in Hokke-e ganmon" 吉祥院法華會願文. *Kanke bunsō* 管家文草 650. *Kanke bunsō kanke kōshū*, p. 599.

Korai fūtei shō 古来風躰抄. *Kodai chūsei geijutsu ron* 古代中世芸術論. Hayashiya Tatsusaburō 林屋辰三郎, ed. *Nihon shisō taikei* 日本思想大系, vol. 23. Tokyo: Iwanami Shoten, 1973.

Kōzen gokoku ron 興禪護國論. *T* 2543.80:1–17.

Kyōgyōshinshō 教行心證. *SCZ*, pp. 8–342.

Mattō shō 末燈鈔. *SCZ*, pp. 579–617.

Naiten jinro shō 内典塵露章. *DNBZ* 3:49–68.

Nakatomi no harae kunge 中臣祓訓解. *KDZ* 5:160–81.

Nomori no kagami 野守鏡. *GR* no. 484, 27:474–514.

Ryō no gige 令義解. *Kokushi taikei*, part 2, no. 2.

Sandaison gyōjō ki 三代尊行状記 (*Ganso Koun Tettsū sandaison gyōjōki* 元祖孤雲徹通三代尊行状記). *SZ* 16:11–19.

Sangoku Buppō dentsū engi 三國佛法傳通縁起. *DNBZ* 101:97–131.

Sanji raishaku 三時禮釋. *DNBZ* 13:131–44.

Senchaku hongan nenbutsu shū 選擇本願念佛集. *SSH*, pp. 310–50.

Shasekishū 沙石集. Watanabe Tsunaya 渡邊綱也, ed. *Nihon koten bungaku taikei* 日本古典文學体系, vol. 85. Tokyo: Iwanami Shoten, 1966. Reprint 1973.

Shichikajō kishōmon 七箇條起請文. *SSH*, pp. 787–93.

Shinran Shōnin goshōsoku shū 親鸞聖人御消息集. *SCZ*, pp. 618–37.

Shōbō genzō 正法眼蔵. *DZZ* 1, 2:1–458.

"Shōji" 生死. *Shōbō genzō*. *DZZ* 2:528–29.

Shōji jissō gi 聲字實相義. *KDZ* 1:521–34.

Shōmyō genryū ki 聲明源流記. *T* 2720.84:864–65.

Shōzōmatsu wasan 正像末和讃. *SCZ*, pp. 443–62.

Sōkonshū 草根集. *Shikashū taisei* 私家集大成 5: *Chūsei* 中世 3. Wakashi Kenkyūkai 和歌史研究会, ed. Tokyo: Meiji Shoin, 1974. Reprint 1983.

Sokushin jōbutsu gi 即身成佛義. *KDZ* 1:506–20.

"Sokushin zebutsu" 即心是仏. *Shōbōgenzō*. *DZZ* 1:53–58.

Songō shinzō meimon 尊號眞像銘文. *SCZ*, pp. 481–509.

Tanni shō 歎異抄. *SCZ*, pp. 673–97.

Teiho Kenzei ki 訂補建撕記. *SZ* 17:15–32.

Yuishin shō mon'i 唯信鈔文意. *SCZ*, pp. 533–69.

Secondary Sources

Abe, Masao. "The Oneness of Practice and Attainment: Implications for the Relation between Means and Ends." In *Dōgen Studies,* ed. William R. LaFleur, pp. 99–111. Kuroda Institute Studies in East Asian Buddhism 2. Honolulu: University of Hawaii Press, 1985.

Abé Ryūichi. *The Weaving of Mantra: Kūkai and the Establishment of Esoteric Buddhist Discourse.* University of Columbia Press, forthcoming.

———. "Saichō and Kūkai: A Conflict of Interpretations." *Japanese Journal of Religious Studies* 22/1–2 (Spring 1995): 103–37.

Adachi Naoya 安達直哉. "Hōshinnō no seijiteki igi" 法親王の政治的意義. In *Shōensei shakai to mibun kōzō* 荘園制社会と身分構造, ed. Takeuchi Rizō 竹内理三, pp. 173–201. Tokyo: Azekura Shobō, 1980.

Adolphson, Mikael S. "Monks, Courtiers and Warriors in Premodern Japan: The Secular Power of Enryakuji in the Heian and Kamakura Eras." Ph.D. dissertation. Stanford University, 1995.

Akamatsu Toshihide 赤松俊秀. "'Akusō' no shinjō to Kamakura Bukkyō" 「悪僧」の信条と鎌倉仏教. In *Bukkyō shisō ronshū* 仏教思想論集, ed. Okuda Jiō Sensei Kiju Kinen Ronbunshū Kankōkai 奥田慈應先生喜寿記念論文集刊行会, pp. 455–69. Kyoto: Heirakuji Shoten, 1976.

———, ed. *Nihon Bukkyōshi* 日本佛教史, vol. 2: *Chūsei-hen* 中世篇. Kyoto: Hōzōkan, 1967.

Andō Toshio 安藤俊雄. "Ichinen sanzen-setsu no keisei" 一念三千説の形成. *Ōtani gakuhō* 大谷學報 36/3 (Dec. 1956): 64–66.

———. *Tendaigaku: Konpon shisō to sono tenkai* 天台学—根本思想とその展開. Kyoto: Heirakuji Shoten, 1968.

———. *Tendaigaku ronshū: Shikan to jōdo* 天台学論集—止観と浄土. Kyoto: Heirakuji Shoten, 1975.

Andrews, Allan. *The Teachings Essential for Rebirth: A Study of Genshin's Ōjō yōshū.* Tokyo: Sophia University, 1973.

Arai Eizō 新井栄蔵, Watanabe Sadamaro 渡辺貞麿, and Mimura Terunori 三村晃功, eds. *Eizan no bunka* 叡山の分化. Kyoto: Sekai Shisōsha, 1989.

Asai Endō 浅井圓道. "Gogihan no keisei katei no kōsatsu: Gogi no happyō made" 五義判の形成過程の考察—五義の発表まで. *Ōsaki gakuhō* 大崎學報 118 (Oct. 1964): 22–44.

———, ed. *Hongaku shisō no genryū to tenkai* 本覚思想の源流と展開. *Hokekyō kenkyū* 法華経研究 11. Kyoto: Heirakuji Shoten, 1991.

———. "Honzon ron no tenkai" 本尊論の展開. In *Chūsei Hokke Bukkyō no tenkai* 中世法華仏教の展開, ed. Kageyama Gyōō 影山発雄, pp. 251–76. *Hokekyō kenkyū* 法華経研究 5. Kyoto: Heirakuji Shoten, 1974.

———. "Ji no hōmon" 事の法門. *Nichiren kyōgaku kenkyū jo kiyō* 日蓮教學研究所紀要 13 (Feb. 1986): 1–11.

———. *Jōko Nihon Tendai honmon shisō shi* 上古日本天台本門思想史. Kyoto: Heirakuji Shoten, 1975.

———. "Jōko Nihon Tendai ni okeru hongaku hōmon tenkaijō no genkai" 上古

日本天台における本覺法門展開上の限界. *IBK* 印度學佛教學研究 16/1 (Dec. 1967): 30–37.

———. "'Musa sanjin' kō" 「無作三身」考. *IBK* 印度學佛教學研究 18/1 (Dec. 1969): 103–9.

———. "Nichiren no ibun to hongaku shisō" 日蓮の遺文と本覚思想. In *Hongaku shisō no genryū to tenkai* 本覚思想の源流と展開, ed. Asai Endō, pp. 285–306. *Hokekyō kenkyū* 法華経研究 11. Kyoto: Heirakuji Shoten, 1991.

———. "Nihon Tendai no busshō ron" 日本天台の仏性論. In *Hokke Bukkyō no butsuda ron to shujō ron* 法華仏教の仏陀論と衆生論, ed. Watanabe Hōyō 渡辺宝陽, pp. 355–76. *Hokekyō kenkyū* 法華経研究 10. Kyoto: Heirakuji Shoten, 1985.

———. "*Onkō kikigaki* kō" 『御講聞書』考. *Seishin* 棲神 48 (Oct. 1975): 19–29.

———. "Shūso ni okeru kannenron daha no shisō" 宗祖における観念論打破の思想. In *Nichiren kyōgaku no shomondai* 日蓮教学の諸問題, ed. Motai Kyōkō Sensei Koki Kinen Ronbunshū Kankōkai 茂田井教亨先生古希記念論文集刊行会, pp. 141–67. Kyoto: Heirakuji Shoten, 1974.

Asai Yōrin 浅井要麟. "Nichiren kyōgakuchū ni kōsaku seru chūko Tendai no shisō oyobi yōsō" 日蓮教學中に交錯せる中古天台の思想及び様相. *Seishin* 棲神 25 (1940): 62–84.

———. *Nichiren Shōnin kyōgaku no kenkyū* 日蓮聖人教學の研究. Kyoto: Heirakuji Shoten, 1945. Reprint 1980.

Astley, Trevor. "A Matter of Principles: A Note on the Recent Conflict between Nichiren Shōshū and Sōka Gakkai." *Japanese Religions* 17/2 (July 1992): 167–75.

Azuma Ryūshin 東隆眞. "*Gyōgōki* to *Gyōjōki*: *Gyōjōki* no sakusha, seiritsu nendai no suitei" 「行業記」と「行状記」—「行状記」の作者・成立年代の推定. *Shūkyō kenkyū* 宗教研究 6 (1964): 101–5.

———. *Keizan Zenji no kenkyū* 瑩山禅師の研究. Tokyo: Shunjūsha, 1974.

Bellah, Robert. *Tokugawa Religion: The Cultural Roots of Modern Japan.* New York: Free Press, Macmillan, 1957. Reprinted with a new introduction, 1985.

Bielefeldt, Carl. *Dōgen's Manuals of Zen Meditation.* Berkeley: University of California Press, 1988.

———. "The One Vehicle and the Three Jewels: On Japanese Sectarianism and Some Ecumenical Alternatives." *Buddhist-Christian Studies* 10 (1990): 5–16.

Bloom, Alfred. *Shinran's Gospel of Pure Grace.* Tucson: University of Arizona Press, 1965.

Bodiford, William M. *Sōtō Zen in Medieval Japan.* Kuroda Institute Studies in East Asian Buddhism 8. Honolulu: University of Hawaii Press, 1993.

———. "Zen and the Art of Religious Prejudice: Efforts to Reform a Tradition of Social Discrimination." *Japanese Journal of Religious Studies* 23/1–2 (Spring 1996): 1–27.

Buswell, Robert E., Jr. *The Formation of Ch'an Ideology in China and Korea: The Vajrasamādhi-sūtra, a Buddhist Apocryphon.* Princeton: Princeton University Press, 1989.

Chan, Chi-wah. "Chih-li (960–1028) and the Formation of Orthodoxy in the Sung T'ien-t'ai Tradition of Buddhism." Ph.D. dissertation. University of California, Los Angeles, 1993.

Chappell, David, ed., and Masao Ichishima, comp. Trans. Buddhist Translation Seminar of Hawaii. *T'ien-t'ai Buddhism: An Outline of the Fourfold Teachings.* Tokyo: Daiichi Shobō, 1983.

Childs, Margaret H. "*Chigo Monogatari:* Love Stories or Buddhist Sermons?" *Monumenta Nipponica* 35/2 (1980): 127–51.

Conger, George Perrigo. *Theories of Macrocosms and Microcosms in the History of Philosophy.* New York: Columbia University Press, 1922.

Davis, Winston. *Dōjō: Magic and Exorcism in Modern Japan.* Stanford: Stanford University Press, 1980.

———. "The Weber Thesis and the Economic Development of Japan." In his *Japanese Religion and Society: Paradigms of Structure and Change,* pp. 115–31. Albany: State University of New York Press, 1992.

DeBary, Wm. Theodore, et al., eds. *Sources of Chinese Tradition,* vol. 1. New York: Columbia University Press, 1960.

DeGroot, J. J. M. *Le Code du Mahayana en Chine: Son influence sur la vie monacal et sur le monde monacal.* Amsterdam: Verhider Kon. Ak. van Wetensch, 1893, pp. 14–88.

Del Campana, Pier P., trans. "*Sandaihihō-shō:* An Essay on the Three Great Mysteries by Nichiren." *Monumenta Nipponica* 26/1–2 (1971): 205–24.

Dobbins, James C. "Buddhist Modernism, Shinran's Teachings, and Shin Buddhism in Medieval Japan." Ms.

———. "Editor's Introduction: Kuroda Toshio and His Scholarship." *Japanese Journal of Religious Studies* 23/3–4 (Fall 1996): 217–32.

———. "Envisioning Kamakura Buddhism." In *Re-visioning "Kamakura" Buddhism,* ed. Richard Payne, pp. 24–42. Kuroda Institute Studies in East Asian Buddhism 11. Honolulu: University of Hawai'i Press, 1998.

———. *Jōdo Shinshū: Shin Buddhism in Medieval Japan.* Bloomington: Indiana University Press, 1989.

———, ed. *The Legacy of Kuroda Toshio.* Special issue. *Japanese Journal of Religious Studies* 23/3–4 (Fall 1996).

Dolce, Lucia D. "Awareness of *Mappō:* Soteriological Interpretations of Time in Nichiren." *Transactions of the Asiatic Society of Japan,* fourth series, 7 (1992): 81–106.

———. "Esoteric Patterns in Nichiren's Thought." *The Japan Foundation Newsletter* 23/5 (Feb. 1996): 13–16.

Dollarhide, Kenneth. "History and Time in Nichiren's *Senji-shō.*" *Religion* 12 (1982): 233–45.

———. *Nichiren's Senjishō: An Essay on the Selection of the Proper Time.* New York: Edwin Mellen Press, 1982.

Donner, Neal. "Chih-i's Meditation on Evil." In *Buddhist and Taoist Practice in Medieval Chinese Society,* ed. David W. Chappell, pp. 49–64. Honolulu: University of Hawaii Press, 1987.

———. "Sudden and Gradual Intimately Conjoined: Chih-i's T'ien-t'ai View." In *Sudden and Gradual: Approaches to Enlightenment in Chinese Thought,* ed. Peter N. Gregory, pp. 201–26. Kuroda Institute Studies in East Asian Buddhism 5. Honolulu: University of Hawaii Press, 1987.

Donner, Neal, and Daniel B. Stevenson. *The Great Calming and Contemplation: A Study and Annotated Translation of the First Chapter of Chih-i's Mo-ho chih-kuan.* Kuroda Institute Classics in East Asian Buddhism. Honolulu: University of Hawaii Press, 1993.

Elliot, Charles. *Japanese Buddhism.* Edward Arnold, 1935; London: Routledge and Kegan Paul; New York: Barnes and Noble, 1969.

Erickson, Carolly. *The Medieval Vision: Essays in History and Perception.* New York: Oxford University Press, 1976.

Etani Ryūkai 惠谷隆戒. "Eizan kaihō fukkō undō no shomondai" 叡山戒法復興運動の諸問題. *IBK* 印度學佛教學研究 9/1 (Jan. 1961): 108–14.

Faure, Bernard. "The Daruma-shū, Dōgen, and Sōtō Zen." *Monumenta Nipponica* 42/1 (1987): 25–55.

Foard, James H. "In Search of a Lost Reformation: A Reconsideration of Kamakura Buddhism." *Japanese Journal of Religious Studies* 7/4 (Dec. 1980): 261–91.

Ford, James L. "A Life Ignored: Jōkei (1155–1213) and 'Old' Kamakura Buddhism Reexamined." Ph. D. dissertation. Princeton University, 1996.

Foucault, Michel. *The Order of Things: An Archaeology of the Human Sciences* (a translation of *Les Mots et les choses*). New York: Vintage Books, 1970.

Franke, Herbert. "The Taoist Elements in the Buddhist *Great Bear Sūtra (Pei-tou ching)*." Asia Major, third series, 3/1 (1990): 75–111.

Fugen Daien 普賢大圓. "Shinshū kyōgaku to hongaku shisō: Toku ni busshōron o chūshin toshite" 眞宗教學と本覺思想—特に佛性論を中心として. *Ryūkoku Daigaku ronshū* 龍谷大學論集 361 (March 1959): 1–20.

———. "Shinshū nyorai ron no tokushoku" 眞宗如来論の特色. *IBK* 印度學佛教學研究 9/2 (March 1961): 516–23.

Fuji Gakurin Kenkyūka 富士学林研究科. *Nikkō Shōnin Minobu rizan shi* 日興上人身延離山史. Fujinomiya, Shizuoka Prefecture: Nichiren Shōshū Fukyōkai, 1961. Reprint 1977.

Fujii Manabu 藤井学. "Nichiren to shingi" 日蓮と神祇. *Nihon shi kenkyū* 日本史研究 44 (1959): 1–25.

Fujita Kōtatsu. "One Vehicle or Three?" trans. Leon Hurvitz. *Journal of Indian Philosophy* 3 (1975): 79–166.

Fukuda Ryōsei 福田亮成. "Kōbō Daishi no hongakuteki shutaikan" 弘法大師の本覚的主体観. In *Bukkyō no rekishi to shisō* 仏教の歴史と思想, ed. Mibu Taishun Hakushi Shōju Kinen Ronbunshū Kankōkai 壬生台舜博士頌寿記念論文集刊行会, pp. 823–37. Tokyo: Daizō Shuppan, 1985.

Fukuyama Toshio 福山敏男. "Monzeki jiin tanjō" 門跡寺院誕生. In *Hiezan 1: 1200 Nen no ayumi* 比叡山I—1200年の歩み, Kageyama Haruki 景山春樹 et al., pp. 171–93. Asahi Karuchā Bukkusu 朝日カルチャーブックス, no. 60. Osaka: Ōsaka Shoseki, 1986.

Funaoka Makoto 船岡誠. *Nihon Zenshū no seiritsu* 日本禅宗の成立. Tokyo: Yoshikawa Kōbunkan, 1987.

Gimello, Robert M. "Apophatic and Kataphatic Discourse in Mahāyāna: A Chinese View." *Philosophy East and West* 26/2 (April 1976): 117–36.

———. "Chih-yen (602-668) and the Foundations of Hua-yen Buddhism." Ph.D. dissertation. Columbia University, 1976.

Girard, Frédéric. *Un Moine de La Secte Kegon a l'Époque de Kamakura, Myōe (1173–1232) et le "Journal de ses Rêves."* Paris: École Francaise d'Extrème-Orient, 1990.

Goddard, Dwight, ed. and pub. *A Buddhist Bible.* Thetford, Vermont, 1932. 2d ed. (revised and expanded) 1938.

Grapard, Allan G. "Institution, Ritual, and Ideology: The Twenty-two Shrine-Temple Multiplexes of Heian Japan." *History of Religions* 23/3 (1984): 246–69.

———. "Linguistic Cubism: A Singularity of Pluralism in the Sannō Cult." *Japanese Journal of Religious Studies* 14/2–3 (1987): 211–34.

————. *The Protocol of the Gods: A Study of the Kasuga Cult in Japanese History.* Berkeley: University of California Press, 1992.

————. "The Shinto of Yoshida Kanetomo." *Monumenta Nipponica* 47/1 (Spring 1992): 27–58.

————. "The Textualized Mountain—Enmountained Text: The *Lotus Sutra* in Kunisaki." *The Lotus Sutra in Japanese Culture,* ed. George J. Tanabe, Jr., and Willa Jane Tanabe, pp. 159–89. Honolulu: University of Hawai'i Press, 1989.

Gregory, Peter N. "The Problem of Theodicy in the *Awakening of Faith.*" *Religious Studies* 22 (1986): 63–78.

————. "Tsung-mi and the Problem of *Hongaku shisō.*" *Komazawa Daigaku Zen kenkyūjo nenpō* 駒澤大學禪研究所年報 5 (March 1994): 100–51.

————. *Tsung-mi and the Sinification of Buddhism.* Princeton: Princeton University Press, 1991.

Groner, Paul. "Annen, Tankei, Henjō, and Monastic Discipline in the Tendai School: The Background of the *Futsū jubosatsukai kōshaku.*" *Japanese Journal of Religious Studies* 14/2–3 (June–Sept. 1987): 129–59.

————. "The *Fan-wang ching* and Monastic Discipline in Japanese Tendai: A Study of Annen's *Futsū jubosatsukai kōshaku.*" In *Chinese Buddhist Apocrypha,* ed. Robert E. Buswell, Jr., pp. 251–90. Honolulu: University of Hawaii Press, 1990.

————. "The *Lotus Sutra* and Saichō's Interpretation of the Realization of Buddhahood with This Very Body." In *The Lotus Sutra in Japanese Culture,* ed. George J. Tanabe, Jr., and Willa Jane Tanabe, pp. 53–74. Honolulu: University of Hawai'i Press, 1989.

————. "A Medieval Japanese Reading of the *Mo-ho chih-kuan:* Placing the *Kankō ruijū* in Historical Context." *Japanese Journal of Religious Studies* 22/1–2 (Spring 1995): 49–81.

————. *Saichō: The Establishment of the Japanese Tendai School.* Berkeley: Berkeley Buddhist Studies Series, 1984.

————. "Shortening the Path: Early Tendai Interpretations of the Realization of Buddhahood with This Very Body." In *Paths to Liberation: The Mārga and Its Transformations in Buddhist Thought,* ed. Robert E. Buswell, Jr., and Robert M. Gimello, pp. 439–73. Kuroda Institute Studies in East Asian Buddhism 7. Honolulu: University of Hawai'i Press, 1992.

————. "The Significance of Ryōgen's (912–984) Revival of the Tendai Examination System." In *Dainikai kokusai Hokekyō gakkai happyō shiryō* 第二回国際法華経学会発表資料, pp. 122–79. Tokyo: Taishō University, 1987.

Grosnick, William H. "The Categories of *T'i, Hsiang* and *Yung:* Evidence that Paramārtha Composed the *Awakening of Faith.*" *Journal of the International Association of Buddhist Studies* 12/1 (1989): 65–92.

Habito, Ruben L. F. *Originary Enlightenment: Tendai Hongaku Doctrine and Japanese Buddhism.* Studia Philologica Buddhica Occasional Paper Series XI. Tokyo: International Institute for Buddhist Studies, 1996.

Hakamaya Noriaki 袴谷憲昭. *Dōgen to Bukkyō: Jūnikanbon Shōbō genzō no Dōgen* 道元と仏教—十二巻本『正法眼蔵』の道元. Tokyo: Daizō Shuppan, 1992.

————. *Hihan Bukkyō* 批判仏教. Tokyo: Daizō Shuppan, 1990.

————. *Hongaku shisō hihan* 本覚思想批判. Tokyo: Daizō Shuppan, 1989.

————. "Sabetsu jishō o umidashita shisōteki haikei ni kansuru shiken" 差別事

象を生み出した思想的背景に関する私見. In his *Hongaku shisō hihan* 本覚思想批判, pp. 134–58. Tokyo: Daizō Shuppan, 1990.

———. "Tennōsei hihan" 天皇制批判. *Komazawa Daigaku Bukkyōgakubu ronshū* 駒澤大學佛教學部論集 20 (Oct. 1989): 373–400.

———. "'Wa' no han-Bukkyōsei to Bukkyō no hansensei" 「和」の反仏教性と仏教の反戦性. In his *Hihan Bukkyō* 批判仏教, pp. 275–304. Tokyo: Daizō Shuppan, 1990.

Hakeda, Yoshito S., trans. with commentary. *The Awakening of Faith*. New York: Columbia University Press, 1967.

———. *Kūkai: Major Works*. New York: Columbia University Press, 1972.

Hall, John Whitney. "Terms and Concepts in Japanese Medieval History: An Inquiry into the Problems of Translation." *Journal of Japanese Studies* 9/1 (Winter 1983): 1–32.

Hanano Michiaki 花野充昭. "Chūko Tendai bunken to nenbutsu shisō" 中古天台文献と念仏思想. In *Eizan Jōdokyō no kenkyū* 叡山浄土教の研究, ed. Satō Tetsue 佐藤哲英, pp. 318–46. Kyoto: Hyakkaen, 1979.

———. "Junsui Nichiren gi kakuritsu no mondaiten: Asai Yōrin-shi no soshogaku ni taisuru gigi" 純粋日蓮義確立の問題点―浅井要麟氏の祖書学に対する疑義. *Gyōun* 暁雲 2 (Dec. 1975): 1–44.

———. "Nichiren kyōgaku to *Shuzenji-ketsu*" 日蓮教学と『修禅寺決』. *Tōyō gakujutsu kenkyū* 東洋学術研究 15/5 (1976): 127–55.

———. "Nichiren no shōdai shisō to Danna-ryū no kanjō genshi kuden" 日蓮の唱題思想と檀那流の灌頂玄旨口伝. In *Nihon-Chūgoku Bukkyō shisō to sono tenkai* 日本・中国仏教思想とその展開, ed. Misaki Ryōshū 三崎良周, pp. 115–58. Tokyo: Sankibō Busshorin, 1992.

———. "Nichiren Shōnin kyōgaku no shisōshiteki kenkyū joron" 日蓮聖人教学の思想史的研究序論. *Gyōun* 暁雲 1 (1974): 97–150.

———. "Nihon chūko Tendai bunken no kōsatsu (1): Musa sanjin shisō no seiritsu to *Sanjū shika no kotogaki* no senja ni tsuite" 日本中古天台文献の考察（一）―無作三身思想の成立と三十四箇事書の選者について. *IBK* 印度學佛教學研究 24/1 (Dec. 1975): 337–42.

———. "Nihon chūko Tendai bunken no kōsatsu (2): Nichiren no *Risshōkan jō* no shingi mondai ni tsuite" 日本中古天台文献の考察（二）―日蓮の『立正観抄』の真偽問題について. *IBK* 印度學佛學教研究 25/2 (March 1977): 830–35.

———. "Nihon chūko Tendai bunken no kōsatsu (4): *Makura sōshi* no shohon ni tsuite" 日本中古天台文献の考察（四）―『枕双紙』の諸本について. *IBK* 印度學佛教學研究 27/2 (March 1979): 814–16.

———. "Nihon chūko Tendai bunken no kōsatsu (5): Kirikami sōden ni tsuite" 日本中古天台文献の考察（五）―切紙相伝について. *IBK* 印度學佛教學研究 28/2 (March 1980): 751–53.

———. "*Sanjū shika no kotogaki* no senja to shisō ni tsuite" 『三十四箇事書』の選者と思想について. *Tōyō gakujutsu kenkyū* 東洋学術研究 14/6 (1975): 154–63; 15/1 (1976): 135–58; 15/2 (1976): 127–56; 16/1 (1977): 134–54.

———. "Shijū kōhai no seiritsu jiki ni kansuru ichi kōsatsu" 四重興廃の成立時期に関する一考察. *Bukkyōgaku ronshū* 仏教学論集 10 (Dec. 1973): 34–53.

Hara Katsurō 原勝郎. "Tōsai no shūkyō kaikaku" 東西の宗教改革. *Geibun* 藝文 2/7 (1911): 1171–86.

Hayami Tasuku 速水侑. *Heian kizoku shakai to Bukkyō* 平安貴族社会と仏教. Tokyo: Yoshikawa Kōbunkan, 1975.

———. *Nihon Bukkyōshi: Kodai* 日本仏教史—古代. Tokyo: Yoshikawa Kōbunkan, 1986.

Hayashi Senshō 林宣正. "Shikan shō Hokke shisō to Senba kyōgaku: Chūko Tendai to Nichiren kyōgaku to no kankei no issetsu" 止觀勝法華思想と仙波教學—「中古天台と日蓮教學との關系」の一節. In *Shimizu Ryūzan Sensei koki kinen ronbunshū* 清水龍山先生古稀記念論文集, ed. Shimizu Ryūzan Sensei Kyōiku Gojūnen Koki Kinenkai 清水龍山先生教育五十年 古稀記念會, pp. 230–61. Tokyo: By the editor, 1940.

Hazama Jikō 硲慈弘. "Kamakura jidai ni okeru shinjō sōmetsu ron ni kansuru kenkyū" 鎌倉時代に於ける心常相滅論に關する研究. 1942. Reprinted in his *Nihon Bukkyō no kaiten to sono kichō* 日本佛教の開展とその基調, vol. 2: *Chūko Nihon Tendai no kenkyū* 中古日本天台の研究, pp. 298–318. Tokyo: Sanseidō, 1948. Reprint 1974.

———. *Nihon Bukkyō no kaiten to sono kichō* 日本佛教の開展とその基調, vol. 1: *Nihon Tendai to Kamakura Bukkyō* 日本天台と鎌倉佛教. Tokyo: Sanseidō, 1948. Reprint 1974.

———. *Nihon Bukkyō no kaiten to sono kichō* 日本佛教の開展とその基調, vol. 2: *Chūko Nihon Tendai no kenkyū* 中古日本天台の研究. Tokyo: Sanseidō, 1948. Reprint 1974.

Heine, Steven. "'Critical Buddhism' *(Hihan Bukkyō)* and the Debate Concerning the 75-fascicle and 12-fascicle *Shōbōgenzō* Texts." *Japanese Journal of Religious Studies* 21/1 (March 1994): 37–72.

Heng-ching Shih. "T'ien-t'ai Chih-I's Theory of Buddha Nature: A Realistic and Humanistic Understanding of the Buddha." In *Buddha Nature: A Festschrift in Honor of Minoru Kiyota,* ed. Paul Griffiths and John Keenan, pp. 153–70. Reno: Buddhist Books International, 1990.

Hibi Senshun 日比宣俊. "Tendai kyōgaku ni okeru busshu no geshu to busshō" 天台教学に於ける仏種の下種と仏性. *Nichiren kyōgaku kenkyūjo kiyō* 日蓮教學研究所紀要 13 (1986): 49–53.

Hirata Toshiharu 平田俊春. *Heian jidai no kenkyū* 平安時代の研究. Tokyo: Yamaichi Shobō, 1943.

———. *Sōhei to bushi* 僧兵と武士. Tokyo: Nihon Kyōbunsha, 1965.

Hirokawa Gyōbin 廣川尭敏, ed. *Kamakura shin Bukkyō to chūko Tendai to no kōshō ni kansuru kenkyū.* Heisei ninen, sannen, yonendo Monbushō kagaku kenkyūhi hojokin ippan kenkyū (C) kenkyū seika hōkokusho 鎌倉新佛教と中古天台との交渉に関する研究—平成2年、3年、4年度文部省科学研究費補助金一般研究（C）研究成果報告書. Tokyo: 1993.

Hirota Tetsumichi 廣田哲通. *Chūsei Hokekyō chūshakusho no kenkyū* 中世法華経注釈書の研究. Tokyo: Kasama Shoin, 1993.

Hiroumi Kōken 弘海高顕. "Kuden hōmon to Daie Zenji: Ryōzen ichie gennen misan no ku o chūshin toshite" 口傳法門と大慧禪師—靈山一會儼然未散の句を中心として. *Tendai gakuhō* 天台學報 24 (Nov. 1982): 158–62.

———. "Tendai kuden hōmon ni okeru gendō usō ni tsuite" 天台口伝法門における還同有相について. *IBK* 印度學佛教學研究 26/2 (March 1978): 707–8.

Hori Ichirō. *Folk Religion in Japan: Continuity and Change*, ed. Joseph M. Kitagawa and Alan L. Miller. Tokyo: University of Tokyo Press; Chicago: University of Chicago Press, 1968.

Hori Nichiko　堀日亨. *Fuji Nikkō Shōnin shōden*　富士日興上人詳伝. 2 vols. *Seikyō Bunko*　聖教文庫, nos. 43 and 51. Tokyo: Seikyō Shinbunsha, 1974.

Hubbard, Jamie, and Paul L. Swanson, eds. *Pruning the Bodhi Tree: The Storm over Critical Buddhism*. Nanzan Library of Asian Religion and Culture 2. Honolulu: University of Hawaiʻi Press, 1997.

Hunter, Jeffrey. "The *Fuju Fuse* Controversy in Nichiren Buddhism: The Debate between Busshō-in Nichiō and Jakushō-in Nichiken." Ph.D. dissertation. University of Madison at Wisconsin, 1989.

Hurvitz, Leon. *Chih-i: An Introduction to the Life and Ideas of a Chinese Buddhist Monk. Mélanges chinois et bouddhiques* 12 (1960-62): 1–372. Brussels: l'Institut Belge des Hautes Études Chinoises.

———, trans. *Scripture of the Lotus Blossom of the Fine Dharma (The Lotus Sūtra)*. New York: Columbia University Press, 1976.

Ienaga Saburō　家永三郎. *Chūsei Bukkyō shisōshi kenkyū*　中世仏教思想史研究. Kyoto: Hōzōkan, 1947. Revised and expanded 1990.

Ikeda Rosan　池田魯参. "Dōgen to chūko Tendai hongaku shisō: *Shōbōgenzō* 'Hokke ten hokke' o tsūro toshite"　道元と中古天台本覚思想—『正法眼蔵法華転法華』を通路として. *Bukkyōgaku*　仏教学 32 (March 1992): 1–20.

———. "Yamanouchi Shun'yū cho *Dōgen Zen to Tendai hongaku hōmon*　山内舜雄著『道元禅師と天台本覚法門』. *Komazawa Daigaku Bukkyōgakubu ronshū*　駒澤大學佛教學部論集 16 (Oct. 1985): 395–414.

Ikegami Songi　池上尊義. "Nichiren to kokka"　日蓮と国家. In *Nichiren to sono kyōdan*　日蓮とその教団, vol. 1, ed. Kawazoe Shōji　川添昭二 et al., pp. 62–84. Kyoto: Heirakuji Shoten, 1976.

Ikeyama Saien　池山一切圓. "Eizan no kyōiku"　叡山の教育. In *Hieizan* II: Sono kokoro to gyō　比叡山 II:そのこころと行, Setouchi Jakuchō　瀬戸内寂聴 et al., pp. 79–110. Asahi Karuchā Bukkusu　朝日カルチャーブックス, no. 69. Osaka: Osaka Shoseki, 1986.

Imaeda Aishin　今枝愛真. "Dōgen no shōgai"　道元の生涯. In *Kōza Dōgen*　講座道元 1: *Dōgen no shōgai to shisō*　道元の生涯と思想, ed. Kagamishima Genryū　鏡島元隆 and Tamashiro Yasushirō　玉城康四郎, pp. 39–109. Tokyo: Shunjūsha, 1979.

———. *Dōgen: Zazen hitosuji no shamon*　道元—座禅ひとすじの沙門. NHK Books, no. 255. Tokyo: Nippon Hōsō Shuppan Kyōkai, 1976.

Inoue Mitsusada　井上光貞. *Nihon Jōdokyō seiritsushi no kenkyū*　日本浄土教成立史の研究. Tokyo: Yamakawa Shuppan, 1956. Revised (*shintei*　新訂) 1989.

Ishida Mizumaro　石田瑞麿. *Jōdokyō no tenkai*　浄土教の展開. Tokyo: Shunjūsha, 1967.

———. *Kairitsu no kenkyū*　戒律の研究, vol. 2. *Nihon Bukkyō shisō kenkyū*　日本仏教思想研究, vol. 2. Tokyo: Hōzōkan, 1986.

———. "Kuden hōmon ni okeru shijū kōhai no seiritsu"　口傳法門における四重興廃の成立. *IBK*　印度學佛教學研究 15/2 (March 1967): 772–75.

———. *Nihon Bukkyō ni okeru kairitsu no kenkyū*　日本仏教における戒律の研究. Tokyo: Zaike Bukkyō Kyōkai, 1963.

———. "Nyobon: Sono furerarenai jittai ni tsuite" 女犯―その触れられない実態について. In *Bukkyō no rekishiteki tenkai ni miru shokeitai* 仏教の歴史的展開に見る諸形態, ed. Furuta Shōkin Hakushi Koki Kinenkai 古田紹欽博士古希記念会, pp. 424–39. Tokyo: Sōbunsha, 1981.

———. *Ōjō no shisō* 往生の思想. *Sāra Sōsho* サーラ叢書, no. 16. Kyoto: Heirakuji Shoten, 1968. Reprint 1986.

Ishihara Toshio 石原斌夫. "Hongaku shisō to Shinran" 本覚思想と親鸞. *IBK* 印度學佛教學研究 35/2 (March 1987): 763–65.

Ishii Shūdō. "Recent Trends in Dōgen Studies." *Komazawa Daigaku Zen kenkyūjo nenpō* 駒澤大學禪研究所年報 1 (March 1990): 264–319.

Itō Zuiei 伊藤瑞叡. "Chūgoku Kegonshū ni okeru hongakuteki shisō: Kegon jūjikyō ni okeru hongakuteki shisō to Kegon kyōgaku ni okeru hongakuteki shisō" 中国華厳宗における本覚的思想―華厳十地経における本覚的思想と華厳教学における本覚的思想. In *Hongaku shisō no genryū to tenkai* 本覚思想の源流と展開, ed. Asai Endō 浅井圓道, pp. 53–92. *Hokekyō kenkyū* 法華経研究 11. Kyoto: Heirakuji Shoten, 1991.

Itō Zuiei and Murakami Masakatsu 村上征勝. "Sandai hihō bonjōji no keiryō bunkengakuteki shin kenkyū: Kurasutā bunseki ni yoru shingi hantei" 三大秘法禀承事の計量文献学的新研究―クラスター分析による真偽判定. *Ōsaki gakuhō* 大崎學報 148 (March 1992): 1–52.

Iwata Kyōen 岩田教圓. "Eshin-ryū shichika kuden hōmon ni tsuite" 惠心流七箇口傳法門に就いて. *Pitaka* ピタカ 4/1 (1936): 31–38.

Kagamishima Genryū. 鏡島元隆. *Dōgen Zenji no in'yō kyōten-goroku no kenkyū* 道元禅師の引用経典・語録の研究. Tokyo: Mokujisha, 1965.

———. *Dōgen Zenji to sono shūhen* 道元禅師とその周辺. Tokyo: Daitō Shuppan, 1985.

———. "Dōgen Zenji to Tendai hongaku homon: *Hokekyō* in'yō ni kanren shite" 道元禪師と天台本覺法門―法華經引用に關連して. *Shūkyō kenkyū* 宗教研究 2 (Jan. 1960): 50–57.

———. "Eisai, Dōgen sōken mondai ni tsuite: Ko shahon *Kenzei ki* hakken ni chinamite" 栄西・道元相見問題について―古写本建撕記発見に因みて. In *Dōgen* 道元, ed. Kawamura Kōdō 河村孝道 and Ishikawa Rikizan 石川力山, pp. 41–57. *Nihon meisō ronshū* 日本名僧論集 8. Tokyo: Yoshikawa Kōbunkan, 1983.

———. "Honshō myōshu no shisōshiteki haikei" 本証妙修の思想史的背景. 1965. Reprinted in *Dōgen* 道元, Kawamura Kōdō 河村孝道 and Ishikawa Rikizan 石川力山, eds., pp. 97–104. *Nihon meisō ronshū* 日本名僧論集 8. Tokyo: Yoshikawa Kōbunkan, 1983. Also reprinted in Kagamishima Genryū 鏡島元隆, *Dōgen Zenji to sono shūhen* 道元禅師とその周辺, pp. 267–75. Tokyo: Daitō Shuppan, 1985.

Kageyama Gyōō 影山尭雄. *Nichiren kyōdanshi gaisetsu* 日蓮教団史概説. Kyoto: Heirakuji Shoten, 1959. Reprint 1989.

———. "Nichiren Shōnin no kai shisō ni tsuite" 日蓮聖人の戒思想について. *Ōsaki gakuhō* 大崎學報 125–26 (July 1971): 3–23.

Kageyama Haruki 景山晴樹. *Hiezan* 比叡山. Kadokawa Sensho 角河選書, no. 75. Tokyo: Kadokawa Shoten, 1975.

———et al. *Hiezan* I: *1200 nen no ayumi* 比叡山I―1200年の歩み. Asahi Karuchā Bukkusu 朝日カルチャーブックス, no. 60. Osaka: Ōsaka Shoseki, 1986.

———. *Hieizanji: Sono kōsei to shomondai* 比叡山寺—その構成と諸問題. Kyoto: Dōbōsha, 1978.

———. "Matarajin shinkō to sono ihō" 摩多羅神信仰とその遺宝. In *Hieizan to Tendai Bukkyō no kenkyū* 比叡山と天台仏教の研究, ed. Murayama Shūichi 村山修一, pp. 317–40. *Sangaku shūkyōshi kenkyū sōsho* 山岳宗教史研究叢書 2. Tokyo: Meichō Shuppan, 1975.

———. "Santō, kuin, jūrokudani" 三塔・九院・十六谷. In *Hieizan to Tendai Bukkyō no kenkyū* 比叡山と天台仏教の研究, ed. Murayama Shūichi 村山修一, pp. 42–62. *Sangaku shūkyōshi kenkyū sōsho* 山岳宗教史研究叢書 2: Tokyo. Meichō Shuppan, 1975.

Kamikawa Michio 上川通夫. "Chūsei jiin no kōzō to kokka" 中世寺院の構造と国家. *Nihonshi kenkyū* 日本史研究 344 (April 1991): 26–60.

Kanmuri Ken'ichi 冠賢一. "Monbushō tōkei sūri kenkyūjo no *Sandai hihō honjō ji* shinsaku-setsu ni taisuru gigi" 文部省統計数理研究所の「三大秘法禀承事」真作説に対する疑義. *Ōsaki gakuhō* 大崎學報 148 (March 1992): 1–14.

Kanno Hiroshi 菅野博史. *Ichinen sanzen to wa nani ka* 一念三千とは何か. Regurusu Bunko レグルス文庫, no. 204. Tokyo: Daisan Bunmeisha, 1992.

Kashiwagi Hiroo 柏木弘雄. *Daijō kishinron no kenkyū: Daijō kishinron no seiritsu ni kansuru shiryōronteki kenkyū* 大乗起信論の研究—大乗起信論の成立に関する資料論的研究. Tokyo: Shunjūsha, 1981.

———. "*Shaku makaen ron* ni okeru hongaku shisō" 『釈摩訶衍論』における本覚思想. In *Hongaku shisō no genryū to tenkai* 本覚思想の源流と展開, ed. Asai Endō 浅井圓道, pp. 3–26. *Hokekyō kenkyū* 法華経研究 11. Kyoto: Heirakuji Shoten, 1991.

Katō Bunnō, Tamura Yoshirō, and Miyasaka Kōjirō, trans., with revisions by W. E. Soothill, Wilhelm Schiffer, and Pier P. Del Campana. *The Threefold Lotus Sutra: Innumerable Meanings, the Lotus Flower of the Wonderful Law, and Meditation on the Bodhisattva Universal Virtue*. Tokyo: Kōsei Publishing Co., 1975.

Katsumata Shunkyō 勝又俊教. "Kōbō Daishi ni okeru hongaku shisō to sono haikei" 弘法大師における本覚思想とその背景. *Buzan gakuhō* 豊山学報 19 (1974): 29–50.

———. *Mikkyō no Nihonteki tenkai* 密教の日本的展開. Tokyo: Shunjūsha, 1970.

Kawai Takaakira 河合陟明. "Hongaku gainen no koperunikusu-teki tenkai" 本學概念のコペルニクス的轉回. *Shūkyō kenkyū* 宗教研究 114 (1943): 910–15.

Kawakatsu Kenryō 川勝賢亮, ed. *Tahōtō to Hokekyō shisō* 多宝塔と法華経思想. Tokyo: Tōkyōdō Shuppan, 1984.

———. "Tendai tahōtō no honzon" 天台多宝塔の本尊. In *Tahōtō to Hokekyō shisō* 多宝塔と法華経思想, ed. Kawakatsu Kenryō 川勝賢亮, pp. 82–95. Tokyo: Tōkyōdō Shuppan, 1984.

Kawamura Kōdō 河村孝道, ed. *Shohon taikō Eihei kaisan Dōgen Zenji gyōjō Kenzei ki* 諸本対校永平開山道元禅師行状建撕記. Tokyo: Daishūkan Shoten, 1975.

Kawazoe Shōji 川添昭二. "Nichiren no shikan to shingon haigeki" 日蓮の史觀と眞言排擊. *Geirin* 藝林 (Feb. 1957): 47–55.

———. "Nichiren no shūkyō keisei ni okeru nenbutsu haigeki no igi" 日蓮の宗教形成に於ける念佛排擊の意義. *Bukkyō shigaku* 佛教史學 4/3–4 (August 1955): 59–71 and 5/1 (Jan. 1956): 45–57.

———. "Nichiren no Zenshū ha ni tsuite" 日蓮の禪宗破について. *Nihon reki-shi* 日本歴史 (July 1953): 13–17.

Kern, H., trans. *The Saddharma-puṇḍarīka or The Lotus of the True Law.* Sacred Books of the East, vol. 21. Oxford: Clarendon Press, 1909.

Kim, Hee Jin. *Dōgen Kigen: Mystical Realist.* Tucson: University of Arizona Press, 1975. Reprint 1980.

Kitagawa, Joseph. "Japanese Religion: An Overview." In *Encyclopedia of Religion,* ed. Mircea Eliade, vol. 7, pp. 520–38. New York: Macmillan, 1987.

Kitagawa Zenchō 北川前肇. "Gyōgakuin Nitchō no kenkyū: Senba yugaku ni tsuite" 行学院日朝の研究—仙波遊学について. *IBK* 印度學仏教學研究 2/2 (March 1974): 761–64.

———. *Nichiren kyōgaku kenkyū* 日蓮教学研究. Kyoto: Heirakuji Shoten, 1987.

———. "Nichiren Shōnin ni okeru 'Juryōhon no hotoke' ni tsuite" 日蓮聖人における「寿量品の仏」について. *Ōsaki gakuhō* 大崎學報 129 (Dec. 1976): 94–118.

Kiyota Minoru. *Shingon Buddhism: Theory and Practice.* Los Angeles: Buddhist Books International, 1978.

———. "The Structure and Meaning of Tendai Thought." *Transactions of the International Conference of Orientalists in Japan* 5 (1960): 69–83.

Kojima Michimasa 小島道正. "Sannō isshin sangan kuden dokugo" 山王一心三観口伝読後. In *Eizan Bukkyō kenkyū* 叡山仏教研究, ed. Eizan Gakkai 叡山学会, pp. 109–24. Kyoto: Nagata Bunshōdō, 1974.

———. "Tendai kuden hōmon to shingi" 天台口伝法門と神祇. In *Bukkyō shisō ronshū* 仏教思想論集, ed. Okuda Jiō Sensei Kiju Kinen Ronbunshū Kankōkai 奥田慈應先生喜寿記念論文集刊行会, pp. 371–87. Kyoto: Heirakuji Shoten, 1976.

Kojima Michimasa 小島道正, Kodera Bun'ei 小寺文頴 and Take Kakuchō 武覚超. "Tendai kuden hōmon no kyōdō kenkyū" 天台口伝法門の共同研究. *IBK* 印度學佛教學研究 23/2 (March 1975): 372–88 and 24/1 (Dec. 1975): 284–91.

Komatsu Kuniaki 小松邦彰. "Nichiren Shōnin to shingon mikkyō" 日蓮聖人と真言密教. *Nichiren kyōgaku kenkyūjo kiyō* 日蓮教學研究所紀要 14 (1987): 1–22.

Komatsu Yasutaka 小松靖孝. "Nichiren no ryōzen ōkei shisō" 日蓮の霊山往詣思想. In *Nichirenshū no shomondai* 日蓮宗の諸問題, ed. Nakao Takashi 中尾堯, pp. 101–18. Tokyo: Yūzankaku, 1975.

Konishi Jin'ichi 小西甚一. *A History of Japanese Literature,* vol 3: *The High Middle Ages,* trans. Aileen Gatten and Mark Harbison, ed. Earl Minor. Princeton: Princeton University Press, 1991.

———. *Michi: Chūsei no rinen* 道—中世の理念. *Nihon no koten* 日本の古典 3. Tokyo: Kōdansha, 1975.

———. "*Michi* and Medieval Writing." In *Principles of Classical Japanese Literature,* ed. Earl Miner, pp. 181–208. Princeton: Princeton University Press, 1985.

———. "Shunzei no yūgenfu to shikan" 俊成の幽玄風と止觀. *Bungaku* 文學 20/2 (1952): 108–16.

Kubota Osamu 久保田収. *Chūsei Shintō no kenkyū* 中世神道の研究. Kyoto: Shintōshi Gakkai, 1959.

Kubota Tesshō 窪田哲正. "Awa Seichōzan gumonjihō gyōja no keifu: Kiyosumidera shūshi saikō" 安房清澄山求聞持法行者の系譜—清澄寺宗旨再考. *Nichiren kyōgaku kenkyūjo kiyō* 日蓮教學研究所紀要 20 (March 1993): 311–34.

———. "Chūko Tendai ni okeru kai shō shikan no hōmon" 中古天台における戒勝止観の法門. *Ōsaki gakuhō* 大崎學報 139 (June 1985): 45–58.

———. "Kaike to kike no kōshō" 戒家と記家の交渉. *Philosophia* フィロソフィア 70 (1982): 231–46.

———. "Shunpan kyōgaku no ichi kōsatsu: Nichiren kyōgaku tenbō no shiten kara" 俊範教学の一考察—日蓮教学展望の視点から. In *Nichiren kyōgaku no shomondai* 日蓮教学の諸問題, ed. Asai Endō Sensei Koki Kinen Ronbunshū Kankōkai 浅井圓道先生古稀記念論文集刊行会, represented by Watanabe Hōyō 渡邊宝陽, pp. 497–522. Kyoto: Heirakuji Shoten, 1997.

Kumoto Noboru 久下陞. "Hōnen Shōnin ni okeru hongaku shisō" 法然上人における本覚思想. In *Hōnen Shōnin kenkyū* 法然上人研究, ed. Bukkyō Daigaku Hōnen Shōnin Kenkyūkai 佛教大学法然上人研究会, pp. 383–426. Tokyo: Ryūbunkan, 1975.

Kurita Osamu 栗田勇. *Saichō to Tendai hongaku shisō: Nihon seishinshi josetsu* 最澄と天台本覚思想—日本精神史序説. Tokyo: Sakuhinsha, 1994.

Kuroda Toshio 黒田俊雄. "Chūsei jisha seiryoku ron" 中世寺社勢力論. In *Iwanami kōza Nihon rekishi* 岩波講座日本歴史 6: *Chūsei* 中世 2, ed. Asao Naohiro 朝尾直弘 et al., pp. 245–95. Tokyo: Iwanami Shoten, 1975.

———. "The Development of the *Kenmitsu* System as Japan's Medieval Orthodoxy." Trans. James C. Dobbins. *Japanese Journal of Religious Studies* 23/3–4 (Fall 1996): 233–69.

———. "The Discourse on the "Land of Kami" *(Shinkoku)* in Medieval Japan: National Consciousness and International Awareness." Trans. Fabio Rambelli. *Japanese Journal of Religious Studies* 23/3–4 (Fall 1996): 353–85.

———. "Historical Consciousness and *Hon-jaku* Philosophy in the Medieval Period on Mount Hiei." Trans. Allan G. Grapard. In *The Lotus Sutra in Japanese Culture*, ed. George J. Tanabe, Jr., and Willa Jane Tanabe, pp. 143–58. Honolulu: University of Hawai'i Press, 1989.

———. "The Imperial Law and the Buddhist Law." Trans. Jacqueline I. Stone. *Japanese Journal of Religious Studies* 23/3–4 (Fall 1996): 271–85.

———. *Jisha seiryoku: Mō hitotsu chūsei no shakai* 寺社勢力—もう一つの中世社会. Tokyo: Iwanami Shoten, 1980.

———. *Nihon chūsei no kokka to shūkyō* 日本中世の国家と宗教. Tokyo: Iwanami Shoten, 1975.

———. *Nihon chūsei no shakai to shūkyō* 日本中世の社会と宗教. Tokyo: Iwanami Shoten, 1990.

———. "Ōbō to Buppō" 王法と仏法. 1983. Reprinted in *Kuroda Toshio chosakushū* 黒田俊雄著作集, 2: 185–96. Kyoto: Hōzōkan, 1994.

———. "Shinto in the History of Japanese Religion." Trans. James C. Dobbins and Suzanne Gay. *Journal of Japanese Studies* 7/1 (1981): 1–21.

———. *Shōensei shakai* 荘園制社会. *Taikei Nihon rekishi* 体系日本歴史 2. Tokyo: Nihon Hyōronsha, 1967.

LaFleur, William R. *The Karma of Words: Buddhism and the Literary Arts in Medieval Japan*. Berkeley: University of California Press, 1983.

———. "Saigyō and the Buddhist Value of Nature." *History of Religions* 13/2 (Nov. 1973): 93–128, and 13/3 (Feb. 1974): 227–48.

Lai, Whalen W. "A Clue to the Authorship of the *Awakening of Faith:* 'Śikṣānanda's' Redaction of the Word *'Nien'.*" *Journal of the International Association of Buddhist Studies* 3/1 (1980): 34–53.

McCullough, Helen Craig, trans. *The Tale of the Heike.* Stanford: Stanford University Press, 1988.

McMullin, Neil. *Buddhism and the State in Sixteenth-Century Japan.* Princeton: Princeton University Press, 1984.

———. "Historical and Historiographical Issues in the Study of Pre-Modern Japanese Religions." *Japanese Journal of Religious Studies* 16/1 (March 1989): 3–40.

———. "The *Lotus Sutra* and Politics in the Mid-Heian Period." In *The Lotus Sutra in Japanese Culture,* ed. George J. Tanabe, Jr., and Willa Jane Tanabe, pp. 119–41. Honolulu: University of Hawai'i Press, 1989.

———. "The Sanmon-Jimon Schism in the Tendai School of Buddhism: A Preliminary Analysis." *Journal of the International Association of Buddhist Studies* 7/1 (1984): 83–105.

———. "The Sutra Lecture and Doctrinal Debate Traditions in Early and Medieval Japan." In *Tendai shisō to Tō-Ajia bunka no kenkyū* 天台思想と東アジア文化の研究, ed. Shioiri Ryōdō Sensei Tsuitō Ronbunshū Kankōkai 塩入良道先生追悼論文集刊行会, pp. 77–95. Tokyo: Sankibō Busshorin, 1991.

Maeda Eun 前田慧雲. *Tendaishū kōyō* 天台宗綱要. *Maeda Eun zenshū* 前田慧雲全集, vol. 2. Tokyo: Shunjūsha, 1931.

Manaka Fujiko 間中富士子. *Kokubungaku ni sesshū sareta Bukkyō* 国文学に摂収された仏教. Tokyo: Bunnichi Shuppan, 1972.

Maraldo, John C. "Tradition, Textuality, and the Trans-lation of Philosophy: The Case of Japan." In *Japan in Traditional and Postmodern Perspectives,* ed. Charles Wei-shun Fu and Steven Heine, pp. 225–43. Albany: State University of New York Press, 1995.

Mass, Jeffrey P. "The Kamakura Bakufu." In *Warrior Rule in Japan,* ed. Marius B. Jansen, pp. 1–43. Cambridge: Cambridge University Press, 1995.

Matsumoto Shirō 松本史朗. "Bukkyō to shingi: Han-Nihonshugiteki kōsatsu" 仏教と神祇—反日本主義的考察. 1986. In his *Engi to kū: nyoraizō shisō hihan* 縁起と空—如来蔵思想批判, pp. 99–119. Tokyo: Daizō Shuppan, 1989.

———. *Engi to kū: Nyoraizō shisō hihan* 縁起と空—如来蔵思想批判. Tokyo: Daizō Shuppan, 1989.

Matsunaga, Alicia and Daigan. *Foundations of Japanese Buddhism.* Vol. 2: *The Mass Movement (Kamakura and Muromachi Periods).* Los Angeles: Buddhist Books International, 1976.

Matsunaga Yūkei 松長有慶. *Mikkyō kyōten seiritsushi ron* 密教教典成立史論. Kyoto: Hōzōkan, 1980.

———. *Mikkyō no rekishi* 密教の歴史. Sāra sōsho サーラ叢書, no. 19. Kyoto: Heirakuji Shoten, 1969

Matsuo Kenji 松尾剛次. *Kamakura shin Bukkyō no seiritsu: Nyūmon girei to soshi shinwa* 鎌倉新仏教の成立—入門儀礼と祖師神話. Tokyo: Yoshikawa Kōbunkan, 1988.

———. *Kanjin to hakai no chūseishi: Chūsei Bukkyō no jissō* 勧進と破戒の中世史—中世仏教の実相. Tokyo: Yoshikawa Kōbunkan, 1995.

Matsuzaki Keisui 松崎恵水. "Kūkai oyobi sono monka no hongaku yōgorei oyobi sono igi" 空海及びその門下の本覚の用語例及びその意義. In *Hongaku shisō no genryū to tenkai* 本覚思想の源流と展開, ed. Asai Endō 浅井圓道, pp. 119–47. *Hokekyō kenkyū* 法華経研究 11. Kyoto: Heirakuji Shoten, 1991.

Matsuzono Hitoshi 松薗斉. "Nikki no ie: Sekkanke o chūshin ni" 日記の家—摂関家を中心に. In *Iwanami Kōza Nihon tsūshi* 岩波講座日本通史 7: *Chūsei* 中世 1, ed. Asao Naohiro 朝尾直弘 et al., pp. 347–64. Tokyo: Iwanami Shoten, 1993.

Mattis, Susan. "Chih-i's Appropriation of Madhyamaka: Changing Conceptions of Truth and the Buddha's Relation to the Phenomenal World." Ph.D. dissertation. Boston College, 1994.

Métraux, Daniel A. *The Soka Gakkai Revolution*. Boston: University Press of America, 1994.

Mibu Taishun 壬生台舜 and Miyasaka Yūshō 宮坂宥勝. *Nihon no Bukkyō: Tendai-Shingon* 日本の仏教—天台・真言. Tokyo: Shunjūsha, 1971.

Misaki Gisen 三崎義泉. "Chūsei biishiki no chūjiku toshite no 'shikanteki bigaku'" 中世美意識の中軸としての "止觀的美學". *Tendai gakuhō* 天台學報 10 (1968): 44–50.

———. "Hiezan no kaihōgyō to sono rironteki konkyo" 比叡山の回峯行とその理論的根拠. *Nihon Bukkyō gakkai nenpō* 日本仏教学会年報 45 (1979): 287–303.

———. "Mono no aware o utau michi to hongaku shisō to no kanren" もののあはれを歌う道と本覺思想との關連. *Tendai gakuhō* 天台學報 29 (Oct. 1987): 35–40.

Misaki Ryōshū 三崎良周. "Godaiin Annen to *Hongaku san*" 五台院安然と本覚讃. In *Hongaku shisō no genryū to tenkai* 本覚思想の源流と展開, ed. Asai Endō 浅井圓道, pp. 149–70. *Hokekyō kenkyū* 法華経研究 11. Kyoto: Heirakuji Shoten, 1991.

Miyamoto Shōson 宮本照尊. "'Sōmoku kokudo shikkai jōbutsu' no busshōronteki igi to sono sakusha" 「草木國土悉皆成佛」の佛性論的意義とその作者. *IBK* 印度學佛教學研究 9/2 (March 1961): 262–91.

Miyazaki Eishū 宮崎英修. *Fuju fuse-ha no genryū to tenkai* 不受不施派の源流と展開. Kyoto: Heirakuji Shoten, 1969.

———. *Nichirenshū no kitōhō* 日蓮宗の祈禱法. Kyoto: Heirakuji Shoten, 1980.

Mizukami Bungi (Fumiyoshi) 水上文義. "Genkōbon *Renge sanmai-kyō* no seiritsu ni tsuite" 現行本「蓮華三昧經」の成立について. *Tendai gakuhō* 天台學報 21 (1979): 118–20.

———. "*Renge sanmai-kyō (Hongakusan)* o meguru ichi-ni no mondai" 蓮華三昧經（本學讚）をめぐる一、二の問題. *Tendai gakuhō* 天台學報 22 (Nov. 1980): 156–58.

———. "*Renge sanmai-kyō* no seiritsu o megutte" 蓮華三昧經の成立をめぐって. *IBK* 印度學仏教學研究 28/1 (Dec. 1979): 164–65.

Mochizuki Kankō 望月歡厚. "Hongaku hōmon ni tsuite: Hokekyō no nimon to hongaku hōmon no seiritsu." 本學法門に就いて—法華經の二門と本學法門の成立. *Nihon Bukkyōgaku kyōkai nenpō* 日本佛教學協會年報 4 (1931): 95–114.

———. "Juryō shoken hongaku sanjin ron" 壽量所顯本覺三身論. *Ōsaki gakuhō* 大崎學報 13 (July 1910): 1–23; 14 (Sept. 1910): 23–43; 15 (Nov. 1910): 8–29.

————. *Nichiren kyōgaku no kenkyū* 日蓮教學の研究. Kyoto: Heirakuji Shoten, 1958. Reprint 1989.

————. *Nichirenshū gakusetsu shi* 日蓮宗学説史. Kyoto: Heirakuji Shoten, 1969.

Mochizuki Shinkō 望月信亨. *Bukkyō kyōten seiritsushi ron* 佛教經典成立史論. Kyoto: Hōzōkan, 1946.

Morrell, Robert E. *Early Kamakura Buddhism: A Minority Report.* Berkeley: Asian Humanities Press, 1987.

————, trans. *Sand and Pebbles (Shasekishū): The Tales of Mujū Ichien, a Voice for Pluralism in Kamakura Buddhism.* Albany: State University of New York Press, 1985.

Morris, Ivan. *The World of the Shining Prince: Court Life in Ancient Japan.* 1964. Reprint, New York: Penguin Books, 1969.

Motai Kyōkō 茂田井教亨. "Chūsei ni okeru Nichiren kyōgaku no tenkai" 中世における日蓮教学の展開. *IBK* 印度學仏教學研究 20/2 (March 1972): 573–77.

————. "Honzon no genri to keitai." 本尊の原理と形態. *Ōsaki gakuhō* 大崎學報 116 (July 1963): 1–22.

Murai Yasuhiko 村井康彦. "Chūkō no so Ryōgen" 中興の祖・良源. In *Hiezan* I: *1200 nen no ayumi* 比叡山 I — 1200年の歩み. Kageyama Haruki 景山春樹 et al., pp. 147–70. Asahi karuchā Bukkusu 朝日カルチャーブックス, no. 60. Osaka: Osaka Shoseki, 1986.

Murano Senchū, trans. *Nyorai metsugo go gohyakusai shi kanjin honzon shō or The True Object of Worship.* Tokyo: The Young East Association, 1954.

Murata Eiden 村田頴田. "Kantō no Tendai dangisho" 関東の天台談義所. In *Tendai kyōgaku no kenkyū* 天台教学の研究, ed. Tada Kōryū Sensei Shōju Kinen Ronshū Kankōkai 多田厚隆先生頌寿記念論集刊行会, pp. 347–63. Tokyo: Sankibō Busshorin, 1991.

Murayama Shūichi 村山修一. "Hieizan no kankyō to sōshiki" 比叡山の環境と組織. In *Hieizan to Tendai Bukkyō no kenkyū* 比叡山と天台仏教の研究, ed. Murayama Shūichi, pp. 13–41. *Sangaku shūkyōshi kenkyū sōsho* 山岳宗教史研究叢書 2. Tokyo: Meichō Shuppan, 1975.

————. *Hieizan shi: Tatakai to inori no seiiki* 比叡山史 — 闘いと祈りの聖域. Tokyo: Tōkyō Bijutsu, 1994.

————, ed. *Hieizan to Tendai Bukkyō no kenkyū* 比叡山と天台仏教の研究. *Sangaku shūkyōshi kenkyū sōsho* 山岳宗教史研究叢書 2. Tokyo: Meichō Shuppan, 1975.

Murozumi Ichimyō 室住一妙. *Gyōgakuin Nitchō Shōnin* 行學院日朝上人. Yamanashi Prefecture: Minobu Kyōhōsha, 1951.

Nagao Gadjin. "On the Theory of the Buddha Body (*Buddha-kāya*)." *The Eastern Buddhist,* new series 6/1 (May 1973): 25–53.

Nakajō Gyōshū 中條暁秀. "Muromachi jidai no Nichiren kyōgaku to hongaku shisō: Gyōgaku Nitchō ni tsuite" 室町時代の日蓮教学と本覚思想 — 行学日朝について. In *Hongaku shisō no genryū to tenkai* 本覚思想の源流と展開, ed. Asai Endō 浅井圓道, pp. 331–68. *Hokekyō kenkyū* 法華経研究 11. Kyoto: Heirakuji Shoten, 1991.

Nakamura Hajime 中村元. "Kichō kōen: Shizen ni ikiru" 基調講演 — 自然に生きる. *Chūgai nippō* 中外日報 (11/22/1989), pp. 7–8.

————. *Ways of Thinking of Eastern Peoples: India, China, Tibet, Japan.* Revised and ed. Philip P. Wiener. Honolulu: University of Hawai'i Press, 1964. Reprint 1985.

Nakanishi Chikai 中西智海 . "Shinran Shōnin ni okeru hongaku to jitsuzon no mondai" 親鸞聖人における本覚と実存の問題 . *Shinshūgaku* 真宗学 35, 36 (Feb. 1967): 97–114.

Nakanishi Zuikō 中西随功. "Kuden hōmon keiseki no kōsatsu" 口伝法門形成期の考察. *Jingen* 尋源 33 (March 1982): 72–89.

———. "Kuden hōmon seiritsu no shakai kiban" 口伝法門成立の社会基盤 . *IBK* 印度學仏教學研究 29/2 (March 1981): 624–25.

———. "Kuden hōmon tenkai no igi" 口伝法門展開の意義 . *IBK* 印度學仏教學研究 30/2 (March 1982): 627–28.

Nara Hiromoto 奈良弘元 . "Genshin no chosaku ni tsuite" 源信の著作について . *Shūkyō kenkyū* 宗教研究 226 (March 1976): 215–16.

Nattier, Jan. *Once Upon a Future Time: Studies in a Buddhist Prophecy of Decline.* Nanzan Studies in Asian Religions 1. Berkeley: Asian Humanities Press, 1991.

Needham, Joseph. *Science and Civilisation in China,* vol. 2: *History of Scientific Thought.* With the research assistance of Wang Ling. London: Cambridge University Press, 1956.

Ng, Yu-kwan. *T'ien-t'ai Buddhism and Early Mādhyamika.* Honolulu: Tendai Institute of Hawaii, Buddhist Studies Program, University of Hawai'i, 1993.

Nishi Giyū 西義雄 . "Shin Kamakura Bukkyō kōki no in'yu: Toku ni chūko Tendai o chūshin toshite no ichi kōsatsu" 新鎌倉仏教興起の因由—特に中古天台を中心としての一考察 . In *Kamakura Bukkyō keisei no mondaiten* 鎌倉仏教形成の問題点 , ed. Nihon Bukkyō Gakkai 日本仏教学会, pp. 1–17. Kyoto: Heirakuji Shoten, 1969.

Nishiguchi Junko 西口順子 . *Onna no chikara: Kodai no josei to Bukkyō* 女の力—古代の女性と仏教 . Tokyo: Heibonsha, 1987.

Nishimura Keishō 西村冏紹 . "*Kanjin ryaku yōshū* seiritsu kō" (matsu) 『観心略要集』成立考 (末) . *IBK* 印度學仏教學研究 37/2 (March 1989): 672–78.

Nitta Masaaki 新田雅章 . "Hongaku hōmon no keisei no shisōshiteki imi" 本覚法門の形成の思想史的意味 . In *Bukkyō no rekishiteki tenkai ni miru shokeitai* 仏教の歴史的展開に見る諸形態 , ed. Furuta Shōkin Hakushi Koki Kinenkai 古田章欽博士古希記念会 , pp. 700–712. Tokyo: Sōbunsha, 1971.

Nomoto Kakujō 野本覚成 . "Genshi kanjō yori kai kanjō e" 玄旨灌頂より戒灌頂へ . In *Tendai shisō to Tō-Ajia bunka no kenkyū* 天台思想と東アジア文化の研究 , ed. Shioiri Ryōdō Tsuitō Ronbunshū Kankōkai 塩入良道先生追悼論文集刊行会 , pp. 703–24. Tokyo: Sankibō Busshorin, 1991.

———. "*Sange yōryakki* no seikaku" 『山家要略記』の性格 . In *Bukkyō no rekishi to shisō* 仏教の歴史と思想 , ed. Mibu Taishun Hakushi Shōju Kinen Ronbunshū Kankōkai 壬生台舜博士頌寿記念論文集刊行会 , pp. 839–62. Tokyo: Daizō Shuppan, 1985.

Nosco, Peter. "Introduction: Neo-Confucianism and Tokugawa Discourse." In *Confucianism and Tokugawa Culture,* ed. Peter Nosco, pp. 3–26. Princeton: Princeton University Press, 1984.

Ogami Kanchū 尾上寛仲 . "Chūko Tendai ni okeru dangisho" 中古天台に於ける談義所. *IBK* 印度學仏教學研究 8/1 (Jan. 1960): 255–58.

———. "Dangisho to Tendai kyōgaku no ryūden" 談義所と天台教学の流伝 . *Eizan gakuhō* 叡山學報 1 (Oct. 1961): 17–31.

———. "Kantō chiiki ni denpa shita Danna-ryū no keitō" 関東地域に傳播した檀那流の系統. *IBK* 印度學仏教學研究 12/1 (Jan. 1964): 229–34.

———. "Kantō ni okeru chūko Tendai: Kanazawa Bunko no shiryō o chūshin to suru Danna-ryū ni tsuite" 関東における中古天台―金沢文庫の資料を中心とする檀那流について. *Kanazawa Bunko kenkyū* 金沢文庫研究 100 (April 1964): 1–6; 101 (May 1964): 1–5.

———. "Kantō no Tendaishū dangisho: Senba dangisho o chūshin toshite" 関東の天台宗談義所―仙波談義所を中心として. Kanazawa Bunko kenkyū 金沢文庫研究 167 (March 1970): 1–7; 168 (April 1970): 10–17; and 169 (May 1970): 10–17.

———. "Kashiwabara dangisho no hatten" 柏原談義所の発展. *IBK* 印度學仏教學研究 23/2 (March 1975): 614–18.

———. "Shinano no Tendaishū dangisho" 信濃の天台宗談義所. *Shinano* 信濃 12/11–12 (Dec. 1960): 613–20.

———. "*Shūman shū* oyobi *Shūen shū* ni tsuite" 宗満集及び宗円集について. *IBK* 印度學仏教學研究 18/2 (March 1970): 701–6.

———. "Yokawa no shūgaku seido" 横川の修学制度. *Tendai gakuhō* 天台學報 11 (1968): 53–63.

Ōhira Kōryū 大平宏龍. "Muromachi jidai no Nichiren kyōgaku to hongaku shisō: Keirin-bō Nichiryū ni tsuite" 室町時代の日蓮教学と本覚思想―慶林坊日隆について. In *Hongaku shisō no genryū to tenkai* 本覚思想の源流と展開, ed. Asai Endō 浅井圓道, pp. 369–95. *Hokekyō kenkyū* 法華経研究 11. Kyoto: Heirakuji Shoten, 1991.

———. "Nichiryū kyōgaku ni okeru chūko Tendai gi" 日隆教学における中古天台義. *IBK* 印度學仏教學研究 32/2 (March 1984): 615–22.

———. "Nichiryū Shōnin no chūko Tendai gi hihan ni tsuite" 日隆聖人の中古天台義批判について. In *Hokke shisō to Nichiryū kyōgaku* 法華思想と日隆教学, ed. Motohashi Sensei Koki Kinen Ronshū Kankōkai 株橋先生古希記念論集刊行会, pp. 577–621. Amazaki: Hokkeshū Kōryū Gakurin, 1979.

Oka Kyōzui 岡教遂. "Danna-ryū ni ranshō seru tōke no shūgi" 檀那流に濫觴せる當家の宗義. *Ōsaki gakuhō* 大崎學報 65 (Dec. 1923): 45–53.

———. "Genshi kimyōdan no enkaku oyobi kyōri jisō no ippan" 玄旨歸命壇の沿革及び教理事相の一斑. *Ōsaki gakuhō* 大崎學報 17 (March 1911): 30–45 and 18 (July 1911): 37–50.

———. "Nihon Tendai kuden hōmon no yurai oyobi hattatsu" 日本天台口傳法門の由来及其發達. *Ōsaki gakuhō* 大崎學報 22 (May 1911): 25–40; 23 (July 1912): 8–35; 24 (Oct. 1912): 27–51; 25 (Nov. 1912): 26–51.

Ōkubo Dōshū 大久保道舟. *Shūtei zōho Dōgen Zenji den no kenkyū* 修訂増補道元禅師伝の研究. Tokyo: Chikuma Shobō, 1966.

Ōkubo Ryōjun 大久保良順. "Edan ryōryū hōmonchū no Dengyō Daishi" 惠檀両流法門中の傳教大師. In *Dengyō Daishi kenkyū bekkan* 傳教大師研究別巻, ed. Fukui Kōjun 福井康順, pp. 71–91. Tokyo: Waseda Daigaku Shuppan, 1980.

———. "Edan ryōryū kengaku (zōden) no yōsō" 惠檀両流兼学（雑伝）の様相. In *Tendai shisō to Tō-Ajia bunka no kenkyū* 天台思想と東アジア文化の研究, ed. Shioiri Ryōdō Tsuitō Ronbunshū Kankōkai 塩入良道先生追悼論文集刊行会, pp. 307–23. Tokyo: Sankibō Busshorin, 1991.

———. "Edan ryōryū ni kansuru shiron" 恵檀両流に関する試論. *Taishō Daigaku kenkyū kiyō* 大正大學研究紀要 48 (1963): 1–13.

———. "Genshi kimyōdan kanjō: Mitsu ni shite mitsu ni arazaru kanjō" 玄旨帰命壇灌頂—密にして密にあらざる灌頂. *Tendai* 天台 4 (Nov. 1981): 37–46.

———. "Jūjukai kanjō no kōki" 重授戒灌頂の興起. *Tendai gakuhō* 天台學報 22 (Nov. 1980): 1–9.

———. "Kanjin ni tsuite: Ōkubo Ryōjun shi kōen" 観心について—大久保良順師講演. *Tendaishū Tōkyō kyōku kenshūkai kiyō* 天台宗東京教区研修会紀要 3 (June 1978): 1–19.

———. "'Namu myōhō isshin kanbutsu' ni tsuite: Tendai Eshin-ryū gojū sōden shōkō" 「南無妙法一心観仏」について—天台恵心流五重相伝小考. In *Tendai kyōgaku no kenkyū* 天台教学の研究, ed. Tada Kōryū Sensei Shōju Kinen Ronshū Kankōkai 多田厚隆先生頌寿記念論集刊行会, pp. 267–78. Tokyo: Sankibō Busshorin, 1990.

———. "*Shuzenji-ketsu* o chūshin to suru ni-san no mondai" 修禅寺決を中心とする二三の問題. *Tendai gakuhō* 天台學報 9 (1967): 1–8.

———. "Tendai genshi kimyōdan kanjō ni tsuite" 天台玄旨帰命壇灌頂について. In *Dengyō Daishi to Tendaishū* 伝教大師と天台宗, ed. Shioiri Ryōdō 塩入良道 and Kiuchi Gyōō 木内尭央, pp. 308–29. *Nihon Bukkyō shūshi ronshū* 日本仏教宗史論集, vol. 3. Tokyo: Yoshikawa Kōbunkan, 1985.

———. "*Tendai Hokkeshū denbōge* ni tsuite" 天台法華宗傳法偈について. In *Dengyō Daishi kenkyū* 傳教大師研究, ed. Dengyō Daishi Kenkyū Henshūkai 傳教大師研究編集會, pp. 115–30. Tokyo: Waseda Daigaku Shuppan, 1973.

———. "Tendai Hokkeshū no dentō" 天台法華集の伝統. *Dainikai kokusai Hokekyō gakkai happyō shiryō* 第二回国際法華経学会発表資料 (1987), pp. 1–13. Tokyo: Taishō University, 1987.

———. "Tendai kuden hōmon no seiritsu to bunkenka: Seikai no *Tendai den Nangaku shin'yō shō* to *Shūen, Shūman* ryōshū no kōsatsu" 天台口伝法門の成立と文献化—政海の天台伝南岳心要抄と宗円・宗満両集の考察. In *Hongaku shisō no genryū to tenkai* 本覚思想の源流と展開, ed. Asai Endō 浅井圓道, pp. 177–222. *Hokekyō kenkyū* 法華経研究 11. Kyoto: Heirakuji Shoten, 1991.

———. "Wakō dōjin kanjō ni tsuite" 和光同塵灌頂について. In *Bukkyō no rekishi to shisō* 仏教の歴史と思想, ed. Mibu Taishun Hakushi Shōju Kinen Ronbunshū Kankōkai 壬生台舜博士頌寿記念論文集刊行会, pp. 657–79. Tokyo: Daizō Shuppan, 1985.

Ono Bunkō 小野文珖. "Kinsei Nichirenshū kyōgaku ni okeru kanjin shisō no tenkai" (1) 近世日蓮教学における観心思想の展開 (1). *Nichiren kyōgaku kenkyūjo kiyō* 日蓮教學研究所紀要 3 (1976): 92–103.

———. "Senba to Nichiren monka to no kōryū: 'Kantō Tendai' to Kantō Nichiren kyōdan" 仙波と日蓮門下との交流—「関東天台」と関東日蓮教団. In *Hongaku shisō no genryū to tenkai* 本覚思想の源流と展開, ed. Asai Endō 浅井圓道, pp. 425–49. *Hokekyō kenkyū* 法華経研究 11. Kyoto: Heirakuji Shoten, 1991.

———. "Udana-in Nichiki: Kindai Nichirenshū no senkakusha" 憂陀那院日輝—近代日蓮宗の先覚者. In *Kindai Nichiren kyōdan no shisōka: Kindai Nichiren kyōdan, kyōgakushi shiron* 近代日蓮教団の思想家—近代日蓮教団・教

学史試論, ed. Nakano Kyōtoku　中濃教篤, pp. 3–69. *Sōsho Nihon kindai to shūkyō* 叢書日本近代と宗教 2. Tokyo: Kokusho Kankōkai, 1977.

Ōno Tatsunosuke　大野達之助. "Dōgen no hongaku shisō" 道元の本覚思想. *Nihon rekishi* 日本歴史 336 (May 1976): 1–10.

Ooms, Herman. *Tokugawa Ideology: Early Constructs, 1570-1680.* Princeton: Princeton University Press, 1985.

Orzech, Charles D. "Seeing Chen-yen Buddhism: Traditional Scholarship and the Vajrayāna in China." *History of Religions* 29/2 (Nov. 1989): 87–114.

Osabe Kazuo　長部和雄. "Kuden hōmon ni okeru hiden no kigen to Tōketsu to no kankei" 口伝法門における秘伝の起原と唐決との関係. *Mikkyō bunka* 密教文化 5 (August 1956): 19–43.

Ōsumi Kazuo. "Buddhism in the Kamakura Period." Trans., adapted, and expanded by James C. Dobbins. In *The Cambridge History of Japan,* vol 3: *Medieval Japan,* ed. Kōzō Yamamura, pp. 544–82. Cambridge and New York: Cambridge University Press, 1990.

Ōtani Gyōkō　庵谷行亨. "Hōchi-bō Shōshin no hongaku shisō hihan" 宝地房証真の本覚思想批判. In *Hongaku shisō no genryū to tenkai* 本覚思想の源流と展開, ed. Asai Endō　浅井圓道, pp. 223–45. *Hokekyō kenkyū* 法華経研究 11. Kyoto: Heirakuji Shoten, 1991.

———. *Nichiren Shōnin kyōgaku kenkyū* 日蓮聖人教学研究. Tokyo: Sankibō Busshorin, 1984.

———. "Nichiren Shōnin kyōgaku ni okeru honmon to kanjin" 日蓮聖人教学における本門と観心. *IBK* 印度學仏教學研究 25/1 (Dec. 1976): 304–6.

———. "Nichiren Shōnin no san'yaku ron" 日蓮聖人の三益論. *IBK* 印度學仏教學研究 28/1 (Dec. 1979): 252–56.

Ōya Tokujō　大屋徳城. "Heian-chō ni okeru sandai seiryoku no kōsō to chōwa" 平安朝に於ける三大勢力の抗争と調和. In his *Nihon Bukkyōshi no kenkyū* 日本佛教史の研究, vol. 2. Kyoto: Tōbō Bunken Kankōkai, 1929.

Ōyama Kōjun　大山公淳. *Mikkyōshi gaisetsu to kyōri* 密教史概説と教理. Kōyasan: Kōyasan Daigaku, 1961. Reprint 1962.

Ozaki Kōjin　尾崎光尋. *Nihon Tendai rongishi no kenkyū* 日本天台論義史の研究. Kyoto: Konjōdō, 1971.

Payne, Richard K. "Introduction." In *Re-visioning "Kamakura" Buddhism,* ed. Richard Payne, pp. 1–23. Kuroda Institute Studies in East Asian Buddhism 11. Honolulu: University of Hawai'i Press, 1998.

Penkower, Linda L. "T'ien-t'ai during the T'ang Dynasty: Chan-jan and the Sinification of Buddhism." Ph.D. dissertation. Columbia University, 1993.

Plutschow, Herbert Eugen. "Is Poetry a Sin? *Honjisuijaku* and Buddhism versus Poetry." *Oriens Extremus* 25/2 (1978): 206–18.

Pye, Michael. *Skilful Means: A Concept in Mahayana Buddhism.* London: Duckworth, 1978.

Ra, Lang Eun. "The T'ien-t'ai Philosophy of Non-duality: A Study in Chan-jan and Chih-li." Ph.D. dissertation. Temple University, 1988.

Rambelli, Fabio. "True Words, Silence, and the Adamantine Dance: On Japanese Mikkyō and the Formation of the Shingon Discourse." *Japanese Journal of Religious Studies* 21/4 (Dec. 1994): 373–405.

Reischauer, A. K., trans. "Genshin's *Ōjō Yōshū:* Collected Essays on Birth into Paradise." *Transactions of the Asiatic Society of Japan.* Second series, 7 (Dec. 1930): 16–97.

Renondeau, Gaston. *La Doctrine de Nichiren.* Ministère de l'Éducation Nationale. Publications du Musée Guimet, Bibliothèque d'Études 58. Paris: Presses Universitaires de France, 1953.

Rhodes, Robert F. "The *Kaihōgyō* Practice of Mt. Hiei." *Japanese Journal of Religious Studies* 14/2–3 (June–Sept. 1987): 185–202.

———, trans. and intro. "Saichō's *Mappō Tōmyō ki:* A Candle for the Latter Dharma." *The Eastern Buddhist* (new series) 13/1 (Spring 1980): 79–103.

Richard, Rev. Timothy, trans., assisted by Yang Wen Hwei. *The Awakening of Faith in the Mahayana Doctrine—The New Buddhism.* 1894. 2d ed. Shanghai: Kelly and Walsh, 1918.

Risshō Daigaku Nichiren Kyōgaku Kenkyūjo 立正大学日蓮教学研究所, ed. *Nichiren kyōdan zenshi* 日蓮教団全史, vol. 1. Kyoto: Heirakuji Shoten, 1984.

Rodd, Laurel Rasplica. *Selected Writings of Nichiren.* Asian Studies at Hawaii 26. Honolulu: University of Hawai'i Press, 1980.

Ruppert, Brian Douglas. "Buddha Relics and Power in Early Medieval Japan." Ph.D. dissertation. Princeton University, 1997.

Sakai Kyōjun 酒井敬淳. "Nichiren Shōnin ni miru taimitsu no eikyō" 日蓮聖人に見る台密の影響. *Tendai gakuhō* 天台學報 25 (1983): 58–62.

Sakamoto Yukio 坂本幸男. "Sōmoku jōbutsu ni tsuite" 草木成仏について. *Ōsaki gakuhō* 大崎學報 109 (Feb. 1959): 15–21.

Sakamoto Yukio 坂本幸男 and Iwamoto Yutaka 岩本裕, eds. *Hokekyō* 法華経. 3 vols. Tokyo: Iwanami Shoten, 1962.

Sanford, James H. "The Abominable Tachikawa Skull Ritual." *Monumenta Nipponica* 46/1 (Spring 1991): 1–20.

———. "Breath of Life: The Esoteric Nenbutsu." In *Esoteric Buddhism in Japan,* ed. Ian Astley, pp. 65–98. SBS Monograph no. 1. Seminar for Buddhist Studies: Copenhagen and Aaarhus, 1994.

Sanford, James H., William R. LaFleur, and Masatoshi Nagatomi, eds. *Flowing Traces: Buddhism in the Literary and Visual Arts of Japan.* Princeton: Princeton University Press, 1992.

Sansom, G. B. *Japan: A Short Cultural History.* 1931. Revised, Stanford: Stanford University Press, 1978.

Sasaki Kaoru 佐々木馨. *Chūsei kokka no shūkyō kōzō* 中世国家の宗教構造. Tokyo: Yoshikawa Kōbunkan, 1988.

Sasaki Kentoku 佐々木憲徳. *Tendai kyōgaku* 天台教學. Kyoto: Hyakkaen, 1951. Reprint 1963.

Satō Hiroo 佐藤弘夫. "Nichiren no kōki no shisō: Ōbō to Buppō to no kankei o chūshin toshite" 日蓮の後期の思想—王法と仏法との関係を中心として. *Nihon shisōshigaku* 日本思想史学 9 (1977): 49–60.

———. *Nihon chūsei no kokka to Bukkyō* 日本中世の国家と仏教. Tokyo: Yoshikawa Kōbunkan, 1987.

———. "Shoki Nichiren no kokkakan: Kamakura kyū Bukkyō to no hikaku ni oite" 初期日蓮の国家観—鎌倉旧仏教との比較において. *Nihon shisōshi kenkyū* 日本思想史研究 10 (1978): 14–28.

Satō Tetsue 佐藤哲英. "Eizan Jōdokyō kobunken no chōsa to kenkyū" 叡山浄土教古文献の調査と研究. In *Bukkyō bunken no kenkyū* 佛教文献の研究, ed. Satō Tetsue, pp. 1–28. Kyoto: Hyakkaen, 1968.

———. *Eizan Jōdokyō no kenkyū* 叡山浄土教の研究. Kyoto: Hyakkaen, 1979.

———. "*Kannon gengi* narabi ni *Gisho* no seiritsu ni kansuru kenkyū" 觀音玄義並びに義疏の成立に關する研究. *IBK* 印度學仏教學研究 5/1 (Jan. 1957): 10–21.

———. "*Maka shikan* no ichinen sanzen-setsu ni taisuru gigi" 摩訶止觀の一念三千説に對する疑義. *IBK* 印度學仏教學研究 7/1 (Dec. 1958): 105–14.

———. "Santai sangan shisō no kigen oyobi hattatsu: Daiichibu, santai sangan shisō no kigen ni kansuru kenkyū" 三諦三觀思想の起原及び發達—第一部、三諦三觀思想の起原に關する研究. *Nihon Bukkyō gakkai nenpō* 日本佛教學會年報 15 (Sept. 1950): 195–225.

———. *Tendai Daishi no kenkyū* 天台大師の研究. Kyoto: Hyakkaen, 1961.

Schalow, Paul Gordon. "Kūkai and the Tradition of Male Love in Japanese Buddhism." In *Buddhism, Sexuality, and Gender,* ed. José Ignacio Cabezón, pp. 215–32. Albany: State University of New York Press, 1992.

Seiryū Sōji 青龍宗二. "Dōgen Zenji no shoki sangaku ni okeru gidan no shinsō ni tsuite" 道元禅師の初期参学における疑団の真相について. *Shūgaku kenkyū* 宗学研究 5 (April 1963): 131–37.

Sekiguchi Shindai 關口眞大. "Ryōzen jikiju to nenge mishō" 靈山直受と拈花微笑. In *Tōyō bunka ronshū* 東洋文化論集, ed. Fukui Hakushi Shōju Kinen Ronbunshū Kankōkai 福井博士頌壽記念論文集刊行會, pp. 577–86. Tokyo: Waseda Daigaku Shuppanbu, 1969.

———. *Shikan no kenkyū* 止観の研究. Tokyo: Iwanami Shoten, 1975.

———. *Tendai shikan no kenkyū* 天台止観の研究. Tokyo: Iwanami Shoten, 1969.

Serizawa Kazuo 芹沢一男. "Gyōgakuin Nitchō to chūko Tendai shisō to no kanren ni tsuite" 行学院日朝と中古天台思想との関連について. *IBK* 印度學佛教學研究 27/1 (Dec. 1978): 152–53.

———. "Kyōhan ron no ichi kōsatsu: Chūko Tendai shisō to Nichiren kyōgaku no hikaku ni oite" 教判論の一考察—中古天台思想と日蓮教学の比較において. *IBK* 印度學佛教學研究 31/2 (March 1983): 657–59.

Setouchi Jakuchō 瀬戸内寂聴 et al. *Hieizan II: Sono kokoro to gyō* 比叡山II—そのこころと行. Asahi Karuchū Bukkusu 朝日カルチャーブックス, no. 69. Osaka: Ōsaka Shoten, 1986.

Shibuya Ryōtai 澁谷亮泰. "Gosaga Jōkō to chūko Tendai no bokkō" 後嵯峨上皇と中古天台の勃興. *Tendai gakuhō* 天台學報 12 (1969): 26–33.

Shigematsu Akihisa 重松明久. *Nihon Jōdokyō seiritsu katei no kenkyū* 日本浄土教成立過程の研究. Kyoto: Heirakuji Shoten, 1964.

Shigyō Kaishū 執行海秀. "Chūko Tendai to Hokke shisō no renkan" 中古天台と法華思想の連関. In *Hokekyō no shisō to bunka* 法華経の思想と文化, ed. Sakamoto Yukio 坂本幸男, pp. 599–621. Kyoto: Heirakuji Shoten, 1965.

———. "Honzon kuden sōjōsho no kenkyū" 本尊口伝相承書の研究. *Ōsaki gakuhō* 大崎學報 96 (1941). Reprinted in his *Kōmon kyōgaku no kenkyū* 興門教学の研究, pp. 283–309. Tokyo: Kaishūsha, 1984.

———. *Kōmon kyōgaku no kenkyū* 興門教学の研究. Tokyo: Kaishūsha, 1984.

———. "Kōmon kyōgaku no shisōteki tenkai no ichi kōsatsu: Kyōgaku no honshitsu o chūshin toshite" 興門教學の思想的展開の一考察—教學の本質を中心として. *IBK* 印度學佛教學研究 14/1 (Dec. 1965): 81–88.

———. "Nichiren kyōgakujō ni okeru *Ongi kuden* no chii" 日蓮教學上に於ける御義口傳の地位. *IBK* 印度學佛教學研究 3/1 (Sept. 1954): 170–71.

————. "Nichiren Shōnin kyōgaku no shisōshiteki kenkyū no ichi kōsatsu: Toku ni chūko Tendai kyōgaku o haikei to shite" 日蓮聖人教学の思想史的研究の一考察—特に中古天台教学を背景として. *Ōsaki gakuhō* 大崎學報 101 (July 1954): 44–58.

————. *Nichirenshū kyōgakushi* 日蓮教學史. Kyoto: Heirakuji Shoten, 1952. Reprint 1985.

————. "Ongi kuden no kenkyū" 御義口傳の研究. *Risshō Daigaku ronsō* 立正大學論叢 1/2 (July 1942): 68–87 and 2/7 (June 1943): 33–64.

Shikii Shūjō 色井秀讓. "Jūjukai kanjō: Sokuji nishin no shōchōteki gyōgi" 重授戒潅頂—即事而真の象徴的行儀. *Tendai* 天台 4 (1981): 26–32. Reprinted in *Dengyō Daishi to Tendaishū* 伝教大師と天台宗, ed. Shioiri Ryōdō 塩入良道 and Kiuchi Gyōō 木内堯央, pp. 297–307. *Nihon Bukkyōshi ronshū* 日本仏教史論集 3. Tokyo: Yoshikawa Kōbunkan, 1985.

————. *Kaikanjō no nyūmonteki kenkyū* 戒觀頂の入門的研究. Osaka: Tōhō Shuppan, 1989.

————. "Kaikanjō to gasshō" 戒觀頂と合掌. *Tendai gakuhō* 天台學報 24 (1982): 11–17.

————, ed. *Tendai Shinseishū shūgaku hanron* 天台真盛宗宗学汎論. Kyoto: Tendai Shinseishū Shūgaku Kenkyūjo, 1961.

Shima Chiryō (a.k.a. "Enrei gakunin" 延嶺學人). "Endon Hōin Songai" 圓頓法印尊海. *Ōsaki gakuhō* 大崎學報 8 (May 1908): 48–59; 9 (Dec. 1908): 20–32.

————. "Taitō kōshō shikō" 台當交渉史稿. *Ōsaki gakuhō* 大崎學報 10 (July 1909): 32–47; 11 (Dec. 1909): 10–16.

Shimaji Daitō 島地大等. "Chūko Tendai no gakugo toshite mitaru hongaku no gainen" 中古天台の學語として見たる本覺の概念. 1916. Reprinted in his *Kyōri to shiron* 教理と史論, pp. 109–17. Tokyo: Meiji Shoin, 1931.

————. "Hongakumon no shinkō" 本覺門の信仰. In his *Shisō to shinkō* 思想と信仰, pp. 530–42. Tokyo: Meiji Shoin, 1928. Reprint 1929.

————. *Nihon Bukkyō hongaku shisō no gaisetsu* 日本佛教本覺思想の概説. In his *Bukkyō taikō* 佛教大綱. Tokyo: Meiji Shoin, 1931.

————. *Nihon Bukkyō kyōgakushi* 日本佛教教學史. Tokyo: Nakayama Shobō, 1933. Reprint 1976.

————. "Nihon ko Tendai kenkyū no hitsuyō o ronzu" 日本古天台研究の必要を論ず. *Shisō* 思想 60 (October 1926): 174–92.

————. "Nihon Tendai no kuden hōmon" 日本天台の口傳法門. 1910. Reprinted in his *Kyōri to shiron* 教理と史論, pp. 53–66. Tokyo: Meiji Shoin, 1931.

————. "Shōdai shisō ni tsuite" 唱題思想に就て. 1922. Reprinted in his *Kyōri to shiron* 教理と史論, pp. 494–510. Tokyo: Meiji Shoin, 1931.

————. "Taimitsu no jisōteki kitō ni tsuite" 台密の事相的祈禱に就いて. 1912. Reprinted in his *Kyōri to shiron* 教理と史論, pp. 175–85. Tokyo: Meiji Shoin, 1931.

————. *Tendai kyōgaku shi* 天台教学史. Tokyo: Ryūbunkan, 1986.

Shimizu Ryūzan 清水龍山. *Nichiren Shōnin no gakusetsu no yurai ni tsuite* 日蓮聖人の學説の由来に就いて. 1919. In *Shimizu Ryūzan chosakushū* 清水龍山著作集, 1:167–368. Osaka: Tōhō Shuppan, 1979.

————. *Tendai Nichiren taishō ronjutsu Hokekyō yōgi* 天台日蓮對照論述法華經要義. Reprinted in *Shimizu Ryūzan chosakushū* 清水龍山著作集, 1:1–368. Osaka: Tōhō Shuppan, 1979.

Shinno Kōryō　新野光亮. "Dōgen Zenji no gidan ni tsuite no ichi kōsatsu"　道元禅師の疑団についての一考察. *IBK* 印度學佛教學研究 20/1 (Dec. 1971): 142–43.

Shioda Gisen　塩田義遜. "Asa daimoku to yū nenbutsu"　朝題目と夕念仏. *Ōsaki gakuhō* 大崎學報 103 (June 1955): 64–68.

———. *Honmon jikan shi* 本門事觀史. *Seishin* 棲神 25 (1940): 1–54.

Shioiri Ryōchū　鹽入亮忠. "Dengyō Daishi no hongaku shisō: Busshinron o chūshin toshite"　傳教大師の本覺思想—佛身論を中心として. *IBK* 印度學佛教學研究 9/1 (Jan. 1961): 22–27.

Shioiri Ryōdō　塩入良道. "'Honzon' zakkō"　「本尊」雑考. *Bukkyō bunka* 仏教文化 (Oct. 1970): 11–20.

Shirato Waka. "Inherent Enlightenment *(hongaku shisō)* and Saichō's Acceptance of the Bodhisattva Precepts." *Japanese Journal of Religious Studies* 14/2–3 (June–Sept. 1987): 113–27.

Shively, Donald H. "Buddhahood for the Nonsentient: A Theme in *Nō* Plays." *Harvard Journal of Asiatic Studies* 20/1–2 (June 1957): 135–61.

Sonoda Kōyū　薗田香融. "Sentokuzō to honzon: Shoshū honzon no shiteki ichi kōsatsu"　先徳像と本尊—諸宗本尊の史的一考察. 1959. Reprinted in his *Heian Bukkyō no kenkyū* 平安佛教の研究, pp. 211–25. Kyoto: Hōzōkan, 1981.

———. "Yama no nenbutsu: Sono kigen to seikaku" 山の念仏—その起源と性格. 1968. Reprinted in his *Heian Bukkyō no kenkyū* 平安佛教の研究, pp. 163–91. Kyoto: Hōzōkan, 1981.

Stevens, John. *The Marathon Monks of Mt. Hiei.* Boston: Shambala Publications, 1988.

Stevenson, Daniel B. "The Four Kinds of Samādhi in Early T'ien-t'ai Buddhism." In *Traditions of Meditation in Chinese Buddhism,* ed. Peter N. Gregory, pp. 45–97. Kuroda Institute Studies in East Asian Buddhism 4. Honolulu: University of Hawai'i Press, 1986.

Stone, Jacqueline. "Chanting the August Title of the *Lotus Sutra: Daimoku* Practices in Classical and Medieval Japan." In *Re-visioning "Kamakura" Buddhism,* ed. Richard K. Payne, pp. 116–66. Kuroda Institute Studies in East Asian Buddhism 11. Honolulu: University of Hawai'i Press, 1998.

———. "An Introduction to the Poetry of Jien." *Journal of Asian Culture* 8 (1984): 207–31.

———. "Rebuking the Enemies of the *Lotus:* Nichirenist Exclusivism in Historical Perspective." *Japanese Journal of Religious Studies* 21/2–3 (June–Sept. 1994): 231–59.

———. "Seeking Enlightenment in the Last Age: *Mappō* Thought in Kamakura Buddhism." *The Eastern Buddhist* 18/1 (Spring 1985): 28–56 and 18/2 (Autumn 1985): 35–64.

———. "Some Disputed Writings in the Nichiren Corpus: Textual, Hermeneutical and Historical and Problems." Ph.D. dissertation. University of California, Los Angeles, 1990.

Sueki Fumihiko　末木文美士. "Akunin shōki-setsu o megutte" 悪人正機説をめぐって. 1982. Reprinted in his *Nihon Bukkyō shisōshi ronkō* 日本仏教思想史論考, pp. 431–38. Tokyo: Daizō Shuppan, 1993.

———. "Amida santai-setsu o megutte"　阿弥陀三諦説をめぐって. *IBK* 印度學佛教學研究 28/1 (Dec. 1979): 216–22.

————. "Annen: The Philosopher Who Japanized Buddhism." *Acta Asiatica* 66 (1994): 69–86.

————. "Chūsei Tendai to hongaku shisō" 中世天台と本覚思想. 1991. Reprinted in his *Nihon Bukkyō shisōshi ronkō* 日本仏教史論考, pp. 312–46. Tokyo: Daizō Shuppan, 1993.

————. *Heian shoki Bukkyō shisō no kenkyū: Annen no shisō keisei o chūshin toshite* 平安初期仏教思想の研究—安然の思想形成を中心として. Tokyo: Shunjūsha, 1995.

————. *"Hōbutsu shū to Shinnyo kan"* 『宝物集』と『真如観』. *Shin Nihon koten bungaku taikei* 新日本古典文学大系 49 (Nov. 1993): 1–4.

————. "Kamakura Bukkyō kenkyū o megutte" 鎌倉仏教研究をめぐって. In his *Nihon Bukkyō shisōshi ronkō* 日本仏教思想史論考, pp. 273–83. Tokyo: Daizō Shuppan, 1993.

————. *"Kanjin ryaku yōshū* no kenkyū" 『観心略要集』の研究. *Tōyō bunka kenkyūjo kiyō* 東洋文化研究所紀要 95 (Nov. 1984): 179–294.

————. *"Kanjin ryaku yōshū* no senja ni tsuite" 『観心略要集』の選者について. *IBK* 印度學佛教學研究 27/1 (Dec. 1978): 330–33.

————. *"Myōgyōshin yōshū* no shomondai" 『妙行心要集』の諸問題. In *Tendai kyōgaku no kenkyū* 天台教学の研究, ed. Tada Kōryū Sensei Shōju Kinen Ronshū Kankōkai 多田厚隆先生頌寿記念論集刊行会, pp. 279–303. Tokyo: Sankibō Busshorin, 1990.

————. "Nihon Bukkyō: Sokushin jōbutsu o chūshin ni" 日本仏教—即身成仏を中心に. *Iwanami kōza: Tōyō shisō* 岩波講座—東洋思想 12: *Tō-Ajia no Bukkyō* 東アジアの仏教, pp. 190–219. Tokyo: Iwanami Shoten, 1988.

————. "A Reexamination of the *Kenmitsu Taisei* Theory." *Japanese Journal of Religious Studies* 23/3–4 (Fall 1996): 446–66.

————. "Tendai hongaku shisō kenkyū no shomondai" 天台本覚思想研究の諸問題. 1987. Reprinted in his *Nihon Bukkyō shisōshi ronkō* 日本仏教史思想論考, pp. 284–311. Tokyo: Daizō Shuppan, 1993.

————. "Two Seemingly Contradictory Aspects of the Teaching of Innate Enlightenment *(Hongaku)* in Medieval Japan." *Japanese Journal of Religious Studies* 22/1–2 (Spring 1995): 3–16.

Sugawara Shinkai 菅原信海. *Sannō Shintō no kenkyū* 山王神道の研究. Tokyo: Shunjūsha, 1992.

Suguro Shinjō 勝呂信静. "Hokekyō chūshaku no dōkō" 法華経注釈の動向. In *Chūsei Hokke Bukkyō no tenkai* 中世法華仏教の展開, ed. Kageyama Gyōō 影山尭雄, pp. 149–85. *Hokekyō kenkyū* 法華経研究 5. Kyoto: Heirakuji Shoten, 1974.

————. "Nichiren ni okeru kaie no shisō to kyōdan no mondai" 日蓮における開会の思想と教団問題. *Nihon Bukkyō gakkai nenpyō* 日本仏教学会年表 39 (March 1974): 355–70.

————. "Shūgaku kenkyūjō no ni, san no mondaiten" 宗学研究上の二・三の問題点. In *Nichiren kyōgaku no shomondai* 日蓮教学の諸問題, ed. Motai Kyōkō Sensei Koki Kinen Ronbunshū Kankōkai 茂田井教亨先生古希記念論文集刊行会, pp. 363–93. Kyoto: Heirakuji Shoten, 1974.

Suzuki Teitarō (D. T. Suzuki), trans. *Açvaghosha's Discourse on the Awakening of Faith in the Mahāyāna.* Chicago, 1900. Authorized facsimile from Ann Arbor: University Microfilms, 1968.

Swanson, Paul L. "Editor's Introduction." *Tendai Buddhism in Japan.* Special issue. *Japanese Journal of Religious Studies* 14/2–3 (June–Sept. 1987): 71–78.

———. *Foundations of T'ien-t'ai Philosophy: The Flowering of the Two Truths Theory in Chinese Buddhism.* Nanzan Studies in Religion and Culture. Berkeley: Asian Humanities Press, 1989.

———. "Understanding Chih-i: Through a Glass, Darkly?" *Journal of the International Association of Buddhist Studies* 17/2 (1994): 337–60.

———. "Zen is Not Buddhism: Recent Japanese Critiques of Buddha-Nature. *Numen* 40 (1993): 115–49.

Taga Munehaya 多賀宗隼. *Eisai* 栄西. Tokyo: Yoshikawa Kōbunkan, 1965.

———. "Kōkaku oyobi *Makura sōshi* ni tsuite" 皇覚および「枕雙紙」について. *Kanazawa Bunko kenkyū* 金沢文庫研究 61 (Nov. 1960): 6–8.

Taira Masayuki 平雅行. "Kamakura Bukkyō ron" 鎌倉仏教論. *Iwanami kōza Nihon tsūshi* 岩波講座日本通史, vol. 8: *Chūsei* 中世 2, ed. Asao Naohiro 朝尾直弘 et al., pp. 255–301. Tokyo: Iwanami Shoten, 1994.

———. "Mappō matsudaikan no rekishiteki igi" 末法・末代観の歴史的意義. In his *Nihon chūsei no shakai to Bukkyō* 日本中世の社会と仏教, pp. 110–54. Tokyo: Hanawa Shobo, 1992.

———. *Nihon chūsei no shakai to Bukkyō* 日本中世の社会と仏教. Tokyo: Hanawa Shobō, 1992.

Taira Ryōshō 平了照. "Eshin Sōzu no *Kanjin ryaku yōshū* ni tsuite" 惠心僧都の觀心略要集について. In *Tōyō bunka ronshū* 東洋文化論集, ed. Fukui Hakushi Shōju Kinen Ronbunshū Kankōkai 福井博士頌寿記念論文集刊行会, pp. 601–13. Tokyo: Waseda Shuppankai, 1969.

———. "Ryōzen dōchō ni tsuite" 靈山同聽について. *Tendai gakuhō* 天台學報 14 (1971): 1–11.

Tajima Tokuon 田島徳音. "Kawataya jūkūtsū ni tsuite" 河田十九通に就いて. *Sange gakuhō* 山家學報 1/4 (1931): 72–86.

Takada Enin 高田惠忍. "Hongaku shisō Taitō kōshō shiron" 本覺思想台當交渉史論. *Ōsaki gakuhō* 大崎學報 26 (Jan. 1913):1–14; 28 (June 1913): 10–31; 29 (July 1913): 17–38.

Takagi Yutaka 高木豊. "'Futari no Nichiren' kaikō: Kanazawa Bunkozō *Rishōin kechimyaku* o Nichiren den no shiryō kara nozokubeki kana no koto" 〈二人の日蓮〉改稿—金沢文庫蔵［理性院血脈］を日蓮伝の史料から除くべき歟のこと. *Ōsaki gakuhō* 大崎學報 135 (March 1982): 22–45.

———. *Heian jidai Hokke Bukkyōshi kenkyū* 平安時代法華仏教史研究. Kyoto: Heirakuji Shoten, 1973.

———. *Kamakura Bukkyōshi kenkyū* 鎌倉仏教史研究. Tokyo: Iwanami Shoten, 1982.

———. "Kiyosumi no Nichiren" 清澄の日蓮. *Kanazawa Bunko kenkyū* 金沢文庫研究 124 (June 1966): 1–6.

———. "Nichiren no shisō no keishō to hen'yō" 日蓮の思想の継承と変容. In *Nichiren* 日蓮, ed. Tokoro Shigemoto 戸頃重基 and Takagi Yutaka 高木豊, *Nihon shisō taikei* 日本思想大系, 14: 573–95. Tokyo: Iwanami Shoten, 1970.

———. *Nichiren: Sono kōdō to shisō* 日蓮—その行動と思想. *Nihonjin no kōdō to shisō* 日本人の行動と思想, no. 4. Tokyo: Hyōronsha, 1970. Reprint 1985.

———. *Nichiren to sono montei* 日蓮とその門弟. Tokyo: Kōbundō, 1965.

———. "Shunpan no hongaku shisō" 俊範の本覚思想. In *Hongaku shisō no genryū to tenkai* 本覚思想の 源流と展開, ed. Asai Endō 浅井圓道, pp. 173–76. *Hokekyō kenkyū* 法華経研究 11. Kyoto: Heirakuji Shoten, 1991.

Takahashi Ken'yū 高橋謙祐. "*Hon'in-myō shō* ni miru Kōmon kyōgaku no shisō haikei ni tsuite" 『本因妙抄』にみる興門教学の思想背景につして. *IBK* 印度學佛教學研究 28/2 (March 1980): 618–19.

———. "Nichiren Shōnin to *Shuzenji-ketsu*" 日蓮聖人と『修禅寺決』. *Nichiren kyōgaku kenkyūjo kiyō* 日蓮教學研究所紀要 5 (March 1978): 81–99.

———. "Shimizu Ryūzan: Nichiki keishōsha no jikaku to kokutaikan" 清水龍山—日輝継承者の自覚と国体観. In *Kindai Nichiren kyōdan no shisōka: Kindai Nichiren kyōdan, kyōgakushi shiron* 近代日蓮教団の思想家—近代日蓮教団・教学史試論, ed. Nakano Kyōtoku 中濃教篤, pp. 233–74. *Sōsho Nihon kindai to shūkyō* 叢書日本近代と宗教 2. Tokyo: Kokusho Kankōkai, 1977.

———. "Tendai gakusō Shinson ni tsuite" 天台学僧信尊について. *Nichiren kyōgaku kenkyūjo kiyō* 日蓮教學研究所紀要 4 (March 1977): 53–65.

Take Kakuchō 武覚超. "Eizan, Mii to Nichiren monka to no kōryū: Shijū kōhai han no seiritsu o megutte" 叡山・三井と日蓮門下との交流—四重興廃判の成立をめぐって. In *Hongaku shisō no genryū to tenkai* 本覚思想の源流と展開, ed. Asai Endō 浅井圓道, pp. 397–423. *Hokekyō kenkyū* 法華研究 11. Kyoto: Heirakuji Shoten, 1991.

———. "Nihon Tendai to Nichiren: Toku ni honmon shisō ni tsuite" 日本天台と日蓮—特に本門思想について. *Eizan gakuin kenkyū kiyō* 叡山学院研究紀要 7 (1984): 53–70.

———. "Tendai Daishi Chigi no honjakuron" 天台大師智顗の本迹論. *Tendai gakuhō* 天台學報 24 (Nov. 1982): 137–43.

———. *Tendai kyōgaku no kenkyū* 天台教学の研究. Kyoto: Hōzōkan, 1988.

Takeshima Hiroshi 竹島寛. "Jiin no shishi sōzoku to kettō sōzoku" 寺院の師資相續と血統相續. 1936. Reprinted in his *Ōchō jidai kōshitsushi no kenkyū* 王朝時代皇室史の研究, pp. 457–515. Tokyo: Meichō Fukyūkai, 1982.

Takeuchi Rizō 竹内理三. "Kuden to kyōmei: Kugyōgaku keifu (hitsuji kuden seiritsu izen)" 口傳と教命—公卿學系譜 (秘事口傳成立以前). *Rekishi chiri* 歷史地理 75/3 (March 1940): 143–57 and 75/4 (April 1940): 257–72.

Tamamuro Taijō 圭室諦成. *Dōgen* 道元. Tokyo: Shinjinbutsu Ōraisha, 1971.

———. *Nihon Bukkyōshi gaisetsu* 日本佛教史概説. Tokyo: Risōsha, 1940.

Tamura Enchō 田村圓澄. "Akunin shōki-setsu no seiritsu" 悪人正機説の成立. *Shigaku zasshi* 史學雜誌 61/11 (Nov. 1952): 1–24.

Tamura Kansei 田村完誓. "Eshin-ryū sanjū shichika kuden hōmon no keisei ni kansuru shiron" 恵心流三重七箇口伝法門の形成に関する試論. In *Bukkyō kyōri no kenkyū* 仏教教理の研究, ed. Tamura Yoshirō Hakushi Kanreki Kinenkai 田村芳朗博士還暦記念会, pp. 351–69. Tokyo: Shunjūsha, 1982.

———. "Minobu Bunko shozō no chūko Tendai kuden bunken ni tsuite" 身延文庫所蔵の中古天台口伝文献について. In *Indo shisō to Bukkyō* インド思想と仏教, ed. Nakamura Hajime Hakushi Kanreki Kinenkai 中村元博士還暦記念会, pp. 643–58. Tokyo: Shunjūsha, 1973.

Tamura Yoshirō 田村芳朗. "Critique of Original Awakening Thought in Shōshin and Dōgen." Trans. Jan Van Bragt. *Japanese Journal of Religious Studies* 11/2–3 (June–Sept. 1984): 243–66.

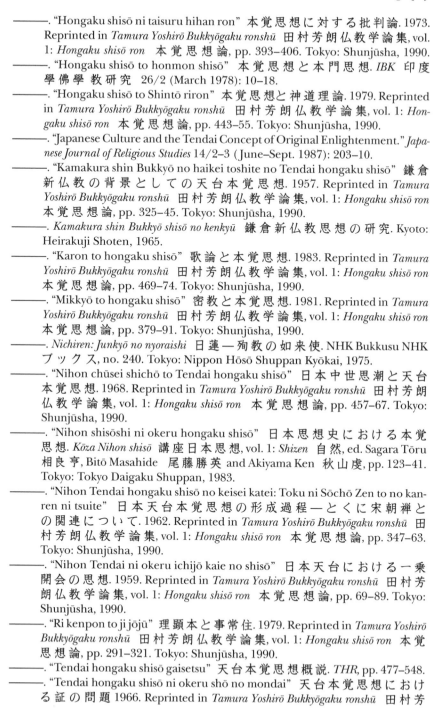

———. "Hongaku shisō ni taisuru hihan ron" 本覚思想に対する批判論. 1973. Reprinted in *Tamura Yoshirō Bukkyōgaku ronshū* 田村芳朗仏教学論集, vol. 1: *Hongaku shisō ron* 本覚思想論, pp. 393–406. Tokyo: Shunjūsha, 1990.

———. "Hongaku shisō to honmon shisō" 本覚思想と本門思想. *IBK* 印度學佛學研究 26/2 (March 1978): 10–18.

———. "Hongaku shisō to Shintō riron" 本覚思想と神道理論. 1979. Reprinted in *Tamura Yoshirō Bukkyōgaku ronshū* 田村芳朗仏教学論集, vol. 1: *Hongaku shisō ron* 本覚思想論, pp. 443–55. Tokyo: Shunjūsha, 1990.

———. "Japanese Culture and the Tendai Concept of Original Enlightenment." *Japanese Journal of Religious Studies* 14/2–3 (June–Sept. 1987): 203–10.

———. "Kamakura shin Bukkyō no haikei toshite no Tendai hongaku shisō" 鎌倉新仏教の背景としての天台本覚思想. 1957. Reprinted in *Tamura Yoshirō Bukkyōgaku ronshū* 田村芳朗仏教学論集, vol. 1: *Hongaku shisō ron* 本覚思想論, pp. 325–45. Tokyo: Shunjūsha, 1990.

———. *Kamakura shin Bukkyō shisō no kenkyū* 鎌倉新仏教思想の研究. Kyoto: Heirakuji Shoten, 1965.

———. "Karon to hongaku shisō" 歌論と本覚思想. 1983. Reprinted in *Tamura Yoshirō Bukkyōgaku ronshū* 田村芳朗仏教学論集, vol. 1: *Hongaku shisō ron* 本覚思想論, pp. 469–74. Tokyo: Shunjūsha, 1990.

———. "Mikkyō to hongaku shisō" 密教と本覚思想. 1981. Reprinted in *Tamura Yoshirō Bukkyōgaku ronshū* 田村芳朗仏教学論集, vol. 1: *Hongaku shisō ron* 本覚思想論, pp. 379–91. Tokyo: Shunjūsha, 1990.

———. *Nichiren: Junkyō no nyoraishi* 日蓮—殉教の如来使. NHK Bukkusu NHK ブックス, no. 240. Tokyo: Nippon Hōsō Shuppan Kyōkai, 1975.

———. "Nihon chūsei shichō to Tendai hongaku shisō" 日本中世思潮と天台本覚思想. 1968. Reprinted in *Tamura Yoshirō Bukkyōgaku ronshū* 田村芳朗仏教学論集, vol. 1: *Hongaku shisō ron* 本覚思想論, pp. 457–67. Tokyo: Shunjūsha, 1990.

———. "Nihon shisōshi ni okeru hongaku shisō" 日本思想史における本覚思想. *Kōza Nihon shisō* 講座日本思想, vol. 1: *Shizen* 自然, ed. Sagara Tōru 相良亨, Bitō Masahide 尾藤勝英 and Akiyama Ken 秋山虔, pp. 123–41. Tokyo: Tokyo Daigaku Shuppan, 1983.

———. "Nihon Tendai hongaku shisō no keisei katei: Toku ni Sōchō Zen to no kanren ni tsuite" 日本天台本覚思想の形成過程—とくに宋朝禅との関連について. 1962. Reprinted in *Tamura Yoshirō Bukkyōgaku ronshū* 田村芳朗仏教学論集, vol. 1: *Hongaku shisō ron* 本覚思想論, pp. 347–63. Tokyo: Shunjūsha, 1990.

———. "Nihon Tendai ni okeru ichijō kaie no shisō" 日本天台における一乗開会の思想. 1959. Reprinted in *Tamura Yoshirō Bukkyōgaku ronshū* 田村芳朗仏教学論集, vol. 1: *Hongaku shisō ron* 本覚思想論, pp. 69–89. Tokyo: Shunjūsha, 1990.

———. "Ri kenpon to ji jōjū" 理顕本と事常住. 1979. Reprinted in *Tamura Yoshirō Bukkyōgaku ronshū* 田村芳朗仏教学論集, vol. 1: *Hongaku shisō ron* 本覚思想論, pp. 291–321. Tokyo: Shunjūsha, 1990.

———. "Tendai hongaku shisō gaisetsu" 天台本覚思想概説. *THR*, pp. 477–548.

———. "Tendai hongaku shisō ni okeru shō no mondai" 天台本覚思想における証の問題 1966. Reprinted in *Tamura Yoshirō Bukkyōgaku ronshū* 田村芳

朗仏教学論集, vol. 1: *Hongaku shisō ron* 本覚思想論, pp. 185–202. Tokyo: Shunjūsha, 1990.

Tanabe, George J., Jr. *Myōe the Dreamkeeper: Fantasy and Knowledge in Early Kamakura Buddhism.* Cambridge: Council on East Asian Studies, Harvard University, 1992.

Tanabe, Willa Jane. "The Lotus Lectures: *Hokke Hakkō* in the Heian Period." *Monumenta Nipponica* 39/4 (Winter 1984): 393–407.

———. *Paintings of the Lotus Sutra.* New York and Tokyo: Weatherhill, 1988.

Tokoro Shigemoto 戸頃重基. *Nichiren kyōgaku no shisōshi kenkyū* 日蓮教学の思想史研究. Tokyo: Fuzan-bō, 1976.

———. *Nichiren no shisō to Kamakura Bukkyō* 日蓮の思想と鎌倉仏教. Tokyo: Fuzan-bō, 1965. Reprint 1975.

———. "Tami no ko no jikaku no keisei to tenkai" 民の子の自覚の形成と展開. In *Nichiren* 日蓮, ed. Tokoro Shigemoto 戸頃重基 and Takagi Yutaka 高木豊, *Nihon shisō taikei* 日本思想大系, vol. 14, pp. 485–516. Tokyo: Iwanami Shoten, 1970.

Tsuji Zennosuke 辻善之助. *Nihon Bukkyōshi* 日本佛教史. 10 vols. Tokyo: Iwanami Shoten, 1944–1955.

Tsumori Kiichi 都守基一. "Ryōzen jōdo shinkō no keifu" 霊山浄土信仰の系譜. *Nichiren kyōgaku kenkyūjo kiyō* 日蓮教學研究所紀要 15 (1988): 23–51.

Udaka Ryōtetsu 宇高良哲. "Chūsei no Kawagoe Senba dangisho ni tsuite" 中世の川越仙波談義所について. *Tendai gakuhō* 天台學報 32 (1990): 59–68.

Ueda Honshō 上田本昌. "Nichiren Shōnin no shingikan: Tenshō Daijin, Hachiman Daibosatsu o chūshin toshite" 日蓮聖人の神祇観―天照大神・八幡大菩薩を中心として. *Seishin* 棲神 40 (Dec. 1967): 17–31.

———. "Nichirenshū to shingi" 日蓮と神祇. In *Bukkyō to kamigami* 仏教と神々, ed. Daihōrin Henshūbu 大法輪編集部, pp. 81–88. Tokyo: Daihōrinkaku, 1988. Reprint 1991.

Ueda Yoshifumi, ed. *Notes on the Inscriptions on Sacred Scrolls: A Translation of Shinran's Songō shinzō meimon.* Shin Buddhism Translation Series. Kyoto: Honganji International Center, 1982.

Uesugi Bunshū 上杉文秀. *Nihon Tendai shi* 日本天台史. 2 vols. Nagoya: Hajinkaku Shobō, 1935. Reprint 1936.

Umehara Takeshi 梅原武 et al., eds. *Shinran, Dōgen, Nichiren* 親鸞・道元・日蓮. *Nihon no koten* 日本の古典 12. Tokyo: Kawade Shobō Shinsha, 1973.

Waddell, Norman, and Abe Masao, trans., with an introduction. "Dōgen's *Bendōwa.*" *The Eastern Buddhist* 4/1 (May 1971): 124–57.

———, trans., with an introduction. "Shōbō genzō Genjō kōan." *The Eastern Buddhist* 5/1 (May 1972): 129–40.

Wai-tao, Bikshu, and Dwight Goddard, trans. "Awakening of Faith: Mahayana Shradhotpadda Shastra." 1936–1937. In *A Buddhist Bible,* ed. and pub., Dwight Goddard, pp. 357–404. 2d ed. (revised and expanded). Thetford, Vermont, 1938.

Watanabe Hōyō 渡辺宝陽. "Daimandara to Hokkedō" 大曼荼羅と法華堂. In *Nichiren to sono kyōdan* 日蓮とその教団, vol. 1, ed. Kawazoe Shōji 川添昭二 et al., pp. 85–114. Kyoto: Heirakuji Shoten, 1976.

———. "Honjaku ron no tenkai" 本迹論の展開. In *Chūsei Hokke Bukkyō no tenkai*

中世法華仏教の展開, ed. Kageyama Gyōō 影山尭雄, pp. 277–304. *Hokekyō kenkyū* 法華経研究 5. Kyoto: Heirakuji Shoten, 1974.

———. "Nichiren Shōnin no busshu ron" 日蓮聖人の仏種論. In *Hokke Bukkyō no butsuda ron to shujō ron* 法華仏教の仏陀論と衆生論, ed. Watanabe Hōyō 渡辺宝陽, pp. 401–23. *Hokekyō kenkyū* 法華経研究 10. Kyoto: Heirakuji Shoten, 1985.

———. *Nichirenshū shingyōron no kenkyū* 日蓮宗信行論の研究. Kyoto: Heirakuji Shoten, 1976.

———. "Nichiren Shōnin no shūkyō ni okeru 'hōbō' no igi" 日蓮聖人の宗教における「謗法」の意義. In *Nichiren Shōnin kenkyū* 日蓮聖人研究, ed. Miyazaki Eishū 宮崎英修 and Motai Kyōkō 茂田井教亨, pp. 87–115. Kyoto: Heirakuji Shoten, 1972.

Watanabe Hōyō and Kitagawa Zenchō 北川前肇. *Nichiren no iitakatta koto* 日蓮のいいたかったこと. Monju sensho もんじゅ撰書, no. 8. Tokyo: Kōdansha, 1985.

Watanabe Shujun 渡邊守順 et al. *Hieizan* 比叡山. Kyoto: Hōzōkan, 1987.

Watanabe Shujun, Amano Denchū 天納傳中 and Mizugami Fumiyoshi (Bungi) 水上文義. "Tendai no monzeki" 天台の門跡. In *Hieizan* 比叡山, Watanabe Shujun 渡邊守順 et al., pp. 241–311. Kyoto: Hōzōkan, 1987.

Watson, Burton, trans. *The Lotus Sutra*. New York: Columbia University Press, 1993.

Wayman, Alex. "The Mirror as a Pan-Buddhist Metaphor-Simile." *History of Religions* 13/4 (May 1974): 251–69.

Williams, Paul. *Mahāyāna Buddhism: The Doctrinal Foundations*. London: Routledge, 1989.

Wilson, Bryan, and Karel Dobbelaere. *A Time to Chant: The Sōka Gakkai Buddhists in Britain*. Oxford: Clarendon Press, 1994.

Yamakawa Chiō 山川智應. "Eizan ni okeru Nichiren Shōnin no shiyū no kenkyū" 叡山における日蓮聖人の師友の研究. In his *Nichiren Shōnin kenkyū* 日蓮聖人研究, 1: 106–69. Tokyo: Shinchōsha, 1929.

———. *Nichiren Shōnin den jikkō* 日蓮聖人傳十講. Tokyo: Jōmyō Zenshū Kankōkai, 1921. Reprint 1975.

———. "*Risshōkan jō* ni taisuru gigi ni tsuite" 「立正觀抄」に對する疑議に就いて. *Seishin* 棲神 24 (Dec. 1938): 26–48.

Yamanaka Kihachi 山中喜八, ed. *Gohonzon shū* 御本尊集 and *Gohonzon shū mokuroku* 御本尊集目録. Tokyo: Risshō Ankoku Kai, 1952. Revised 1974. Reprint 1981.

Yamanouchi (Yamauchi) Shun'yū 山内舜雄. *Dōgen Zen to Tendai hongaku hōmon* 道元禅と天台本覚法門. Tokyo: Daizō Shuppan, 1985.

———. "*Shōbōgenzō shō* to Tendai hongaku hōmon" 『正法眼蔵抄』と天台本覚法門. *Komazawa Daigaku Bukkyōgakubu ronshū* 駒澤大學佛教學部論集 17 (Oct. 1986): 70–112.

———. "Tendai kyōgaku to Dōgen" 天台教学と道元. In *Kōza Dōgen* 講座道元, vol. 6: *Bukkyōgaku to Dōgen* 仏教学と道元, ed. Kagamishima Genryū 鏡島元隆 and Tamashiro Yasushirō 玉城康四郎, pp. 2-24. Tokyo: Shunjūsha, 1980.

Yamasaki Taikō. *Shingon: Japanese Esoteric Buddhism*. Trans. and adapted by Richard and Cynthia Peterson, ed. Yasuyoshi Morimoto and David Kidd. Boston: Shambala, 1988.

Yasuji Kirimura, ed. *Outline of Buddhism.* Tokyo: Nichiren Shōshū International Center, 1981.

Yoshino Hiroko 吉野裕子. *Kamigami no tanjō: Eki, gogyō to Nihon no kamigami* 神々の誕生―易・五行と日本の神々. Tokyo: Iwanami Shoten, 1990.

Yūki Reimon 結城令聞. "Shotō Bukkyō no shisōshiteki mujun to kokka kenryoku to no kōsaku" 初唐佛教の思想史的矛盾と國家權力との交錯. *Tōyō bunka kenkyūjo kiyō* 東洋文化研究所紀要 25 (1961): 1–28.

Index

acquired enlightenment (*shikaku*), 346, 358; in *Awakening of Faith*, 6; Danna school and, 104; Dōgen's view of, 74–75; rejected by new Kamakura founders, 393n. 48; term used in Tendai doctrinal classification, 37, 353

actuality (*ji*): associated with origin teaching, 171, 200, 381n. 114; constant abiding of, 29, 201–203, 207–209, 225–226; emphasis on in original enlightenment thought, 37–38, 42, 43, 85–86, 172; esoteric Buddhist view of, 28, 225; Hua-yen view of, 10, 31; importance in Tendai thought, 29, 33; meaning in esoteric Buddhism, 28–29, 68; Nichiren's view of, 68, 264, 266, 272; nonduality with principle, 38, 85, 200–201, 203–204; Taimitsu view of, 28–29; T'ien-t'ai view of, 10, 27–28, 31

Agui school, 140, 149

Aizen Myōō, 247, 277, 279, 331

Akamatsu Toshihide, 222–223

ālaya-vijñāna (store consciousness), 5–6, 7

Amida, 33, 86, 132, 133–134, 159–160, 167; exclusive devotion to, 57; four kinds of, 175, 417n. 76; nonduality of practitioner and, 174–175, 192

Amoghavajra, 5, 27

Andō Toshio, 360

Anne, 112

Annen, 21, 26, 27, 30, 129, 344, 378n. 84; doctrinal classification, 23, 24; "four ones" concept, 23; influence of Kūkai on, 12; on *Lotus Sūtra*, 254, 434n. 78; on precepts, 19, 128, 234

Anraku school, 36, 134, 366

aristocratic monks, 84, 110–113, 114, 140, 145–146, 224

art, 113, 279

Asai Endō, 72

Asai Yōrin, 69–71, 76, 91, 239, 318, 326

Ashikaga Mochiuji, 327, 453n. 92

Aśvaghoṣa, 5

Avīci hell, 193–194, 255, 296

Awakening of Faith in the Mahāyāna (*Ta-sheng ch'i-hsin lun*), 5, 6, 14; commentaries on, 11; Fa-tsang's commentary on, 7, 13, 14; influence, 9, 41; original enlightenment concept in, 37, 38, 39, 82; water and waves metaphor, 208

Awataguchi Jōmyō, 146, 174; debate texts, 118; as founder of Gyōsen-bō lineage, 138, 402n. 52; and "fourfold rise and fall," 169; and "*shikan* surpasses the *Lotus*" doctrine, 311; succession dispute, 138–139, 141; and "threefold seven great matters," 176–177

Azuma kagami (Mirror of the East), 56, 148

bakufu: conflict with Gotoba, 243; establishment of, 55; Nichiren's relationship with, 242, 251, 258, 260–261, 262, 299; patronage of Buddhist monks, 57